# Writings of Edward the Sixth, William Hugh, Queen Catherine Parr, Anne Askew, Lady Jane Grey, Hamilton, and Balnaves

EDWARD VI.

# WRITINGS

## OF

## EDWARD THE SIXTH,

WILLIAM HUGH, QUEEN CATHERINE PARR,
ANNE ASKEW, LADY JANE GREY,
HAMILTON, AND BALNAVES.

LONDON:
THE RELIGIOUS TRACT SOCIETY,
56, PATERNOSTER-ROW;
AND SOLD BY JSBEI 21, BERNERS-STREET;
EDINBURGH; AND OTHER BOOKSELLERS.
1831.

# WRITINGS

OF

# EDWARD THE SIXTH,

WILLIAM HUGH, QUEEN CATHERINE PARR.

ANNE ASKEW, LADY JANE GREY,

HAMILTON, AND BALNAVES.

---

LONDON:
THE RELIGIOUS TRACT SOCIETY,
56, PATERNOSTER-ROW;
SOLD ALSO BY NISBET, 21, BERNERS-STREET; OLIPHANT, EDINBURGH; AND OTHER BOOKSELLERS.

1831.

# CONTENTS.

### EDWARD THE SIXTH.

| | Page |
|---|---|
| Some Account of King Edward the Sixth | 1 |
| Some Particulars of Sir John Cheke | 22 |
| King Edward the Sixth, against the Pope's Supremacy | 25 |
| ———————————, A Short Catechism | 49 |
| Extracts from the Primer of King Edward the Sixth | 80 |

### HUGH.

| | |
|---|---|
| Some Account of William Hugh | 2 |
| The Troubled Man's Medicine. | |
| Book I. To comfort a man being in trouble, adversity, or sickness. | 3 |
| II. To teach a man gladly to die | 39 |

### CATHERINE PARR.

Some Account of Queen Catherine Parr................. 1
Letter to Lady Wriothesley, comforting her for the loss of her Son 14
Prayers or Meditations; wherein the mind is stirred patiently to suffer all afflictions here, to set at naught the vain prosperity of this world, and always to long for everlasting felicity. Collected out of certain holy works, by the most virtuous and gracious princess, Catherine, queen of England, France, and Ireland......................................... 15
The Lamentation or Complaint of a Sinner, made by the most virtuous and gracious lady, queen Catherine, (Parr,) bewailing the ignorance of her blind life led in superstition.... 29
Chap. I. Of an humble confession of sins to the glory of God 32
II. A lamentation of a sinner, with a hearty repentance in faith, to obtain absolution and remission through the merits of Christ........................ 36
III. What true faith worketh in the soul of a sinner.... 38
IV. Of the great love of God towards mankind, and of the inward beholding of Christ crucified........ 41
V. Of the glorious victories of Christ over all enemies. 43
VI. That we ought to submit ourselves to the school of the cross, and still look and learn in the book of the cross .................................... 47
VII. A christian bewailing the miserable ignorance and blindness of men............................. 49
VIII. Of the fruits and rules of true christianity for men to follow ................................... 52
IX. Of the fruits of infidelity, and offence of weaklings. 54
X. Of carnal gospellers, by whose evil living, God's truth is shamefully slandered ...................... 56
XI. Of the virtuous properties of God's children, of whom every one attendeth his vocation............... 59
XII. The conclusion, with a christian exhortation to the amendment of life........................... 62

## CONTENTS.

### ANNE ASKEW.

|   | Page |
|---|---|
| Short Account of Anne Askew | 2 |
| John Bale to the Christian readers | 3 |
| Her First Examination | 10 |
| Her Latter Apprehension and Examination | 21 |
| The Ballad she made and sang in Newgate | 33 |
| Her Martyrdom | 36 |

### LADY JANE GREY.

| | |
|---|---|
| Some Account of Lady Jane Grey | 2 |
| Her communication with Dr. Feckenham | 19 |
| Letter I. To Bullinger | 22 |
| —— II. To the same | 25 |
| —— III. To the same | 26 |
| —— IV. To Queen Mary | 28 |
| —— V. To her Father | 32 |
| —— VI. To Harding | 34 |
| ——VII. To her sister, lady Catherine | 41 |
| An effectual Prayer made in time of trouble | 42 |
| Letter from John Banks to H. Bullinger | 44 |
| Last hours of the duke of Suffolk | 46 |
| A CERTAIN GODLY SUPPLICATION by certain inhabitants of Norfolk and Suffolk | 49 |

### PATRICK HAMILTON.

| | |
|---|---|
| Brief Account of Patrick Hamilton | 2 |
| John Frith unto the Christian Reader | 3 |
| Patrick's Places, a treatise of the law and the gospel | 4 |

### BALNAVES.

The Confession of Faith, containing how the Troubled Man should seek refuge at his God, thereto led by faith; with the declaration of the article of Justification at length. The order of good works which are the fruits of faith; and how the faithful and justified man should walk and live in the perfect and true christian religion, according to his vocation. Compiled by M. Henry Balnaves, of Halhill, and one of the lords of session and council of Scotland, being a prisoner within the old palace of Roane. In the year of our Lord, 1548. Directed to his faithful brethren, being in like trouble or more. And to all true professors and favourers of the sincere word of God.

| | |
|---|---|
| The Epistle Dedicatory by the Publisher | 3 |
| Original Preface, by Knox | 6 |
| The Author, unto the faithful readers | 12 |
| Confession of Faith, declaring the article of Justification | 13 |
| A Brief Summary of this Book | 113 |

# SOME ACCOUNT

OF

# KING EDWARD VI.

EDWARD THE SIXTH was the son of Henry VIII. by his third wife, Jane Seymour. He was born at Hampton-court, October 12th, 1537, where he was christened with much ceremony on the 15th of the same month. The birth of a prince had been long desired, but the joy with which the intelligence was received by the court and the nation, was abated by the death of the queen, his mother, on the 24th, twelve days after the birth of her son.\* Henry was much afflicted, and showed that he was not insensible to the loss he had sustained; even the festivities of the ensuing Christmas were not allowed to put aside the outward tokens of respect to her memory.

The care which Henry VIII. evinced for the welfare of his children, with his anxiety to place them under the charge of learned and pious instructors, are circumstances which prove the character of that monarch, with all his faults, to have been very different from the representations of those who cannot forgive the part he took in freeing this country from the iron bands of popery. At the early age of six years, prince Edward was committed to the charge of able preceptors, the principal of whom was Sir Anthony Cook, a sincere favourer of the gospel, whose own children manifested their father's suitableness for such a trust. Another of his early tutors was Dr. Richard Cox, moderator of the school of Eton, afterwards dean of Christ Church and chancellor of the university of Oxford, and lastly bishop of Ely. When Dr. Cox received an ecclesiastical appointment which often required him to be absent from his noble pupil, Sir John Cheke, then professor of Greek at Cambridge, where he had, with much difficulty, introduced a more correct

---

\* Some historians have by mistake stated October the 14th as the day of queen's Jane's death, the error, probably at first unintentional, has been copied from one to another. By this the Romanists have strengthened their legend of Henry's desiring that the life of the child might be preserved by the death of his mother, which they still repeat. The falsehood of that statement is clearly proved by a book among the records of the Herald's college, (see Strype's Memorials,) which gives all the particulars relative to the queen's funeral, and the various ceremonies of attendance on the corpse, from her decease to the interment. An original letter from her physicians to the council is also in existence, dated the 24th, which describes her declining state, from an illness incident to her condition, and mentions her being supposed to be near death. There is also a letter extant from the queen herself, written after the birth of her son.

pronunciation of that language,* was appointed tutor to the prince. These excellent and learned men gave full attention to their important charge. The manner in which their labours were blessed is thus described by William Thomas, afterwards clerk of the council, himself a learned man. In a work entitled The Pilgrim, he says, " If ye knew the towardness of that young prince, your hearts would melt to hear him named, and your stomach abhor the malice of them that would him ill. The beautifullest creature that liveth under the sun; the wittiest, the most amiable, and the gentlest thing of all the world. Such a capacity in learning the things taught him by his schoolmasters, that it is a wonder to hear say. And finally, he hath such a grace of posture, and gesture in gravity, when he comes into a presence, that it should seem he were already a father, and yet passes he not the age of ten years. A thing undoubtedly much rather to be seen than believed." Sufficient proof still remains of the progress made by prince Edward under these instructors, from numerous letters written by him in Latin and in French, some as early as his ninth year, also by several Latin orations or themes, preserved in the British Museum. At this period of his life the prince chiefly resided in Hertfordshire. Of his tutors, Cheke appears to have been the most constantly with him, but the early formation of his habits and temper probably had devolved principally upon Cook and Cox. The prince afterward told Cardan he had had two masters, Moderation and Diligence, designating Cox by the former, and Cheke by the latter appellation. Curio, the Italian reformer, addressing Cheke and Cook, said, " that by their united prayers, counsels, and industry, they had formed a king of the highest, even of divine hopes." But, in the history of this excellent prince, Cranmer must never be forgotten. The watchful care of that excellent prelate, and his anxiety for the progress of the reformation, were continually exercised for the benefit of the heir to the crown, and for his advancement in true religion and sound learning. It is however evident, that more than mere natural docility prepared the youthful prince to receive the instructions of his able and pious preceptors. The effects of divine influence upon his heart were manifest during the whole of his short yet interesting course. Without this, human teachers would have planted and watered in vain.

We have not many anecdotes of the youthful days of this excellent prince; but one which is characteristic of his piety, and evidences the principles in which he was trained, has been preserved by Fuller. When engaged with some companions in amusements suitable for his age, he wished to take down from a shelf something above his reach. One of his playfellows offered him a

* Gardiner's zeal against every kind of reformation, and especially any which promoted the study of the scriptures in the original, was shown by his decided opposition to this improvement, he threatened expulsion to all who should favour it.

large bible to stand upon, but perceiving it to be a bible, Edward refused such assistance with much indignation. He sharply reproved the offerer, adding, it was unfit that he should trample under his feet that which he ought to treasure up in his head and heart.

Fox says, that there was not wanting in the prince any diligence to receive that which his instructors would teach him. So that in the midst of all his play and recreation, he would always observe to keep the hours appointed to his study, using the same with much attention, till time called him again from his book to pastime. In this, his study and keeping of his hours, he so profited, that Cranmer, beholding his towardness, his readiness in both tongues, in translating from Greek to Latin, from Latin to Greek again, in declaiming with his school-fellows without help of his teachers, and that extempore, wept for joy, declaring to Dr. Cox, his schoolmaster, that he would never have thought it to have been in the prince except he had seen it himself.

Fox then mentions prince Edward's exact knowledge of the various parts of his own realm, Scotland, and France; also his minute acquaintance with the names and characters of all the magistrates and gentlemen who bore any authority. A manuscript in the British Museum relates how a schoolmaster, named Herne, incited his unwilling scholars to apply themselves more diligently to their books, and to improve in learning, by emulating the example of their prince.

While prince Edward was in the tenth year of his age, and was thus preparing for the duties which lay before him, Henry VIII. died, on January 28th, 1547. The office of protector devolved upon the earl of Hertford, one of the young king's maternal uncles. The appointment of this nobleman to that important office became a means of promoting the reformation. His piety appears from a devout prayer which he seems to have used constantly with reference to the important charge which devolved upon him. It is as follows:—

"Lord God of hosts, in whose only hand is life and death, victory and confusion, rule and subjection, receive me, thy humble creature, into thy mercy, and direct me in my requests, that I offend not thy high majesty. O my Lord and my God, I am the work of thy hands; thy goodness cannot reject me. I am the price of thy Son's death, Jesu Christ; for thy Son's sake thou wilt not lose me. I am a vessel for thy mercy: thy justice will not condemn me. I am recorded in the book of life, I am written with the very blood of Jesus; thy inestimable love will not cancel then my name. For this cause, Lord God, I am bold to speak to thy Majesty. Thou, Lord, by thy providence hast called me to rule; make me therefore able to follow thy calling. Thou, Lord, by thine order hast committed an anointed king to my governance; direct me therefore with thy hand, that I err not from thy good pleasure. Finish in me, Lord, thy beginning, and begin in me that thou wilt finish.

"By thee do kings reign, and from thee all power is derived. Govern me, Lord, as I shall govern; rule me, as I shall rule. I am ready for thy governance; make thy people ready for mine. I seek thy only honour in my vocation; amplify it, Lord, with thy might. If it be thy will that I shall rule, make thy congregation subject to my rule. Give me power, Lord, to suppress whom thou wilt have to obey.

"I am by appointment thy minister for thy king, a shepherd for thy people, a sword-bearer for thy justice: prosper the king, save thy people, direct thy justice. I am ready, Lord, to do that thou commandest; command that thou wilt. Remember, O, God, thine old mercies; remember thy benefits showed heretofore. Remember, Lord, me thy servant, and make me worthy to ask. Teach me what to ask, and then give me that I ask. None other I seek to, Lord, but thee, because none other can give it me. And that I seek is thine honour and glory.

"I ask victory, but to show thy power upon the wicked. I ask prosperity, but for to rule in peace thy congregation. I ask wisdom, but by my counsel to set forth thy cause. And as I ask for myself, so, Lord, pour thy knowledge upon all them which shall counsel me. And forgive them, that in their offence I suffer not the reward of their evil.

"If I have erred, Lord, forgive me; for so thou hast promised me. If I shall not err, direct me; for that only is thy property. Great things, O my God, hast thou begun in my hand; let me then, Lord, be thy minister to defend them. Thus I conclude, Lord, by the name of thy Son Jesus Christ. Faithfully I commit all my cause to thy high providence, and so rest to advance all human strength under the standard of thy omnipotency."

The coronation took place on the 28th of February. The usual grant of a general pardon followed; thus the prosecutions for religion commenced during the latter years of the preceding reign, under the act of six articles, were terminated. Although that and other persecuting acts were not regularly repealed till some months after, many were released from prison, and a number of learned and pious individuals were allowed to return from exile, whose assistance gave new vigour to the efforts for reformation. But the most remarkable circumstance connected with the coronation, was the address of archbishop Cranmer to the youthful monarch. The prelate therein gave the following charge, which the king did not forget, as his subsequent conduct shows. This address was found among the collections of archbishop Usher.

"Most dread and royal sovereign; the promises your highness hath made here, at your coronation, to forsake the devil and all his works, are not to be taken in the bishop of Rome's sense; when you commit any thing distasteful to that see, to hit your majesty in the teeth, as pope Paul the third, late bishop of

Rome, sent to your royal father, saying, 'Didst thou not promise, at our permission of thy coronation, to forsake the devil and all his works, and dost thou run to heresy? For the breach of this thy promise, knowest thou not, that it is in our power to dispose of thy sword and sceptre to whom we please?' We, your majesty's clergy, do humbly conceive, that this promise reacheth not at your highness's sword, spiritual or temporal, or in the least at your highness swaying the sceptre of this your dominion, as you and your predecessors have had them from God. Neither could your ancestors lawfully resign up their crowns to the bishop of Rome or his legates, according to their ancient oaths then taken upon that ceremony.

"The bishops of Canterbury, for the most part, have crowned your predecessors, and anointed them kings of this land; yet it was not in their power to receive or reject them; neither did it give them authority to prescribe them conditions to take or leave their crowns, although the bishops of Rome would encroach upon your predecessors, by their act and oil, that in the end they might possess those bishops with an interest to dispose of their crowns at their pleasure. But the wiser sort will look to their claws and clip them.

"The solemn rites of coronation have their ends and utility; yet neither direct force or necessity: they are good admonitions to put kings in mind of their duty to God, but no increasement of their dignity; for they are God's anointed; not in respect of the oil which the bishop useth, but in consideration of their power, which is ordained; of the sword, which is authorized; of their persons, which are elected of God, and endued with the gifts o his Spirit, for the better ruling and guiding of his people.

"The oil, if added, is but a ceremony: if it be wanting, tha king is yet a perfect monarch notwithstanding, and God's anointed, as well as if he was inoiled. Now for the person or bishop that doth anoint a king, it is proper to be done by the chiefest. But if they cannot, or will not, any bishop may perform this ceremony.

"To condition with monarchs upon these ceremonies, the bishop of Rome (or other bishops owning his supremacy) hath no authority; but he may faithfully declare what God requires at the hands of kings and rulers, that is, religion and virtue. Therefore, not from the bishop of Rome, but as a messenger from my Saviour Jesus Christ, I shall most humbly admonish your royal majesty, what things your highness is to perform.

"Your majesty is God's vicegerent, and Christ's vicar within your own dominions, and to see, with your predecessor Josiah, God truly worshipped, and idolatry destroyed; the tyranny of the bishops of Rome banished from your subjects, and images removed. These acts are signs of a second Josiah, who reformed the church of God in his days. You are to reward virtue, to revenge sin, to justify the innocent, to relieve the poor, to procure peace, to repress violence, and to execute justice throughout your realms. For precedents on those kings who performed not these things, the old law shows how the Lord revenged his quarrel; and on those kings who fulfilled these things, he poured forth his blessings in abundance. For example, it is written of Josiah, in the book of the Kings, thus: 'Like unto him there was no king, that turned to the Lord with all his heart, according to all the law of Moses; neither after him arose there any like him.' This was to that prince a perpetual fame of dignity, to remain to the end of days.

"Being bound by my function to lay these things before your royal highness; the one, as a reward if you fulfil; the other, as a judgment from God if you neglect them; yet I openly declare, before the living God, and before these nobles of the land, that I have no commission to denounce your majesty deprived, if your highness miss in part, or in whole, of these performances: much less to draw up indentures between God and your majesty; or to say you forfeit your crown, with a clause for the bishop of Rome, as have been done by your majesty's predecessors, king John and his son Henry of this land. The Almighty God of his mercy let the light of his countenance shine upon your majesty, grant you a prosperous and happy reign, defend you, and save you; and let your subjects say, Amen.

"GOD SAVE THE KING."

The piety of the youthful monarch was manifested at the coronation. Bale relates, upon the authority of credible witnesses, that when three swords were brought to be carried in the procession, as emblematical of his three kingdoms, the king said there was one yet wanting. The nobles inquiring what it was, he answered, THE BIBLE, adding, "That book is the sword of the Spirit, and to be preferred before these swords. That ought in all right to govern us, who use them for the people's safety by God's appointment. Without that sword we are nothing, we can do nothing, we have no power. From that we are what we are this day. From that we receive whatsoever it is that we at present do assume. He that rules without it, is not to be called God's minister, or a king. Under that we ought to live, to fight, to govern the people, and to perform all our affairs. From that alone we obtain all power, virtue, grace, salvation, and whatsoever we have of divine strength." When the pious young king had thus expressed himself, he commanded the bible to be brought with the greatest reverence, and carried before him.

His affection for Cranmer, and his pious feelings, appear from the following letter written by him to the archbishop, originally in Latin.

"Revered godfather, although I am but a child, yet I am not unmindful of the services and the kindnesses you daily perform and manifest towards me. I have not forgotten your kind letters delivered to me on St. Peter's eve. I was unwilling to answer them until now, not from neglect or forgetfulness, but that, as I daily meditated on them, and committed their contents faithfully to memory, at length having well considered them I might reply the more wisely. I do indeed embrace and venerate the truly paternal affection towards me which is expressed in them—may your life be prolonged for many years, and may you continue to be a respected father to me by your godly and wholesome counsels. For I consider that godliness is to be desired and embraced by me above all things, since St. Paul has said, Godliness is profitable to all things."

Cranmer's reply is as follows: it was also written in Latin.

"My beloved son in Christ—I am as much concerned for your welfare as my own; therefore when I learn that you are safe and well, I feel myself to be so also. My absence cannot be so unpleasant to you, as your letters are pleasing to me. They show that you possess a disposition worthy of your rank, and a preceptor suitable for such a disposition. From your letters I perceive that you so cultivate learning that heavenly truths are not among the things you least care for, and whoso careth for those things, shall not be overcome by any cares. Go on, therefore, in the way upon which you have entered, and adorn your native land, that the light of virtue which I behold in you may hereafter enlighten all your England," &c.

His tutor (probably Dr. Cox) says in a letter to the archbishop, "Your godson is merry and in health, and of such towardness in learning, godliness, gentleness, and all honest qualities, that both you and I, and all in this realm, ought to think him to be, and take him for, a singular gift sent of God," &c.

The education of Edward VI. inspired the protestants with great hopes of the progress of the truth, but they were not wholly devoid of apprehensions respecting the influence of the papists at court. Bale says, "Many things I conclude concerning prince Edward, whom I doubt not but the Lord hath sent for the singular comfort of England. Not that I timorously define any thing to come concerning him; considering it only in the Lord's power. But I desire of the same Lord to preserve his bringing up from the contagious drinks of those false physicians. And this is to be prayed for of all men." That many such prayers were offered by the protestants there can be no doubt; the frequent references to the youthful monarch by Latimer and other reformers, show the pleasure mixed with anxiety, with which they regarded his advance in life. Latimer, in his sermon on the plough, notices how the papists "whispered the king in his ear," alluding no doubt particularly to the crafty Gardiner, who also laboured earnestly to persuade the protector and the council to leave all matters concerning religion in their present state, during the king's minority.

Happily for England, the intrigues of Gardiner were not successful. The reformation advanced steadily from the commencement of the reign of Edward VI. That it proceeded not to the full extent which might have been desirable, is accounted for by the peculiar state of parties in the English court at that time; also by the political situation of the country with regard both to foreign and domestic affairs. That much remained imperfect may readily be admitted, but at no previous period of English history, and not often at any subsequent time, was true religion more generally prevalent through all ranks than in the reign of Edward VI. To enter into the details of the progress of the reformation would be impossible in the present brief account, which is rather intended to give some particulars of the private character of king Edward than of the public proceedings of his reign.*

The decision with which the protector and his counsellors proceeded with the work of reformation from the first, is shown by a letter from John ab Ulmis to Bullinger, written at Oxford on Ascension day, 1546. He says, "England is adorned and enlightened by the word of God, and the number of the faithful increases largely every day. The mass, so dear to papists, begins to give way; in many places it is already dismissed and condemned by divine authority, images are extirpated throughout the land, nor does the least spark remain which can afford hopes to the papists, or give them an occasion for confirming their errors respecting idols, or an opportunity of drawing aside the people from our Saviour. The marriage of the clergy is allowed and sanctioned by the royal approbation. Peter Martyr has demonstrated to general satisfaction, from the scriptures, and the writings of orthodox divines, that purgatory is only a cross to which we have been hitherto subjected. The same result has taken place respecting the eucharist, or the holy supper of the Lord—that it is a commemoration of Christ, and a solemn showing forth of his death, not a sacrifice."

As early as 1548, though but eleven years of age, we find king Edward seriously attending to the duties of the kingly office, by studying the state and condition of his realm, with an earnest desire to promote its safety and peace. In acquiring this knowledge, among other persons, he made considerable use of William Thomas already mentioned, whose natural abilities and attainments fitted him to impart information upon these subjects. Thomas planned a series of discourses to illustrate a number of principles or propositions which he stated. Of these he gave a list, desiring the king to point out such as he most wished to have discussed without delay. These "Common-places of State," as they were entitled, are enumerated by Strype. It is hardly necessary to say that they differ most widely from the principles which Machiavel prepared for the instruction of an Italian prince, not long before that period. The following may be mentioned: 10. Whether religion, beside the honour of God, be not also the greatest stay of civil order?—23. How much good ministers are

* Some account of the progress of the reformation during the reign of king Edward will be found in the life of Cranmer, prefixed to the writings of that reformer in the present collection.

to be rewarded and the evil punished?—80. Whether princes ought to be contented with reasonable victories, and so to leave? The discourses of Thomas, it is true, were founded chiefly upon human policy, but there are points in them which indicate a better spirit; as for example, the religion of a prince whose amity is sought, is stated to be a matter for consideration. "A prince in battle," must also "examine whether his cause be lawful and just; for in a just cause shall God assist him." In a discourse concerning his majesty's outward affairs, we find the following paragraph. "Albeit that our quarrel is in God, and God our quarrel, who never faileth them that trust in him; yet forasmuch as wickedness reigneth in the midst of us, like as we should not mistrust the goodness of God, so ought we neither to neglect that policy which may help us to avoid the like captivity, that for wickedness happened to the elect people of Israel." Similar references to divine truths will not be found in political instructions at many periods of our history, and the reader will easily suppose that when such principles were recognised in private official documents, those of a public nature would not be deficient in their mention of Him who has declared, "By me kings reign."

The attendance of Cheke upon his royal pupil was interrupted for a time, the cause of which does not distinctly appear; but the fruits of his former instructions still remained. Among other interesting documents respecting king Edward, still in existence, is a journal, wherein are written down brief remarks concerning such affairs as from time to time came before him. Cheke is said to have advised him to keep a diary, observing, "That a dark and imperfect reflection upon affairs floating in the memory, was like words dispersed and insignificant; whereas a view of them in a book, was like the same words digested and disposed in good order, and so made significant." The king also kept in his own custody copies of all public records, and other matters which came under the consideration of the council.

Cheke returned to his attendance upon the king, early in 1550: he was in some danger of being involved in the protector's disgrace, but escaped the storm, and stood afterwards more secure in the royal favour. He used his increasing interest at court to favour religious and learned men, foreigners as well as English. Ridley, as we shall hereafter see, called him, "one of Christ's special advocates, and one of his principal proctors." Ascham also urged upon him the opportunity which he enjoyed, with Cecil and Cook, of favouring good matters relative either to religion or learning, and told him that they were expected to use these opportunities as they were able. Ascham's letters show that Cheke was not indifferent to these important subjects. The beneficial influence of Cheke also appeared from the kind reception given to Bucer, Fagius, and Martyr, when driven to England by the persecutions which followed the promulgation of the Interim in Germany. A number of letters and other documents which still exist, show the advantages which resulted to the English reformation from the assistance of these refugees, under whose advice many improvements were introduced into the revised service book.

Cranmer as well as Cheke encouraged the resort of the foreign protestants to England. On the decease of Bucer, application was made to Melancthon to supply his place; the king's death, however, intervened before a final arrangement was effected. Even foreigners who did not visit England were fully aware of the value of this pious king, as appears from many passages in their writings. Bullinger, in particular, addressed him in the preface to a decade of his sermons, in a manner which at once showed his own faithfulness, and his opinion of the christian principles of the monarch. He urged him, "To hold it as an undoubted truth that true prosperity was to be obtained by him no other ways, than by submitting himself and his whole kingdom to Christ, the highest Prince, and by framing all matters of religion and justice throughout his dominions according to the rule of God's word; not stirring one inch from that rule; propagating the kingdom of Christ, and trampling upon that of antichrist, as he had so happily begun." In another dedication he urges the king to proceed with firmness, and in the fear of God, not imitating the politic courses then adopted in Germany. The foreign protestants were anxious to engage the co-operation of Edward, and offered to wave some minor points of discipline if a general union could be effected. In order to counteract this, the romanists sent emissaries who pretended to be opposed to popery, while they were secretly supported by Gardiner in their attempts to excite discord in England.

The king was solicitous for the welfare and comfort of these learned refugees, who were a good deal inconvenienced by some manners and customs of England. Hearing that Bucer had suffered in health for the want of a stove (or heated room) which he had been accustomed to in Germany, he sent him twenty pounds to defray the expense of constructing one previously to the next winter. Bucer in return wrote a book as a new year's gift for the king. It was entitled, "Concerning the kingdom of Christ." A summary of the contents is given by Burnet. It contained much advice on the subject of reformation, and probably occasioned a general discourse on that subject, which the king wrote about the year 1551. Bucer and his countrymen were also a good deal annoyed by the papists, who still abounded in the universities. The king's esteem for these exiles further appeared by his desire to retain Peter Martyr when the city of Strasburg requested him to return to them. After Bucer's decease, kind attention was shown to the interests of his widow. The persecutions consequent upon the Interim, which had driven Bucer and his associates from their own countries, excited much sympathy among English protestants. There also was ground for apprehensions of the revival of popery at home. Under these circumstances, to the petition in the liturgy, "Give peace in our time," was added the response,

"Because there is none other that fighteth for us but thou, O Lord."

The political events of the reign of Edward VI. need only to be noticed very briefly in this sketch. The intrigues of the papists, combined with the popular feelings, which were excited by various recent changes affecting the state of society in England, led to commotions in several districts during the year 1549, particularly in Norfolk, Cornwall, and Devonshire. These were suppressed with considerable difficulty.* The duke of Somerset, though earnest for the doctrines as well as the outward advantages of the reformation, weakened his influence as lord protector, by various proceedings calculated to render him unpopular. His authority was also assailed by political rivals. One of these, his own brother, the lord admiral, a very unworthy character, endeavoured to supplant the protector with the king, by secretly supplying the latter with money, flattering his youthful vanity, and endeavouring to excite his evil passions. The political intrigues of the admiral at length called for severe measures, and he was condemned and executed as a traitor, in 1549. Before the close of that year, the protector himself was displaced from his office and imprisoned, chiefly by the intrigues of the earl of Warwick, afterwards the duke of Northumberland, who succeeded to the direction of public affairs, and outwardly adopted the measures of reformation pursued by Somerset, though with more worldly views. Somerset was pardoned, and released from confinement in the following year, but again engaging in the intrigues of those turbulent times, he was condemned and executed in January, 1552. The political changes in those days were seldom unattended with bloodshed, and usually were followed by numerous executions.

We resume the personal history of king Edward. The king, now about thirteen years of age, continued his studies. We find him at this time reading Aristotle's Ethics; the philosophical works of Cicero he had previously read. Both Greek and Latin were now become familiar to him. Nor was he less occupied in theological studies. The active part taken by Cheke in some of the public disputations with the romanists, is a sufficient proof that his pupil was interested in those subjects. In a letter to Sturmius, dated December, 1550, Ascham, speaking of the king, says, " that his nature equalled his fortune; but his virtue, or to speak as a christian, the manifold grace of God in him, exceeded both. He did to admiration outrun his age in his desires of the best learning, in his study of the truest religion, in his will, his judgment, and his constancy." The dowager queen of Scots, who visited the English court about the same time, said that she found more wisdom and solid judgment in young king Edward, than she would have looked for in any three princes that were in Europe.

* See Cranmer, p. 50. Becon, p. 209.

His favourite companion was Barnaby Fitzpatrick, a young gentleman of Ireland, brought up with him from childhood. In 1551, the youthful monarch sent his companion to Paris to attend the French court, that he might acquire knowledge which would be useful in future life. The anxiety Edward felt for his favourite's best interests is shown in a letter to him, dated December 20, 1551. It is as follows: " We have received your letters of the 8th of this present month, whereby we understand how you are well entertained, for which we are right glad, and also how you have been once to go on pilgrimage. For which cause we have thought good to advertise you, that hereafter, if any such chance happen, you shall desire leave to go to Mr. Pickering,* or to Paris for your business. And if that will not serve, declare to some man of estimation with whom you are best acquainted, that, as you are loth to offend the French king, because you have been so favourably used, so with safe conscience you cannot do any such thing, being brought up with me, and bound to obey my laws; also that you had commandment from me to the contrary. Yet if you are vehemently procured, you may go, as waiting on the king, not as intending to the abuse, nor willingly seeing the ceremonies, and so you look not on the mass. But in the mean season, regard the scripture, or some good book, and give no reverence to the mass at all. Furthermore remember, when you may conveniently be absent from the court, to tarry with sir William Pickering, to be instructed by him how to use yourself." After some further directions as to his conduct, the king tells him not to forget his learning, "chiefly reading of the scriptures." Fuller observes upon this and other letters of the king to Fitzpatrick, that familiar epistles communicate truth to posterity, presenting history unto us with a true face of things, though not in so fine a dress as other kinds of writings. Ascham, in one of his letters to Sturmius, speaks of the impression which must have been made in France by the duke of Suffolk and the other noble youths who had been educated with the king, and who had visited that country. He also mentions the abilities and acquirements of the princess Elizabeth in the highest terms.

About this period, a learned Italian, named Cardan, visited England on his return from Scotland to the continent. He had some interviews with the king, and has left the following testimony respecting the youthful monarch. "All the graces were combined in him. He possessed the knowledge of many languages while yet a child. In addition to English, his native tongue, he was well acquainted both with Latin and French, nor was he ignorant of the Greek, Italian, and Spanish, and perhaps of more. Nor was he ignorant of logic, of the principles of natural philosophy, or of music: he played well upon the lute. A beautiful specimen of mortality; his seriousness manifested royal majesty; his disposition was suitable to his exalted rank. In

* The English ambassador.

sum, that child was so educated, possessed such abilities, and caused such expectations, that he appeared a miracle. This is not said as mere rhetorical expressions, nor does it exceed the truth, but in fact falls short of it." Cardan adds, " He was a marvellous boy ; he had learned seven languages, as I was told. With his own, French, and Latin, he was thoroughly acquainted." He also relates a conversation he had with Edward, in which the latter showed that he was not to be satisfied with the imperfect statements then made on astronomical subjects.

The king's continued attention to matters of state is described by Fox, who relates that he was as well informed with respect to his affairs beyond sea, as those who were personally concerned in the negotiations. Also, that in the reception of ambassadors he would give answers to every part of their orations, to the great wonder of those that heard him, doing that in his tender years, by himself, which many princes at their mature age are seldom wont to do but by others. He was very anxious for the due administration of justice, arranging such hours and times as he considered would best forward the despatch of poor men's causes, without long delays and attendance. His attention to economy is manifest from many documents; it did not arise from a sordid desire of accumulation, but from a wish to spare his subjects as much as possible, and at the same time to extricate himself from a heavy load of debt which consumed his pecuniary resources.

He took great pleasure in active exercises, particularly riding, leaping, and shooting with the long-bow, as appears from his own journal, as well as the records of others.

The reign of Edward VI. furnishes the rare instance of a prince who could bear to hear truths faithfully told, and who listened to preachers that did not hesitate to speak to him with sincerity and truth. Fox says, " Few sermons or none in his court, especially in the lord protector's time, but he would be at them." Again, " Never was he present at any such discourses but he would take notes of them with his own hand." Latimer's sermons supply several instances of bold, uncompromising fidelity ; he preached at court during several lent seasons in succession. In a discourse preached by Lever in 1550, we find equal faithfulness. It appears that there were some about the court who endeavoured to turn the king from his laudable studies and pursuits to the usual light and frivolous pastimes of courts; this indeed is plainly shown by his own journal. Lever boldly adverted to the subject in the following terms :

" It is not unlike, but if your majesty, with your council, speak unto your nobles for provision now to be made for the poor people, ye shall find some, that setting afore your eyes the hardness of the matter, the tenderness of your years, and the wonderful charges that should be requisite, will move and counsel you to quiet yourself, to take your ease, yea, to take your pastime, in hawking, hunting, and gaming." And then turning his speech to such a one, he thus accosted him, " Thou hast no taste nor savour how delicious God is unto a pure conscience in godly exercise of good works. But all that thou regardest and feelest is voluptuous pleasures in worldly vanities; and therefore thou dost not perceive, how that they which be endowed with a special grace of God, may find more pleasure and pastime in godly governance, to keep together and save simple men, than in hawking and hunting, to chase and kill wild beasts. Yea, a godly king shall find more pleasure in casting lots for Jonah, to try out offenders which trouble the ship of this commonwealth, than in casting dice at hazard, to allow and maintain by his example such things as should not be suffered in a commonwealth. Yea, surely a good king shall take far more delight in edifying with comfort, and decking with good order, the congregation of his people, the church and house of God, the heavenly city of Jerusalem, than in building such houses as seem gay and gorgeous, and are indeed but vile earth, stones, timber, and clay. Such like answer ought your majesty and all noblemen to make, if ye find any of your counsellors more carnal than spiritual, more worldly than godly."

Knox also preached with equal faithfulness in 1552, shortly before the removal of the court from Westminster, boldly reproving the ill-conduct of the duke of Northumberland and the marquess of Winchester, even to their faces, as he states in his Faithful Admonition. Instead of incurring the royal displeasure by this conduct, a living in the city of London was offered him; he declined it from scruples respecting conformity, but he was still retained as one of the six itinerating preachers appointed by the king. Latimer was too aged and infirm to undertake the regular discharge of public duties; but we find him dwelling with archbishop Cranmer, and as a gift of twenty pounds, then a considerable sum, was ordered for him by the king at an early part of his reign, we may be assured that a suitable provision was continued to him.

Strype has given a minute and painful delineation of vices common at that period. It must be remembered they arose from principles implanted in the days of popery. The tares which had been plentifully sown now were apparent. To these evils the reformers continually refer with much sorrow; they doubtless tended to bring down divine displeasure upon the land. The profligate conduct of many among the nobility, even of some who professedly were attached to the reformation, shows most clearly the effects of divine grace, which alone enabled this pious monarch and others to resist the contagion of evil example.

Some good, however, could be said of the English nobility. Ascham, writing to Sturmius, says that the nobles of England never were more attached to learning. He adds, " Our illustrious king excels those of his own age, and even passes belief in understanding, industry, perseverance, and erudition. I do not learn this from the report of others, but from my own personal knowledge—and to witness it has afforded me much pleasure. I can say that the virtues appear to have taken up their abode in him." In reference to his listening to good counsels, Cheke, in a letter to the duke of Somerset, says, "Wherefore, as his majesty hath always learned, so I trust he laboureth daily to avoid the ground of all error, that self-pleasing which the Greeks do call *Philautia*; when a man delighteth in his own reason and despiseth other men's counsel, and thinketh no man's foresight to be so good as his, nor any man's judgment compared to his own."

Considerable anxiety prevailed respecting a suitable matrimonial alliance for the king. A union with Mary, the young queen of Scotland, had originally been designed. After this was relinquished, some progress was made in a treaty with the royal family of France—the French king at that time was in some respects a favourer of the reformation; but the English protestants in general were much against a foreign alliance. Latimer spoke with his accustomed plainness from the pulpit, advising the king "to choose one that is of God, that is, of the household of faith; and such a one as the king can find in his heart to love, and lead his life in pure and chaste espousage with. Let him choose a wife that fears God. Let him not choose a proud wanton; one full only of rich treasures and worldly pomp." Besides the proposed marriage with a French princess, which at one period was in a considerable degree of forwardness, alliances were at other times proposed with a daughter of the duke of Somerset, and with the lady Jane Grey. John ab Ulmis, writing to Bullinger, in June, 1551, respecting lady Jane, says, "A report becomes common, and is current among the nobility, that the king is to espouse this illustrious young female. If that should come to pass, how happy the union! and how beneficial to the church may we expect it to prove!"

In 1552, his beloved tutor was afflicted with the sweating sickness, a contagious disease which carried off considerable numbers. The king was anxious for Cheke's recovery. He sought it by earnest prayer. When told by the physicians that they despaired of his tutor's recovery, he replied, "No, Cheke will not die this time, I begged his life this morning in my prayer, and obtained it." Nor was this confident expectation disappointed. The recovery of Cheke was regarded by the pious reformers as a national mercy. They knew not the darker hour which approached, both with respect to the tutor and his royal pupil.

In the year 1552, the king was attacked by the measles and the small-pox. From the effects of these maladies he never recovered, though in a letter to Fitzpatrick he speaks of himself as fully restored to health. In April that year, he removed to Greenwich for the change of air, and continued to reside there the short remainder of his life, with the exception of a progress in the summer. During the ensuing winter he was afflicted with a cough, and symptoms of consumption appeared: but he was not less intent upon the welfare of his kingdom as to matters connected with religion. We find, early in 1553, a catechism set forth by the royal authority, which is generally known as " King Edward's Catechism." This valuable summary of the doctrines of the reformation is generally supposed to have been the work of dean Nowell, who enlarged it after the accession of queen Elizabeth; it will be found in the present collection. The king was earnest to procure uniformity as to doctrine, and one of his latest memorandums connected with the public concerns of religion has distinct reference to this point. With this view he had articles of religion prepared, which are very similar to the thirty-nine articles, set forth in the reign of queen Elizabeth. At that period the principle of full toleration in matters of religion was not understood or recognised even by protestants. But an important step towards religious liberty may be here remarked; although a declaration of assent to these articles was required of all who were public teachers in the church, the royal command to this effect did not direct any compulsory measures to enforce subscription, nor any severe proceedings, unless the articles were openly withstood or gainsaid, in which case the council were to be informed, that such further order might be taken as appeared requisite. Upon this principle the king seems to have proceeded with regard to his sister the princess Mary, as though he went so far as to prevent the performance of the mass at her court, he records in his journal that upon her answering that her soul was God's, and her faith she would not change, nor dissemble her opinion with contrary doings; it was told her that " he constrained not her faith, but willed her not as a king to rule, but as a subject to obey; and that her example might breed too much inconvenience." How different were Mary's proceedings towards her sister Elizabeth when she succeeded to the throne! The alternate obstinacy and compliances of Mary in her correspondence with her father and brother on this subject, appear from her letters yet extant, some of which evince mental reservation worthy of the followers of Loyola; doubtless they were written under the counsel of her spiritual advisers. These discussions with his sister evidently were injurious to the king's health.

The king's illness gave rise to ambitious projects on the part of the bold and unprincipled duke of Northumberland. He grasped at the succession to the crown, and resolved to secure it, if possible, to his own family. His designs were furthered by the king's sincere attachment to the truth, which made him deeply apprehensive of the consequences, if a bigoted papist like his sister Mary should succeed to the throne. He therefore listened to a plan suggested by Northumberland, whereby both the king's sisters should be passed by as illegitimate, on the ground of the marriages of their mothers having been declared void, and by passing over other branches who had a nearer right to the throne, the succession should be settled upon the lady Jane Grey, who, as Northumberland had arranged, was to marry one of his sons, the lord Guildford Dudley. Her mother, lady Frances Brandon, duchess of Suffolk, was grandaughter of Henry VII.

As the spring of 1553 advanced, reports of the king's death were frequent; the anxiety of the nation at large appears from many passages in the writings of the reformers. Feeling his strength decline, Edward became increasingly anxious to secure a protestant successor. He drew up a paper with his own hand, directing the order of succession to the throne, by which the crown devolved upon the lady Jane Grey. An instrument was then prepared by which the principal counsellors declared their assent to this settlement. The judges hesitated for some time, but, with one exception, were finally induced to consent. Northumberland's conduct was such as to make them apprehensive of personal violence. He urged this measure forward; archbishop Cranmer opposed it, and argued much with the king against such a proceeding, in the presence of two of the nobility. He also desired to have a private conference with Edward upon the subject, but this was not allowed, and the duke of Northumberland told him at the council board, that "it became him not to speak to the king as he had done." Cranmer for some time refused to be a party to this instrument, and urged much in behalf of the lady Mary's right. He was silenced, and told that the judges and king's counsel learned in the law were of opinion the alteration could lawfully be made. Cranmer then absented himself from the council, and still refused to sign till the king personally entreated him not to stand out. At length his affection for his royal master, and the authority of the principal law officers prevailed; he reluctantly added his signature. Only one of the judges, justice Hales, refused his assent; but this did not save him from being an object of persecution and suffering in the ensuing reign. The regular instrument, signed by the king and his counsellors, bears date June 21.

Another public document completed by Edward at this time, excites more pleasing reflections. At the commencement of his last sickness, bishop Ridley preached before him, and said much upon the duty of all persons to be charitable according to their ability, especially those who were of high rank. After this sermon, the king sent for the bishop, and commanded him to sit down, and be covered. He then went over the principal arguments mentioned in the sermon, desiring Ridley, that as he had shown what was his duty, he would now show in what manner he should perform it. Ridley was affected, even to tears, at this pleasing conduct of the king, and asked leave to consult with the mayor and aldermen of London upon the subject. Edward approved of this, and desired that they would consider the best manner of relieving the poor.

They did so; and Ridley returned in a few days with a plan, dividing the poor into three parts; the poor by impotency, the poor by casualty, and the thriftless poor; again subdividing them into nine classes. After this, the king ordered the Grey Friars monastery, with the lands belonging to it, to be endowed as a school, (now Christ's Hospital;) St. Bartholomew's for sick and maimed persons; Bridewell and Bethlehem, for idle, dissolute characters, and the insane; provision also was made for the relief of poor housekeepers. He hastened the appropriation of these endowments to the laudable purposes just mentioned; and on signing the charters, upon the 26th of June, 1553, when he was so weak as scarcely to be able to hold the pen, he thanked God for sparing his life until he had executed his design. The reader will recollect that all these noble foundations have continued to the present time, as well as several free schools founded by him.

The above is the account given respecting the origin of these noble foundations, by bishop Ridley himself to Grafton the historian. A letter from bishop Ridley to secretary Cecil, contains some further information respecting one of these establishments. He writes thus on the 29th of May: "Good Mr. Cecil, I must be suitor to you, in our Master Christ's cause: I beseech you be good unto him. The matter is this, alas, he hath been too long abroad, as you do know, without lodging, in the streets of London, both hungry, naked, and cold. Now, thanks be to almighty God, the citizens are willing to refresh him, and to greet him with both meat, drink, clothing, and firing; but alas, sir, they lack lodging for him, for in some one house I dare say they are fain to lodge three families under one roof. Sir, there is a wide, large, empty house of the king's majesty's, called Bridewell, that would wonderfully well serve to lodge Christ in, if he might find such good friends in the court to procure in his cause. Surely I have such a good opinion in the king's majesty, that if Christ had such faithful and trusty friends that would heartily speak for him, he should undoubtedly succeed at the king's majesty's hands. Sir, I have promised my brethren the citizens to move you in this matter, because I do take you for one that feareth God, and would that Christ should be no more abroad in the streets. There is a rumour that one goeth about to buy that house of his majesty to pull it down. If there be any such thing, for God's sake speak you in our Master's name. I have written to M. Gates more at large in this matter, I join you with him and all that love and look for Christ's final benediction at the latter day. If M. Cheke is almost recovered, God be blessed. Were he amongst you I would surely make him in this business one of Christ's special advocates, or rather one of his principal protectors, and surely I would not be sent away. And thus I wish you in Christ, and well to fare."*

* Ridley's anxiety to promote these good works, appears from a sermon of Lever's, preached in 1550. He says that, "a number of poor,

The king now evidently drew near his end. When there appeared no longer to be hopes of life, the physicians were dismissed, and some remedies suggested by a female empiric were tried, but without success. The physicians were recalled in a few days, but the royal sufferer rapidly declined, and on the 6th of July breathed his last. "His manner of death," as the council reported to sir Thomas Hoby, "was such toward God, as assureth us that his soul is in place of eternal rest."

Fox relates, "About three hours before his death, this godly child, his eyes being closed, speaking to himself, and thinking that none heard him, made this prayer which follows:

"'Lord God, deliver me out of this miserable and wretched life, and take me among thy chosen. Howbeit, not my will, but thy will be done. Lord, I commit my spirit to thee. O Lord! thou knowest how happy it were for me to be with thee, yet for thy chosen's sake send me life and health, that I may truly serve thee. O my Lord God bless thy people, and save thine inheritance. O Lord God, save thy chosen people of England. O my Lord God, defend this realm from papistry, and maintain the true religion, that I and my people may praise thy holy name, for thy Son Jesus Christ's sake.'

"Then turned he his face, and seeing who was by him, said unto them, 'Are ye so nigh? I thought ye had been further off.' Then Dr. Owen, one of his physicians, who gave this account, to satisfy him, said, 'We heard you speak to yourself, but what you said we know not.' He then (after his fashion) smilingly said. 'I was praying to God.' The last words of his pangs were these: 'I am faint, Lord, have mercy upon me, and take my spirit.' And thus he yielded up the ghost."

The untimely decease of Edward, and the political circumstances of that day, caused reports to be spread of his having fallen a victim to poison. For this there was no real foundation. The opinions which then prevailed are stated in a letter of Terentian, an Italian, who had accompanied Peter Martyr to England, (Ep. Helv. Reform. lxxvi.) He says, "On the 6th of July died that holy Josiah, our earthly hope; of consumption as the physicians state, of poison as is said, for the papists spread this report that they may heap every sort of odium upon Northumberland, and, to say the truth, there are considerable grounds for suspicion; but if I may say what I think, I would rather believe the papists themselves to be the authors of such wickedness, for they manifest no appearance of sorrow, and no inquiry is made respecting such a crime."

feeble, halt, blind, lame, sickly, with idle vagabonds and dissembling caitiffs mixed among them, lay, and crept begging in the miry streets of London and Westminster,"—adding, "but now I trust that a good overseer, a godly bishop I mean, will see that they in these two cities shall have their need relieved and faults corrected, to the good ensample of all other towns and cities."

Strype says, "His funeral was solemnized at Westminster, Aug. 8, 1553. Whereat were expressed, by all sorts of people, such signs of sorrow for his death, by weepings and lamentations, as the like was scarce ever seen or heard upon the like occasion."

Burnet relates, "Day, bishop of Chichester, preached the funeral sermon for king Edward. It was intended by queen Mary that all the burial rites should have been according to the old forms that were before the reformation. But Cranmer opposed this vigorously, and insisted upon it, that as the king himself had been a zealous promoter of the reformation, so the English service was then established by law. Upon this he stoutly hindered any other way of officiating, and himself performed all the offices of the burial; to which he joined the solemnity of a communion. In these, it may be easily imagined, he did every thing with a very lively sorrow; since as he had loved the king beyond expression, so he could not but look on his funeral as the burial of the reformation, and in particular as a step to his own."

Bale relating the above, remarks how much Edward had the welfare of his people at heart, and says that he had often observed him at public prayers when the words, O Lord save thy people, were repeated, joining most fervently with clasped hands and eyes lifted up to heaven.

To enlarge upon the excellences of this our "British Josiah," would not be difficult, but it is unnecessary. Enough has been related to show, that although his rank and situation exposed him to many temptations, he was preserved from evil, and ever anxious for the discharge of his peculiar duties. But the most important feature in his character is, that he was a follower of the truth, "a saint of God," one of whom the world was not worthy.

Many letters and other writings of Edward VI. have been preserved. The greater part of these have been printed by Burnet and Strype. Though interesting as illustrations of his character, they are not desirable for the present collection. The treatise on the papal supremacy is a specimen of his productions; it is supposed to have been written by this prince at the age of twelve years. A sufficient memorial of Edward VI. will never be wanting so long as the protestant faith is professed in England.

The original of his journal is in the British Museum; it has been printed by Burnet, but there are very few observations of the king on the events he notes down. One of these notices refers to the execution of the unhappy Joan Bocher.* Another contains evidence

---

* For some account of the undeserved sufferings of this friendless and persecuted female, see life of Cranmer, p. 49. The entry respecting her in king Edward's journal does not notice the interference which the archbishop is said to have made on this occasion. It is as follows: "May 2, 1549. Joan Bocher, otherways called Joan of Kent, was burned for holding that Christ was not incarnate of the virgin Mary; being condemned before, but kept in hope of conversion; and the 30th

of the deceitful course adopted by bishop Gardiner. "The duke of Somerset, with five others of the council, went to the bishop of Winchester, to whom he made this answer: 'I having deliberately seen the Book of Common Prayer, although I would not have made it so myself, yet I find such things in it as satisfieth my conscience, and therefore I will both execute it myself, and also see others my parishioners to do it.'" The journal contains various notices, which show the interest Edward took in the affairs of the protestants in Germany, and the anxiety caused by the designs of the Romanists respecting the princess Mary; but, though valuable as an historical document, it contains very little relating to the internal progress of the reformation. The principal circumstances relative to the fall and execution of the duke of Somerset are mentioned, and the active endeavours of Northumberland to occupy the young king's attention by a succession of amusements, while the death of his excellent uncle was urged forward, are very apparent. From memorandums written by the king still extant, it is evident that in allowing the proceedings against his uncle to go forward, he considered that he was sacrificing his personal regard and feelings for the due course of justice and the welfare of the kingdom. Hayward describes him as often lamenting the unhappy situation in which the necessity for consenting to his uncle's death placed him.

The extended circulation of the bible must ever be considered as one of the principal glories of king Edward's reign. The free use of the scriptures now was permitted to all; and no less than thirty-four editions of the whole Bible, or of the New Testament, were printed during the six years Edward VI. was upon the throne, besides separate editions of detached parts, and innumerable other writings setting forth the truths of the gospel.

Among the most valuable memorials of his reign, the first book of Homilies may be mentioned. These discourses have been so often printed, and are circulated in so many forms, that it is unnecessary to advert to them further, or to include any portion of them in the present collection. Nowell's Catechism, in its original form, supplies an important summary of the doctrines of the reformation, as set forth at this period, and as such it is given in this work. A selection of prayers from the Primer authorized by king Edward, also shows the principles of truth then taught in our land. The serious reader cannot peruse them without pleasure and profit, and they may without impropriety be considered as productions of the youthful monarch, though not immediately from his pen.

of April the bishop of London and the bishop of Ely were to persuade her; but she withstood them, and reviled the preacher that preached at her death." Deep indeed must have been the dreadful prejudices that authorized religious persecution, when king Edward could thus record such an event. The preacher was a dissembling papist, Dr. Scory; the sufferer told him to go and read the scriptures, and we cannot be surprised that she expressed herself in strong terms.

## SOME PARTICULARS OF SIR JOHN CHEKE.

A few additional particulars respecting sir John Cheke may be added to those contained in the foregoing account of his royal pupil, as he was an important character among the British reformers. He was born in Cambridge, in 1514, where he afterwards studied, and became very eminent for his knowledge in the learned languages, particularly the Greek tongue, which till then had been almost wholly neglected. He was appointed tutor to prince Edward in 1544. During the reign of his royal pupil, he ever exerted his influence in promoting true religion and learning, and was often called to discharge duties of importance.

On the accession of queen Mary, Cheke was imprisoned for the part he had taken relative to lady Jane Grey, but was pardoned and liberated in September, 1554. Foreseeing the rapid approach of romish persecution he procured leave to travel, but remaining at Strasburg, and associating with the protestant exiles, his whole property was confiscated.

Early in 1556, he went to Brussels to see his wife, being encouraged to venture thither by a treacherous invitation from two of queen Mary's counsellors. With the credulity then common, even in some of the most distinguished characters of the age, he had recourse to astrological calculations, and being encouraged thereby, proceeded on his journey. It is unnecessary to make any observations upon the delusions of that art, the fate of Cheke is a sufficient commentary thereon. By order of king Philip he was waylaid, seized, and conveyed to the nearest port, where he was put on board a ship and brought to the Tower of London. It soon appeared that religion was the cause of this treatment. Feckenham and others were sent to reason with him, and he was unable to withstand the usual argument of "turn or burn." After some conferences with cardinal Pole, he submitted to return to the church of Rome. The triumph of the papists was great, while they took every occasion to mortify their new convert. They obliged Cheke to be continually with their leading men, and even to be present at the examinations and condemnations of several protestants. But Cheke, although he thus manifested his frailty like many others, was not like them hardened in his shame. Remorse and vexation of spirit preyed upon him; he pined away, and died in September, 1557.

Strype has minutely recorded the particulars of Cheke's life and writings. We may add an extract from one of his letters to his royal pupil, printed by Harrington; it was written during his sickness, already mentioned, when his recovery was despaired of. He thus urges attention to the most important concerns: " Because I am departing, my sovereign lord, unto the King of all kings, Almighty God, and must by his appointment leave you, whom of long time I have done my best to bring up in virtue and good learning; and you are now coming to a government of yourself, in which state I pray God you may always be served with them that will faithfully, truly, and plainly give you counsel, I have thought it my duty, for a memory of my last will, and for a token of my well-wishing unto you, which now remains with me as it has heretofore done—to require you, yea, and in God's behalf to charge you, that, forasmuch as years both have and will diminish in you the fear of man, to have yet before your eyes continually the fear of God. By the which if you do not direct, order, and temper all your doings and sayings, be you well assured neither to have good success in the great charge that He hath committed to you, neither in the end to enjoy that joyful place which is promised to them that fear him For if God do extremely punish men of low estate, and of low degree, for wanting of that necessary jewel, which in scripture hath so many promises, how severely will he punish kings and princes failing therein, in whom the lack thereof must needs be perilous both to themselves and to the commonwealth." After other cautions and serious admonitions, Cheke urges, " For your divinity, I would wish you would diligently continue the reading of the New Testament, with Sapientia, Ecclesiasticus, and the Proverbs."

To the above we may subjoin an extract of a letter written by Cheke in 1549 relating to a charge in private life, his ward, mistress Penelope Pye, daughter of sir William Pye.

"You are to have in mind whose you are: first, the child of God; secondly, the daughter of sir William Pye; thirdly, the charge of your father's friends. Each of these respects hath sundry considerations, both of comforts and helps that they minister, of duties that they lay upon you, and of means and orders how to use them.

" In that you pertain to God, these are your comforts—that he is able to defend and uphold you; that his purpose of preserving you is constant and from eternity; that his foresight for you cannot be deceived; that his care for you never ceaseth; that his promises are infallible; and that whatsoever happeneth is by his ordinance; and whatsoever happeneth by his ordinance, howsoever it seemeth to sense, it is indeed good for you that are his; that he shall continually guide you, he shall prosperously bless you, he shall eternally save you.

" Your duties to him are, that you depend wholly upon him; that you have full faith and affiance in him; that you reverently love him; that you lovingly fear him; that you honour him, and frame yourself as he himself has appointed; that you make his commandments the rule of your life, and charity the mark that you are his. The means of attaining and using these, stand in hearing the word of God, in prayer, and in conversation.

" In hearing the word of God, whether it be by the voice of others pronouncing, or by yourself reading, you are ever to think that God speaketh to you. In prayer, either public or private, you are to remember that you speak to God. In conversatio" either open or secret, in close place or in hidden thought, you are not to forget that you walk in the eye and sight of God. In hearing God speak to you in his word, know that He speaketh that made you, that seeth you, that shall judge you, that hath power to damn and save you; whose word is, to the believing and obedient, the savour of life unto life; but to the unbelieving and disobedient, it is the savour of death unto death; therefore hear it humbly with reverence. Know, that he speaketh to you that loved you, that chose you, that adopted you, that redeemed you, that preserveth you daily, and will save you for ever; therefore hear it with love and joyfulness. Know, that he speaketh to you that is perfectly wise, infallibly true, and unchangeably constant; therefore hear it with heedfulness, belief, and assurance. Know, that he speaketh that will have account how you heard him; therefore hear it with care, that you may receive it to fruit. This that you well do, do it often and with diligence.

"In prayer, when you speak to God, know that you have attained the honour to be admitted to the presence and speech of the unspeakable Majesty, infinitely passing the highest princes; therefore pray with humbleness. Know, that you speak to your Father that loveth you, to him that calleth you, to him that hath promised to hear you, to him that joyeth in hearing you; therefore pray with love and confidence. Know, that you speak to him that understandeth the bottom of your heart, and regardeth none but hearty prayer; pray, therefore, with a clean heart, which he seeth; with a true, unfeigned heart, which he understandeth; with a loving heart, which he embraceth; with a bold, assured heart, which he encourageth; and with a whole heart, which he challengeth.

"In your conversation, know that it extendeth to God, to yourself, and to others: to God, in the rules of religion; to yourself, in the precepts of virtue; to others, in the duties of obedience, kindness, truth, and charity.

"Of religion, you are to keep those rules that God in his own word hath delivered, knowing that none other can please God; and therein remember a wise and godly meaning of your late natural father, who heartily wished that, without spending time in variance of questions, the people might be diligently instructed in two things, the one, of sufficiency of salvation by Christ alone; the other, the sufficiency of doctrine in the only word of God."

He tells her, "For the hiding of sins, there is no covering but God's mercy; and the mercy of God, as it is gotten with humble repentance and true faith, so is it lost by desperation, and driven away by presumption." Cheke then proceeds to urge those duties which were peculiarly incumbent upon her, cautioning her against the papists, and adding, "In all your doings, therefore, and in all advices, either given you by others or conceived by yourself, cast this in mind, to think what your father would have liked had he lived."

# KING EDWARD THE SIXTH

## HIS OWN ARGUMENTS AGAINST THE POPE'S SUPREMACY.

WHEREIN SEVERAL POPISH DOCTRINES AND PRACTICES CONTRARY TO GOD'S WORD ARE ANIMADVERTED ON, AND THE MARKS OF ANTICHRIST ARE APPLIED TO THE POPE OF ROME.

*Translated out of the original, written with the king's own hand in French, and still preserved.*

---

Edward the Sixth, by the Grace of God, King of England, France, and Ireland, Defender of the Faith, and on Earth, after God, Head of the Church of England, and of Ireland.

To his most dear and well-beloved Uncle, Edward, Duke of Somerset, Governor of his Person, and Protector of his Kingdoms, Countries, and Subjects.

AFTER having considered, my dear and well-beloved uncle, how much they displease God, who waste all their time on the follies and vanities of this world, spending it in trifling sports and diversions, from whence comes no profit or benefit to themselves, or mankind; I have determined to employ myself about the doing something, which will be, as I hope, profitable to myself, and acceptable unto you. Having then considered, that we see many papists not only curse us, but call and name us heretics, because we have forsaken their antichrist, and its traditions, and followed the light which God hath been pleased to afford us; we are inclined to write something to defend us against their contumelies, and lay them, as it is just, upon their own backs. For they call us heretics, but alas! they are so themselves, whilst they forsake the pure voice of the gospel, and follow their own imaginations; as is most evident from Boniface the third, who thought, when he was made the universal bishop, that the falling away, which St. Paul speaks of in his second epistle to the Thessalonians, and second chapter, had happened in himself. For St. Paul saith, We beseech you, brethren, by the coming of our Lord, that ye be not soon shaken in mind, or be troubled, neither by spirit, nor by word, nor by letter, as that the day of Christ is at hand. Let no man deceive you by any means; for that day shall not come, except there come a falling away first, and that man of sin be revealed, the son of perdition; who exalteth himself above all that is called God, so that he, as God, sitteth in the temple of God, &c.

Notwithstanding, he followed his own proud imaginations and fancies, and did not forsake his errors, which he knew to be very wicked.

Considering then by your life and actions, that you have a great affection to the Divine word, and the sincere religion, I dedicate this present work to you, praying you to take it in good part. God give you his perpetual grace, and show his benignity upon you for ever.

*From our Palace at Westminster, in London, this last day of August,* 1549.[*]

---

[*] From the date set down by himself, it appears that the following treatise was written by king Edward when only twelve years of age. He began it December 13th, 1548, and finished it March 14th following.

A

## SMALL TREATISE

AGAINST THE

# PRIMACY OF THE POPE.

We may easily find and perceive by the experience of the world, that human nature is disposed to all evils, and entangled by all manner of vices. For what nation is there in the earth in which there is not some vice, and many disorders? And principally in this age, because now there is such an exaltation of the great empire of antichrist; which is the source of all evil, the fountain of all abomination, and true son of the devil. For when God had sent his only Son to heal our infirmities, and to reconcile the world unto himself by his death; the devil instantly changed the institutions of Christ into human traditions, and perverted the holy scriptures to his purposes and designs, by his minister the pope. And therefore, if the astrologers, who maintain that all things shall return to their own elements, say a truth, the pope shall descend into hell; for he cannot belong unto God, or be his servant, whilst, under the pretence of religion, and the command of God, he usurps unto himself the authority of Christ, as appears in all his works. Therefore it seemed best to me, in this little book, first to condemn the papacy, and afterwards the doctrine of the pope. Though I am not ignorant that it is a difficult task, because there are many that will contradict it: notwithstanding, we will condemn the supremacy of the pope; from these following reasons.

## THE FIRST PART.

First then, whereas the papists say, that Rome is the mother of all other churches, and therefore the bishop of

Rome ought to be superior to all other bishops, I answer, that is impossible; because the first promise was made unto the Jews: now Rome was then heathen, and Jerusalem was christian; for St. Paul, writing to the Romans, says, Through their fall, salvation is come unto the Gentiles.

And because the papists cannot prove Rome to have been the mother of all the other churches, they therefore say the bishop of Rome hath received his power from St. Peter: to whom had been given the same authority with Christ, and remains in the said bishop of Rome to this day; which they endeavour to prove out of these following texts, Thou art Peter, and upon this rock I will build my church, saith Christ; and a little after, And I will give thee the keys of the kingdom of heaven; and they allege that other place of scripture, where Peter says to Christ, Lord, thou knowest that I love thee: saying, that he that loves Christ is the chiefest, and Peter loving Christ more than any of the other apostles loved him, is thereby the chief and principal of the apostles.

Again, they affirm that he only was commanded to feed the sheep of Christ, and to be the fisher of men; and that he was the first speaker, and made answer to Jesus, Behold, here are two swords; from whence the papists conclude, that Peter had a temporal and a spiritual sword.

They allege also some human reasons, that as the bees have one king, so all christians ought to have one pope. And that as there was of old amongst the Jews, a principal priest or bishop, as Moses and Aaron, so now it is necessary there should be a bishop of the bishops.

Here are two great falsehoods in these few words: the one is, that the authority and supremacy over the church was given to St. Peter: the other, that Peter was at Rome.

To the first, where they say that that authority was given him by these words, Thou art Peter, &c. I answer, that if you remark the preceding and following words in that chapter of the gospel, you will find that Christ did not speak of Peter, as he was barely a man, but as he was a believer. For the foregoing words are, how Peter had said, Thou art the Son of God: by which it is evident, that Christ did not say, that Peter was the foundation of the church, but spoke of the faith of Peter. The following words declare how that Christ called Peter, Satan; but the church of God is not founded upon Satan, therefore it is not founded upon Peter: for if the church was founded upon St. Peter, it would have a weak foundation: and like that house which was built on a sandy foundation, which could not stand long, but, the floods came, and the winds blew, and beat upon that house; and it fell. In like manner would the church fall, if it had so poor a foundation. By which one may see that these words in the text, Thou art Peter, and upon this stone will I build my church, must not be understood of Peter, but of the faith of Peter, upon which the church is founded. But he was a frail and weak vessel, and denied Christ thrice.

Their second text is, that the keys of heaven were given to St. Peter. To which I answer, That the keys were given not only to Peter, but also to the other apostles. And by this argument I answer, that he was not principal; because the rest received the same authority of the keys, that was committed to him. On which account St. Paul calls St. Peter the pillar, not the foundation of the church; his companion, not his governor, Gal. ii. And what are the keys of heaven? The authority of pardoning sins? No, it is the preaching of the gospel of God the Father, the gospel, I say, of God; not the pope's or devil's. And as when a door is open, every one who will, may enter therein; so when God sent his gospel, he opened truth, which is the gate of heaven: and gave unto men an understanding of the scriptures, which if they obeyed, they should thereby be saved, 2 Cor. ii. By which we see that the gospel and the truth of the scriptures are the only gates that conduct men to the kingdom of God.

Whence St. Paul says, Rom. x. Whosoever shall call upon the name of the Lord, shall be saved: how then shall they call on him in whom they have not believed? And how shall they believe in him of whom they have not heard? And how shall they hear without a preacher? And a little after, he saith, So then faith cometh by hearing, and hearing by the word of God. And in the fourth chapter to the Romans, he also saith, But to him that worketh not, but believeth on Him that justifieth the ungodly, his faith is counted for righteousness. Moreover, we will prove that the preaching of the gospel is the key of heaven: in the tenth chapter to the Romans Paul affirms that, Whoever calls upon the name of the Lord, shall be saved; and that the preaching of the gospel is the door that leads to the invocation of the name of God; whence it follows, that the preaching of the gospel is the way and entrance of salvation.

Again, Paul affirms that faith justifies, and that the preaching of the gospel causes faith, which I have showed before, whence it follows that the true preaching of the word is the door and entrance to justification. Like as ground which is sowed may produce fruit, if the seed be not cast into ground which is full of thistles, or thorns, or stones; and yet although it be sowed in such ground, it will a little meliorate the earth. So, if the word of God be sowed in the hearts of honest people, or such as have a zeal for truth, it will confirm them in all goodness; but if any be obstinate and perverse, they cannot impute the fault unto the scriptures, which is really in themselves.

Therefore we ought to do our utmost endeavours to cause the gospel to be preached throughout all the world; as it is written, All power is given unto me in heaven and in earth: go ye therefore, and teach all nations, baptizing them in my name, Matt. xxviii. Mark xvi. Luke xxiv.

Since then it is proved that the keys of heaven is the authority of preaching; and that the authority of preaching was given to all the apostles, I cannot see how, by that text, any more authority was given to Peter than to the other disciples: and St. Paul says, he himself was not a whit behind the very chiefest apostles.

Then, if he said true, St. Peter was not above him: and if I were asked which of them was the better, I should say Paul, because he preached more than they all.

But we ought to account certainly, that the Spirit of God was poured out upon them all; and that the same Spirit of God which filled St. Peter, filled also St. Paul: from whence may be proved, that neither of them was superior to the other.

Again, the papists say, that after Christ was raised from the dead, he asked who loved him, and that Peter answered, he loved him, and therefore, say they, he was the chief apostle.

By which reason, every good man ought to have the supremacy over every other, because each good and pious person loves God; for it is the duty and office of every true christian. Now the question is not, whether Peter was faithful, pious, good, a holy and true christian? but whether he was principal, head, governor, and king, above and over the rest of the apostles, and ministers of Jesus Christ?

For, if the pope would have the authority of St. Peter, which was to preach, I would be content to give it him. But he regards but little the precept of God; for Jesus departed into a mountain alone, when he perceived the Jews would make him a king and emperor: and the pope by wrong, or violence, or deceit, hath made all nations subject unto him.

Jesus wore a crown of thorns, and a purple robe was thrown upon him in derision, and all the multitude mocked and spit upon him—but the pope decks himself with a triple crown, and is adored by kings, princes, emperors, and all estates of persons. Jesus washed his disciples' feet—and kings kiss the feet of the pope. Jesus paid tribute—but the pope receives, and pays none. Jesus opened his mouth and taught the people—the pope takes his ease and rest in his castle of St. Angelo. Jesus healed all diseases—the pope rejoices in blood and massacres. Christ bore his cross upon his shoulders—the pope is borne upon the shoulders of men. Christ came with peace and poverty into the world—the pope delights in stirring up war amongst the kings and princes of the earth. Christ came meekly, humbly, and compassionately, sitting upon an ass—but the pope rides in all pomp and splendour. Christ was a lamb—the pope is a wolf. Christ was poor—the pope would have all christian kingdoms under his power and command. Christ drove the money-changers and sellers out of the temple—the pope receives them in. Jesus instituted the sacrament in commemoration of himself—the pope formed the mass, a master-piece of imposture. Jesus ascended into heaven—and the pope falls into hell. God hath commanded that we should have no other God but him—and the pope makes himself to be honoured like unto a great God. God forbids us to commit idolatry—and the pope is the author of image-worship. God hath prohibited swearing in vain—but the pope allows his friends perjury. God hath commanded the use of festivals in good works, prayers, and devotions—but the pope allows pomp, games, idleness, and mimicry to be exercised on those days in churches. God hath forbidden murder, and killing any person—and it is a matter of great compassion and sorrow, to see how cruelly the pope persecutes christians. God foretold this persecution in Matthew xxiv. Many false prophets, said Christ, shall arise at that time; and because iniquity shall abound, the love of many shall wax cold;

but the gospel shall be preached in all the world; when ye therefore shall see the abomination of desolation, spoken of by Daniel the prophet, stand in the holy place, then let them which be in Judea, flee into the mountains. And is not this come to pass now? Yea, for there are many wolves in sheep's clothing; who under the pretence of religion, obscure the true doctrine of Christ; and almost all abominations were introduced into the holy place, that is to say, brought into the church of God.

But to return to our matter, God hath forbid adultery—notwithstanding, the pope, who will be obedient to his father the devil, commands his priests to keep several concubines and harlots, rather than join themselves to any in marriage. God hath forbid stealing from either man, woman, or child—but the pope is such an old thief, that he robs even God of his honour, and transfers it to himself. God hath forbid bearing false witness against any one—but the pope cries that all is good grist which comes to his mill. God hath commanded us to be content with what is our own—but the pope will have every house pay him a tribute; to conclude, he is in every thing opposite to God. But I cannot blame him, for he fulfils the command of Paul, which says, Children, obey your parents, and the demon of hypocrisy is his father, to whom he pays all obedience. The devil walketh about as a roaring lion, saith St. Peter, seeking whom he may devour. And does not the pope do the same? Yea certainly, for he not only ordains wicked and unjust laws; but he pursues to death, all who have a true zeal and love towards God.

But to return to the primacy of Peter. I ask, how many kingdoms St. Peter had under his dominion? For it was impossible that all kingdoms should be under him, when St. James was then bishop of Jerusalem, and that city was not then christian. Neither can I see how Peter should be the chief: for St. Paul says to the Corinthians concerning the apostles, All are yours, and you are Christ's, and Christ is God's. Likewise, St. Peter calls himself by no other title but Peter an apostle of Jesus Christ, by which it is manifest, that we are not Peter's, but Peter is ours. Again, when Paul came to Antioch, he withstood Peter to his face, because he was to be blamed: which he would not have done if Peter had possessed any such authority, or could not have lied, as they say. But, as I have said thereupon, Paul, seeing the dissimulation of Peter, said unto him, If thou, being a Jew, livest after the manner of Gentiles, and not as do the Jews, why compellest thou the Gentiles to live as do the Jews? We who are Jews by nature, and not sinners of the Gentiles, knowing that a man is not justified by the works of the law, but by the faith of Jesus Christ, even we have believed in Jesus Christ, that we might be justified by the faith of Christ, and not by the works of the law. Let us then see how it is possible that Peter should be chief; for if he was principal, who loved Christ the best, it is evident that St. John would be the chiefest of the apostles, for Christ appointed him to take care of his mother, and John lay in the bosom of Jesus, whilst he supped.

But to the matter in hand. I ask, whether a lawful council can be called but by the pope? To which, I am sure, the papists will answer negatively. Then I ask, if the pope can call a council before his election? To which, I know, they will reply, He cannot. If then no council is lawful without a pope, and that none who is labouring to be elected pope can assemble a council, then the council which confirms the pope as superior over the church, is not lawful; because it was not convocated by a pope, there being then none elected.

But, being thus driven from that argument, they fly to another, and say, that Christ commanded Peter to feed his sheep: but he commanded all the rest to do the same, saying, Go ye therefore and teach all nations, baptizing them in my name. But the pope does not obey the commandment of Jesus Christ; for he doth not feed his sheep, but devours them, like a roaring lion who walks about to seek his prey. Now I wish the pope would obey the commandment which God gave unto St. Peter. For I should not regret his having authority to preach Christ to all the world, but he leaves the preaching of the gospel, and usurps the authority of being Head of the Church, which of right belongs to none but Christ.

It is true, the pope is primate of the church, but it is not the divine or catholic church but the diabolical one; for he transgresses the commandment given in general to St. Peter and the rest of the apostles. For when Christ sent his twelve disciples to preach the gospel of repentance and the kingdom of God, he said, Behold, I send you forth as sheep amongst wolves: but the bishop of Rome is like a wolf amongst sheep, eating and devouring the poor sheep of Christ; and when they are hid by fear, he takes the voice of a sheep to betray and devour them. He excuses himself from preaching, upon its being too low and mean an office for him, saying, He hath lower officers and ministers for that work; whilst he is taken up with seeing and attending to the singing of the masses. But I answer to the first, That if the office of preaching was not below St. Peter, who had received all his authority and power from Christ himself, methinks those who call themselves the successors of Peter, should not esteem the office too mean for them.

St. Paul writes to Timothy what every bishop ought to be ; A bishop, saith he, must be blameless, the husband of one wife, sober, of good behaviour, given to hospitality, apt to teach, not given to wine, no striker, not given to filthy lucre, but one that ruleth well his own house, having his children in subjection with all gravity. Now let us arraign the pope before St. Paul, and examine whether by St. Paul's rule he be guilty or not. The first command to a bishop is, to be blameless ; but we have proved that the bishop of Rome transgresses all the commandments of God, by which he stands guilty. The second is, that he be the husband of one wife, in which the bishop of Rome errs mightily; for he allows concubines, and counts filthiness better than lawful and honest marriage. The third is, that he should be sober, and full of wisdom and virtue, which the bishop of Rome very little observes. The fourth is, that he be liberal, given to hospitality, not greedy of filthy lucre ; but the bishop of Rome is full of avarice and oppression. The fifth is, that he be apt to teach ; but our diabolical father accounts maintaining the glory of God by preaching, as too mean an office for him ; notwithstanding his predecessor Peter either preached the gospel, or sinned against God in not observing that commandment, Go ye, and preach the gospel over all the world. But he will imprison, slay, and burn those who do preach the word, and would himself be their executioner, if he did not find others to do it in his stead; by which we may see that he loves himself more than he loves God. What shall I say more? He disobeys all the orders of St. Paul : give verdict therefore whether he be guilty or innocent.

But now we will proceed to their other arguments, and first, to their maintaining Peter to be the chief, for which they allege his being commanded to feed the sheep. To which I answer, that all the apostles were commanded as well as he, to feed the sheep of Christ, in these words of the gospel, Go ye all and preach, &c. for the preaching of the gospel signifies nothing else but feeding his sheep. And their other argument is not more substantial, when they say Peter was a fisher of men; for I say, Andrew and John were, by the same authority, made fishers of men: for fishers of men are really nothing but preachers of Christ.

Now, if the preaching of the gospel be unlawful without authority from Peter or the pope, then the preaching of St. Paul was not lawful, because he did not receive his authority from Peter; notwithstanding the pope accounts himself a God, saying, I cannot lie, therefore I have spoken truth. To which I answer, that if he be not greater than Peter, he may lie; for Peter denied Christ thrice, Peter then lied thrice: and St. Paul afterwards reproved him for his dissimulation.

But the bishop of Rome lies notoriously, if in nothing else, but in his pretending to be the head of the christian church, and having the keys of heaven. For, if the pope have the keys of heaven, I make this query, When the pope is dead, and none hath the keys, how can any soul enter into heaven? no person till he be elected pope having the keys; whence it must follow, that the pope being dead, heaven's gates are closed! But it is a folly to say, that the pope hath the keys of heaven and hell, when Christ is our only Mediator, our Gate, Head, Shepherd, Redeemer, and Sovereign Lord; who after he had taught, instructed, done many miracles, and suffered death, for us, and pronounced salvation to all that believe on his name, and from the power of his passion faithfully believe to be saved, ascended into heaven with great honour and glory, and is seated on the right hand of God his Father, where he intercedes for us; remaining for ever with his blessed Father, and the Holy Ghost, one God in Trinity, and three Persons in unity, full of power and virtue, and free from vice and sin; remaining with us by his Spirit, and being in every respect equal with his Father, till he shall come in glory to be Judge of all the world: whose goodness is inscrutable, mercy inexpressible, and glory most inestimable. He is our Governor and Master; he is our Shepherd and Redeemer; and we are his subjects and sheep; we are ransomed by his blood, and washed by the waters of baptism, to show that we are his sheep; none else is our pastor or Lord: neither the pope, nor any on earth can be our head; else we should become a monster having two heads. Paul writing to the Corinthians, says, that all is ours; Peter, Apollos, and all the other apostles were ours, and we are Christ's, and Christ is God's; whereby it appears, that Peter is not a head, but a minister unto us. Therefore, we must esteem God our spiritual Father, who, by the passion of Christ, took from us all the pains of death and hell, to all who believe in him; that is the spirit of adoption, whereby we cry, Abba, Father. If the pope then will be called our spiritual father, we shall have three fathers, whereof the one is carnal, and two spiritual: neither can the pope be so, for as Christ is the immaculate Lamb, and only Son of God, endued with all power; on the other side, the pope is an unclean and ravenous wolf, and only son of the devil his father, from whom he hath received his authority and office.

But I would fain know, whether the pope be our spiritual, carnal, or diabolical father? In the first place, I see not how he can be our carnal father, because he lives celibate, and makes a profession of chastity. Neither can he be our spiritual father, being so addicted to the world and worldliness; then it follows that he must be our diabolical father! Let us therefore conclude, that as it was said of Christ, Thou art my Son, this day have I begotten thee; God will say to the pope, Thou art my enemy, this day have I destroyed thee. And as Christ was of the order of Melchisedek, so the pope is of the order diabolic. But as christianity is spiritually very good, and well designed; yet if there be not good order to preserve it, it must decay. As the body of a man could not be healthy with two heads, four arms, or four feet; so these christian countries could never well subsist under the distraction of two equal sovereigns. But some may question me then, and say, What then, you would not have any kings or emperors? But to that I answer, that God, who sent his only Son down into the world, made him king over it, putting all spiritual and temporal authority into his hands; he by his sovereignty hath placed kings to be his lieutenants over the earth; but he hath not ordained any supreme bishop: for we find none so authorized by the holy scripture. Now, if the papists say, that the pope is heir to him, I would advise him then, to stay till Christ were dead before they seized upon his kingdom; because no heirs take the possession of their inheritances, till after the death of their predecessors.

Moreover, the papists say, that as under the old law there was a high priest or archbishop of the Jews, so there ought now to be a head or supreme minister amongst christians. To which I answer, that the priesthood of Aaron and Moses represented the supremacy of our Saviour Christ, not the pope. For Christ, who came down to the earth, and suffered death for us, says of himself, that he was our Messias, and that he was the true Bread which came down from heaven, and our only Shepherd. For St. John testifies that, he says, I am the door; he that entereth not by me into the sheepfold, but climbeth up some other way, is a thief; but he that entereth in by the door is the Shepherd of the sheep. To Him the porter openeth, and the sheep hear his voice: and he calleth his own sheep by name, and leadeth them out, and the sheep follow him, for they know his voice; and a stranger will they not follow. But the pope, not coming by Christ, is an abominable thief. Therefore all true and good sheep ought to fly from him: for he comes to devour, not feed them; to prey upon them, not instruct them. But the papists, being thus scourged with their own rod, that is, with their own argument, say further, that after the disciples had preached about the cities, after they returned to Jesus, he asked them, whether they had any sword with them? and that they answered, Here are two swords. Now they urge further, that one of the swords signifies the spiritual, the other the temporal power; which reason, as shall be showed hereafter, is foolish and vain. For first, we ought to consider from whence the apostles came; they had been sent to preach Christ to all people, and to show the light to those that sat in darkness. Secondly, we must consider the power Christ had on earth; for he said himself, that his kingdom was not of this world; and there are two sorts of authority, the one spiritual, the other temporal. On which account St. Paul writes in his first epistle to the Corinthians, As the body is one, and hath many members, for several uses; so there are also in the church of Christ, amongst the spiritual ministers; first, apostles; secondly, prophets; thirdly, teachers; and some temporal ministers, as kings, emperors, governors, and lieutenants. Now Christ was a spiritual minister, as he testifies of himself, saying, My kingdom is not of this world. And again, when two brethren came unto him and requested him to divide their inheritance between them, he answered, Man, who made me a judge, or a divider over you? The third thing to be considered, is, that Christ spake to the disciples concerning the swords ironically. Fourthly, that all the apostles answered together, Behold, here are two swords. Fifthly, you may observe in the text, that the apostles understood not what Christ meant.

By all which we may easily understand that text; for after the apostles had been sent to preach the gospel of truth, when they returned to Jesus, he said unto them, Had you any sword with you then? as much as to say, When I sent you first out, you would have staves with you, but now what do you think, hath not my grace kept you from all evil? Or else, What need have you of a sword? Then his disciples, not Peter only, not understanding what Christ said, answered, there were two swords.

By which we see Christ spoke ironically, and that all the disciples made answer, not Peter alone; as if he should say, I have two swords, the one signifying my temporal authority, and the other signifying my spiritual jurisdiction: neither would nor could Christ give a temporal authority, forasmuch as he was a spiritual minister. And the papists err extremely in one argument, where they say, that Cephas is a head, whereas in truth, Cephas is a stone; but when these their arguments are weakened, then they cry It is probable, that Peter was the chief apostle, because he spake first at that time, concerning our dispute, and so answered in behalf of all the apostles.

But it is more likely he was not the prince over the rest, for St. Paul says, For I suppose I was not a whit behind the very chiefest apostles, 2 Cor. xi. For in nothing I am behind the very chiefest apostles, 2 Cor. xii : in which number Peter is comprised. Now, we must not dispute what is most probably true, but what is most certainly true. Nevertheless, let us examine whether it be probable or not; for Andrew sometimes spake first, and it is not to be doubted but that each of them sometimes spake first; but it does not therefore follow, that he who speaks sometimes first, must be bishop of the bishops. His first speaking at that time, may signify that he was of a very courageous spirit; or else that he could have desired to have been the greatest. But Christ said, They that humble themselves like a little child, shall be the greatest in the kingdom of heaven ; neither is there any lofty proud title in the kingdom or church of Christ, as you may see in that magnificate in Luke, (Luke i.) for God loves humility; and Christ says, in Mark, If any man desire to be first, the same shall be last of all, and servant unto all. And in another evangelist he saith, Whoso receiveth one such little child in my name, receiveth me ; and unless ye become as little children, ye shall not be fit for the kingdom of heaven, Matt. xviii. Nor does Peter attribute so high a title to himself, as the pope takes upon him. For he writes thus in his epistle, Peter a servant and an apostle of Jesus Christ, and no more. But the pope, what does he say? " Paul the third, by the grace of God, the most holy pope and father, deputy to Peter, and vicar to Christ, king of kings, prince of princes, bishop of the bishops, and God on earth !" Behold therefore, how he calls himself God, and blasphemes Christ. Behold how he is filled and puffed up with pride and vanity. Behold how large and fair a name and title he takes, though he be a venomous serpent ; calling himself the most Holy Father, whereas he is a detestable thief, and contaminated with all uncleanness. He calls himself the pope, which word signifies, father unto all nations, whilst he brings them to destruction. Nay, he calls himself the vicar of Christ, and deputy of St. Peter, and God upon earth ; whilst he is vicar to Beelzebub, deputy to Lucifer, and a terrestrial demon ; for he would seem to be very good, whilst he is very wicked. And it is no wonder if the ministers of the devil appear brave and triumphant outwardly, for St. Paul writes to the Corinthians, No marvel what false apostles and deceitful workers can transform themselves into ; Satan himself being transformed into an angel of light.

Wherefore you may easily discern the true ministers of the word from the false antichrists; because the true apostles walk after the Spirit of God, and the false walk after the flesh. Let us therefore see whether the pope be the minister of God, or the devil: which I fear he will prove; proclaiming himself a good man, a most holy bishop, a king of kings: whereas he is the tyrant of tyrants. All others exercise their tyranny over bodies, but this wolf and tyrant exercises his tyranny over the souls of men, constraining the poor and simple lambs of God to forsake their faith, whereby they are saved, to follow his abominable traditions and diabolical precepts ; which if they refuse to obey, to wit, adoring images, and offering to his idols and devils, he burns, racks, and torments them, or forces them to a costly recantation.

During the reign of my late father the king,* when the pope's name was blotted out of our books, he stopped the mouths of christians with his six articles, as if he would choke them. And at this day in France, before any one is burnt, a little before the execution, they cut out his tongue, that he may not speak.

Considering then that the pope is the minister of Lucifer, I am in good hopes, that as Lucifer fell from heaven into hell, so the pope his vicar will fall from the great glory of his papacy, into contemptible derision.

For David hath said in his psalms, With the pure thou wilt show thyself pure, and with the froward thou wilt show thyself froward. Again, the pope hath taken God's honour away from him; therefore I hope God will divest him of his honours and glory. As the virgin Mary saith, He hath put down the mighty from their seats, and exalted them of low degree. Take heed of thyself then, O pope, for if thou tumblest, thou wilt have a terrible fall. As a man who is got up into a high tower, would have a huge leap if he should fall down; so thou who hast exalted thyself into the heavens, wouldest fall down into the abyss of hell: as Christ foretold of Tyre and Sidon.

But to return to the pope's primacy. I know very well that the scripture speaks of one God, one faith, one baptism, but no mention of one pope. Now, if Peter had been a God on earth, and vicar of Christ, we should have been baptized into his name. But Paul, who affirms himself to be inferior to none of the other apostles, will not allow us to be baptized in his name. Nay, he is so far from having us baptized in the name of Peter, that he will not have it said, I am of Peter, or of Paul, or of Apollos.

And now that the papists cannot prove by the scriptures that we ought to have one pope, they run to similitudes; saying, that as the creatures in the earth, as the bees, have a king over them, so all christians ought to have one king and pope. To which I will answer three ways: First, that their reason is not extracted from the holy scripture, but from their own invention. Secondly, That all the bees which are in the world, or in christendom, have not a king. Thirdly, That if all bees have their king, so have we, namely, Jesus Christ.

But the papists will then say, that if we condemn the papacy, we shall condemn our forefathers as heretics. I

* Henry VIII.

## Against the Primacy of the Pope.

will answer to that, as God answered Elijah, when he said to the Lord that the children of Israel had forsaken his covenant, and were unjust and wicked, Yet I have left me seven thousand in Israel, all the knees which have not bowed to Baal. Neither must we imagine, but that there have been many christians in the world, some of whom have spoken openly against the papacy, and others that have kept their knowledge and sentiments to themselves; but the papists will not suffer us to know more than our fathers. But I know very well, that our religion consists not of old customs, or the usage of our fathers; but in the holy scriptures, and the divine word; and that (if you think antiquity and custom makes a thing good) is older than the world: for God is the Word, who was without beginning, and shall continue without end; and if you think truth ought to be followed and obeyed, all truth is contained in that book. Our religion ought not to be steered or governed by our forefathers; for Ezekiel saith, Walk ye not in the statutes of your fathers, for they were polluted. Moreover, our God, and Saviour, and Redeemer, Jesus Christ, said, I am the way, and the truth, and the life; he did not say, I am the old custom.

The papists then say, that though Christ did not indeed ordain the pope, yet he left it to the church to do it. To which I ask, how Peter then was elected the universal bishop? For all things necessary to our salvation are written in the bible, as St. Paul testifies in his epistle to Timothy, where he says, But continue thou in the things which thou hast learned, &c. And that from a child thou hast known the holy scriptures, which are able to make thee wise unto salvation, through faith which is in Christ Jesus.

## THE SECOND PART.

BUT to what purpose do we go about to prove that Peter is not the head of the church? For allow he had been so, that does not conclude that the bishop of Rome is the principal head: for the papists themselves cannot prove that Peter was ever at Rome. By the scripture they cannot prove it; nor by any true history: therefore the bishop of

Rome loses one of his great titles, Papa ex jure divino, (pope by divine right,) for no authority can be ex jure divino, unless it be confirmed by the scripture.

Well then, we have him in a great plunge, since he must be forced to say, Paul, pope by human traditions; for if he be not bishop by the divine word, but only by human traditions, then all kings, princes, and other magistrates, may abrogate the statutes and institutions made by their fathers, as we have seen before.

If every one then had known this, the pope had been poor long ago. Now the papists say, that the bishop of Rome was instituted by the primitive church; but no more than Mahomet, for they began near the same age, and the pope was elected when all manner of wicked errors were advanced in christendom.

Nevertheless, to prove that Peter was at Rome, they produce the Clementine epistles, but we will prove them counterfeited, and falsified by the papists. For in them it is written that Peter was at Rome, in the second year of the reign of Claudius, and lived there twenty-five years. But Christ was crucified in the eighteenth year of Tiberius, and he reigned five years after the crucifixion: Caius Caligula reigned four years; and Claudius two; which makes it eleven years before Peter went to Rome: and in the eighteenth year of our Lord, Paul found St. Peter in Jerusalem;[*] by which we see their history is false. And we will prove that it is not true that Clement wrote those epistles unto James, for James was dead before Clement was bishop.

Moreover, St. Peter was the bishop of the Jews, and not of the Gentiles: for St. Paul glories in several places that he was the apostle of the Gentiles. Again, St. Paul, writing to the Galatians, says, that he went up to Jerusalem to see Peter. Therefore it is most probable that Peter·dwelt for the most part in Jerusalem, or in the adjacent cities. And here we may see the craft of the devil, and the power of God. For notwithstanding the devil, to establish his power, invented the Clementine epistles; though they were counterfeited by the papists, yet I say, God by his goodness and clemency towards his elect, hath caused the said epistles to be so written, that every one who hath read history, may plainly comprehend and understand, that they

[*] Gal. i. 18.

were feigned by serpentine subtilty, and by some abominable and obdurate papists.

In several other instances also, we may discover their false subtilty; for notwithstanding that the holy scripture saith, Idols are senseless things, and without life; they have often framed images, which sometimes rolled their eyes, sometimes turned their heads, sometimes moved their hands, and sometimes their whole bodies: by which means they made people believe, that an image, made of wood, heard and understood them; all of it being made so to the life, that, as they turned them, they made the head and eyes of the image to turn also. But, as Daniel with ashes or sand proved that the idol Bel did not eat, but his priests, so by the holy scriptures, the confession of several persons, and by observation and experience, they have been proved to have been mere machines, and other instruments.

## THE THIRD PART.

SINCE we see that Peter neither was the chief, nor was it Rome; considering that they say the pope cannot lie, we will examine whether they themselves have not acknowledged that no person ought to be the primate of the church.

For Gregory the first hath written, that none ought to be pope. Gregory was then bishop of Rome, and Maurice was emperor, and there were many heresies in chrisendom; and the bishop and patriarch of Constantinople at that time pretended to be the universal bishop, who was much favoured by Maurice: but Gregory declared then in his writings, that there ought to be no principal in the church.

And now the papists are overthrown by this; they say that by the consent of the general councils and doctors, a universal bishop was established under the name of pope: whereas for four or five hundred years after Christ, there was no person in the world that was distinguished or called by that name. Moreover, when there were several contentions about the papacy, all learned persons detested the opinion that there must be a pope: and sometimes the very bishops of Rome themselves abhorred it. And St. Cyprian, writing concerning the unity of the church, saith, "There is one bishop, of whom every bishop holds a share.

For as there are many beams in the sun, yet the brightness is but one: many branches in a tree, several streams from a fountain; in like manner the church is but one; which being illuminated by the brightness of our Lord, who extends his beams throughout all the world, yet nevertheless the clarity* is but one, namely, Jesus Christ." Likewise the same Cyprian, being bishop of Carthage, calls the bishop of Rome his companion. Moreover, St. Jerome, bishop of Rome, (ep. ad Evag.) humbles the style of primate; saying, If there be any question of the authority of a primate of the church, also there are bishops of nations and cities, it follows not therefore that there is a primate over all the world, for the world is much greater than any city. And also in the council of Carthage it was decreed, that none should be called the first or primate of the bishops.

What shall I say more? It was consented and agreed by all, for six hundred years after Christ, that none ought to be pope. (August. Epist. 28. ad Const.) How could Peter then have been primate, or the pope his successor? For Peter in his epistles does not command, but prays and beseeches the ministers of God. Likewise, when he is accused for having communicated with the Gentiles, he does not burn his accusers, as the pope does his: but excuses himself, and shows a submission.

Again, when he was sent to Samaria by his brethren and companions, he readily obeyed their decree, and went down to that city.

## THE FOURTH PART.

Of this detestable and diabolical pope, the holy scriptures, in several places, give us a plenary demonstration; some of which I shall show unto you. As first, in the seventh of Daniel, it is set down how that Daniel, who was beloved by Belshazzar, saw a vision, which appeared to him thus; I saw, says Daniel, in my vision by night, and behold, the four winds of the heaven strove upon the great sea, and four great beasts came up out of the earth. The first was like a lion, and had eagle's wings; and I beheld till the wings thereof were plucked, and a man's heart was given to it. The second beast was like unto a bear, and it raised up itself on one side; and they said thus unto it,

* Light, brightness.

Arise, devour much flesh. The third was like unto a leopard, which had upon the back of it four wings of a fowl, and the said beast had also four heads. After this I beheld the fourth beast, which was dreadful and terrible, and strong exceedingly; and it had great iron teeth, and devoured every thing, and it had ten horns. And behold, there came up among them another little horn, before whom there were three of the first horns plucked up by the roots; and it had eyes, and a mouth speaking blasphemies. And I beheld till I saw the Ancient of Days did sit, and I beheld, saith Daniel, till the judgment was set for the horn, and till the beast was slain, and his body given to the burning flame: and it shall be for a time, times, and a half. Now the four winds, and the four beasts, as Melancthon, Oecoampadius, and all learned writers say, signify the four monarchies; the first was that of the Assyrians, whereof Nebuchadnezzar was emperor, who, after he had been made like unto the beasts for a long season, had the understanding of a man given him again. The second signified the empire of the Persians, which was a dominion of great cruelty. The third notified the Grecian empire, which was immediately raised to its grandeur; and the four wings and four heads signify the four emperors which succeeded Alexander, and divided amongst them the Grecian monarchy; for Seleucus was made king of Syria, Ptolemy got Egypt, Antigonus Asia, and Cassander Greece. The fourth beast signifies the terrible monarchy of the Romans, out of which arises a little horn, which is antichrist; and antichrist hath two eyes, namely, the pope and Mahomet; for notwithstanding that the pope doth not speak against Christ, as Mahomet doth, nevertheless I answer, that the pope is as much, or rather more, an antichrist than Mahomet. For as he who flatters us is our enemy, though he seems to be our friend; so the pope, who styles himself the servant of the servants of God, is the enemy of Christ; whilst under the shadow of religion, he puts in practice all hypocrisy, idolatry, dissimulation, and all sort of traditions. His time shall be a time, times, and a half; that is to say, his days shall be shortened, for the number of seven stands for a perfect number in scripture; for St. Paul says, the just fall seven times a day, that is, often. Now the half of seven is three and a half; therefore we must interpret by that imperfect time, that those days shall be shortened. St. Paul also, in two epistles, prophesies of the pope; first, writing to the Thessalonians, he says, Now we beseech you, brethren, by the coming of our Lord, that ye be not soon shaken in mind, or be troubled, neither by spirit, nor by word, nor by letter, as that the day of Christ is at hand. Let no man deceive you by any means, for that day shall not come, except there come a falling away first, and that man of sin be revealed, the son of perdition; who opposeth and exalteth himself above God, so that he as God sitteth in the temple of God, showing himself as God. And now ye know what withholdeth, that he might be revealed in his time. For the mystery of iniquity doth already work; only he who now letteth, will let until he be taken out of the way. Again, St. Paul, writing to Timothy, speaks thus: Now the Spirit speaketh expressly, that in the latter times some shall depart from the faith; giving heed to doctrines of devils, speaking lies in hypocrisy, forbidding to marry, and commanding to abstain from meats, which God hath created to be received with thanksgiving of them which believe. Now let every one be asked, if the pope hath not forbidden certain meats, at certain times, and they must all confess he hath, for most folks have felt it; or, perchance, I should not be a liar if I said, that almost all folks have felt it.

And concerning the prohibition of marriage, ask their own priests. St. Peter tells us, that there shall come in the last days scoffers, &c. St. John, in the Apocalypse, says, Seven angels poured out the vials of God's wrath upon the earth; and the signification is probable to be thus—The first vial to be the Assyrian monarchy, when the people of Israel became captive to Nebuchadnezzar.* The second the Persian monarchy. The third vial the monarchy of the Grecians, which Alexander first established. The fourth was the Roman monarchy, which the apocalypse, because of its grandeur, says, the fourth vial was poured upon the sun. The fifth is our antichrist the pope. The sixth vial is the dominion of Mahomet. The seventh vial signifies the end of the world, and the day of judgment.

In the following chapter he declares, that one of the seven angels came and talked with him, and showed him the state, honour, and riches of the pope: for he says, he saw a woman sit upon the beast, full of names of

* It is hardly necessary to say that these interpretations of prophecy do not appear to be correct.

blasphemy, having seven heads and ten horns; and the woman was arrayed in purple, and scarlet colour, and decked with gold ; having a golden cup in her hand, full of abominations, and filthiness of her fornications: and upon her forehead was written, Babylon the mother of harlots, and abominations of the earth, Rev. xvii. The seven heads signify the seven hills which antichrist dwells on ; for Rome is built upon seven mountains. The seven horns are the number of the kings who made war with the Lamb, and the Lamb overcame them, for he is Lord of lords, and King of kings; then another angel came down from heaven, crying, Babylon is fallen, and is become the habitation of devils. Thence I hope, that the kingdom of antichrist shall be destroyed: for though the wicked may prosper for a time, their dominion shall not last; but those who study the law of the Lord, their prosperity shall last for ever. St. Paul, writing to Timothy, says, This know also, that in the last days, men shall be lovers of their own selves, covetous, boasters, proud, blasphemers, &c. 2 Tim. iii. And the prophet Isaiah saith, that Christ shall smite the earth, with the rod of his mouth, and with the breath of his lips shall he slay the wicked, Isaiah xi.

Since we see then that the reign of antichrist shall not last for ever, we must wait for the destruction of Babylon, and submit ourselves to the will of the Lord.

## THE CONCLUSION AND FIFTH PART.

In the first part of our book, we have proved and declared that Peter was not primate of the church, by confuting all the papistical reasons for it.

In the second, we have proved that they cannot produce and allege any true testimony, that St. Peter was at Rome.

In the third part, we have proved from themselves, that they have said they ought not to have the primacy.

In the fourth part, we have explained the prophecies speaking of antichrist. Since then the pope is that wicked one, very son of the devil, an antichrist, and an abominable tyrant, let us pray unto the Lord to preserve those still in the light who have seen it: and that he will show the sincere, pure, and true light unto those who sit in darkness: that all the world may glorify God in this life, and be partakers of the eternal kingdom of heaven in the world to come, by the merits of Jesus Christ our Saviour ; to whom, with the Father, and the Holy Ghost, be all honour, glory, dominion, and praise, for ever and ever. Amen.

---

The original manuscript is written in French, by the king's own hand, and is entitled "L'Encontre les abus du Monde," that is, Against the abuses of the world, meaning, as Strype observes, the abuses imposed upon the faith and worship of christians by the pope, whom he calls Antichrist.

It is authenticated to be the king's own composition, by a note written at the end by his instructor in the French language ; when translated, it is as follows :

"Just as a good painter can represent the visage, look, countenance, and bulk of a prince; so by the writings, words, and actions of a prince, one may easily understand what spirit is in him, and to what he is addicted. As one may see by the writings of this young king, who composed and wrote this book, being not yet full twelve years old, and without the help of any person living ; except as to the subject, which he had heard of many, and the remembrance which he had of books that he had read. For, from the time he began to write the said book and until he had finished it, the said book was always in my keeping, even to the present time."

A very few corrections of small importance have been made by the French instructor.

# A SHORT CATECHISM,

OR,

## PLAIN INSTRUCTION,

CONTAINING

THE SUM OF CHRISTIAN LEARNING, SET FORTH BY THE KING'S MAJESTY'S AUTHORITY, FOR ALL SCHOOLMASTERS TO TEACH.

### 1553.

---

*An Injunction given by the King our Sovereign Lord, his most excellent Majesty, to all Schoolmasters and Teachers of Youth, within all his Grace's realms and dominions, for authorizing and establishing the use of this Catechism.*

Edward the Sixth, by the grace of God, King of England, France, and Ireland; Defender of the Faith; and of the Church of England, and also of Ireland, the Supreme Head:—To all Schoolmasters and Teachers of Youth.

When there was presented unto us, to be perused, a short and plain order of Catechism, written by a certain godly and learned man, we committed the debating, and diligent examination thereof, to certain bishops, and other learned men, whose judgment we have in great estimation. And because it seemed agreeable with the scriptures, and the ordinances of our realm, we thought it good, not only for that agreement to put it forth abroad to print: but also, for the plainness and shortness, to appoint it out for all schoolmasters to teach. That the yet unskilful and young age, having the foundations laid, both of religion and good letters, may learn godliness together with wisdom; and have a rule for the rest of their life, what judgment they ought to have of God, to whom all our life is applied; and how they may please God, wherein we ought, with all the doings and duties of our lives to travail.

We will therefore and command, both all and each of you, as ye tender our favour, and as ye mind to avoid the just punishment of transgressing our authority, that ye truly and diligently teach this Catechism in your schools, immediately after the other brief Catechism which we have already set forth: that young age, yet tender and wavering, being by authority and instructions of true religion stablished, may have a great furtherance to the right worshipping of God, and good helps to live in all points according to duty. Wherewith being furnished, by better using, due godliness toward God, the Author of all things; obedience toward their king, the shepherd of the people; loving affection to the commonweal, the general mother of all; they may seem not born for themselves, but be profitable and dutiful toward God, their king, and their country.

Given at Greenwich the 20th of May, the 7th year of our reign

EDWARD SIXTH.

During the reign of king Edward VI., efforts were for the first time made for the catechetical instruction of young persons in the doctrines of truth, set forth especially for their use, in the English tongue. Several works were published with this design, the latest and most complete was the Short Catechism, approved by the synod in 1552. It was set forth by the king's authority, and one of the latest public acts of king Edward, was an injunction to all schoolmasters and teachers of youth to use the same. On queen Mary's accession to the throne, much opposition was made to this catechism. In the first convocation, Dr. Weston, a zealous papist, brought in a bill, declaring it to be pestiferous, full of heresies, and unauthorized by the late synod. All present, excepting six, agreed with him. Philpot then stood up and defended the catechism, desiring that some of the learned men concerned in the setting forth that book, might be called before them, and suffered to defend it; but this of course was not allowed.

Weston, who had himself subscribed to it in the former synod, afterwards charged Ridley with being the author. The latter declared he was not, though he admitted having perused and approved it. Ponet, bishop of Winchester in queen Elizabeth's reign, is supposed by Tanner and some others to have written this catechism, but there appears no doubt that the author was Dr. Alexander Nowell, then head master of Westminster school, subsequently an exile in queen Mary's reign, and dean of St. Paul's under queen Elizabeth.

It was published and set forth under his own name, in a revised and considerably enlarged form, after his return from exile, and was then approved by the convocation, and finally in 1570 set forth by authority. In each form it was printed both in English and Latin. Of the first edition, usually known as King Edward's catechism, Strype says, " It was certainly written by Alexander Nowell, as I find by comparing Nowell's catechism and this together. The speakers are the same in both. And in many places the very same questions and answers are given verbatim, only Nowell's catechism published under queen Elizabeth is much larger."

Ridley probably refers to this work in his Farewell to his Friends, and in his letter to the Brethren. (See Ridley, p. 141, 186.) Ponet may have been supposed to be the author, from the license to Day in 1553, which allows him to print this catechism, also containing permission "to print all the works and books devised or compiled" by Ponet.

The catechism is given in the present collection in its original form, as one of the most important pieces connected with the history of the reformation. The anxiety felt by the papists on account of the numerous catechisms set forth in the reformed churches, is shown by the introduction to the Catechism of the Council of Trent, which, after complaining of "the mighty volumes" of the heretics, and the infinite number of "their little books," states, " As many *catechisms* as there are provinces in Europe, nay, almost as many as the cities, are circulated, all of which abound with heresies, whereby the minds of the simple are deceived."

# THE
# CATECHISM.

It is the duty of them all, whom Christ hath redeemed by his death, that they not only are servants to obey, but also children to inherit: and so to know which is the true trade of life, and that God liketh; that they may be able to answer to every demand of religion, and to render account of their faith and profession.

And this is the plainest way of teaching, which not only in philosophy, Socrates, but also in our religion, Apolinarius, hath used: that both by certain questions, as it were by pointing, the ignorant might be instructed, and the skilful put in remembrance, that they forget not what they have learned. We, therefore, having regard to the profit, which we ought to seek in teaching of youth, and also to shortness, that in our whole schooling there should be nothing, either overflowing or wanting, have conveyed the whole sum into a dialogue, that the matter itself might be the plainer to perceive, and we the less stray in other matters, beside the purpose.

Thus then beginneth the master to appose* his scholar.

*Master.* Since I know, dear son, that it is a great part of my duty, not only to see that thou art instructed in good letters, but also earnestly and diligently to examine, what sort of religion thou followest in this thy tender age: I thought it best to appose thee by certain questions, to the intent I may perfectly know, whether thou hast well or ill travailed therein. Now therefore, tell me, my son, what religion that is, which thou professest.

*Scholar.* That, good master, do I profess, which is the religion of the Lord Christ: which in the eleventh of the Acts is called the christian religion.

*M.* Dost thou then confess thyself to be a follower of christian godliness and religion, and a scholar of our Lord Christ?

*S.* That, forsooth, do I confess, and plainly and boldly profess; yea, therein I account the whole sum of all my glory, as that which is both of more honour, than that the

* Examine.

slenderness of my understanding may attain unto it: and also more approaching to God's majesty, than that I, by any feat of utterance, may easily express.

*M.* Tell me then, dear son, as exactly as thou canst, in what points thou thinkest that the sum of christian religion standeth.

*S.* In two points, that is to say, true faith in God, and assured persuasion, conceived of all those things which are contained in the holy scriptures; and in charity, which belongeth both to God and to our neighbour.

*M.* That faith which is conceived by hearing and reading of the word; what doth it teach thee concerning God?

*S.* This doth it principally teach: that there is one certain nature, one substance, one ghost,* and heavenly mind, or rather an everlasting Spirit, without beginning or ending, which we call God: whom all the people of the world ought to worship with sovereign honour, and the highest kind of reverence. Moreover, out of the holy words of God, which by the prophets and the beloved of almighty God, are in the holy books published, to the eternal glory of his name, I learn the law and the threatenings thereof; then the promises and the gospel of God. These things, first written by Moses and other men of God, have been preserved whole and uncorrupted, even to our age; and since that, the chief articles of our faith have been gathered into a short abridgement, which is commonly called the creed, or symbol of the apostles.

*M.* Why is this abridgement of the faith termed a symbol?

*S.* A symbol is as much as to say, a sign, mark, privy token, or watch-word, whereby the soldiers of the same camp are known from their enemies. For this reason the abridgement of the faith, whereby the christians are known from them that are no christians, is rightly named a symbol.

*M.* First, tell me somewhat what thou thinkest of the law, and then afterward of the creed, or symbol.

*S.* I shall do, good master, with a good will, as you command me. The Lord God hath charged us by Moses, that we have none other God at all, but him; that is to say, that we take him alone, for our one only God, our Maker, and Saviour. That we reverence not, nor worship any portraiture, or any image whatsoever, whether it be painted, carved, graven, or by any means fashioned,

* Spirit.

howsoever it be. That we take not the name of our Lord God in vain; that is, either in a matter of no weight, or of no truth. Last of all, this ought we to hold stedfastly and with devout conscience: that we keep holily and religiously the sabbath day; which was appointed out from the others for rest and service of God.

*M.* Very well. Now hast thou rehearsed unto me the laws of the first table; wherein is, in a sum, contained the knowledge and true service of God. Go forward, and tell me, what are the duties of charity, and our love toward men.

*S.* Do you ask me, master, what I think of the other part of the law, which is commonly called the second table?

*M.* Thou sayest true, my son: that is it indeed, that I would fain hear of.

*S.* I will in few words despatch it, as my simple knowledge will serve me. Moses hath knit it up in a short sum; that is, that with all loving affection we honour and reverence our father and mother. That we kill no man. That we commit no adultery. That we steal nothing. That we bear false witness against none. Last of all, that we covet nothing that is our neighbour's.

*M.* How is that commandment, of the honouring father and mother, to be understood?

*S.* Honour of father and mother contains love, fear, and reverence: yea, and it further stands in obeying, succouring, defending, and nourishing them, if need require. It binds us also most humbly, and with most natural affection, to obey the magistrates, to reverence the ministers of the church, our schoolmasters, with all our elders and betters.

*M.* What is contained in that commandment, Do not kill?

*S.* That we hate, wrong, or revile no man. Moreover it commands us, that we love even our foes; do good to them that hate us: and that we pray for all prosperity and good to our very mortal enemies.

*M.* The commandment of not committing adultery, what thinkest thou it contains?

*S.* This commandment contains many things: for it forbiddeth not only to talk with another man's wife, or any other woman unchastely; but also to touch her, or with lustful look to behold her; or by any unhonest mean to woo her, either by ourselves, or any other in our behalf: finally, herein is debarred all kind of filthy and straying lust.

*M.* What thinkest thou of the commandment, not to steal?

*S.* I shall show you as briefly as I have done the rest, if it please you to hear me. It commands us, to beguile no man, to occupy no unlawful wares, to envy no man his wealth, and to think nothing profitable, that either is not just, or differs from right and honesty: briefly, rather willingly to lose that which is thine own, than wrongfully take that which is another's, and turn it to thine own commodity.

*M.* How may that commandment be kept, of bearing no false witness.

*S.* If we neither ourselves speak any false or vain lie; nor allow it in others, either by speech or silence, or by our present company. But we ought always to maintain truth, as place and time serve.

*M.* Now remains the last commandment, of not coveting any thing that is our neighbour's: what means that?

*S.* This law, generally, forbids all sorts of evil lusts; and commands us to bridle and restrain all greedy unsatiable desire of our will, which holds not itself within the bounds of right and reason: and it wills that each man be content with his estate. But whosoever covets more than right, with the loss of his neighbour, and wrong to another, he breaks and bitterly looses the bond of charity and fellowship among men. Yea, and upon him, unless he amend, the Lord God, the most stern revenger of the breaking his law, shall execute most grievous punishment. On the other side, he that lives according to the rule of these laws, shall find both praise and bliss; and God also his merciful and bountiful good Lord.

*M.* Thou hast shortly set out the ten commandments. Now, then, tell me, how all these things, that thou hast particularly declared, Christ hath in few words contained, setting forth unto us in a sum, the whole pith of the law?

*S.* Will you that I knit up in a brief abridgement, all that belongs both to God and to men?

*M.* Yea.

*S.* Christ saith thus; Thou shalt love the Lord thy God with all thy heart, with all thy soul, with all thy mind, and with all thy strength. This is the greatest commandment in the law. The other is like unto this. Thou shalt love thy neighbour as thyself. Upon these two commandments hang the whole law, and the prophets.

*M.* I will now, that thou tell me further, what law is that, which thou speakest of; that which we call the law of nature, or some other besides?

*S.* I remember, master, that I learned of you long ago, that it was ingrafted by God in the nature of man, while nature was yet sound and uncorrupted. But after the entrance of sin, although the wise were somewhat, after a sort, not utterly ignorant of that light of nature, yet was it by that time so hid from the greatest part of men, that they scarce perceived any shadow thereof.

*M.* What is the cause, that God willed it to be written out in tables: and that it should be privately appointed to one people alone?

*S.* I will show you. By original sin and evil custom, the image of God in man was so darkened at the beginning, and the judgment of nature so corrupted, that man himself does not sufficiently understand, what difference is between honesty and dishonesty, right and wrong. The bountiful God, therefore, minding to renew that image in us, first wrought this by the law written in tables, that we might know ourselves; and therein, as it were in a glass, behold the filth and spots of our soul, and stubborn hardness of a corrupted heart; that by this mean, yet acknowledging our sin, and perceiving the weakness of our flesh, and the wrath of God fiercely bent against us for sin, we might the more fervently long for our Saviour Christ Jesus: who by his death and precious sprinkling of his blood, hath cleansed and washed away our sins; pacified the wrath of the Almighty Father; by the holy breath of his Spirit createth new hearts in us; and reneweth our minds after the image and likeness of their Creator, in true righteousness and holiness. Which thing neither the justice of the law, nor any sacrifices of Moses, were able to perform.

And that no man is made righteous by the law, it is evident; not only thereby, that the righteous liveth by faith: but also hereby, that no mortal man is able to fulfil all that the law of both the tables commands. For we have hinderances that strive against the law; as the weakness of the flesh, froward appetite, and lust naturally engendered. As for sacrifices, cleansings, washings, and other ceremonies of the law, they were but shadows, likenesses, images, and figures of the true and everlasting sacrifice of Jesus Christ, done upon the cross. By the benefit whereof alone, all the sins of all believers, even from the beginning of the world, are pardoned by the only mercy of God, and by no desert of ours.

*M.* I hear not yet, why Almighty God's will was, to declare his secret pleasure to one people alone, which was the Israelites.

*S.* Truly, that had I almost forgotten. I suppose it was not done, as though the law of the ten commandments did not belong generally to all men: forasmuch as the Lord our God is not only the God of the Jews, but also of the Gentiles. But rather, this was meant thereby, that the true Messiah, which is our Christ, might be known at his coming into the world; who must needs have been born of that nation, and none other, for true performance of the promise. For the which cause, God's pleasure was to appoint out for himself one certain people, holy, sundered from the rest, and, as it were, peculiarly his own; that by this means his divine word might be continually kept holy, pure, and uncorrupted.

*M.* Hitherto thou hast well satisfied me, dear son: now let us come to the christian confession, which I will that thou plainly rehearse unto me.

*S.* It shall be done. "I believe in God, the Father Almighty; Maker of heaven and earth. And in Jesus Christ, his only Son, our Lord: which was conceived by the Holy Ghost: born of the virgin Mary: suffered under Pontius Pilate: was crucified: dead and buried. He went down to hell: the third day he rose again from the dead. He went up to heaven: sitteth on the right hand of God, the Father almighty: from thence shall he come, to judge the quick and the dead. I believe in the Holy Ghost. I believe the holy universal church; the communion of saints; the forgiveness of sins; the rising again of the flesh; and the life everlasting."

*M.* All these, my son, thou hast rehearsed generally and shortly. Therefore, thou shalt do well to set out largely all that thou hast spoken particularly; that I may plainly perceive what thy belief is concerning each of them. And first, I would hear of the knowledge of God; afterwards, of the right serving of him.

*S.* I will with a good will obey your pleasure, dear master, as far as my simple knowledge will suffer me. Above all things we must stedfastly believe and hold; that God almighty, the Father, in the beginning, and of nothing, ade and fashioned this whole frame of the world; and all things whatsoever are contained therein; and that they all are made by the power of his word, that is, of Jesus Christ, the Son of God; which is sufficiently approved by witness of scriptures. Moreover, that when he had thus shapen all creatures, he ruled, governed, and saved them by his bounty and liberal hand; hath ministered, and yet also ministereth most largely, all that is needful for maintenance and preserving of our life; that we should so use them, as behoves mindful and godly children.

*M.* Why dost thou call God, Father?

*S.* For two causes; the one, for that he made us all at the beginning, and gave life unto us all. The other is more weighty, for that by his Holy Spirit and by faith he hath begotten us again; making us his children; giving us his kingdom and the inheritance of life everlasting, with Jesus Christ, his own true and natural Son.

*M.* Seeing then God hath created all other things to serve man, and made man to obey, honour, and glorify him; what canst thou say more of the beginning and making of man?

*S.* Even that which Moses wrote. That God shaped the first man of clay; and put into him soul and life. Then, that he cast Adam into a dead sleep, and brought forth a woman, whom he drew out of his side, to make her a companion with him of all his life and wealth. And therefore was man called Adam, because he took his beginning of the earth; and the woman called Eve, because she was appointed to be the mother of all living.

*M.* What image is that, after the likeness whereof thou sayest that man was made?

*S.* That is most absolute righteousness, and perfect holiness; which most nearly belongeth to the very nature of God, and most clearly appeared in Christ, our new Adam. Of the which in us, there scarcely are to be seen any sparkles.

*M.* What! are there scarcely to be seen?

*S.* It is true. For they do not now so shine, as they did in the beginning, before man's fall; forasmuch as man, by the darkness of sins and mist of errors, hath corrupted the brightness of this image. In such sort hath God in his wrath wreaked him upon the sinful man.

*M.* But, I pray thee, tell me, wherefore came it thus to pass?

*S.* I will show you. When the Lord God had made the

frame of this world, he himself planted a garden, full of delight and pleasure, in a certain place eastward, and called it Eden. Wherein, beside other passing fair trees, not far from the midst of the garden, was there one especially, called the tree of life, and another, called the tree of knowledge of good and evil.

Herein the Lord, of his singular love, placed man; and committed unto him the garden to dress, and look unto; giving him liberty to eat of the fruits of all the trees of paradise, except the fruit of the tree of knowledge of good and evil. The fruit of this tree, if ever he tasted, he should without fail die for it. But Eve, deceived by the devil counterfeiting the shape of a serpent, gathered of the forbidden fruit; which was for the fairness to the eye to be desired; for the sweetness in taste to be reached at; and pleasant for the knowledge of good and evil; and she ate thereof, and gave unto her husband to eat of the same. Which doing, they both immediately died; that is to say, were not only subject to the death of the body, but also lost the life of the soul, which is righteousness.

And forthwith, the image of God was defaced in them; and the most beautiful proportion of righteousness, holiness, truth, and knowledge of God, was confounded, and in a manner utterly blotted out. There remained the earthly image, joined with unrighteousness, guile, fleshly mind, and deep ignorance of godly and heavenly things. Hereof grew the weakness of our flesh; hereof came this corruption, and disorder of lusts and affections; hereof came that pestilence; hereof came that seed and nourishment of sins, wherewith mankind is infected, and it is called sin original. Moreover, thereby nature was so corrupted, and overthrown, that unless the goodness and mercy of almighty God had holpen us by the medicine of grace, even as in body we are thrust down into all wretchedness of death; so, must it needs have been, that all men, of all sorts, should be thrown into everlasting punishment, and fire unquenchable.

*M.* Oh the unthankfulness of men! But what hope had our first parents, and from thenceforth the rest, whereby they were relieved?

*S.* When the Lord God had both with words and deeds chastised Adam and Eve, for he thrust them both out of the garden with a most grievous reproach, he then cursed the serpent, threatening him, that the time should one day come, when the Seed of the woman should break his head. Afterwards, the Lord God established that same glorious and most bountiful promise: first, with a covenant made between him and Abraham, by circumcision, and in Isaac his son; then again, by Moses; last of all, by the oracle of the holy prophets.

*M.* What meaneth the serpent's head, and that Seed which God speaketh of?

*S.* In the serpent's head lieth all his venom, and the whole pith of his life and force. Therefore, do I take the serpent's head to betoken the whole power and kingdom or more truly, the tyranny of the old serpent, the devil. The Seed, as St. Paul does plainly teach, is Jesus Christ the Son of God, very God and very man; conceived by the Holy Ghost, of Mary, the blessed, pure, and undefiled maid; and was so born and fostered by her, as other babes are, saving that he was most far from all infection of sin.

*M.* All these foundations that thou hast laid, are most true. Now, therefore, let us go forward to those his doings wherein lieth our salvation and conquest against that old serpent.

*S.* It shall be done, good master. After that Christ Jesus had delivered in charge to his apostles that most joyful, and in all points heavenly doctrine, the gospel which, in Greek, is called euangelion, in English, good tidings, and had, as by sealing, established the same with tokens, and miracles innumerable, whereof all his life was full; at length was he sore scourged, mocked with scorning and spitting in his face; last of all, his hands and feet bored through with nails; and he fastened to a cross. Then he truly died, and was truly buried; that by his most sweet sacrifice he might pacify his Father's wrath against mankind; and subdue him by his death who had the authority of death, which was the devil. Forasmuch, not only the living, but also the dead, were they in hell, or elsewhere, they all felt the power and force of this death; to whom, lying in prison, as Peter saith, Christ preached though dead in body, yet alive in spirit.

The third day after, he uprose again, alive in body also, and with many notable proofs, the space of forty days he abode among his disciples, eating and drinking with them. In whose sight he was conveyed away in a cloud up into heaven; or rather, above all heavens; where he now sitteth at the right hand of God the Father; being made Lord of all things, be they in heaven, or in earth; King of all kings; our everlasting and only high Bishop; our only Mediator: only Peacemaker between God and men. Now, since that he is entered into his glorious majesty, by sending down his Holy Spirit unto us, as he promised, he lighteneth our dark blindness; moveth, ruleth, teacheth, cleanseth, comforteth, and rejoiceth our minds, and so will he still continually do; till the end of the world.

*M.* Well, I see, thou hast touched the chief articles of our religion, and hast set out, as in a short abridgement, the creed that thou didst rehearse. Now therefore, I will demand of thee questions of certain points.

*S.* Do as shall please you, master; for you may more perfectly instruct me in those things that I do not thoroughly understand, and put me in remembrance of that I have forgotten; and print in my mind deeper such things, as have not taken stedfast hold therein.

*M.* Tell me then. If by his death we get pardon of our sins; was not that enough, but that he must also rise again from the dead?

*S.* It was not enough, if you have respect either to him or to us. For unless he had risen again, he should not be taken for the Son of God. For which cause also, while he hung upon the cross, they, that saw him, upbraided him and said, " He hath saved others, but cannot save himself; let him now come down from the cross, and we will believe him." But now, uprising from the dead to everlasting continuance of life, he hath showed a much greater power of his Godhead, than if, by coming down from the cross, he had fled from the terrible pains of death. For to die is common to all men, but to loose the bonds of death, and by his own power to rise again, that properly belongeth to Jesus Christ, the only begotten Son of God, the only author of life.

Moreover, it was necessary that he should rise again with glory, that the sayings of David and other prophets of God might be fulfilled, which told before, that neither his body should see corruption, nor his soul be left in hell. As for us, we neither had been justified, nor had any hope left to rise again, had not he risen again, as Paul in divers places plainly shows. For, if he had remained in the prison of death, in the grave, and been holden in corruption, as all men beside, how could we have hoped for safety by him, who saved not himself? It was meet therefore and needful for the part that he had in hand, and for the chief stay of our safeguard, that Christ should first deliver himself from death, and afterwards assure us of safety by his uprising again.

*M.* Thou hast touched, my son, the chief cause of Christ's rising again. Now would I fain hear thy mind of his going up into heaven. What answer thinkest thou is to be made to them that say, it had been better for him to tarry here with us now present to rule and govern us? For besides other diverse causes, it is likely that the love of the people toward their prince, especially being good and gracious, should grow the greater by his present company.

*S.* All these things which he should do if present, that is to say, if he were in company among us, he doth them absent. He ruleth, maintaineth, strengtheneth, defendeth, rebuketh, punisheth, correcteth, and performeth all such things, as do become such a prince, or rather God himself. All those things, I say, he performeth, which belong either to our need or profit, honour or commodity.

Besides this, Christ is not altogether so absent from the world, as many suppose. For albeit the substance of his body be taken up from us; yet is his Godhead perpetually present with us, although not subject to the sight of our eyes. For things that are not bodily, cannot be perceived by any bodily mean. Who ever saw his own soul? No man. Yet what is there more present, or what to each man nearer, than his own soul? Spiritual things are not to be seen, but with the eye of the Spirit. Therefore he, that in earth will see the Godhead of Christ, let him open the eyes, not of his body, but of his mind, but of his faith, and he shall see Him present, whom eye hath not seen; he shall see Him present, and in the midst of them, wheresoever two or three be gathered together in his name; he shall see Him present with us, even unto the end of the world. What said I? Shall he see Christ present? Yea, he shall both see and feel him, dwelling within himself in such sort, as he doth his own proper soul. For Christ dwelleth and abideth in the mind and heart of him who fasteneth all his trust in him.

*M.* Very well; but our confession is, that he is ascended up into heaven. Tell me, therefore, how that is to be understood?

*S.* So use we commonly to say of him that has attained to any high degree or dignity, that he is ascended up, or advanced into some high room, some high place or state; because he hath changed his former case, and is become of more honour than the rest. In such a case is Christ gone up, as he before came down. He came down from highest honour to deepest dishonour, even the dishonour and vile state of a servant, and of the cross. And likewise, afterwards he went up from the deepest dishonour, to the highest honour, even that same honour which he had before. His going up into heaven, yea, above all heavens, to the very royal throne of God, must needs be evident by most just reason, that his glory and majesty might in comparison agreeably answer to the proportion of his baseness and reproachful estate. This Paul teaches us, in his writings to the Philippians, He became obedient even unto death; yea, the very death of the cross. Wherefore, God hath both advanced him to the highest state of honour; and also given him a name above all names; that at the name of Jesus every knee should bow, of all things in heaven, earth, and hell.

But although he is already gone up into heaven, nevertheless, by his nature of Godhead, and by his Spirit, he shall always be present in his church, even to the end of the world. Yet this proves not that he is present among us in his body. For his Godhead hath one property, his manhood another. His manhood was created, his Godhead uncreated. His manhood is in some one place of heaven; his Godhead is in such sort each-where, that it filleth both heaven and earth.

But to make this point plainer, by a similitude, or comparing of like to like, there is nothing that doth more truly, like a shadow, express Christ, than the sun, for it is a fit image of the light and brightness of Christ. The sun alway keeps the heavens, yet do we say, that it is present also in the world; for without light there is nothing present, that is to say, nothing to be seen of any man; for the sun with his light full fills all things. So, Christ is lifted up above all heavens, that he may be present with all, and fully furnishes all things, as St. Paul doth say.

But as touching the bodily presence of Christ here in earth, if it be lawful to place in comparison great things with small, Christ's body is present to our faith; as the sun, when it is seen, is present to the eye: the body whereof, although it do not bodily touch the eye, nor be presently with it together here in earth; yet is it present to the sight, notwithstanding so large a distance of space between. So, Christ's body, which at his glorious going up was conveyed from us; which hath left the world, and is gone unto his Father; is a great way absent from our mouth, even when we receive with our mouth the holy sacrament of his body and blood. Yet is our faith in heaven, and beholds that Sun of righteousness, and is present together with him in heaven, in such sort as the sight is in heaven with the body of the sun; or in earth the sun with the sight. And as the sun is present to all things by his light; so is Christ also in his Godhead. Yet neither can the light of the sun be sundered from the body; nor from his immortal body the Godhead of Christ. We must therefore so say, that Christ's body is in some one place of heaven, and his Godhead every where, that we neither of his Godhead make a body, nor of his body, a God.

*M.* I see, my son, thou art not ignorant after what sort Christ is rightly said to be from us in body, and with us in spirit. But this one thing would I know of thee. Why is Christ our Lord thus conveyed away from the sight of our eyes, and what profit we take by his going up to heaven?

*S.* The chief cause thereof was to pluck out of us that false opinion, which sometime deceived the apostles themselves; that Christ should in earth visibly reign, as kings and ruffling\* princes of the world. This error he minded to have utterly suppressed in us, and that we should think his kingdom to consist in higher things. Which he therefore thought fitter, because it was more for our commodity and profit that some such kingdom should be set up, as the foundations thereof should rest upon our faith. Wherefore, it was necessary that he should be conveyed away from us, past perceiving of all bodily sense; that by this means our faith might be stirred up, and exercised to consider his government and providence, whom no sight of bodily eyes can behold.

And forasmuch as he is not king of some one country alone, but of heaven and earth, of quick and dead, it was most convenient that his kingdom should be otherwise governed, than our senses may attain unto. For else he should have been constrained, sometimes to be carried up to heaven, sometimes to be driven down to the earth; to remove sometimes into one country, sometimes into another: and, like an earthly prince, to be carried hither and thither,

\* Proud, turbulent.

by divers changes of affairs. For he could not be presently with all at once, unless his body were so turned into Godhead, that he might be in all, or in many places together; as Eutyches, and certain like heretics, held opinion.

If it so were, that he might be each where present with all, at one very instant of time; then were he not man, but a ghost: neither should he have had a true body, but a fantastical: whereof should have sprung forthwith a thousand errors; all which he hath despatched by carrying his body up whole to heaven. In the mean season he, remaining invisible, governeth his kingdom and commonwealth, that is, his church, with sovereign wisdom and power. It is for men to rule their commonwealths by a certain civil policy of men; but for Christ and God, by a heavenly Godlike order.

But all that I have hitherto said, contains but a small parcel of the profit that we take by the carrying up of Christ's body into heaven. For there are many more things that here might be rehearsed, whereof large store of fruit is to be gathered. But especially this may not be left unspoken—that the benefits are such and so great, which come unto us by the death, rising again, and going up of Christ, as no tongue either of men or angels is able to express. And that you may know my mind herein, I will rehearse certain of the chief; whereunto, as it were two principal points, the rest may be applied.

I say therefore, that both by these and other doings of Christ, two commodities do grow unto us; the one, that all the things that ever he hath done for our profit and behoof, he hath done them, so that they are as well our own, if we will cleave thereunto with stedfast and lively faith, as if we had done them ourselves.

He was nailed to the cross; we were also nailed with him, and in him our sins were punished. He died and was buried; we likewise with our sins are dead and buried, and that in such sort, that all remembrance of our sins is utterly taken out of mind. He is risen again, and we are also risen again with him; that is, are so made partakers of his rising again and life, that from henceforth death hath no more rule over us. For the same Spirit is in us, that raised up Jesus from the dead. Finally, as he is gone up into heavenly glory, so are we lifted up with him. Albeit that these things do not now appear, yet then shall they all be brought to light, when Christ, the Light of the world, shall show himself in his glory, in whom all our bliss is laid up in store. Moreover, by his going up are granted us the gifts of the Holy Ghost; as Paul doth sufficiently witness, Eph. iv.

The other benefit which we take by the doings of Christ is, that Christ is set for an example unto us, to frame our lives thereafter. If Christ hath been dead; if he hath been buried for sin; he was so but once. If he be risen again; if he be gone up to heaven; he is but once risen, but once gone up. From henceforth he dieth no more, but liveth with God, and reigneth in everlasting continuance of glory. So, if we are dead; if we are buried to sin; how shall we hereafter live in the same? If we are risen again with Christ; if by stedfast hope we live now in heaven with him; heavenly and godly things, not earthly and frail, we ought to set our care upon. And even as heretofore we have borne the image of the earthly man; so, from henceforward let us bear the image of the heavenly.

As the Lord Christ never ceases to do us good, by bestowing upon us his Holy Spirit, by garnishing his church with so many notable gifts, and by perpetually praying to his Father for us; like reason ought to move us to aid our neighbour with all our endeavour, to maintain, as much as in us lies, the bond of charity. And to honour Christ our Lord and Saviour; not with wicked traditions and cold devices of men, but with heavenly honour and spiritual indeed, most fit for us that give it, and him that shall receive it; even as he hath honoured and doth honour his Father: for he that honoureth him, honoureth also the Father; of which he himself is a substantial witness.

*M.* The end of the world, holy scripture calls the fulfilling and performance of the kingdom and mystery of Christ, and the renewing of all things. For, says the apostle Peter, 2 Pet. iii. We look for a new heaven and a new earth, according to the promise of God: wherein dwelleth righteousness. And it seems reason that corruption, unstedfast change, and sin, whereunto the whole world is subject, should at length have an end. Now, by what way, and what fashion of circumstances, these things shall come to pass, I would fain hear thee tell.

*S.* I will tell you, as well as I can, according to the witness of the same apostle; The heavens shall pass away like a storm: the elements shall melt away: the earth and all the works therein shall be consumed with fire: as though he should say, As gold is wont to be fined, so shall the whole world be purified with fire, and be brought to its full perfection. The lesser world, which is man, following the same, shall likewise be delivered from corruption and change. And so for man this greater world, which for his sake was first created, shall at length be renewed, and be clad with another hue, much more pleasant and beautiful.

*M.* What then remaineth?

*S.* The last and general doom. For Christ shall come: at whose voice all the dead shall rise again, perfect and sound, both in body and soul. The whole world shall behold him sitting in the royal throne of his majesty: and after the examination of every man's conscience, the last sentence shall be pronounced. Then the children of God shall be in perfect possession of that kingdom of freedom from death, and of everlasting life, which was prepared for them, before the foundations of the world were laid. And they shall reign with Christ for ever. But the ungodly, who believed not, shall be thrown from thence into everlasting fire, appointed for the devil and his angels.

*M.* Thou hast said enough of the again rising of the dead. Now, it remains that thou speak of the holy church; whereof I would very fain hear thy opinion.

*S.* I will rehearse that in few words shortly, which the holy scriptures set out at large and plentifully. Before that the Lord God had made the heaven and earth, he determined to have for himself a most beautiful kingdom and holy commonwealth. The apostles and the ancient fathers, that wrote in Greek, called it Ecclesia, in English, a congregation or assembly: into which he hath admitted an infinite number of men, that should all be subject to one King, as their sovereign and only one head: him we call Christ, which is as much as to say, Anointed. For the high bishops, and kings among the Jews, who in figure betokened Christ, whom the Lord anointed with his Holy Spirit, were wont by God's appointment, at their consecration, to have material oil poured on them.

To the furnishing of this commonwealth belong all they, as many as do truly fear, honour, and call upon God, wholly applying their mind to holy and godly living: and all those that, putting all their hope and trust in him, do assuredly look for the bliss of everlasting life. But as many as are in this faith stedfast, were forechosen, predestinated, and appointed out to everlasting life, before the world was made.

Witness hereof, they have within in their hearts the Spirit of Christ, the author, earnest, and unfailable pledge of their faith. Which faith only is able to perceive the mysteries of God: only bringeth peace unto the heart: only taketh hold on the righteousness that is in Christ Jesus.

*M.* Doth then the Spirit alone, and faith, sleep we ever so soundly, or stand we ever so reckless and slothful, so work all things for us, as without any help of our own to carry us idle up to heaven?

*S.* I use, master, as you have taught me, to make a difference between the cause and the effects. The first, principal, and most perfect cause of our justifying and salvation, is the goodness and love of God; whereby he chose us for his, before he made the world. After that, God granteth us to be called by the preaching of the gospel of Jesus Christ, when the Spirit of the Lord is poured into us; by whose guiding and governance we are led to settle our trust in God, and hope for the performance of all his promises. With this choice is joined, as companion, the mortifying of the old man; that is, of our affections and lusts.

From the same Spirit also cometh our sanctification, the love of God and of our neighbour, justice, and uprightness of life. Finally, to say all in sum, whatsoever is in us, or may be done of us, pure, honest, true, and good; that altogether springs out of this most pleasant root, from this most plentiful fountain, the goodness, love, choice, and unchangeable purpose of God. He is the cause, the rest are the fruits and effects. Yet the goodness, choice, and Spirit of God, and Christ himself, are also causes conjoined and coupled each with other; which may be reckoned among the principal causes of our salvation. As oft therefore as we use to say, that we are made righteous and saved by only faith, it is meant thereby, that faith, or rather trust alone, doth lay hand upon, understand, and perceive our righteous-making to be given us of God freely: that is to say, by no deserts of our own, but by the free grace of the almighty Father.

Moreover, faith doth engender in us the love of our neighbour; and such works as God is pleased withal. For if it be a lively and true faith, quickened by the Holy Ghost, it is the mother of all good saying and doing. By this short tale is it evident, whence and by what means we attain to be made righteous. For, not by the worthiness of our deservings, were we either heretofore chosen, or long ago saved; but by the only mercy of God, and pure grace of Christ our Lord; whereby we were in him made to those good works, that God hath appointed for us to walk in. And although good works cannot deserve to make us righteous before God; yet do they so cleave unto faith, that neither can faith be found without them, nor good works be any where without faith.

*M.* I like very well this short declaration of faith and works; for Paul plainly teaches the same. But canst thou yet further depaint\* me out that congregation, which thou callest a kingdom, or commonwealth of christians: and so set it out before mine eyes, that it may severally and plainly be known asunder from each other fellowship of men?

*S.* I will prove how well I can do it. Your pleasure is, master, as I take it, that I point you out some certain congregation, that may be seen.

*M.* That it is indeed; and so it shall be good for you to do.

*S.* That congregation is nothing else but a certain multitude of men; which, wheresoever they are, profess the pure and upright learning of Christ, and that in such sort as it is faithfully set forth in the holy testament by the evangelists and apostles; which in all points are governed and ruled by the laws and statutes of their King and High bishop, Christ, in the bond of charity; which use his holy mysteries, that are commonly called sacraments, with such pureness and simplicity, as touching their nature and substance, as the apostles of Christ used, and left behind in writing.

The marks therefore of this church are; first, pure preaching of the gospel; then brotherly love, out of which, as members all out of one body, spring good will of each to the other: thirdly, upright and uncorrupted use of the Lord's sacraments, according to the ordinance of the gospel: last of all, brotherly correction and excommunication, or banishing those out of the church, that will not amend their lives. This mark the holy fathers termed discipline. This is that same church that is grounded upon the assured rock, Jesus Christ, and upon truth in him. This is that same church, which Paul calls the pillar and upholding stay of truth. To this church belong the keys, wherewith

\* Describe.

heaven is locked and unlocked; for that is done by the ministration of the word; whereunto properly appertains the power to bind and loose; to hold for guilty, and forgive sins. So that whosoever believeth the gospel preached in this church, he shall be saved; but whosoever believeth not, he shall be damned.

*M.* Now, would I fain hear thy belief of the Holy Ghost.

*S.* I confess him to be the third person of the Holy Trinity. And since he is equal with the Father and the Son, and of the very same nature, he ought equally to be worshipped with them both.

*M.* Why is he called holy?

*S.* Not only for his own holiness, but for that by him are made holy the chosen of God, and members of Christ. And therefore have the scriptures termed him the Spirit of sanctification, or making holy.

*M.* Wherein consisteth this sanctification?

*S.* First, we are newly begotten by his inward motion. And therefore said Christ, we must be new-born of water, and of the Spirit. Then by his inspiration are we adopted, and as it were by choice made the children of God. For which cause he is not causelessly called the Spirit of adoption. By his light, are we enlightened to understand God's mysteries. By his judgment, are sins pardoned and retained. By his power, is the flesh with her lusts kept down and tamed. By his pleasure, are the manifold gifts dealt among the holy. Finally, by his means, shall our mortal bodies be raised again to life. Therefore, in the Author of so great gifts, we do not without a cause believe, honour, and call upon him.

*M.* Well, thou hast now said sufficiently of the Holy Ghost. But this would I hear of thee, why it immediately follows, that we believe the holy universal church, and the communion of saints?

*S.* These two things I have always thought to be most fitly coupled together. Because the fellowships and incorporations of other men proceed, and are governed by other means and policies; but the church, which is an assembly of men called to everlasting salvation, is both gathered together, and governed by the Holy Ghost, of whom we even now made mention. Which thing, since it cannot be perceived by bodily sense or light of nature, is, by right and for good reason, here reckoned among things that are known by belief.

And therefore, this calling together of the faithful is called universal, because it is bound to no one special place. For God, throughout all coasts of the world, hath them that worship him; which, though they are far scattered asunder by divers distance of countries and dominions, yet are they members most nearly joined of that same body, whereof Christ is the head; and have one spirit, faith, sacraments, prayers, forgiveness of sins, and heavenly bliss, common among them all; and are so knit with the bond of love, that they endeavour themselves in nothing more, than each to help the other, and to build together in Christ.

*M.* Seeing thou hast already spoken of the knowledge of God and his members: I would also hear what is the true service of God?

*S.* First, we must consider that the right and true knowledge of God, is the principal and only foundation of God's service. The same knowledge, fear doth foster and maintain, which in scriptures is called, The beginning of wisdom. Faith and hope are the props and stays, whereupon lean all the rest that I have rehearsed. Furthermore, charity, which we call love, is like an everlasting bond, by the strait knot whereof all other virtues are bound in one together, and their force increased. These are the inward parts of God's service; that is to say, which consist in the mind.

*M.* What hast thou to say of the sabbath, or the holy day, which even now thou madest mention of, among the laws of the first table?

*S.* Sabbath is as much to say, as "rest." It was appointed for only honour and service of God, and it is a figure of that rest and quietness which they have that believe in Christ. For our trust in Christ doth set our minds at liberty from all slavish fear of the law, sin, death, and hell; assuring us in the mean season, that by him we please God, and that he hath made us his children, and heirs of his kingdom; whereby there groweth in our hearts peace and true quietness of mind; which is a certain foretaste of the most blessed quiet, which we shall have in his kingdom.

As for those things that are used to be done on the sabbath day, as ceremonies and exercises in the service of God, they are tokens and witnesses of this assured trust.

And meet it is, that faithful christians, on such days as are appointed out for holy things, should lay aside unholy works, and give themselves earnestly to religion and serving of God.

*M.* What are the parts of that outward serving God, which thou saidst even now did stand in certain bodily exercises; which are also tokens of the inward serving him?

*S.* First, to teach and hear the learning of the gospel; then, the pure and natural use of the ceremonies and sacraments; last of all, prayer made unto God by Christ, and in the name of Christ, which without fail obtaineth the Holy Ghost, the most assured author of all true serving of God, and upright religion.

*M.* Tell me what thou callest sacraments?

*S.* They are certain customary, reverent doings and ceremonies, ordained by Christ, that by them he might put us in remembrance of his benefits, and we might declare our profession, that we be of the number of them which are partakers of the same benefits, and which fasten all their affiance in him: that we are not ashamed of the name of Christ, or to be termed Christ's scholars.

*M.* Tell me, my son, how these two sacraments are ministered; baptism, and that which Paul calleth the supper of the Lord?

*S.* Him that believeth in Christ, professeth the articles of the christian religion, and mindeth to be baptized, (I speak now of them that be grown to ripe years of discretion, since for the young babes their parents' or the church's profession sufficeth,) the minister dippeth in, or washeth with pure and clean water only, in the name of the Father, and of the Son, and of the Holy Ghost: and then commendeth him by prayer to God, into whose church he is now openly, as it were, enrolled, that it may please God to grant him his grace, whereby he may answer in belief and life agreeably to his profession.

*M.* What is the use of the Lord's supper?

*S.* Even the very same that was ordained by the Lord himself, Jesus Christ. Who, as St. Paul saith, the same night that he was betrayed, took bread: and when he had given thanks, brake it, and said; This is my body, which is broken for you; do this in remembrance of me. In like manner, when supper was ended, he gave them the cup, saying, This cup is the new testament in my blood. Do this, as oft as ye shall drink thereof, in the remembrance of me. This was the manner and order of the Lord's supper, which we ought to hold and keep; that the remembrance of so great a benefit, the passion and death of Christ, be always kept in mind: that after that the world is ended, he may come and make us to sit with him at his own board.

*M.* What does baptism represent and set before our eyes?

*S.* That we are by the Spirit of Christ new born, and cleansed from sin; that we are members and parts of his church, received into the communion of saints. For water signifieth the Spirit. Baptism is also a figure of our burial in Christ, and that we shall be raised up again with him in a new life, as I have before declared in Christ's resurrection.

*M.* What declares and betokens the supper unto us; which we solemnly use in the remembrance of the Lord?

*S.* The supper, as I have showed a little before, is a certain thankful remembrance of the death of Christ; forasmuch as the bread represents his body, betrayed to be crucified for us; the wine stands in stead and place of his blood, plenteously shed for us. And even as by bread and wine our natural bodies are sustained and nourished; so by the body, that is, the flesh and blood of Christ, the soul is fed through faith, and quickened to the heavenly and godly life.

*M.* How come these things to pass?

*S.* These things come to pass by a certain secret mean and lively working of the Spirit; when we believe that Christ hath, once for all, given up his body and blood for us, to make a sacrifice and most pleasant offering to his heavenly Father; and also when we confess and acknowledge him our Saviour, High bishop, Mediator, and Redeemer, to whom is due all honour and glory.

*M.* All this thou dost well understand. For methinks thy meaning is, that faith is the mouth of the soul; whereby we receive this heavenly meat, full both of salvation and immortality, dealt among us by the means of the Holy Ghost. Now, since we have treated of the sacraments, pass forward to the other parts of God's service.

*S.* I will do your commandment. There remain two things belonging to the perfection of God's service. First, our Lord Jesus Christ's will was, that there should be teachers and evangelists; that is to say, preachers of the gospel, to this intent, that his voice might continually be heard to sound in his church. He that covets as all ought

o covet, to bear the name of a christian, may have no
doubt that he ought, with most earnest affection and fervent
desire, endeavour himself to hear and soak* into his mind
the word of the Lord: not like the words of any man, but
like, as it is indeed, the word of almighty God.

Secondly. Because all that is good, and that ought of a
christian to be desired, cometh unto us from God, and is
by him granted; therefore of him we ought to require all
things: and by thanksgiving acknowledge them all received
of him. Which he so well liketh, that he esteemeth it instead of a passing pleasant sacrifice; as it is most evident
by the witness of the prophets and apostles.

*M.* Hast thou any certain and appointed manner of
praying?

*S.* Yea, forsooth; even the very same that our Lord
taught his disciples, and in them all other christians. Who
being on a time required to teach them some sort of prayer,
taught them this. When ye pray, said he, say, Our Father
which art in heaven, hallowed be thy name. Thy kingdom
come. Thy will be done in earth, as it is in heaven. Give
us this day our daily bread, and forgive us our trespasses,
as we forgive them that trespass against us. And lead us
not into temptation. But deliver us from evil: for thine is
the kingdom, power, and glory, for ever. Amen.

*M.* How thinkest thou, Is it lawful for us, to use any
other words of prayer?

*S.* Although in this short abridgement are sufficiently
contained all things that every christian ought to pray for;
yet hath not Christ in this prayer tied us up so short, as
that it were not lawful for us to use other words and manner of prayer. But he hath set out in this prayer certain
principal points, whereunto all our prayers should be referred. But, let each man ask of God, as his present need
requireth. Whatsoever ye ask the Father in my name,
saith Christ, he shall give it you.

*M.* Forasmuch as there is in all this prayer nothing
doubtful, or beside the purpose: I would hear thy mind
of it.

*S.* I do well perceive what the words do signify.

*M.* Thinkest thou then, that there is in it nothing dark,
nothing hid, nothing hard to understand?

*S.* Nothing at all. For neither was it Christ's pleasure
that there should be any thing in it dark, or far from our

* Imbibe.

capacity, especially since it belongs equally to all, and it is as necessary for the simple as the learned.

*M.* Therefore declare unto me in few words each part by itself?

*S.* When I say, Our Father which art in heaven: this do I think with myself, that it cannot be, but that he must hear me, and be pleased with my prayers. For I am his son, although unprofitable and disobedient, and he on the other side is my most bountiful Father, most ready to take pity and pardon me.

*M.* Why dost thou say, he is in heaven? Is he in some one certain and limited place in heaven? What means that, which he saith of himself, I fill both heaven and earth? again, The heaven is my seat and the earth my footstool?

*S.* Hereof have I spoken somewhat before, whereunto I will join this that follows. First of all, as oft as we do say, Which art in heaven, it is as much to say as, heavenly and divine; for we ought to think much higher of our heavenly Father than of our earthly.

He is also said to be in heaven for this cause, that in that high and heavenly place, the notable and wonderful works of God do the more clearly and gloriously show themselves; and he is now declared to be in everlasting and full felicity; whereas we abide, yet banished in earth full wretchedly. Moreover, as the heaven, by unmeasurable wideness of compass, contains all places, the earth, and the sea; and no place is there that may be hid from the large reach of heaven, since it is at every instant of time to every thing present; so, hereby may we understand, that God is likewise present to each thing and in each place. He seeth, heareth, and governeth all things, he being himself a Spirit and most far from all earthly and mortal state. Witness whereof Jeremiah the prophet. Am not I, saith the Lord, a God near unto you? And am not I a God far off? Shall any man be able to shroud himself in such a corner, that I cannot espy him?

This is a pithy sentence to drive fear into us, that we offend not that Lord of so large a dominion; whereby also we are persuaded assuredly to believe, that God will hear, whensoever we shall stand in need. For he is at all times, and in all places present. This foundation then laid, and so sweet and pleasant entrance prepared, there follows the first part of the Lord's prayer; wherein we require, that not only we, but also all others whosoever, may in holiness honour, reverence, and worship his name.

*M.* How is that to be done?

*S.* I shall show you. Then we do that, when leaving all those that have the name of gods, be they in heaven or in earth, or worshipped in temples, in divers shapes and images; we acknowledge him alone, our Father; pray to the true God, and Jesus Christ, his only Son, whom he hath sent; and by pure unfeigned prayer call upon him alone with uprightness of life and innocency.

*M.* Thou hast said very well. Proceed.

*S.* In the second part we require, that his kingdom come. For we see not yet all things in subjection to Christ. We see not the stone hewn off from the mountain without work of man, which altogether bruised and brought to nought the image, which Daniel describes; that the only rock, Christ, may obtain and possess the dominion of the whole world, granted him of his Father.

Antichrist is not yet slain. For this cause do we long for and pray, that it may at length come to pass and be fulfilled, that Christ may reign with his saints, according to God's promises. That he may live and be Lord in the world, according to the decrees of the holy gospel; not after the traditions and laws of men, or pleasure of worldly tyrants.

*M.* God grant his kingdom may come, and that speedily.

*S.* Moreover, since it is the children's duty to frame their life to their father's will, and not the father's to bow to the children's pleasure; forasmuch as our will is commonly by exciting of affections, and stirring of lusts, drawn to do those things that God is displeased with; it is reason, that we hang wholly upon the beck of our heavenly Father, and wholly submit ourselves to his heavenly government. Wherefore, for this cause, we mortal men do pray, that we may in like case be obedient to his commandment, as are the sun and moon, and other stars in heaven, which by ordinary courses, and by enlightening the earth with incessant beams, execute the Lord's will continually. Or that we, as the angels and other divine spirits, in all points obey him; who bestow all their travail diligently, to accomplish his godly commandments.

Next after that, he teacheth us to ask of our heavenly Father our bread: whereby he meaneth not meat only, but also all things else, needful for maintenance and preserving of life: that we may learn, that God alone is author of all things; who maketh the fruits of the earth both to grow and increase to plenty. Wherefore, it is meet that we call upon him alone in prayer; who, as David saith, alone feedeth and maintaineth all things.

*M.* Some suppose this place to mean that bread which Christ maketh mention of in the sixth of John. That is, of the true knowledge and taste of Christ, who was born and died for us; wherewith the faithful soul is fed. The reason whereupon they gather this, is the Greek word, (EPIOUSION,) whereby they understand, supernatural, spiritual, heavenly, and divine. This meaning I refuse not, for both these expositions may fitly agree with this place; but why calleth he it daily bread, which is also signified by this word?

*S.* We ask daily bread, that might be always present and accompany us continually; to slake and satisfy our thirsty desire, and unsatiate stomach; lest otherwise we should be, as Christ saith, careful for to-morrow; because the morrow shall care for itself. For it shall not come without its own discommodity and care; wherefore, it is not reason, that one day should increase the evil of another. It shall be sufficient for us daily to ask, that which our most bountiful Father is ready daily to give.

Now follows the fifth request, wherein we beseech the Father to forgive us our trespasses and faults, that we have committed. This request, doubtless, is very necessary, since there is no man living free from sin. Here, therefore, must we cast away all trust of ourselves. Here, must we pluck down our courage. Here, must we pray our most merciful Father, for the love of Jesus Christ, his most dear and obedient Son, to pardon, forgive, and utterly blot out of his book, our innumerable offences.

Here, ought we, in the mean season, to be mindful of the covenant we make with God. That it may please God so to forgive us our trespasses, as we ourselves forgive them that trespass against us. Therefore, it is necessary that we forgive and pardon all men all their offences, of what sort or condition soever they are. If we forgive men their faults, our heavenly Father shall forgive us ours.

*M.* Were these things, my son, thus used, there should not at this day thus violently reign so many brawls, so many contentions, so many and such heinous disagreements, enmities, and hatreds of one man to another. But now, whereas each man so standeth in his own conceit, that he will not lose an inch of his right, either in honour or wealth; it oft befalls, that they lose both their wealth, their honour, and their life itself withal. Yea, they put from themselves, and turn away, the favour of God and everlasting glory.

But thou, my son, must not be ignorant of Christ's commandment; nor of that which Paul teaches, that thou suffer not thyself to be overcome of evil, that is, suffer not thyself so to be seduced by any other man's offence, as to repay evil for evil, but rather overcome evil with good. I mean by doing him good, that hath done thee evil; by using him friendly, that hath showed himself thy most cruel foe. Now, go forward to the sixth request.

*S.* I will, with a good will, as you command me. Forasmuch as we are feeble, weak, subject to a thousand perils, a thousand temptations, easy to be overcome, ready to yield to every light occasion, either to men fraught with malice, or to our own lusts and appetites, or finally, to the crafty malicious serpent, the devil; therefore, we beseech our Father, that he bring us into no temptation, no such hard escape and peril; nor leave us in the very plunge of danger; but, if it come to that point, that he rather take us away from the present mischief and engines of the devil, the author and principal cause of all evil, than suffer us to run headlong into destruction. Now, have you, good master, in few words all that you have taught me, unless peradventure, somewhat be overslipped in the rehearsal.

*M.* Because thine is the kingdom, power, and glory, for ever. Amen. Why was it Christ's pleasure to knit up our prayer with this clause in the end?

*S.* Partly, that we should declare our assured trust to obtain all things, that we have before required. For there is nothing which, if it be asked with faith, he is not able or not willing to give, who ruleth and governeth all things, who is able to do all things, who is garnished with endless glory.

These things, when we rehearse of God, our Father, there remaineth no cause to doubt, or suspect that we shall receive denial. Partly, by so saying, we teach ourselves how meet it is to make our suit to God, since beside him none glistereth with such shining glory, none hath dominion so large, or force so great, to be able to stay him from giving that he hath appointed, according to his pleasure; or to take away that which he hath already given us. And there is no evil of ours so great, that may not be put away by his exceeding great power, glory, and wisdom.

*M.* I like well, my son, this thy short declaration; and I see nothing left out, that ought to have been spoken.

*S.* But yet this one thing will I add thereto. The chief and principal thing required in prayer is, that without all doubting we stedfastly believe, that God, our Father, will grant what we do ask: so, that it be neither unprofitable for us to receive, nor unfit for him to give. For he that is not assured, but doubtful, let him not think, as James saith, to get anything at the hands of God.

*M.* I see now, my dear son, how diligently and heedfully thou hast applied thy mind to those things that I have taught thee; how godly and upright a judgment thou hast of God's true service; and of the duties of neighbours one to another. This remains, that from henceforth thou so frame thy life, that this heavenly and godly knowledge decay not in thee, nor lie soul-less and dead, as it were in a tomb of the flesh. But rather see that thou wholly give thyself, continually and earnestly, to these godly studies. So, thou shalt live, not only in this present life, but also in the life to come, which is much better and more blessed than this life present. For godliness, as Paul saith, hath a promise, not in this life only, but in the other. It is convenient, therefore, that we earnestly follow godliness, which plainly openeth the way to heaven, if we will seek to attain thereto.

And the principal point of godliness is, as thou hast declared even now very well, to know God only; to covet him only as the chief felicity; to fear him, as our Lord; to love and reverence him, as our Father, with his Son, our Saviour Jesus Christ. This is he, who hath begotten and regenerated us. This is he, who at the beginning gave us life and soul: who maintaineth, who blesseth us with life of everlasting continuance. To this godliness is directly contrary godlessness. As for superstition and hypocrisy, they counterfeit indeed, and resemble it: whereas, nevertheless they are most far different from all true godliness; and therefore we ought to avoid them, as a pestilence, as the venom, and most contagious enemies of our soul and salvation.

The next point of godliness is, to love each man as our brother. For if God did at the beginning create us all; if he doth feed and govern us; finally, if he be the cause and author of our dwelling in this wide frame of the world; the name of brother must needs most fitly agree with us.

And with so much straiter bond shall we be bound together, as we approach nearer to Christ, who is our brother, the first begotten and eldest; whom he that knoweth not, he that hath no hold of, is unrighteous indeed, and hath no place among the people of God. For Christ is the root and foundation of all right and justice, and he hath poured into our hearts certain natural lessons; as, Do that, saith he to another, that thou wouldst have done unto thyself.

Beware therefore, thou do nothing to any man, that thou thyself wouldest not willingly suffer. Measure always another by thine own mind, and as thou feelest in thyself. If it grieve thee to suffer injury, if thou think it wrong that another man doth to thee; judge likewise the same in the person of thy neighbour, that thou feelest in thyself; and thou shalt perceive, that thou dost no less wrongfully in hurting another, than others do in hurting thee.

Here, if we would stedfastly fasten our feet; hereunto if we would earnestly travail; we should attain to the very highest top of innocency. For the first degree thereof is, to offend no man. The next, to help all men as much as in us lieth; at least to will and wish well to all. The third, which is accounted the chief and most perfect, is to do good, even to our enemies that wrong us.

Let us, therefore, know ourselves, pluck out the faults that are in us, and in their place plant virtues; like unto the husbandmen, that first use to stub and root out the thorns, brambles, and weeds, out of their fallow land and unlooked to; and then each where therein scatter and throw in to the earth good and fruitful seeds, to bring forth good fruit in their due season. Likewise let us do. For first, let us labour to root out froward and corrupt lusts; and afterwards plant holy and fit conditions for christian hearts. Which, if they are watered, and fattened with the dew of God's word, and nourished with warmth of the Holy Ghost, they shall bring forth, doubtless, the most plentiful fruit of immortality and blessed life; which God hath by Christ prepared for his chosen, before the foundations of the world were laid. To whom be all honour and glory. Amen.

Bishop Randolph observes, " This Catechism, published in the time of king Edward VI., was the last work of the reformers of that reign; whence it may fairly be understood to contain, as far as it goes, their ultimate decision, and to represent the sense of the church of England as then established."

# THE PRIMER

OF

# KING EDWARD VI.

PRIMERS are books intended to assist private devotion; also designed for the instruction of children and young persons, and for family use. Such compilations were common in the church of Rome previously to the reformation and during its progress. They were, however, almost entirely in Latin, so as to be intelligible only to those acquainted with that language. If others learned prayers from their contents, it was merely to repeat them by rote in a language they understood not. While popery prevailed in England, Primers in the vulgar tongue were not allowed. In the year 1519, six men and a woman were burned at Coventry, the accusation against whom was having taught their children to repeat the Lord's prayer and the commandments in English; while the children were admonished by the persecutors not to meddle again with the Lord's prayer, the belief, or the commandments in English, if they wished to escape a similar fate! (*See the narrative and authorities in Fox's Acts and Monuments.*)

The reformers were not indifferent to the important subject of education and popular instruction. As early as 1529, an elementary book of this description had been published in English, as appears from its being prohibited with other protestant works, in a proclamation issued that year. But when the reformation had proceeded further, the subject was revived, and in 1535, an English Primer was set forth by authority. From the size and contents of this work it evidently was designed for general use, as a complete manual of devotion, and not merely for elementary instruction—this was the more important as the public services were still continued according to the church of Rome. It was edited by Dr. Marshal, archdeacon of Nottingham, but Cranmer doubtless assisted in the work. Strype (*Memorials*, I. i. ch. xxxi.) has given a very particular account of this book and its contents, which were designed, as he states, "to make the common people understand their prayers and divine worship, and to cure some gross errors in religion, that were then by popish craft generally entertained by the vulgar, by putting superstitious books into their hands—the good design therefore was, that the laity might be furnished with a better direction for prayers and devotions than they usually had before." This Primer was chiefly a collection of small tracts containing admonitions and instructions as well as devotions for ordinary christians, and whatever may be thought concerning the utility of such works in times of greater light and knowledge, they were then doubtless of much use to many. The best proof of this was the offence taken by the papists, who when they regained a portion of their influence some years after, caused several of these pieces to be prohibited, although as a whole the work was far from being free from Romish errors. It contained, however, cautions against the worship of the virgin and other superstitious practices.

A smaller Primer in English was soon afterwards published by Hilsey, bishop of Rochester, but this, and others which were printed later in the reign of Henry VIII., were not wholly freed from Romish doctrines. The best is that which was printed in 1546, the last year of Henry. It has been reprinted, and is not uncommon. The Latin Romish Primers were also from time to time reprinted; the most popular in England seems to have been the one "according to Salisbury use." An edition of this, printed in the last year of queen Mary, is in Latin and English in parallel columns. So far the papists conceded to the popular desire for instruction, but it contains the grossest errors of popery.

During the reign of Edward VI. the primers were printed in English, and in the successive editions, alterations may be found marking the progress of religious knowledge. The most complete was set forth immediately after the publication of the revised and improved edition of the Common Prayer. An exclusive privilege was given to William Seres, dated 4th of March, 1552, (1553,) to print all books of private prayers, called Primers.

In the prayers for the general use of more than one person, this edition was conformed to the Common Prayer; and various improvements and additions were introduced into those intended for the use of single individuals.

The subsequent history of the protestant English Primer is very brief, and the causes of its disuse are not difficult to ascertain. In the reformation under Elizabeth a greater degree of uniformity as to public and social formularies of devotion was required, than ever had been deemed requisite by the earlier reformers, and, indeed, more than has been enforced by the church of Rome, which, in social worship, allows almost unbounded liberty. Thus the Primer was neglected by the more strict adherents to the public formularies of that day, and of course was not used by those who opposed such uniformity. The more general diffusion of religious knowledge, and the variety of devotional works issued from the press, also rendered the Primer less requisite for families, while being rather a book of devotion than of elementary instruction, it became less important in religious education, for which other assistance was provided.

Although there may not be at the present day any necessity for urging the use of the Primer, according to the original design of the compilers, yet the excellent private prayers it contains will be acceptable and useful to many; they certainly are valuable remains of the British reformers, and in the last edition of king Edward's reign, from which the following pages are reprinted, they exhibit the principles which those who were then in authority desired to convey into every house, and to inculcate on every heart, throughout the land. They manifestly prove the importance which the reformers attached to *personal religion*, and show that it was not forgotten or neglected amidst their more public labours.

EXTRACTS FROM

# THE PRIMER;

OR,

## BOOK OF PRIVATE PRAYER, NEEDFUL TO BE USED OF ALL CHRISTIANS.

AUTHORIZED AND SET FORTH BY ORDER OF KING EDWARD VI., TO BE TAUGHT, LEARNED, READ, AND USED, OF ALL HIS SUBJECTS.

Printed A. D. 1553.

**GRACES TO BE SAID BEFORE DINNER AND SUPPER.**

### GRACE BEFORE DINNER.

The eyes of all look up and trust in thee, O Lord, thou givest them meat in due season. Thou openest thine hand, and fillest with thy blessing every living thing. Good Lord, bless us, and all thy gifts which we receive of thy bounteous liberality, through Christ our Lord. Amen.

The King of eternal glory make us partakers of his heavenly table. Amen.

God is charity;[*] and he that dwelleth in charity[*] dwelleth in God, and God in him. God grant us all to dwell in him. Amen.

### GRACE AFTER DINNER.

The God of peace and love vouchsafe always to dwell with us; and thou, Lord, have mercy upon us. Glory, honour, and praise be to thee, O God, who hast fed us from our tender age, and givest sustenance to every living thing; replenish our hearts with joy and gladness, that we, always having sufficient, may be rich and plentiful in all good works, through our Lord Jesus Christ. Amen.

### GRACE BEFORE SUPPER.

O Lord Jesus Christ, without whom nothing is good, nothing is holy; we beseech thee to bless us and our supper; and with thy blessed presence to cheer our hearts; that in all our meats and drinks, we may taste or savour of thee, to thy honour and glory. Amen.

[*] Love.

### GRACE AFTER SUPPER.

Blessed is God in all his gifts; and holy in all his works. Our help is in the name of the Lord, who hath made both heaven and earth. Blessed be the name of our Lord, from henceforth, world without end.

Most mighty Lord and merciful Father, we yield thee hearty thanks for our bodily sustenance, requiring also, most entirely, thy gracious goodness, so to feed us with the food of thy heavenly grace, that we may worthily glorify thy holy name in this life, and afterwards be made partakers of the life everlasting, through our Lord Jesus Christ. Amen. Lord save thy church, our king and realm; and send us peace in Christ. Amen.

### GRACE BEFORE SUPPER.

Christ, who at his last supper, promised his body to be crucified, and his precious blood to be shed for our sins, bless us and our supper. Amen.

### THANKS AFTER DINNER OR SUPPER.

All ye whom God hath here refreshed with this sufficient repast, remember your poor and needy brethren; of whom some lie in the streets, sore, sick, naked, and cold; some are hungry and so dry, that they would be glad of the least draught of your drink, and of the smallest paring of your bread. They are your own flesh, and brethren in Christ; bought as dearly with his precious blood as you were; but yet our Lord has dealt more easily with you than with them, and more austerely with them than with you; relieve them therefore according to your power; and give to God all glory, honour and praise, for ever and ever. Amen.

---

### BEFORE THOU PRAY.

First; Examine thine own conscience with what kind of temptation or sin thou art most encumbered withal; and pray earnestly to God for remedies thereto. Asking of him all things needful both for soul and body; privately for thine own self and thy family, and generally for all the christian congregation. If any of you lack wisdom (that is, any gift of grace) let him ask of God who giveth to all men indifferently, and casteth no man in the teeth,* and it shall be given him.

* Giveth to all

Secondly; Upon consideration of thine own lack, and the common lack* of the congregation, remember that God commandeth thee by prayer to call upon him for remedy, aid, and help, saying: "Ask, seek, knock; watch and pray;" call upon me, saith God, " in the day of tribulation."

Thirdly; Consider that God doth not only command thee to pray, but also promiseth graciously to hear and grant all thine honest, lawful, and godly requests and petitions; saying, "Ask, and ye shall have; knock, and it shall be opened unto you; every one that asketh, hath, &c. "Call upon me," saith God, "in the day of trouble, and I will deliver thee."

Fourthly; Thou must stedfastly believe God's promises; and trust undoubtedly, both that he can and will perform them. "Ask in faith," saith St. James, " nothing doubting;" for why shouldest thou doubt, seeing that the holy scripture testifies of God, that he is faithful, just, and true, in all his words and promises; saying, "The Lord is faithful in all his words. He will ever be mindful of his covenant. The truth of the Lord endureth for ever."

Fifthly; Thou must ask of God all thy petitions and requests, for his mercy and truth sake; for Christ Jesus' sake, and in his blessed and holy name. "Save me, O God," saith David, "for thy name's sake." "No man cometh unto the Father, but by me," saith Christ. " Verily, verily, I say unto you, whatsoever you ask of the Father in my name, he will give it you." Mark, that he saith, "In my name."

Sixthly; Thou must never ask for worldly and corruptible things, pertaining to this transitory life, such as bodily health, wealth, or strength, without employing in thy prayer such conditions as these, "If it be thy will, O Lord; if it stand with thine honour and glory; if it be for my soul's health, profit, and advantage; if not, thy will be done and not mine." All these things your heavenly Father knoweth that ye have need of, before ye ask of him. With this condition prayed Christ, saying, "Father, if it be possible, let this cup pass from me; nevertheless, not as I will, but as thou wilt." With this condition prayed David for his return in his exile.

Seventhly; Thou must not appoint any certain time to God for granting thy requests; but utterly commit that to his godly will and pleasure, who knows best what time of granting thy requests is most commodious and profitable for thee.

* General need.

Finally; Thou must in any wise take heed, when thou prayest, that thou art in love and charity with all men; or else, all these aforesaid things profit nothing at all. For, like as a surgeon cannot heal a wound perfectly, so long as any iron remains in it, even so, prayer cannot profit, so long as the mind is cankered and defiled with guile, fraud, deceit, rancour, hatred, malice, and such other like wretchedness; for brotherly reconciliation must needs go before prayer. As Christ saith, "If thou offerest thy gift at the altar, and there rememberest that thy brother hath aught against thee, leave there thine offering before the altar, and go thy way; first be reconciled to thy brother, and then come, and offer thy gift."

Prepare thyself therefore to prayer with the eight aforesaid considerations; and, being adorned and garnished with faith, hope, charity, meekness, soberness, equity, pity, and godliness, go in Christ's name, and pray unto God with all diligence. And that thy prayer may be more effectual, let it be joined always with temperate fasting, and charitable alms to thy needy neighbour.

And in thy faithful prayers remember that thou pray for our sovereign.

### THE SUM.
*Pray because*

1. Thou hast need.
2. God commands thee.
3. Of God's promises.
4. Pray in faith of God's promise.
5. Ask all things in Christ's name.
6. Ask worldly and temporal things conditionally.
7. Appoint God no time; but abide his pleasure.
8. In any wise pray in charity.
9. Ask things pertaining to thy salvation, remission of sin, and life everlasting, without condition. For these hath God certainly promised to all them that with a true, faithful, and obedient heart, do come unto him in earnest and continual prayer.

### A PRAYER
CONTAINING IN IT ALL THE AFORESAID PREPARATIONS UNTO PRAYER.

O gracious Lord, and most merciful Father, who hast, from the beginning of mine age, hitherto delivered me from innumerable perils and dangers, both of soul and body; I most heartily thank thee. And yet, forasmuch as I feel in myself so many faults and imperfections, such readiness to evil, and such frowardness and slackness to do good, I quake and tremble for fear of thy fierce wrath, and strict judgment. But when I consider with myself, that thou commandest me by prayer to crave of thee all things necessary for soul and body, I conceive a little hope of recovery of that which I stand in need of. And it fully comforteth me, and maketh me not a little joyful, when I remember, that thou, O Father, not only commandest me to pray, but also, of thine exceeding great mercy, promisest graciously to hear my lamentable suit; and mercifully to grant to me my lawful and needful requests. And my faith, confidence, and sure trust is, that thou art true and just in all thy words and promises, and both canst and wilt perform them, and grant me mine honest petitions. Howbeit, for all that, I will not presume to ask them in mine own name, neither for mine own merit nor deserving; but for Christ Jesus' sake; and in his blessed and holy name; and for thy mercy and truth's sake. But, touching all those things that pertain to this my corruptible body and transitory life, I humbly beseech thy fatherly goodness to grant me them, so far as they agree unto thy holy will, pleasure, honour, and glory, and may be best suited to my improvement, profit, and advantage. Nevertheless, I beseech thee, good Lord, grant me them, not at such time as I fancy to be best; but at such time, as shall appear most meet to thy godly Majesty, unto whose protection I fully and wholly commit both me and all mine. Moreover, seeing that thou regardest no prayer, unless it be made in love and charity, I humbly beseech thy gracious goodness, that I may alway pray in charity, make my petitions and requests in charity, use thy gracious gifts and benefits in charity, and lead all my whole life and conversation in charity. And, finally, I heartily pray thee, that I may daily, through the assistance of thy Holy Spirit, more and more mortify all my carnal desires and sinful affections. And vouchsafe to prosper both me and mine, and all the christian congregation, in all our honest and godly affairs: increase also thy gracious gifts in us; and confirm us and establish us so in grace, that we may go forward in all goodness; grant this most merciful Father for Jesus Christ's sake, our only Mediator and Advocate. So be it.

### THE BEGINNING OF PRAYER.

At the beginning of morning and evening private prayer, thou shalt daily read, meditate, weigh, and deeply consider out of these sentences of holy scripture that follow. And then from the bottom of thine heart add the confession of thy sins, and the prayer following.

### SENTENCES OF HOLY SCRIPTURE.

Ezek. xviii. 21—23. Ezek. xviii. 30. Zech. i. 3. Luke xiii. 3. Luke xv. 10. Matt. iii. 2. Psalm li. 17. Isaiah lv. 7. Joel ii. 12, 13. Psalm lxxxv. 4. Jer. xxxi. 18. 1 John i. 9.

### A CONFESSION OF SINS.

Almighty and most merciful Father, I have erred and strayed from thy ways like a lost sheep. I have followed too much the devices and desires of my own heart. I have offended against thy holy laws. I have left undone those things which I ought to have done; and I have done those things which I ought not to have done; and there is no health in me. But thou, O Lord, have mercy upon me a miserable offender. Spare thou me, O God, which confess my faults; restore thou me, that am penitent; according to thy promises, declared unto mankind in Christ Jesu our Lord. And grant, O most merciful Father, for his sake, that I may hereafter live a godly, righteous, and sober life, to the glory of thy holy name. Amen.

### ADD TO THIS CONFESSION THIS PRAYER.

Almighty God, the Father of our Lord Jesus Christ, which desirest not the death of a sinner, but rather that he may turn from his wickedness, and live; and hast given power and commandment to thy ministers, to declare and pronounce to thy people, being penitent, the absolution and remission of their sins; and pardonest and absolvest all them which truly repent, and unfeignedly believe thy holy gospel; I beseech thee to grant me true repentance and thy Holy Spirit; that those things may please thee which I do at this present, and that the rest of my life hereafter may be pure and holy; so that at the last I may come to thy eternal joy through Jesus Christ our Lord. Amen.*

---

* On reference to the decree of the council of Trent, De Pœnitentia, the reader will perceive that this prayer shows how decidedly the British reformers were opposed to the church of Rome respecting the

*The following Prayers are from a subsequent part of the Primer, entitled,* SUNDRY GODLY PRAYERS FOR DIVERSE PURPOSES.

### FOR GENTLEMEN.

Albeit whatsoever is born of flesh is flesh, and all that we receive of our natural parents is earth, dust, ashes, and corruption; so that no child of Adam hath any cause to boast himself of his birth and blood, begotten in sin, conceived in uncleanness, and born by nature the children of wrath ; yet, forasmuch as some for wisdom, godliness, virtue, valour, eloquence, learning, and policy, are advanced above the common sort of people, unto dignities and temporal promotions, as men worthy to have the superiority in a christian commonwealth; and, by this means, have obtained among the people a more noble and worthy name: we most entirely beseech thee, from whom cometh the true nobility to so many as are born of thee, and are made thy sons through faith, whether they are rich or poor, noble or simple, to give a good spirit to our superiors; that, as they are called gentlemen in name, so they may show themselves in all their doings, gentle, courteous, loving, merciful, and

---

ministration of what the latter calls the sacrament of penance, and absolution. The ninth, tenth, and fifteenth canons of that decree are as follows :—"IX. If any one say, that the sacramental absolution of the priest is not a judicial act, but merely a ministration of pronouncing and declaring the remission of sins to him that confesses his offences, provided he do but believe he is forgiven ; or if the priest absolve him not seriously (with intention) ; or that the confession of the penitent is not required that the priest may absolve him—let him be accursed!"—" X. If any one say, that priests who are in mortal sin, have not the power of binding and loosing ; or that priests are not the only ministers of absolution, but that it is said to all the faithful in Christ, ' Whatsoever thou shalt bind on earth shall be bound in heaven; and whatsoever thou shalt loose on earth, shall be loosed in heaven ;' also, ' Whosesoever sins ye remit, they are remitted unto them ; and whosesoever sins ye retain, they are retained'—so that by the power of these words, the open sins of any, may be absolved by any one, through rebuke alone, if the offender submit when rebuked, and in like manner secret sins may be absolved upon voluntary confession—let him be accursed!"
—" XV. If any one say, that the keys [power]were given to the church only for absolving [loosing], and not for binding [or still holding a sinner to be guilty], and therefore that priests when they impose penances [or punishments] upon those who confess, act beyond the bounds of their authority, and contrary to the institution of Christ ; also, that it is a fiction that when eternal punishment is taken away by the power of the keys, there does not, for the most part, still remain a temporal penalty to be expiated —let him be accursed !"

liberal unto their inferiors, living among them as natural fathers among their children; not oppressing them, but favouring, helping, and cherishing them: not destroyers, but fathers of the commonalty; not enemies to the poor, but aiders, helpers, and comforters of them—that when thou shalt call them from this vale of wretchedness, they, having first shown gentleness to the common people, may receive gentleness again at thy merciful hand, even everlasting life; through Jesus Christ our Lord. Amen.

### FOR LANDLORDS.

The earth is thine, O Lord, and all that is contained therein; notwithstanding, thou hast given the possession thereof to the children of men, to pass over the time of their short pilgrimage in this vale of misery. We heartily pray thee, to send thy Holy Spirit into the hearts of them that possess the grounds, pastures, and dwelling places of the earth; that they, remembering themselves to be thy tenants, may not rack, and stretch out the rents of their houses and lands; nor yet take unreasonable fines and incomes, after the manner of covetous worldlings; but so let them out to others, that the inhabitants thereof may be able both to pay the rents, and also honestly to live, to nourish their families, and to relieve the poor. Give them grace also to consider that they are but strangers and pilgrims in this world, having here no dwelling-place, but seeking one to come; that they, remembering the short continuance of their life, may be content with that is sufficient, and not join house to house, nor couple land to land, to the impoverishment of others, but so behave themselves in letting out their tenements, lands, and pastures, that after this life they may be received into everlasting dwelling-places; through Jesus Christ our Lord. Amen.

### FOR LABOURERS, AND MEN OF OCCUPATIONS.

As the bird is born to fly, so is man born to labour; for thou, O Lord, hast commanded in thy holy word, that man shall eat his bread in the labour of his hands, and in the sweat of his face: yea, thou hast given commandment, that if any man will not labour, the same should not eat; thou requirest of us, also, that we withdraw ourselves from every brother that walketh inordinately,\* and giveth not his mind unto labour; so that thy godly pleasure is that

\* Disorderly.

no man be idle, but every man labour according to his vocation and calling. We most humbly beseech thee to engrave in the hearts of labourers and workmen a willing disposition to travail for their living, according to thy word; and to bless the labourer's pains, and travails of all such as either till the earth, or exercise any other handicraft; that they, studying to be quiet, and to meddle with their own business, and to work with their own hands, and through thy blessing enjoying the fruits of their labours, may acknowledge thee, the giver of all good things, and glorify thy holy name. Amen.

### FOR RICH MEN.

Albeit, Lord, thou art the giver of all good things, and through thy blessing men become rich, that are godly and justly rich; yet we are taught in thy divine scriptures, that riches, and the cares of worldly things smother and choke up thy holy word; and that it is more easy for a camel to go through the eye of a needle, than for a rich man to enter into the kingdom of heaven. Again, that they which will be rich, fall into temptations and snares, and into many foolish and noisome lusts, which whelm men into perdition and destruction, (for covetousness is the root of all evil,) we, therefore, perceiving by thy blessed word so many incommodities, yea pestilences of man's salvation to accompany riches, most entirely beseech thee to bless such as thou hast made rich, with a good, humble, loving, and free mind; that they, remembering themselves to be thy dispensers and stewards, may not set their minds upon the deceitful treasures of this world, which are more brittle than glass, and more vain than smoke, nor yet heap up thick clay against themselves; but liberally and cheerfully bestow part of such goods, as thou hast committed unto them, upon their poor neighbours; make for themselves friends of this wicked mammon; be merciful to the needy; be rich in good works; and ready to give and to distribute to the necessity of the saints, laying up in store for themselves a good foundation, against the time to come; that they may obtain everlasting life, through Jesus Christ, thy Son, our Lord. Amen.

### FOR POOR PEOPLE.

As riches, so likewise poverty is thy gift, O Lord; and as thou hast made some rich to despise the worldly goods, so hast thou appointed some to be poor, that they may receive thy benefits at the rich man's hands. And as the godly rich are well beloved of thee, so in like manner are the poor, that bear the cross of poverty patiently and thankfully; for good and evil, life and death, poverty and riches, are of thee, O Lord; we therefore most humbly pray thee, to give a good spirit to all such as it hath pleased thee to burden with the yoke of poverty; that they may, with a patient and thankful heart, walk in their state, like to that poor Lazarus of whom we read in the gospel of thy wellbeloved Son, who chose rather patiently and godly to die, than unjustly or by force to get any man's goods, and by no means envy, murmur, or grudge against such as it hath pleased thee to endue with more abundance of worldly goods: but knowing their state, although ever so humble and base, to be of thee their Lord God, and that thou wilt not forsake them in this their great need, but send them things necessary for their poor life, may continually praise thee, and hope for better things in the world to come; through Jesus Christ our Lord. Amen.

### THE PRAYER OF A TRUE SUBJECT.

As it is thy godly appointment, O Lord God, that some should bear rule in this world to see thy glory set forth, and the common peace kept; so it is thy pleasure again, that some should be subjects and inferior to others in their vocation; although before thee there is no respect of persons. And, forasmuch as it is thy godly will and pleasure to appoint and set me in the number of subjects, I beseech thee to give me a faithful heart unto the high powers; that there may be found in me no disobedience, no unfaithfulness, no treason, no falsehood, no dissimulation, no insurrection, no commotion, no conspiracy, nor any kind of rebellion in word or in deed, against the civil magistrates; but all faithfulness, obedience, quietness, subjection, humility, and whatsoever else becometh a subject; that I, living here in all lowliness of mind, may at the last day, through thy favour, be lifted up into everlasting glory; where thou, most merciful Father, with thy Son, and the Holy Ghost, livest and reignest, very God, for ever and ever. Amen.

### OF ALL CHRISTIANS.

Albeit, O heavenly Father, all we that unfeignedly

profess thy holy religion, and faithfully call on thy blessed name, are thy sons, and heirs of everlasting glory: yet, as all the members of a body have not one office, so likewise we, being many, and making one body, whereof thy dearly beloved Son is the head, have not all one gift, neither are we all called to one office, but as it hath pleased thee to distribute, so receive we. We therefore most humbly pray thee to send thy Spirit of love and concord among us; that, without any disorder or debate, every one of us may be content with our calling; quietly live in the same; study to do good unto all men, by the true and diligent exercise thereof, without too much seeking of our own private gain; and so order our life, in all points, according to thy godly will, that by well doing we may stop the mouths of such foolish and ignorant people as report us to be evil doers; and cause them, through our good works, to glorify thee our Lord God in the day of visitation. Amen.

A PRAYER SUITABLE FOR ALL MEN; AND TO BE SAID AT ALL TIMES.

Most merciful Father, grant me to covet with an ardent mind those things which may please thee; to search them wisely, to know them truly, and to fulfil them perfectly, to the laud and glory of thy name. Order my living so that I may do that which thou requirest of me; and give me grace that I may know it, and have will and power to do it; that I may obtain those things which are most convenient for my soul. Gracious Lord, make my way sure and straight to thee, so that I fall not between prosperity and adversity; but that in prosperous things I may give thee thanks, and in adversity be patient; so that I be not lift up with the one, nor oppressed with the other. And that I may rejoice in nothing but that which moveth me to thee; nor be sorry for any thing but for those things which draw me from thee; desiring to please nobody, nor fearing to please any besides thee. Most loving Father, let all worldly things be vile unto me, for thee; and be thou my most special comfort above all. Let me not be merry with the joy that is without thee; and let me desire nothing besides thee; let all labour delight me which is for thee; and let all the rest weary me which is not in thee. Make me to lift up my heart oftentimes to thee; and when I fall, make me to think on thee and be sorry, with a stedfast purpose of amendment. Loving Lord, make me humble, without feigning; cheerful, without lightness; sad, without mistrust; sober, without heaviness; true, without doubleness; fearing thee, without desperation; trusting in thee, without presumption; telling my neighbours their faults meekly, without dissimulation; teaching them with words and examples, without any mockings; obedient without arguing; patient without grudging; and pure without corruption. Give me also, I beseech thee, a watchful spirit, that no curious thought withdraw me from thee. Let it be so strong, that no filthy affection draw me backwards; so stable, that no tribulation break it. Grant me also to know thee; diligent to seek a godly conversation; to please, and finally hope to embrace thee, for the precious blood sake of that immaculate Lamb, our only Saviour Jesus Christ, to whom, with thee, O Father, and the Holy Ghost, three Persons and one God, be all honour and glory, world without end. Amen.

THE FOLLOWING ARE AMONG
## GENERAL PRAYERS
TO BE SAID FOR THE GRACE AND FAVOUR OF GOD.

Whosoever liveth without thy grace and favour, O most gracious and favourable Lord, although for a time he walloweth in all kinds of fleshly pleasures, and abound with too much worldly riches, yet is he nothing else but the wretched bond-slave of Satan, and a vile heap of sin. All his pleasure is extreme poison, all his wealth is nothing else but plain beggary. For what felicity can there be where thy grace and favour wanteth? But where thy grace and favour is present, though the devil roar, the world rage, the flesh assail, there is true blessedness, unfeigned pleasure, and continual wealth. Pour down, therefore, thy heavenly grace, and fatherly favour upon us: that we, being assured of thy favourable goodness towards us, may rejoice and glory in thee, and have cheerful hearts, whensoever we are most assailed with any kind of adversity; be it poverty or sickness, loss of friends, or persecution for thy name's sake, to whom be glory for ever. Amen.

FOR THE GIFT OF THE HOLY GHOST.

So frail is our nature; so vile is our flesh; so sinful is

our heart; so corrupt are our affections; so wicked are all our thoughts, even from our childhood upwards, that of ourselves we can neither think, breathe, speak, or do any thing that is praiseworthy in thy sight, O heavenly Father; yea, except thou dost assist us with thy merciful goodness, all things are so far out of frame in us, that we see nothing present in ourselves but thy heavy displeasure and eternal condemnation. Vouchsafe, therefore, O loving Father, to send thy Holy Spirit unto us, which may make us new creatures; put away from us all fleshly lusts; fill our hearts with new affections and spiritual motions; and so, altogether renew us both in body and soul, through his godly inspiration, that we may die unto the old Adam, and live unto thee in newness of life, serving thee our Lord God in holiness and righteousness all the days of our life. Amen.

### FOR THE TRUE KNOWLEDGE OF OURSELVES.

It is written in thy holy gospel, most loving Saviour, that thou camest into this world, not to call the righteous, that is, such as justify themselves, but sinners unto repentance. Suffer me not, therefore, O Lord, to be in the number of those, who boasting their own righteousness, their own works and merits, despise that righteousness which cometh by faith, which alone is allowable before thee. Give me grace to acknowledge mine own self as I am, even the son of wrath by nature, a wretched sinner, and an unprofitable servant; and wholly to depend on thy merciful goodness with a strong and unshaken faith; that in this world thou mayest continually call me unto true repentance, seeing I continually sin, and, in the world to come, bring me unto everlasting glory. Amen.

### FOR A PURE AND CLEAN HEART.

The heart of man naturally is corrupt and unsearchable through the multitude of sins, which lie buried in it, insomuch that no man is able to say, My heart is clean, and I am clear from sin. Remove from me, therefore, O heavenly Father, my corrupt, sinful, stony, stubborn, and unfaithful heart. Create in me a clean heart, free from all noisome and ungodly thoughts. Breathe into my heart by thy Holy Spirit, godly and spiritual motions; that out of the good treasure of the heart, I may bring forth good things, unto the praise and glory of thy name. Amen.

#### FOR A QUIET CONSCIENCE.

The wicked are like a raging sea, which is never in quiet; neither is there any peace to the ungodly: but such as love thy law, O Lord, they have plenty of peace; they have quiet minds, and contented consciences, which is the greatest treasure under the sun; given of thee to so many as seek it at thy hand, with true faith and continual prayer. Give me, O Lord, that joyful jewel, even a quiet mind and a contented conscience; that I, being free from the malicious accusations of Satan, from the crafty persuasions of the world, from the subtle enticements of the flesh, from the heavy curse of the law, and fully persuaded of thy merciful goodness toward me, through faith in thy Son Jesus Christ, may quietly serve thee, both bodily and ghostly, in holiness and righteousness, all the days of my life. Amen.

#### FOR FAITH.

Forasmuch as nothing pleaseth thee that is done without faith, appear it before the blind world ever so beautiful and commendable, but it is counted in thy sight sinful and worthy of condemnation: yea the self sin and condemnation. This is most humbly to desire thee, O Father, for Christ's sake, to breathe into my heart by thy Holy Spirit, this most precious and singular gift of faith, which worketh by charity. Whereby also we are justified, and received into thy favour; that I, truly believing in thee, and fully persuaded of the truth of thy holy word, may be made thy son, and inheritor of everlasting glory, through Jesus Christ our Lord. Amen.

#### FOR CHARITY.

Thy cognizance and badge whereby thy disciples are known, O Lord and Saviour Jesu Christ, is charity or love, which cometh out of a pure heart, a good conscience, and of faith unfeigned. I pray thee, therefore, give me this christian love and perfect charity, that I may love thee my Lord God, with all my heart, with all my mind, with all my soul, and with all my strength; doing always of very love that only which is pleasant in thy sight. Again, that I may love my neighbour and christian brother as myself; wishing as well to him as to myself; and ready at all times to do for him whatsoever lieth in my power, that when we shall all stand before thy dreadful judging place, I, being known by thy badge, may be numbered among thy disciples, and so, through thy mercy, receive the reward of eternal glory. Amen.

### FOR PATIENCE.

When thou livedst in this world, O Lord Christ, thou showedst thyself a true mirror of perfect patience, suffering quietly, not only the venomous words, but also cruel deeds of thy most cruel enemies; forgiving them, and praying for them which most despitefully handled thee. Give me grace, O most meek and loving Lamb of God, to follow this thy patience; quietly to bear the slanderous words of mine adversaries; patiently to suffer the cruel deeds of mine enemies; to forgive them; to pray for them; yea, to do good to them; and by no means to go about once to avenge myself, but rather to give place unto wrath, seeing that vengeance is thine, and thou wilt reward: seeing also, that thou helpest them to their right that suffer wrong; that I, thus patiently suffering all evils, may afterwards dwell with thee in glory. Amen.

### FOR HUMILITY.

What have we, O heavenly Father, that we have not received? Every good gift, and every perfect gift, is from above, and cometh down from thee, which art the Father of lights. Seeing then all that we have is thine, whether it pertain to the body or the soul, how can we be proud, and boast ourselves of that which is none of our own? Seeing also, that as to give, so to take away, thou art able; and wilt whensoever thy gifts are abused, and thou not acknowledged to be the Giver of them. Take, therefore, away from me all pride and haughtiness of mind; graft in me true humility, that I may acknowledge thee the Giver of all good things, be thankful unto thee for them, and use them unto thy glory, and the profit of my neighbour. Grant also, that all my glory and rejoicing may be in no earthly creatures, but in thee alone, which doest mercy, equity, and righteousness upon earth. To thee alone be all glory. Amen.

### FOR MERCIFULNESS.

Thy dearly beloved Son in his holy gospel exhorteth us to be merciful, even as thou our heavenly Father, art merciful, and promisest that if we be merciful to other, we shall obtain mercy of thee, who art the Father of mercies and God of all consolation. Grant, therefore, that forasmuch as thou art our Father, and we thy children, we may resemble thee in all our life and conversation; and that, as thou art beneficial and liberal, not only to the good, but also to the evil, so we likewise may show ourselves merciful, gentle, and liberal to so many as have need of our help; that at the dreadful day of doom we may be found in the number of those merciful, whom thou shalt appoint by thy only begotten Son to go into everlasting life; to whom with thee and the Holy Ghost be all honour and praise. Amen.

### FOR TRUE GODLINESS.

In thy law, O thou Maker of heaven and earth, thou hast appointed us a way to walk in, and hast commanded that we should turn neither on the right hand nor on the left, but do according to thy good will and pleasure, without adding of our own good intents and fleshly imaginations. As thou hast commanded, so give me grace, good Lord, to do. Let me neither follow my own will, nor the fancies of other men, neither let me be beguiled with the mask of old customs, long usages, fathers' decrees, ancient laws, nor anything that fighteth with thy holy ordinances and blessed commandment; but faithfully believe, and stedfastly confess that to be the true godliness, which is learned in thy holy Bible: and according unto that, to order my life unto the praise of thy holy name. Amen.

### FOR THE TRUE UNDERSTANDING OF GOD'S WORD.

O Lord, as thou alone art the Author of the holy scriptures, so likewise can no man, although he be ever so wise, politic, and learned, understand them, except he be taught by thy Holy Spirit, who alone is the schoolmaster to lead the faithful unto all truth. Vouchsafe, therefore, I most humbly beseech thee, to breathe into my heart thy blessed Spirit, who may renew the senses of my mind, open my wits,* reveal unto me the true understanding of thy holy mysteries, and plant in me such a certain and infallible knowledge of thy truth, that no subtle persuasion of man's wisdom may pluck me from thy truth; but that as I have learned the true understanding of thy blessed will, so I

* Mind.

may remain in the same continually, come life, come death; unto the glory of thy blessed name. Amen.

#### FOR A LIFE AGREEABLE TO OUR KNOWLEDGE.

As I have prayed unto thee, O heavenly Father, to be taught the true understanding of thy blessed word, by thy Holy Spirit, so I most entirely beseech thee, to give me grace to lead a life agreeable to my knowledge. Suffer me not to be of the number of those, who profess that they know God with their mouth, but deny him with their deeds. Let me not be like unto that son who said unto his father that he would labour in his vineyard, and yet laboured nothing at all, but went abroad loitering idly. Make me rather like unto that good and fruitful land, which yieldeth again her seed with great increase; that men seeing my good works, may glorify thee, my heavenly Father. Amen.

#### FOR A GOOD NAME.

Nothing becometh the professor of thy name better, O heavenly Father, than so to behave himself according to his profession, that he may be well reported of them that are of the household of faith. Yea, such sincerity and pureness of life ought to be in those who profess thy holy name, that the very adversaries of thy truth should be ashamed once to mutter against them.

Give me grace, therefore, I most entirely desire thee, so to frame my life according to the rule of thy blessed word, that I may give no occasion to speak evil of me; but rather so live in my vocation, that I may be an example to others to live godly and virtuously, unto the honour and praise of thy glorious name. Amen.

#### FOR A COMPETENT LIVING.

Although I doubt not of thy fatherly provision for this my poor and needy life, yet forasmuch as thou hast both commanded and taught me by thy dear Son to pray unto thee for things necessary for this my life; I am bold at this present to come unto thy divine Majesty, most humbly beseeching thee, that as thou hast given me life, so thou wilt give me meat and drink to sustain the same: Again, as thou hast given me a body, so thou wilt give clothes to cover it; that I, having sufficient for my living, may the more freely, and with the quieter mind, apply myself unto thy service and honour. Amen.

#### FOR A PATIENT AND THANKFUL HEART IN SICKNESS.

Whom thou lovest, O Lord, him dost thou chasten, yea every son that thou receivest, thou scourgest, and in so doing thou offerest thyself unto him, as a father unto his son. For what son is he whom the father chasteneth not? Grant, therefore, I most heartily pray thee, that whensoever thou layest thy cross on me, and visitest me with thy loving scourge of sickness, I may by no means strive against thy fatherly pleasure; but patiently and thankfully abide thy chastisement, ever being persuaded, that it is for the health both of my body and soul; and that by this means thou workest my salvation; subduest the flesh unto the spirit; and makest me a new creature; that I may, hereafter, serve thee more freely, and continue in thy fear unto my life's end. Amen.

#### FOR STRENGTH AGAINST THE DEVIL, THE WORLD, AND THE FLESH.

O Lord God, the devil goeth about like a roaring lion, seeking whom he may devour; the flesh lusteth against the spirit; the world persuadeth unto vanities; that we may forget thee, our Lord God, and so be condemned for ever. Thus are we miserably on every side besieged of cruel and restless enemies, and likely at every moment to perish, if we be not defended with thy godly power against their tyranny. I, therefore, poor and wretched sinner, despairing of my own strength, which indeed is none, most heartily pray thee to endue me with strength from above, that I may be able, through thy help, with strong faith to resist Satan; with fervent prayer to mortify the raging lusts of the flesh; with continual meditation of thy holy law, to avoid the foolish vanities and transitory pleasures of this wicked world; that I, through thy grace, being set at liberty from the power of mine enemies, may live and serve thee in holiness and righteousness all the days of my life. Amen.

#### FOR THE GLORY IN HEAVEN.

The joys, O Lord, which thou hast prepared for them that love thee, no eye hath seen, no ear hath heard, neither is any heart able to think. But as the joys are great and unspeakable, so are there few that do enjoy them. For strait is the gate and narrow is the way that leadeth unto life, and few there be that find it. Notwithstanding, O heavenly Father, thou hast a little flock, to whom it is thy pleasure to give the glorious kingdom of heaven. There is a certain number of sheep, that hear thy voice, whom no man is able to pluck out of thy hand, who shall never perish, to whom also thou shalt give eternal life. Make me, therefore, O Lord, of that number, whom thou from everlasting hast predestinate to be saved; whose names also are written in the book of life. Pluck me out of the company of the goats which shall stand on thy left hand, and go into damnation; and place me among those thy sheep which shall stand on thy right hand and be saved. Grant me this, O merciful Father, for thy dear Son's sake, Jesus Christ our Lord. So shall I, enjoying this singular benefit at thy hand, and being placed in thy glorious kingdom, sing perpetual praises to thy godly Majesty, who livest and reignest with thy dearly beloved Son, and the Holy Ghost, one true and everlasting God, world without end. Amen.

### A THANKSGIVING UNTO GOD FOR ALL HIS BENEFITS.

Thy benefits toward me, O most loving Father, are so great and infinite, whether I have respect unto my body or unto my soul, that I find not in myself how to recompense any part of thine unspeakable goodness towards me. But thou who needest none of my goods, knowing our poverty, yea our nothingness, requirest of us for a recompense of thy kindness, only the sacrifice of praise and thanksgiving. O Lord and merciful Father, what worthy thanks am I, poor and wretched sinner, able to give thee? Notwithstanding, trusting on thy mercy and favourable kindness, I offer unto thee, in the name of Christ, the sacrifice of praise, ever thanking thee most heartily for all thy benefits which thou hast bestowed upon me, thy most unprofitable servant, from the beginning of my life unto this present hour; most humbly beseeching thee to continue thy lovingkindness towards me; and to give me grace so to walk, worthy of this thy fatherly goodness, that when thou shalt call me out of this careful life, I may enjoy that thy most singular and last benefit, which is everlasting glory, through Jesus Christ our Lord, to whom, with thee and the Holy Ghost, be all honour and praise for ever and ever Amen.

#### A PRAYER NECESSARY TO BE SAID AT ALL TIMES.

O bountiful Jesu, O sweet Saviour, O Christ the Son o. God, have pity upon me, mercifully hear me, and despise not my prayers. Thou hast created me of nothing; thou hast redeemed me from the bondage of sin, death, and hell, neither with gold nor silver, but with thy most precious body once offered upon the cross, and thine own blood shed once for all, for my ransom; therefore cast me not away, whom thou by thy great wisdom hast made; despise me not whom thou hast redeemed with such a precious treasure: nor let my wickedness destroy that which thy goodness hath builded. Now whilst I live, O Jesu, have mercy on me, for if I die out of thy favour, it will be too late afterward to call for thy mercy; whilst I have time to repent, look upon me with thy merciful eyes, as thou didst vouchsafe to look upon Peter thine apostle; that I may bewail my sinful life, and obtain thy favour, and die therein. I acknowledge that if thou shouldest deal with me according to strict justice, I have deserved everlasting death. Therefore I appeal to thy high throne of mercy, trusting to obtain God's favour, not for my merits, but for thy merits, O Jesu, who hast given thyself an acceptable sacrifice to thy Father; to appease his wrath, and to bring all sinners truly repenting, and amending their evil life, into his favour again. Accept me, O Lord, among the number of them that shall be saved; forgive my sins; give me grace to lead a godly and innocent life; grant me thy heavenly wisdom, inspire my heart with faith, hope, and charity; give me grace to be humble in prosperity, patient in adversity, obedient unto my rulers, faithful unto them that trust me, dealing truly with all men; to live chastely, to abhor adultery, fornication, and all uncleanness; to do good after my power unto all men; to hurt no man; that thy name may be glorified in me, during this present life, and that I afterward may obtain everlasting life, through thy mercy and the merits of thy passion. Amen.

#### A PRAYER IN PROSPERITY.

Most merciful Father, which hast of thy gracious mercy, without my deserving, endued me abundantly with many gracious gifts, both spiritually and bodily; and hast hitherto preserved me from innumerable perils and dangers, both (

soul and body; and hast, at this present, bestowed upon me bodily health, wealth, and abundance of worldly substance; I most heartily thank thee; beseeching thee most humbly so to illuminate my mind, that I may in all things be thankful unto thee for thy great benefits; and also, during my life, may freely bestow thy gracious gifts, to the glorifying of thy holy name, the advancement of thy honour, and profit of my neighbour. Grant this, most merciful Father, for thy Son Jesus Christ's sake, our only Saviour and Mediator. Amen.

### A PRAYER IN ADVERSITY.

Almighty God, who for mine ingratitude and sinful life hast worthily punished me with much affliction and adversity, I most humbly beseech thee to give me grace utterly to detest and abhor my former wretched and sinful life; and to study daily for the amendment of the same; and that I may fully be persuaded that this affliction hath not chanced to me by casualty or misfortune, but by thy foreknowledge, counsel, permission, and determinate pleasure; and that thou beatest me with this thy rod of fatherly correction, not to the intent to cast me clean out of thy favour; but because thou wouldest thereby nurture me and reclaim me, to unfeigned repentance for my former life; to be more circumspect of godly life hereafter; to exercise my faith in thy godly promises; to try me, whether I will be patient and constant in adversity; to make me abhor the vain pleasures of this life; and, finally, with fervent and continual desire to long for the life everlasting. Wherefore, I most heartily pray thee, vouchsafe to increase and strengthen my faith, hope, charity, and meekness, and that I may, without murmur or grudge, patiently bear this thy fatherly chastisement; especially grant me, that I may daily increase more and more in fervent love towards thee: for thy holy word saith, that to them that love God, all things shall happen for the best; whether it be prosperity or adversity, health or sickness, life or death. In consideration whereof, I submit me wholly to thee; and fully surrender and resign all my will to thy most godly will and pleasure; which I nothing doubt shall end this my affliction so as shall be meetest and most agreeable to thy honour and glory, and to my most perfect wealth and everlasting salvation; through Jesus Christ our only Saviour, Redeemer, Advocate, and Mediator. Amen.

#### A PRAYER TO BE SAID WHEN THE SICK PERSON IS JOYFUL AND GLAD TO DIE.

O Lord Jesu Christ, I beseech thy mercy and goodness, that thou wilt strengthen and conduct my soul in the great journey which approacheth unto me. I believe thou for my sake didst die, and rise again; and that thou, through thy mercy, shalt forgive me all my sins; and that thou hast promised me everlasting life. Of this my belief, O Lord, shalt thou be witness with all thine elect. This shall also be my last will; in this faith, O Lord, do I die upon thine incomparable mercy. And if through pain and smart, impatience, or other temptation, I should or would shrink from this faith, O Lord, I beseech thee, let me not stick in such unbelief and blasphemy; but strengthen and increase my faith, to the intent that sin, hell, and the devil may not hurt me. For thou art stronger and mightier than all they. To this do I stedfastly trust; Lord, let me not be confounded. Amen.

#### A PRAYER.

Laud, honour, and thanks be unto thee, most merciful Lord Jesu Christ, for thy holy incarnation, for thy pains and bitter passion, through the which I know that thou art my Redeemer and Saviour; and believe that thou hast overcome sin, hell, and the devil; so that they cannot hurt me. To this do I only trust; upon this do I build; upon this standeth all my hope; in this trust and confidence will I be found. Only, O Lord, be propitious and merciful unto me, even as I, according to thy faithful promises, do nothing doubt. O Lord, leave me not in this great distress, but deliver me from evil. Amen.

#### A PRAYER FOR THEM THAT LIE IN EXTREME PANGS OF DEATH.

O pitiful Physician, and Healer both of body and soul, Christ Jesu! Vouchsafe to cast thy merciful eyes upon thy poor and sinful creature, who lieth here captive, and bound with sickness, turning his weakness to thy glory, and to his health. And vouchsafe, good Lord, to send him patience and endurance, that he may stedfastly continue to the end: And that he may, with a true and perfect faith, fight manfully against all temptations of the devil, when he may no longer continue. So be it.

## 104     King Edward VI.—Primer.

[Instead of the Dirige, a service for the dead highly esteemed in the church of Rome, and strongly imbued with its doctrinal errors, the Primer contains under the same title, a selection from the Psalms, and other appropriate parts of scripture, with the following prayers intended for use in the house of mourning.]

---

O merciful God, the Father of our Lord Jesus Christ, who is the resurrection and the life ; in whom whosoever believeth shall live, though he die ; and whosoever liveth and believeth in him, shall not die eternally: Who also hath taught us, by his holy apostle Paul, not to be sorry as men without hope, for them that sleep in him ; we meekly beseech thee, O Father, to raise us from the death of sin unto the life of righteousness, that when we shall depart this life, we may sleep in him, and, at the general resurrection in the last day, receiving again our bodies, and rising again in thy most gracious favour, we may, with all thine elect saints, obtain eternal joy. Grant this, O Lord God, by the means of our Advocate, Jesus Christ ; who, with thee and the Holy Ghost, liveth and reigneth one God for ever. Amen.

---

Almighty God, we give thee hearty thanks for those thy servants, whom thou hast delivered from the miseries of this wretched world, from the body of death, and all temptation ; and hast brought their souls, which they committed into thy holy hands, into sure consolation and rest : Grant, we beseech thee, that at the day of judgment, we, with all thy elect departed out of this life, may fully receive thy promises, and be made perfect altogether, through the glorious resurrection of thy Son, Jesus Christ, our Lord. Amen.[*]

[*] King Edward the Sixth's Primer is accessible to any person who wishes to see the whole of its contents ; two editions having been recently printed.

# THE TROUBLED MAN'S MEDICINE;

IN TWO BOOKS, THE ONE COMFORTING A MAN BEING IN
TROUBLE, ADVERSITY, OR SICKNESS; THE OTHER
TO TEACH A MAN TO DIE BOTH
PATIENTLY AND GLADLY.

VERY PROFITABLE TO BE READ OF ALL MEN, WHEREIN THEY
MAY LEARN PATIENTLY TO SUFFER ALL
KINDS OF ADVERSITY.

MADE AND WRITTEN

## BY WILLIAM HUGH,

TO A FRIEND OF HIS.

*First printed,* 1546.

WILLIAM HUGH was a native of Yorkshire. He was educated at Corpus Christi college, Oxford. In 1543, he took the degree of master of arts. At that time he was almost wholly occupied as tutor. Afterwards falling under the notice of lady Denny, he was appointed her chaplain, and enabled to pursue his studies with less interruption through her assistance. He was the author of a small work, entitled, "The Troubled Man's Medicine," which went through several editions in the sixteenth century. He also translated into English, "The Book of Bertram, the priest, intreating of the body and blood of Christ." This able and ancient argument against transubstantiation was of considerable use in removing the errors of popery in England. Another work, in which he combated the popish error that infants dying unbaptized would not be saved, he dedicated to queen Catharine Parr. Hugh died at Oxford in 1549, from breaking a blood vessel.

The Troubled Man's Medicine is inserted in the present collection, having been a popular work during the reformation. It also presents a specimen of a species of writing different from other reformers of that day, although it afterwards prevailed to a considerable extent, namely, attempting to illustrate scriptural arguments by reference to facts of ancient history. Although inferior in force to more simple scriptural argumentation, it was preferable to the scholastic reasonings so commonly brought forward by the Romish divines. It marks a change in the writings of theologians, and, under the divine blessing, would have considerable effect upon many nobility and gentry of that day who had entered upon literary studies. It appeared desirable to include one piece of this description in the present collection, and we cannot but remark the clearness with which the author states the scripture doctrine of justification by faith only, when he returns to the bible from his quotations out of human literature. The whole is here reprinted, excepting a few expressions which would now be obsolete.

# THE TROUBLED MAN'S MEDICINE.

## BOOK I.

### TO COMFORT A MAN BEING IN TROUBLE, ADVERSITY, OR SICKNESS.

PART THE FIRST.

*The results of abundance and wealth, and those of poverty and adverse fortune, should cause us to endure the latter with thanksgiving.*

MOST gentle friend Urban, I plainly perceive, not so much by your letters as by the report of other men, that you are not joyful, neither of a quiet mind, but rather unquieted, sad, and pensive, in that fortune, which in her inconstancy, as you say, only is constant, doth not, according to her old tenure, favour you, in that the world, which for the most part is not theirs that are of God, good, and virtuous, does not, as it has done, smile upon you.

As all things are common among them which are trusty and faithful friends, so, doubtless, are the very affections of the mind, which at length is well known of me, not by hearing but by proof, not by reading but by experience. For as your joyful and prosperous state made me to rejoice, so your adverse fortune and sadness causes me likewise to be sad. Wherefore it shall be expedient, and my part, to find some way or means whereby this heaviness, wherewith both our minds as yet are equally occupied, may be set aside, or at the least restrained. To increase your substance with cattle, gold, or silver, my mind is willing, but my power is impotent. To teach you how these things may be procured I have not learned.

But that medicine only which learned men have counted most present to a sick and sorrowful heart, I will endeavour, though peradventure not skilfully, yet friendly to minister.

The medicine is brotherly counsel and friendly communication.

This, saith Plutarch, writing to Apollonius, is to a sick mind the best physician. Words and voices, saith Horace in his epistles, do mitigate grief and put away the greatest part of sorrow.

Surely I think that as the diseases of the body are healed by confections made of herbs and other things proceeding out of the apothecary's shop; so the diseases of the mind are only to be cured with comfortable and unfeigned words, flowing out of a friendly and faithful heart.

Isocrates, in his Oration of Peace, saith, "I would ye should chiefly know, that whereas many sundry remedies are found of the physicians against the sickness and maladies of the body; against the disease of the mind there is none, saving friendly words." Wherefore Apollo, accounted chief, and of the physicians in manner the god, in Ovid, complains grievously, that the disease of his mind could be cured with no herbs, and that the arts which did profit every man could not refrain his troublous affection.

I would wish the muses were so favourable unto me that I might gather such herbs in their gardens, that would well purge your mind of this heaviness; as it is not to be approved in any man, who is partaker of reason, but especially in a man of Christ's religion; howbeit, alas, so great is the blindness of our foolish nature, we think those things which are not lamentable, are to be lamented; and those which are not horrible in reality, are greatly to be feared.

In this point I may compare us to unwise children, which vehemently fear them that use evil-favoured visors, thinking that they are spirits, devils, and enemies of their health; whereas if they had the wit boldly to pull off the visors, they should see hidden under them gentle countenances, and faces of their friends, kinsmen, or, peradventure, most loving fathers.

Or else we may be justly likened unto raging Ajax, who in his fury and madness used the hogs which God had prepared for his sustenance and wholesome nourishment, as though they had been his deadly enemies, and ordained to his utter destruction.

What childishness or worse than madness is it, to bewail, and not to take in good worth, adversity, misfortune, or poverty, which happen to us, not by chance, but by the providence and will of our heavenly Father, who worketh every thing for the best towards them that love him, as St. Paul saith to the Romans, ch. viii. who formeth and fashioneth us according to his own will, who maketh us rich and poor, sick and whole, fortunate and miserable, at his pleasure, and all for our good, profit, and advantage. Lest thou be deceived, I would not have thee imitate the common sort, ascribing worldly miseries to the stars, to fate and fortune; playing therein the part of the dog, which bites the stone that is hurled at him, not blaming the hurler thereof; but rather imitate the example of David, who blamed not Shimei railing at him outrageously, but imputed his despites unto the Lord, by whom he was thought to be sent, and attributed them, with thanks, to God, of whom, by the testimony of scripture, cometh both death and life, riches and poverty, good and evil. This witnesseth the Psalmist, saying, The Lord doth advance and suppress, the Lord maketh the rich and eke the poor.

But thou wilt say, peradventure, If we were certain that our misfortunes and miseries were sent unto christian men by God, they would be much more tolerable; but when we see our cattle die by stinging of serpents, or by contagion, from which they might have been safe if they had been diligently observed; or when we fall into diseases, whereof we might have been clear, if unwholesome meats and diet, infected places or persons had been avoided; or when we are robbed or suffer other losses by negligence of our servants, or evil will of our neighbours; or where we see that we might have been in good case if this chance or that chance had been escaped, if this thing or that thing had not been done—finally, when we see ourselves, by such or like chances as I have spoken of, come to misery, we think it rather to be imputed to evil fortune, than to the hand of God, by the same mean seeking or working our welfare.

Truly, whosoever is of this opinion, in my judgment, seems to be ignorant that God is provident and careful for men. Also to lack the knowledge of his most holy and wholesome scriptures. In Matthew x. it is written, that a sparrow, which is a bird of small estimation, cannot fall to the ground, without our heavenly Father, neither a hair of a man's head. And shall we, which are the sheep of his pasture, his people, and his sons, whom he regardeth a thousand times more than the sparrows, think that the loss of those things which we have enjoyed, be they riches, health, or any other worldly things, either the miss of them which we have desired, can chance without his will and godly providence?

Who so foolish as to think that while God regards the hairs of our heads, which are neither greatly profitable nor necessary, he will contemn and neglect things which pertain to the sustaining and necessity of the whole body.

Who knows not that Job's substance decayed by divers chances, as by tempests and thunders, by thieves and robbers, his children destroyed by the falling of a house? which things to the infidel would have seemed bare chance, and not afflicted by any godly power, yet in deed, as it is manifest in the history, these were nothing else but means or instruments which the Lord used to the performance of his will.

Holy Job, of all christian men much to be followed, after he had lost all, and was brought to extreme misery, did not accuse his carpenters for building of a ruinous house, neither did he cry out upon fortune as the unfaithful do, nor yet found fault at his herdmen, in that they drove not his cattle diligently into the safe stables, but, considering the true cause of his calamities and wretchedness, said, Naked I came from my mother's womb, and naked I shall go hence. The Lord did give me wealth, and the Lord hath taken it away; as it pleased the Lord, so it is done; his name be blessed.

David, in his Psalms, evidently shows that our calamities come none otherwise but by the will and permission of God, which trieth us as the gold is tried in the fiery furnace, being never the worse therefore, but better and purer. Thou, saith he, O Lord, hast proved us, and as silver is wont with fire, thou hast examined us; thou hast brought us into snares, and laid tribulations upon our backs. Thou hast made men our enemies, and set them in our necks; we have passed by fire and water. Jeremiah, in ch. iii. of his Lamentations, confirms this, pronouncing such words, Who saith that it should be done, the Lord not commanding? Do not good and evil proceed from the mouth of the Highest? The Gentiles, as blind as they were, of this thing were not altogether ignorant.

The Greek poet, Hesiod, asks what is the cause that some men are vile, some noble, some rich, other some poor? he maketh answer himself, and saith, The will of the mighty God—which saying I would wish to be as well believed of christian men, as it was truly spoken by a blind heathen.

Seeing therefore that misfortunes, lack or loss of riches,

health, and such things, come not rashly, but by the providence of our celestial Father; why should we not take them well, and, after the example of Job, blessing his name, and giving him thanks for them? Specially considering that adversities chancing to them which love the Lord, are not tokens of his anger, neither arguments that he casteth us off, but of a fatherly love rather, and a friendly care. Thou shalt perceive, if thou read diligently the holy histories, that the more part of those whom God hath chosen to be of his little flock, have been wretched in the respect of the world, and miserable, tossed, and turmoiled with manifold misfortunes, distracted and unquieted with continual sorrows.

Let Elijah the prophet be for an example, whom God loved so well that he vouchsafed to communicate his counsel and mysteries unto him.

What quietness, I pray you, or wealth, what riches or surety had he, for all the friendship that was betwixt God and him? Truly so much wealth, that he had never a house to put his head in. Such plenty of meat and drink, that if the ravens and the angel had not fed him, he had perished with hunger. Such quietness, that he could not tell which way to turn him, nor whither to flee from the persecution of Ahab, Baal's priests, and cruel Jezebel. Such joy in this world, that he desired oft to die before he died. What should I speak of Elisha, Jeremiah, and, in short, of the greatest part of God's prophets, which were ever wrapped in woe and deadly anguish, the world seldom or never ministering any cause of gladness, comfort, or solace? I will not speak of the apostles, who, besides that they were poor, and beggarly all the days of their life, for God's word were troubled, threatened, mocked, scourged, and at the last, to the sight of men, miserably died.

Our master Christ, the Son of God, would be an abject among the people, and subject to afflictions innumerable; showing thereby that neither his kingdom, nor the kingdom of those who are of his household, is in this world. He saith to his apostles, Because ye are not of the world the world doth hate you, John xv. which doubtless loves and chiefly favours them that are her own children, and children of darkness, regarding more this temporal life, than the life which is promised to them that cleave wholly to the Lord our God.

Scripture, not dissembling with us, but telling plainly whereto we should cleave, teaches that they which are

God shall, as in the stead of a recognizance,* suffer afflictions, adversities, and troubles. All they that will live virtuously in Christ shall be afflicted, 2 Tim. iii. Jeremiah, speaking in the person of God, ch. xxv. saith, In the city wherein my name is invocated I will begin to punish; as for you, (meaning the wicked,) ye shall be as innocents, and not touched. And, The time is, that judgment must begin at the house of God, 1 Peter iv. Christ suffered for us, leaving us an example that we should follow his footsteps.

O that we might have seen the kind heart of Christ, when he was punished, hanged, and crucified, not for his own cause, but for ours, how willingly he suffered, giving us an example, that we might follow his footsteps; doubtless we should, with more courage and fortitude, for our own sakes, suffer troubles than we do. Lo, we that live are mortified for Christ, that the life of Christ may appear in our carnal bodies, 2 Cor. iv. If any man, saith Christ, will come after me, let him forsake himself, take his cross on his back and follow me; for otherwise he is not meet for me. Every member, doubt ye not, of Christ's body shall have the cross, either of poverty or persecution, sickness or imprisonment, injuries or of slanders, or of like things.

Happy is he that followeth Christ manfully and faileth not, for he at length shall be eased of his heavy burden; he at length shall find perpetual rest and eternal quietness.

We must be here, not as inhabitants and home-dwellers, but, as Paul saith, as strangers. Not as strangers only, but, after the mind of Job, as painful soldiers, appointed of our captain, Christ, to fight against the devil, the world, flesh, and sin. In the which fight, except we behave ourselves lawfully and strongly, by the sentence of scripture, we shall not be crowned. Let us, therefore, arm ourselves with the weapons prescribed by St. Paul unto the Ephesians, and other places of scripture, to Christ's soldiers, and with a bold courage contemn the darts of the devil and worldly miseries, endeavouring to overthrow our minds, and weaken our faith toward God. For our Captain with a glorious victory shall gloriously deliver us.

In worldly wars there are and have been many of courage, not unlike to Jason, Hercules, and Theseus, who

* A badge or mark of distinction worn by the followers of noblemen.

covet to enterprise upon dangerous places, and perilous enemies, whereby they may have, by their manful conflict, praise or a garland of bay boughs, honour or temporal promotions.

And shall we, whose reward shall be not a garland made of green boughs that lightly withereth, but a crown of glory that ever shall flourish; not temporal preferments which endure not, but inheritance in heaven that shall be continual, shall we be loth stoutly to withstand the world?

It chances oft that the presence of one whom a man lightly loves shall move him to contend and fight fiercely with his adversary, little or nothing regarding his life, but rather careful, lest with shame he take a foil in her presence whom he loves; and shall the presence of our spouse Christ, whose eyes continually look on the hearts and minds, nothing move us? For a man to have taken a foil before his earthly love had been no loss of body nor soul, but a little shame, and that not durable. But to take a foil of poverty, miseries, sickness, losses, lack, or other misfortunes, and not to keep our minds still above them, with contempt of their assaults, besides that the presence of God shall shame us, not the body, but the soul (except the grace of God after raise us) shall utterly perish.

Look therefore that we fight merrily and boldly, despising all misfortunes that hurt or threaten hurt to our mortal bodies.

But either I am deceived, or I hear you saying, Sir, it is quickly spoken, but it is not so lightly done. It is hard, and by the sentence of philosophers, against nature, for men to be content with those things which hurt and damage their bodies, and as you require us with contempt to fight against them, doubtless it is very hard, and for our strength and power a thing impossible.

What then! shall we play the part of Demosthenes, cast away our weapons and despair? No, not so, but, mistrusting our own power, let us flee to God, as unto a holy anchor, and safe refuge, desiring help of him, who, by promise made, shall aid, assist, and defend us. Call on me, saith he, in the day of trouble, and I will deliver thee. The Lord is nigh to all them that are of a troubled heart, and fear him. In thine infirmity despise not the Lord, but pray unto him, and he shall heal thee, as it is written in the book of Ecclesiasticus. There is no doubt, therefore, but we shall have his help, if we faithfully call for it

And in him that comforteth, if the words of Paul are true, we shall be able to do all things; and nothing shall be impossible for us, being faithful. Therefore, let us say with Hezekiah, 2 Chron. xxxii. Play we the men, and comfort ourselves, for the Lord is with us, our helper, and fighteth for us. The Lord (as he saith in 2 Sam. xxii.) is our rock and our strength, our saviour and refuge, our buckler, our advancer, and the horn of our health.

Let us then not fear, nor cease constantly to withstand the cruel enforcements of adversity, ever keeping our minds and faith toward God unwounded, unharmed, and not discouraged by them, thinking still that they are sent of God; who by infirmity worketh strength, by ignominy glory, by poverty perpetual riches, by death life; who doth wound and heal, striketh and maketh whole, as it is in the Psalms. And for none other end, but as they were sent to Job, to exercise and prove us, that his glory may appear in us, and that we may avoid the greater evils, sin and thraldom to the devil and hell.

The afflictions, believe me, that we count evils, encumbering our flesh, are nothing in respect of those evils wherewith the ungodly are cumbered, living in infidelity and sin, under the ire of God, under the power of the devil, being servants to iniquity, to whom, saith the Lord, is no peace; whose minds and conscience, as Isaiah writes, are ever like to a fervent sea that cannot rest, whose floods redound to conculcation[*] and mourning. That these greater, I say, and more heinous evils may be avoided, these little, or rather not at all to be esteemed evils, are inflicted of God; also that we may at length, after all our strife, with our Captain, Christ, royally triumph.

If we would well consider for what purpose God hath created us, we should bear with afflictions and adverse fortune much more than we do.

All things in this world are made to serve man. The sheep to clothe him, the ox to feed him, the horse to carry him, the herbs and trees, some to nourish him, some to cure him being diseased, some to deliver him, the sun and moon to give him light, so, in conclusion, all other things under heaven, in one duty or other, serve man; and as all these things were made to serve man, so man was made to serve God in holiness and pureness of life, and to this end, doubtless, poverty with other afflictions doth

[*] Laying waste.

much more conduce than wealth or carnal quietness. In this respect we ought to wish, and thank God for adversity rather than for wealth.

The one causes us to forget him, the other to remember him; the one to despise him, the other to call upon him and worship him; the one provokes to incontinency and naughtiness, the other to temperance and soberness; the one calleth us to all kinds of vice, the other to virtue and pureness of life. What, I pray you, made David an adulterer and cruel murderer, but wealth and quietness? Jeroboam, brought to wealth and prosperous state, became a wicked and a shameful idolater. Oh perilous abundance of goods and satiety of meats and quietness, which destroyed with so many souls those goodly cities Sodom and Gomorrah. Nothing else made Uzziah proud, and, by reason thereof, to be stricken with leprosy, but the before-named.

What made the young man covetous and loth to follow Christ when he was bid, but worldly wealth, which he then enjoyed?

You see in the gospel how the men that were bidden to the king's supper could not come, worldly riches and business keeping them back. They which came and filled up the places at the feast were wretched, sick, and lame beggars.

Christ bewailed Jerusalem because that by her wealthiness and abundance of things she forgot his visitation.

What else brought the rich glutton to forget God, himself, and his mortality, to incontinency, drunkenness, gluttony, and at the last to the place where is mourning and gnashing of teeth, but wealth, prosperity, and worldly quietness? Thus you see that the effects of riches and wealth are nothing else, for the most part, but murder, adultery, drunkenness, idolatry, covetousness, gluttony, contempt of God, pride, and incontinency. What christian man will not fear, chiefly considering the fragility of our nature, which, as it is written in Genesis, even from our young age is ever inclined to the worst, to possess much riches, or to enjoy worldly wealth, seeing that they draw men so entirely from God, so far into vice and mischief.

If we are sick in body, having our wits, we will not touch those meats which we think may move or increase our disease, though they are ever so dainty or precious. And shall we not fear to wallow in worldly wealth, which to our souls is so dangerous that nothing can be more pernicious?

We read of some heathen philosophers, of which sort was Bias, who gave and cast away their goods, whereby they might more quietly study for the knowledge of things.

Crates was glad of his shipwreck and poverty, Anaxagoras of his imprisonment, Plato of his exile from the king's court, because their minds were more quiet thereby and fitted for the study of philosophy.

And shall we that are christian men think the lack or loss of worldly things is to be lamented, which are, or may be, the cause of quietness of conscience, and of a mind more fitted for the serving of God, whereto we were created?

But you will say, peradventure, What, sir! you speak as though men might not both be wealthy and virtuous. Know you not that St. Paul said, Phil. iv. that he might suffer penury, or lawfully have abundance? Moreover that he will have the rich men commanded, 1 Tim. vi. not to cast away their riches, neither to cease honestly to procure them; but that they put no trust in them. Have you not also learned by the Old Testament, that Abraham, Isaac, Joseph, with divers others, had the world at will, and yet were godly, and, as far as we can judge, are now in the hand of God, where the souls of just men are? Indeed, I grant that men may lawfully procure riches and enjoy the same, so that they do it it not at the impulse of avarice or ambition, nor putting any trust in them.

I confess also that some men have been, are, and shall be both wealthy and virtuous, else God forbid, but in my judgment it is but one amongst many. It is a very rare thing, and wonderful hard, yea so hard, that Christ, who cannot lie, saith, Easier it is for a camel to enter through a needle's eye than for a rich man to enter into the kingdom of heaven. We must, saith scripture, enter into the kingdom of God by many tribulations, of which how void the wealthy man is, at least of such as seem to be sent of God, who seeth not? The way to heaven is strait, sharp, and painful, Matt. vii. The way of the wealthy man is large, soft, and pleasant. I think that St. James, speaking the words, James v. which I will repeat, thought the more part of rich and wealthy men to be children of the world, and carnal. Go to, you rich men, saith he, weep and howl like dogs, in the wretchedness that shall come upon you. Your riches are putrefied, and your precious garments eaten of the moths, your gold and silver is rusty, and the rust of it shall be a witness against you, and shall eat your flesh like as it were fire. You have laid up wrath for yourselves against the last days. You have eaten and drunk upon the earth, and nourished your hearts with pleasures.

I dare to say, having respect to the divine wisdom of St. James, to the histories of old time, and to the rich men that are in our time, whose lives commonly, if a wise man apply to the rule of the gospel, shall seem so little to agree unto it, that St. James thought very few rich men should escape, whom this saying shall not touch.

St. Paul, knowing the nature of wealth and riches, willeth us, having nourishment and wherewith we may be clothed, to be content, for they that will be made rich fall into temptation, into the snare of the devil, into many desires, noisome and unprofitable, which drown men in the sea of death and perdition, 1 Tim. vi.

Seeing therefore it is a hard thing for the rich, worldly-quiet, and wealthy men to be saved, and that but few of them, as it should seem, do enter into God's kingdom, methinks we christians have no great cause to be sorry for any temporal things lost, nor to covet those which we have not yet possessed. But, saying with the psalmist, It is good for me, O Lord, that thou hast humbled me, set nought by them, which rather entice us into sin and perdition.

If Hercules had feared that he should have been cast away with a shirt made by woman's hand, he would never have worn shirt so long as he had lived. And shall not we fear to be wrapt in worldly wealth, which in manner is no less dangerous for our souls than was Dejanira's shirt for Hercules's body?

As we have partly considered the abundance of things and wealth, so we will consider poverty also and adverse fortune, whose works and effects, if they are conferred together, shall be found the contrary. For, as is said before, that worldly success draws men from God, and allures them to vice, the devil, and sin; so adverse fortune, retaining us commonly in honest behaviour, and in the favour of God, stops up the windows and doors which lead men unto wickedness and God's displeasure. It stops up the windows to adultery, to the contempt of God, and pride,

Finally, in a manner, to all those vices whereunto they were set wide open by wealth.

If ye desire to have a proof, read scripture, mark well the manner of David's life, who, so long as he was poor, tossed with afflictions, troubled with the persecutions of Saul, beset on every side with dangers, driven from place to place, from post to pillar, sustaining hunger and cold, having few or no friends, lodging, or substance, lived in the fear of God, loving him, calling upon him night and day, trusting him, and void of all vices.

Jeroboam, so long as he was but a poor man, nor yet advanced to his kingdom, lived in the laws of God without reprehension. But upon what vices these two stumbled after they came to wealth you heard before. Thus you see how wealth layeth blocks in the way that leadeth to heaven; adversity in the way that leadeth to fearful damnation. Wherefore our loving Father, ever correcting the children whom he loveth, giveth adversity as the better of these two, for the most part to his elect, as a medicine to them which have offended, lest they fall again; to them which have not greatly trespassed, (howbeit every man is a sinner and deserveth evil,) as a medicine preservative, lest they should slide. Which medicine, though it seem to us at the first more bitter than gall, yet if we flavour it with the sweetness of his commandments and pleasant promises, we shall find it more delicious than the honeycomb.

It is written, Proverbs iii. My dear son, thou shalt not neglect the correction of the Lord, neither shalt thou be discouraged when thou art reproved; whom the Lord loveth he correcteth; the child which he receiveth he scourgeth. If ye suffer chastisement, God doth offer himself to you, as unto his children. What child is there but his father chastiseth him? By this scripture you may see that our adversities and afflictions are not tokens of God's displeasure towards us, but of his good will and love. Wherefore, they ought not to discourage, but rather encourage us; not to make us sad, but merry; not sorrowful, but joyful; in that he of goodness will vouchsafe to take us as his children, to subdue our flesh, to strengthen our souls.

By troubles, as Saint Paul saith, he was strengthened to vanquish our enemies, 2 Cor. xii.

Whereby we shall be meet at the last to have with him quietness which his Son Jesus Christ with the effusion of his blood bought for us, where shall be no death, no wailing, no weariness, no sickness, no hunger, no thirst, no chafing, no corruption, no necessity, no sorrows.

Let us therefore suffer willingly and gladly, the correction of our heavenly Father, and afflictions, even as his only Son did, whom he spared not, but permitted to be scourged, to abide hunger and cold, to be in worse case for lodging than the foxes in the field, or the birds of the air, and at the length to suffer a most ignominious death. Let us, in all our afflictions, comfort ourselves with the example of him, remembering that the disciple is not above the master, nor the servant above his lord, neither yet the inferior members above their head.

Our head is Christ, in that he hath not abhorred afflictions, they may not be in any case disdained of us.

I marvel that we disdain them, that we should have great pleasure and delight in. We would be wonderfully well content to handle the table at the which Christ did sit, the garments or vestures he used, or other like relics, as being consecrated with his holy touching, much better methinks we ought to be apayed* to handle afflictions as relics; which, besides that they were oft hallowed by His most holy touching, he also commanded to be fingered of us, specially seeing that more rewards and merits come by the handling of them than by the aforenamed.

Do we not disdain them, I say, but rather, as Paul willeth, let us glory in our troubles, for trouble worketh patience, patience worketh proof, proof worketh hope, which shall not confound us, Rom. v.

I will not yet cease to speak more of the precepts of God, as touching this point. Son, thou coming to the service of God, prepare thyself to tentation, sustain the sustentations of the Lord, and be joined unto him. Sustain, whereby at the last thy life may be increased, Eccl. vii.

Thus ye see that the children of God are commanded still to bend themselves to tentation and adversity, which follows them no otherwise than the shadow followeth the body.

Now mark the end that is promised to our afflictions, if we bear them as we ought to do. Truly I say unto you, saith Christ to his friends, you shall weep and lament; they which are of the world shall joy, you shall be sorry; but this sorrow of yours shall be turned into solace, John xvi. I do think that the afflictions which we suffer here are

* Rewarded.

nothing in comparison of the glory we shall have in the world to come, Rom. viii. Our exceeding tribulation, which is for a moment and light, prepareth an exceeding and an eternal weight of glory unto us, while we look not on the things which are seen, but on the things which are not seen; for things which are seen, are temporal; but things which are not seen, are eternal, 1 Cor. iv. Although the earthly house of this our habitation, Paul meaneth the body, be corrupted, we know that we shall have a building of God, a house not made with man's hand, but everlasting in heaven, 2 Cor. v. Who, hearing these promises, is so stony hearted, that he will not take in good part whatsoever shall befall, be it ever so heinous, horrible, and perilous to his mortal members?

Few men will refuse to suffer for the space of a whole year the physician's tortures, now his veins to be cut, now painfully to be bathed, now to take most bitter medicine, otherwise to fast, and to be punished many other ways, that his body which is mortal, after these sorrows being delivered of his sickness, may joy for a time.

Much less a christian heart should be loth to sustain troubles, misfortune, and miseries here for a while, that the soul which is immortal may after joy for ever, with joys, not such as the poet Pindar attributes unto happy souls, piping, playing, or singing, pleasant gardens, gorgeous houses, and goodly spectacles, playing at dice, tennis, or tables, or other like; but such as neither ear hath heard, as St. Paul witnesses, nor eye hath seen, with such joys as faith taketh not, hope toucheth not, charity apprehendeth not; they pass all desires and wishes; gotten they may be, rightly esteemed they cannot be.

Blessed is that man, saith St. James, who suffereth temptation and trouble, for after his proof he shall receive the crown which God hath promised to them which love him. Every castigation seemeth to have no pleasure, but rather grief, howbeit, at the last it shall give a quiet fruit of righteousness to them which have been troubled by it, Heb. xii.

Who, I say, hearing these comfortable promises, will not joyfully say with St. Paul, What thing in the world shall separate us from the love of God? Shall trouble or persecution? Shall nakedness or dangers? Shall the sword or hunger? as who say, None of all these, neither death nor life, angels nor princes, things that are present, neither that are to come, height, strength, nor depth shall separate us from the love of God which is in Jesus Christ our Lord, Rom. viii.

But, to conclude, seeing that poverty, troubles, miseries, and afflictions are vanquishers of vice, and maintainers of virtue; seeing that they are appointed of God our Father to them that love him, and not as tyrannical torments, but as fatherly corrections and friendly medicines; also that God hath promised to those who patiently bear them, perpetual quietness, joy, and endless solace; why should we not with thanksgiving be very glad of them? If we are otherwise affected, let us not think the contrary; but we are disposed much like unto those who labour of violent agues, whose true taste being taken from them by the reason of their disease, they cannot endure with such meats as are most wholesome, and conducible to their health, but desire those which make most against them, and increase their sickness.

Wherefore if we chance so to feel ourselves, cease we not to solicit the Lord with prayers, that he will vouchsafe to take this spiritual ague from us, whereby we may with judgment reject the sweet but poisonous baits and dainties of the devil, and the world; and taste those meats which are most wholesome and profitable for our souls.

### Part the Second.

*How the Gentiles were moved to endure adversities, and how much more readily Christian men should suffer them.*

It is to be wondered, friend Urban, if these things cannot move christian men to suffer adversities, and despise worldly success as a very vain vanity, seeing that the infaithful Gentiles were moved to endure adversities by things of much less importance.

Some of them, as Socrates and Diogenes, considering that worldly wealth could not cause a quiet and joyful mind, and that it was a thing of no worth, neglected it, as a thing of no price, and set it at nought.

Whose consideration, Plutarch, as it appears by his similitude, approved as not untrue. "Likewise," saith he, 'as a man going to the sea, and first carried toward the great ship in a little boat, there beginning to feel sickness, desires much to be at the greater vessel, supposing to find ease therein; where he is worse troubled with the same grief than he was before: even so a man, being in a vile state and poor case, and not well content therewith, covets advancement to higher condition, his goods also to be increased. To the which things if he attain, he shall be more unquiet than he was before in his former misery."

If you require examples, look to Alexander the Great, king of Macedonia, who, possessing in a manner all the kingdoms, riches, and wealth in the world, for all that was so little quiet, that when he heard Democritus speaking of many other worlds, wept bitterly, that he had not yet wholly conquered one of them. Of the other part, poor Diogenes, glad to use, instead of a house, a tun to lie in, and compelled by poverty to live with cold herbs and water, his mind being instructed with learning and virtues, was never unquiet, never filled with care; no, he thought himself richer than Alexander, to whom he was bold to say, at such time as he offered to give him what he would desire, that he was in better case, and had less need than he, for as for him his lot pleased him, but as for Alexander, he could not be satisfied with the kingdom of Macedonia, no not with the kingdoms of the whole earth.

Alexander, marvelling at the security and quietness of his mind, said, "And if I were not Alexander himself, I would wish to be none other, but even Diogenes." I think truly, if he were alive and here again, knowing so much as he knoweth now, that he would no more wish to be Alexander still, but Diogenes, crying out against the vain desires of the world, with this or some other like oration.

"Whither is the blind error of men ravished? at things which are substantial, true, and profitable, no man doth marvel; things that are hurtful, trifling, and uncertain, every man with great labour seeks after. Why do men importunately desire empires, preferments, riches, or other worldly things? Let all men learn by me, that as these things are vain and transitory, so they make men never the better, but rather worse; never the quieter, but rather more unquiet. I was once, of all emperors and rulers the richest, subduing valiantly barbarous nations, and people innumerable, yet these things so little made me quiet, that by the reason of them, my mind was troubled with all kinds of unquietness. Now ambition and insatiable desire of more regions, rule, and empires, occupied my mind painfully; now mad rage and ire provoked by drunkenness, which by the reason of abundance of goods I was addicted to, punished me, and with violence sometime moved me to the murder of my friends. Now unlawful lusts, now envy vexed me, otherwise the hellish furies fleeing about my conscience, and not suffering the memory of my murder, or other evil facts, to be obliterated, so sorely grieved me, that I would now and then have pierced my heart with a sword, or have pined myself to death, if I had not been hindered. Once, as a fool, I preferred the state of Alexander before the condition of poor Diogenes, but then I judged like unwise Midas, then I knew not that the virtues of the mind alone cause true quietness, worldly success nothing profiting, but greatly diminishing the same."

What can be more true than such an oration? Whom would it not move, if it were spoken by the mouth of Alexander, as he would speak it doubtless if he might return to us, to esteem the world according to this worthiness? Moreover you may see by the example of Agamemnon, how little quietness worldly wealth brings. He was so much disquieted with his high state, that he lamented his chance in that he was king, and ruler over so many people.

Laertes, who to the sight of the world lived wealthily and wondrous quiet, yet was not quiet indeed, as Plutarch witnesses.

On the other side, Metrocles, vile and beggarly, in winter covering his body with a tub for lack of house, and in summer taking up his lodging in the porches of temples, faring not so well as the dogs of the city, yet was of so quiet a mind, that his quietness among writers shall be had in perpetual memory. Dettus, about to be burned, such was the virtue of his mind, was said not to be unquieted at all.

Thus I say, some of the wise Gentiles, considering and seeing that true quietness proceedeth only of virtue, esteemed worldly wealth not of a straw.

Yet we christian men, such is our lack of true wisdom, who know or ought to know, if we remember as I have spoken before, that there is no quietness to them which are of God, but quietness of mind and conscience; which is procured only by virtue, pureness of life, and by hope specially. Which as St. Paul saith, cometh of proof, proof of patience, patience of troubles, and so consequently, our quietness must come by troubles—what do we not attempt, to obtain worldly vanities, running by sea and by land, by rocks and sands, by Scilla and Syrtes, by fire and sword, as saith the poet, fearing no dangers, nor perils, like men out of our wits, seeking fire in the sea, and requiring water of the dry pumice stone?

Oh blindness! what, I pray you, have we gotten when we have procured riches or worldly preferments, whose purchasing commonly is painful, the keeping full of busy fear, the use dangerous, the loss deadly?

What, I say, have we got? tranquillity of mind? no, truly, but access of unquietness; for the more our goods grow, the more groweth care.

Miserable, saith the poet, is the keeping of much money. In the which respect, Horace desired his friend, after he had made him rich, to take his goods from him again.

What then; hast thou satisfied thy appetite that thou hadst to worldly things? nothing less. For as he which hath the dropsy, the more he drinks, the more he thirsts; so the worldly man, the more he hath, the more he covets. Hast thou increase of virtues? no, rather an expulsion of them all. What then hast thou? truly a bait to all vice and mischief. And if thou take not very good heed, an instrument to work thine own confusion.

Oh perilous and most pestilent harlot, I mean the world, which is transfigured in pleasures, and abundance of riches of the earth, in pleasures and voluptuousness. And I call her not only a harlot, but the most filthy and most dirty quean, whose face is foul, horrible, sharp, bitter, and cruel. And in this most, wherein all they are counted without forgiveness whom she deceiveth. And although her countenance be so filthy and so wild, so barbarous and so cruel; yet many are snared by her, and when they see all things in her body full of peril, full of death, full of mischief; yet she is desired of them, and counted to be loved and coveted. Notwithstanding that she maketh no man better, wiser, or more temperate, no man more favourable, gentle, or prudent.

Finally, she changeth no angry person into a man meek of behaviour, neither teaches the voluptuous man sobriety, nor the impudent shamefacedness, neither at any time by her is gotten any kind of virtue to the soul. No, rather like Circe, who, as Homer writes, changed by enchantments Ulysses' men into hogs, dogs, and other brute beasts, she makes them which are virtuous to be vicious; and of reasonable men, beasts unreasonable. Whereunto may we impute the fault, that some which have been meek and gentle, as it often befalls, by reason of ire and furiousness are changed from men, as though it were into raging lions, but to the enchanting Circe, the world?

What makes them which have been modest, sober, and temperate, as we have many examples, for their drunkenness and beastly intemperance, most like unto the unclean and filthy hogs?—that enchanting Circe, the world!

What takes our understandings from us, by reason of pride, and causes us shamefully to forget ourselves and our mortal state? That enchanting Circe, the world!

To be short, this same enchanting Circe, the world, changes even for the most part of them that have to do with her vile ornaments, except it be some spiritual Ulysses, into mere brutes, if ye have respect to heavenly wisdom.

Horace, considering her enticing charms, calls her riches and ornaments matter of great evil, and counsels them which are loth to be wicked, to hurl them into the sea.

Let us therefore not sorrow for the lack or loss of riches, or other worldly things that are so perilous, but rather prepare ourselves, partly to follow the counsel of Horace, though he were a heathen, not in casting away of our goods if we have them, but living as though we had them not, and giving them away, rather than that our souls, which God hath dearly bought, should take hurt by them. Remembering that Christ saith, Matt. v. It is better to go to heaven having but one eye or one arm, than to the fire of hell with two eyes or two arms.

It is better with poverty and affliction to be favoured of God, than with wealth and prosperity to have his displeasure. Let the children of the world and the devil, who is the prince of the world, seek their wealth; it is proper unto them, and let them enjoy it. Let us which are of Christ, seek and inquire for heavenly wealth, which by God's promise shall be peculiar to us.

Let the Cretians, Epicureans, Bœotians, with such other barbarous and carnal people, care for things that are pleasant for the body, and pertain to this present transitory life; let us which are (or ought to be) spiritual, care for things that pertain to the spirit, and life to come. But I will return again to the Gentiles, for I began to declare with what things they were moved to the contempt of the world. There were others of them, of the which sort I have named two or three before, whom the desire of knowledge moved to despise worldly things utterly; perceiving that it was hard and unfit for them, having the use an abundance of temporal goods, attentively to apply to their studies.

In this point who does not see them to be commended above the more part of us christians? who, although our religion requires minds more alienated from the world, and addicted to the contemplation of spiritual things, yet our whole minds and strength are wholly intent to things that are vain and earthly, scarcely believing the saying of Christ, No man can serve two masters, God and the world, Matt. vi. Neither regarding the saying of St. Paul, No man serving in the ways of God entangleth himself with worldly business, 2 Tim. ii. that is to say, in my judgment, no man is chiefly and wholly given to the purchasing and disposing of carnal and earthly things, and also to the commandments, wherein God requires our love with all our hearts, minds, and souls, not bestowing any part of it on these temporal clouds and vain shadows, Matt. xix. It is a shame that the mere knowledge of natural and vile things, should obtain of the Gentiles, what neither the knowledge of heavenly things, neither the care of our souls, nor the commandments nor the promises of God, can obtain of us that are christian men.

Others of the Gentiles, in whose number was Aristides, who were moved with no hope of good things, that should befall after this life, yet they, even for very virtue's sake only, fancied not, but neglected, worldly wealth. Chiefly seeing it for the most part came to the worst and naughty fellows, while to the best and most virtuous came miseries and troubles.

The thing is partly declared by the answers of poverty and riches in Aristotle's problem. It was asked of Riches why he used to dwell with the worst, holding the best as though they were disdained? He answered, that his mind was once to have tarried ever with them that were good; but Jupiter, envying this his purpose, put out his eyes, and since he lost his sight, it was ever his lot lightly to happen on the worst. It was also asked of Poverty, why she did still visit the good men, and pass by them that were wicked and naughty? She answered that good men could tell how to entreat her.

You shall read that such murderers as Tantalus, ambitious as Crœsus, covetous persons as Crassus, sycophants as Cillicon, had great abundance of wealth.

On the other part, such just and good men as Aristides,

Cato Uticensis, Fabius Maximus, Anaxagoras, and Plato, were ever in great need and troubles, indigence and afflictions. Truly, though scripture doth not provoke me, yet charity partly moveth me, to think that God had his elect even among the Gentiles, and that he would have them afflicted like as those which openly profess him.* Many naughty fellows, saith the Greek poet Callimachus, are rich and wealthy; the good miserable and poor. But with these things we must not be moved. The consideration of the thing was sufficient to set the mind of Aristides at utter defiance with the world and his ornaments.

Yet we, knowing by God's word, as by the 21st chapter of Job, by the 30th Psalm, by the 22d chapter of Jeremiah, that evil men do live wealthy, advanced and comforted with all kinds of dainties, extolled as the cedars of Libanus, that all things do prosper with them, and their seed after them, on the other side, that good men are afflicted, punished, and vexed, yet had we rather be numbered among the wealthy and wicked, and to be imitators of their sect, than among the godly, who by their patience and sorrows shall penetrate the heavens. We had rather with wealthy Nabal and his temporal pleasures, descend to the devil; than with poor Christ and his temporal troubles, ascend into the kingdom of God his Father.

But it is said in scripture, Proverbs xiv. The extremity of joy is occupied with mourning.

Once it shall repent us sorely, not without the singing of Lysimachus's song. King Lysimachus, by chance of wars, being taken of the Scythians, in his captivity was so sore pressed with thirst that he was glad to sell his kingdom for a draught of drink. Afterwards, remembering for how short a pleasure he had sold a thing most precious, he cried out and wept, saying, "Alas, how mad was I, to sell a noble empire for the satisfying of my affection, and greedy belly!" I fear it will be some of our end at the last, who have the world in such estimation, to sing likewise this sorrowful song.

Oh we miserable and brainless fools, which would for vain pleasures and transitory wealth lose the royal

* This was the opinion of Zuinglius, but the study of the scriptures, when our minds are not absorbed by classical pursuits, shows us the deficiencies of even the best among the heathens, when tried by gospel principles and practice. When Hugh speaks of Aristides and others as just and good, he means in the common acceptation of the words, not in the scriptural sense.

kingdom of God, with the eternal pleasures which he hath prepared for them that love him and renounce the world. Than which world, alas, what is more vain? Man, the best part of it, is compared of scripture to the flower of grass; the grass shall be withered, and the flower shall fall down. O happy souls, which in all your afflictions have been faithful and constant; to you the spring of the Lord shall ever be flourishing and green. Woe be unto these false illusions of the world, baits of perdition, hooks of the devil; which have so shamefully deceived us, and seduced us from the right path of the Lord, into the by-ways of confusion, and briers of perpetual punishment, where our weeping shall never cease, nor the furies of our conscience shall ever wax old.

At the last, friend Urban, seeing that as wealth and riches cause unquietness of mind; so adverse fortune and poverty to a christian man's heart inferreth deep quietness—seeing that as wealth stayeth and hindereth us from the contemplation of heavenly and spiritual things, so adversity taketh the stay and the hinderance away;—seeing that as the nature of worldly success is to make us to be numbered among the unjust, so is the nature of afflictions to induce us to the number of them that are good, godly, and virtuous— let us love poverty, and embrace afflictions, as things most expedient and necessary for us; let us fear and beware of wealth, as a thing, except we have grace to use it, most deadly, devilish, and dangerous.

### Part the Third
*An Exhortation to flee to God in troubles, and the comfort to be found in his word.*

But thou wilt say, perchance, Sir, if ye were in my case, your mind would be troubled no less than mine; I have wife and children, a family, which the law of nature and honesty binds me to nourish. I have neither money nor other goods to defend them. Besides that my body hath no such health, as is necessary for a needy and poor man. I am chafed also with slanders and injuries, as though these things before were nothing. Whom, I pray you, would not these things discourage, and in manner make as a man desperate?

If the case be as thou sayest, beware well, and take diligent heed, lest the devil use thee, as he doth his, and the children of damnation, being in like anguish. Beware he bring thee not to damnable mistrust. Neither let him lead thee to any unhonest crafts, as theft, perjury, adultery, murder, deceit, or such like, for the unlawful augmenting of thy substance, so making that which God hath offered thee as a mean whereby thou mightest the rather approach unto him, a mean to perdition and hell fire. But if thou art in these miseries, remember that they come not rashly, but even of the Lord. There is no evil, saith scripture, befalls to thee or any other in the city, which the Lord hath not wrought, Amos iii. Of the Lord, I say, who, as it is written in the third chapter of the Apocalypse, chastiseth all the children that he loveth, whereby he may with a fatherly affection correct them. While we are judged of the Lord, we are corrected, lest we be condemned with them of this world, 1 Cor. xi. Remembering these things, let us in all our miseries comfort our hearts, and say unto our heavenly Father as did Crates to Fortune after his shipwreck. Crates after he had lost by shipwreck all that he had, said this with a merry cheer: Go to, Fortune, I know what thou meanest. I am sure thou dost intend none other, but to call me to philosophy. Go to, I am well content to come thither as thou callest me.

Even so say we to our heavenly Father when we are afflicted, Go to, most bountiful Father, I know what thou meanest, I know thou dost none other but call me to repentance. Lo, I come willingly thither as thou dost call me.

Permit not the devil, I say, thine enemy, to bring thee, being needy and poor, to desperation; but flee from him lightly to God's word, as to a most strong fortress. For there, by reading or hearing the promises of God, thou shalt be sufficiently armed against him.

Read the sixth chapter of Matthew, where Christ himself pronounceth these words to them which are his faithful, I say unto you, be not careful for your lives what you shall eat, or what you shall drink; nor yet for your bodies what you shall put on. Is not the life more worth than meat, and the body more of value than raiment? Behold the fowls of the air, for they sow not, neither reap, nor yet carry into their barns, yet your heavenly Father feedeth them.

Which of you, though he took thought therefore, could put one cubit to his stature? Why care ye then for raiment? Consider the lilies of the field, how they do grow; they labour not, neither spin, and yet for all that, I say unto you, that even Solomon in all his royalty was not arrayed like unto one of these. Wherefore, if God so clothe the grass which is to day in the field, and to-morrow shall be cast into the furnace, shall not he much more do the same for you, O ye of little faith? Therefore take no thought, saying, What shall we eat, or what shall we drink, or wherewith shall we be clothed? After all these things seek the Gentiles, for your heavenly Father knoweth that ye have need of all these things. But rather seek first the kingdom of God and the righteousness thereof, and all these shall be ministered unto you. Thus, by promise made by the mouth of Christ, wherein never was found deceit, nor guile, we shall lack nothing, if we are faithful, that is necessary for us. I have been young, saith the prophet, and I have waxed old, yet I never saw the just left, nor his seed begging their bread, Ps. xxxvii. Cast thy cogitations on the Lord, and he shall nourish thee, Ps. lv. Be you careful for no worldly thing, but with prayer and obsecration* let your petitions be known of God, Phil. iv.

He that giveth seed to the sower shall give us both meat and drink, 2 Cor. ix. Comfort we ourselves therefore, believing these promises, and never despairing utterly.

But, because we believe those things the better whereof we have proof, I will bring examples whereby ye shall see that God both will, and is able to perform so much for his faithful, as he hath promised.

Samson, almost lost for thirst, after the conflict that he had with the Philistines, prayed to God and found drink in an ass's jaws. Hagar in the wilderness, despairing of her own life and her child's for lack of victuals, and with many salt tears laying the child far from her lest her motherly eyes should see it die, was fed of God, and comforted beyond her expectation. The poor woman of Sarepta, looking to die with her child, the day after the prophet came to her house, had her oil and meal so augmented, that she lacked not till the time of plenty returned. Therefore wheresoever any lack happeneth, be it of corn, or such other necessaries, despair we not; calling to remembrance this example, let us think with ourselves that God is able at all times to increase our corn, lying in the barn, grow-

* Supplication.

ing in the field, being bread in the oven, yea, or in thy mouth, at his pleasure, as well as he did the oil or meal of the woman of Sarepta, or the oil of the debtor's wife by his prophet Elisha. But if it so befall, that no hope be left of our temporal nourishment, yet have we no just cause to despair, remembering that scripture saith, Man doth not only live in bread, but in every word that proceedeth from the mouth of God. The omnipotent God did use armour and weapons, yet not necessarily as instruments, by the which he gave to his people Israel many victories, yet his power alone was the chiefest author of the same.

So, though he use meats and drinks as means whereby he nourishes us, yet the principal cause of our sustentation is his virtue and godly power; and as he often gave victories to the Israelites, their hands and weapons not moved at all, so hath he also fed, and can do so again, his faithful, though worldly meat and drink are not utterly ministered. A better proof needs not than the example of Moses and Elijah, whom he sustained with his heavenly power the space of forty days, without the ministration of any worldly feeding. Therefore, as David said, My sword shall not save me, neither yet will I trust in my bow. So say we, Our meats and drinks shall not save us, neither will we trust in worldly things; for the power of God sustaineth us, and in him will we trust, by whom all things do consist, Col. i. Who sustaineth all things with the word of his power, Heb. i. Who openeth his hand, and filleth every beast with his blessing, Ps. cxlv. whose hand being open, all things are filled with goodness; whose face being turned away, all things are troubled; whose Spirit being withdrawn, all things shall fail and be brought into dust, Ps. civ. Who saveth man and beast, Ps. xxxvi. Who covereth the heavens with clouds, prepareth rain for the ground, and bringeth forth grass in the mountains; who giveth to beasts their meat, and to the young of the ravens calling upon him, Ps. cxlvii. In him, to whom all these things are justly ascribed, do we live, move, and be, Acts xvii. In whom, of whom, and by whom, all things are, to whom be glory for ever, Rom. xi.

If ye have respect to the foregoing examples, ye shall perceive that the Lord, after he hath brought us even to the extremity, as the Psalmist saith, can and will, if it be expedient, deliver us; not only from hunger and thirst, but from all other miseries, harms, and adversities, from persecution and drowning, from fire and our enemies, from sickness, slanders, and death.

Who delivered David, so often unjustly persecuted, from the bloody hands of Saul? Or the three children, thrust into the hot furnace, from burning? Noah from drowning? Lot from the vengeance that lighted on Sodom and Gomorrah? Daniel from the hungry mouths of the lions? The Israelites from the Egyptians their enemies, from servitude, and intolerable bondage? Joseph from slanders? Peter from his bands and imprisonment?

Who restored so many lepers to cleanness amongst the Jews? Peter's mother-in-law from her ague to health? So many lame to their limbs, so many blind to their sight? Was it not the mighty hand of God which is not yet shortened, neither weakened, but as strong as ever it was? And though it please him to defer our deliverance, as it befell to Joseph and to Israel when oppressed with the Egyptians, whereby his glory may be more clearly shown; yet let us think none other but he hath both power and will to help and save us from all miseries whatsoever they are, if it stand with our souls' health and his glory.

If it do not, he will not if he love us. If he will not, let us take it in good worth, and conform our wills to his. Playing the part of a wise patient, who would be glad to have his disease, and the cause thereof, expelled by keeping a hard diet, and receiving of bitter medicines for a month, and no longer if it might be; but in case his sickness cannot be healed, except he use those bitter medicines and hard diet a whole year, he will rather do so in hope of health afterward, than by refusing them be sick all the days of his life.

Even so, if our souls cannot be clear of such diseases and botches as shall displease the eyes of God, except we use adversities so long as we live, as spiritual medicines ministered to us by God; let us be well contented in hope that we shall, after this life, which is but a year, or rather but a minute of an hour in comparison of the time that is to come, have health everlasting, no more in danger of any maladies.

Therefore, in such prayers as we make in our afflictions, let us follow the example of David, who in his most trouble said, If it please the Lord, he will deliver me, but if he say, Thou dost not please me, I am ready and willing. Follow we the example of our master Christ, who said in his prayer that he made a little before his death, Father, if it be possible that I may escape this passion, howbeit, not as I will, but as thou wilt.

Let us behave ourselves in our afflictions, as did the three children threatened of Nebuchadnezzar. The Lord, say they, that we worship, can deliver us from the fire, if it please him; but if it please him not, be it known to thee, O king, that we will not worship thy gods, neither thy image made of gold.

Learn we also the lesson taught us in the Lord's prayer, O Father, thy will be fulfilled. And if our carnal affections, at any time will rise against us, stirred up of the flesh and the devil our enemies, upbraiding us, and endeavouring to shame us with our afflictions, to make us blaspheme God, as though he had forgotten us, make we answer to them, as Aristides did to his countrymen, when they upbraided him with poverty, Cease to object my poverty and afflictions against me, which are uncomely and unpleasant only for them unto whom they befall against their wills. I, counting myself no better than my master Christ, am well content and pleased with them.

Or, if the same pricks and goads of the devil, affections I mean, will at any time move us to that which is not godly nor honest, for advantage or money sake, for preferment, health of the body, or any other commodity or comfort, whereof we seem to have need; let us make answer to them as did Marcus Curius to the Samnites offering him money.

Marcus Curius was once a man of much nobility, riches, and renown among the Romans, howbeit at the length (as it fortuned) he became a very poor man, insomuch that his meat for the most part was only roots, cold herbs, and worts.

It chanced that the ambassadors of the Samnites, then being at Rome, and hearing of his poverty whom they had known once to be famous and wealthy, came to his house to visit him, where they found him in a poor chamber, poorly arrayed, and seething coleworts for his dinner. They, after much communication, about to depart, gently offered to give him money, the which he refused disdainfully with these words, "Keep your money to yourselves, you Samnites, for he that can be content with such apparel, and such fare, hath no need of it." Even so say we to our affections, ambassadors of the devil and the world. Let the world keep his goods and his prosperous things himself, for he that can be content to live as did his master Christ hath no need of them. But what need these profane examples seeing that we have better in holy scripture. Let us answer them as Job did his friends, Although the Lord kill me, yet I will hope in him still.

Though it please God so extremely to punish us, even to the end of our lives, as he did Lazarus, with hunger, cold, and lack of lodging, boils, blotches, and grievous sickness, yet we are not discouraged, calling to remembrance this his promise, "He that will persevere even to the end shall be saved." I am sure if Lazarus were here again, knowing so much as he knoweth, though a hundred times as many evils should vex his body as did once, yet he would not be grieved therewith.

Let our strength be, as Isaiah saith, in hope and silence. Whatsoever chance, be we quiet and keep silence, even as our Master did, being as a sheep before the shearer, or led toward the slaughterhouse, when the Jews buffeted him and spat in his face.

He that committeth himself to God, saith scripture, keepeth silence; him that keepeth silence doth God so beat, that he may amend him; so cast him down that he may raise him; so slayeth him that he may make him alive. Let us therefore be cheerful, looking for the Lord, whose coming doubtless shall come and will not tarry. But what should I say "will come," who hath promised to be with us still, even to the end of the world, who as scripture witnesseth, when all our friends, father, and mother, forsake us, he receiveth us, neither will ever leave us fatherless and motherless, for such is his promise, but be with us continually, in all our troubles, and at the last, as he did Lazarus, with others of his sort, clearly deliver us; in the mean space do we feed ourselves joyfully with hope.

The proverb saith, meaning of worldly things, Hope nourisheth outlaws; much more should the hope of Christ's promises nourish us, for the hope of worldly things is fallible. But the hope of God's promises cannot be deceived, neither shall it ever shame us. I have hoped in thee, O Lord, saith David, and I shall never be confounded. Moreover, let us comfort ourselves, considering that the man itself is the immortal soul. The body is but a case, after the mind of Socrates, a house, or a prison rather, as Paul nameth it; and the man itself is no better for corporeal commodities, neither the worse for corporeal incommodities.

But, by the judgment of holy Chrysostom, like as a horse is nothing the better for his golden bridle, silver saddle, precious trappings, or other ornaments, but for his swiftness, pace, and strength; no more is our interior man for riches, wealth, health of the body, liberty, or other like, but for the virtue of the mind, and grace of God. Wherefore, if we be never the better for riches, let us not fear poverty; nor for health, let us not fear sickness; nor for good name, let us not fear slanders; nor for liberty, let us not fear bondage; nor for this common life, let us not fear death. "We are better," saith Chrysostom, "for the virtue of the mind, which is to think uprightly of God, and to live justly among men." All the other exterior things may be plucked away from us; this cannot, no not by the devil, except we ourselves willingly consent.

The devil, although he took from Job all his goods, whereby he might provoke him to blaspheme God; although he took his health to slake the constancy of his mind; his children to make him speak evil of the Godhead; yet could he never take this from him. But in withdrawing all worldly things, he heaped up the great riches of virtue, of the love and favour of God, through patience. Job was hurt of the devil, and of his afflictions, as one Prometheus was of his enemy.

Prometheus was a man that had a great swelling in his back, deforming his person very much. It befell that his enemy falling out with him, thrust a dagger into the same deformed place; that done, he departed, thinking that he had slain him. Howbeit, Prometheus had so little harm by his wound, that whereas his back could be cured before with no physic or surgery, then it was made whole. So he received commodity and health of him that intended his destruction and death. Likewise truly it befell to Job, if the thing be advisedly pondered.

Suffer me, I pray you, to speak this by the way, seeing that Job for all these cruel torments of the devil, for all these misfortunes and punishments, was never much the worse, who had not yet received the law, neither the redemption of Christ, nor the grace of his resurrection,[*] much less should we, who are weaponed with all these things, with like evils be harmed.

What were the apostles worse for their hunger, thirst,

[*] Only seeing them as afar off, Christ not having then suffered, Job xix. 25, 26.

and nakedness? Lazarus for his botches, poverty, and sickness? Joseph for his slanders? Abel for the cruel death he suffered? Were they not more noble and excellent for these among men, and prepared they not for themselves, through these, crowns of glory with God? Therefore, let us ever be joyful in Christ, and care for no worldly miseries, for lack or loss of goods, for slanders or imprisonment, for sickness, banishment, or death.

But if it befall that all our goods are taken from us, let us say with Job, and without sorrow, Naked we came into the world, and naked we shall go hence.

If we are slandered, put we the saying of the Lord before our eyes, Cursed are you when men speak well by you; be you glad and rejoice when they reject your name. If we are banished, remember that we have no dwelling place here, but look for one that is to come. If we fall into great sickness, use that saying of the apostle, Though this our exterior man be corrupted, yet the interior is daily renewed. Art thou shut in prison? and hangeth cruel death over thy head? set before thee John beheaded, and so great a prophet's head given in reward of pleasure, to a dancing wench.

Hast thou notably offended, and therefore in thy conscience art thou troubled with the despair of God's mercy? For the avoiding of this spiritual trouble, think with thyself that thy heavenly Father doth sweetly expostulate with thee after this sort:

"What now, my dear child? why ceaseth not thy spirit at the last to be afflicted? why dost thou unwisely derogate from the multitude of my mercies? Whom dost thou think that I am? Phalaris the tyrant? Manlius? Seleucus? or some cruel Scythian? Or else of mercies the Father, and of all consolation the God, long suffering and of much mercy?

"Art thou not taught by my Son Jesus to call me thy Father? Have not I promised that I would be thy Father by my prophet Jeremiah, and that thou shouldest be my son? Why dost thou not therefore ask me forgiveness, well hoping for pardon? Who is it of you, although ye are evil, who will not forgive his son, acknowledging his faults, being suppliant, desiring pardon, and promising amendment, notwithstanding he hath provoked him to ire a hundred times? And thinkest thou that I, which am the Father of mercies, of whom all fatherliness in heaven and earth is amed, Eph. iii. who possess the riches of goodness, patience, and long suffering, not to be ready to forgive my children truly repenting? Be of good comfort, my child, be of good comfort, mistrusting not my mercy, which surpasses not only man's mercy, how great soever it be, but all mine own works.

"Also judgment without mercy shall they feel whose hearts are obdurate, hardened, and will not repent; who delight still in their sins and will never leave their wickedness; who contemn my words and trust me not. From them indeed health* must needs be far away, Psa. cxix.

"But as for thee, repent, and the kingdom of heaven shall draw nigh. Matt. iii. Trust, and thy faith shall save thee. Matt. ix. I would have all men to be saved, and no man to perish, 1 Tim. ii. My fashion is ever to recreate, thinking lest he perish utterly which is abject or cast down.

"It is not my will, believe me, that one of these my little ones be cast away, Matt. xviii. whom I ever loved so well, that I would vouchsafe to give my only Son for them. John iii. But thy trespasses are great, wherefore thou art not lightly persuaded to trust in my mercy.

"Christ Jesus came into the world to save sinners. 1 Tim. i. He came to call sinners, and not the just, and to save that which was lost. Matt. ix.

"I know that thou an offender shouldest offend, and as a transgressor, I called thee from thy mother's womb; yet for my name's sake will I make my fury afar off. Isa. xliii. Thy good works can be of no such perfection that they may be able to save thee; nor can thy evil works, so that you repent with a full purpose to renew thy life, hurl thee into the hell fire. For I am, I am which put away thine iniquities for mine own sake, and thy sins will not I remember. Isa. xliii. I am, dear son, I am which put away thy sins for myself, for myself, and will give my glory to none other. Is. xlviii. Suppose thy sins to be as red as scarlet, they shall be made as white as snow, Isa. i. which I have scattered as clouds, and as a mist have I dispersed them.

"Turn to me, I say, for I have redeemed thee. I have redeemed thee which have pity upon all men, and for repentance behold not men's sins. I would thou shouldest know that I thy Lord am meek and gentle. Neither can I turn my face from thee, so that thou wilt return to me. It is commonly said, that if a man dismiss his wife, and

* Salvation.

she departing marries another husband, shall he return to her any more? Shall not she be as a polluted and a defiled woman? Thou hast sinned with many lovers, Jer. iii. yet for all that, am I ready to return to thee, so that thou wilt return to me. Such is my facility,* so gentle I am, such is my benignity, so great is my mercy, which thy most loving Brother and Advocate Christ, that washed thee from thy sins in his blood, hath purchased, continually praying for thee. Hast thou not heard how merciful I showed myself to David, to the Ninevites, and to Ahab? To Magdalen, to the thief, to the publican and others innumerable? Why dost thou not open the examples of them, as a table or glass wherein thou mayest well learn how exorable† I am; how ready and willing to forgive? Consider with thyself how heinous faults I have pardoned them. Go to, therefore, be of good cheer, lift up thine eyes, mistrust me no longer, turn to me and thou shalt be saved, commend thy spirit into my hands, and the prince of this world shall have nothing to do with thee, for by me, the God of truth, thou art truly redeemed, Isa. xlv."

Whensoever deadly despair shall trouble thy conscience, set this oration before thine eyes, which is nothing else indeed but God's own word, written by his most holy prophets and apostles.

Finally, thou art so tossed and troubled that it should seem that God had wholly forgotten thee. Read the forty-ninth of Isaiah, where thou shalt find these words; Sion said, (he meaneth God's elect,) the Lord hath left me, and the Lord hath also forgotten me. Can the mother forget her infant, and not pity the child she hath brought forth? but whether she can or no, I cannot, O Sion, forget thee. Alas, how should he forget them that believe in him, with whom, as it seemeth by his own words, he suffereth? Whatsoever is done to one of these little ones which believe in me, the same is done unto me, Matt. xxv. He that toucheth you, toucheth the very ball of mine eye. Zech. ii. And this should be no little consolation for the faithful, seeing that they have God himself as companion and partaker of their sorrows. For all our afflictions and griefs of the mind, let us require remedies of God's word, which without fail can mitigate all pains that occupy the hearts of them which believe in him.

* Readiness, easiness to be entreated.     † Easy to be entreated.

Wherefore it is not vain that Christ saith in the gospel, Come unto me all ye that labour and are laden, and I shall refresh you. Neither without a cause, that David who had oft experience of the comfort received of God's word, said this, How sweet are thy words, O Lord, to my mouth, more delighting my taste than the honeycomb! Psa. xix.

Whatsoever is written, it is written for our learning, that by patience and comfort of the scriptures, we may have hope, Rom. xv. By this you may gather that our comfort is to be required of scripture. Believe me, though the most heinous waves and tempests of this sea, the world, are raised up, threatening drowning to Peter's ship, yet if it be fastened with the anchor of God's word, well, they may move it, but overwhelm it they cannot.

And among all other things let us have in mind those scriptures wherein we are ascertained, that our bodies after this common death shall rise again, wonderfully glorified by the same power that formed them first. Those also wherein is promised the eternal felicity that shall be given to all them, who, after the example of Christ, suffer adversities, and overcome the devil and the world with theirs, for they shall abundantly comfort the believing people. Lo, saith the Lord, mentioning the resurrection and renewing of our bodies, I will put breath into you, and you shall be quickened. I will give you sinews, and cover you with flesh and skin; I will put into you a spirit, and you shall live and know that I am the Lord, Ezek. xxxvii.

We look for Jesus Christ our Saviour, who shall transfigure our vile bodies, and conform them to his glorious body, by the same virtue, wherewith he is able to subdue all things, Phil. iii. Doubtless, like as a grain of wheat sown in the ground is first putrefied and brought as into a thing of nought, yet after that springeth up freshly with a goodlier form than it had before—so man's body, sown in the ground after this temporal life, is first corrupted, and in manner brought to nothing, yet at the last by his power, which did create all things of nothing, it shall rise again with a form of much more excellency than ever was the first. Though this thing be wonderful, yet incredible it is not; for he that was able to make all the world, with his creatures, of nothing, must needs be able to make our bodies again of something. For the matter of our bodies shall ever remain in grass, worms, dust, stones, or some other form, even to the last day. And then surely, even as

Lazarus and Christ, of whom we are members, and therefore must needs at the last rise with him, being our Head, were resuscitated from their sleep—so I may call this corporal death—in like case shall the bodies of all men arise, some into the resurrection of judgment, some of life.

But this word " sleep," friend Urban, brings me in remembrance of a question which you moved to me at our last being together, and forasmuch as I could not then for lack of opportunity conveniently give you an answer, by these letters you shall know my mind, howbeit very briefly, for I purpose to defer the reasoning of the matter to our next meeting.

Your question was, whether that the soul of man, after this temporal death, sleepeth, as doth the body, void both of pain and pleasure, unto the day of judgment or no? I answer, that it is as much against the nature of the soul to sleep, as it is against the nature of the sun to be a dark body, or the fire to be without heat.

The soul of man, being a heavenly spirit, is so lively and constant, so strong and vigilant a substance, that naturally it cannot but perpetually persevere in operation. For of its own nature it is a very operation and motion itself, which never ceaseth, but like as the sun, which way soever he is moved, shineth and inflameth, so the soul of man, whithersoever it is brought, liveth and moveth continually. Yea, and though the body, which of nature is gross and drowsy, is oppressed with sleep, yet the soul is still occupied in the memory, in the understanding, or in other of the more excellent powers, as by dreams every man may see. Much less can it sleep, when it is wholly delivered from the sluggish body. Therefore, as the body sleepeth, so the soul cannot; forasmuch as it is a substance accommodated to continual moving, and cannot be weary.

Truly the error of those is great who persuade themselves that the soul, separate from the body, shall sleep unto the last day; and this error is old, and was confuted by Origen, and others of his time. Neither was it ever since received into the church, unto such time as a pestilent kind of men, whose madness is execrable, brought it of late days into the world again. But as all others of their opinions are perverse, abhorrent from the truth, and devilish, so is this. Declaring its patrons not to be taught in Christ's school, but in Galen's rather, who affirmed the death of the soul necessarily to follow the death of the body.

But leaving these vain fantasies, let us give ear to God's word.

It is written, Eccl. xii. The dust shall return to his earth, from whence it came, and the spirit to God which gave it. Where I hope it shall be so far from death and sleep, that it shall live delighted with joys unspeakable.

He that heareth my word, saith Christ, and believeth in him which sent me, hath life everlasting, and he shall not come into condemnation, but he shall pass from death to life, John v. Mark that he saith not, from death to sleep, but from death to life.

The parable in the 16th chapter of Luke doth well prove their false opinion. Where it is written, that Lazarus after his death used joy and gladness; on the other part, that the rich glutton was grieved and tormented. If the souls of men should sleep, neither should any joy have been attributed to Lazarus, nor punishment to the glutton.

What will they say to these words which Christ spoke to the thief, This day thou shalt be with me in paradise? Will they make us believe that paradise is a dormitory or a place to sleep in? In case it be, a man would think that Christ is or was once asleep therein. For he saith, Thou shalt be with me in paradise. St. Paul was rapt, 2 Cor. xii. into paradise, and there heard words which a man may not lawfully speak. These words he heard not with the ears of his body; for it lay prostrate on the ground, Acts ix. but of the soul, which part of Paul was ravished into paradise, where he did hear and see mysteries. Therefore, I cannot believe that paradise is a sleeping place; seeing that Paul was so occupied there in hearing of secret things. Moreover, whereas St. Paul desired to die, and to be with Christ, methinks he should rather have wished for the prolongation of his life, if the soul should continually sleep to the last day. For in this world, after a sort, we have the fruition of God, as though it were by a glass, as St. Paul himself teaches. But after this life, if these opinions be true, we shall have no fruition of God at all, except it be through dreams, unto the day of judgment. Therefore, St. Paul's wish, if we credit these antichrists, must seem to be foolish.

The Lord saith that he is the God of Abraham, the God of Isaac, the God of Jacob, not the God of the dead, but of the living. Betwixt the dead and these men's sleepers, I see no difference.

If Saul had been taught by any of the old prophets,

that the souls of men should sleep, he would not have gone about so busily to have raised up Samuel.*

Therefore, I say, believe not these false deceivers, who endeavour not only to persuade the sleep of souls, but also to make vain the resurrection of the dead, and so to abolish an article of our faith, and to make our religion vain.

And hereafter when you shall read or hear any such scriptures as is a part of 1 Thess. iv. where is mentioned the sleep of the dead, ascribe it to the bodies, which indeed shall sleep to the day of judgment, and then shall arise again, the souls joined to them, and awake from their sleep undoubtedly. Therefore saith Job, I know that my Redeemer doth live, and in the last day I shall rise from the earth, and in my flesh shall see my Saviour, Job xix.

Oh that happy and joyful last day, at the least, to the faithful, when Christ by his covenant shall grant unto them which shall overcome and keep his works even to the end, that they may ascend and sit in seats with him, as he hath ascended, and sitteth in the throne with his Father, Rev. ii. iii. where sorrow shall be turned into gladness that no man shall take from them. Then, as Isaiah writeth, They which are redeemed, shall return and come unto Sion, praising the Lord, and eternal joy shall be over their heads; they shall obtain mirth and solace, sorrow and wailing shall be utterly vanquished. Then, the sun shall no more give them light, nor the moon disperse the darkness for them; but the Lord our God shall be their light and comfort continually. Then doubt ye not, if we are only constant here in the love and faith of God, we shall have for earthly poverty, heavenly riches; for hunger and thirst, satiety of the pleasant presence of God; for bondage, liberty; for sickness, health; for death, life everlasting.

For this time, friend Urban, I shall desire you to take this poor letter, howsoever it be, in good worth, and hereafter if it shall please God to call me to a more quiet living, as ye know I am yet compelled necessarily to bestow in manner all my time and study in teaching of young scholars, I will write to you more largely of this argument, and peradventure, God, the author of all good things, giving me grace, more learnedly. Then fare you well. At Oxford, the 15th day of March.

* The author quotes 1 Peter iii. in the sense in which it was then commonly, but erroneously understood.

## BOOK II.

#### TO TEACH A MAN GLADLY TO DIE.

*Extract from the Dedication.*

IN the dedication to lady Denny the author says, " I was bold to dedicate this little book unto your gentleness, which book for that purpose I have written, that men might learn to die patiently, to leave the world willingly, and to go unto Christ gladly. How necessary such a thing is among the people, albeit I would wish that one or other should take the matter in hand, that can handle it more wisely and learnedly than I have here done, they which have been at the point of death, or they that have searched the consciences of men being about to die, can best express. The devil, doubtless, which at all times is busied and earnestly occupied in seeking the destruction of man's soul, in the day of death showeth his diligence most, now bringing a man in love with the world and his commodities, provoking him to hate death, and to resist, as much as lieth in him, the will of God; now leading him to despair, to the mistrust of God's promises, and impatience.

" Is it not needful then to have something written and ready, especially among the unlearned, whereby they may learn to despise death, to contemn the world, to obey the will of God? whereby they may be reduced from murmuring to patience, from despair and mistrust to a firm and constant faith in the promises of God?

" Whether this book shall perform so much or no, I cannot tell; yet thus much I dare say, that he which heareth or readeth it, with a mind and purpose to learn the said things, shall not utterly lose his labour.

The occasion why I write this book declamation-wise is this:—It happened to me not long ago to visit a friend lying on his death bed, whom, after my poor knowledge and learning, I exhorted to die christianly. His friends that then were present, in a while after, earnestly required me to write the same exhortation, even as I had pronounced it unto the sick; declaring that so it should most move the readers, hearers, and such as should need like consolation.

I, thinking no less with myself, was content herein to satisfy their requests. The thing written I determined to give to your ladyship, not for that I thought so slender and simple a thing worthy of your worship, but that I might, as I said before, show some argument of a thankful mind. This I beseech your ladyship, howsoever it be, take in good worth, not looking so much to the smallness of the gift, as unto the mind of the giver thereof."

### ADDRESS TO ONE WHOSE SICKNESS IS THOUGHT TO BE UNTO DEATH.

By certain arguments a man may easily conjecture, dearly beloved, that the last sleep, which to a true christian of all sleeps ought to be most pleasant, by little and little creepeth upon your mortal limbs. If my judgment deceive me not, you, ere it be long, shall walk the same way, which for the crimes of our first father Adam, needs must be trodden of all his posterity. Of all, I say; the escape or evasion of death being granted to no man; wherefore you ought the less to be grieved.

Scripture saith, All we shall die, and as water shall slide into the ground, 2 Sam. xiv. Like as there is one entrance for every man into this present life, so one passage and departure.

Therefore we are admonished in the Book of Wisdom not to fear the judgment of death, but rather to remember things that have happened before our time, and those which shall succeed. That is to say, that none of our progenitors could ever escape the blow of death, neither shall any of our posterity. In Gen. iii. we are admonished that we are dust, and into dust we shall return, by reason of death, which for the fault and disobedience of our first formed parent, with his inevitable dart, striketh and deadly woundeth all men. He woundeth mortally, not the wretched only, the needy and miserable, but the fortunate also, the wealthy, and the noble, Rom. v. Yea, kings, rulers, and the richest emperors, which in power and dignity, riches, renown, and glory, excel, and in their time rule the world according as they list. Not the unlearned only, the rude and barbarous, but those also who in learning and manners are most instructed. Not the overcome and careful captives, but also the puissant conquerors themselves.

Alexander, a king most victorious, by whose power and furious wars Asia with Europe was manfully subdued, no man being able to resist him, could find no weapon to conquer death. The notable wisdom of Solomon, the deep learning of Aristotle or of Galen, could not by any means avoid death. Tully's eloquence could not move him. The riches of Crassus could not corrupt him. He favoured not the beauty of fair Absalom, neither spared he the strength of strong Samson.

One night, saith the poet, tarrieth for every body, and the way of death must once be trodden of all men. Like as all the stars that come from the east, though they are ever so goodly and bright, yet at the last they go to the west, and there, according to the diversity of their circles, some slowly, some speedily, withdraw themselves out of our sight, even so all men which come from the east, that is to say their nativity, are born into the world; although they glister and shine here for a season, yet at the last they must needs, some sooner, some later, according to the duration which they have received of God, fall in the west of death, depart and withdraw themselves from the sight of men. Therefore, the wise man Simonides, at such time as Pausanias, a noble captain, desired to learn some good and fruitful lesson, bade him remember that he was mortal. Therefore also, Philip the king of Macedonia, wallowing in worldly wealth and prosperity, commanded his chamberlain that he should every day, at his uprising, sadly* repeat these words, " Remember, king Philip, and forget not that thou art a man to mortality subject." All flesh is grass, and every man is the flower of grass; the grass shall be withered, and the flower shall be dried away, Isa. xl. The man, saith Job, that is born of a woman liveth but a short time, replenished with many miseries, fadeth as a flower, and is worn away, vanishing as a shadow.

Wherefore, not without a cause the life of man is compared of Lucian to a bubble in the water; of Pindar to the shadow of a dream; of Eschylus to the shadow of vain smoke. Truly, if death should chance but to a few, and to the unluckiest, we should seem to have a just cause heavily

* Seriously

to take death, as I think you partly do. But seeing that he doth as well knock at the rich man's door as at the poor, at the happy man's door as at the unhappy; at the strong man's door, as at the weak; at the king's towers, as at the shepherd's cots; why should we not take well a thing importing such necessity?

How unreasonable is it for a man to take heavily his death more than his birth; considering that the one is appointed for man as well as the other, the one as common as the other, the one as necessary as the other, and of them both death is the better! In being sorry to die, we shall seem to lament in that our lot is mortal, and that we are not angels or equal with God, which is a great point of foolishness, mixed with impiety.

If we are troubled with such as are calamities indeed, to have two or three companions we count in a manner a comfort sufficient. Much more we should be comforted as touching death, seeing that we have not two or three, but all men, of what estate or degree soever they are of, as companions and partakers of the same; yea even the very saints themselves, and those that were highly favoured of God.

Moses, who was admitted to the secrets and mysteries of God, died. David, whom God pronounced to be a man after his heart's desire, died. John the evangelist, most tenderly beloved of his Master, died. John Baptist, than whom, by the sentence of Christ, none greater hath risen among the children of men, died. And not saints only, but the dearly beloved Son of God, Christ, being both God and man, a Lamb most innocent, and without spot, that he might pay our ransom, deliver sinful wretches from thraldom, and pacify his Father's wrath, was content to die the most ignominious death of the cross.

And shall we sinners that were begotten in sin, born in sin, and have lived in sin all the days of our lives, be aggrieved to put off these our vile and sinful bodies?

Christ, when he was in the shape of God, and thought it no robbery to be equal with God, made himself of no reputation, taking upon him the shape of a servant, and became like another man, and in apparel was found as a man, humbled himself, and became obedient unto death, that he might advance us to the kingdom of his Father; and shall we, being but worms, dust and clay, be loth to die, whereby we may enjoy the same advancement.

Sisigambis, the mother of Darius, king of Persia, for the very love she bare toward Alexander, forasmuch as he used her somewhat gently in her captivity, was wondrous willing by death to follow him after his decease. And shall we christians be sorry to follow Christ, who in captivity hath reteined us well and not evil,* but bursting utterly all his bands, hath clearly delivered us? Sisigambis vehemently desired to follow Alexander, who was her enemy indeed more than her friend; and shall we be unwilling to follow Christ, who is our friend most faithful and assured? She desired to follow him which made her poor, and shall not we covet to follow Christ, who hath impoverished himself to make us rich? She was content to follow him that made her of a free woman and a queen a bond handmaid, and shall we by our wills refuse to follow Christ, who hath made us of vile slaves and beggarly captives free men and kings? She would needs follow Alexander, although she could not tell where to find him, nor in his presence how to be entreated; and shall we be loth to follow Christ, whom we know certainly to be at the right hand of his Father? Where we shall be sure, if we die faithful, to find him, and for ever to dwell with him, with most gentle entertainment.

She would follow him that did not look, call, nor send for her; and shall not we willingly follow Christ, when his pleasure shall be to call for us?

Christ, I say, our Lord and our God, our life, as it is written, and the length of our days, calleth us, and forasmuch as the days of men are determined of God, as Job saith, Job xiv. we may not ascribe our death to the stars or destiny, but unto the calling of God, in whom we live, move, and be; of whom cometh both death and life; who hath appointed our terms that we cannot pass; with whom is the number of our months; without whom a hair cannot fall on the ground from our heads, much less the whole bodies, Matt. x. For he that worketh all things for himself, hath power both of death and life.

I can much commend the common people, forasmuch as they seem to imitate St. Cyprian, in using this phrase, When it shall please God to call me to his mercy, and such like. Wherein they declare themselves not to be of their opinion, who think that men are not cared for, nor governed of God; but that all things do chance even by very fortune.

* Hath remembered us for good.

Which opinion, if it were true, God should either be ignorant of many things, or else abhorrent from his creatures. And therefore should he seem either not true or not good.

But, this matter being left, I will return to my purpose. Seeing that it is appointed for all men to die when it shall please God to call them, let us be content joyfully to depart thither, and when our heavenly and most bountiful Father shall call us, remembering ever that we ought to work, not our own wills, but the will of God, according to the prayer that we customably use, by the command of Christ.

How preposterous and perverse is it to desire, that the will of God may be fulfilled in heaven and in earth, and yet, when he willeth us to depart from this world, that we should, by our wills, resist him; and, like untoward and stubborn servants, are rather drawn with the bands of necessity, than with love or obedience, due to the will of God.

There are none of us but we will wish deliverance from this Egypt, with its captivity and troubles; and to dwell with God in the land of promise, where is all joy and quietness. Yet after that God hath brought us even to the gate of the said land—for as the course of our life is a race toward death, so death is the gate of everlasting life—we are loth to enter in by it; we would gladly be honoured with heavenly rewards, but we are unwilling to go where they are.

What should we pray so oft, Let the kingdom of heaven come, if we are so much delighted with earthly bondage? why do we pray that the day of the kingdom may be hastened, if we are more desirous here to serve the devil, than to reign in heaven with Christ? But let us break our own wayward wills, conforming them to the will of God, showing ourselves willing at all times to pay that we owe.

What other thing is it to die, than to pay such things as were for a time liberally lent us? what honest heart will not, and that willingly, at the least if ability fail not, pay again money to him who gently did lend it at his need, whensoever it shall be required?

And shall we hesitate to pay to the earth, the mother of us all, our bodies of whom we borrowed them, and our souls to God our Father, who bountifully did lend them? God forbid. No, we ought to be much more ready to pay our souls to God, than the debtor to pay his money. For of the payment of the money few or no commodities ensue, but after the paying of our souls to God, innumerable pleasures and infinite commodities succeed. For then at the length they are happily brought from darkness to light, from fear to security, from travail to quietness, from a thousand dangerous rocks and waves into a sure haven; from the use of vain, vile, filthy, and transitory things, to the fruition of the eternal Deity of God.

What christian man will not be glad of such an exchange? what loving child will not heartily covet deliverance from the misery, bondage, and tyranny of this world, and to dwell with his most merciful Father in heaven? Oh blindness! what cause have we, I pray you, to hate death, by whose means we are made of bondmen free, of strangers home dwellers, of beasts like unto angels?

If that a great ruler happen to call any of us to a king's or emperor's court, promising to do for us, to set us out with temporal riches, to endue us with worldly possessions; we think ourselves very fortunate. And when God, the ruler of all rulers, and king of all kings, shall call us to his court, and give us inheritance and possessions, not in earth, but in heaven, which are constant, and shall never be taken from us, by storms or tempests, by craft or subtilty of the law, by oppression or tyranny, by death, the devil, or sin, shall we think ourselves unfortunate? No, truly, if we are well in our senses, but rather count that time, whensoever it shall come, of all times to be the most happy, forasmuch as then, the kingdom of God, the reward of life, the joy of eternal health, perpetual gladness, possession of paradise, that was once lost, are even at hand. Then, for earthly things, heavenly; for little things, great; for transitory things, eternal, shall take place.

Who then, I pray you, will fear death, but he that hath no faith, that lacketh hope; that would not go to Christ; and believeth not that he beginneth then to reign with Christ, when he beginneth to leave this world?

O that we had a spark of the grace and faith that Simeon had, who, being a just and faithful man, was assured by a godly responsion,[*] that he should not die before he had seen Christ. Whom after that he had seen in the temple, and known in spirit, he knew certainly that he should shortly be called of God, and die. Therefore he, being marvellous glad, took the child in his arms, and

[*] Revelation from God.

blessing God, cried out and said, Now dismiss thy servant, O Lord, according to thy word, in peace; for mine eyes have seen thy saving health.

Here did Simeon prove and testify, that free tranquillity, true peace, and firm security, do happen to the servants of God, when they are drawn from this troublesome world, and brought to the gate of the everlasting mansion.

Peradventure you will say unto me, Sir, as for Simeon I cannot blame him, though he was well content to die, forasmuch as he was a man of a great age, and, as they say commonly, even at the pit's bank. I am but a young man. I might have lived yet many years with no small comfort of my friends; by the common course my time was not yet come.

I grant, indeed, you are a man of no great age, but what day, I pray you, can we appoint for any man's death? Every day may be a last day if it stand with the pleasure of God. We see that some die in their birth, some in their cradles, some in the flower of their age, some in their old age, some when they are rich, other some when they are poor; so that we may plainly understand that God doth give to every man his life upon that condition that he surrender it again whensoever it shall please him to require it.

But among all others, saith the Greek poet Menander, most happy are they, and best beloved of God, that die when they are young. Which saying, as it is very wise, so it is very true. And yet a man may easily perceive it, if he have respect to the spiritual evils and temporal incommodities that occupy this life; for they commonly depart, not yet infected with so much malice, entangled with so much vice, corrupted with so much wickedness, as their elders. Not yet so far separated from God by the reason of sin, and made members utterly and limbs of the devil.

It befalls for the most, that men, after they come to a ripe and complete age, are wholly drawn from God, from virtue, from simplicity and integrity of life, to sin, wickedness, and ungodly living. The rich by injurious handling the poor, by oppression, ingurgitation,* and filthy incontinency. The poor by picking, lying, desperation, and blaspheming the name of God: I speak of many but not of all. The worldly wise by craft, deceit, and subtilty. The learned oft by heresy, ambition, and devilish doctrines. I will not speak of envy, malice, rancour, and adultery, which at ripe

* Gluttony and drunkenness.

age increase in growing, and, as Scylla and Charybdis, hurl the greatest part of men into the horrible sea of perdition.

The Holy Ghost teacheth by Solomon, that they which please God best are quickly and speedily taken from this world, lest they should be polluted with the wickedness of the same. He was taken away, saith he, lest malice should change his understanding, for his soul did please God, and he hath made haste to bring him from the midst of iniquity. Enoch pleased God, and he was not found afterward, for God had taken him away.

Therefore, to please God is to be counted worthy of him; to be delivered from this world, and to be brought thither as the devout soul of the prophet coveted to come, saying, How dearly beloved are thy habitations, O God of virtues; my soul desireth, and maketh haste to thy halls, Ps. lxxxiv. Those trees are not best that are most durable, but those of whom doth spring most profitable fruit. Neither are those songs most commendable that are longest, but that most delight the ears of men. Even so the longest life is not chiefest, but that which is most virtuous, and least defaced with vice.

Let us further ponder these temporal displeasures and incommodities, and then judge whether death, when or in what age soever it befalls, is better than life, according to the words of Ezekiel, or not.

Consider of what calamities, chances, miseries, and perils, men are in danger. No man living is happy on every part; no man is utterly content with his lot; whether that reason or chance, as saith Horace, hath offered it unto him. Therefore, no man, according to Solon's words, is happy indeed before he is buried. For this cause Socrates, with others of his sect, desired ever desirously to die; esteeming death not to be miserable, but the end of all miseries; not troublous, but the end of all troubles.

Better, saith Ezekiel, is death than life, and eternal rest than continual sorrows; for every part of this life doubtless is replenished with unpleasantness, full of sorrow, unquieted with cares, troublesome, and vexed with diseases.

What trade of life soever a man shall follow, saith Crates, he shall be sure to find bitterness therein. In the fields are labours; at home, cares; in a strange country, fear, if a man have ought; in the sea, fear with jeopardies; in youth, foolishness; in age, feebleness; in marriage, unquietness; in lacking a wife, solitariness; if a man have children, he hath care; if he have none, he is half maimed; so that one of these two, saith he, is to be wished, either not to be born, or quickly to die.

The wretchedness of this world hath compelled even the holiest men, being wearied therewith, to wish for death. Jonah, in his travail, said, that it was better for him to die than to live. Elias in his life-time often coveted, and not unadvisedly, to yield up the ghost.

Neither can I see any cause why all of us, who have any hope of another life to come, should not wish for the same thing: seeing that no man liveth who laboureth not under the want both of spiritual and temporal things. Though a man have ever so much excellency in honours, abundance in riches, delight in pleasures, nothing can satisfy him truly, or bring asleep his desires, appetites, and insatiable lusts, no more than the daughters of Danaus can fill their bottomless tubs. Is it not better, therefore, to change this life, to leave this strange country, and go where is all excellency of honours, abundance of all good things; where perpetual pleasures shall ever be in thy right hand even to the end. Where thy Divinity shall be seen, loved, and reserved for ever.

Death of itself indeed is somewhat formidable; and the way to death, as saith the philosopher, is painful. Yet if we consider the premises, and that death is nothing else but a gate, whereby men enter into life, we shall see it to be amiable, and much to be embraced. I marvel what evil spirit hath so blinded and bewitched the minds of men, and made them mad, so shamefully doting, forasmuch as they can persuade themselves to be best here to live still in these rotten tents, open to all sharp winds and bitter storms, in these ruinous houses, in these stinking prisons, I mean our bodies, and to hate death as it were a venomous and poisonous serpent, seeing it is so friendly a thing, inferring a great sea of commodities and pleasures; seeing it is, and only it, the finisher of our filthy and painful imprisonment, a consummation of our labours and grievous wars, and arriving at the safe haven and end of our peregrination, a laying away of a heavy burden, a termination of all sickness, an evasion of all dangers, a return into our country, an entrance into glory. If we are wise let us be well content to die, and cheerfully give a farewell to this miserable world, continually unquieted with troubles, and troubled with unquietness; subject to sundry evils, and the false illusions of vain fortune; for truly it hath much more gall than honey; much more bitterness than sweetness. The which is well signified by this fable of Homer:—Jupiter, saith he, sitting in heaven, and having before him two great tuns, the one of felicity, the other of misery, against a little spoonful of happiness poureth out a great ladleful of unhappiness. Meaning thereby that fortune and misfortune among men do not equally part the stake.

Eschylus, recounting with himself the continual tossing and turmoiling of men's bodies and minds, crieth out after this sort: Oh how unjust are those men, how foolish, that hate death, seeing it is a remedy most present for all evils, and the chiefest expeller of all anxieties!

Many of the heathen, for this cause, thought death of all things most to be desired. How much more ought the same to be embraced of us, which are well assured by holy scripture of the immortality of the soul, of a better life to come, and that death is none other but an entrance into that life which is true, permanent, and constant!

Let the wicked Sadducees, which deny the resurrection of the flesh, take heavily their death; for they look for none other life after this. Let us which are sure that our bodies shall arise again freshly renewed, esteem death as a thing most pleasant.

Let those which have had no schoolmaster but Aristotle, who affirms death of all terrible things to be most terrible, fear death.

Let us, which have learned of St. Paul, that to die is a gain; that whether we live or die, we are of the Lord; and that Christ hath died, that he might be ruler both over the quick and the dead, heartily say, with David, Deliver, O Lord, deliver our souls out of prison, that they may confess thy name.

Besides a thousand incommodities and displeasures of this present slippery life, this doth also accede, that our sins daily renewed, augmented, and increased, we more and more provoke the Lord to ire. And the innocency of life, if we have any, is wholly endangered, rather than the which should decay St. Paul desired to die; Better, saith he, it is for me to die, than any man should make vain my glory.

Therefore let us not love the world, for indeed it will not love us very much if we are true christians, neither the things that are therein, or else the charity of the Father cannot abide in us; for all things in the world, which is wholly set in malice, are either concupiscence of the flesh, concupiscence of the eyes, or pride of life.

To conclude, if death were only an abolisher of worldly displeasures, it were a thing not utterly to be abhorred. But, forasmuch as with worldly miseries it putteth away those that are spiritual, and further leadeth us to eternal blessedness, why should we not much wish for it, covet and desire it?

Curtius, and the Decii of Rome, affecting the vain glory of the world, vowed themselves, no man commanding, willingly to death. And shall we, christians, die impatiently, whereby we may attain to the true and heavenly glory, God commanding and calling us? Or shall we, rather, following the example of St. Paul, wish for the dissolution of our bodies, and to be with Christ?

What thing in the world is of such excellency that it may justly so allure you, being a wise, and, as I take you, a faithful man, that you should be loth to leave it? Riches? uncertain, false, and vain, the use whereof is vanity, which shall not profit you in the day of obduction* and vengeance, to be short, very smoke.—Friends? untrusty, dissemblers, fools, in whom is no health, every man is a hypocrite, and wicked, and every mouth hath spoken foolishness.—Parents? you shall have a Father in heaven who loveth and tendereth you more than these earthly parents.—Wife, brethren, and children? you shall dwell with your brother Christ, who loveth and careth for you much more than all those care, who hath spent, not his money or other external things for your sake, but his most precious blood. So much hath he esteemed you, so vehemently hath he loved you before the beginning of the world; yea, and loveth you still.—Pleasures? you shall have the presence of God, which so far passeth all other pleasures as the brightness of the sun excelleth the light of a candle.—Honours? vain and inconstant, for all things here are vanity.—Your body? a corruptible prison, which burdeneth the soul, and depresseth the sense, musing on many things. From the which prison the soul, being the very man itself, for the body is but a case, desireth more to be delivered than the prisoners from their imprisonment and chains, and as fervently covets access unto God, as the chafed hart, boiling with heat, desires the sweet flowing water.

Is it your country? A strange country; for so long as

* Trouble, overwhelming.

we live here we are strange from Christ: here we have no permanent city, but look for one that is to come.

Here we are aliens, as David said, none otherwise than all our forefathers; abiding in the reign of the tyrant the devil, that is to say, in the world beset with a thousand enemies. First, the foul, crooked serpent himself afar off and nigh, by fines and strokes, with all kinds of weapons, never ceaseth endeavouring to oppugn us.

The world disquiets us, and labours still to subvert us; the flesh, as much as lieth in him, cowardly betrays us, and aids busily the aforesaid enemies. Now poverty, now riches, and care of things gotten, molest us night and day. With how many grievous sicknesses are men's bodies vexed! What injuries, slanders, despites, usually grieve us! Now we must prepare ourselves to fight with avarice and uncleanness; now with ire, ambition, and other carnal vices. To be short, the mind of man is beset with so many enemies that scantly is he able to resist.

If avarice be prostrate, unlawful lust offers us battle. If lust be subdued, ambition draws his sword. If ambition be cast down, ire provokes us; pride sets in his foot, drunkenness approaches, envy breaketh concord, emulation cutteth amity away. I will not speak of desperation, of the deaf beating of consciences, of the furies of the mind, with such others, which with horrible enforcements furiously assail innumerable, for what should I fight with the monster hydra?

Who can number the sands in the sea? or the stars fixed in the high heavens? which, I think, pass not much the number of men's enemies.

Seeing, therefore, that man daily suffereth so many persecutions and dangers, should we desire to stand still in the midst of our enemies, among so many sharp swords? or shall we covet by death quickly to flee to Christ, our defender and helper? Specially seeing that Christ himself instructeth us, and saith, "Truly, truly, I say unto you, that you shall weep and lament. The world shall rejoice; you shall be sorry, but this sorrow of yours shall be turned into gladness."

Who will not be desirous to want heaviness, and to enjoy perfect gladness? When this sorrow shall be turned into gladness, he declares, saying, I will see you again, and your hearts shall be joyful, and this mirth shall no man take from you. Therefore, seeing that to see Christ is to be glad; and that we shall not be glad indeed till such time as we shall see him, what blindness or rather madness is it here to delight in pain, tears, and pensiveness; and not rather to covet to come unto the joy which no man shall take from us!

Let us play the wise men, and be glad at the vocation of God, to leave this painful peregrination, to depart from this labyrinth, and be transferred to our country, and to our most loving Father's house, where is no sickness, no sorrows, no weariness, no hunger, no cold, no labour, no mourning, no jeopardies, no enmity, no care; to be short, no adversity at all; but much tranquillity and pleasure that shall ever endure, and deep quietness. Where we shall have for false riches, true inheritance; for dissembling friends, Abraham, Isaac, the blessed virgin Mary, Peter, Paul, and the angels of God, which, as the proverb is, shall ever love. Whose faithfulness and love shall never be changed from us. Who, considering these things, will not say with the prophet, that the day of death is better than the day of birth? Who will not confess that he which dieth in the Lord maketh the change between Glaucus and Diomedes, that is to say, receiveth for brass, silver; and for copper, pure beaten gold?

But peradventure you will say unto me, Sir, as for this world, howsoever it be, I know it, and of its good things I am a partaker, but whither I shall go hence as yet I know not, nor what I shall have after this life; therefore to leave a certainty for a thing uncertain, how should I but be sorry?

Hearken then, I pray you, and give ear a little; and I shall declare unto you by God's infallible word, both whither you shall go hence, and what you shall have after this life. The body, saith Ecclesiastes, shall return to the earth, from whence it came, and the soul to God which gave it, Ecc. xii. The souls of just men are in the hands of God, and the torment of death shall not touch them. Many mansions, saith Christ, are in the house of my Father; if it were otherwise, I would have told you. I go to prepare a place for you, and if I go to prepare a place for you, I will come again and take you to myself, that you may be where I am, John xiv.

Trust therefore, and you shall be sure by this promise to come thither where Christ is. Every man that heareth the

## The Troubled Man's Medicine. 53

word of Christ, and believeth in him that sent him, hath life everlasting. He cometh not into judgment, but passeth from death to life, John v.

We know, saith Paul, that if the earthly house of this our habitation be dissolved, we shall have a building of God, a house not made with man's hands, but everlasting in heaven, 2 Cor. v. That dwelling, doubtless, shall happen to the faithful, which Christ of his great mercy promised to the thief, with these most comfortable words, This day thou shalt be with me in paradise.

Therefore seeing it is so, that the souls of just and faithful men are in the hand of God, as you are assured by scripture, where the torment of death shall not touch them; seeing Christ hath prepared a place for them, and that they shall dwell even there as Christ himself dwelleth; seeing that we shall have, after the dissolution of these our earthly bodies, an everlasting mansion in heaven, doubt no more whither you shall go after this life, but be ready; repent and believe, and you shall enter, accompanied of the five wise virgins, into the joyous marriage mentioned in Matthew.

What the faithful shall have after this life, St. Paul in the 1 Cor. ii. sufficiently declares. The eye, saith he, hath not seen, the ear hath not heard, neither the heart of man hath thought, the excellency of the good things that God hath prepared for them that love him.

Again to the Romans; The passions, troubles and afflictions we suffer here, are not worthy of the glory which shall be revealed in us in the time to come. Thus St. Paul, who was rapt into the third heaven, and saw secrets which a man may not lawfully speak, hath taught you what the souls of good men shall enjoy after this life; that is glory, and such excellency of pleasures, as the senses and understanding of man cannot comprehend.

But if St. Paul had spoken nothing of the matter, yet a reasonable man might partly conceive the great and invisible things that good men shall possess in the other life, from these present things little and visible. Forasmuch as our vile and corruptible bodies, by the benignity of God, receive so many commodities, benefits, and pleasures, of the heavens, the earth, and the sea; of the light and darkness, of heat and cold; of the rain, winds, and dew; of birds, beasts, and fishes; of herbs, plants, and trees of the earth — to be short, of the ministry of all creatures, serving us successively in their due times, whereby they may alleviate our weariness, what, how great, and innumerable shall those be which he hath prepared for those that love him, in the heavenly country, where we shall see him face to face?

If he do so much and so great things for us, being in prison, what shall he do for us in the palace! Seeing that the works of God are so great and innumerable, wondrous and delectable, which the good and the evil both receive, how great shall those be, which the good shall receive being alone! Seeing that he performeth so much for his friends, and his enemies, yet being together, what shall he do for his friends separately! Seeing that he comforteth us so much in the day of tears, how much shall he comfort us in the day of marriage! Seeing that the prison containeth such things, what manner of things shall our country contain!

The eye, as it is said before, hath not seen, the ear hath not heard, nor the heart of man can think the excellency of those things, which God hath prepared for his friends. According to the great multitude of his magnificence, is the multitude of his pleasantness, which he hath laid up for them that fear him. Therefore, let us not doubt whither we shall go, neither what we shall have, being faithful, in the other world. Forasmuch as we may certainly know, not by scripture only, but also by the leading of natural reason. All such doubt put away, desire we most heartily and fervently access to those things which God hath prepared for his friends, musing some such godly meditation as is this, which St. Augustine hath in his soliloquies:

"The heart desireth not so much, O Lord, the wells of sweet water, as my soul desireth to be with thee. My soul hath sorely thirsted for thee, O Lord, the well of life. O when shall I come and appear before thy glorious face? O well of life, and vein of living waters, when, when shall I come from the earth, that desert without way, unto the waters of thy sweetness, that I may see thy virtue, and satisfy my thirst with the waters of thy mercy? I am athirst, O Lord, and thou art the well of life, fill me with thy waters, I beseech thee. I do thirst for thee, O Lord, the living God; when shall I come and appear before thy face? Shall I never see that day? that day, I mean, of pleasantness and mirth; that day which the Lord hath made, that we might be glad and joyful in it? O day most bright, fair, calm, void of all storms, tempests, and troublesome winds, having no eventide nor falling down of the sun, in the which I shall hear the voice of praise, the voice of exultation and confession.

"In the which day I shall here enter into the joy of the Lord thy God; where are great, inscrutable, and marvellous things, whereof there is no number. Enter into joy without heaviness, into joy which containeth eternal gladness, where shall be all good things and no evil, where a man shall have what he will, and nothing that he will not, where life shall be sweet and amiable, where shall be no enemy impugning us, but safe security, sure tranquillity, quiet jocundity,* pleasant felicity, happy eternity, eternal blessedness—and the blessed Trinity; of the Trinity the Unity, of the Unity the Deity, of the Deity, blessed fruition.

O joy above all joys, O joy passing all other, O joy besides which there is no joy. When shall I enter, that I may see my Lord that dwelleth in thee, and the great vision? What is it that hindereth me so long? alas, how long shall it be said to me, Where is thy God, and where is thine expectation? Art not thou, O Lord God? We look for Jesus Christ, who shall reform the bodies of our humiliation, and conform them to his.

"When shall he return from the marriage, that he may lead us to his marriage? Come, O Lord, and tarry not. Come, sweet Jesus, come and visit us in peace; come and bring us from prison, that we may be glad before thee with perfect hearts; come, Thou which art desired of all nations; show thy face, and we shall be saved; come, my own light, my Redeemer, and bring my soul from prison, that it may confess thy name. How long shall I, poor wretch, be tost in the floods of my mortality, crying to thee, O Lord, and thou hearest me not? Hear my cry, I beseech thee, from this troublesome sea, and bring me to the port of felicity.

"Oh happy are they which have passed the dangers of this jeopardous sea, and have attained to thee, O surest haven. Happy, thrice happy are they which have passed from the sea to the banks; from banishment to their country; from prison to the heavenly palace, where they rejoice with continual quietness, that they have sought by many tribulations! O happy, and happy again, which are eased of the burden of their evils, and, being sure of immarcessible† glory, inhabit the kingdom of comeliness! O everlasting kingdom! O kingdom of all worlds, where is light that never faileth, and the peace of God that passeth all sense;

* Joy, pleasant mirth.     † Unfading.

in the which peace, the souls of saints do rest, where everlasting happiness covereth their heads with joy and exultation. Where sorrow and mourning can have no place. Oh how glorious is thy kingdom, good Lord, in the which thy saints do reign, clothed with light as it were with a garment, having on their heads crowns of precious stones.

"O kingdom of everlasting blessedness, where thou, O Lord, the hope of saints, and diadem of glory, art looked upon of thy holy ones, face to face, making them glad on every side, in thy peace that passeth all sense. There is joy without end, gladness without sadness, health without sickness, mirth without sorrow, increase without labour, light without darkness, life without death, all good things without all evil things, where youth never waxeth old, where life hath no end, where beauty never fadeth, where love is never cold, where joy doth never decrease, where sorrow is never felt, where wailing is never heard; where no evil is to be feared; for there the highest felicity is possessed. That is to say, ever to see thy face, O Lord of powers.

Therefore, happy are they which have already attained unto such joys. Unhappy are we, forasmuch as we do yet travel in a strange country as banished men, suspiring* unto thee, being the port of the sea. O country, O our sweet country afar off, we look towards thee; from this unquiet ocean we do salute thee with tears; we desire and sue to come unto thee. O Christ, God of God, the hope of mankind, our refuge and virtue, whose light afar off among the dark clouds, over the stormy seas, as the beam of a star of the sea, doth irradiate our eyes, that we may be directed to the safe haven—govern our ship with thy right hand, and with the stern† of thy cross, lest we perish in the floods, lest the tempests of the sea drown us, lest the depth swallow us up. With the hook of thy cross, draw us unto thee from this tempestuous sea. O thou, our only comfort, whom we see afar off, as the Morning Star, and the Sun of justice,‡ with our eyes scant able to weep any longer. Unto thee, standing upon the bank, and looking for us, we thy redeemed, we thy banished men, whom thou hast bought again with thy precious blood, do cry.

"Thou, O Lord of health, art hope of all coasts of the earth, afar off, and in the sea. We do waver in the troublous surges, O most bountiful Lord, behold our jeopardies; save us, sweet Lord, for thy name's sake; grant us that we

* Desiring fervently. † Helm. ‡ Righteousness.

may so keep a mean betwixt Scylla and Charybdis, that we may eschew both the dangers, and happily come to port, our ship and our merchandise safe." (Aug. Solil. cap. xxxv.)

Let us, I say, now and then, all hate of death excluded, muse some such godly meditation, earnestly desiring of God, not temporally to live, but to die; not to continue here in banishment among our enemies, but to be delivered, and dwell in our country with Christ; not to endure here in these dangerous wars, but through death to come unto peace most pleasant.

Yet, peradventure one scruple is left behind that troubleth your conscience, and suffereth not your mind as yet to be quiet. You will say unto me, " Sir, I remember that among many things, I heard you say that the souls of just men are in the hands of God, and the torment of death shall not touch them. I am not just, no, not so much as a dream or a shadow of a just man, but rather a sinner most miserable, who have been accustomed, even from my young age, to heap vice upon vice, and with detestable transgression continually to exasperate my Lord God. Wherefore, the judgment of scripture, and not without a cause, troubleth my conscience, causeth it to fear, condemneth it, and pulleth it in pieces. All offences, says it, shall be gathered together, and all those that work iniquity, they shall be sent into the furnace of fire, where shall be mourning and gnashing of teeth, Matt. xiii. Again, they which have done well shall go into everlasting life, they that have done evil into everlasting fire, Matt. xxv. Neither adulterers, fornicators, robbers, covetous persons, nor worshippers of images, with such other, shall inherit the kingdom of God, 1 Cor. vi. This is the sentence of God's word, this repelleth me from his kingdom and from paradise, whereof you made mention; this maketh me afraid, and with shame utterly putteth me back; this confoundeth me, and chaseth me clean away."

Doubtless, you do very well, in that you confess your own uncleanness. For if that any of us should say that we have not offended, we should deceive ourselves, 1 John i. All men have swerved, and are made unprofitable, neither is there any that doeth good, no, not one, Rom. iii. We have wandered, verily, all of us, as it were sheep, every one after his own way, Isa. liii. being servants unprofitable, and by nature the children of wrath, neither is any good, God only excepted, Matt. xix. Wherefore, in his sight no man shall be able to justify himself, nor yet to abide him, if he observe our iniquities, for in his sight the very stars are not clean; but what then? shall we, being brought to this strait, cowardly despair? God forbid. Well, what shall we do? Whither shall we flee? Where is our refuge? Let us flee unto Christ, as unto a sure sanctuary, safe refuge, and puissant defender. Unto Christ! How dare we be so bold, whose precepts we have never obeyed, whose laws we have seldom, or never kept, whom we have disdained to love again, notwithstanding that he hath ever been our lover most faithful and true? He, being full of mercy, calleth us unto him of his own accord. Come hither to me, saith he, all you that labour and are laden with sin, and I shall refresh you, Matt. xi.

Let us be bold therefore to sue to his mercy; and of his holy oracles, which are written for our consolation and learning, let us require comfort. For they, such is the virtue of them, can easily erect men's minds, and quiet troubled consciences; they, as most wholesome medicines, shall give us present health; they shall pronounce mercy to the penitent sinner, and pardon to the captives; they shall declare us to be no more under the rigour of the law, but under grace and mercy; they shall teach us that God is pacified, and that our sins are forgiven us for his Son's sake. You are freely justified, saith Paul, by grace through the redemption that is in Jesus Christ, whom God hath set forth to be the obtainer of mercy through faith in his blood, to declare his righteousness, for the remission of sins that are gone before, in the sufferance of God, to declare his righteousness in this time, that he may be righteous, and the justifier of him which is of the faith of Jesus Christ, Rom. iii.

By grace, as he saith to the Ephesians, we are saved through faith, and that not of ourselves, it is the gift of God, and that not of our own works, lest any man should glory, Eph. ii. Wherefore, seeing it is so, that we are freely justified by faith in Christ Jesus, we shall have no just cause to despair, but rather to be at peace with God, through Christ, by whom we have entrance into this grace wherein we do stand; yea and to glory in the hope of the sons of God, Rom. v.

Scripture saith not, Happy are those that sin not; but, Happy they whose sins are hidden, and whose iniquities are forgiven. Yea, and to him which worketh not, yet believeth in Him that justifieth the wicked, faith is imputed to him for justice, according to the purpose of the grace of God, Rom. iv.

Doubtless, if our justification should depend on the innocency of our own lives, we should perish, how many soever we are, Rom. viii. But seeing that God who is rich in mercy, for the great love that he hath loved us with, when we were dead by sin, and hath quickened us with Christ, and that not of our deserving, lest any man should glory, Eph. ii. but by the mere grace of God, purchased by the blood of Christ, which is made our redemption, our justice, our prudence, and sanctification, 1 Cor. i. why should we not, being penitent and faithful, laying our sins upon his back, who hath taken away our diseases, and hath carried with him our infirmities, Isa. liii. and further putting him in remembrance of his promise made to sinners, both by his prophets and his apostles—boldly call on his mercy for his Son's sake? Especially considering that he is much more prone of his own nature to forgive, than we are to ask forgiveness, yea, and because that you do partly mistrust him, methinks I should hear him, being somewhat angry, sweetly expostulate with thee, after this sort:

"What now, my dear child? Why ceaseth not thy spirit at the last to be afflicted? Who dost thou think that I am? A cruel tyrant, or else of mercies the Father, and of all consolation? 2 Cor. i. The God, long suffering, and of much mercy? "Art not thou taught by my Son Jesus to call me thy Father? Matt. vi. Have not I promised by my prophet Jeremiah that I would be thy Father, and thou shouldest be my son? Why dost thou not therefore ask me forgiveness, well hoping for pardon? Who is it of you, although you are evil, that will not forgive his son, lamenting his faults, being suppliant, desiring pardon, and promising amendment, notwithstanding that he hath provoked him to anger a hundred times? And thinkest thou that I, which am the Father of mercies, of whom all fatherliness in heaven and in earth is named, which possess the riches of goodness, patience, and longanimity, am not to be ready to forgive my children truly repenting? Rom. ii.

"Be of good comfort, my child, be of good comfort, mistrusting not my mercy, which surpasseth not only man's mercy, how great soever it be, but my own works also. Judgment without mercy shall they feel, whose hearts are obdurate, hardened, and will not repent; which delight still in their sins, and will never leave their wickedness; which contemn my word, and trust me not; from them, indeed, health must needs be far away. But, as for thee, repent, and the kingdom of heaven shall draw nigh, Matt. iii. Trust, and thy faith shall save thee, Matt. ix.

"For as Moses hath exalted the serpent in the desert, so hath my Son been exalted, that every man, believing in him, might be saved, and have life everlasting, John iii.

"I would have all men to be saved and no man to perish, 1 Tim. ii. my fashion is ever to raise him up, lest he perish utterly, which is cast down. It is not my will, believe me, that one of these little ones be cast away, whom I have ever loved so well that I would vouchsafe to give my only Son for them, Matt. xviii. But thy trespasses are great, wherefore thou art not persuaded to trust in my mercy.

"Christ Jesus came into the world to save sinners, 1 Tim. i. He is thine Advocate, and an atonement for thy sins, and not for thine only, but for the sins of the whole world, 1 John ii. He came to call transgressors, not the just, and to save that which was lost, Matt. ix.

"I am, dear son, I am he that putteth away thy sins for myself, and will give my glory to none other. Suppose thy sins be as red as scarlet, they shall be made as white as snow; I have scattered them as clouds, and as mists have dispersed them. Turn to me, for I have redeemed thee. Such is my facility, so gentle I am, such is my benignity, so great is my mercy, which thy most loving brother and Advocate, Christ, that washed thee from thy sins in his blood, hath purchased, continually praying for thee. Why dost thou not open the examples of my word, as a table, or glass, wherein thou mayest well learn how exorable I am, how ready and willing to forgive? Consider with thyself how heinous faults I have pardoned them, Jer. iii. Go to, therefore, be of good cheer, lift up thine eyes, mistrust me no longer, turn to me and thou shalt be saved, Isa. xlv. Commend thy spirit into my hands, and the prince of this world shall have nothing to do with thee, for by me, the Lord of truth, thou art truly redeemed."[*]

Who, hearing these words of his heavenly Father, as they are His words indeed, so sweetly alluring him, so earnestly comforting him, so pleasantly drawing him to

[*] Some other arguments are used which have been already given, p. 33 and 34.

himself, will any more doubt of his mercy? Despair you not utterly, dear friend, nor yet be you sorrowful for anything; but if your false enemy the devil approach, objecting against you the multitude and grievousness of your sins, turn to God, and say unto him, Turn away thy face from my sins, good Lord, and look on the face of thy Christ Jesus.

Thy sins, saith your enemy, in number pass the sands of the sea. Answer, The mercy of God is much more plenteous.—How canst thou hope for the reward of justice, being altogether unjust? Christ Jesus is my justice.—Shalt thou, being covered with sins, enter into rest with Peter and Paul? Nay, but with the thief, who heard on the cross, This day thou shalt be with me in Paradise.—How hast thou this trust, who never didst good? I have a good Lord, an exorable Judge, and a gracious Advocate.—Thou shalt be drawn to hell. My head is in heaven already, and from it the inferior members cannot be severed.—Thou shalt be damned. Thou art a false accuser, no judge; a damned spirit, no condemner.—Many legions of devils do wait for thy soul. I should despair indeed if I had not a Defender, which hath overcome your tyranny.—God is unjust if he give for evil deeds everlasting life. He is just and keepeth his promise, and I have already appealed from his justice to his mercy.—Thou dost flatter thyself with vain hope. The truth cannot lie; to make false promises belongeth unto thee.—What thou leavest here thou seest, but what thou shalt have thou seest not. Things which are seen are temporal, but things which are not seen are eternal.—Thou goest hence laden with evil deeds, and naked of all good works. I shall desire God to exonerate me of mine evils, and to cover me with his goodness.—God heareth no sinners. Yet he heareth them that repent, and for sinners he died.—Thy repentance is too late. It was not too late for the thief.—The thief had a stedfast faith, thine is wavering. I desire God, that he will increase my faith.—Thou dost falsely persuade thyself to find God merciful, which punisheth thee with pains after this sort. Herein he playeth the part of a gentle physician.—Why would he that death should be so bitter? He is the Lord, he willeth nothing but that which is good. And why should I, a servant unprofitable, refuse to suffer that which the Lord of glory hath suffered?—It is a miserable thing to die. Blessed be the dead that die in the Lord.—But the death of sinners is most wretched. He is no longer a sinner which hath acknowledged his fault, with repentance and hope of mercy.—Thou shalt leave this world. I shall go from painful banishment into my country.—Look what a heap of good things thou leavest behind thee. Yet a great deal more evil.—Thou leavest thy riches. They are the world's, I do carry all that is mine away with me.—What canst thou carry with thee? thou hast nothing that is good. That is truly mine, mine own, that Christ hath freely forgiven me.—Thou must forsake thy wife and thy children. They are the Lord's, I do commend them to him.—It is a hard thing to be drawn from thy dearly beloved. They shall shortly follow me.—Thou art plucked from thy pleasant friends. I hasten to friends more pleasant.

Thus thou are taught, not to give place to the devil, endeavouring to overthrow thee, but boldly to repel every dart that he can hurl at thee. Neither let the care for thy friends, wife, and children, trouble thee, mistrusting not but God shall provide as well for them, and peradventure better, in thine absence, than he did in thy life-time. For thou must consider that thine own power hath not all this while sustained thee or them, and procured things necessary, but God, in whom we live, move, and are, hath done it. God, which feedeth, nourisheth, and saveth both man and beast, which royally clotheth the grass in the field, covereth the heavens with clouds, careth for the birds of the air, and prepareth meat for the very chickens of the ravens, shall much more regard thy friends, being his people, confessing his name.

Call to remembrance how mercifully he provided for the poor widow and her children, spoken of in 2 Kings iv. By the benignity of God, this poor woman with her children was much better provided for after the death of her husband, though he were a holy man, than she was before. God is even the same God now that he was then, and can do as much for christian men now, in these days, as he could then for the Jews. And he, doubtless, if thou fear him, will regard thy wife, children, and friends, no less than he did the wife and children of this prophet.

Further, call to remembrance how that they, many times, who are left of their friends rich, and in great honours, are after brought to poverty, yea, and to the beggar's staff. On the other side, that they which are left poor and beggarly of their friends, at the length come to great riches, authority, and honour. Wherefore I do think, as I oft have said, not I, but the prophet, that both riches and poverty come of God. And that men shall have what it shall please God to give them. Yet I will not blame an honest provision for men's children. Therefore commit them to God, for they are his, let them cast their care on the Lord, and he by his promise shall nourish them.

And to you that are his friends here, to you I speak. What meaneth this your heaviness? Why do you sorrow after this sort; to what purpose do you trouble yourselves with weepings? why do ye, as it were in a manner draw into dispute the will of God with your unjust complaints? Do ye think him to be a meet matter of lamenting, sorrowing, and wailing, because he is delivered from dangers to safety, from bondage to liberty, from diseases to immortality, from earthly things to heavenly, from men to the company of God's angels? Wherein hath he offended you, that you so envy the good which hath befallen him? If ye do not envy, what needs all these tears? I am sure if ye knew to what felicity he is going, you would banquet, and be joyful, at the least if ye love his welfare.

Christ said to his disciples, when they were sad that he would depart, If ye loved me you would be glad, forasmuch as I go to my Father. Wherein he declared, that we ought not to be sad, but joyful, at the departure of our friends from hence. What, I pray you, shall you lose by the death of your friend, but that he shall be out of your sight, and that but a time? nevertheless you may at all times, in the mean space, in your minds and memories, see him, talk with him, and embrace him. Mourn no more for him, for he offers you no cause of mourning, but if ye will needs mourn, mourn for yourselves, in that ye are are not so nigh the port of our sweet country, flowing with milk and honey, as he is. This mourning is more fit for the Scythians, and such other barbarous people who know not the condition of faithful souls, than for you which know, or might all this while have learned.

Let them, I pray you, weep and howl like brutes, let them cut their ears and noses as they were wont to do, at the death of their friends. Let us be joyful. Let Admetus, Orpheus, and such other infidels, mourn at the death of their friends, and require them again of Proserpine. Let not us require our friends of God again, though we might have them, since it must be with the loss of their wealth and prosperous being.

Were you not to be counted unreasonable, and to your friend no friend, if you should require him to dine or dwell with you, having nothing in your house but horsebread,* and stinking water, where he may go to a friend more faithful than you are, and have at all times all kinds of dainties? And will you be counted reasonable, who would by your wills hinder this your friend, going to the house of his most faithful friend Christ, where he shall have heavenly dainties, and meat of the holy angels, in comparison of which, your cheer is worse than horsebread and stinking water indeed. Mourn no more for him, I say, but be glad that your friend shall attain to such felicity.

What other thing is it for us christians to mourn at the death of our friends, than to give an occasion to the infidels to reprehend and accuse us, forasmuch as we do deny the thing in deed, that we do profess with our mouths? For in words we say that the soul of man is immortal, and that there is another life better than this. In our mourning we seem to show ourselves to be of another opinion.

What profit is it, I pray you, to pronounce virtue in words, and in deeds to destroy the truth? St. Paul doth reprove and blame them which are heavy in the departure of their friends, saying, I would not have you ignorant, O brethren, as touching them that sleep, that ye be not sad, as others that have no hope. It belongeth to them to weep, and to be sorry at the death of their friends, which have no hope of another life to come, and not to us which believe that our souls are immortal, and that our bodies shall arise again. Mourn no more for him therefore, but prepare and make ready yourselves to follow him, living virtuously, for that ye know not the day or hour.

Now to you again, my friend. See that you are joyful in God, and let not this short affliction of your body disquiet your mind. But sauce it rather, and make it pleasant with the hope of everlasting blessedness, remembering that as you shall be quickly delivered from this sickness, so you shall no more hereafter be subject to any sorrows, pains, or pensiveness. It should never grieve a man to fare evil at dinner, knowing that he shall have a supper most dainty

* Bread made of beans and other coarse sorts of grain, for the food of horses.

and delicate. When your pangs shall be most urgent, set this saying of St. Paul before your eyes, Things which are seen, and that we suffer here, are temporal, and last for a while, but things which are not seen, and that we shall have, are eternal. In hope therefore of these eternal things, willingly compose your body to sleep, for so this corporeal death is named in scripture. The patriarchs were ever said to have slept with their fathers, when they died, and not without a cause, for that our bodies shall arise again in the last day, as though it were from a sleep indeed. At the blowing of a trumpet, saith Paul, the dead shall rise uncorrupt; and from heaven, saith the same Paul, we look for our Lord Jesus Christ, which shall transform our vile bodies, and conform them to his glorious body. If we believe that Jesus died and rose again, even so those also which are asleep through Jesus, shall God bring with him, 1 Thess. iv. Oh! bringing most blessed, goodly, and pleasant, when the bodies that now are sown in corruption, shall arise in uncorruption. That now are in dishonour, shall rise in glory. That now are sown in weakness, shall rise in power. That now are sown natural bodies, shall rise spiritual. When these corruptible shall put on incorruption, and these mortal shall put on immortality; death is clearly swallowed up in victory, 1 Cor. xv.

Oh how joyous shall that day be to the faithful! when men's bodies, made like to the body of Christ, shall inhabit the kingdom which God hath prepared for those that fear him, before the beginning of the world, where they shall have joy and everlasting gladness, whereas they, being like to the angels of God, shall shine as the sun in the kingdom of their Father.

At the last, sweet friend, forasmuch as I have declared unto you that all men must die, and that when it shall please God.—Further, that in dying we do no other, but as all the saints, yea, and Christ himself, hath done, with whom we shall rise again. And that death is but a due repaying of things, that were for a time liberally lent us; to the earth our bodies, and our souls to God our most bountiful Father. That nothing here is of such excellency, that it should allure a wise man, and him that hopeth for another life to come, to tarry long with it; that good men have ever desired to die, and to be with God, forasmuch as death is the end of all miseries, the finisher of all sorrows, and an entrance into perpetual bliss.

Further, in that I have declared unto you whither you shall go, and what you shall have after this life, and that God most mercifully hath forgiven you your sins, for that you are repentant and faithful, and that he will provide for yours, if they fear him, as well or better than he did in your days.

Finally, that this body of yours shall rise again from the earth gloriously in the last day, through his power that gave its first fashion—for that these things are so, I say, quiet your mind, and prepare yourself, as doth the swan with song of heart and pleasure, to die, and to the accomplishment of God's will, all fear of death being excluded.

Think only of immortality, being willing and glad to depart hence to God that calleth you. Which, as the servants of God should always be ready to do, so at this time most ready, forasmuch as this miserable world, beset with the horrible tempests, storms, and troublesome whirlwinds of all kinds of evil, beginneth to decay.

Moreover, as grievous things have already befallen to nations, so more grievous things are to be looked for, in that sin daily increaseth among men more and more, provoking the justice of God. Therefore, I cannot but think it a great gain quickly to depart hence. If the posts of the house were perished, and the trembling roof should threaten ruin to be at hand, would you not, being in health, depart with all speed? If a troublesome and stormy tempest suddenly risen on the sea, should threaten plain shipwreck, and the drowning of you and your company, would you not make haste to the port?

Lo, the world decayeth, and the end of things threateneth plain falling down; and shall not you give thanks to God, and for your own part be glad that you shall be delivered in time, from such ruins, plagues, and tempests as hang over the heads of men?

Think, sweet friend, I beseech you, and think again, that so long as we are here, we are very strangers; and that we ought chiefly to embrace that hour, which shall appoint every one of us to his own house, and restore us, delivered from all snares of the world, to paradise, and the heavenly kingdom.

Who, being in a strange country, will not covet to return to his own country? Who, sailing towards his friends, will not covet a quick and prosperous wind, that he may the rather embrace his well beloved? We count paradise our country, the patriarchs to be our parents and friends. Why then do we not fervently desire speedily to see the patriarchs at paradise, where a great company of our friends look for us, and a wonderful number of our parents, brethren, and sisters tarry for us; we being sure of their immortality, and wishing that we had the same? At the sight and meeting of these, oh how great gladness shall happen both to us and them! How great pleasure of the heavenly kingdom, without fear of death, and with the eternity of life! How high and perpetual felicity! There is the glorious company of the apostles; there is the laudable number of the glad prophets; there is the innumerable host of martyrs crowned, and triumphing with the victory of their strifes and passions. There are those which have broken the concupiscency of their flesh, with the strength of continence. There are the merciful enjoying their rewards, who by feeding the poor, and helping the needy, have wrought the works of justice; and keeping the commandments of God, have transferred their earthly patrimonies into heavenly treasures: this is the joyous company; to this no earthly company is to be compared. To Him which hath bought you a place in this company with the price of his blood, I do betake you. Commit yourself to his hands, for he shall never fail you. Farewell.

**PRECIOUS IN THE SIGHT OF THE LORD, IS THE DEATH OF HIS SAINTS.**

*The conclusion of this book, teaching all men gladly to die.*

I suppose that by this doctrine, every christian man shall be contented, and will be instructed in the time of death to put away from them these aforesaid impediments, so that I trust in God they shall not hinder him, nor draw him back from a joyful and glad will to receive this corporeal death, but shall wait for it patiently, and with a good will, whensoever our dear Father calleth him thereto. For by it, as it were thorough and entire, he leadeth us unto another life a thousand fold better, and so delivereth us from all misery and displeasure, from all dangers, and out of the hands of all our enemies, being certified by our faith, that all things which could hurt or hinder us, whether it were sin, death, devil, or hell, are altogether vanquished and overcome, being turned to our profit.

The account is passed, the Judge is appeased, all debts are pardoned, forgotten quite, satisfied and paid, and there is nothing found damnable in us, because we are in Jesus Christ, and in his faith, as it is said sufficiently before.

But it is always to be noted, and this should we keep well in memory, that we have all these things only by Jesus Christ, who is our head, and we his members, I mean, those that are christians, not all they that bear the name, for, by a loving faith, we trusted, and do rest in and upon him, and his blessed word, knowing that he is Lord of lords, almighty Emperor above all that are in heaven, hell, or earth who hath given us all these things of his mere liberality, without any deserving of us, but through his love and kindness; and hath obtained it for us of his celestial Father, by his precious blood. Because we believe this is true, and know that it is so, all fear and dread goeth from us, and by this means God worketh again in us a ferventness, and such a love toward him, that we turn all things to his praise and honour who hath showed us such kindness and love, being of nature his very enemies.

Therefore, let us continually apply ourselves again to please Him, and to leave all that we know doth displease him. But because that by reason of the sinful and filthy flesh, we are daily troubled and inclined to evil, which doth withdraw and hinder us so to do, therefore, let us call for his help, and desire with the apostle Paul, as is said before, that this mortal body may die and be destroyed, to the intent that we may serve God, and be obedient evermore unto him without any hinderance. And as long as we have here to travail, bearing this sinful flesh about with us, let us resist daily, and fight against the evil inclinations thereof, to the intent that we may hold it under the bridle, and so continue as valiant captains—in and by our Head, Jesus Christ. The which God our celestial Father grant eternally.

# SOME ACCOUNT
## OF
# QUEEN CATHERINE PARR,

The last Consort of Henry VIII.

CATHERINE PARR, the sixth and surviving queen of king Henry VIII., was born in Westmoreland. She was the daughter of sir Thomas Parr, of Kendal,* and married first to Edward Burgh, secondly to John Neville, lord Latimer. After his decease, she became the wife of Henry, in July 1543.

She was early instructed in literature; a plan frequently adopted with females of rank in the sixteenth century; in England, it was promoted by the example of the monarch in the education of his daughters. Udal writes thus in a dedicatory epistle to queen Catherine herself. " Now, in this gracious and blissful time of knowledge, in which it hath pleased God almighty to reveal and show abroad the light of his most holy gospel, what a number is there of noble women, especially here in this realm of England; yea, and how many in the years of tender virginity, not only as well seen, and as familiarly traded in the Latin and Greek tongues, as in their own mother language; but also in all kinds of literature and arts, made exact, studied, and exercised, and in the holy scripture and theology so ripe, that they are able aptly, wisely, and with much grace, either to indite or to translate into the vulgar tongue, for the public instruction and edifying of the unlearned multitude! Neither is it now a strange thing to hear gentlewomen, instead of most vain communication about the moon shining in the water, to use grave and substantial talk in Latin and Greek, with their husbands, of godly matters. It is now no news in England, for young damsels in noble houses, and in the courts of princes, instead of cards and other instruments of idle trifling, to have continually in their hands, either psalms, homilies, and other devout meditations, or else Paul's epistles, or some book of holy scripture matters; and as familiarly to read or reason thereof, in Greek, Latin, French, or Italian, as in English. It is now a common thing to see young virgins so nursed and trained in the study of letters, that they willingly set all other vain pastimes at nought, for learning's sake. It is now no news

* He left his two daughters £800 each, but in case their brother died, and they became co-heiresses of his estates, then the whole of the £1600 was to be paid to the abbey of Clairvaux, to purchase copes and vestments for performing the Romish ceremonials. Such an arrangement gives some idea of the pomp of those services, when it is remembered that the sum is equal to more than ten times t' amount at the present day.

at all to see queens and ladies of most high state and progeny, instead of courtly dalliance, to embrace virtuous exercises of reading and writing, and with most earnest study, both early and late, to apply themselves to the acquiring of knowledge, as well in all other liberal arts and disciplines, as also most especially of God and his most holy word."

Of the number thus described, was Catherine Parr, also lady Bacon and her sisters, the daughters of sir Anthony Cook, the princesses Mary and Elizabeth, lady Jane Grey, and many others. Nor were these acquirements to be found only amongst persons of quality. One instance at least is recorded of their being found in a tradesman's wife. From the monument of Elizabeth Lucar, daughter of one Paul Withipol, and wife of Emanuel Lucar, a merchant tailor of London, given by Stow in his Survey, it appears that she wrote three hands very fairly, that she understood Latin, Spanish, and Italian, writing and speaking them with perfect utterance and readiness; that she sung and played well upon the viol, lute, and virginals; besides this she was not deficient in accomplishments peculiar to her sex, being excellently skilled in all kinds of needlework. Her moral qualities were also most praiseworthy, and above all, to use the simple expressions of her epitaph, "Reading the scriptures to judge light from dark, Directing her faith to Christ the only mark." She died in 1537, aged only twenty-seven. From various records of that day, it appears that the females who thus acquired learning were not on that account negligent as to the domestic duties incumbent upon them as daughters, wives, and heads of families.

An anecdote of Catherine Parr related by Strype, would, however, indicate that in early life she did not very willingly enter into the domestic employments then usually attended to, even by females of rank. Some astrologer having cast her nativity, told her she was born to sit in the highest seat of imperial majesty, having all the eminent stars and planets in her house, which she took such notice of, that when her mother used sometimes to call her to work, she would say, " My hands are ordained to touch crowns and sceptres, not needles and spindles!" Upon the mischievous absurdity of such a prognostication it is unnecessary to remark. Many other females must have been born under the same siderial aspect who *never* rose to a throne.

We must not forget that, as is noticed by Udal, the learning of that period ever had especial reference to scriptural knowledge, and the study of the doctrines of truth. Historians of infidel or latitudinarian principles have treated the literary acquirements of the higher ranks at that day as contemptible, or at best pedantic; but the christian estimates them more correctly. The writings of queen Catherine Parr alone, are sufficient to manifest the real value of those acquirements, and the subsequent part of this sketch will show the important services she was thereby enabled to render to the reformation. From her early youth she studied the scriptures, although a considerable time elapsed, as appears from her own writings, before she was freed from the mental bondage of popery.

When elevated to the throne, queen Catherine Parr was placed in a dangerous and arduous station. She did not hesitate openly to manifest her attachment to the doctrines of the gospel, and rendered all the services in her power to the reformers. Udal states that the translation of the paraphrases of Erasmus on the New Testament, a copy of which was ordered to be placed in every parish church in the kingdom, was executed by her means. Udal was then master of Eton school, the queen engaged him in this work, well knowing his ability to superintend and take part in the same. In 1545, previously to the work being printed, he wrote an epistle dedicatory to the queen, in which he mentions, that "at her exceeding great costs and charges, she had hired workmen to labour in the vineyard of Christ's gospel, and procured the whole paraphrase of Erasmus upon all the New Testament to be diligently translated into English, by several men whom she employed upon this work." He further said, that he trusted the king would not allow it to remain buried in silence, but would cause it to be set abroad in print, to the use that she had designed; "that is, to the commodity and benefit of good English people, now a long time sore thirsting and hungering after the sincere and plain knowledge of God's word."

The translators of this paraphrase were for the most part persons of rank and ability; some portion, Strype concludes, was the work of queen Catherine herself, the paraphrase on the gospel by St. John was begun by the princess Mary, but was finished by her chaplain, Dr. Malet, "she being cast into sickness partly by overmuch study in this work;" upon which it has been observed, that probably the translation of some Romish legendaries or rituals might have been more agreeable to her. It is likely, however, that she undertook this paraphrase desiring to please her father, who at that time was disposed to favour such works. A letter written by the queen to the princess respecting this translation, shows the interest she took therein.

The queen evinced considerable judgment in selecting this work of Erasmus to be put forth by authority. It was written by him in his best days, and very fully comprised the opinions of the best early divines on doctrinal subjects; it also exposed the errors and superstitious abuses of popery, and being the work of Erasmus, carried with it an authority to all, except the most bigoted of the papists, which any production exclusively written by the English Reformers would not have possessed, even had there been time, which there was not, to prepare such a work; while its passing through the hands of men well affected to gospel truth, was an assurance to the protestants that its contents were not at variance with the scriptures—the paraphrase on the Revelation was not the work of Erasmus, but of Leo Jude. Queen Catherine also doubtless had reason to judge that this work was most likely to be acceptable to the king.

The papists were not indifferent to the exertions of queen Catherine Parr in promoting the reformation. She had many around her at court of the same principles as herself, and early in the year 1546, when for a time bishop Gardiner, the duke of Norfolk, the lord chancellor Wriothesley, and other romanists had gained a portion of influence at court, that party made a vigorous effort for her destruction. To this persecution, Ann Askew fell a victim; the narrow escape of the queen is best given in the words of Fox, which includes many interesting historical particulars. He says,

"About the year 1546, after the king returned from Boulogne, he was informed that queen Catherine Parr, at that time his wife, was very much given to the reading and study of the holy scriptures; and that she for that purpose had retained divers well learned and godly persons, to instruct her thoroughly in the same, with whom she used to have private conference touching spiritual matters. Commonly, but especially in Lent, every day in the afternoon, for the space of an hour, one of her chaplains made some collation to her and to her ladies, and gentlewomen of her chamber, or others that were disposed to hear; in which sermons they oftimes touched such abuses as in the church then were rife. Which things as they were not secretly done, so neither were their preachings unknown unto the king. Whereof at the first, and for a great time, he seemed very well to like. Which made her the more bold, being indeed become very zealous toward the gospel, and the professors thereof, frankly to debate with the king, touching religion, and therein flatly to discover herself; oftentimes wishing, exhorting, and persuading the king, that as he had, to the glory of God and his eternal fame, begun a good and a godly work in banishing that monstrous idol of Rome, so he would thoroughly perfect and finish the same, cleansing his church of England clean from the dregs thereof, wherein as yet remained great superstition.

"And albeit the king grew towards his latter end very stern and opinionate, so that of few he could be content to be taught, but worst of all to be contended withal by argument; notwithstanding, toward her he refrained his accustomed manner, as appeared by great respects, either for the reverence of the cause, whereunto of himself he seemed well inclined, if some others could have ceased from seeking to pervert him, or else for the singular affection which until a very small time before his death, he always bore unto her. For never handmaid sought with more careful diligence to please her mistress, than she did with all painful endeavour apply herself, by all virtuous means, in all things to please his humour.

"Moreover, besides the virtues of the mind, she was endued with very rare gifts of nature, as singular beauty, favour, and comely personage, being things wherein the king was greatly delighted; and so enjoyed for the king's favour, to the great likelihood of the setting at large of the gospel within this realm at that time, had not the malicious practice of certain enemies professed against the truth, which at that time also were very great, prevented the same, to the utter alienating of the king's mind from religion, and almost to the extreme ruin of the queen and certain others with her, if God had not marvellously succoured her in that distress.

"The king's majesty, as you have heard, misliked to be contended withal in any kind of argument. This humour of his, although not in smaller matters, yet in causes of religion as occasion served, the queen would not stick now and then to oppose in reverent terms and humble talk, entering with him into discourse, with sound reasons of scripture. The which the king was so well accustomed unto in those matters, that at her hands he took all in good part, or at the least never showed countenance of offence thereat; which did not a little appal her adversaries to hear and see. During which time, perceiving her so thoroughly grounded in the king's favour, they durst not for their lives once open their lips unto the king in any respect to touch her, either in her presence, or behind her back: and so long she continued this her accustomed usage, not only of hearing private sermons, as is said, but also of her free conference with the king in matters of religion, without all peril, until at the last, by reason of his sore leg, the anguish whereof began more and more to increase, he waxed sickly, and therewithal froward, and difficult to be pleased.

"In the time of this his sickness, he had left his accustomed manner of coming and visiting of the queen: and therefore she, according as she understood him by such assured intelligence as she had about him, to be disposed to have her company, sometimes being sent for, other sometimes of herself would come to visit him, either at after dinner or after supper, as was most fit for her purpose. At which times she would not fail to use all occasions to move him, according to her manner, zealously to proceed in the reformation of the church. The sharpness of the disease had sharpened the king's accustomed patience, so that he began to show some tokens of misliking; and contrary unto his manner, upon a day, breaking off that matter, he took occasion to enter into other talk, which somewhat amazed the queen. To whom, notwithstanding, in her presence, he gave neither evil word nor countenance, but knit up all arguments with gentle words and loving countenance; and after other pleasant talk, she for that time took her leave of his majesty. Who after his manner, bidding her 'Farewell, sweet heart,' for that was his usual term to the queen, licensed her to depart.

"At this visitation, the bishop of Winchester, Gardiner, was present, as also at the queen's taking her leave, and he had very well printed in his memory the king's sudden interrupting of the queen in her tale, and falling into other matter, and thought that if the iron were beaten whilst it was hot, and that the king's humour were holpen, such misliking might follow towards the queen, as might both overthrow her and all her endeavours; and he only awaited some occasion to renew into the king's memory the former misliked argument. His expectation in that behalf did not fail; for the king at that time showed himself no less prompt and ready to receive any information, than the bishop was maliciously bent to stir up the king's indignation against her. The king, immediately upon her departure from him, used these or like words; 'A good hearing it is when women become such clerks; and a thing much to my comfort, to come in mine old days to be taught by my wife!'

"The bishop hearing this, seemed to mislike that the queen should so much forget herself, as to take upon her to stand in any argument with his majesty, whom he to his face extolled for his rare virtues, and specially for his learned judgment in matters of religion, above not only princes of that and other ages, but also above doctors professed in divinity; and said that it was an unseemly thing for any of his majesty's subjects to reason and argue with him so malapertly, and grievous to him for his part and other of his majesty's counsellors and servants, to hear the same; and that they all, by proof, knew his wisdom to be such, that it was not needful for any to put him in mind of any such matters. He inferred, moreover, how dangerous and perilous a matter it is, and ever hath been, for a prince to suffer such insolent words at his subjects' hands; who as they take boldness to contrary their sovereign in words, so want they no will, but only power and strength, to overthrow them in deeds.

"Besides this, he said, that the religion by the queen so stiffly maintained, did not only disallow and dissolve the policy and politic government of princes, but also taught the people that all things ought to be in common, so that what colour soever they pretended, their opinions were indeed so odious, and for the prince's estate so perilous, that, saving the reverence they bare unto her for his majesty's sake, they durst be bold to affirm that the greatest subject in this land, speaking those words that she did speak, and defending those arguments that she did defend, had with impartial justice, by law, deserved death.

"Howbeit, for his part he would not, and durst not, without good warrant from his majesty, speak his knowledge in the queen's case, although very apparent reasons made for him, and such as his dutiful affection towards his majesty, and the zeal and preservation of his estate, would scarcely give him leave to conceal, though the uttering thereof might, through her and her faction, be the utter destruction of him, and of such as indeed did chiefly tender the prince's safety, without his majesty would take upon him to be their protector, and as it were their buckler. Which, if he would do, as in respect of his own safety he ought not to refuse, he, with others of his faithful counsellors, could within a short time disclose such treason, cloaked with this cloak of heresy, that his majesty should easily perceive, how perilous a matter it is to cherish a serpent within his own bosom. Howbeit, he would not for his part willingly deal in the matter, both for reverent respect aforesaid, and also for fear lest the faction was grown already too great there, with the prince's safety to discover the same. And therewithal, with heavy countenance and whispering together with them of that sect there present, he held his peace.

"These and such other kinds of Winchester's flattering phrases, marvellously whetted the king both to anger and displeasure towards the queen, and also to be jealous and mistrustful of his own estate, for the assurance whereof princes use not to be scrupulous to do any thing. Thus then Winchester, with his flattering words seeking to frame the king's disposition after his own pleasure, so far crept into the king at that time, and with doubtful fears he with other his fellows so filled the king's mistrustful mind, that before they departed the place, the king, to see belike what they would do, had given commandment, with warrant, to certain of them for that purpose, to consult together about the drawing of certain articles against the queen, wherein her life might be touched; which the king by their persuasions pretended to be fully resolved not to spare, provided there should be any rigour or colour of law to countenance the matter. With this commission they departed for that time from the king, resolved to put their pernicious practice to as mischievous an execution.

"During the time of deliberation about this matter, they failed not to use all kind of policies, and mischievous practices, as well to suborn accusers, as otherwise to betray her, in seeking to understand what books, by law forbidden, she had in her closet. And the better to bring their purpose to pass, because they would not upon the sudden, but by means deal with her, they thought it best, at the first, to begin with some of those ladies whom they knew to be great with her, and of her blood. The chiefest whereof, as most of estimation, and privy to all her doings, were these: the lady Herbert, afterward countess of Pembroke, and sister to the queen, and chief of her privy chamber; the lady Lane, being of her privy chamber, and also her cousin german; the lady Tyrwhit of her privy chamber, and, for her virtuous disposition, in very great favour and credit with her.

"It was devised that these three above named, should first of all have been accused and brought to answer unto the six articles, and upon their apprehension in the court, their closet and coffers should have been searched, that somewhat might have been found, whereby the queen might be charged; which being found, the queen herself presently should have been taken, and likewise carried by barge by night unto the Tower. This platform thus devised, the king was forthwith made privy unto the device by Winchester and Wriothesley, and his consent thereunto demanded. Who, belike to prove the bishop's malice, how far it would presume, like a wise politic prince, was contented to give his consent, and to allow of every circumstance, knowing notwithstanding in the end what he would do. And thus the day, the time, and the place of these apprehensions aforesaid were appointed; which device yet after was changed.

"The king at that time lay at Whitehall, and used very seldom, being not well at ease, to stir out of his chamber or privy gallery; and few of his council, but by especial commandment, resorted unto him, these only excepted; who by reason of this practice, used oftener than of ordinary to repair unto him. This purpose was handled so secretly, that it grew now within few days of the time appointed for the execution of the matter, and the poor queen knew not nor suspected any thing at all; and therefore used after her accustomed manner, when she came to visit the king, still to deal with him touching religion, as she did before.

"The king all this while gave her leave to utter her mind at the full without contradiction; not upon any evil mind or misliking, to have her speedy despatch, but rather to try out the uttermost of Winchester's fetches. Thus, after her accustomed conference with the king, when she had taken her leave of him, the time and day of Winchester's final day approaching fast upon, it chanced that the king of himself, upon a certain night after her being with him, and her leave taken of him, in misliking her religion, did break the whole practice unto one of his physicians, either doctor Wendy, or else Owen, but rather Wendy as is supposed; pretending unto him, as though he intended not any longer to be troubled with such a doctress as she was, and also declaring what trouble was in working against her by certain of her enemies, but yet charging him withal, upon peril of his life, not to utter it to any creature living; and thereupon declared unto him the parties above named with all circumstances, and when and what the final resolution of the matter should be.

"The queen all this while compassed about with enemies and persecutors, perceived nothing of all this, nor what was working against her, and what traps were laid for her by Winchester and his fellows; so closely was the matter conceived. But see what the Lord God, who from his eternal throne of wisdom seeth and despatcheth all the inventions of Ahitophel, and comprehendeth how the wily beguile themselves, did for his poor handmaid, in rescuing her from the pit of ruin, whereinto she was ready to fall unawares.

"For as the Lord would, so came it to pass, that the bill of articles drawn against the queen, and subscribed with the king's own hand, falling from the bosom of one of the aforesaid counsellors, was found and taken up of some godly person, and brought immediately unto the queen. Who reading there the articles comprised against her, and perceiving the king's own hand unto the same, for the sudden fear thereof, fell instantly into a great melancholy and agony, bewailing and taking on in such sort, as was lamentable to see, as certain of her ladies and gentlewomen yet alive, who were then present about her, can testify.

"The king hearing what perplexity she was in, almost to the peril and danger of her life, sent his physicians unto her. Who seeing what extremity she was in, did what they could for her recovery. Then Wendy, who knew the cause better than the other, and perceiving by her words what the matter was, according to that the king before had told him; for the comforting of her heavy mind, began to break with her in secret manner touching the said articles devised against her, which he himself, he said, knew right well to be true; although he stood in danger of his life, if ever he were known to utter the same to any living creature. Nevertheless, partly for the safety of her life, and partly for the discharge of his own conscience, having remorse to consent to the shedding of innocent blood, he could not but give her warning of that mischief that hanged over her head, beseeching her most instantly to use all secrecy in that behalf, and exhorted her somewhat to frame and conform herself unto the king's mind, saying he did not doubt, but if she would so do, and show her humble submission unto him, she should find him gracious and favourable unto her.

"It was not long after this, but the king hearing of the dangerous state wherein she yet still remained, came unto her himself. Unto whom after that she had uttered her grief, fearing lest his majesty, she said, had taken displeasure with her, and had utterly forsaken her; he like a loving husband, with sweet and comfortable words, so refreshed and appeased her careful mind, that she upon the same began somewhat to recover, and so the king after he had tarried there about the space of an hour, departed.

"After this, the queen remembering with herself the words that master Wendy had said unto her, devised how by some good opportunity she might repair to the king's presence. And so first commanding her ladies to convey away their books, which were against the law, the next night following, after supper, she, waited upon only by the lady Herbert, her sister, and the lady Lane, who carried the candle before her, went unto the king's bedchamber, whom she found sitting and talking with certain gentlemen of his chamber. Whom when the king did behold, very courteously he welcomed her, and breaking off the talk, which before her coming he had with the gentlemen aforesaid, began of himself, contrary to his manner before accustomed, to enter into talk of religion, seeming, as it were, desirous to be resolved by the queen of certain doubts which he propounded.

"The queen perceiving to what purpose this talk did tend, not being unprovided in what sort to behave herself towards the king, with such answers resolved his questions as the time and opportunity present did require, mildly and with a reverent countenance answering again after this manner.

"'Your majesty, doth right well know, neither I myself am ignorant, what great imperfection and weakness by our first creation, is allotted unto us women, to be ordained and appointed as inferior and subject unto man as our head, from which head all our direction ought to proceed, and that as God made man to his own shape and likeness, whereby he being endued with more special gifts of perfection, might rather be stirred to the contemplation of heavenly things, and to the earnest endeavour to obey his commandments; even so also made he woman of man, of whom and by whom she is to be governed, commanded, and directed. Whose womanly weakness and natural imperfection, ought to be tolerated, aided, and borne withal, so that by his wisdom such things as are lacking in her, ought to be supplied.

" ' Since therefore God hath appointed such a natural difference between man and woman, and your majesty being so excellent in gifts and ornaments of wisdom, and I, a seely, poor woman, so much inferior in all respects of nature unto you; how then comes it now to pass, that your majesty in such diffuse causes of religion, will seem to require my judgment? Which when I have uttered and said what I can, yet must I, and will I, refer my judgment in this and all other cases to your majesty's wisdom, as my only anchor, supreme head and governor here in earth next under God, to lean unto.'

" ' Not so, by St. Mary,' quoth the king; ' you are become a doctor, Kate, to instruct us, as we take it, and not to be instructed, or directed by us.'

" ' If your majesty take it so,' quoth the queen, ' then hath your majesty very much mistaken me, who hath ever been of the opinion to think it very unseemly and preposterous for the woman to take upon her the office of an instructor or teacher to her lord and husband, but rather to learn of her husband, and to be taught by him. And where I have with your majesty's leave heretofore been bold to hold talk with your majesty, wherein sometimes in opinions there hath seemed some difference, I have not done it so much to maintain opinion, as I did it rather to minister talk, not only to the end your majesty might with less grief pass over this painful time of your infirmity, being intentive to our talk, and hoping that your majesty should reap some ease thereby; but also that I, hearing your majesty's learned discourse, might receive to myself some profit thereof. Wherein I assure your majesty I have not missed any part of my desire in that behalf, always referring myself in all such matters unto your majesty, as by ordinance of nature it is convenient for me to do.'

" ' And is it even so, sweet heart?' quoth the king. ' And tended your arguments to no worse end? Then perfect friends we are now again, as ever at any time heretofore;' and kissing her, he added this saying, that it did him more good at that time to hear those words of her own mouth, than if he had heard present news of a hundred thousand pounds in money fallen unto him. And with great signs and tokens of marvellous joy and liking, with promises and assurances, never again in any sort more to mistake her, entering into other very pleasant discourses with the queen and the lords, and gentlemen standing by, in the end, being very far in the night, he gave her leave to depart. Whom in her absence, to the standers by, he gave as singular and as effectuous commendations, as before time to the bishop and the chancellor, who then were neither of them present, he seemed to mislike of her.

"Now then, the king's mind was clean altered, and he detested in his heart, as afterwards he plainly showed, this tragical practice of those cruel Caiphases; who nothing understanding of the king's well reformed mind, and good disposition toward the queen, were busily occupied about thinking and providing for their next day's labour, which was the day determined to have carried the queen to the Tower.

"The day, and almost the hour appointed being come, the king being disposed in the afternoon to take the air, waited upon with two gentlemen only of his bedchamber, went into the garden, whither the queen also came, being sent for by the king himself, the three ladies above named alone waiting upon her. With whom the king at that time disposed himself to be as pleasant as ever he was in all his life before. When suddenly, in the midst of their mirth, the hour determined being come, in comes the lord chancellor into the garden with forty of the king's guard at his heels, with purpose indeed to have taken the queen, together with the three ladies aforesaid, whom they had before purposed to apprehend alone, even then unto the Tower.* Whom then the king sternly beholding, breaking off his mirth with the queen, stepping a little aside, he called the chancellor unto him. Who upon his knees spake certain words unto the king, but what they were, for that they were softly spoken, and the king a good distance from the queen, it is not well known, but it is most certain that the king's replying unto him was, knave, for his answer; yea, arrant knave, beast, and fool; and with that the king commanded him presently to avaunt out of his presence. Which words, although they were uttered somewhat low, yet were they so vehemently whispered out by the king, that the queen with her ladies did easily overhear them; which had been not a little to her comfort, if she had known at that time the whole cause of his coming so perfectly as after she knew it. Thus departed the lord chancellor out of the king's presence as he came, with all his train, the whole mould of all his device being utterly broken.

"The king, after his departure, immediately returned to the queen. Whom she perceiving to be very much chafed, albeit coming towards her he enforced himself to put on a merry countenance, with as sweet words as she could utter, endeavoured to qualify the king's displeasure, with request unto his majesty in the behalf of the lord chancellor, whom he seemed to be offended withal; saying, for his excuse, that albeit she knew not what just

* Fuller says, "Whither had she been sent, *vestigia nulla retrorsum*, (alluding to Esop's fable of no footsteps being found pointing backwards from the lion's den,) without doubt she had followed the way of his former wives in that place."

cause his majesty had at that time to be offended with him, yet she thought that ignorance, not will, was the cause of his error, and so besought his majesty, if the cause were not very heinous, at her humble suit to take it.

"'Ah! poor soul,' quoth he, 'thou little knowest how evil he deserveth this grace at thy hands. Of my word, sweet heart, he hath been towards thee an arrant knave, and so let him go.' To this the queen in charitable manner replying in few words, ended that talk; having also by God's only blessing, happily for that time and ever, escaped the dangerous snares of her bloody and cruel enemies for the gospel's sake."

This attempt of Gardiner's, with some other practices of his about this period, in favour of popery, caused the king to order his name to be erased from the list of his executors, and to take some other steps which facilitated the progress of the reformation at the commencement of the reign of Edward VI.

Among other services Catherine Parr at this time rendered to the cause of learning and truth, was the preventing the confiscation of the colleges at Cambridge by her intercession, which were placed at the king's disposal by a recent act, while many about the court were anxious to obtain their revenues.

There can be no doubt that by the example and efforts of queen Catherine, much outward decorum, at least, was introduced into the court while she presided; and in many instances more than an external profession of religion. Her own constant attention to the observances of religion, appears not only from the foregoing narrative of Fox, but also from the little devotional works compiled by her, especially her prayers and meditations, several editions of which were printed in 1545 and the two following years, in a form particularly well suited to be a convenient manual for constant use.* Ballard has remarked, that the dreadful alarm she must have felt at the attempt of Gardiner for her destruction, seems to have awakened all the divine faculties of her soul, and to have made her more earnest in preparation for eternity.

Fuller observes of queen Catherine, that she was "one of great piety, beauty, and discretion. Next to the bible she studied the king's disposition, observing him to her utmost. And need she had of a nimble soul to attend at all times on his humour, whose fury had now got the addition of frowardness thereunto. She was rather nurse than wife unto him, who was more decayed by sickness and intemperance than old age."

The history of queen Catherine Parr, after the decease of Henry, is short and melancholy. The provision he made for her, though a mark of his affection and esteem, was but a slender provision for one of her rank.† Thus left an unprotected female in

---

* These are published by the Religious Tract Society.
† Four thousand pounds in addition to her jointure.

dubious times, it is not surprising that she should listen to the addresses of a man of rank and power, earlier than modern ideas of propriety would countenance. She married in the same year Sir Thomas Seymour, lord admiral of England, uncle to king Edward and brother to the protector, the duke of Somerset. It appears that she was the more inclined to this union by the revival of an early affection for that able, but ambitious and unprincipled individual. Ambition, indeed, appears to have been his chief inducement to this alliance, which was disapproved by his brother, though the young king wrote a congratulatory letter to the queen, assuring her that suitable provision should be made for them if at any time need required.

With the lord admiral she lived but a short time, and that very unhappily. He was a scorner of the truth, and though he did not prevent her continuing openly to manifest her regard for the gospel, he did not hesitate to show his own indifference, by continually absenting himself from the public services she instituted for the benefit of their family. Latimer openly spoke of this in one of his sermons before king Edward. (See Latimer, p. 62.)

This pious female was soon released from her trials. She died in September, 1548, soon after giving birth to a daughter; not without strong suspicions that she was poisoned by her husband, who was desirous of marrying the princess Elizabeth. His ambitious and cruel practices, however, soon met with a just reward. To use the words of Latimer, "he died very dangerously, irksomely, horribly." He had been in practice, if not in profession, an open infidel. Some lines, however, written by him a short time before his execution, evince a mind aware of the cause of his situation; he says, "Forgetting God to love a king, hath been my rod." Her daughter, thus left an orphan, died at an early age.

Her writings consist of a small manual of Prayers or Meditations, which is reprinted in the following pages. There is also a compilation, chiefly from scripture, entitled Psalms. These are fifteen in number, and are reflections on various subjects connected with christian life. But the most valuable of her writings was, " Queen Catherine Parr's Lamentation of a Sinner, bewailing the ignorance of her blind life." This was published after her decease by lord Burleigh, who found it among her papers, and it is reprinted in the present collection. Some letters written by her will be found in Strype and Haynes. She also translated an exposition of the fifty-first Psalm made by Jerome of Ferraria. The part she took in the translation of the Paraphrase of Erasmus has been already noticed.

Such was Catherine Parr, one of those queens whom God has been pleased to constitute nursing mothers to his church—a main instrument in protecting and advancing the English reformation at a most critical period; one who, it cannot be doubted, was a real follower of Christ.

The following consolatory letter, written by Catherine Parr, shows her piety, and her attention to the precepts of the gospel, for it was addressed to the wife of one of her bitter opponents.

### Letter of Queen Catherine Parr to Lady Wriothesley, comforting her for the loss of her only son.

GOOD my lady Wriothesley, understanding it hath pleased God of late to disinherit your son of this world, of intent he should become partner and chosen heir of the everlasting inheritance, for which calling and happy vocation ye may rejoice, yet when I consider you are a mother by flesh and nature, doubting how you can give place quietly to the same; inasmuch as Christ's mother, endued with all godly virtues, did utter a sorrowful natural passion of her Son's death, whereby we have all obtained everlastingly to live—therefore amongst other discreet and godly consolations given unto you, as well by my lord your husband, as other your wise friends, I have thought with mine own hand to recommend unto you my simple counsel and advice; desiring you not so to utter your natural affection by inordinate sorrow, that God have cause to take you as a murmurer against his appointments and ordinances. For what is excessive sorrow but a plain evidence against you, that your inward mind doth repine against God's doings, and a declaration that you are not contented, that God hath put your son by nature, but his by adoption, in possession of the heavenly kingdom? Such as have doubted of the everlasting life to come, do sorrow and bewail the departure hence, but those which are persuaded that to die here is life again, do rather hunger for death, and count it a felicity, than to bewail it as an utter destruction.

How much, madam, are you to be counted godly wise, that will and can prevent, through your godly wisdom, knowledge, and humble submission, that thing which time would at length finish. If you lament your son's death, you do him great wrong, and show yourself to sorrow for the happiest thing that ever came to him, being in the hands of his best Father. If you are sorry for your own commodity, you show yourself to live to yourself. And as of his towardness you could but only hope, his years were so young which could perform nothing, it seemeth that he was now a meet and pleasant sacrifice for Christ.

Wherefore, good my lady Wriothesley, put away all immoderate and unjust heaviness, requiring you with thanksgiving to frame your heart, that the Father in heaven may think you are most glad and best contented to make him a present of his spiritual, and your only natural son; glorifying him more in that it hath pleased his majesty to accept and able him to his kingdom, than that it first pleased him to comfort you with such a gift; who can at his pleasure recompense your loss with such a like jewel, if gladly and quietly you submit, and refer all to his pleasure.

# PRAYERS,

OR

# MEDITATIONS;

WHEREIN THE MIND IS STIRRED PATIENTLY TO SUFFER ALL AFFLICTIONS HERE, TO SET AT NOUGHT THE VAIN PROSPERITY OF THIS WORLD, AND ALWAYS TO LONG FOR THE EVERLASTING FELICITY. COLLECTED OUT OF CERTAIN HOLY WORKS, BY THE MOST VIRTUOUS AND GRACIOUS PRINCESS CATHERINE, QUEEN OF ENGLAND, FRANCE, AND IRELAND.

A. D. 1546.

---

"If ye be risen again with Christ, seek the things which are above, where Christ sitteth on the right hand of God. Set your affection on things that are above, and not on things which are on the earth," Col. iii.

---

Most benign Lord Jesus, grant me thy grace, that it may alway work in me, and persevere with me unto the end.

Grant me that I may ever desire and will that which is most pleasant and most acceptable to thee.

Thy will be my will, and my will be to follow alway thy will.

Let there be alway in me one will, and one desire with thee; and that I have no desire to will or not to will, but as thou wilt.

Lord, thou knowest what thing is most profitable and most expedient for me.

Give, therefore, what thou wilt, as much as thou wilt, and when thou wilt.

Do with me what thou wilt, as it shall please thee, and shall be most to thine honour.

Put me where thou wilt, and freely do with me in all things after thy will.

Thy creature I am, and in thy hands, lead and turn me where thou wilt.

Lo, I am thy servant, ready to do all things that thou commandest; for I desire not to live to myself, but to thee.

Lord Jesus, I pray thee, grant me grace, that I may never set my heart on the things of this world, but that all worldly and carnal affections may utterly die and be mortified in me.

Grant me above all things that I may rest in thee, and finally quiet and pacify my heart in thee.

For thou, Lord, art the very true peace of heart, and the perfect rest of the soul, and without thee all things are grievous and unquiet.

My Lord Jesus, I beseech thee, be with me in every place, and at all times; and let it be to me a special solace, gladly, for thy love, to lack all worldly solace.

And if thou withdraw thy comfort from me at any time, keep me, O Lord, from desperation, and make me patiently to abide thy will and ordinance.

O Lord Jesus, thy judgments are righteous, and thy providence is much better for me than all that I can imagine or devise.

Wherefore, do with me in all things as it shall please thee, for it may not but be well, all that thou doest.

If thou wilt that I be in light, be thou blessed; if thou wilt that I be in darkness, be thou also blessed.

If thou vouchsafe to comfort me, be thou highly blessed; if thou wilt I live in trouble and without comfort, be thou likewise ever blessed.

Lord, give me grace gladly to suffer whatsoever thou wilt shall fall upon me, and patiently to take at thy hand good and bad, bitter and sweet, joy and sorrow; and for all things that shall befall unto me, heartily to thank thee.

Keep me, Lord, from sin, and I shall dread neither death nor hell.

Oh what thanks ought I to give unto thee, who hast suffered the grievous death of the cross, to deliver me from my sins, and to obtain everlasting life for me.

Thou gavest us most perfect example of patience, fulfilling and obeying the will of thy Father, even unto the death.

Make me, wretched sinner, obediently to use myself after thy will in all things, and patiently to bear the burden of this corruptible life. For though this life be tedious, and as a heavy burden for my soul, yet, nevertheless, through thy grace, and by example of thee, it is now made much more easy and comfortable, than it was before thy incarnation and passion.

Thy holy life is our way to thee, and by following of thee we walk to thee who art our Head and Saviour. And yet, except thou hadst gone before, and showed us the way to everlasting life, who would endeavour to follow thee? seeing we are yet so slow and dull, having the light of thy blessed example and holy doctrine to lead and direct us.

O Lord Jesus, make that possible, by grace, which is impossible to me, by nature.

Thou knowest well that I may little suffer, and that I am anon cast down and overthrown with a little adversity; wherefore, I beseech thee, O Lord, to strengthen me with thy Spirit, that I may willingly suffer for thy sake all manner of trouble and affliction.

Lord, I will acknowledge unto thee all mine unrighteousness, and I will confess unto thee all the unstableness of my heart.

Oftentimes a very little thing troubleth me sore, and maketh me dull and slow to serve thee.

And sometimes I purpose to stand strongly, but when a little trouble cometh, it is to me great anguish and grief, and of a very little thing riseth a grievous temptation to me

Yea, when I think myself to be sure and strong, and that, as it seemeth, I have the upper hand, suddenly I feel myself ready to fall with a little blast of temptation.

Behold, therefore, good Lord, my weakness, and consider my frailness, best known to thee.

Have mercy on me, and deliver me from all iniquity and sin, that I be not entangled therewith.

Oftentimes it grieveth me sore, and in a manner confoundeth me, that I am so unstable, so weak, and so frail, in resisting sinful motions.

Which, although they draw me not always to consent, yet nevertheless, their assaults are very grievous unto me.

And it is tedious to me to live in such battle, albeit, I perceive that such battle is not unprofitable unto me. For thereby I the better know myself, and mine own infirmities, and that I must seek help only at thy hands.

O Lord God of Israel, the lover of all faithful souls, vouchsafe to behold the labour and sorrow of me, thy poor creature.

Assist me in all things with thy grace, and so strengthen me with heavenly strength, that neither my cruel enemy, the fiend, neither my wretched flesh, which is not yet subject to the spirit, have victory or dominion over me.

Oh what a life may this be called where no trouble nor misery lacketh! where every place is full of snares of mortal enemies!

For one trouble or temptation overpast, another cometh speedily; and the first conflict enduring, a new battle suddenly ariseth.

Wherefore, Lord Jesus, I pray thee, give me grace to rest in thee above all things, and to quiet me in thee above all creatures; above all glory and honour, above all dignity and power, above all cunning and policy, above all health and beauty, above all riches and treasure, above all joy and pleasure, above all fame and praise, above all mirth and consolation, that man's heart may take or feel besides thee.

For thou, Lord God, art best, most wise, most high, most mighty, most sufficient, and most full of all goodness, most sweet, and most comfortable, most fair, most loving, most noble, most glorious; in whom all goodness most perfectly is. And therefore, whatsoever I have besides thee, it is nothing to me; for my heart may not rest nor fully be pacified but only in thee.

O Lord Jesus, most loving spouse, who shall give me wings of perfect love, that I may fly up from these worldly miseries, and rest in thee? O when shall I ascend to thee, and see and feel how sweet thou art? When shall I wholly gather myself in thee, so perfectly that I shall not, for thy love, feel myself, but thee only, above myself, and above all worldly things; that thou mayest vouchsafe to visit me in such wise as thou dost visit thy most faithful lovers. Now, I often mourn and complain of the miseries of this life, and with sorrow and great heaviness suffer them. For many things happen daily to me which oftentimes trouble me, make me heavy, and darken mine understanding. They hinder me greatly, and put my mind from thee, and so encumber me many ways, that I cannot freely and clearly desire thee, nor have thy sweet consolations, which with thy blessed saints are always present. I beseech thee, Lord Jesus, that the sighings and inward desires of my heart may move and incline thee to hear me.

O Jesus, King of everlasting glory, the joy and comfort of all christian people that are wandering as pilgrims in the wilderness of this world, my heart crieth to thee by still desires, and my silence speaketh unto thee, and saith, How long tarrieth my Lord God to come to me!

Come, O Lord, and visit me; for without thee I have no true joy; without thee my soul is heavy and sad.

I am in prison, and bound with fetters of sorrow, till thou, O Lord, with thy gracious presence, vouchsafe to visit me, and to bring me again to liberty and joy of spirit, and to show thy favourable countenance unto me.

Open my heart, Lord, that I may behold thy laws, and teach me to walk in thy commandments.

Make me to know and follow thy will, and to have always in my remembrance thy manifold benefits, that I may yield due thanks to thee for them.

But I acknowledge and confess for truth, that I am not able to give thee worthy thanks for the least benefit that thou hast given me.

O Lord, all gifts and virtues that any man hath in body or soul, natural or supernatural, are thy gifts and come of thee, and not of ourselves, and they declare the great riches of thy mercy and goodness unto us.

And though some have more gifts than others, yet they all proceed from thee, and without thee the least cannot be had.

O Lord, I account it for a great benefit, not to have many worldly gifts, whereby the laud and praise of men might blind my soul, and deceive me.

Lord, I know that no man ought to be abashed or miscontent that he is in a low estate in this world, and lacketh the pleasure of this life, but rather to be glad and rejoice thereat. For so much as thou hast chosen the poor and meek persons, and such as are despised in the world, to be thy servants and familiar friends.

Witness thy blessed apostles, whom thou madest chief pastors and spiritual governors of thy flock, who departed from the council of the Jews, rejoicing that they were counted worthy to suffer rebuke for thy name.

Even so, O Lord, grant that I, thy servant, may be as well content to be taken as the least, as others are to be greatest; and that I be as well pleased to be in the lowest place as in the highest; and as glad to be of no reputation in the world, for thy sake, as others are to be noble and famous.

Lord, it is the work of a perfect man never to sequester his mind from thee, and among many worldly cares to go without care; not after the manner of an idle or dissolute person, but by the prerogative of a free mind, alway minding heavenly things, and not cleaving by inordinate affection to any creature.

I beseech thee, therefore, my Lord Jesus, keep me from the superfluous care of this world, that I be not disquieted with bodily necessities, and that I be not taken with the voluptuous pleasures of the world, or of the flesh.

Preserve me from all things which hinder my soul's health, that I be not overthrown with them.

O Lord God, who art sweetness unspeakable, turn into bitterness to me all worldly and fleshly delights, which might draw me from the love of eternal things, to the love of short and vile pleasure.

Let not flesh and blood overcome me, nor yet the world with his vain glory deceive me, nor the fiend with his manifold crafts supplant me; but give me spiritual strength in resisting them, patience in suffering them, and constancy in persevering to the end.

Give me, for all worldly delectations, the most sweet consolation of thy Holy Spirit; and, for all fleshly love, endue my soul with fervent love of thee.

Make me strong inwardly in my soul, and cast out thereof all unprofitable cares of this world, that I be not led by unstable desires of earthly things, but that I may repute all things in this world, as they are, transitory, and soon vanishing away, and myself also with them drawing towards an end.

For nothing under the sun may long abide, but all is vanity and affliction of spirit.

Give me, Lord, therefore, heavenly wisdom, that I may learn to seek and find thee, and above all things to love thee.

Give me grace to withdraw me from them that flatter me, and patiently to suffer them that unjustly grieve me.

Lord, when temptation or tribulation cometh, vouchsafe to succour me, that all may turn to my spiritual comfort, and patiently to suffer, and alway to say, Thy name be blessed.

Lord, trouble is now at hand, I am not well, but I am greatly vexed with this present affliction. O most glorious Father, what shall I do? Anguish and trouble are on every side; help now, I beseech thee, in this hour, thou shalt be lauded and praised when I am perfectly made meek before thee.

The Lord is strong enough to take this trouble from me, and to assuage the cruel assaults thereof, that I be not overcome with them, as thou hast oftentimes done before this time; that when I am clearly delivered by thee, I may with gladness say, The right hand of Him that is highest hath made this change.

Lord, grant me thine especial grace, that I may come thither where no creature shall hinder me, nor keep me from the perfect beholding of thee.

For as long as any transitory thing keepeth me back, or hath rule in me, I may not truly ascend to thee.

O Lord, without thee nothing may long delight or please. For if any thing should be liking and savoury, it must be through help of thy grace, seasoned with the Spirit of thy wisdom.

O everlasting Light, far passing all things, send down the beams of thy brightness from above, and purify and lighten the inward parts of my heart.

Quicken my soul and all the powers thereof, that it may cleave fast, and be joined to thee, in joyful gladness of spiritual desires.

O when shall that blessed hour come, that thou shalt visit me and gladden me with thy blessed presence; when shalt thou be to me all in all? Verily, until that time come, there can be no true joy in me.

But alas, the old man, that is my carnal affections, live still in me, and are not crucified nor perfectly dead.

For yet striveth the flesh against the spirit, and moveth great battle inwardly against me, and suffereth not thy kingdom of my soul to live in peace.

But thou, good Lord, who hast the lordship over all, and power of the sea, to assuage the rages and surges of the same, arise and help me, destroy the power of mine enemies, which always make battle against me. Show forth the greatness of thy goodness, and let the power of thy right hand be glorified in me; for there is to me none other hope nor refuge, but in thee only, my Lord, my God; to thee be honour and glory everlasting.

O Lord, grant me that I may wholly resign myself to thee, and in all things to forsake myself, and patiently to bear my cross and to follow thee.

O Lord, what is man, that thou vouchsafest to have mind of him, and to visit him?

Thou art alway one, alway good, alway righteous; and holily, justly, and blessedly disposing all things after thy wisdom.

But I am a wretch, and of myself alway ready and prone to evil, and do never abide in one state, but many times do vary and change.

Nevertheless, it shall be better with me, when it shall please thee; for thou, O Lord, only, art he that mayest help me, and thou mayest so confirm and stablish me, that my heart shall not be changed from thee, but be surely fixed, and finally rest and be quieted in thee.

I am nothing else, of myself, but vanity before thee; an unconstant creature and a feeble; and therefore, whereof may I rightfully glory, or why should I look to be magnified?

Whoso pleaseth himself without thee, displeaseth thee; and he that delighteth in men's praisings, loseth the true praise before thee. The true praise is to be praised of thee; and the true joy is to rejoice in thee.

Wherefore, thy name, O Lord, be praised, and not mine. Thy works be magnified, and not mine, and thy goodness be always lauded and blessed.

Thou art my glory, and the joy of my heart; in thee shall I glory, and joy in thee, and not in myself, nor in any worldly honour or dignity, which compared to thy eternal glory is but a shadow and very vanity.

O Lord, we live here in great darkness, and are soon deceived with the vanities of this world; and are soon grieved with a little trouble; yet, if I could behold myself well, I should plainly see that what trouble soever I have suffered, it hath justly come upon me, because I have sinned, and grievously offended thee. To me, therefore, confusion and despite is due; but to thee laud, honour, and glory.

Lord, send me help in my troubles, for man's help is little worth.

How often have I been disappointed, where I thought I should have found friendship! And how often have I found it where I least thought!

Wherefore it is a vain thing to trust in man, for the true trust and health of man is only in thee.

Blessed be thou, Lord, therefore, in all things that

happen unto us, for we are weak and unstable, soon deceived, and soon changed from one thing to another.

O Lord God, most righteous Judge, strong and patient, who knowest the frailty and malice of man; be thou my whole strength and comfort in all necessities, for mine own conscience, Lord, sufficeth not.

Wherefore, to thy mercy I do appeal, seeing no man may be justified, nor appear righteous in thy sight, if thou examine him after thy justice.

Oh blessed mansion of thy heavenly city! oh most clear day of eternity which the night may never darken! This is the day, alway clear and joyful; always sure, and never changing its state.

Would to God this day might shortly appear and shine upon us, and that these worldly fantasies were at an end.

This day shineth clearly to thy saints in heaven, with everlasting brightness; but to us pilgrims on earth it shineth obscurely, and as through a mirror or glass.

The heavenly citizens know how joyous this day is; but we outlaws, the children of Eve, weep and wail the bitter tediousness of our day, that is, of this present life, short and evil, full of sorrow and anguish; where man is oftentimes defiled with sin, encumbered with affliction, disquieted with troubles, wrapped in cares, busied with vanities, blinded with errors, overcharged with labours, vexed with temptations, overcome with vain delights and pleasures of the world, and grievously tormented with penury and want.

O when shall the end come of all these miseries? When shall I be clearly delivered from the bondage of sin?

When shall I, Lord, have only mind on thee, and fully be glad and joyful in thee?

When shall I be free without hinderance, and be in perfect liberty, without grief of body and soul?

When shall I have peace without trouble? peace within and without, and on every side stedfast and sure?

O Lord Jesus, when shall I stand and behold thee, and have full sight and contemplation of thy glory?

When shalt thou be to me all in all, and when shall I be with thee in thy kingdom that thou hast ordained for thine elect people from the beginning?

I am left here poor, and as an outlaw, in the land of mine enemies, where daily are battles and great misfortunes.

Comfort mine exile, assuage my sorrow, for all my desire

is to be with thee. It is to me an unpleasant burden, what pleasure soever the world offereth me here.

I desire to have inward fruition in thee, but I cannot attain thereto.

I covet to cleave fast to heavenly things, but worldly affections pluck my mind downward.

I would subdue all evil affections, but they daily rebel and rise against me, and will not be subject unto my spirit.

Thus I, wretched creature, fight in myself, and am grievous to myself, while my spirit desireth to be upward, and contrary, my flesh draweth me downward.

Oh what suffer I inwardly! I go about to mind heavenly things, and straight a great rabble of worldly thoughts rush into my soul.

Therefore, Lord, be not long away, nor depart in thy wrath from me. Send me the light of thy grace, destroy in me all carnal desires.

Send forth the hot flames of thy love to burn and consume the hot fantasies of my mind.

Gather, O Lord, my senses and the powers of my soul together in thee, and make me to despise all worldly things, and by thy grace strongly to resist and overcome all motions and occasions of sin. Help me, thou everlasting truth, that no worldly guile nor vanity hereafter have power to deceive me. Come also, thou heavenly sweetness, and let all bitterness of sin flee far from me.

Pardon me and forgive me as oft as in my prayer my mind is not surely fixed on thee.

For many times I am not there where I stand or sit, but rather there whither my thoughts carry me.

For there I am where my thought is, and there as customably is my thought, there is that I love.

And that oftentimes cometh into my mind which by custom pleaseth me best, and delighteth me most to think upon; accordingly as thou dost say in thy gospel, Where a man's treasure is, there is his heart.

Wherefore, if I love heaven I speak gladly thereof, and of such things as are of God, and of that which appertaineth to his honour, and to the glorifying of his holy name.

And if I love the world, I love to talk of worldly things, and I joy anon in worldly felicity, and sorrow and lament soon for worldly adversity.

If I love the flesh, I imagine oftentimes that which pleaseth the flesh.

If I love my soul, I delight much to speak and to hear of things that are for my soul's health.

And whatsoever I love, of that I gladly hear and speak, and bear the images of them still in my mind.

Blessed is that man, who for the love of the Lord setteth not by the pleasures of this world, and learneth truly to overcome himself, and with the fervour of spirit crucifieth his flesh, so that in a clean and a pure conscience he may offer his prayers to thee, and be accepted to have company of thy blessed angels; all earthly things being excluded from his heart.

Lord, and holy Father, be thou blessed now and ever ; for as thou wilt, so is it done, and that thou dost is alway best.

Let me, thy humble and unworthy servant, joy only in thee, and not in myself, nor in any thing else beside thee.

For thou, Lord, art my gladness, my hope, my crown, and all mine honour.

What hath thy servant but that he hath of thee, and that without his desert. All things are thine, thou hast created and made them.

I am poor, and have been in trouble and pain ever from my youth, and my soul hath been in great heaviness through manifold passions that come of the world and of the flesh ; wherefore, Lord, I desire that I may have of thee the joy of inward peace.

I ask of thee, to come to that rest which is ordained for thy chosen children, that are fed and nourished with the light of heavenly comforts, for without thy help I cannot come to thee.

Lord, give me peace, give me inward joy, and then my soul shall be full of heavenly melody, and devout and fervent in lauding and praising thee.

But if thou withdraw thyself from me, as thou hast sometime done, then may not thy servant run the way of thy commandments as I did before.

For it is not with me as it was when the lantern of thy spiritual presence did shine upon my head, and I was defended under the shadow of thy wings from all perils and dangers.

O merciful Lord Jesus, ever to be praised, the time is come that thou wilt prove thy servant, and rightful it is that I shall now suffer somewhat for thee.

Now is the hour come that thou hast known from the

beginning, that thy servant for a time should outwardly be set at naught, and inwardly to lean to thee; and that he should be despised in the sight of the world, and be broken with affliction, that he may after arise with thee in a new light, and be clarified and made glorious in thy kingdom of heaven.

O holy Father, thou hast ordained it so to be, and it is done as thou hast commanded.

This is thy grace, O Lord, to thy friend, to suffer him to be troubled in this world for thy love, how often soever it be, and of what person soever it be, and in what manner soever thou wilt suffer it to fall unto him. For without thy will or sufferance what thing is done upon earth?

It is good to me, O Lord, that thou hast meekened me, that I may thereby learn to know thy righteous judgments, and to put from me all manner of presumption and stateliness of heart. It is very profitable for me that confusion hath covered my face, that I may learn thereby rather to seek to thee for help and succour, than to man.

I have thereby learned to dread thy secret and terrible judgments, who scourgest the righteous with the sinner, but not without equity and justice.

Lord, I yield thanks to thee that thou hast not spared my sins, but hast punished me with scourges of love, and hast sent me affliction and anguish, within and without.

No creature under heaven may comfort me but thou, Lord God, the heavenly physician of man's soul, who strikest and healest, who bringest a man nigh to death, and afterward restorest him to life again, that he may thereby learn to know his own weakness and imbecility and the more fully to trust in thee, O Lord.

Thy discipline is laid upon me, and thy rod of correction hath taught me, and under that rod I wholly submit me. Strike my back and my bones as it shall please thee, and make me to bow my crooked will unto thy will.

Make me a meek and a humble disciple, as thou hast sometime done with me, that I may walk after thy will.

To thee I commit myself to be corrected; for better it is to be corrected by thee here than in time to come.

Thou knowest all things, and nothing is hid from thee that is in man's conscience.

Thou knowest all things to come before they befall; and it is not needful that any man teach thee, or warn thee of any thing that is done upon the earth.

Thou knowest what is profitable for me, and how much tribulations help to do away the rust of sin in me.

Do with me after thy pleasure; I am a sinful wretch, to none so well known as to thee.

Grant me, Lord, to know that which is necessary to be known; to love that which is to be loved; to desire that which pleaseth thee; to regard that which is precious in thy sight; and to refuse that which is vile before thee.

Suffer me not to judge thy mysteries after my outward senses, nor to give sentence after the hearing of the ignorant, but by true judgment to discern things spiritual; and above all things alway to search and follow thy will and pleasure.

O Lord Jesus, thou art all my riches, and all that I have, I have it of thee.

But what am I, Lord, that I dare speak to thee? I am thy poor creature, and a worm most abject.

Behold, Lord, I have naught, and of myself I am naught worth; thou art only God, righteous and holy; thou orderest all things, thou givest all things, and thou fulfillest all things with goodness.

I am a sinner, barren and void of all godly virtue. Remember thy mercies, and fill my heart with plenty of thy grace, for thou wilt not that thy works in me should be made in vain.

How may I bear the misery of this life except thy grace and mercy do comfort me?

Turn not thy face from me, defer not the visiting of me, withdraw not thy comforts, lest haply my soul be made as dry earth, without the water of grace.

Teach me, Lord, to fulfil thy will, to live meekly and worthily before thee, for thou art all my wisdom and knowledge, thou art he that knowest me as I am, that knewest me before the world was made, and before I was born or brought into this life. To thee, O Lord, be honour, glory, and praise, for ever and ever. Amen.

PRAISE BE TO THE GOD ETERNAL. AMEN.

*A Prayer for the King and Queen's Majesties.*

O LORD Jesu Christ, most high, most mighty, King of kings, Lord of lords, the only Ruler of princes, the very Son of God, on whose right hand sitting, dost from thy throne behold all the dwellers upon earth: with most lowly hearts we beseech thee, vouchsafe with favourable regard to behold our most gracious sovereigns, the king and queen's majesties, and so replenish them with the grace of thy Holy Spirit, that they alway incline to thy will and walk in thy way: keep them far from ignorance, and through thy gift let prudence and knowledge alway abound in their royal hearts. So instruct them, O Lord Jesu, reigning upon us in earth, that their majesties alway obey thy Divine Majesty in fear and dread. Endue them plentifully with heavenly gifts. Grant them in health and wealth long to live. Heap glory and honour upon them. Gladden them with the joy of thy countenance. So strengthen them that they may vanquish and overcome all their and our foes, and be dreaded and feared of all the enemies of their realms.

# THE LAMENTATION OR COMPLAINT OF A SINNER,

MADE BY THE MOST VIRTUOUS AND RIGHT GRACIOUS LADY

## QUEEN CATHERINE, (PARR,)

BEWAILING THE IGNORANCE OF HER BLIND LIFE, LED IN SUPERSTITION.

VERY PROFITABLE TO THE AMENDMENT OF OUR LIVES.

Set forth and put in print at the instant desire of the right gracious lady, Catherine, duchess of Suffolk, and the earnest request of the right honourable lord William Parr, marquess of Northampton.

First printed 1548.

---

### TO THE READER.

William Cecil having taken much profit by the reading of this treatise following, wisheth unto every christian by the reading thereof, like profit, with increase from God.

Most gentle and christian reader, if matters should be rather confirmed by their reporters, than the reports warranted by the matters, I might justly bewail our time, wherein evil deeds are well worded, and good deeds called evil. But sincere truth is, that things are not good for their praises, but are praised for their goodness. I do not move thee to like this christian treatise, because I have mind to praise it; but I exhort thee to mind it; and, for the goodness, thou shalt allow it; for whose liking I labour not to obtain, only, moved by mine example, their judgment I regard, chiefly confirmed by the matter. Truly, our time is so disposed to grant good names to evil fruits, and excellent terms to mean works, that neither can good deeds enjoy their due names, being defrauded by the evil; neither excellent works can possess their worthy terms, being forestalled by the mean; insomuch that men seek, rather, how much they can, than how much they ought to say; inclining more to their pleasure, than to their judgment, and to show themselves rather eloquent, than the matter good; so that neither the goodness of the cause can move them to say more, neither the evilness less. For, if the excellency of this christian contemplation, either for the goodness appearing herein to marvel, either for the profit ensuing hereupon to the reader, should be with due commendation followed; I, of necessity, should either travail to find out new words, the old being anticipated by evil matters, or wish that the common speech of praising were spared, until convenient matters were found to spend it; such is the plenty of praising and scarceness of deserving.

Wherefore, lacking the manner in words, and not the matter in deed of high commendation, I am compelled to keep in my judgment with silence, trusting that whom my report could not have moved to like this present treatise, the worthiness of the matter shall compel to give it honour.

Any earthly man would soon be stirred to see some mystery of magic, or practice of alchymy, or, perchance, some enchantment of elements; but thou, who art christened, hast here a wonderful mystery of the mercy of God, a heavenly practice of regeneration, a spiritual enchantment of the grace of God. If joy and triumph be showed, when a king's child is born into the world, what joy is sufficient, when God's child is regenerated from heaven. The one is flesh, which is born of flesh; the other is spirit, which is born of Spirit. The one, also, shall wither like the grass of the earth in short time; the other shall live in heaven beyond all time. If the finding of one lost sheep be more joyful than the having of ninety and nine; what joy is it, to consider the return of a stray child of almighty God, whose return teacheth the ninety and nine to come to their fold! Even such cause of joy is this, that the angels in heaven take comfort herein. Be thou, therefore, joyful, when a noble child is newly born; show thyself glad when the lost sheep hath won[*] the whole flock; be thou not sad where angels rejoice.

Here mayest thou see one, if the kind may move thee, a woman; if degree may provoke thee, a woman of high estate; by birth made noble, by marriage most noble, by wisdom godly, by a mighty king, an excellent queen; by a famous Henry, a renowned Catherine; a wife to him that was a king to realms; refusing the world wherein she was lost, to obtain heaven, wherein she may be saved; abhorring sin, which made her bound, to receive grace, whereby she may be free; despising flesh, the cause of corruption, to put on the Spirit, the cause of sanctification; forsaking ignorance, wherein she was blind, to come to knowledge, whereby she may see; removing superstition, wherewith she was smothered, to embrace true religion, wherewith she may revive.

The fruit of this treatise, good reader, is thine amendment; this only had, the writer is satisfied. This good lady thought no shame to detest her sin to obtain remission; no vileness to become nothing, to be a member of Him who is all things in all; no folly to forget the wisdom of the world, to learn the simplicity of the gospel at the last; no displeasantness to submit herself to

[*] Returned to.

the school of the cross, the learning of the crucifix, the book of our redemption, the very absolute library of God's mercy and wisdom. This way, thought she, her honour increased, and her state permanent, to make her earthly honour heavenly, and neglect the transitory for the everlasting.

Of this I would have thee warned, that the profit may ensue. These great mysteries and graces are not well perceived, except they are surely studied; neither are they perfectly studied, except they are diligently practised; neither profitably practised without amendment. See and learn hereby what she hath done, then mayest thou practise and amend that thou canst do; so shalt thou practise with ease, having a guide, and amend with profit, having a zeal. It is easier to see these, than to learn; begin at the easiest to come to the harder; see thou her confession, that thou mayest learn her repentance; practise her perseverance, that thou mayest have like amendment; despise thyself in eschewing vice, that thou mayest please God in asking grace; let not shame hinder the confession, which hindered not the offence. Be thou sure, "if we acknowledge our sins, God is faithful to forgive us, and to cleanse us from all unrighteousness." Obey the prophets saying, "Declare thy ways to the Lord."

Thus far thou mayest learn to know thyself: next this, be thou as diligent to relieve thyself in God's mercy, as thou hast been to relieve thyself in thine own repentance. For God hath concluded all things under sin, because he would have mercy upon all; who hath also borne our sins in his body upon the tree, that we should be delivered from sin, and should live unto righteousness, by whose stripes we are healed. Here is our anchor; here is our shepherd; here we are made whole; here is our life, our redemption, our salvation, and our bliss; let us, therefore, now feed, by this gracious queen's example, and be not ashamed to become in confession publicans, since this noble lady will be no pharisee.

And, to all ladies of estate, I wish as earnest mind, to follow our queen in virtue as in honour, that they might once appear to prefer God before the world, and be honourable in religion, who now are honourable in vanities; so shall they, as in some virtuous ladies of right high estate it is with great comfort seen, taste of this freedom of remission of the everlasting bliss, which exceeds all thoughts and understandings, and is prepared for the holy in spirit. For the which, let us, with our intercession, in holiness and pureness of life, offer ourselves to the heavenly Father, an undefiled host.* To whom be eternal praise and glory, throughout the earth, without end. Amen.†

* Sacrifice, victim. Romans xii. 1.
† Sir William Cecil, the author of this preface, was the great lord Burleigh, he owed his first introduction to Henry VIII. to the successful disputation with two Romish priests. During a long and active life he constantly laboured to promote the reformation.

# THE LAMENTATION OF A SINNER.

### The First Chapter.

*Of an humble confession of sins to the glory of God.*

When I consider, in the bethinking of mine evil and wretched former life, mine obstinate, stony, and untractable heart, to have so much exceeded in evilness, that it hath not only neglected, yea contemned, and despised God's holy precepts and commandments; but, also, embraced, received, and esteemed, vain, foolish, and feigned trifles, I am partly, by the hate I owe to sin, which hath reigned in me, and partly, by the love I owe to all christians, whom I am content to edify; even, with the example of mine own shame, forced, and constrained, with my heart and words, to confess and declare to the world, how ingrate, negligent, unkind, and stubborn, I have been to God my Creator, and how beneficial, merciful, and gentle, he hath been always to me his creature, being such a miserable and wretched sinner.

Truly, I have taken no little small thing upon me. First, to set forth my whole stubbornness and contempt in words; the which is incomprehensible in thought, as it is in the nineteenth Psalm, Who understandeth his faults? Next this, to declare the excellent beneficence, mercy, and goodness of God, which is infinite, and unmeasurable. Neither can all the words of angels and men make relation thereof, as appertaineth to his most high goodness. Who is he, that is not forced to confess the same, if he consider what he hath received of God, and doth daily receive? Yea, if men would not acknowledge and confess the same, the stones would cry it out. Truly, I am constrained and forced to speak, and write thereof, to mine own confusion and shame, but to the glory and praise of God. For he, as a loving Father, of most abundant and high goodness, hath heaped upon me innumerable benefits; and I, contrary, have heaped manifold sins, despising that which was good, holy, pleasant, and acceptable in his sight, and choosing that which was delicious, pleasant, and acceptable, in my sight.

And no marvel it was that I so did, for I would not learn to know the Lord, and his ways, but loved darkness better than light, yea, darkness seemed to me light. I embraced ignorance, as perfect knowledge, and knowledge seemed to me superfluous and vain. I regarded little God's word, but gave myself to vanities, and shadows of the world. I forsook him, in whom all truth is and followed, the vain, foolish imaginations of my heart. I would have covered my sins with the pretence of holiness; I called superstition godly meaning, and true holiness error. The Lord did speak many pleasant and sweet words unto me, and I would not hear; he called me diversely, but through frowardness, I would not answer.

Mine evils and miseries are so many, and so great, that they can accuse me even to my face. Oh, how miserably and wretchedly am I confounded, when, for the multitude and greatness of my sins, I am compelled to accuse myself! Was it not a marvellous unkindness, when God did speak to me, and also call to me, that I would not answer him? What man, so called, would not have heard? Or what man, hearing, would not have answered? If an earthly prince had spoken, or called, I suppose there are none, but would willingly have done both. Now, therefore, what a wretch and caitiff am I, that, when the Prince of princes, the King of kings, did speak many pleasant and gentle words unto me, and also called me so many and sundry times, that they cannot be numbered; and yet, notwithstanding these great signs and tokens of love, I would not come unto him, but hid myself out of his sight, seeking many crooked and by-ways, wherein I walked so long, that I had wholly lost his sight. And no marvel, or wonder, for I had a blind guide, called Ignorance, who dimmed so mine eyes, that I could never perfectly get any sight of the fair, goodly, straight, and right ways of his doctrine; but continually travelled, uncomfortably, in foul, wicked, crooked, and perverse ways; yea, and because they were so much haunted of many, I could not think, but that I walked in the perfect and right way, having more regard to the number of the walkers, than to the order of the walking; believing also, most assuredly, with company, to have walked to heaven, whereas, I am most sure, they would have brought me down to hell.

I forsook the spiritual honouring of the true living God, and worshipped visible idols, and images made of men's hands, believing, by them, to have gotten heaven; yea, to say the truth, I made a great idol of myself, for I loved myself better than God. And, certainly, look, how many things are loved, or preferred, in our hearts, before God, so many are taken and esteemed for idols, and false gods. Alas! how have I violated this holy, pure, and most high precept and commandment of the love of God! Which precept bindeth me to love him with my whole heart, mind, force, strength, and understanding: and I, like unto an evil, wicked, and disobedient child, have given my will, power, and senses, to the contrary, making, almost, of every earthly and carnal thing, a god!

Furthermore, the blood of Christ was not reputed by me sufficient for to wash me from the filth of my sins; neither such ways, as he had appointed by his word; but I sought for such riffraff as the bishop of Rome hath planted in his tyranny and kingdom, trusting, with great confidence, by the virtue and holiness of them, to receive full remission of my sins. And so I did, as much as was in me, obfuscate\* and darken the great benefit of Christ's passion, than the which, no thought can conceive anything of more value. There cannot be done so great an injury and displeasure to almighty God, our Father, as to tread under foot Christ, his only begotten and well beloved Son. All other sins in the world, gathered together in one, are not so heinous and detestable in the sight of God. And no wonder, for, in Christ crucified, God doth show himself most noble and glorious, even an almighty God, and most loving Father, in his only dear and chosen blessed Son.

And, therefore, I count myself one of the most wicked and miserable sinners in the world, because I have been so much contrary to Christ my Saviour. St. Paul desired to know nothing, but Christ crucified; after he had been rapt into the third heaven, where he heard such secrets, as were not convenient and meet to utter to men, but counted all his works and doings as nothing to win Christ. And I, most presumptuously thinking nothing of Christ crucified, went about to set forth mine own righteousness, saying, with the proud pharisee, "Good Lord, I thank thee, I am

\* Obscure.

not like other men: I am none adulterer, nor fornicator, and so forth;" with such like words of vain glory, extolling myself, and despising others; working as an hired servant for wages, or else for reward; and not, as a loving child, only for very love, without respect of wages or reward, as I ought to have done. Neither did I consider how beneficial a Father I had, who did show me his charity and mercy, of his own mere grace and goodness, that, when I was most his enemy, he sent his only begotten and well-beloved Son into this world of wretchedness and misery, to suffer most cruel and sharp death for my redemption. But my heart was so stony and hard, that this great benefit was never truly and lively printed in my heart, although, with my words it was oft rehearsed, thinking myself to be sufficiently instructed in the same, and being, indeed, in blind ignorance; and yet I stood so well in mine own judgment and opinion, that I thought it vain to seek the increase of my knowledge therein.

Paul calleth Christ the wisdom of God; and, even the same Christ, was, to me foolishness. My pride and blindness deceived me, and the hardness of my heart withstood the growing of truth within it. Such were the fruits of my carnal and human reason—to have rotten ignorance in price for ripe and seasonable knowledge; such, also, is the malice and wickedness that possesseth the hearts of men; such is the wisdom and pleasing of the flesh. I professed Christ in my baptism, when I began to live, but I swerved from him after baptism, in continuance of my living, even as the heathen, which never had begun.

Christ was innocent, and void of all sin; and I wallowed in filthy sin, and was free from no sin. Christ was obedient unto his Father, even to the death of the cross; and I disobedient, and most stubborn, even to the confusion of truth. Christ was meek and humble in heart, and I most proud and vain-glorious. Christ despised the world, with all the vanities thereof, and I made it my god, because of the vanities. Christ came to serve his brethren, and I coveted to rule over them. Christ despised worldly honour, and I much delighted to attain the same. Christ loved the base and simple things of the world, and I esteemed the most fair and pleasant things. Christ loved poverty, and I wealth. Christ was gentle and merciful to the poor, and I hard-hearted and ungentle. Christ prayed for his enemies, and I hated mine. Christ rejoiced in the conversion of sinners, and I was not grieved to see their reversion* to sin. By this declaration, all creatures may perceive how far I was from Christ, and without Christ; yea, how contrary to Christ, although I bare the name of a christian: insomuch that, if any man had said, I had been without Christ, I would have stiffly denied and withstood the same; and yet, indeed, I neither knew Christ, nor wherefore he came.

As concerning the effect and purpose of his coming, I had a certain vain and blind knowledge, both cold and dead, which may be had with all sin; as doth plainly appear by this my confession and open declaration.

## The Second Chapter.
*A Lamentation of a Sinner, with a hearty repentance in Faith, to obtain absolution and remission, through the merits of Christ.*

WHAT cause now have I to lament, sigh, and weep, for my life and time so evil spent! With how much humility and lowliness ought I to come, and acknowledge my sins to God, giving him thanks, that it hath pleased him, of his abundant goodness, to give me time of repentance! For I know my sins, in the consideration of them, to be so grievous, and, in the number, so exceeding, that I have deserved, very often, eternal damnation. And for the deferring of God's wrath, so manifoldly due, I must incessantly give thanks to the mercy of God; beseeching also, that the same delay of punishment cause not his plague to be the sorer, since mine own conscience condemns my former doings. But his mercy exceedeth all iniquity. And if I should not thus hope, alas, what should I seek for refuge and comfort? No mortal man is of power to help me; and, for the multitude of my sins, I dare not lift up mine eyes to heaven, where the seat of judgment is, I have so much offended my God. What! shall I fall in desperation? Nay, I will call upon Christ, the Light of the world, the Fountain of life, the Relief of all careful consciences, the Peacemaker between God and man, and the only health and comfort of all true repentant sinners.

He can, by his almighty power, save me, and deliver me out of this miserable state, and hath will, by his mercy, to save even the whole sin of the world. I have no hope nor

* Turning again

confidence in any creature, neither in heaven nor earth, but in Christ, my whole and only Saviour. He came into the world to save sinners, and to heal them that are sick; for he said, The whole have no need of the physician. Behold, Lord, how I come to thee, a sinner sick, and grievously wounded; I ask not bread, but the crumbs that fall from the children's table. Cast me not out of thy sight, although I have deserved to be cast into hell fire.

If I should look upon my sin, and not upon thy mercy, I should despair; for, in myself, I find nothing to save me, but a dunghill of wickedness to condemn me. If I should hope, by mine own strength and power, to come out of this maze of iniquity and wickedness, wherein I have walked so long, I should be deceived. For I am so ignorant, blind, weak, and feeble, that I cannot bring myself out of this entangled and wayward maze; but, the more I seek means and ways to wind myself out, the more I am wrapped and tangled therein.

So that I perceive my striving therein to be hinderance, my travail to be labour spent in going back. It is the hand of the Lord that can, and will, bring me out of the endless maze of death. For, without I be prevented by the grace of the Lord, I cannot ask forgiveness, nor be repentant, or sorry for them. There is no man can avow that Christ is the only Saviour of the world, but by the Holy Ghost; yea, as St. Paul saith, no man can say, The Lord Jesus, but by the Holy Ghost. The Spirit helpeth our infirmity, and maketh continual intercession for us, with such sorrowful groanings as cannot be expressed.

Therefore, I will first require, and pray the Lord, to give me his Holy Spirit, to teach me to avow, that Christ is the Saviour of the world, and to utter these words, 'The Lord Jesus;" and, finally, to help mine infirmities, and to intercede, or entreat for me. For I am most certain and sure, that no creature, in heaven or earth, is of power, or can, by any mean, help me; but God, who is omnipotent, almighty, beneficial. and merciful, wellwilling, and loving, to all those that call, and put their whole confidence and trust in him. And, therefore, I will seek none other means, nor advocate, but Christ's holy spirit; who is only the Advocate and Mediator between God and man, to help and relieve me.

## THE THIRD CHAPTER.

*What true Faith worketh in the soul of a Sinner.*

BUT now, what maketh me so bold and hardy, to presume to come to the Lord with such audacity and boldness, being so great a sinner? Truly, nothing, but his own word. For he saith, "Come to me, all ye that labour, and are burdened, and I shall refresh you." What gentle, merciful, and comfortable words are these to all sinners! Were he not a frantic, mad, beastlike, and foolish man, that would run for aid, help, or refuge to any other creature? What a most gracious, comfortable, and gentle saying was this, with such pleasant and sweet words to allure his very enemies to come unto him! Is there any worldly prince, or magistrate, that would show such clemency and mercy to their disobedient and rebellious subjects, having offended them? I suppose they would not with such words allure them, except it were to call those whom they cannot take, and punish them being taken. But even as Christ is Prince of princes, and Lord of lords, so his charity and mercy exceedeth and surmounteth all others. Christ saith, If carnal fathers do give good gifts to their children when they ask them, how much more shall your heavenly Father, being in substance all holy, and most highly good, give good gifts to all them that ask him.

It is no small nor little gift that I now require, neither think I myself worthy to receive such a noble gift, being so ingrate, unkind, and wicked a child. But when I behold the benignity, liberality, mercy, and goodness of the Lord, I am encouraged, boldened, and stirred to ask such a noble gift. The Lord is so bountiful and liberal, that he will not have us satisfied and contented with one gift, neither to ask simple and small gifts; and therefore he promiseth and bindeth himself by his word, to give good and beneficial gifts to all them that ask him with true faith, without which nothing can be done acceptable or pleasing to God; for faith is the foundation and ground of all other gifts, virtues, and graces; and therefore I will pray and say, Lord, increase my faith.

For this is the life everlasting, O Lord, that I must believe thee to be the true God, and him whom that thou didst send, Jesus Christ. By this faith I am assured, and by this assurance I feel the remission of my sins. This is it that maketh me bold, this is it that comforteth me, this is it that quencheth all despair.

I know, O my Lord, thine eyes look upon my faith. St. Paul saith, We are justified by faith in Christ, and not by the deeds of the law; for if righteousness come by the law, then Christ died in vain. St. Paul meaneth not here a dead, human, and historical faith, gotten by human industry; but a supernatural and lively faith, which worketh by charity, as he himself plainly expresses. This dignity of faith is no derogation to good works; for out of this faith spring all good works, yet we may not impute to the worthiness of faith or works our justification before God, but ascribe and give the worthiness of it wholly to the merits of Christ's passion, and refer and attribute the knowledge and perceiving thereof only to faith; whose very true and only property it is to take, apprehend, and hold fast the promises of God's mercy, which maketh us righteous; and to cause me continually to hope for the same mercy, and in love to work all manner of ways allowed in the scripture, that I may be thankful for the same.

Thus I feel myself to come, as it were, in a new garment before God; and now by his mercy to be taken as just and righteous, who, of late, without his mercy, was sinful and wicked; and by faith to obtain his mercy, the which the unfaithful cannot enjoy. And although St. John extolleth charity in his epistle, saying, that God is charity, and he that dwelleth in charity dwelleth in God. Truly, charity maketh men live like angels, and of the most furious, unbridled, and carnal men, maketh meek lambs.

Yea, with how fervent a spirit ought I to call, cry, and pray to the Lord to make his great charity to burn and flame my heart, being stony and evil affected, that it never would conceive nor regard the great, inestimable charity and love of God, in sending his only begotten and dear beloved Son into this vale of misery, to suffer the most cruel and sharp death of the cross for my redemption. Yea, I never had this unspeakable and most high charity and abundant love of God printed and fixed in my heart duly, till it pleased God of his mere grace, mercy, and pity, to open mine eyes, making me to see and behold with the eye of lively faith, Christ crucified to be mine only Saviour and Redeemer. For then I began, and not before, to perceive and see mine own ignorance and blindness; the cause thereof was that I would not learn to know Christ my Saviour and Redeemer.

But when God, of his mere goodness, had thus opened mine eyes, and made me see and behold Christ, the Wisdom of God, the Light of the world, with a supernatural sight of faith, all pleasures, vanities, honour, riches, wealth, and aids of the world, began to wax bitter unto me. Then I knew it was no illusion of the devil, nor false, nor human doctrine I had received. When such success came thereof, that I had in detestation and horror that which I erst so much loved and esteemed, being of God forbidden that we should love the world, or the vain pleasures and shadows in the same, then began I to perceive that Christ was my only Saviour and Redeemer; and the same doctrine to be all divine, holy, heavenly, and infused by grace into the hearts of the faithful, which never can be attained by human doctrine, knowledge, or reason, although they should travail and labour for the same to the end of the world. Then began I to dwell in God by charity, knowing, by the loving charity of God in the remission of my sins, that God is charity, as St. John saith. So that of my faith, whereby I came to know God, and whereby it pleased God, even because I trusted in him, to justify me, sprang this excellent charity in my heart.

I think no less, but many will wonder and marvel at this my saying, that I never knew Christ for my Saviour and Redeemer until this time. For many have this opinion, saying, Who knoweth not there is a Christ? Who, being a christian, doth not confess him his Saviour? And thus believing their dead, human, historical faith and knowledge, which they have learned in their scholastical books to be the true infused faith and knowledge of Christ, which may be had, as I said before, with all sin, they used to say, by their own experience of themselves, that their faith doth not justify them. And true it is, except they have this faith, which I have declared here before, they shall never be justified.

And yet it is not false that by faith only I am sure to be justified. Even this is the cause that so many impugn this office and duty of true faith, because so many lack the true faith. And even as the faithful are forced to allow this true faith, so the unfaithful can, in nowise probably, entreat thereof; the one feeling in himself that which he saith, the other not having in him for to say.

I have certainly no curious learning to defend this matter withal, but a simple zeal and earnest love to the truth inspired of God, who promiseth to pour his Spirit upon all flesh; which I have, by the grace of God, whom I most humbly honour, felt in myself to be true.

## The Fourth Chapter.

*Of the great Love of God towards mankind, and of the inward beholding of Christ crucified.*

LET us therefore now, I pray you, by faith, behold and consider the great charity and goodness of God, in sending his Son to suffer death for our redemption when we were his mortal enemies; and after what sort and manner he sent him.

First, It is to be considered, yea, to be undoubtedly and with a perfect faith believed, that God sent him to us freely; for he did give him, and sold him not. A more noble and rich gift he could not have given. He sent not a servant or a friend, but his only Son, so dearly beloved; not in delights, riches, and honours, but in crosses, poverties, and slanders; not as a Lord, but as a servant, yea, and, in most vile and painful sufferings, to wash us, not with water, but with his own precious blood; not from mire, but from the puddle and filth of our iniquities. He hath given him not to make us poor, but to enrich us with his divine virtues, merits, and graces; yea, and in him he hath given us all good things, and finally himself, and with such great charity as cannot be expressed.

Was it not a most high and abundant charity of God to send Christ to shed his blood, to lose honour, life, and all for his enemies? Even in the time when we had done him most injury he first showed his charity to us with such flames of love, that greater could not be showed. God in Christ hath opened unto us, although we are weak and blind of ourselves, that we may behold in this miserable estate the great wisdom, goodness, and truth, with all the other godly perfections which are in Christ. Therefore inwardly to behold Christ crucified upon the cross is the best and goodliest meditation that can be.

We may see also in Christ crucified the beauty of the soul better than in all the books of the world: for who that with a lively faith seeth and feeleth in spirit that Christ, the Son of God, is dead for the satisfying and purifying of the soul, shall see that his soul is appointed for the very tabernacle and mansion of the inestimable and incomprehensible majesty and honour of God. We see also in Christ crucified how vain and foolish the world is, and how that Christ, being most wise, despised the same. We see also how blind it is, because the same knoweth not Christ, but persecuteth him. We see also how unkind the world is, by the killing of Christ in the time he did show it most favour. How hard and obstinate was it that would not be mollified with so many tears, such sweat, and so much bloodshed of the Son of God, suffering with such great and high charity?

Therefore he is now very blind that seeth not how vain, foolish, false, ingrate, cruel, hard, wicked, and evil the world is. We may also in Christ crucified weigh our sins, as in a divine balance, how grievous and how weighty they are, seeing they have crucified Christ; for they would never have been counterpoised but with the great and precious weight of the blood of the Son of God. And therefore God, of his high goodness, determined that his blessed Son should rather suffer bloodshed than our sins should have condemned us. We shall never know our own misery and wretchedness but with the light of Christ crucified; then we shall see our own cruelty, when we feel his mercy; our own unrighteousness and iniquity, when we see his righteousness and holiness. Therefore, to learn to know truly our own sins is to study in the book of the crucifix, by continual conversation in faith; and to have perfect and plentiful charity is to learn, first by faith, the charity that is in God towards us.

We may see also in Christ upon the cross how great the pains of hell, and how blessed the joys of heaven are; and what a sharp and painful thing it shall be to them that shall be deprived of that sweet, happy, and glorious joy, Christ. Then this crucifix is the book wherein God hath included all things, and hath most compendiously written therein all truth profitable and necessary for our salvation. Therefore let us endeavour ourselves to study this book, that we, being enlightened with the Spirit of God, may give him thanks for so great a benefit.

## THE FIFTH CHAPTER.

*Of the glorious Victories of Christ over all Enemies.*

IF we look further into this book we shall see Christ's great victory upon the cross, which was so noble and mighty that there never was other so noble or mighty, that there never was, neither shall be such. If the victory and glory of worldly princes were great because they did overcome great hosts of men, how much was Christ's greater, which vanquished not only the prince of this world, but all the enemies of God; triumphing over persecution, injuries, villanies, slanders, yea, death, the world, sin, and the devil, and brought to confusion all carnal prudence!

The princes of the world never did fight without the strength of the world: Christ contrarily went to war even against all the strength of the world. He fought, as David did with Goliath, unarmed of all human wisdom and policy, and without all worldly power and strength. Nevertheless, he was fully replenished and armed with the whole armour of the Spirit; and in this one battle he overcame for ever all his enemies. There was never so glorious a spoil, neither a more rich and noble, than Christ was upon the cross, who delivered all his elect from such a sharp and miserable captivity. He had in his battle many stripes, yea, and lost his life, but his victory was so much the greater. Therefore, when I look upon the Son of God with a supernatural faith and light, so unarmed, naked, given up, and alone, with humility, patience, liberality, modesty, gentleness, and with all other his divine virtues, beating down to the ground all God's enemies, and making the soul of man so fair and beautiful; I am forced to say that his victory and triumph was marvellous; and therefore Christ well deserved to have this noble title, Jesus of Nazareth, King of the Jews.

But if we will particularly unfold and see his great victories, let us first behold how he overcame sin with his innocency, and confounded pride with his humility; quenched all worldly love with his charity, appeased the wrath of his Father with his meekness, and turned hatred into love with his so many benefits and godly zeal.

Christ hath not only overcome sin, but rather he hath killed the same; inasmuch as he hath satisfied for it himself with the most holy sacrifice and oblation of his precious body in suffering most bitter and cruel death. Also after another sort, that is, he giveth all those that love him so much spirit, grace, virtue, and strength, that they may resist, impugn, and overcome sin, and not consent, neither suffer it to reign in them. He hath also vanquished sin, because he hath taken away the force of the same; that is, he hath cancelled the law, which was in evil men the occasion of sin. Therefore sin hath no power against them that are, with the Holy Ghost, united to Christ; in them there is nothing worthy of damnation. And although the dregs of Adam do remain, that is, our concupiscences, which indeed are sins, nevertheless they are not imputed for sins, if we be truly planted in Christ. It is true, that Christ might have taken away all our immoderate affections, but he hath left them for the great glory of his Father, and for his own greater triumph. As for example: when a prince fights with his enemies, which sometime had the sovereignty over his people, and subduing them, may kill them if he will, yet he preserves and saves them; and whereas they were lords over his people, he makes them after to serve whom they before had ruled. Now, in such a case the prince shows himself a greater conqueror in that he hath made them which were rulers to obey, and the subjects to be lords over them to whom they served, than if he had utterly destroyed them upon the conquest. For now he leaves continual victory to them whom he redeemed, whereas otherwise the occasion of victory was taken away where none were left to be the subjects. Even so, in like case, Christ hath left in us these concupiscences, to the intent they should serve us to the exercise of our virtues, where first they did reign over us to the exercise of our sin. And it may be plainly seen, that whereas first they were such impediments to us that we could not move ourselves towards God, now, by Christ, we have so much strength, that notwithstanding the force of them, we may assuredly walk to heaven. And although the children of God sometime do fall by frailty into some sin, yet, that falling maketh them to humble themselves, and to acknowledge the goodness of God, and to come to him for refuge and help.

Likewise Christ, by his death, hath overcome the prince of devils with all his host, and hath destroyed them all. For, as Paul saith, it is verified that Christ should break the serpent's head, prophesied by God. And although the devil tempt us, yet if by faith we are planted in Christ, we shall not perish, but rather by his temptation take great force and might. So it is evident that the triumph, victory, and glory of Christ is the greater, having in such sort subdued the devil; that whereas he was prince and lord of the world, holding all creatures in captivity, now Christ useth him as an instrument to punish the wicked, and to exercise and make strong the elect of God, in christian warfare.

Christ likewise hath overcome death in a more glorious manner, if it be possible, because he hath not taken it away; but leaving universally all subject to the same. He hath given so much virtue and spirit, that whereas afore we passed thereto with great fear, now we are bold through the Spirit, for the sure hope of the resurrection, that we receive it with joy. It is now no more bitter, but sweet; no more feared, but desired; it is no death, but life.

And also it hath pleased God that the infirmities and adversities do remain to the sight of the world; but the children of God are by Christ made so strong, righteous, whole, and sound, that the troubles of the world are comforts of the spirit, the passions of the flesh are medicines of the soul; for all manner of things work to their commodity and profit; for they in spirit feel that God their Father doth govern them, and disposeth all things for their benefit; therefore they feel themselves sure. In persecution, they are quiet and peaceful; in trouble, they are without weariness, fears, anxieties, suspicions, miseries; and, finally, all the good and evil of the world worketh to their commodity.

Moreover, they see that the triumph of Christ hath been so great, that not only he hath subdued and vanquished all our enemies and the power of them, but he hath overthrown and vanquished them after such a sort, that all things serve to our health. He might and could have taken them all away, but where then should have been our victory, palm, and crown? For we daily have fights in the flesh, and by the succour of grace have continual victories over sin; whereby we have cause to glorify God who, by his Son, hath weakened our enemy the devil, and by his Spirit giveth us strength to vanquish his offspring.

So do we acknowledge daily the great triumph of our Saviour, and rejoice in our own fights; the which we can no wise impute to any wisdom of this world, seeing sin to increase by it; and where worldly wisdom most governeth, there most sin ruleth; for as the world is enemy to God, so also the wisdom thereof is adverse to God, and, therefore, Christ hath declared, and discovered the same to be foolishness. And, although he could have taken away all worldly wisdom, yet he hath left it for his greater glory, and the triumph of his chosen vessels. For before, whereas it was our ruler against God, now, by Christ, we are served of it for God, as of a slave in worldly things; albeit, in supernatural things, the same is not to be understood. And further, if, at any time men would impugn, and gainsay us with the wisdom of the world, yet we have, by Christ, so much supernatural light of the truth, that we make a mock of all those that repugn the truth.

Christ also, upon the cross, hath triumphed over the world. First, because he hath discovered the same to be naught; and that, although it was covered with the veil of hypocrisy, and the vesture of moral virtues. Christ hath showed, that, in God's sight, the righteousness of the world is wickedness, and he hath yielded witness, that the works of men, not regenerated by him in faith, are evil; and so Christ hath judged and condemned the world for naught. Furthermore, he hath given to all his so much light and spirit, that they know it, and dispraise the same; yea and tread it under their feet, with all vain honours, dignities, and pleasures; not taking the fair promises, neither the offers which it presents, nay, they rather make a scorn of them. And, as for the threatenings and force of the world, they nothing fear.

Now, therefore, we may see how great the victory and triumph of Christ is, who hath delivered all those the Father gave him from the power of the devil, cancelling upon the cross the writing of our debts. For he hath delivered us from the condemnation of sin, from the bondage of the law, from the fear of death, from the danger of the world, and from all evils in this life, and in the other to come. And he hath enriched us, made us noble, and most highly happy, after such a glorious and triumphant way, as cannot with tongue be expressed; and, therefore, we are forced to say, his triumph is marvellous.

It is also seen and known, that Christ is the true Messiah; for he hath delivered man from all evils, and by him man hath all goodness, so that he is the true Messiah. Therefore, all other helpers are but vain and counterfeited saviours; seeing that, by this, our Messiah, Christ, wholly and only, we are delivered from all evils, and by him we have all goodness. And that this is true, it is evident and clear, because the very true christian is a christian by Christ. And the true christian feeleth inwardly, by Christ, so much goodness of God, that even troublous life and death are sweet unto him, and miseries are happiness. The true christian, by Christ, is disburdened from the servitude of the law, having the law of grace, graven by the Spirit, inhabiting his heart, and from sin that reigned in him, from the power of the infernal spirits, from damnation, and from every evil; and is made a son of God, a brother of Christ, heir of heaven, and lord of the world; so that, in Christ and by Christ, he possesses all good things.

But let us know that Christ yet fighteth in spirit in his elect vessels, and shall fight even to the day of judgment; at which day shall that great enemy, death, be wholly destroyed, and shall be no more. Then shall the children of God rejoice in him, saying, O death, where is thy victory and sting? there shall be then no more trouble nor sin; nay, rather, none evil, but heaven for the good, and hell for the wicked. Then shall wholly be discovered the victory and triumph of Christ, who, according to Paul, shall present unto his Father the kingdom, together with his chosen saved by him.

It was no little favour towards his children, that Christ was chosen of God to save us, his elect, so highly by the way of the cross. Paul calleth it a grace, and a most singular grace. We may well think, that he, having been to the world so valiant a captain of God, was full of light, grace, virtue, and spirit; therefore, he might justly say, "It is finished." We, seeing then that the triumph and victory of our Captain Christ is so marvellous, glorious, and noble, to the which war we are appointed; let us force ourselves to follow him, with bearing our cross, that we may have fellowship with him in his kingdom.

## The Sixth Chapter.

*That we ought to submit ourselves to the school of the cross, and still look and learn in the book of the cross.*

Truly, it may be most justly verified, that to behold Christ crucified in spirit, is the best meditation that can be. I certainly never knew mine own miseries and wretchedness so well by book, admonition, or learning, as I have done by looking into the spiritual book of the cross. I lament much I have passed so many years, not regarding that divine book; but I judged, and thought myself to be well instructed in the same; whereas now I am of this opinion, that if God would suffer me to live here a thousand years, and I should study continually in the same divine book, I should not be filled with the contemplation thereof. Neither hold I myself contented, but always have a great desire to learn and study more therein. I never knew mine own wickedness, neither lamented for my sins truly, until the time God inspired me with his grace, that I looked in this book; then I began to see perfectly, that mine own power and strength could not help me, and that I was in the Lord's hand, even as the clay is in the potter's hand; then I began to cry and to say:

"Alas! Lord, that ever I have so wickedly offended thee, being to me, from the beginning, so gracious, and so good a Father, and, most specially, now thou hast declared and showed thy goodness unto me, when, in the time, I have done thee most injury, to call me, and also to make me know, and take thee for my Saviour and Redeemer."

Such are the wonderful works of God, to call sinners to repentance, and to make them to take Christ, his well-beloved Son, for their Saviour; this is the gift of God, and of all christians to be required and desired. For, except this great benefit of Christ crucified be felt and fixed surely in man's heart, there can no good work be done acceptable before God; for in Christ is all fulness of the Godhead, and in him are hid all the treasures of wisdom and knowledge: even he is the water of life, whereof whosoever shall drink, he shall never more thirst, but it shall be in him a well of water, springing up into everlasting life. St. Paul saith, There is no damnation to them that are in Christ, which walk not after the flesh, but after the Spirit. Moreover he saith, If, when we were enemies, we were reconciled to God, by the death of his Son, much more, seeing we are reconciled, we shall be preserved by his death. It is no little or small benefit we have received by Christ, if we consider what he hath done for us, as I have perfectly declared heretofore. Wherefore, I pray the Lord, that this great benefit of Christ crucified may be stedfastly fixed and printed in all christians' hearts, that they may be true lovers of God, and work as children, for love, and not as servants, compelled with threatenings, or provoked with hire.

The sincere and pure lovers of God do embrace Christ with such fervency of spirit, that they rejoice in hope, are bold in danger, suffer in adversity, continue in prayer, bless their persecutors. Further, they are not wise in their own opinion, neither high-minded in their prosperity, neither abashed in their adversity, but humble and gentle always to all men. For they know, by their faith, they are members all of one body, and that they have all possessed one God, one faith, one baptism, one joy, and one salvation. If these pure and sincere lovers of God were thickly sown, there should not be so much contention and strife growing on the fields of our religion as there is. Well, I shall pray to the Lord to take all contention and strife away, and that the sowers of sedition may have mind to cease their labour, or to sow it among the stones, and to have grace to sow gracious virtues, where they may both take root, and bring forth fruit, with sending also a godly unity and concord amongst all christians, that we may serve the Lord in true holiness of life.

### THE SEVENTH CHAPTER.

*A christian bewailing the miserable ignorance and blindness of men.*

THE example of good living is required of all christians; but especially in the ecclesiastical pastors and shepherds. For they are called in scripture, workmen with God, disbursers of God's secrets, the light of the world, the salt of the earth; at whose hands all others should take comfort in working, knowledge of God's will, and sight to become children of light, and to taste of seasonable wisdom. They have, or should have, the Holy Spirit, abundantly to pronounce and set forth the word of God, in verity and truth. If ignorance and blindness reign amongst us, they should, with the truth of God's word, instruct and set us in the truth, and direct us in the way of the Lord.

But thanks be given unto the Lord, that hath now sent us such a godly and learned king, in these latter days, to reign over us; that, with the virtue and force of God's word, hath taken away the veils and mists of errors, and brought us to the knowledge of the truth, by the light of God's word; which was so long hid and kept under, that the people were nigh famished, and hungred, for lack of spiritual food. Such was the charity of the spiritual curates and shepherds. But our Moses, and most godly wise governor and king, hath delivered us out of the captivity and bondage of Pharaoh. I mean by this Moses, king Henry the eighth, my most sovereign favourable lord and husband; one, if Moses had figured any more than Christ, through the excellent grace of God, meet to be another expressed verity of Moses's conquest over Pharaoh.* And I mean by this Pharaoh, the bishop of Rome, who hath been, and is a greater persecutor of all true christians, than ever was Pharaoh of the children of Israel; for he is a persecutor of the gospel and grace, a setter forth of all superstition and counterfeit holiness, bringing many souls to hell with his alchemy and counterfeit money, deceiving the poor souls under the pretence of holiness; but so much the greater shall be his damnation, because he deceiveth and robbeth under Christ's mantle. The Lord keep and defend all men from his jugglings and sleights, but especially the poor, simple, and unlearned souls. And this lesson I would all men had of him, that, when they began to mislike his doing, then only begin they to like God, and certainly not before.

As for the spiritual pastors and shepherds, I think they will cleave and stick to the word of God, even to the death; to vanquish all God's enemies, if need shall require; all respects of honour, dignity, riches, wealth, and their private commodities, laid apart; following also the examples of Christ, and his chosen apostles, in preaching and teaching sincere and wholesome doctrine, and such things as make for peace, with godly lessons, wherewith they may edify others; that every man may walk after his vocation in holiness of life, in unity and concord, which unity is to be desired of all true christians.

It is much to be lamented, the schisms, varieties, contentions, and disputations that have been, and are in the world about the christian religion, and no agreement nor concord of the same among the learned men. Truly, the devil hath been the sower of the seed of sedition, and shall be the maintainer of it, even till God's will be fulfilled.

---

* Although these expressions are too favourable for one who was such a slave to his appetites and lusts, yet it must not be forgotten that to Henry the eighth we are indebted, as an instrument, for the scriptures in our own language, and for the beginning of the reformation. He was a coarse instrument, yet well suited to break the iron ands of popery.

There is no war so cruel and evil as this, for the war with sword killeth but the bodies, and this slayeth many souls; for the poor unlearned persons remain confused, and almost every one believeth and worketh after his own way; and yet there is but one truth of God's word, by the which we shall be saved. Happy are they that receive it, and most unhappy are they which neglect and persecute the same. For it shall be more easy for Sodom and Gomorrah, at the day of judgment, than for them. And not without just cause, if we consider the benevolence, goodness, and mercy of God, who hath declared his charity towards us, greater, and more inestimable, than ever he did to the Hebrews. For they lived under shadows and figures, and were bound to the law. And Christ, we being his greatest enemies, hath delivered us from the bondage of the law, and hath fulfilled all that was figured in their law, and also in their prophecies; shedding his own precious blood to make us the children of his Father, and his brethren, and hath made us free, setting us in a godly liberty; I mean not license to sin, as many are glad to interpret the same, when christian liberty is godly entreated of.

Truly, it is no good spirit that moveth men to find fault at every thing, and when things may be well taken, to pervert them into an evil sense and meaning. There are in the world many speakers of holiness and good works, but very rare and seldom is declared, which are the good and holy works. The works of the Spirit are almost never spoken of, and, therefore, very few know what they are. I am able to show the ignorance of the people to be great, not in this matter alone, but in many others, the which were most necessary for christians to know. Because I have had just proof of the same, it makes me thus much to say, with no little sorrow and grief in my heart, for such a miserable ignorance and blindness amongst the people.

I doubt not but we can all say, "Lord, Lord;" but I fear God may say unto us, This people honoureth me with their lips, but their hearts are far from me. God desireth nothing but the heart, and saith, He will be worshipped in spirit and truth. Christ condemned all hypocrisy and feigned holiness, and taught sincere, pure, and true godliness; but we, worse than frantic, or blind, will not follow Christ's doctrine, but trust to men's doctrines, judgments, and sayings, which bedims our eyes, and so the blind lead the blind, and both fall into the ditch. Truly, in my simple and unlearned judgment, no man's doctrine is to be esteemed, or preferred, like unto Christ and the apostles; nor to be taught, as a perfect and true doctrine, but even as it doth accord and agree with the doctrine of the gospel.

But yet, those that are called spiritual pastors, (although they are most carnal, as very evidently and plainly appears by their fruits,) are so blinded with the love of themselves, and the world, that they extol men's inventions and doctrines before the doctrine of the gospel. And when they are not able to maintain their own inventions and doctrines with any jot of the scripture, then they most cruelly persecute them that are contrary to the same. Are such the lovers of Christ? Nay, nay, they are the lovers of the wicked mammon, neither regarding God, nor his honour. For filthy lucre hath made them almost mad, but frantic they are doubtless. Is not this miserable state of spiritual men in the world much to be lamented of all good christians? But yet I cannot allow, neither praise all kind of lamentation, but such as may stand with christian charity.

## THE EIGHTH CHAPTER.

*Of the fruits and rules of true christianity for men to follow.*

CHARITY suffereth long, and is gentle, envieth not, upbraideth no man, casteth frowardly no faults in men's teeth, but referreth all things to God; being angry without sin, reforming others without slanders, carrying ever a storehouse of mild words to pierce the stony-hearted men. I would that all christians, like as they have professed Christ, would so endeavour themselves to follow him in godly living. For we have not put on Christ to live any more to ourselves in the vanities, delights, and pleasures of the world, and the flesh; suffering the concupiscence and carnality of the flesh to have its full swing, for we must walk after the Spirit, and not after the flesh; for the spirit is spiritual, and coveteth spiritual things, and the flesh carnal, and desireth carnal things. The men, regenerate by Christ, despise the world and all the vanities and pleasures thereof; they are no lovers of themselves, for they feel how evil and infirm they are, not being able to do any good thing without the help of God, from whom they acknowledge all goodness to proceed.

They flatter not themselves with thinking every thing to be good and holy which shineth to the world; for they know all external and outward works, be they ever so glorious and fair to the world, may be done of the evil as well as of the good. And, therefore, they have in very little estimation the outward show of holiness, because they are all spiritual, casting up their eyes upon heavenly things; neither looking nor regarding the earthly things, for they are to them vile and abject. They have also the simplicity of the dove, and the policy of the serpent; for, by simplicity, they have a desire to do good to all men, and to hurt no man, no, though they have occasion given; and, by policy, they give not, nor minister any just cause to any man, whereby their doctrine might be reproved. They are not, also, as a reed shaken with every wind; but, when they are blasted with the tempests and storms of the world, then remain they most firm, stable, and quiet, feeling in spirit, that God, as their best Father, doth send, and suffer all things for their benefit and commodity. Christ is to them a rule, a line, and example of christian life; they are never offended at any thing, although occasion be ministered unto them. For, like as Christ, when Peter would have withdrawn him from death, answered, and said, "Go back from me, Satan, for thou offendest me;" that is, As much as lieth in thee, thou givest me occasion with thy words to make me withdraw myself from death, although I yield not thereto; for this, thy procurement, cannot extinguish the burning desire I have to shed my blood for my chosen. Even so the perfect men are never offended at anything; for, although the world were full of sin, they would not withdraw themselves from doing of good, nor wax cold in the love of the Lord. And much less would they be moved to do evil, yea rather, they are so much the more moved to do good.

The regenerated by Christ are never offended at the works of God, because they know, by faith, that God doth all things well; and that he cannot err, either for want of power, or by ignorance, or malice; for they know him to be almighty, and that he seeth all things, and is most abundantly good. They see, and feel in spirit that of the will most highly perfect, cannot but proceed most perfect works. Likewise, they are not offended at the works of men; for, if they are good, they are moved by them to take occasion to follow them, and to acknowledge the goodness of God, with giving of thanks, and praising his name daily the more. But if they are indifferent, and such as may be done with good and evil intents, they judge the best part, thinking they may be done to a good purpose, and so they are edified. But, if they are so evil, that they cannot be taken in good part by any means, yet they are not offended, although occasion be given; nay, rather, they are edified, inasmuch as they take occasion to be better, though the contrary be ministered to them.

Then begin they to think and say thus; If God had not preserved me with his grace, I should have committed this sin and worse. Oh how much am I bound to confess and acknowledge the goodness of God! They go also thinking and saying further; He that hath sinned, may be one of God's elect; peradventure the Lord hath suffered him to fall, to the intent he may the better know himself. I know he is one of them that Christ hath shed his blood for, and one of my christian brethren; truly, I will admonish and rebuke him, and, in case I find him in despair, I will comfort him, and show him the great goodness and mercy of God in Christ; and, with godly consolations, I will see if I can lift him up. And thus ye may see how the men, regenerated by Christ, of every thing, win and receive fruit.

### The Ninth Chapter.
*Of the fruits of infidelity, and offence of weaklings*

And contrariwise, the younglings, and imperfect, are offended at small trifles, taking every thing in evil part, grudging and murmuring against their neighbour; and so much the more, as they show themselves fervent in their so doing, they are judged of the blind world, and of themselves, great zeal-bearers to God. If this were the greatest evil of these younglings, it were not the most evil; but I fear they are so blind and ignorant, that they are offended also at good things, and judge nothing good, but such as they embrace and esteem to be good, with murmuring against all such as follow not their ways. If there are any of this sort, the Lord give them the light of his truth, that they may increase and grow in godly strength. I suppose, if such younglings and imperfect had seen Christ and his disciples, eat meat with unwashen hands, or not to have fasted with the pharisees, they would have been offended, seeing him to be a breaker of men's traditions. Their affections dispose their eyes to see through other men, and they see nothing in themselves; where charity, although it be most full of eyes, to see the faults of others, whom it coveteth to amend, thinketh none evil, but discreetly and rightly interpreteth all things, by the which every thing is taken more justly and truly.

Now, these superstitious weaklings, if they had been conversant with Christ, and had seen him lead his life, sometime with women, sometime with Samaritans, with publicans, sinners, and with the pharisees, they would have murmured at him. Also, if they had seen Mary pour upon Christ the precious ointment, they would have said, with Judas, This ointment might have been sold, and given to the poor. If they also had seen Christ, with whips, drive out of the temple those that bought and sold, they would forthwith have judged Christ to have been troubled and moved with anger, and not by zeal of charity. How would they have been offended, if they had seen him go to the Jews' feast, heal a sick man upon the sabbath day, practise with the woman of Samaria, yea, and show unto her of his most divine doctrine and life! They would have taken occasion to have hated and persecuted him, as the scribes and pharisees did; and even so should Christ, the Saviour of the world, have been to them an offence and ruin.

There are another kind of little ones imperfect, which are offended after this sort and manner. As when they see one that is reputed and esteemed holy, to commit sin, forthwith they learn to do that, and worse, and wax cold in doing of good, and confirm themselves in evil; and then they excuse their wicked life, publishing the same with the slander of their neighbour. If any man reprove them, they say, Such a man did this, and worse. So it is evident that such persons would deny Christ, if they saw other men do the same. If they went to Rome, and saw the enormities of the prelates, which are said to reign there amongst them, I doubt not, if they saw one of them sin, who was reputed and taken for holy, their faith would be lost, but not the faith of Christ, which they never possessed; but they should lose that human opinion which they had of tne goodness of the prelates. For, if they had the faith of Christ, the Holy Ghost should be a witness unto them; the which should be mighty in them, that, in case all the world would deny Christ, yet they would remain firm and stable in the true faith.

The pharisees also took occasion of the evil of others, to wax haughty and proud, taking themselves to be men of greater perfection than any others because of their virtue; even as the pharisee did when he saw the publican's submission. And so they are offended with every little thing, judging evil, murmuring against their neighbour; and, for the same, they are of many reputed, and taken for the more holy and good, whereas, indeed, they are the more wicked. The most wicked persons are offended even at themselves; for, at their little stability in goodness, and of their detestable and evil life, they take occasion to despair, where they ought the more to commit themselves to God, asking mercy for their offences; and, forthwith, to give thanks, that it hath pleased him of his goodness to suffer them so long a time.

But what needs it any more to say that evil men are offended even at the works of God? They see God suffer sinners, therefore, think they, sin displeases him not. And, because they see not the good rewarded with riches, oftentimes they imagine that God loveth them not. It seemeth to them God is partial, because he hath elected some, and some reproved. And therefore they say, that the elected are sure of salvation; taking, by that, occasion to do evil enough, saying, Whatsoever God hath determined, shall be performed. If also they see the good men oppressed, and the evil men exalted, they judge God to be unjust, taking occasion to live evil, saying, Inasmuch as God favoureth the naughty men, let us do evil enough, to the intent he do us good. If then the wicked be offended, even at God, it is no wonder if they are offended at those that follow and walk in his paths and ways.

### The Tenth Chapter.

*Of carnal gospellers, by whose evil living, God's truth is shamefully slandered.*

I WILL now speak with great dolour and heaviness in my heart, of a sort of people which are in the world, that are called professors of the gospel, and, by their words, do declare and show they are much affected to the same. But, I am afraid, some of them do build upon the sand, as Simon Magus did, making a weak foundation. I mean, they make not Christ their chief foundation; professing his doctrine, of a sincere, pure, and zealous mind; but either because they would be called gospellers, to procure some credit and good opinion of the true and very favourers of Christ's doctrine; or to find out some carnal liberty, or to be contentious disputers, finders, or rebukers of other men's faults; or else, finally, to please and flatter the world. Such gospellers are an offence, and a slander to the word of God, and make the wicked to rejoice and laugh at them, saying, Behold, I pray you, their fair fruits. What charity, what discretion, what godliness, holiness, or purity of life is among them? Are not they great avengers, foul gluttons, slanderers, backbiters, adulterers, fornicators, swearers, and blasphemers, yea, and wallow and tumble in all sins? These are the fruits of their doctrine.

And thus it may be seen how the word of God is evil spoken of, through licentious and evil living; and yet the word of God is all holy, pure, sincere, and godly, being the doctrine and occasion of all holy and pure living. It is the wicked that pervert all good things into evil, for an evil tree cannot bring forth good fruit; and, when good seed is sown in a barren and evil ground, it yieldeth no good corn; and so it fareth by the word of God. For, when that is heard, and known of wicked men, it bringeth no good fruit; but when it is sown in good ground, I mean the hearts of good people, it bringeth forth good fruit abundantly; so that the want and fault is in men, and not in the word of God. I pray God, all men and women may have grace to become meet tillage for the fruits of the gospel, and to leave only the jangling of it. For, only speaking of the gospel makes not men good christians, but good talkers, except their facts and works agree with the same; so then their speech is good, because their hearts are good. And even as much talk of the word of God, without practising the same in our living, is evil and detestable in the sight of God; so it is a lamentable thing to hear, how there are many in the world that do not well digest the reading of scripture, and do commend and praise ignorance, and say, " That much knowledge of God's word is the original of all dissension, schisms, and contention; and makes men haughty, proud, and presumptuous, by reading of the same."

This manner of saying is no less than a plain blasphemy against the Holy Ghost. For the Spirit of God is the author of his word, and so the Holy Ghost is made the author of evil, which is a most great blasphemy, and, as the scripture saith, a sin that shall not be forgiven in this world, neither in the other to come. It were all our parts and duties to procure and seek all the ways and means possible, to have more knowledge of God's word set forth abroad in the world, and not to allow ignorance, and to discommend knowledge of God's word, stopping the mouths of the unlearned with subtle and crafty persuasions of philosophy and sophistry, whereof comes no fruit, but a great perturbation of the mind to the simple and ignorant, not knowing which way to turn them. For, is it not extreme wickedness to charge the holy, sanctified word of God with the offences of man? Or, to allege the scriptures to be perilous learning, because certain readers thereof fall into heresies?

These men might be enforced by this kind of argument, to forsake the use of fire, because fire burneth their neighbour's house; or to abstain from meat and drink, because they see many are surfeited. Oh blind hate! They slander God for man's offence, and excuse the man whom they see offend, and blame the scripture which they cannot improve. Yea, I have heard of some who have very well understood the Latin tongue, that when they have heard learned men persuade to the credit and belief of certain unwritten verities, as they call them, which are not in scripture expressed, and yet taught as doctrine apostolic, and necessary to be believed; they have been of this opinion, that the learned men have more epistles written by the apostles of Christ, than we have abroad in the canon of the Old and New Testament, or are known of any, but only to them of the clergy. Which belief I did not a little lament in my heart to hear, that any creature should have such a blind, ignorant opinion.

Some kind of simplicity is to be praised; but this simplicity, without the verity, I can neither praise nor allow. And thus it may be seen, how we, that are unlettered, remain confused, unless God, of his grace, enlighten our hearts and minds with a heavenly light and knowledge of his will; for we are given, of ourselves, to believe men better than God. I pray God to send all learned men the Spirit of God abundantly, that their doctrine may bring forth the fruits thereof. I suppose there never was more need of good doctrine to be set forth in the world, than now in this age; for the carnal children of Adam are so wise in their generation, that, if it were possible, they would deceive the children of light. The world loveth his own, and, therefore, their facts and doings are highly esteemed of the world; but the children of God are hated, because they are not of the world; for their habitation is in heaven, and they do despise the world as a most vile slave.

The fleshly children of Adam are so politic, subtle, crafty, and wise, in their kind, that the elect should be deceived, if it were possible. For they are clothed with Christ's garment in outer appearance, with a fair show of all godliness and holiness in their words; but they have so shorn, nopped, and turned Christ's garment, and have so disguised themselves, that the children of light, beholding them with a spiritual eye, do account and take them for men which have sold their master's garment, and have stolen a piece of every man's garment; yet, by their subtle art, and crafty wits, they have so set those patches and pieces together, that they do make the blind world and carnal men to believe it is Christ's very mantle

## THE ELEVENTH CHAPTER.

*Of the virtuous properties of God's children, of whom every one attendeth his vocation.*

BUT the children of light know the contrary; for they are led by the Spirit of God to the knowledge of the truth, and therefore they discern and judge all things right, and know from whence they come, even from the bishop of Rome and his members, the headspring of all pride, vain glory, ambition, hypocrisy, and feigned holiness.

The children of God are not abashed, although the world hate them; they believe they are in the grace and favour of God, and that he, as a best father, doth govern them in all things, putting away from them all vain confidence and trust in their own doings; for they know they can do nothing but sin, of themselves. They are not so foolish and childish, as not to give God thanks for their election, which was before the beginning of the world; for they believe most surely they are of the chosen; for the Holy Ghost doth witness to their spirit, that they are the children of God, and, therefore, they believe God better than man. They say, with St. Paul, Who shall separate us from the love of God? Shall tribulation, anguish, persecution, hunger, nakedness, peril, or sword? As it is written, For thy sake are we killed all day long, and are accounted as sheep appointed to be slain; nevertheless, in all these things we overcome, through Him that loveth us. For I am sure, that neither death, nor life, neither angels, nor rule, neither power, neither things present, neither things to come, neither quantity or quality, neither any creature, shall be able to depart us from the love of God, which is in Christ Jesus our Lord.

They are not, by this godly faith, presumptuously inflamed; nor, by the same, become they loose, idle, or slow in doing of godly works, as carnal men dream of them; so much the more fervent they are in doing most holy and pure works, which God hath commanded them to walk in. They wander not in men's traditions and inventions, leaving the most holy and pure precepts of God undone, which they know they are bound to observe and keep. Also, they work not like hirelings, for need, wages, or reward; but, as loving children, without respect of lucre, gain, or hire; they are in such liberty of spirit, and joy so much in God, that their inward consolation cannot be expressed with tongue. All fear of damnation is gone from them, for they have put their whole hope of salvation in His hands, who will and can perform it; neither have they any post or pillar to lean to, but God, and his smooth, unwrinkled church; for he is to them all, in all things, and to him they lean, as a most sure square pillar, in prosperity and adversity; nothing doubting of his promises and covenants, for they believe most surely they shall be fulfilled.

Also, the children of God are not curious in searching the high mysteries of God, which are not meet for them to know. Neither do they go about with human and carnal reasons to interpret scripture, persuading men, by their subtle wits and carnal doctrine, that much knowledge of scripture maketh men heretics, without they temper it with human doctrine, sophistry, philosophy, and logic, wherewith to be seduced, according to the traditions of men, after the ordinances of the world, and not after Christ, as

St. Paul doth most diligently admonish us; which arts are not convenient and meet to be made checkmate with scripture; for the scriptures are so pure and holy, that no perfection can be added unto them; for, even as fine gold doth excel all other metals, so doth the word of God all men's doctrines. I beseech the Lord to send the learned and unlearned such abundance of his Holy Spirit, that they may obey and observe the most sincere and holy word of God, and show the fruits thereof, which consist chiefly in charity and godly unity—that, as we have professed one God, one faith, and one baptism, so we may be all of one mind, and one accord, putting away all biting and gnawing; for, in backbiting, slandering, and mis-reporting our christian brethren, we show not ourselves the disciples of Christ whom we profess. In Him was most high charity, humility, and patience, suffering most patiently all ignominy, rebukes, and slanders, praying to his eternal Father for his enemies with most perfect charity; and, in all things, he did remit his will to his Father's, as the scripture doth witness, when he prayed in the mount. A godly example and lesson for us to follow at all times and seasons, as well in prosperity as in adversity; to have no will but God's will, committing and leaving to him all our cares and griefs, and to abandon all our policies and inventions; for they are most vain and foolish, and, indeed, very shadows and dreams.

But we are yet so carnal and fleshly, that we run headlong, like unbridled colts without snaffle or bridle. If we had the love of God printed in our hearts, it would keep us back from running astray. And, until such time as it please God to send us this bit to hold us in, we shall never run the right way, although we speak and talk ever so much of God and his word. The true followers of Christ's doctrine have always a respect and an eye to their vocation. If they are called to the ministry of God's word, they preach and teach it sincerely, to the edifying of others, and show themselves in their living followers of the same. If they are married men, having children and family, they nourish and bring them up, without all bitterness and fierceness, in the doctrine of the Lord, in all godliness and virtue; committing the instruction of others, which appertain not to their charge, to the reformation of God, and his ministers, which chiefly are kings and princes, bearing the sword even for that purpose to punish evil doers. If they are children, they honour their father and mother, knowing it to be God's commandment, and that he hath thereto annexed a promise of long life. If they are servants, they obey and serve their masters with all fear and reverence, even for the Lord's sake, neither with murmuring nor grudging, but with a free heart and mind.

If they are husbands, they love their wives as their own bodies; after the example as Christ loved the congregation, and gave himself for it, to make it to him a spouse without spot or wrinkle. If they are women married, they learn of St. Paul to be obedient to their husbands, and to keep silence in the congregation, and to learn of their husbands at home. Also, they wear such apparel as becometh holiness and comely usage with soberness; not being accusers or detractors; not given to much eating or delicate meats, and drinking of wine; but they teach honest things, to make the young women sober-minded, to love their husbands, to love their children, to be discreet, chaste, housewifely, good, and obedient unto their husbands, that the word of God be not evil spoken of. Verily, if all sorts of people would look to their own vocation, and ordain the same, according to Christ's doctrine, we should not have so many eyes and ears to other men's faults as we have. For we are so busy and glad to find and espy out other men's doings, that we forget, and can have no time to weigh and ponder our own; which, after the word of God, we ought first to reform, and then we shall the better help another to take the straw out of his eyes.

But, alas! we are so much given to love and to flatter ourselves, and so blinded with carnal affections, that we can see and perceive no fault in ourselves; and, therefore, it is a thing very requisite and necessary for us, to pray all, with one heart and mind to God, to give us a heavenly light and knowledge of our own miseries and calamities; that we may see them, and acknowledge them truly before him.

### The Twelfth Chapter.

*The conclusion, with a christian exhortation to the amendment of Life.*

If any man shall be offended at this my lamenting the faults of men which are in the world, fantasing with themselves, that I do it either of hatred or of malice to any sort or kind of people, verily, in so doing, they shall do me great wrong; for, I thank God, by his grace, I hate no creature—yea, I would say more, to give witness of my conscience, that neither life, honour, riches, neither whatsoever I possess here, which appertaineth to mine own private commodity, be it ever so dearly beloved of me, but most willingly and gladly I would leave it to win any man to Christ, of what degree, or sort soever he were. And yet is this nothing, in comparison to the charity that God hath showed me, in sending Christ to die for me. No, if I had all the charity of angels, and apostles, it should be but like a spark of fire, compared to a great heap of burning coals.

God knoweth of what intent and mind I have lamented mine own sins and faults to the world. I trust nobody will judge that I have done it for praise or thanks of any creature; since, rather, I might be ashamed, than rejoice in rehearsal thereof. For, if they knew how little I esteem and weigh the praise of the world, that opinion were soon removed and taken away; for, I thank God, by his grace, I know the world to be a blind judge, and the praises thereof to be vain and of little moment; and, therefore, I seek not the praises of the same, nor to satisfy it, none otherwise than I am taught by Christ to do, according to christian charity. I would to God we would all, when occasion doth serve, confess our faults to the world, all respects of our own commodity laid apart. But, alas! self-love doth so much reign among us, that, as I have said before, we cannot espy our own faults. And although, sometimes we find our own guilt, either we are favourable to interpret it no sin, or else we are ashamed to confess ourselves thereof; yea, and we are sorely offended and grieved to hear our faults charitably and godly told us of others, putting no difference between charitable warning and malicious accusing.

Truly, if we sought God's glory, as we should do in all things, we should not be ashamed to confess ourselves to digress from God's precepts and ordinances, when it is manifest we have done, and daily do so. I pray God, our own faults and deeds condemn us not at the last day, when every man shall be rewarded according to his doings. Truly, if we do not redress and amend our living according to the doctrine of the gospel, we shall receive a terrible sentence of Christ the Son of God, when he shall come to judge and condemn all transgressors, and breakers of his precepts and commandments, and to reward all his obedient and loving children. We shall have no man of law to make our plea for us, neither can we have the day deferred; neither will the Judge be corrupted with affection, bribes, or reward; neither will he hear any excuse or delay; neither shall this saint, or that martyr, help us, be they ever so holy; neither shall our ignorance save us from damnation; but yet wilful blindness, and obstinate ignorance, shall receive greater punishment, and not without just cause. Then shall it be known who hath walked in the dark; for all things shall appear manifest before him; no man's deeds shall be hidden, no, nor words nor thoughts. The poor and simple observers of God's commandments shall be rewarded with everlasting life, as obedient children to the heavenly Father; and the transgressors, adders to, and diminishers from, the law of God, shall receive eternal damnation for their just reward. I beseech God we may escape this fearful sentence, and be found such faithful servants, and loving children, that we may hear the happy, comfortable, and most joyful sentence ordained for the children of God, which is:

Come hither, ye blessed of my Father, and receive the kingdom of heaven prepared for you before the beginning of the world.

Now unto the Father, the Son, and the Holy Ghost, be all honour and glory, world without end. Amen.

# THE EXAMINATIONS

## OF

# ANNE ASKEW,

LATELY MARTYRED IN SMITHFIELD, BY THE ROMISH POPE'S UPHOLDERS.

*(Written by herself, and published by John Bale. Some further particulars are added from Fox and Strype.)*

---

The verity of the Lord endureth for ever.—Psalm cxvii.
Anne Askew stood fast by this verity of God to the end.

---

FAVOUR IS DECEITFUL, AND BEAUTY IS A VAIN THING. BUT A WOMAN THAT FEARETH THE LORD IS WORTHY TO BE PRAISED. SHE OPENETH HER MOUTH TO WISDOM, AND IN HER LANGUAGE IS THE LAW OF GRACE.—Prov. xxxi.

Printed A. D. 1546.

The persecution urged forward by bishop Gardiner and his associates during the latter years of Henry VIII., was aimed at queen Catherine Parr, and several of her attendants, with others of rank at court. The narrow escape of the queen has been related; but one of her attendants, Mrs. Anne Askew, and a gentleman of the royal household, named Lascels, were burned.

Anne Askew* was the second daughter of Sir William Askew, of Kelsey in Lincolnshire. A marriage was planned between the eldest sister and the heir of a neighbouring gentleman named Kyme, but she died before the union took place. Sir William, unwilling to lose an advantageous match, compelled his second daughter to marry Kyme. The marriage was against her will, but when it had taken place, she demeaned herself like a christian wife, and became the mother of two children. After a time, by the study of the scriptures, she was convinced of the errors of popery, and became a true follower of Christ. Her husband, being a bigoted papist, was much enraged at this change, and after a series of ill treatment, by the advice of his priests, violently drove her from his house. She came to London, where she attended upon the queen, and sought a divorce on the ground of her husband's conduct, considering that his cruel usage had released her obligations, according to the principle laid down by St. Paul, 1 Cor. vii. 15.

Anne Askew's beauty, learning, and piety, procured her much esteem from the queen's friends, while she was hated by Gardiner and his party. Her conduct was irreproachable. A strong testimony in her favour was borne by a papist, according to the following relation from Strype. " A great papist of Wickham college, called Wadloe, a cursitor of the chancery, hot in his religion, and thinking not well of her life, got himself lodged at the next house to her. For what purpose need not be opened. But the conclusion was, that instead of speaking evil of her, he gave her the praise to sir Leonil Throgmorton, for the devoutest and godliest woman that ever he knew. For, said he, at midnight she beginneth to pray, and ceaseth not for many hours after, when I, and others are at sleep or at work."

In 1546, she was accused of heresy, and made an undaunted profession of the truth, an account of which being penned by her own hand, was conveyed to Bale, and printed by him in Germany. Bale accompanied it with severe reflections upon the conduct of the Romanists towards her, which it does not appear necessary to reprint, as the affecting narrative is a sufficient comment upon the proceedings of her persecutors.

* Her name is also spelled Ascue and Ayscough.

# JOHN BALE TO THE CHRISTIAN READERS.

Among other most singular offices, diligent reader, which the Lord hath appointed to be done in the earnest spirit of Elias, by the forerunners of his latter appearance, this is one very special to be noted, They shall turn the hearts of their ancient elders into the children, Mal. iv. and the unbelievers of their time to the wisdom of those righteous fathers, as did John Baptist before his first coming, Luke i. That is, saith Bede, "The faith and fervent zeal of the prophets and apostles shall they plant in their hearts, which shall in those days live, and be among men conversant, and then will break forth (saith he, as a very true prophet) such horrible persecution, as will first of all take from the world those mighty Elias's, by triumphant martyrdom, to the terrifying of others in the same faith, of whom some shall become, through that occasion, most glorious martyrs unto Christ also; and some very wicked apostates, forsaking his lively doctrine." For, by the said Bede's testimony in the beginning of the same chapter, two most certain signs shall we then have that the latter judgment day is at hand; the return of Israel's remnant unto their Lord God, and the horrible persecutions of antichrist.

Confer with this treated scripture and former prophecy of that virtuous man Bede, the world's alteration now, with the terrible turmoilings of our time; and, as in a most clear mirror, ye shall well perceive them at this present to be in most quick working. And as concerning the Israelites or Jews, I have both seen and known of them in Germany, most faithful christian believers. Neither is it in the prophecy, Hos. iii. that they should at that day be all converted, any more than they were at John Baptist's preaching, Luke i. For as Isaiah reporteth, Though the posterity of Jacob be as the sea sand, innumerable, yet shall but a remnant of them convert them unto their Lord God, Isa. x. And though the Lord hath sifted that house of Israel, as bruised corn in a sieve, among all other nations, Amos ix. yet shall not that remnant of theirs perish, but at that day be saved, through the only election of grace, Rom. xi.

Now concerning the aforesaid forerunners, in this most wonderful change of the world before the latter end thereof; I think within this realm of England, besides other nations abroad, the spirit of Elias was not all asleep in good William Tindal, Robert Barnes, and such others more, whom antichrist's violence hath sent hence in fire to heaven, as Elias went before in the fiery chariot, 2 Kings ii.

These turned the hearts of the fathers unto the children, such time as they took from a great number of our nation, by their godly preachings and writings, the corrupted belief of the pope and his master workers, which were no fathers but cruel robbers and destroyers, John x. reducing them again to the true faith of Abraham and Peter, Gen. xv. and Matt. xvi. The pure belief in Christ's birth and passion, which Adam and Noah sucked out of the first promise of God, Jacob and Moses out of the second, David and the prophets out of the third, and so forth, the apostles and fathers out of the other scriptures, so firmly planted they in the consciences of many, that no cruel kind of death could avert them from it. As we have for example their constant disciples, and now strong witnesses of Jesus Christ, John Lascels and ANNE ASKEW, with their other two companions, very glorious martyrs before God, though they are not so before the wrong judging eyes of the world, whom the bloody remnant of antichrist put unto most cruel death in Smithfield at London, in the year of our Lord 1546, in July.

If they only, as was John Baptist, are great before the Lord, by the holy scriptures' allowance, who are strongly adorned with the graces of his Spirit, as faith, force, understanding, wisdom, patience, love, long sufferance and such like; I dare boldly affirm these four mighty witnesses also to be the same, so well as the martyrs of the primitive or apostles' church. For these had those virtues as strongly as they, and as boldly objected their bodies to the death, for the undefiled christian belief, against the malignant synagogue of Satan as ever did they, for no tyranny admitting any created or corruptible substance for their eternal living God.* If the blind babes, to prove them unlike, do object against me the miracles showed at their deaths more than at these, as that unfaithful generation is ever desirous of wonders, Matt. xii. I would but know of them what miracles were showed when John Baptist's head was cut off in the prison?

* Not believing the sacramental bread to be the real body of Christ.

Mark vi. and when James the apostle was beheaded at Jerusalem? Acts xii. These two were excellent before God, though they were but miserable wretches, light fellows, seditious heretics, busy knaves, and vile beggars, in the sight of noble king Herod and his honourable council of prelates.

If to maintain their purpose, they allege of Stephen, that he at his death beheld heaven open; I ask them again, what they were who saw it more than his own person? Sure I am, that their wicked predecessors there present saw it not. For they stopped their ears when he told them thereof, Acts vii. If they yet bring forth the other histories of apostles and martyrs, I answer them, that all they are of no such authority as these before spoken of. The pope's martyrs, indeed, were much fuller of miracles than ever were Christ's, as himself told us they should be so, Matt. xxiv. Yet friar Forest, John Fisher, and Thomas More wrought no miracles, though many are now registered in their lives and legends by the friars of France, Italy, Spain, and others. And as for the holy maid of Kent with doctor Bocking, though they wrought great wonders by their life, yet none appeared at their deaths. Of his own chosen martyrs Christ looketh for none other miracle, but that only they persevere faithful to the end, Matt. x. and never deny his verity before men, Luke xii. For that worthy victory of the sinful world, standeth in the invincibleness of faith, and not in miracles and wonders, as those wavering understandings suppose, 1 John v.

Right wonderfully will this appear in the two mighty conflicts hereafter following, which the faithful servant of Jesus, ANNE ASKEW, a gentlewoman, very young, dainty, [delicate,] and tender, had with that outraging synagogue in her two examinations, about the twenty-fifth year of her age, which she sent abroad by her own hand-writing. The handlings of her other three companions shall be showed in other several treatises at leisure. For the glory and great power of the Lord, so manifestly appearing in his elect vessels, may not now perish at all hands, and be unthankfully neglected, but be spread the world over, as well in Latin as English, to the perpetual infamy of such wilfully cruel and spiteful tyrants. Nothing at all shall it terrify us, nor yet in any point hinder us of our purpose, that our books are now in England condemned and burned by the bishops and priests, with their frantic affinity, the great antichrist's upholders, which seek by all practices possible to turn over the king's most noble and godly enterprize. But it will from henceforth occasion us to set forth in the Latin also that which before we wrote only in English, and so make their spiritual wickedness and treason known much farther off. What availed it Jehoiakim to burn Jeremiah's prophecy, by the ungracious counsel of his prelates? Jer. xxxvi. Or yet Antiochus to set fire on the other scriptures, as told in the book of Maccabees.

After the apostles were brought before the council, and straitly commanded to cease from preaching, they preached much more than before, Acts iv. In most terrible persecution of the primitive church, were the examinations and answers, torments and deaths, of the constant martyrs written, and sent abroad all the world over, as Eusebius testifies in his ecclesiastical history. Their copies abound yet every where. Great slaughter and burning hath been here in England for John Wickliff's books ever since the year of our Lord 1382, yet have not one of them thoroughly perished. I have at this hour the titles of one hundred and forty-four of them, which are many more in number. For some of them under one title comprehend two books, some three, some four; yea, one of them containeth twelve. I think not the contrary, but ere the world is at a full end, God will so glorify that twenty times condemned heretic,[*] execrated, cursed, spitted, and spatled at, that all your popish writers before his time and after, will be reckoned but vile swineherds to him, for the good favour he bare to Christ's holy gospel. A very madness is it to strive against God, when he will have the long hidden iniquities known. As the wise man, Gamaliel, said, Acts v. If this enterprise that is now taken against you be of God, ye shall never be able with all your tyrannous practices to dissolve it.

Now concerning that blessed woman, ANNE ASKEW, who lately suffered the tyranny of this world for righteousness' sake. In Lincolnshire was she born, of a very ancient and noble stock; sir William Askew, a worthy knight, being her father. But no worthiness in the flesh, nor yet any worldly nobleness availeth to God-ward, before whom is no acceptation of person, Acts x. It is only faith, with his true love and fear, which makes us the accepted, noble, and worthy children unto God, John i. Whereof, by his gift,

[*] Wickliff.

she had wonderful abundance. Such a one was she as was Lydia, the purple-seller, whose heart the Lord opened, by the godly preaching of Paul at Thyatira, Acts xvi. For she gave diligent heed to his word when it was once taught without superstition, and would no longer be a false worshipper or idolater after the wicked school of antichrist; but became from thenceforth a true worshipper, worshipping her Lord God, (which is a Spirit and not bread,) in spirit and in verity, according to that word of his, John iv. The gospel of Christ she bare in her heart, as did the holy maid Cecilia, and never after ceased from the study thereof, nor from godly communication and prayer, till she was by most cruel torments taken from this wretched world.

I do here as to her, dear friends in the Lord, as did the faithful brethren in France, at the cities of Lyons and Vienne, by a like faithful young woman called Blandina, who was there put to death with three mighty companions among others more, as this was, for her christian belief, about the year of our Lord 170, in the primitive spring of their christianity.* They wrote unto their brethren in the lands of Asia and Phrygia, very far off, her mighty strong sufferings for Christ's faith, which they knew nothing of before. I write here unto you in England the double process of this noble woman whereof ye are not ignorant, forsomuch as it was there so manifestly done among you. I have coupled these two examples together, because I find them in so many points agree. Blandina was young and tender, so was Anne Askew also. But that which was frail of nature in them both, Christ made most strong by his grace. Blandina had three earnest companions in Christ, Maturus, Sanctus, and Attalus, fervently faithful as herself. So had Anne Askew three fire fellows; a gentleman called John Lascels, her instructor a priest, and a tailor called John Adams, men in Christ's verity most constant unto the end. With Blandina were in prison to the number of ten, who denied the truth, and were clearly forsaken of God for it. How many fell from Christ besides Crome and Shaxton, when Anne Askew stood fast by him, I am uncertain.† But I counsel them as St. John counselled the Laodiceans, in the miserable estate they are now in, to buy them thorough tried gold of Christ, lest they perish altogether, Rev. iii. If they had not

* See History of the Church of Christ, Vol. I.
† See Fox, Acts and Monuments.

still remained in that channel, whom Christ commanded John in no wise to measure, Rev. xi. they had never so shamefully blasphemed, like as Bede also toucheth in his former prophecy.

Prompt was Blandina, and of most strong courage, in rendering her life for the liberty of her faith; no less lively and quick was Anne Askew in all her imprisonings and torments. Great was the love Blandina had to Christ; no less was the love of Anne Askew. Blandina never fainted in torment; no more did Anne Askew in spirit, when she was so terribly racked of Wriothesly the chancellor, and Rich, that the strings of her arms and eyes were perished. Blandina derided the cruelty of the tyrants; so did Anne Askew the madness of the bishops and their speechmen. Red burning plates of iron and of brass had Blandina put to her sides; so had Anne Askew the flaming brands of fire. Full of God and his verity was Blandina; so was Anne Askew to the very end. Christ wonderfully triumphed in Blandina; so did he in Anne Askew, when she made no noise on the rack, and so earnestly afterward rejoiced in him. Blandina was given forth to wild beasts to be devoured; so was Anne Askew to cruel bishops and priests, whom Christ calleth ravening wolves, devourers, and thieves, Matt. vii. John x. Blandina upon the scaffold boldly reprehended the pagan priests for their error; so did Anne Askew, when she was fast tied to the stake, with courage rebuke that blasphemous apostate Shaxton, with the bishops' and priests' generation, for their manifest maintenance of idolatry.

Blandina, at the stake, showed a visage unterrified; so did Anne Askew, a countenance stout, mighty, and earnest. Indefatigable was the spirit of Blandina; so was the spirit of Anne Askew. The love of Jesus Christ, the gift of the Holy Ghost, and hope of the crown of martyrdom, greatly mitigated the pain in Blandina; so did those three worthy graces the terror of all torments in Anne Askew. The strong spirit of Christ gave courage to Blandina; the same mighty Spirit, and not the pope's desperate spirit, made Anne Askew both to rejoice and to sing in the prison. So bold was Blandina, saith Eusebius, that she communed with Christ unseen. I suppose Anne Askew's latter examination will show her not to be much less. Gentle was Blandina to the christian believers, and terrible to their adversaries; so was Anne Askew, very lowly to true teachers, but scornful and high stomached to the enemies of truth. Many were converted by the sufferings of Blandina; a far greater number by the burning of Anne Askew. Though Blandina were young, yet was she called the mother of martyrs; many men have supposed Anne Askew, for her christian constancy, to be no less. Blandina prayed for her persecutors; so did Anne Askew most fervently. The ashes of Blandina, and of other martyrs, were thrown into the flood of the Rhone; what was done with the ashes of Anne Askew and her companions, I cannot yet tell.

All these former reports of Blandina, and many more besides, hath Eusebius in his Ecclesiastical History, and others also have the same. And, as touching Anne Askew, these two examinations, with her other known handlings in England, are sufficient witnesses for her. Thus the fire hath not taken Anne Askew wholly from the world, but left her here unto it, more pure, perfect, and precious than before. So that concerning her it may well be said, as Paul verifies, 2 Cor. xii. The strength of God is here made perfect by weakness. When she seemed most feeble, then was she most strong; and gladly she rejoiced in that weakness, that Christ's power might strongly dwell in her. Thus the Lord chooseth the foolish of this world to confound the wise, and the weak to deface the mighty; yea, things despised, and thought very vile, to bring things to nought which the world hath in most high reputation. I think if this martyr were rightly conferred* with those canonized martyrs which have had, and yet still have censings and singings, massings and ringings in the pope's English church, cause with cause, and reason with reason, as haply hereafter they shall be, she should be a great blemish unto them. An example of strong sufferance might this holy martyr be unto all them that the Lord shall after like manner put forward in this horrible fury of antichrist, to the glory of his persecuted church. Amen.

* Compared.

# THE FIRST EXAMINATION

### OF

# MISTRESS ANNE ASKEW,

BEFORE THE INQUISITORS, 1545. WRITTEN BY HERSELF.

To satisfy your expectation, good people, this was my first examination in the year of our Lord, 1545, and in the month of March.

First, Christopher Dare examined me at Sadler's hall, being one of the quest,* and asked if I did not believe that the sacrament hanging over the altar, was the very body of Christ really. Then I demanded this question of him, Wherefore St. Stephen was stoned to death? and he said he could not tell. Then I answered, that no more would I assoil† his vain question.

Secondly, he said that there was a woman which did testify that I should read, how God was not in temples made with hands. Then I showed him the seventh and seventeenth chapters of the Acts of the Apostles, what Stephen and Paul had said therein. Whereupon he asked me how I took those sentences? I answered, that I would not throw pearls among swine, for acorns were good enough.

Thirdly, he asked me, wherefore I said that I had rather read five lines in the bible, than hear five masses in the temple? I confessed that I said no less, not for the dispraise of either the epistle or gospel, but because the one did greatly edify me, and the other nothing at all. As St. Paul doth witness in the fourteenth chapter of his first epistle to the Corinthians, where he saith, If the trumpet giveth an uncertain sound, who will prepare himself to the battle?

Fourthly, he laid unto my charge that I should say, if an ill priest ministered, it was the devil and not God.

My answer was, that I never spake such thing. But this was my saying—that whosoever he were that ministered unto me, his ill conditions could not hurt my faith, but in spirit I received, nevertheless, the body and blood of Christ.

* Or inquisitors appointed to enforce the act of six articles. See the life of Cranmer, page 28.
† Explain, reply to.

Fifth, he asked me what I said concerning confession? I answered him my meaning, which was as St. James saith, that every man ought to acknowledge his faults to other; and the one to pray for the other.

Sixthly, he asked me what I said to the king's book?* And I answered him, that I could say nothing to it, because I never saw it.

Seventhly, he asked me if I had the Spirit of God in me? I answered, If I had not, I was but a reprobate or cast away. Then he said he had sent for a priest to examine me, who was there at hand. The priest asked me what I said to the sacrament of the altar, and required much to know therein my meaning. But I desired him again to hold me excused concerning that matter. None other answer would I make him, because I perceived him to be a papist.

Eighthly, he asked me, if I did not think, that private masses did help souls departed. I said, it was great idolatry to believe more in them, than in the death which Christ died for us.

Then they had me thence unto my lord mayor, and he examined me, as they had before, and I answered him directly in all things as I answered the quest before. Besides this, my lord mayor laid one thing to my charge, which was never spoken of me, but of them; and that was, whether a mouse eating the host, received God or no. This question did I never ask, but indeed they asked it of me, whereunto I made them no answer, but smiled.†

Then the bishop's chancellor rebuked me and said, that

\* See Cranmer, p. 33. 86.

† Strype on Loud's authority, relates this more particularly. "My lord mayor, sir Martin Bowes, sitting with the council, as most meet for his wisdom, and seeing her standing upon life and death, said, 'I pray you, my lords, give me leave to talk with this woman;' leave was granted. *L. M.* Thou foolish woman, sayest thou that the priests cannot make the body of Christ? *A. A.* I say so, my lord; for I have read that God made man; but that man can make God I never yet read, nor ever shall read it, as I suppose. *L. M.* No! Thou foolish woman, after the words of consecration, is it not the Lord's body? *A. A.* No; it is but consecrated bread, or sacramental bread. *L. M.* What if a mouse eat it after the consecration? What shall become of the mouse? What sayest thou, thou foolish woman? *A. A.* What shall become of her, say you, my lord? *L. M.* I say, that mouse is damned. *A. A.* Alack poor mouse!—By this time my lords heard enough of my lord mayor's divinity; and perceiving that some could not keep in their laughing, proceeded to the butchery and slaughter they intended before they came thither."

I was much to blame for uttering the scriptures. For St. Paul, he said, forbade women to speak, or to talk of the word of God. I answered him, that I knew Paul's meaning as well as he, which is 1 Cor. xiv. that a woman ought not to speak in the congregation by the way of teaching. And then I asked him, how many women he had seen go into the pulpit and preach? He said he never saw any. Then I said, he ought to find no fault in poor women, except they had offended against the law.

Then the lord mayor commanded me to ward. I asked him if sureties would not serve me, and he made me short answer, that he would take none. Then was I had to the compter, and there remained twelve days, no friend being admitted to speak with me. But in the mean time there was a priest sent unto me, who said that he was commanded of the bishop to examine me, and to give me good counsel, which he did not. But first he asked me for what cause I was put in the compter, and I told him, I could not tell. Then he said, it was great pity that I should be there without cause, and concluded that he was very sorry for me. Secondly he said, it was told him that I should deny the sacrament of the altar. And I answered again, that what I had said, I had said. Thirdly, he asked me if I were shriven. I told him No. Then he said he would bring one to me to shrive me. And I told him so that I might have one of these, that is to say, Dr. Crome,* sir William, Whitehead, or Huntington, I was contented, because I knew them to be men of wisdom; as for you, or any other, said I, I will not dispraise, because I know you not. Then he said, I would not have you think but that I, or any other that shall be brought you, shall be as honest as they, for if we were not, you may be sure the king would not suffer us to preach. Then I answered by the saying of Solomon; By communing with the wise, I may learn wisdom, but by talking with a fool, I shall take scathe,†

---

* Dr. Crome was a person of some eminence among the reformers. He was troubled under the act of six articles, and afterwards in queen Mary's reign; he escaped by making some explanations and retractations, but was always suspected by the Romanists. At this time, 1546, he was called to account by Bonner for a sermon preached at Mercers' chapel, wherein he had urged that Christ was the only sufficient sacrifice for the sins of the whole world, and that he had offered himself once for all. Crome thereby condemned the popish doctrine respecting the mass.

† Harm, injury.

Prov. xiii. Fourthly he asked, if the host should fall and a beast did eat it, whether the beast did receive God or no? I answered, seeing you have taken the pains to ask this question, I desire you also to take so much pains more as to assoil it yourself, for I will not do it, because I perceive you come to tempt me. And he said it was against the order of schools, that he which asked the question, should answer it. I told him I was but a woman, and knew not the course of schools. Fifthly, he asked me, if I intended to receive the sacrament at Easter, or no? I answered, that else I were no christian woman, and that I did rejoice that the time was so near at hand; and then he departed thence with many fair words.

The twenty-third day of March, my cousin Britain came into the compter unto me, and asked there whether I might be bailed or no? Then went he immediately unto my lord mayor, desiring him to be so good unto me, that I might be bailed. My lord answered him, and said that he would be glad to do the best that in him lay. Howbeit he could not bail me without the consent of a spiritual officer, requiring him to go and speak with the chancellor of London. For he said, like as he could not commit me to prison without the consent of a spiritual officer, no more could he bail me without consent of the same.

So upon that, he went to the chancellor, requiring of him as he did before of my lord mayor. He answered him, that the matter was so heinous, that he durst not of himself do it, without my lord of London were made privy thereunto. But he said he would speak unto my lord in it, and bade him repair unto him the next morrow, and he should well know my lord's pleasure. And upon the morrow after, he came thither, and spake both with the chancellor and with the bishop of London. The bishop declared unto him that he was very well contented that I should come forth to a communication, and appointed me to appear before him the next day after, at three of the clock at afternoon. Moreover, he said unto him, that he would there should be at the examination such learned men, as I was affectioned to, that they might see, and also make report, that I was handled with no rigour. He answered him, that he knew no man that I had more affection to, than to another. Then said the bishop, Yes; as I understand, she is affectioned to doctor Crome, sir William, Whitehead, and Huntington, that they might hear the matter, for she did know them to be learned and of godly judgment. Also he required my cousin Britain, that he should earnestly persuade me to utter even the very bottom of my heart, and he sware by his fidelity, that no man should take any advantage of my words, neither yet would he lay ought to my charge for any thing that I should there speak: but if I said any manner of thing amiss, he, with others more, would be glad to reform me therein, with most godly counsel.

On the morrow after, the bishop of London sent for me at one of the clock, his hour being appointed at three, and as I came before him, he said he was very sorry for my trouble, and desired to know my opinion in such matters as were laid against me. He required me also, in anywise, boldly to utter the secrets of my heart, bidding me not to fear in any point, for whatsoever I did say within his house, no man should hurt me for it. I answered, Forsomuch as your lordship appointed three of the clock, and my friends will not come till that hour, I desire you to pardon me giving answer till they come. Then said he, that he thought it meet to send for those four men which were aforenamed and appointed. Then I desired him not to put them to the pains, for it should not need, because the two gentlemen which were my friends, were able enough to testify what I should say. Anon after he went into his gallery with master Spillman, and willed him in anywise that he should exhort me to utter all that I thought. In the mean while he commanded his archdeacon to commune with me, who said unto me, Mistress, wherefore are you accused? I answered, Ask my accusers, for I know not as yet. Then took he my book out of my hand, and said, Such books as this is, have brought you to the trouble you are in. Beware, saith he, beware, for he that made it was burnt in Smithfield. Then I asked him if he were sure that it was true that he had spoken. And he said he knew well the book was of John Frith's making. Then I asked him if he were not ashamed for to judge of the book before he saw it within, or yet knew the truth thereof. I said also that such unadvised and hasty judgment, is a token apparent of a very slender wit. Then I opened the book and showed it him. He said he thought it had been another, for he could find no fault therein. Then I desired him no more to be so swift in judgment, till he thoroughly knew the truth, and so he departed. Immediately after came my cousin Britain in with divers others, as master Hall of Gray's Inn, and such others like. Then my lord of London persuaded my cousin Britain as he had done oft before, which was that I should utter the bottom of my heart in anywise. My lord said after that unto me, that he would I should credit the counsel of my friends in his behalf, which was, that I should utter all things that burdened my conscience; for he ensured me that I should not need to stand in doubt to say anything. For like as he promised them, he said, he promised me, and would perform it; which was, that neither he, nor any man for him, should take me at advantage of any word I should speak; and therefore he bade me say my mind without fear. I answered him, that I had nought to say; for my conscience, I thanked God, was burdened with nothing.

Then brought he forth this unsavoury similitude, that if a man had a wound, no wise surgeon would minister help unto it, before he had seen it uncovered. In like case, said he, can I give you no good counsel, unless I know wherewith your conscience is burdened. I answered, that my conscience was clear in all things; and for to lay a plaster unto the whole skin, it might appear much folly.

Then you drive me, said he, to lay to your charge your own report, which is this; you did say, He that doth receive the sacrament by the hands of an ill priest, or a sinner, receiveth the devil and not God. To that I answered, that I never spake such words. But as I said before, both to the quest and to my lord mayor, so say I now again, that the wickedness of the priest should not hurt me, but in spirit and faith I receive no less the body and blood of Christ. Then said the bishop unto me, What a saying is this, In spirit? I will not take you at advantage. Then I answered, My lord, without faith and spirit I cannot receive him worthily.

Then he laid unto me, that I should say that the sacrament remaining in the pix was but bread. I answered that I never said so, but indeed the quest asked me such a question, whereunto I would not answer, I said, till such time as they had answered me this question of mine, wherefore Stephen was stoned to death? They said they knew not. Then said I again, no more would I tell them what it was.

Then my lord laid it unto me, that I had alleged a certain text of the scripture. I answered, that I alleged none other but St. Paul's own saying to the Athenians, in the seventeenth chapter in the Acts of the Apostles, that God dwelleth not in temples made with hands. Then asked he me what my faith and belief was in that matter? I answered him, I believe as the scripture doth teach me.

Then inquired he of me, What if the scripture doth say that it is the body of Christ? I believe, said I, as the scripture doth teach me. Then asked he again, What if the scripture doth say that it is not the body of Christ? My answer was still, I believe as the scripture informeth me. And upon this argument he tarried a great while, to have driven me to make him an answer to his mind. Howbeit I would not, but concluded this with him, that I believe therein and in all other things, as Christ and his holy apostles did leave them. Then he asked me why I had so few words? And I answered, God hath given me the gift of knowledge, but not of utterance; and Solomon saith, That a woman of few words is a gift of God, Prov. xix.

Thirdly, my lord laid unto my charge, that I should say that the mass was idolatry. I answered him, No; I said not so. Howbeit the quest did ask me, whether private masses relieved souls departed or no? Unto whom then I answered, What idolatry is this, that we should rather believe in private masses than in the healthsome death of the dear Son of God! Then said my lord again, What an answer is that! Though it were but mean, said I, yet it was good enough for the question.

Then I told my lord that there was a priest which heard what I said there, before my lord mayor and them. With that the chancellor answered, who was the same priest—So she spake it in very deed before my lord mayor and me.

Then were there certain priests, as doctor Standish and others, which tempted me much to know my mind. And I answered them always thus: That I have said to my lord of London, I have said. Then doctor Standish desired my lord to bid me say my mind concerning the same text of St. Paul. I answered, that it was against St. Paul's learning that I, being a woman, should interpret the scriptures, especially where so many wise learned men were.

Then my lord of London said he was informed, that one should ask of me if I would receive the sacrament at Easter, and I made a mock of it. Then I desired that mine accuser might come forth, which my Lord would not. But he said again unto me, I sent one to give you good counsel, and at the first word you called him papist. That

I denied not, for I perceived he was no less; yet made I none answer unto it.

Then he rebuked me, and said, that I should report, that there were bent against me threescore priests at Lincoln. Indeed, quoth I, I said so. For my friends told me, if I came to Lincoln, the priests would assault me and put me to great trouble, as thereof they had made their boast; and when I heard it, I went thither indeed, not being afraid, because I knew my matter to be good. Moreover, I remained there six days, to see what would be said unto me. And as I was in the minster reading in the bible, they resorted unto me by two and by two, by five and by six, minding to have spoken unto me, yet went they their ways again without words speaking.

Then my lord asked if there were not one that did speak unto me. I told him yes, that there was one of them at the last which did speak to me indeed. And my lord then asked me what he said. And I told him his words were of small effect, so that I did not now remember them. Then said my lord, There are many that read and know the scripture, and yet do not follow it, nor live thereafter. I said again, My lord, I would wish that all men knew my conversation and living in all points, for I am so sure, myself, this hour, that there are none able to prove any dishonesty by me. If you know any that can do it, I pray you bring them forth. Then my lord went away, and said, he would entitle somewhat of my meaning, and so he wrote a great circumstance. But what it was, I have not all in memory, for he would not suffer me to have the copy thereof. Only I remember this small portion of it.

Be it known, saith he, to all men, that I Anne Askew do confess this to be my faith and belief, notwithstanding my reports made before to the contrary. I believe that they which are houseled[*] at the hands of a priest, whether his conversation be good or not, do receive the body and blood of Christ in substance really. Also I do believe, that after the consecration, whether it be received or reserved, it is no less than the very body and blood of Christ in substance. Finally, I do believe in this, and in all other sacraments of holy church, in all points, according to the old catholic faith of the same. In witness whereof, I, the said Anne, have subscribed my name.

There was somewhat more in it, which because I had

[*] Those who receive the sacrament of the altar.

not the copy, I cannot now remember. Then he read it to me, and asked me if I did agree to it. And I said again, I believe so much thereof, as the holy scripture doth agree unto; wherefore I desire you, that you will add that thereunto. Then he answered, that I should not teach him what he should write. With that, he went forth into his great chamber and read the same bill before the audience, which inveigled and willed me to set to my hand, saying also, that I had favour shown me. Then said the bishop, I might thank others, and not myself for the favour that I found at his hand. For he considered, he said, that I had good friends, and also that I was come of a worshipful stock.

Then answered one Christopher, a servant unto master Denny, Rather ought you, my lord, to have done it in such case for God's sake than for man's. Then my lord sat down, and took me the writing, to set thereto my hand, and I wrote after this manner; I Anne Askew do believe all manner of things contained in the faith of the catholic church.

[And forasmuch as mention here is made of the writing of Bonner, which this godly woman said before she had not in memory, therefore I thought in this place to infer the same, both with the whole circumstance of Bonner, and with the title thereunto prefixed by the register, and also with her own subscription; to the intent the reader seeing the same subscription neither to agree with the time of the title above prefixed, nor with the subscription after the writing annexed, might the better understand thereby what credit is to be given hereafter to such bishops, and to such registers. The tenour of Bonner's writing proceeds thus:*—

"The true copy of the confession, and belief of Anne Askew, otherwise called Anne Kyme, made before the bishop of London, the twentieth day of March, in the year of our Lord God, after the computation of the church of England, 1545, and subscribed with her own hand, in the presence of the said bishop and others, whose names hereafter are recited, set forth, and published at this present, to the intent the world may see what credence is now to be given unto the same woman, who in so short a time hath most damnably altered and changed her opinion and belief, and therefore rightly in open court arraigned and condemned. (Ex Regist.)

* This, and some subsequent particulars, were added by Fox.

"Be it known to all faithful people, that as touching the blessed sacrament of the altar, I do firmly and undoubtedly believe, that after the words of consecration be spoken by the priest according to the common usage of this church of England, there is present really the body and blood of our Saviour Jesus Christ, whether the minister which doth consecrate, be a good man or a bad man, and that also, whensoever the said sacrament is received, whether the receiver be a good man or a bad man, he doth receive it really and corporeally. And moreover, I do believe, that whether the said sacrament be then received of the minister, or else reserved to be put into the pix, or to be brought to any person that is impotent or sick, yet there is the very body and blood of our said Saviour; so that whether the minister or the receiver be good or bad, yea, whether the sacrament be received or reserved, always there is the blessed body of Christ really.

"And this thing with all other things touching the sacrament, and other sacraments of the church, and all things else touching the christian belief, which are taught and declared in the king's majesty's book, lately set forth for the erudition of the christian people, I Anne Askew, otherwise called Anne Kyme, do truly and perfectly believe, and so here presently confess and acknowledge. And here I do promise, that henceforth I shall never say or do anything against the premises, or against any of them. In witness whereof, I, the said Anne, have subscribed my name unto these presents. Written the twentieth day of March, in the year of our Lord God, 1545. (Ex Regist.)

"By me Anne Askew, otherwise called Anne Kyme.

"Witnesses.—Edmund, bishop of London. John, bishop of Bath. Owen Oglethorp, doctor of divinity. Richard Smith, doctor of divinity. John Rudde, batchelor of divinity. William Pie, batchelor of divinity. John Wymsley, archdeacon of London. John Cook, Robert John, Francis Spillman, Edward Hall, Alexander Brett, Edmund Buts, with divers other more being then present."

Here mayest thou note, gentle reader, in this confession, both in the bishop and his register, a double sleight of false conveyance. For although the confession purporteth the words of the bishop's writing, whereunto she set her hand, yet by the title prefixed before, mayest thou see that both she was arraigned and condemned before this was registered, and also that she is falsely reported to have put to her hand; which indeed by this her own book appears not so to be, but after this manner and condition—I Anne Askew do believe all manner of things contained in the faith of the catholic church, and not otherwise. It followeth more in the story.]

Then because I added unto it the catholic church, he flung into his chamber in a great fury. With that my cousin Britain followed him, desiring him for God's sake to be a good lord unto me. He answered, that I was a woman, and that he was nothing deceived in me. Then my cousin Britain desired him to take me as a woman, and not to set my weak womanish wit to his lordship's great wisdom.

Then went in unto him Dr. Weston, and said, that the cause why I did write there the catholic church, was, that I understood not the church was written before. So with much ado, they persuaded my lord to come out again, and to take my name with the names of my sureties, which were my cousin Britain, and master Spillman of Gray's Inn.

This being done, we thought that I should have been put to bail immediately according to the order of the law. Howbeit, he would not suffer it, but committed me from thence to prison again, until the next morrow, and then he willed me to appear in the Guildhall, and so I did. Notwithstanding, they would not put me to bail there neither, but read the bishop's writing unto me as before, and so commanded me again to prison. Then were my sureties appointed to come before them on the next morrow in Paul's church, which did so indeed. Notwithstanding, they would once again have broken off with them, because they would not be bound also for another woman at their pleasure, whom they knew not, nor yet what matter was laid unto her charge. Notwithstanding, at the last, after much ado and reasoning to and fro, they took a bond of them of recognisance for my forthcoming. And thus I was at last delivered.

Written by me ANNE ASKEW.

# THE LATTER APPREHENSION AND EXAMINATION

OF THE WORTHY MARTYR OF GOD,

## MISTRESS ANNE ASKEW,

WRITTEN BY HERSELF, A. D. 1546. PRINTED A. D. 1547.

---

I will pour out my spirit upon all flesh, (saith God,) your sons and your daughters shall prophesy. And whosoever call on the name of the Lord shall be saved.—Joel ii.

---

I DO perceive, dear friend in the Lord, that thou art not yet persuaded throughly in the truth concerning the Lord's supper, because Christ said unto his apostles; Take, eat, this is my body which is given for you.

In giving forth the bread as an outward sign or token to be received with the mouth, he minded them, in a perfect belief to receive that body of his which should die for the people, or to think the death thereof to be the only health and salvation of their souls. The bread and the wine were left us for a sacramental communion, or a mutual participation of the inestimable benefits of his most precious death and bloodshedding, and that we should in the end thereof be thankful together for that most necessary grace of our redemption. For, in the closing thereof, he said thus; This do ye in remembrance of me. Yea, so oft as ye shall eat it, or drink it. Luke xxii. and 1 Cor. xi. Else should we have been forgetful of that we ought to have in daily remembrance, and also have been altogether unthankful for it; therefore it is meet that in our prayers we call unto God, to graft in our foreheads the true meaning of the Holy Ghost concerning this communion. For St. Paul saith, The letter slayeth; the Spirit is it only that giveth life, 2 Cor. iii. Mark well John vi. where all is applied unto faith, note also the 2 Cor. iv. and in the end thereof ye shall find plainly that the things which are seen are temporal, but they that are not seen are everlasting. Yea, look in Hebrews iii. and ye shall find that Christ, as a son, and no servant, ruleth over his house, whose house are we, and not the dead temple, if we hold fast the confidence and rejoicing of that hope to the end. Wherefore, as saith the Holy Ghost, To day if ye shall hear his voice, harden not your hearts, &c. Ps. xcv.

*The sum of my examination before the king's council at Greenwich.*

Your request as concerning my prison fellows, I am not able to satisfy, because I heard not their examinations; but the effect of mine was this:—I, being before the council, was asked of M. Kyme. I answered that my lord chancellor knew already my mind in that matter. They with that answer were not contented, but said, it was the king's pleasure that I should open the matter unto them. I answered them plainly that I would not so do. But if it were the king's pleasure to hear me, I would show him the truth. Then they said, it was not meet for the king to be troubled with me. I answered, that Solomon was reckoned the wisest king that ever lived, yet misliked he not to hear two poor common women, much more his grace, a simple woman, and his faithful subject. So in conclusion I made them no other answer in that matter. Then my lord chancellor asked me of my opinion in the sacrament. My answer was this, I believe that so oft as I, in a christian congregation, do receive the bread in remembrance of Christ's death, and with thanksgiving, according to his holy institution, I receive therewith the fruits also of his most glorious passion. The bishop of Winchester bade me make a direct answer. I said I would not sing a new song of the Lord in a strange land. Then the bishop said, I spake in parables. I answered, it was best for him, for if I show the open truth, said I, ye will not accept it. Then he said, I was a parrot. I told him again I was ready to suffer all things at his hands, not only his rebukes, but all that should follow besides, yea and that gladly.

Then had I divers rebukes of the council, because I would not express my mind in all things as they would have me. But they were not in the mean time unanswered, which now to rehearse were too much, for I was with them there about five hours. Then the clerk of the council conveyed me from thence to my lady Garnish.*

The next day I was brought again before the council. Then would they needs know of me what I said to the sacrament. I answered, that I already had said what I could say. Then after divers words they bade me go by. Then came my lord Lisle, my lord of Essex, and the bishop of Winchester, requiring me earnestly that I should confess

* Prison.

the sacrament to be flesh, blood, and bone. Then said I to my lord Parr and my lord Lisle, that it was great shame for them to counsel contrary to their knowledge. Whereunto in few words they said, that they would gladly all things were well.

Then the bishop said, he would speak with me familiarly. I said, so did Judas, when he unfriendly betrayed Christ. Then desired the bishop to speak with me alone. But that I refused. He asked me why? I said, that in the mouth of two or three witnesses, every matter should stand according to Christ's and Paul's doctrine, Matt. xviii. 2 Cor. xiii.

Then my lord chancellor began to examine me again of the sacrament. Then I asked him how long he would halt on both sides? Then would he needs know where I found that. I said in the scripture, 1 Kings xviii. Then he went his way. Then the bishop said, I should be burnt. I answered, that I had searched all the scriptures, yet could I never find there, that either Christ or his apostles put any creature to death. Well, well, said I, God will laugh your threatenings to scorn, Psalm ii. Then was I commanded to stand aside. [Then came M. Paget to me with many glorious words, and desired me to speak my mind to him. I might, he said, deny it again if need were. I said that I would not deny the truth. He asked me how I could avoid\* the very words of Christ; Take, eat, this is my body, which shall be broken for you. I answered, that Christ's meaning was there as in these other places of the scripture; I am the door, John x. I am the vine, John xv. Behold the Lamb of God, John i. The rock stone was Christ, 1 Cor. x. and such other. Ye may not here, said I, take Christ for the material thing that he is signified by; for then ye will make him a very door, a vine, a lamb, and a stone, clean contrary to the Holy Ghost's meaning. All these indeed do signify Christ, like as the bread doth his body in that place. And though he did say there, Take, eat this in remembrance of me, yet did he not bid them hang up that bread in a box, and make it a god, or bow to it.]† Then came to me doctor Cox and doctor Robinson. In conclusion we could not agree.

Then they made me a bill about the sacrament, willing

\* Make of no effect.

† This statement respecting Paget is omitted in Fox. He was one of the principal ministers of state at that period, but a worldly timeserving character, and having joined himself to queen Mary, was laid aside on queen Elizabeth's accession.

me to set my hand thereunto, but I would not. Then on the Sunday I was sore sick, thinking no less than to die. Therefore I desired to speak with master Latimer, but it would not be. Then was I sent to Newgate in my extremity of sickness; for in all my life before was I never in such pain. Thus the Lord strengthen you in the truth. Pray, pray, pray.

---

*The confession of me, Anne Askew, for the time I was in Newgate, concerning my belief.*

I find in the scripture, that Christ took the bread and gave it to his disciples, saying, Take, eat, this is my body which shall be broken for you, meaning in substance, his own very body, the bread being thereof only a sign or sacrament. For, after like manner of speaking, he said he would break down the temple, and in three days build it up again, signifying his own body by the temple, as St. John declares, John ii. and not the stony temple itself. So that the bread is but a remembrance of his death, or a sacrament of thanksgiving for it, whereby we are knit unto him by a communion of christian love, although there are many that cannot perceive the true meaning thereof, for the veil that Moses put over his face before the children of Israel, that they should not see the clearness thereof, Exod. xxxiv. and 2 Cor. iii. I perceive the same veil remaineth to this day. But when God shall take it away, then shall these blind men see. For it is plainly expressed in the history of Bel in the bible, that God dwelleth in no thing material. O king, saith Daniel, be not deceived, for God will be in nothing that is made with hands of men, Dan. xiv.[*] Oh, what stiff-necked people are these, that will always resist the Holy Ghost! But as their fathers have done, so do they, because they have stony hearts.

Written by me, ANNE ASKEW, that neither wish death, nor fear his might, and as merry as one that is bound towards heaven.

Truth is laid in prison, Luke xxi. The law is turned to wormwood, Amos vi. And there can no right judgment go forth, Isa. lix.

---

[*] The reader will remember that this is one of the apocryphal additions to Daniel.

O forgive us all our sins, and receive us graciously. As for the works of our hands, we will no more call upon them. For it is thou Lord that art our God. Thou showest ever mercy unto the fatherless.

O, if they would do this, saith the Lord, I should heal their sores, yea with all my heart would I love them.

O Ephraim, what have I to do with idols any more? whoso is wise shall understand this. And he that is rightly instructed will regard it; for the ways of the Lord are righteous. Such as are godly will walk in them, and as for the wicked, they will stumble at them, Hosea xiv.

Solomon, saith St. Stephen, builded an house for the God of Jacob. Howbeit, the Highest of all dwelleth not in temples made with hands; as saith the prophet, Heaven is my seat, and the earth is my footstool. What house will ye build for me? saith the Lord; or what place is it that I shall rest in? Hath not my hand made all things? Acts vii.

Woman, believe me, saith Christ to the Samaritan, the time is at hand, that ye shall neither in this mountain, nor yet at Jerusalem, worship the Father. Ye worship ye wot not what, but we know what we worship. For salvation cometh of the Jews. But the hour cometh, and is now, wherein the true worshippers shall worship the Father in spirit and verity, John iv.

Labour not, saith Christ, for the meat that perisheth; but for that which endureth unto life everlasting, which the Son of man shall give you; for him God the Father hath sealed, John vi.

*The sum of the condemnation of me, Anne Askew, at the Guildhall.*

They said to me there that I was a heretic, and condemned by the law, if I would stand in mine opinion. I answered that I was no heretic, neither yet deserved I any death by the law of God. But, as concerning the faith which I uttered and wrote to the council, I would not, I said, deny it, because I knew it true. Then would they needs know, if I would deny the sacrament to be Christ's body and blood. I said, Yea; for the same Son of God that was born of the virgin Mary, is now glorious in heaven, and will come again from thence at the latter day, like as he went up, Acts i. And as for that ye call your God, it is but a piece of bread. For a more proof thereof, mark it when you list, let it lie in the box but three months, and it will be mouldy, and so turn to nothing that is good. Whereupon I am persuaded that it cannot be God.

After that, they willed me to have a priest; and then I smiled. Then they asked me if it were not good. I said, I would confess my faults unto God, for I was sure that he would hear me with favour, and so we were condemned without a quest.*

My belief which I wrote to the council was this—That the sacramental bread was left us to be received with thanksgiving, in remembrance of Christ's death, the only remedy of our soul's recovery; and that thereby we also receive the whole benefits and fruits of his most glorious passion. Then would they needs know whether the bread in the box were God or no. I said, God is a Spirit, and will be worshipped in spirit and truth, John iv. Then they demanded, Will you plainly deny Christ to be in the sacrament? I answered, that I believed faithfully the eternal Son of God not to dwell there. In witness whereof, I recited again the history of Bel, Dan. xiv. Acts vii. and xvii. and Matt. xxiv. concluding thus, I neither wish death, nor yet fear his might; God have the praise thereof with thanks.

### *My letter sent to the lord chancellor.*

The Lord God, by whom all creatures have their being, bless you with the light of his knowledge. Amen.

My duty to your lordship remembered, &c. It might please you to accept this my bold suit, as the suit of one, which upon due consideration is moved to the same, and hopeth to obtain. My request to your lordship is only that it may please the same to be a mean for me to the king's majesty, that his grace may be certified of these few lines which I have written concerning my belief. Which when it shall be truly conferred with the hard judgment given me for the same, I think his grace shall well perceive me to be weighed in an uneven pair of balances. But I remit my matter and cause to almighty God, who rightly judgeth all secrets. And thus I commend your lordship to the governance of him, and fellowship of all saints. Amen.

By your handmaid, ANNE ASKEW.

* Without a jury; persons accused under the act of six articles were entitled to a trial by jury.

### *My faith briefly written to the king's grace.*

I Anne Askew, of good memory, although God hath given me the bread of adversity, and the water of trouble, yet not so much as my sins have deserved, desire this to be known unto your grace. That forasmuch as I am by the law condemned for an evil doer, here I take heaven and earth to record, that I shall die in my innocency. And according to that I have said first, and will say last, I utterly abhor and detest all heresies. And as concerning the supper of the Lord, I believe so much as Christ hath said therein, which he confirmed with his most blessed blood. I believe also so much as he willed me to follow and believe, yea so much as the catholic church of him doth teach. For I will not forsake the commandment of his holy lips. But, look, what God hath charged me with his mouth, that have I shut up in my heart; and thus briefly I end for lack of learning.

ANNE ASKEW

---

### *The effect of my examination and handling, since my departure from Newgate.*

On Tuesday I was sent from Newgate to the sign of the Crown, where master Rich and the bishop of London, with all their power and flattering words, went about to persuade me from God, but I did not esteem their glosing pretences. Then came there to me Nicholas Shaxton, and counselled me to recant as he had done. I said to him, that it had been good for him never to have been born, with many other like words. Then master Rich sent me to the Tower, where I remained till three of the clock. Then came Rich and one of the council, charging me upon my obedience to show unto them if I knew man or woman of my sect. My answer was, that I knew none. Then they asked me of my lady of Suffolk, my lady of Sussex, my lady of Hertford, my lady Denny, and my lady Fitzwilliams. I said, if I should pronounce anything against them, that I were not able to prove it. Then said they unto me, that the king was informed that I could name, if I would, a great number of my sect. I answered, that the king was as well deceived in that behalf, as dissembled with in other matters.

Then commanded they me to show how I was maintained in the compter; and who willed me to stick by my opinion. I said that there was no creature that therein did strengthen me. And as for the help that I had in the compter, it was by the means of my maid. For, as she went abroad in the streets, she made her moan to the prentices, and they by her did send me money, but who they were I never knew. Then they said, that there were divers gentlewomen that gave me money—but I knew not their names. Then they said, that there were divers ladies that had sent me money. I answered, that there was a man in a blue coat which delivered me ten shillings, and said that my lady of Hertford sent it me. And another in a violet coat, gave me eight shillings, and said my lady Denny sent it me. Whether it were true or no, I cannot tell. For I am not sure who sent it me, but as the men did say. Then they said there were of the council that did maintain me. And I said, No.

Then they did put me on the rack, because I confessed no ladies or gentlewomen to be of my opinion,\* and thereon they kept me a long time. And because I lay still and did not cry, my lord chancellor and master Richt† took pains to rack me with their own hands till I was nigh dead.

Then the lieutenant caused me to be loosed from the rack. Straightway I swooned, and then they recovered me again. After that I sat two long hours reasoning with my lord chancellor upon the bare floor, where he with many flattering words, persuaded me to leave my opinion. But, my Lord God, I thank his everlasting goodness, gave me grace to persevere, and will do, I hope, to the very end. Then was I brought to a house, and laid in a bed, with as weary and painful bones as ever had patient Job, I thank my Lord God therefore. Then my lord chancellor sent me word, if I would leave my opinion, I should want nothing, if I would not, I should forth to Newgate and so be burned. I sent him again word, that I would rather die, than to break my faith.

Thus the Lord open the eyes of their blind hearts, that the truth may take place. Farewell, dear friend, and pray, pray, pray.

Fox adds, Touching the order of her racking in the Tower, thus it was. First, she was led down into a dungeon, where sir Anthony Knevet the lieutenant, commanded

\* See life of queen Catherine Parr.
† Fox says, it was sir John Baker.

his gaoler to pinch her with the rack. Which being done so much as he thought sufficient, he went about to take her down, supposing he had done enough. But Wriothesly the chancellor, not contented that she was loosed so soon confessing nothing, commanded the lieutenant to strain her on the rack again. Which because he denied to do, tendering the weakness of the woman, he was threatened therefore grievously of the said Wriothesly, saying, that he would signify his disobedience unto the king; and so consequently upon the same, he and master Rich throwing off their gowns, would needs play the tormentors themselves, first asking her if she were with child. To whom she answering again, said, Ye shall not need to spare for that, but do your will upon me; and so quietly and patiently praying unto the Lord, she abode their tyranny, till her bones and joints were almost plucked asunder, in such sort, that she was carried away in a chair. When the racking was past, Wriothesly and his fellow took their horses toward the court.

In the mean time, while they were making their way by land, the good lieutenant taking boat, sped in all haste to the court, to speak with the king before the other, and so did. Who there making his humble suit to the king, desired his pardon, and showed him the whole matter as it stood, and of the racking of mistress Askew, and how he was threatened by the lord chancellor, because at his commandment, not knowing his highness' pleasure, he refused to rack her, which he for compassion could not find in his heart to do, and therefore humbly craved his highness' pardon. Which when the king had understood, he seemed not very well to like their so extreme handling of the woman, and also granted to the lieutenant his pardon, willing him to return and see to his charge. Great expectation was in the mean season among the warders and other officers of the Tower, waiting for his return, whom when they saw come so cheerfully, declaring unto them how he had sped with the king, they were not a little joyous, and gave thanks to God therefore.

---

*Anne Askew's answer unto John Lascel's letter.*

O friend most dearly beloved in God; I marvel not a little what should move you to judge in me so slender a faith as to fear death, which is the end of all misery. In the Lord I desire you not to believe of me such wickedness. For I doubt it not, but God will perform his work in me, like as he hath begun. I understand the council is not a little displeased that it should be reported abroad, that I was racked in the Tower. They say now, what they did there, was but to fear me; whereby I perceive they are ashamed of their uncomely doings, and fear much, lest the king's majesty should have information thereof. Wherefore they would no man to noise it. Well, their cruelty God forgive them.

Your heart in Christ Jesus. Farewell, and pray.

*The answer of Anne Askew against the false surmises of her recantation.*

I have read the process, which is reported of them that know not the truth, to be my recantation. But as sure as the Lord liveth, I never meant thing less than to recant. Notwithstanding this, I confess, that in my first troubles I was examined of the bishop of London about the sacrament. Yet had they no grant of my mouth, but this, that I believed therein as the word of God did bind me to believe; more had they never of me. Then he made a copy which is now in print, and required me to set thereunto my hand: but I refused it. Then my two sureties did will me in no wise to stick thereat, for it was no great matter, they said.

Then with much ado, at the last I wrote thus: I Anne Askew do believe this, if God's word do agree to the same, and the true catholic church. Then the bishop being in great displeasure with me, because I made doubts in my writing, commanded me to prison; where I was awhile, but afterwards by the means of friends, I came out again. Here is the truth of that matter. And as concerning the thing that ye covet most to know, resort to the sixth of John, and be ruled always thereby. Thus fare ye well, quoth Anne Askew.

*The confession of the faith which Anne Askew made in Newgate before she suffered.*

I Anne Askew, of good memory, although my merciful

Father hath given me the bread of adversity, and the water of trouble; yet not so much as my sins have deserved—confess myself here, a sinner before the throne of his heavenly majesty, desiring his eternal mercy. And forsomuch as I am by the law unrighteously condemned for an evil doer concerning opinions, I take the same most merciful God of mine, who hath made both heaven and earth, to record, that I hold no opinions contrary to his most holy word. And I trust in my merciful Lord, who is the giver of all grace, that he will graciously assist me against all evil opinions, which are contrary to his blessed verity. For, I take him to witness, that I have, and will, unto my life's end, utterly abhor them to the uttermost of my power.

This is the heresy which they report me to hold—that after the priest hath spoken the words of consecration, there remaineth bread still. But they both say, and also teach it for a necessary article of faith, that after those words are once spoken, there remaineth no bread, but even the selfsame body that hung upon the cross on Good Friday, both flesh, blood, and bone! To this belief of theirs, say I, Nay: for then were our common creed false, which saith, that he sitteth on the right hand of God the Father Almighty, and from thence shall come to judge the quick and the dead. Lo! this is the heresy that I hold, and for it must suffer the death. But, as touching the holy and blessed supper of the Lord, I believe it to be a most necessary remembrance of his glorious sufferings and death. Moreover, I believe as much therein as my eternal and only Redeemer, Jesus Christ, would I should believe.

Finally, I believe all those scriptures to be true, which he hath confirmed with his most precious blood. Yea, and as St. Paul saith, those scriptures are sufficient for our learning and salvation that Christ hath left here with us; so that I believe we need no unwritten verities to rule his church with. Therefore, look what he hath said unto me with his own mouth in his holy gospel, that have I with God's grace closed up in my heart, and my full trust is, as David saith, that it shalt be a lantern to my footsteps, Psal. cxix.

There are some do say that I deny the eucharist or sacrament of thanksgiving; but those people do untruly report of me. For I both say and believe it, that if it were ordered like as Christ instituted and left it, a most singular comfort it were unto us all. But, as concerning your mass, as it is now used in our days, I do say and believe it to be the most abominable idol that is in the world. For my God will not be eaten with teeth, neither yet dieth he again. And upon these words that I have now spoken, will I suffer death.

O Lord, I have more enemies now than there are hairs on my head: yet, Lord, let them never overcome me with vain words, but fight thou, Lord, in my stead; for on thee cast I my care. With all the spite they can imagine, they fall upon me which am thy poor creature. Yet, sweet Lord, let me not set by them which are against thee; for in thee is my whole delight. And, Lord, I heartily desire of thee, that thou wilt of thy most merciful goodness forgive them that violence which they do and have done unto me. Open also thou their blind hearts, that they may hereafter do that thing in thy sight which is only acceptable before thee, and to set forth thy verity aright, without all vain fantasies of sinful men. So be it, O Lord, so be it.

By me, ANNE ASKEW.

---

Fox adds, Hitherto we have intreated of this good woman. Now it remaineth that we touch somewhat as concerning her end and martyrdom. After that she, being born of such stock and kindred, that she might have lived in great wealth and prosperity, if she would rather have followed the world than Christ, now had been so tormented, that she could neither live long in so great distress, neither yet by her adversaries be suffered to die in secret; the day of her execution being appointed, she was brought into Smithfield in a chair, because she could not go on her feet, by means of her great torments from the extremity she suffered upon the rack. When she was brought unto the stake, she was tied by the middle with a chain that held up her body. When all things were thus prepared to the fire, Dr. Shaxton who was then appointed to preach, began his sermon. Anne Askew hearing, and answering again unto him, where he said well, confirmed the same; where he said amiss, there she said, He misseth, and speaketh without the book.

The sermon being finished, the martyrs,[*] standing there tied at three several stakes ready to their martyrdom, began their prayers. The multitude and concourse of the people was exceeding, the place where they stood being railed

[*] John Lascels, a gentleman of the king's household; Nicholas Belenian, a priest; John Adams, a tailor; and Anne Askew.

about to keep out the press. Upon the bench under St. Bartholomew's church, sat Wriothesly, chancellor of England, the old duke of Norfolk, the old earl of Bedford, the lord mayor, with divers others more. Before the fire should be set unto them, one of the bench hearing that they had gunpowder about them, and being afraid lest the fagots, by strength of the gunpowder, would come flying about their ears, began to be afraid; but the earl of Bedford declared unto him how the gunpowder was not laid under the fagots, but only about their bodies to rid them out of their pain, which having vent, there was no danger to them of the fagots, so he diminished that fear.

Then Wriothesly, lord chancellor, sent to Anne Askew, letters offering to her the king's pardon, if she would recant. Who, refusing once to look upon them, made this answer again; that she came not thither to deny her Lord and Master. Then were the letters likewise offered unto the others, who in like manner following the constancy of the woman, denied not only to receive them, but also to look upon them. Whereupon the lord mayor commanding fire to be put to them, cried with a loud voice, Fiat justitia! Let justice be done!

And thus the good Anne Askew with these blessed martyrs, being troubled so many manner of ways, and having passed through so many torments, having now ended the long course of her agonies, being compassed with flames of fire, as a blessed sacrifice unto God, she slept in the Lord, A. D. 1546, leaving behind her a singular example of christian constancy for all men to follow.

---

*The Ballad which Anne Askew made and sang when she was in Newgate.*

Like as the armed knight
Appointed to the field,
With this world will I fight,
And faith shall be my shield.

Faith is that weapon strong
Which will not fail at need;
My foes therefore among
Therewith will I proceed.

As it is had in strength
   And force of Christ his way,
It will prevail at length
   Though all the devils say, Nay.

Faith in the fathers old
   Obtained righteousness,
Which makes me very bold
   To fear no world's distress.

I now rejoice in heart,
   And hope bids me do so,
That Christ will take my part,
   And ease me of my woe.

Thou say'st Lord, Whoso knock
   To them thou wilt attend;
Undo therefore the lock,
   And thy strong power send.

More enemies now I have,
   Than hairs upon my head,
Let them not me deprave,
   But fight thou in my stead.

On thee my care I cast,
   For all their cruel spite,
I set not by their haste
   For thou art my delight

I am not she that list
   My anchor to let fall,
For every drizzling mist;
   My ship's substantial.

Not oft use I to write,
   In prose, nor yet in rhyme,
Yet will I show one sight,
   That I saw in my time.

I saw a royal throne
   Where justice should have sit,
But in her stead was one
   Of moody, cruel wit.

Absorpt was righteousness
   As of the raging flood;
Satan in fierce excess
   Sucked up the guiltless blood.

*Her latter Apprehension and Examination.* 35

> Then thought I, Jesus, Lord,
>  When thou shalt judge us all,
> Hard is it to record
>  On these men what will fall.
>
> Yet Lord, I thee desire,
>  For that they do to me,
> Let them not taste the hire
>  Of their iniquity.

God hath chosen the weak things of the world, to confound things which are mighty. Yea, and things of no reputation for to bring to nought things of reputation; that no flesh should presume in his sight, 1 Cor. i.

---

Strype has recorded a few additional particulars respecting Anne Askew, from the relation of John Loud, a learned man of some eminence in those days, who being himself suspected of heresy, narrowly escaped the flames. His mind having been awakened to a sense of the truth, he resorted to those who were imprisoned for religion at that time. Among them was William Morrice, gentleman usher to the king, the father of archbishop Cranmer's secretary, who was possessed of considerable property in Essex.* To him Loud frequently obtained admittance privately at night, incurring all the discomforts and dangers of visiting the prison, that he might converse about religion. Loud however escaped, and lived till 1579.

Loud says of Anne Askew, " I must needs confess of her, now departed to the Lord, that the day before her execution, and the same day also, she had an angel's countenance and a smiling face. For I was with Lascels, sir George Blage,† and the other (Belenian the priest, then

---

\* It is hardly necessary to say that Cranmer took no part in these persecutions. He was at that time himself in considerable danger, but protested against Gardiner's proceedings.

† The arrest of sir George Blage was one means of stopping this persecution. He was one of the king's privy chamber, and was apprehended by the lord chancellor Wriothesly, on the Sunday before Anne Askew suffered, for an irreverent observation upon the popish consecrated wafer, made in conversation after a sermon preached that day by Dr. Crome. On the Monday, he was condemned under the act of six articles, and ordered to be burned on the Wednesday! This proceeding excited much alarm at court, but the king learning the cause from the earl of Bedford, was much enraged, and ordered a pardon to be issued

burned,) and with me were three of the Throckmortons, sir Nicholas being one, and Mr. Kellum the other. By the same token, one unknown to me said, 'Ye are all marked that come to them, take heed of your lives.' Master Lascels, a gentleman of a right worshipful house of Gatford, in Nottinghamshire, mounted up into the window of the little parlour at Newgate, and there sat, and by him sir George. Master Lascels was merry and cheerful in the Lord, being come from hearing the sentence of his condemnation, and said these words, 'My lord bishop would have me confess the Roman church to be the catholic church, but that I cannot, for it is not true.'

"When the hour of darkness came, and their execution, Mrs. Anne Askew had been so racked that she could not stand, but was holden up between two sergeants, sitting there in a chair. And after the sermon was ended, they put fire to the reeds; the council looking on, and leaning in a window by the hospital, and among them sir Richard Southwell, (whose tutor Loud was.) And before God, (he declares,) at the first putting to of the fire, there fell a little dew, or a few pleasant drops upon us that stood by, a pleasing noise from heaven, God knows whether. I may truly term it a thunder crack, as the people did in the gospel, John xii. 29. or an angel, or rather God's own voice. But to leave every man to his own judgment, methought it seemed rather, that the angels in heaven rejoiced to receive their souls into bliss, whose bodies their popish tormentors cast into the fire."

Bale relates the same circumstance from the narrative of some Dutch merchants then present. It caused considerable discussion at the time, and the papists urged that it was a testimony of the martyrs' damnation! This opinion Bale controverts with much ability

immediately. "Ah! my pig!" was the familiar exclamation of the monarch on seeing his rescued favourite. "Yea," answered sir George, on again hearing the appellation usually given him by the king, "if your majesty had not been better to me than your bishops, your pig had been roasted ere now!"

# THE PRECIOUS REMAINS

## OF THE

# LADY JANE GREY,

CONTAINING SOME ACCOUNT OF HER LIFE, HER LETTERS, AND OTHER PIECES.

# SOME ACCOUNT

OF

# LADY JANE GREY.\*

LADY JANE GREY was an illustrious personage of the blood royal of England, by both parents—her grandmother on her father's side, (Henry Grey, marquis of Dorset,) being queen consort to Edward IV.; and her grandmother on her mother's, (lady Frances Brandon,) being daughter to Henry VII. queen dowager of France, and mother to Mary queen of Scots. Lady Jane had no brothers, she was the eldest of three daughters, and was born in 1537, at Bradgate, her father's seat in Leicestershire. She very early gave astonishing proofs of her uncommon abilities, insomuch that, upon a comparison with Edward VI., who was nearly of the same age, and thought a kind of miracle, the superiority has been given to her in every respect. Her genius appeared in the works of her needle, and the beautiful character in which she wrote; besides which she played admirably on various instruments of music, and accompanied them with a voice exquisitely sweet in itself, assisted by all the graces that art could bestow. These, however, were only the inferior ornaments of her character; she was far from priding herself on them, while through the rigour of her parents in exacting such great attention to them, they became her grief more than her pleasure.

Her father had himself some taste for letters, and was a great patron of the learned. He had two chaplains, Harding†

---

\* There are several biographical sketches of Lady Jane Grey extant, which have supplied the substance of the present account. The most recent, "Howard's Lady Jane Grey and her times," contains numerous historical particulars relative to her family and contemporaries, which the author has collected with considerable industry. To the present sketch some letters are added, which have not before been accessible to the English reader.

† Harding was a learned divine of Oxford. He professed the protestant religion on the accession of Edward VI., and became chaplain to the duke of Suffolk. When queen Mary came to the throne, he

and Aylmer,* both men of distinguished learning, whom he employed as tutors to his daughter; and under whose instructions she made such proficiency as surprised them both. Her own language she spoke and wrote with peculiar accuracy; the French, Italian, Latin, and, it is said, Greek, were as natural to her as her own; she not only understood them, but spoke and wrote them with the greatest freedom: she was versed likewise in Hebrew, Chaldee, and Arabic, and all this while a mere child. She had also a sedateness of temper, a quickness of apprehension, and a solidity of judgment, which enabled her not only to become the mistress of languages, but of sciences; so that she thought, spoke, and reasoned, upon subjects of the greatest importance, in a manner that surprised all. She was brought up in piety as well as learning. Her early letters show that she lived in the fear of God, and that she followed the protestant faith from principle. As Burnet observes, She read the scriptures much, and acquired great knowledge in divinity.

With these endowments she had so much mildness, humility, and modesty, that she set no value upon those acquisitions; she was naturally fond of literature, and that fondness was much heightened as well by the severity of her parents in the feminine part of her education, as by the gentleness of her tutor Aylmer in this. When mortified and confounded by the unmerited chiding of the former, she returned with double pleasure to the lessons of the latter, and sought in Demosthenes and Plato, who were her favourite authors, the delight that was denied her in all other scenes of life, in which she mingled but little, and seldom with any satisfaction. It is true, her alliance to the crown, as well as the great favour in which the marquis of Dorset, her father, stood with Henry VIII. and Edward VI. unavoidably brought her sometimes to court, and she received many marks of Edward's attention,

returned to popery, in consequence of which his former pupil addressed a letter to him written in severe terms, but such as he deserved for his apostasy. After the restoration of the protestant faith, Harding retired to the continent, and engaged in a warm and lengthened controversy with bishop Jewell.

* Aylmer was an active preacher of the reformation; he boldly opposed popery on the accession of queen Mary. He then withdrew to the continent, where he remained till Elizabeth came to the throne. In 1576 he was appointed bishop of London. He is noticed in the life of Becon.

yet she seems to have continued for the most part in the country, at Bradgate.

Here she was with her beloved books in 1550, when the famous Roger Ascham* called on a visit to the family in August. All the rest being engaged in hunting, he went to wait upon Lady Jane in her apartment, and found her reading the "Phædon" of Plato in the original Greek. Astonished at this, after the first salutations, he asked her, why she lost such pastime as there needs must be in the park, at which smiling, she answered, "I wist all their sport in the park is but a shadow to that pleasure that I find in Plato. Alas! good folk, they never felt what true pleasure meant."

This naturally leading him to inquire how a lady of her age had attained to such a depth of pleasure, both in the language and philosophy of Plato, she made the following very remarkable reply: "I will tell you, and I will tell you a truth, which perchance you will marvel at. One of the greatest benefits which ever God gave me is, that he sent me such sharp and severe parents, and so gentle a schoolmaster. For when I am in presence either of father or mother, whether I speak, keep silence, sit, stand, or go, eat, drink, be merry or sad; be sewing, playing, dancing, or doing any thing else, I am so sharply taunted, so cruelly threatened, yea, presently sometimes with pinches, nips, and bobs, and other ways, which I will not name for the honour I bear them, so without measure misordered, that I think myself in hell, till time come that I must go to M. Aylmer, who teaches me so gently, so pleasantly, with such fair allurements to learning, that I think all the time nothing while I am with him; and when I am called from him, I fall to weeping, because whatsoever I do else but learning, is full of grief, trouble, fear, and wholly misliking unto me. And thus my book has been so much my

* Ascham was an eminent scholar of the university of Cambridge, and particularly well skilled in Greek. In 1548, he was appointed tutor to the princess (afterwards queen) Elizabeth; afterwards he was Latin secretary to Edward VI. He continued to be a protestant in the reign of Mary, but was allowed to continue unmolested, and indeed patronized, on account of his abilities. To his other attainments, he added that of writing a most beautiful hand. He was re-appointed Latin secretary and tutor to queen Elizabeth. Ascham died in 1568. His last words were, "I am suffering much pain, I sink under my disease; but this is my confession, this is my faith, this prayer contains all that I wish for, 'I desire to depart hence, and to be with Christ.'"

pleasure, and brings daily to me more and more pleasure; in respect of it all other pleasures in very deed are but trifles and troubles unto me." What reader is not affected with Ascham's account of this interview? We may also observe that although lady Jane was treated as a child by her harsh parents, yet learned and pious men, such as Ascham, Bucer, and Bullinger, regarded her as far beyond her years in piety and learning.

At this time Ascham was going to London to attend sir Richard Morrison on an embassy to the emperor Charles V. In a letter written the December following, to the dearest of his friends, having informed him that he had lately had the honour and happiness of being admitted to converse familiarly with this young lady at court, and that she had written a very elegant letter to him, he proceeds to mention this visit at Bradgate, and his surprise thereon, not without some degree of rapture. Thence he takes occasion to observe, that she both spoke and wrote Greek to admiration; and that she had promised to write him a letter in that language, upon condition that he would send her one first from the emperor's court.

This rapture rose much higher while he was penning a letter addressed to her the following month. In the letter speaking of these interviews, he assures her, that among all the agreeable varieties which he had met with in his travels abroad, nothing had occurred to raise his admiration like that incident in the preceding summer, when he found her, a young maiden by birth so noble, in the absence of her tutor, and in the sumptuous house of her most noble father, at a time, too, when all the rest of the family both male and female, were amusing themselves with the pleasures of the chase; "I found," continues he, "the divine maid diligently studying the divine Phædon of the divine Plato in the original Greek. Happier, certainly, in this respect, than in being descended, both on the father and mother's side, from kings and queens."[*]

John ab Ulmis, writing from Bradgate in June 1551, to Bullinger, spoke in very high terms of lady Jane. He says, "From the learned epistle, written to you by the daughter of this prince, you will easily perceive the respect and esteem she entertains towards you. Surely there never lived any one more to be respected than this young female if her family be considered, more learned if we regard her

[*] Ascham, Ep. ad. Sturmium, i. 4, iii. 7.

age, or more excellent if we consider her in both. She is greatly praised by all the nobility, and they talk of her being espoused to the king. If that event should take place, how happy would the union be, and how beneficial to the church! But God will direct concerning these things; he only causes to prosper, he cares for, remembers, foresees, and disposes of all things agreeably to his will."

About this time some changes happened in the family; for her maternal uncles, Henry and Charles Brandon, both dying at Bugden, the bishop of Lincoln's palace, of the sweating sickness, her father was created duke of Suffolk, October 1551. Dudley, earl of Warwick, was also created duke of Northumberland the same day; and in November the duke of Somerset was imprisoned for a conspiracy against him as privy counsellor. From that time lady Jane appears to have been occasionally at court. In the summer of 1552 the king made a great progress through some parts of England, during which lady Jane went to pay her duty to his majesty's sister, the lady Mary, at Newhall in Essex. During this visit, her piety, and zeal against popery, prompted her to reprove the lady Ann Wharton, for making a courtesy to the host, or consecrated wafer, enclosed in a box, suspended, as was then usual, over the altar. Lady Jane observing her companion courtesy, asked if the princess were coming. Her companion replied No, but she made obeisance to Him that made us all. Why, said lady Jane, how can that be he that made us all, for the baker made him? which being carried by some officious person to the ear of the princess, was retained in her heart, so that she never loved lady Jane afterwards; and indeed the events of the following year were not likely to work a reconciliation

Another anecdote of her is related by Aylmer. He says, that having received from the lady Mary goodly apparel of tinsel cloth of gold and velvet, laid on with parsement lace of gold, when she saw it she said, "What shall I do with it?" Wear it, said a gentlewoman standing by. Nay, answered she, it were a shame to follow my lady Mary against God's word, and leave my lady Elizabeth who followeth God's word.

The dukes of Suffolk and Northumberland, who were now, after the fall of Somerset, grown to the height of their wishes in power, upon the decline of the king's health in 1553, began to think how to prevent that reverse of fortune, which, as things then stood, they foresaw must happen upon his death. To obtain this end, no other remedy was judged sufficient, but a change in the succession of the crown, and transferring it into their own families.

What other steps were taken preparatory to this bold attempt, may be seen in the general histories. Those excellent and amiable qualities which had rendered lady Jane dear to all who had the happiness to know her, joined to her near affinity to the king, subjected her to become the chief tool of an ambition notoriously not her own.

Upon this very account she was married to the lord Guildford Dudley, fourth son to the duke of Northumberland, without being acquainted with the real design of the match, which was celebrated with great pomp in the latter end of May, 1553; at the same time her younger sister, and the sister of her husband, were married to the lords Herbert and Hastings. These marriages were so much to the king's satisfaction that he contributed largely to the expense of them from the royal wardrobe. In the mean time, though the populace were very far from being pleased with the exorbitant greatness of the duke of Northumberland, yet they could not help admiring the beauty and innocence which appeared in lord Guildford and his bride. Lady Jane then removed from her father's house to the residences of the Dudleys—Durham house in London, and Sion house in the country. From her letter to queen Mary, she seems to have spent some days of this short period with her mother.

The pomp and splendour attending these nuptials was the last gleam of joy that shone in the palace of Edward, who grew so weak in a few days after, that Northumberland thought it high time to carry his project into execution. Accordingly, in the beginning of June, he broke the matter to the young monarch; who at length yielded to overlook his sisters, and to set aside his father's will; agreeably to which, a deed of settlement being drawn up in form of law by the judges, was signed by his majesty and all the lords of the council. Judge Hales however to the last refused his assent, and Cranmer was only induced to comply by the express commands of king Edward, and the assurance of the law officers of the crown, that such a proceeding was lawful.

The next step was to concert the most proper method for carrying this settlement into execution, and, till that was done, to keep it as secret as possible. To this end Northumberland directed letters to the lady Mary in her brother's name, requiring her attendance at Greenwich, where the court then was; but she discerned the real object of this invitation, and two days before the death of her brother, she retired to Norfolk, from whence she could escape by sea if she found it requisite to do so. The king expired July 6, 1553, but the two dukes, Suffolk and Northumberland, found it necessary to conceal his decease, that they might have time to gain the city of London, and to procure the consent of lady Jane, who was so far from being concerned in this business, that, as yet, she was unacquainted with the pains that had been taken to procure her the title of queen.

The Tower and city of London being secured, the council quitted Greenwich and came to London; and July 10, in the forenoon, the two last-mentioned dukes repaired to Sion house, where the lady Jane resided with her husband as part of the Northumberland family. There the duke of Northumberland, with much solemnity, explained to his daughter in law the disposition the late king had made of his crown by letters-patent; the clear sense the privy-council had of her right; the consent of the magistrates and citizens of London; and, in conclusion, himself and other nobles fell on their knees, and paid their homage to her as queen of England. Lady Jane, somewhat astonished at their discourse, but not at all moved by their reasons, or in the least elevated by such unexpected honours, returned them an answer to this effect: That the laws of the kingdom and natural right standing for the king's sisters, she would beware of burdening her weak conscience with a yoke which belonged to them; that she understood the infamy of those who had permitted the violation of right to gain a sceptre; that it were to mock God and deride justice to scruple at the stealing of a shilling, and not at the usurpation of a crown.

"Besides," said she, "I am not so young, nor so little read in the guiles of fortune, to suffer myself to be taken by them. If she enrich any, it is but to make them the subject of her spoil; if she raise others, it is but to pleasure herself with their ruins; what she adored but yesterday, is to-day her pastime; and, if I now permit her to adorn and crown me, I must, to-morrow, suffer her to crush and tear me to pieces. Nay, with what crown does she present me! a crown which hath been violently and shamefully wrested from Catharine of Arragon, made more unfortunate by the punishment of Ann Boleyn, and others that wore it after her; and why then would you have me add my blood to theirs, and be the third victim from whom this fatal crown may be ravished with the head that wears it? But in case it should not prove fatal unto me, and that all its venom were consumed, if fortune should give me waranties of her constancy, should I be well advised to take upon me these thorns which would lacerate, though not kill me outright; to burden myself with a yoke, which would not fail to torment me, though I were assured not to be strangled with it? My liberty is better than the chain you proffer me, with what precious stones soever it be adorned, or of what gold soever framed. I will not exchange my peace for honourable and precious jealousies, for magnificent and glorious fetters; and, if you love me sincerely, and in good earnest, you will rather wish me a secure and quiet fortune, though mean, than an exalted condition exposed to the wind, and followed by some dismal fall." Lady Jane herself described the principal circumstances attending her elevation to the throne in a letter to queen Mary, see p. 28.

However she was at length prevailed upon by the exhortations of her father, the intercession of her mother, the artful persuasions of Northumberland, and, above all, by the earnest desires of her husband, whom she tenderly loved, to yield her assent to what had been done, and what remained to do. And thus, with a heavy heart, she suffered herself to be conveyed by water to the Tower, where she entered with all the state of a queen, attended by the principal nobility, and, what is very extraordinary, her train was supported by the duchess of Suffolk, her mother, in whom, if in any of this line, the right of succession remained. About six in the afternoon, she was proclaimed with all due solemnities in the city; the same day she also assumed the regal title, and proceeded afterwards to exercise many acts of sovereignty: but, passing over the transactions of her short reign of fourteen days, which are the subjects of general history, we may proceed to her behaviour on her fall, which was occasioned rather by the general apprehensions of Northumberland's tyranny than by any affection for Mary.

Queen Mary was no sooner proclaimed, than the duke of Suffolk, who then resided with his daughter in the Tower, went to her apartment, and, in the softest terms he could, acquainted her with the situation of their affairs, and that, laying aside the state and dignity of a queen, she must again return to that of a private person; to which, with a settled and serene countenance, she made this answer: "I better brook this message than my former advancement to royalty; out of obedience to you and my mother, I have grievously sinned, and offered violence to myself. Now I do willingly, and as obeying the motions of my soul, relinquish the crown, and endeavour to salve those faults committed by others, if at least so great a fault can be salved, by a willing relinquishment and ingenuous acknowledgment of them."*

Burnet observes, She had a mind wonderfully raised above the world; and at the age wherein others are but imbibing the notions of philosophy, she had attained to the practice of the highest precepts of it. She was neither lifted up with the hope of a crown, nor cast down when she saw her palace made, afterwards, her prison; but carried herself with an equal temper of mind, in those great inequalities of fortune which so suddenly exalted and depressed her.

Thus ended her reign, but not her misfortunes. She was separated from her husband by the command of bishop Gardiner. They were placed separately in confinement, being stripped of every penny they possessed. She saw the father of her husband, with all his family, and many of the nobility and gentry, brought prisoners to the Tower, for supporting her claim to the crown; and this grief must have met with some accession from his being soon after brought to the block. Before the end of the month, she had the mortification of seeing her father, the duke of Suffolk, in the same circumstances with herself; but her mother, the duchess, not only remained exempt from all punishment, but had such interest with the queen, as to procure the duke his liberty, on the last day of the month. Lady Jane and her husband, being still in confinement, were, November 3, 1553, carried from the

---

* The suddenness of this change is shown by the following circumstance. Lady Jane had signified her willingness to stand godmother to the son of a gentleman pensioner, named Underhill. She sent lady Throckmorton as her proxy, who left the Tower in the afternoon to attend the christening, her mistress then being regarded as queen. On her return in the evening, she found the ensigns of royalty all reved, and her mistress a prisoner!

Tower to Guildhall, with Cranmer and others, and arraigned for high treason. They pleaded guilty. Lady Jane manifested the utmost coolness and presence of mind upon this occasion. Neither the pressure of the crowd, the clash of arms of the numerous guard, nor the solemn ceremonies observed in passing sentence, seemed to affect or overcome her. After her return, she had in fact to comfort those whose business it was rather to have comforted her. Judge Morgan, who pronounced sentence of death upon lady Jane, afterwards became raving mad, in which state he died, incessantly calling out that the lady Jane should be taken from his sight.

It is not easy to ascertain what were Mary's intentions towards lady Jane Grey and her husband. She addressed a letter to queen Mary, applying for mercy, and the author by whom this letter is printed, states that the queen resolved to pardon her at that time, but was induced afterwards to order her execution in consequence of the part taken by her father in Wyatt's insurrection. Several little indulgences were granted to them, which tended to alleviate the severity of their confinement, and which would imply a design of mercy towards them; but the conduct of Mary and her counsellors in other cases, also shows that this might be done to promote an object she had much at heart, namely, to induce the prisoners to profess the Romish faith. But lady Jane had counted the cost of following the truth, promises and threats were both disregarded, she evidently expected to suffer; she was, however, kept some months in suspense.

In January, 1554, the proposed marriage of the queen with Philip of Spain, had excited so much disgust in the nation, that sir Thomas Wyatt and others took arms with a view to prevent a union from which they anticipated many calamities to England. This hasty and ill-concerted insurrection was soon suppressed. No religious question was mixed with it, and many of the protestants were most active in opposing it, but the duke of Suffolk endeavoured to promote these proceedings, and the death of his daughter and her husband was resolved on. The news made no great impression upon lady Jane; the bitterness of death was passed; she had expected it, and was so well prepared to meet her fate, that she was very little discomposed.

Bishop Ponet expressly declares, that several of the council who had been most active in setting up lady Jane against queen Mary, were now active in causing her execution! The day first fixed for her death was Friday, February 9, and she had, in some measure, taken leave of the world by writing a letter to her unhappy father, who she heard was more disturbed with the thoughts of being the author of her death, than with the apprehension of his own. While she was in this frame of mind, Dr. Feckenham, abbot of Westminster, came to her from the queen, who was very desirous she should die professing herself a papist, as her father-in-law had done.* The abbot was the queen's confessor, and a very fit instrument, if any had been fit for the purpose, having, with an acute wit, and a plausible tongue, a great tenderness in his nature.

Lady Jane received him with much civility, and behaved towards him with so much calmness and sweetness of temper, that he could not help being overcome with her distress; so that, either mistaking, or pretending to mistake her meaning, he procured a respite of her execution till the 12th. When he acquainted her with it, and wished to enter upon a more formal conference, she told him, that he had entirely misunderstood her sense of her situation; that, far from desiring her death might be delayed, she expected and wished for it as the period of her miseries, and as her entrance into eternal happiness.†

Feckenham went to this conference with great hope and exultation. He appears to have thought that it would be no difficult matter to triumph over a dejected and heart-broken young female. But he found it quite otherwise. Yet lady Jane was still anxious to decline the proposed dispute; telling him that now she had no time to spare—that controversy might be fit for the living, but not for the dying—and, therefore, the truest sign of his having that compassion for her, of which he made such strong professions, would be to leave her undisturbed in her intercourse with God.

* The duke of Northumberland was beheaded August 22nd. He had been confined in a part of the Tower of London, called Beauchamp's tower. Some years since a curious device and inscription was discovered on one of the walls of this room, which there is strong reason to believe had been carved by this unhappy nobleman. The name of his daughter-in-law "JANE" had also been cut by him in two places. He appears to have been willing to do any thing to save his life.

† Banks, in a letter written at this time, Ep. Helv. Ecc. Ref. lxxix. states, that lady Jane had desired a brief interval, "that those enticements which invited her to wish for life, might be repressed, and entirely cut down by the sword of the word of God."

With this humble request the confessor's presumptuous hopes forbad compliance; particularly as several individuals had been purposely admitted, before whom he was anxious to display his powers.

The account of this conference states, that Feckenham had with her a long and tedious disputation; but, like the other priests who had preceded him in attempting to bring her back to popery, he found himself in all holy gifts much her inferior. He even acknowledged himself fitter to be her disciple than her teacher; and he besought her to deliver to him some brief account of her faith, which he might hereafter keep, and as a faithful witness publish to the world. To this she is stated to have willingly condescended; telling him to question her in what points of religion soever it pleased him, and promised that she would give answers, such as she would be ever ready to seal with her blood. This catechising argument, for such it was, took place in the Tower publicly, before an assemblage of the noble and learned; during which, lady Jane bore herself with such a modest humility, yet so honourably stout in all things, which either concerned her God, or her religion, that she engaged all the hearts of her auditory, while Feckenham lost much of that good opinion of his learning, which for a long time he had enjoyed. On this, we are told, that finding his own weakness, and his inability to repel her truth with his scholastic fallacies, he lost his temper, and dared to use to her speeches unsuitable for his gravity; an insult, however, which she only answered with smiles and patience. Some notes of this conference were drawn up by lady Jane herself, and will be found in the following pages.

When Feckenham was about to depart, he said, "Madam, I am sorry for you and your obstinacy, and now I am assured you and I shall never meet again." She replied, "It is most true, sir, we shall never meet again, except God turn your heart; for I stand undoubtedly assured that unless you repent and turn to God, you are in a sad and desperate case; and I pray to God in his mercy to send you his Holy Spirit, for he hath given you of his great gift of utterance, if it please him to open your heart to the truth."

Between the announcement of the order for her execution, and its fulfilment, the lieutenant of the Tower, sir John Gage, evidently impressed with love and respect for the unhappy sufferers, was anxious to procure some memorial of his illustrious prisoners; and accordingly he presented to them a " vellum book of a small thickish size,* being the devotions of some English protestant of quality, who was cast into prison wrongfully, according to his own opinion. It was illuminated by some foreigner, but hath since been abused: and is now imperfect in two places." Such is the description of the book in the Harleian catalogue, to which is added a note; " I will not affirm that this manual was written by the direction of Edward Seymour, duke of Somerset, and protector of England, upon his first commitment to the Tower of London, and that the last five prayers were added after his second commitment, which ended in his execution. But if this were so, it is easy to apprehend how it might come into the hands of that noble, but unfortunate lady, the lady Jane Grey; but that this book was in the lady Jane's hands, or possession, and was also looked into by her husband, appears from three notes, written on the lower margins."

The probability is, that the book had been borrowed by the illustrious sufferers; and other materials not being allowed, was made by them the means of communicating their last wishes and farewells to their friends. The first note is evidently addressed by lord Guildford to his father-in-law. " Your loving and obedient son wisheth unto your grace, long life in this world, with as much joy and comfort as ever I wished to myself; and in the world to come joy everlasting. Your most humble son till his death. G. DUDDELEY."

A few pages farther on, is a note from lady Jane, addressed to the duke of Suffolk: " The Lord comfort your grace, and that in his word, wherein all his creatures only are to be comforted. And though it hath pleased God to take away two of your children, yet think not, I most humbly beseech your grace, that you have lost them; but trust that we, by leaving this mortal life, have won an immortal life. And I for my part, as I have honoured your grace in this life, will pray for you in another life. Your grace's most humble daughter, JANE DUDDELEY."

Lady Jane also addressed sir John Gage in the following words: " Forasmuch as you have desired so simple a woman to write in so worthy a book, good master

* It is now in the British Museum, Harl. Coll. No. 2342.

lieutenant, therefore I shall, as a friend, desire you, and as a christian require you, to call upon God to incline your heart to his laws, to quicken you in his way, and not to take the word of truth utterly out of your mouth. Live still to die, that by death you may purchase eternal life; and remember how the end of Methusael, who, as we read in the scriptures, was the longest liver that ever was of a man, died at the last. For, as the preacher saith, there is a time to be born and a time to die; and the day of death is better than the day of our birth. Yours, as the Lord knoweth, as a friend. JANE DUDDELEY."

On the 11th of February she was, for the most part, occupied in religious exercises and meditations, but in the course of the evening she took up a new testament in Greek, " in which after she had read awhile, and closing the book, she found at the end of it some leaves of clean paper unwritten; which," says the author quoted, " as it were awakening and exciting her zeal, to some good and charitable office, she took pen and ink, and on these waste leaves wrote a most learned and godly exhortation; which she had no sooner finished, than she closed up the book, and delivered it to one of her attendants, mistress Tylney, or mistress Ellen, desiring her to bear it to her sister, lady Herbert, as the last token of her love and remembrance."

After finishing this exhortation to her sister, she was not permitted to remain in peace, but was again assailed by two bishops and two learned doctors, who held her in deep conference upwards of two hours, striving with all their powers of eloquence and persuasion to induce her to recant, and die in the Romish faith; in this, however, they were, as before, totally unsuccessful; for " her faith being built upon the rock, Christ, was by no worldly persuasion or comfort to be either moved or shaken; so that, after the expense of time, and the loss of much speech, they left her, as they said, a lost and forsaken member; but she, as before, prayed for them, and with a most charitable patience endured their worst censures."

The queen intended that lady Jane and her husband should suffer together on Tower-hill, but the council, fearful of the effect her appearance might have upon the people, ordered that she should suffer within the walls of the Tower. In the morning, the lord Guildford earnestly desired the officers, that he might take his last farewell of her; which, though they willingly gave permission, yet upon notice, she advised the contrary, assuring him that such a meeting would rather add to his afflictions than increase the quiet wherewith they had prepared their souls for the stroke of death; that he demanded a lenitive, which would put fire into the wound, and that it was to be feared her presence would rather weaken than strengthen him; that he ought to take courage from his reason, and derive constancy from his own heart; that if his soul were not firm and settled, she could not settle it by her eyes, nor confirm it by her words; that he should do well to remit this interview to the other world; that there, indeed, friendships were happy, and unions indissoluble, and that theirs would be eternal, if their souls carried nothing with them of terrestrial, which might hinder them from rejoicing. All she would do was to give him a farewell out of a window, as he passed to the place of his dissolution, which he suffered on the scaffold on Tower-hill with much christian meekness. His body was then carried back to the Tower in a cart. It is related that lady Jane was then sitting in her chamber, but on hearing the rumbling of the cart she arose and went to the window, though entreated by her attendants not to do so. She beheld his remains, and said, " O Guildford, Guildford, the anterepast is not so bitter that you have tasted, and that I shall soon taste, as to make my flesh tremble; it is nothing compared to the feast that you and I shall this day partake of in heaven."

She then sat down and wrote in her tablets three short sentences. The first was in Greek, and may be thus translated; " If his slain body shall give testimony against me before men, his blessed soul shall render an eternal proof of my innocence before God." She here adverted to her not having desired the crown. The second sentence was in Latin; " The justice of men took away his body, but the divine mercy has saved his soul." The third was in English; " If my fault deserved punishment, my youth and my imprudence were worthy of excuse; God and posterity will show me favour."

About an hour after she was led to the scaffold within the Tower. She was attended by Feckenham, but was observed not to give much heed to his discourses, keeping her eyes stedfastly fixed on a book of prayers, which she had in her hand. After some short recollection, she saluted those who were present with a countenance perfectly composed; then taking leave of Feckenham, she said,

"God will abundantly requite you, good sir, for your humanity to me, though your discourses gave me more uneasiness than all the terrors of my approaching death." She exhibited a countenance so gravely settled with all modest and comely resolution, that not the slightest trace of fear or grief could be observed in her words or actions.

When she mounted upon the scaffold, she said to the people standing thereabout, "Good people, I am come hither to die, and by a law I am condemned to the same. The fact against the queen's highness was unlawful, and the consenting thereunto by me; but touching the procurement and desire thereof by me, or on my behalf, I do wash my hands thereof in innocency before God, and the face of you good christian people this day;" and therewith she wrung her hands wherein she had her book. Then said she, "I pray you all, good christian people, to bear me witness that I die a true christian woman, and that I do look to be saved by no other means, but only by the mercy of God in the blood of his only Son Jesus Christ; and I do confess, that when I did know the word of God, I neglected the same, and loved myself and the world; and therefore this plague and punishment is happily and worthily happened unto me for my sins; and yet I thank God of his goodness, that he has thus given me a time and respite to repent. And now, good people, while I am alive, I pray you assist me with your prayers." Then kneeling down, she turned to Feckenham, saying, Shall I say this psalm? and he said, Yea. Then said she the fifty-first psalm in English, in most devout manner, to the end; and then she stood up and gave her attendant, mistress Ellen, her gloves and handkerchief, and her book to master Brydges (Gage?) of the Tower, and then she untied her gown, and the executioner pressed upon her to help her off with it, but she desiring him to let her alone, turned towards her two gentlewomen, who helped her off therewith, also her neckerchief, giving her a fair handkerchief to knit about her eyes.[*]

Then the executioner kneeled down and asked her forgiveness, whom she forgave most willingly. Then he willed her to stand upon the straw, which doing she saw the block; then she said, I pray you dispatch me quickly. Then she kneeled down, saying, Will you take it off before

---

[*] Her gloves were sent to Bullinger, as a memorial of his beloved correspondent. See Lit. Helvet. Reform. p. 351.

I lay me down? and the executioner said, No madam. Then tied she the handkerchief about her eyes, and feeling for the block, she said, What shall I do? Where is it? where is it? One of the standers-by guiding her thereunto, she laid her head upon the block, and then stretched forth her body, and said, Lord, into thy hands I commend my spirit; and so finished her life, in the year of our Lord God 1554, the 12th day of February.

It was long after called black Monday, as being the commencement of a week in which forty-seven persons were executed, and some of them quartered alive, in the streets of London! This excessive severity excited general indignation, and Knox in his bold and courageous manner observed, " I find that Jezebel, that cursed idolatress, caused the blood of the prophets to be shed, and Naboth to be martyred unjustly, for his own vineyard. But I think she never erected half so many gallows in all Israel as Mary hath done in London alone." Bishop Gardiner had publicly advised the queen to proceed rigorously, in a sermon he preached before her on the preceding Sunday.

Such was the life and death of lady Jane Grey. It affords a pleasing proof that the doctrines of the gospel can support in the time of trial, and the hour of death. These doctrines were set forth in the English reformation. Although not condemned as a heretic, she was a protestant, a follower of Christ, and a martyr to the cause of truth. As such, " the precious remains of lady Jane Grey" claim a place among the writings of the British Reformers. The principal pieces appeared in a printed form within a few months of her decease. They were also inserted by Fox in his Acts and monuments. The letter to queen Mary is an important document respecting the British Reformers, as the contents plainly show that the proceedings which led to lady Jane's brief pageant of royalty, originated entirely from the political motives of her relatives, and that none of the protestant clergy were active in devising or promoting those measures.

*The communication had between lady Jane Grey and Dr. Feckenham, abbot of Westminster.*

*Feckenham.* Madam, I lament your heavy case, and yet I doubt not but that you bear this sorrow of yours with a constant and patient mind.

*Jane.* You are welcome unto me, sir, if your coming be to give christian exhortation. And as for my heavy case, I thank God, I do so little lament it, that rather I account the same for a more manifest declaration of God's favour towards me, than ever he showed me at any time before. And therefore there is no cause why either you or others, who bear me good will, should lament or be grieved with my case, being a thing so profitable for my soul's health.

*F.* I am here come to you at this present, sent from the queen and her council, to instruct you in the true doctrine of the right faith, although I have so great confidence in you, that I shall have, I trust, little need to travail with you much therein.

*J.* I heartily thank the queen's highness, who is not unmindful of her humble subject; and I hope likewise that you no less will do your duty therein, both truly and faithfully, according to that you were sent for.

*F.* What is then required of a christian?

*J.* That he should believe in God the Father, in God the Son, and in God the Holy Ghost, three persons one God.

*F.* Is there nothing else to be required or looked for in a christian, but to believe in him?

*J.* Yes; we must also love him with all our heart, with all our soul, and with all our mind, and our neighbour as ourself.

*F.* Why, then faith only justifies not, or saves not.

*J.* Yes, verily, faith, as Paul saith, only justifieth.

*F.* Why, St. Paul saith, If I have all faith, without love, it is nothing.

*J.* True it is; for how can I love him whom I trust not? or how can I trust him whom I love not? Faith and love go both together, and that love is comprehended in faith.

*F.* How shall we love our neighbour?

*J.* To love our neighbour is to feed the hungry, to clothe the naked, and give drink to the thirsty, and to do to him as we would be done to.

*F.* Why, then it is necessary unto salvation to do good works also; it is not sufficient only to believe.

*J.* I deny that, and I affirm that faith only saveth; but it is meet for a christian to do good works, in token that he follows the steps of his Master, Christ, yet may we not say that they profit to our salvation; for when we have done all, we are unprofitable servants, and faith only in Christ's blood saves us.

*F.* How many sacraments are there?

*J.* Two—the one, the sacrament of baptism; and the other, the sacrament of the Lord's supper.

*F.* No; there are seven.

*J.* By what scripture find you that?

*F.* Well, we will talk of that hereafter. But what is the signification of your two sacraments?

*J.* By the sacrament of baptism, I am washed with water, and regenerated by the Spirit,* and that washing is a token to me that I am the child of God. The sacrament of the Lord's supper offered unto me, is a sure seal and testimony that I am by the blood of Christ, which he shed for me on the cross, made partaker of the everlasting kingdom.

*F.* Why, what do you receive in that sacrament? Do you not receive the very body and blood of Christ?

*J.* No, surely; I do not so believe. I think that at that supper I neither receive flesh nor blood, but only bread and wine, which bread, when it is broken, and the wine, when it is drunken, puts me in mind how that for my sins the body of Christ was broken, and his blood shed on the cross; and with that bread and wine I receive the benefits that come by the breaking of his body, and shedding of his blood on the cross for my sins.

*F.* Why, does not Christ speak these words, Take, eat, this is my body? Require you plainer words? does he not say it is his body?

*J.* I grant he saith so; and so he saith, I am the vine, I am the door; but he is never the more for that a door nor a vine. Does not St. Paul say, He calleth those things that are not, as though they were? (Rom. iv.) God forbid that I should say that I eat the very natural body and blood of Christ; for then either I should pluck away my redemption, or else there were two bodies or two Christs, or twelve bodies, when his disciples did eat his body, and it suffered not till the next day. So finally one body was tormented on the cross; and if they did eat another body, then had he two bodies; or, if his body were eaten, then

---

* The latter part of this communication has been corrected from Harl. MS. 425 in the British Museum.

it was not broken upon the cross. Or, if it were broken upon the cross, it was not eaten of his disciples.

*F.* Why, is it not as possible that Christ by his power could make his body both to be eaten and broken, as to be born of a virgin, as to walk upon the sea, having a body, and other such-like miracles as he wrought by his power only?

*J.* Yes, verily; if God would have done at his supper any miracle, he might have done so; but I say, that he minded to work no miracle, but only to break his body, and to shed his blood on the cross, for our sins. But I pray you answer me to this one question, Where was Christ when he said, Take, eat, this is my body? was he not at the table when he said so? he was at that time alive, and suffered not till the next day. What took he but bread? what brake he but bread? and what gave he but bread? Yea, what he took, that he brake; and look what he brake, he gave; yea, and what he gave, he did eat: and yet all this while he himself was alive, and at supper before his disciples, or else they were deceived.

*F.* You ground your faith upon such authors as say and unsay, both with a breath, and not upon the church, to whom you ought to give credit.

*J.* No, I ground my faith upon God's word, and not upon the church; for if the church be a good church, the faith of the church must be tried by God's word, and not God's word by the church, nor yet my faith. Shall I believe the church because of antiquity, or shall I give credit to the church that takes away from me the one half of the Lord's supper, and will suffer no layman to receive it in both kinds? But surely I think if they deny it to us, then deny they to us part of our salvation. And I say, that it is an evil church, and not the spouse of Christ, but the spouse of the devil, that alters the Lord's supper, and both takes from it, and adds to it. To that church, say I, God will add plagues, and from that church will he take their part out of the book of life. Do they learn that of St. Paul, when he ministered to the Corinthians in both kinds? Shall I believe this church? God forbid!

*F.* That was done for a good intent of the church, to avoid a heresy that sprung upon it.

*J.* Why, shall the church alter God's will and ordinance for good intent? How did king Saul? The Lord God forbid.[*]

[*] The Harl. MS. 425 ends thus—"With these and such like he would have had me lean to the church, but it would not be. There were many other things whereof we reasoned, but these are the chief points, &c."

To this M. Feckenham gave me a long, tedious, yet eloquent reply, using many strong and logical persuasions to compel me to lean to their church; but my faith had armed my resolution to withstand any assault that words could then use against me. Of many other articles of religion we reasoned, but these formerly rehearsed were the chief, and most effectual.

JANE DUDLEY.

After this, Feckenham took his leave, saying, that he was sorry for her; for I am sure, quoth he, that we two shall never meet.

True it is, said the lady Jane, that we shall never meet, except God turn your heart; for I am assured, unless you repent, and turn to God, you are in an evil case; and I pray God, in the bowels of his mercy, to send you his Holy Spirit, for he hath given you his great gift of utterance, if it pleased him also to open the eyes of your heart.

## LETTER I.

### *Jane Grey to Henry Bullinger.*[*]

MOST LEARNED SIR,—I give you never ceasing thanks, and will continue to do so while I live. I never can say that I have done so enough; for it does not appear that I can ever return your great kindnesses—unless you may perhaps consider me to thank you, while I bear them in mind. And there is sufficient cause; for I receive letters from you most ably and excellently written, which indeed are most acceptable to me, because you, at so great a distance, and in your advanced age, laying aside more important affairs, have condescended to write to me who am unworthy to receive letters from one so learned; and also because your writings afford no common pleasure, but teach, warn, and instruct, in what is pious and holy. Especially they point out those things which are best suited to my age, sex, and the rank of our family. In these, as in all the writings which you have set forth for the especial benefit of the

[*] Written at the age of fourteen. The autographs of this and the two following letters were preserved in the public library at Zurich. The two first were printed by Hottinger in his Hist. Eccles. p. ix. They are all included in the Ep. ab Ecc. Helv. Ref. Tiguri, 1742. The riginals are in Latin.

christian public, not only your learning appears, but also it is evident that you are a prudent and pious adviser; who savour only of that which is good, who think of nothing but what pertains to God, who command nothing but what is useful, and produce nothing but what is right, kind, and worthy of a father so much to be respected.

Happy indeed am I to have such a friend and prudent adviser, (as Solomon has said, in the multitude of counsellors there is safety*) and that I am so intimate, and in such strict friendship with so pious a divine; one who is a valiant contender for the truth. Deeply indeed am I indebted to God, and especially that since he has bereaved me of the pious Bucer,† that learned man and holy father, who always, and by all means, was ready to impart whatever was needful to direct and form my conduct, who led me forward in all probity, piety, and sound learning, exciting me by the application of his best counsels—I am deeply indebted, I say, that He has given you to me in the place of Bucer. You will, I trust, continue to urge me forward as you have begun, for I am inclined to linger and delay. Nothing more to be desired could have befallen me, than that I should be considered worthy to receive the letters and salutary counsels of such honoured men, whose virtues cannot be too highly spoken of, and that the same advantage has befallen me as Blesilla, Paulla, and Eustachium, whom St. Jerome taught, as it is said, and led to the knowledge of divine truths by his discourses; such also as was enjoyed by that woman in ancient times, to whom St. John wrote his hortative and pious epistle; or such as the mother of Severus enjoyed, who availed herself of the counsels of Origen, and followed his admonitions; none of whom sought to acquire for themselves praise and advantages from personal beauty, noble connections, or wealth, but rather derived glory and happiness from the counsels of those wise men; so that persons conspicuous for singular erudition and exalted piety, did not disdain to lead them, as it were by the hand, to whatever is excellent, and to supply whatever might best promote their eternal salvation, and the happiness of their lives. Again and again would I entreat you to do the same for me, since you are not to be accounted the least among them, for learning, ability, or piety.

* Prov. xi. 14. Lady Jane quotes the original Hebrew.
† Bucer died at Cambridge in February, 1551.

I, who so boldly make this request, must appear to you too forward, but if you will consider the cause, namely, that I seek to derive from your kindness supplies which may avail to form my conduct, and tend to maintain my faith in Christ my Saviour, your kindness will neither permit, nor will your wisdom incline you to consider what I do as deserving of censure.

I often, as it were, gather sweet flowers in a pleasant garden, from that work so replete with real and sincere religion which you lately sent to my father and myself.* My father also, when his important affairs permit, employs himself in diligently perusing the contents. We ought indeed to give continual thanks to you, and to God for you, that we both derive fruit from thence. We can hardly think it right that we should receive with unthankful hearts so many and such great gifts from you, and many others like you, whom Germany has produced. For we mortals, in our dealings with fellow-mortals, are accustomed, as is equitable, to requite kindnesses by kindnesses, and to prove ourselves mindful of those who bestow benefits upon us. How much the more then ought we to manifest our sense of the divine goodness, since we cannot make any return, but can only receive with gratitude what God bestows, and express heartfelt thanks for the same.

I now come to notice the praises which your letters contain—as I cannot consider them my due, so neither ought I to acknowledge them. Whatever the divine goodness has bestowed upon me, I would attribute entirely to the real source, to the great and only Author of all that I possess which has any appearance of good. Pray to Him in my name continually, that he may so guide me in all my ways, that I may not be found acting unworthy of his great kindness.

My father intended to write, that he might thank you for your noble labours, and the kind manner in which you have inscribed a decade of your sermons to him, thus publishing them under his auspices, but he has been called to a remote part of the country by the king's affairs. He will, however, write to you as soon as his public occupations allow. In conclusion, you will still farther increase my obligations to you, if you will point out to me, as I am now beginning to learn Hebrew, the method whereby I may pursue that course of study to the greatest advantage.

Farewell, thou ornament of the christian church, and

* Bullinger's Decades, or Sermons.

may God long preserve thee a surviver to us and to his church.

Your most devoted, JANE GREY.

## LETTER II.

*Jane Grey to Henry Bullinger.**

I CANNOT allow myself, without great ingratitude, to seem unmindful of my duty, and unworthy of your favours, most learned sir; but must, on all occasions, return you my best thanks for your services, which have been very many. Yet assuredly I do it with humiliation, because the intimate friendship which you wish me to share with you, and so many benefits conferred by you on one wholly undeserving of them, seem to call for more than thanks; nor can I satisfactorily discharge my obligation by so inadequate a return as words.

It distresses me not a little when I now consider how unfit I am to indite a letter that is to be presented to so great a man. For certainly I neither should desire, nor venture to disturb your seriousness with my weak and childish trifles, nor to offend your eloquence by such barbarisms, did I not know that I could no otherwise gratify you, or had I any doubt of your accustomed and well experienced kindness towards me.

Now concerning the letter which I received last from you, accept the following. After that I had read it once and again, for once reading did not seem sufficient, I seemed to have derived as much profit from your excellent and truly pious precepts as I had with difficulty attained from the daily study of the best authors. You persuade me to embrace the true and pure faith in Christ my Saviour. I will strive to satisfy you in this particular, as God shall enable me; but I acknowledge it to be the gift of God, and therefore ought to promise only as the Lord shall impart. Yet I will not cease to pray, with the apostles, that He would daily increase this to me by his grace. To this, God helping me, I will also add, as you enjoin, purity of life, as far as my, alas! too feeble strength can attain thereto. I entreat in the mean time that you, of your christian affection, would daily make mention of me in your prayers.

* Written in her fifteenth year.

I will enter upon the study of the Hebrew language in that method which you so clearly direct.

Farewell; and may God protect you in the engagement which you have taken upon you, and eternally prosper you. 1552.

Yours, most ready to every pious duty,

JANE GREY.

## LETTER III.

### *Jane Grey to Henry Bullinger.**

MOST LEARNED SIR,—The late recollection of a duty ought not to be blamed, if it has not been omitted through negligence. For I am far distant; opportunities for sending letters are few; and it is late before I hear of them. But now, since I have that messenger, by whose means my letters are usually delivered to you, and yours to me, I ought not to be wanting in my duty; but should endeavour with the utmost diligence, by writing to you, to return thanks in the best manner, in words and in deed. For so great is your reputation with all, such is your seriousness, as I hear, in preaching, and such your uprightness of life, as they who are acquainted with you report, that foreign and distant nations, as well as the country in which you dwell, are excited, not merely by your words, but also by your example, to lead good and happy lives. For you are not only, as James hath it, a diligent herald and preacher of the gospel, and of the sacred precepts of God, but also a true " doer" and performer thereof; holding forth in your life those things which you command and teach; by no means " deceiving your own self." Nor are you " like unto those who behold their natural face in a glass," and having gone away, " straightway forget" what was the appearance thereof: you both preach true and sound doctrine, and by your manner of life are an example and pattern to others, to follow that which you teach and perform.

But why do I write these things to you, when such is my unskilfulness as to be unable either worthily to commend your piety, or to speak in adequate terms of your holiness of life, nor can I set forth your doctrines as they ought to

* Written about the time of her marriage.

be regarded and admired. To speak of you as the truth demands, I had need of the powers of Demosthenes or Cicero, for your merits require a space of time, readiness of powers, and ability of speech to set them forth, which a child cannot possess. For as it would appear, God has looked upon you with such complacency as to fit you for usefulness in this world, and for a place in his kingdom hereafter. In the prison of this life you pass your earthly course as dead to the world, even while you live. And you not only live first to Christ, without whom there can be no life, and afterwards to yourself, but you also live for many others, whom you earnestly endeavour, by the will of God, to lead on to that immortality, which you will attain when departed from this world. I will not cease to implore of almighty God, the author and giver of all good things, that your pious labours may be effectual. Nor will I cease to plead that you may be long continued in this life.

These things I have written to you with more boldness than prudence, but you have rendered me such service, by kindly writing to me when unknown to you, assisting me with what was needful to adorn my mind, and to improve my judgment, that I should be justly chargeable with neglect, and forgetful of my duty, if I did not, in every way, show myself mindful of your worth.

Moreover, I hope that you will pardon this my unfeminine boldness, who, though a young girl, thus address a man, and, although ignorant, presume to write to one so learned. Forgive also my rashness in thus disturbing you with my trifles, frivolities, and childish scribbling, while engaged in matters of importance,—which pardon, if I obtain, I shall consider myself deeply indebted to your goodness. But if I have offended in this matter, it is to be ascribed to my regard for you rather than to that forwardness which never should be manifested by our sex, or to that rashness which contends against better judgment. For when I read your works, or think of you, my perception is so overcome by your attainments that I do not so much consider what is suitable to myself as what is due to you.

My mind is indeed involved in many hesitations when I consider my youth, my sex, and scanty measure of learning, or rather my imbecility, each of which alone, and much more when considered together, would deter me from writing. But, on the other hand, when I contemplate your virtues, your celebrity, and the kindness you have shown towards me, the higher consideration yields to the inferior—namely, what is becoming from me towards you; and what is due to you, prevails above every other consideration.

Be pleased to salute in my name that illustrious and learned man, Bibliander, so much signalized for erudition and piety, although he is a stranger to me. For I hear in our country such a report of his learning, and understand that his name is so noted every where for the singular gifts bestowed upon him by God, that, although I have attained but little knowledge, I am compelled to admire the piety and sincerity of this divinely commissioned man. And I pray that such pillars of the church may long prosper and be continued. I shall not cease my best wishes for you, thanking you for the kindness shown to me, and offering my fervent desires for your welfare so long as my life shall be spared.

Farewell, learned sir,
Your most devoted, JANE GREY.

## LETTER IV.

### *From Lady Jane Grey to Queen Mary.*

(Written in August, 1553.*)

MY fault is so great, that but for the goodness and

* This letter is printed by Pollini, in his "Ecclesiastical history of the English revolution," written in Italian, and printed at Rome in 1594. He states that the lady Jane was compelled by her relations to assume the crown, as she explained in a letter written to queen Mary in August, 1553, a copy of which had come to his hands by means of a person worthy of credit, who at that time procured a copy of it in London. He does not mention in what language the letter was written, but it seems from internal evidence to have been written in Italian, in which language both lady Jane and queen Mary were well skilled; it therefore appears here under the disadvantage of a translation. The Rev. H. Soames, who has printed the greater part of the letter in Italian, observes, that "The student of English history is much obliged to Pollini for the preservation of this interesting letter, which bears every mark of genuineness. In general, however, Pollini's work is worthless."

It is a valuable document, the contents are supported by other testimonies. It is inserted here as a strong proof, if any were wanting, that the brief pageant of lady Jane Grey was entirely a political device of Northumberland and his adherents, and that it was not planned or carried into effect by the real leaders of the Reformation, Cranmer and his associates, who are not even mentioned by the unhappy victim of ambition.

clemency of the queen, I could have no hope in asking forgiveness, nor that I should find pardon. For I have given ear to those who at that time appeared to be wise, not only to me, but also to a great part of this realm; but they have made known the contrary, as at present is seen, not only to my great hurt and to their own, but by the common disgrace and blame of all men—they having with such shameful boldness made so dishonourable an attempt to give to another what was not their own to bestow, neither did it become me to accept; rightly and justly then do I blush and am ashamed, while I ask pardon for such a crime. Nevertheless I trust in God, that as at this time I know and confess my lack of wisdom, for which I deserve heavy punishment, unless the great mercy of your highness prevent, so likewise, from many tokens I have hope of your great clemency, knowing that the error charged upon me was not wholly my own. My crime is great, and I confess it to be so, nevertheless, I am accounted more guilty than in truth I am. For although I took upon me that of which I was unworthy, yet no one can say that I ever sought to obtain it for myself, nor ever solaced myself therein, nor accepted of it willingly.

For when it was publicly reported that there was no longer any hope of the king's life, as the duchess of Northumberland before had promised that I should remain in the house with my mother, so having soon after learned this from her husband who first told it to me, she was no longer willing that I should leave my house, saying that if God willed to call the king to his mercy, and there was at that time no hope of his life, it would be needful for me to go immediately to the Tower, since his majesty had made me heir of his kingdom. Which being thus suddenly told unto me, I was greatly moved; it disturbed my mind, and after some time it oppressed me still more.

But notwithstanding, I gave little heed to these words, and did not delay going from my mother. So that the duchess of Northumberland was much displeased with me and with the duchess my mother, saying that if she had resolved to keep me in the house, she had also kept her son, with whom she thought I would assuredly have gone. She continued to be much displeased with me. In truth I remained in her house two or three nights, but at length obtained leave to go to Chelsea for my recreation. While there, shortly after, although unwell, I was summoned by the council, who gave me to understand that I must go the same night to Sion, to receive that which had been ordered respecting me by the king.

The person by whom this news was brought unto me was the lady Sidney, my sister-in-law, daughter of the duchess of Northumberland; she told me with seriousness more than common, that it was needful I should go with her, and I did so. When we arrived, we found no one; but shortly after, there came the duke of Northumberland, the marquess of Northampton, the earls of Arundel, Huntingdon, and Pembroke, who, with unaccustomed kindness and condescension, did me such reverence as was not fitting to my state, for they knelt before me, and in many other ways made semblance to honour me. They also acknowledged me as their sovereign mistress, so that they caused me extreme confusion. After a time they brought to me the duchess Frances my mother, the duchess of Northumberland, and the marchioness of Northampton. The duke of Northumberland, as president of the council, then made known the death of king Edward, showing what cause we had to rejoice for his virtuous and praise-worthy life, and also for his joyful departure. He furthermore took comfort to himself, and to all present, by praising much the goodness and wisdom of his late highness, for the great care he had manifested in the last hours of his life touching his kingdom, having prayed to God to defend it from the popish faith, and to deliver it from the rule of his evil sisters. He then said that his majesty had well weighed an act of parliament, wherein it was formerly enacted* that whosoever should acknowledge the lady Mary, that is, your highness, or the lady Elizabeth, and take them for rightful heirs to the crown of England, should be held for traitors, one of them having formerly been disobedient to her father Henry the eighth, and to himself, touching the truth of religion, and declared enemies of the word of God; also that both were illegitimate. Wherefore in no manner would he that they should be heirs of his crown, he being able in every way to disinherit

* Northumberland referred to an act passed in 1536, whereby both Mary and Elizabeth were declared illegitimate, and unable to succeed to the crown. This act had not been repealed, although in fact it was set aside by the act passed just before the death of Henry VIII., declaring that the succession should devolve upon those princesses in case Edward had no children. The reasons here assigned are in substance contained in the proclamation issued by lady Jane's supporters.

them. He therefore before his death gave charge to his council, that for the duty they owed unto him, for the love they bare to the realm, and for the affection they ought to have for their country, they should obey this his last will. The duke also said, that I was the heir named by his majesty to succeed to the crown, and that my sisters should in like manner succeed me, if I died without issue.

Hearing these words, all the lords of the council kneeled before me, saying that they rendered the honour due to me, I being heir to the crown, of true and direct lineage; and that it became them in every way to observe what they had deliberately promised to the king, to shed their own blood freely, and to offer their own lives to death in this cause. The which things I heard with extreme grief of mind; how I was carried out of myself, amazed, and troubled, I leave it to those lords to testify who were present, and saw me, overcome by sudden and unlooked for sorrow, fall to the ground weeping very bitterly. I then declared to them how unable I was; I deeply lamented the death of so noble a prince, and turning myself to God, I humbly prayed and besought him that if what had been given me was mine by law and right, his divine Majesty would grant me such grace and spirit that I should govern to his glory and service, and to the good of this realm.

On the next day, as is known to every one, I was conducted to the Tower. Shortly after the lord treasurer, the marquess of Winchester, presented to me the jewels, with them he brought the crown, although neither by me nor by any one in my name had this been asked.* He further willed me to put the crown upon my head, that it might be seen whether it became me or not. The which with many excuses I refused to do, nevertheless he told me that I should take it to me without fear, and that another would be made to crown my husband with me. This was heard by me with a troubled mind, also with much grief

---

* In the Harleian Coll. No. 611, is an order from queen Mary to the marquess of Winchester, who was still lord treasurer, dated 20th September, referring to "certain our jewels and stuff" delivered to him on the 20th July by lady Jane Grey, "which she before had received of you the 12th of the same month." It appears that some articles were missing, and he is commanded to use diligence for their recovery. The list is curious; among the missing articles are "a little piece of a broken ring of gold;" "three French crowns, one of them broken;" "four old half-pence of silver;" "sixteen pence, two farthings, and two half-pence;" "a pair of knives;" "two shaving cloths;" "fourteen pair of gloves of divers sorts."

and displeasure of heart. After this nobleman was gone, when talking of many things with my husband, he assented to what had been said, and asked to be made king—he desired to be made by me, by act of parliament.* But afterwards I called the earls of Arundel and Pembroke, and said to them, that if the crown belonged to me, I would be content to make my husband a duke, but I would never consent to make him king. This my resolution caused his mother, when it was reported to her, to find occasion for much wrath and disdain. She became very angry with me, and was so displeased, that she persuaded her son not to sleep with me any longer. He did so, declaring to me moreover that he would not in any way be made a duke, but king. So that I was constrained to send to him the earls of Arundel and Pembroke, who negotiated with him to come to me, otherwise I knew that the next morning he would have gone to Sion.

And thus, in truth, was I deceived by the duke and the council, and ill treated by my husband and his mother. Moreover, as sir John Gates has confessed, the duke was the first to persuade the king to make me his heir. As to the rest, for my part I do not know what the council may have determined, but I know for certain in this time poison was twice given to me, the first time in the house of the duke of Northumberland, and since that, here in the Tower. Of this I have sure and certain testimony, besides that the skin has since that time peeled from my body.

All these things I have willed to say in testimony of my innocence, and for the unburdening of my conscience.

## LETTER V.

*A letter of the Lady Jane written to her father on the 9th of February, 1554.*

FATHER,—although it hath pleased God to hasten my death by you, by whom my life should rather have been lengthened; yet can I so patiently take it, that I yield God more hearty thanks for shortening my woful days, than if all the world had been given unto my possessions, with life lengthened at my own will, and albeit I am very well assured of your impatient dolours, redoubled many ways, both in

---

* He actually assumed the title. It appears from MS. Harl. Coll. No. 523, that "the king" had written to the regent of the Low Counties, desiring her in all *his* affairs to give full credit to sir Philip Hoby.

bewailing your own woe, and especially, as I am informed, my woful state, yet, my dear father, if I may without offence rejoice in my own mishap, herein I may account myself blessed, that, washing my hands with the innocence of my fact, my guiltless blood may cry before the Lord, Mercy to the innocent.

And yet though I must needs acknowledge that being constrained, and, as you know well enough, continually assayed, yet in taking upon me I seemed to consent, and therein grievously offended the queen and her laws; yet do I assuredly trust that this my offence towards God is so much the less, in that, being in so royal estate as I was, mine enforced honour blended never with mine innocent heart. And thus, good father, I have opened unto you the state wherein I at present stand; my death at hand, although to you perhaps it may seem woful, yet to me there is nothing that can be more welcome than from this vale of misery to aspire to that heavenly throne of all joy and pleasure, with Christ our Saviour; in whose stedfast faith, if it may be lawful for the daughter so to write to the father, the Lord that hitherto hath strengthened you, so continue to keep you, that at the last we may meet in heaven with the Father, the Son, and the Holy Ghost.

I am,
Your obedient daughter till death,
JANE DUDLEY.

---

When the lady Jane's father was flourishing in freedom and prosperity in the time of king Edward, there belonged unto him a certain learned man, student and graduate of the university of Oxford, who then being chaplain to the said duke, and a sincere preacher, as he appeared, of the gospel, according to the doctrine of that time set forth and received, shortly after the state of religion began to alter by queen Mary, he altered also in his profession with the time, and of a protestant became a friend and defender of the pope's proceedings.

At whose sudden mutation and inconstant mutability, this christian lady being not a little aggrieved, and most of all lamenting the dangerous state of his soul in sliding so away for fear from the way of truth, wrote her mind unto him in a sharp and vehement letter, which, as it appears to proceed of an earnest and zealous heart, so would that it might take such effect with him as to reduce him to repentance,* and to take better hold again for the health and wealth of his own soul. The copy of the letter is as follows:

---

## LETTER VI.

*A letter of the Lady Jane Grey to master Harding,† late chaplain to the duke of Suffolk, her father, and then fallen from the truth of God's most holy word.*

So oft as I call to mind the dreadful and fearful saying of God, That he which layeth hold upon the plough and looketh back, is not meet for the kingdom of heaven; and on the other side, the comfortable words of our Saviour Christ to all those that, forsaking themselves, do follow him, I cannot but marvel at thee, and lament thy case, who seemedst sometime to be the lively member of Christ, but now the deformed imp of the devil; sometime the beautiful temple of God, but now the stinking and filthy kennel of Satan; sometime the unspotted spouse of Christ, but now the unshamefaced paramour of antichrist; sometime my faithful brother, but now a stranger and apostate; sometime a stout christian soldier, but now a cowardly runaway.‡

Yea, when I consider these things, I cannot but speak to thee, and cry out upon thee—Thou seed of Satan, and not of Judah, whom the devil hath deceived, the world hath beguiled, and the desire of life subverted and made thee of a christian an infidel; wherefore hast thou taken the testament of the Lord in thy mouth? wherefore hast thou preached the law and the will of God to others? wherefore hast thou instructed others to be strong in Christ,

* Harding was alive when this was printed.
† He was afterwards the opponent of bishop Jewell. See Jewell's life prefixed to his writings.
‡ Some persons have supposed this letter was not written by lady Jane Grey, on account of the strong expressions it contains. But the usages of those times allowed expressions in the mouths of females of rank, which would now scarcely be heard even amongst the lowest classes, while the subject was too momentous to allow any trifling, or to render phraseology of much importance. Nor should it be forgotten that this letter was printed in 1554, and that Harding lived many years after, during which time he was engaged in bitter controversies with the protestants, whom he would doubtless have accused of falsehood had this letter not been really addressed to him by his former pupil. Banks transmitted it on the 15th March 1554, to Bullinger, with other pieces written by lady Jane, which he had collected and translated into Latin for the Swiss reformer.

When Fox inquired of Aylmer for communications respecting lady Jane, Aylmer told him of her letter to Harding, already in print, recommending him to insert it in his work, adding, "You will say it was piously and prudently written, and perhaps learnedly too."

when thou thyself dost now so shamefully shrink, and so horribly abuse the testament and law of the Lord?* When thou thyself preachest, not to steal, yet most abominably stealest, not from men, but from God; and committing most heinous sacrilege, robbest Christ thy Lord of his right members, thy body and soul; and choosest rather to live miserably with shame, to the world, than to die, and gloriously with honour, to reign with Christ, in whom even in death is life. Why dost thou now show thyself most weak, when indeed thou oughtest to be most strong? The strength of a fort is unknown before the assault; but thou yieldest thy hold before any battery be made.

Oh wretched and unhappy man! what art thou but dust and ashes? And wilt thou resist thy Maker that fashioned thee, and framed thee? Wilt thou now forsake Him that called thee from the custom-gathering among the Romish anti-christians, to be an ambassador and messenger of his eternal word? He that first framed thee, and since thy first creation and birth preserved thee, nourished and kept thee, yea, and inspired thee with the spirit of knowledge, I cannot say of grace, shall he not now possess thee? Darest thou deliver up thyself to another, being not thine own, but his? How canst thou, having knowledge, or how durst thou, neglect the law of the Lord, and follow the vain traditions of men? and whereas thou hast been a public professor of his name, become now a defacer of his glory?

Wilt thou refuse the true God, and worship the invention of man, the golden calf, the harlot of Babylon, the Romish religion, that abominable idol the most wicked mass? Wilt thou torment again, rend and tear the most precious body of our Saviour Christ with thy bodily and fleshly teeth? Wilt thou take upon thee to offer up any sacrifice unto God for our sins, considering that Christ offered up himself, as Paul saith, upon the cross, a lively sacrifice once for all? Can neither the punishment of the Israelites, which for their idolatry they so oft received, nor the terrible threatenings of the prophets, nor the curses of God's own mouth, make thee fear to honour any

* This man, a little before king Edward died, was heard openly in his sermons in London to exhort the people with great vehemence, that if trouble came, they should never shrink from the true doctrine of the gospel which they had received, but should rather take it for a trial sent of God to prove them, whether they would abide by it or no. All which to be true they can testify that heard him, and who are yet alive; who, also foreseeing the plague to come, were then much confirmed by his words.—*Fox.*

other god than Him? Dost thou so regard Him that spared not his dear and only Son for thee, so diminishing, yea, utterly extinguishing his glory, that thou wilt attribute the praise and honour due unto him, to the idols, which have mouths and speak not, eyes and see not, ears and hear not, which shall perish with them that made them?

What saith the prophet Baruch, when he recited the epistle of Jeremy written to the captive Jews? Did he not forewarn them that in Babylon they should see gods of gold, silver, wood, and stone, borne upon men's shoulders, to cast fear before the heathen? But be not ye afraid of them, saith Jeremiah, nor do as others do; but when you see others worship them, say you in your hearts, It is thou, O Lord, that oughtest only to be worshipped; for as for those gods, the carpenter framed them and polished them; yea, gilded be they, and laid over with silver and vain things, and cannot speak. He showeth, moreover, the abuse of their deckings: how the priests took off their ornaments, and apparelled their women withal; how one holdeth a sceptre, another a sword in his hand, and yet can they judge in no matter, nor defend themselves, much less any other, from either battle or murder; nor yet from gnawing of worms, nor any other evil thing. These, and suchlike words, Jeremiah spake unto them, whereby he proved them to be but vain things, and no gods; and at last he concluded thus, Confounded be all they that worship them.

They were warned by Jeremiah; and thou, as Jeremiah, hast warned others, and art warned thyself, by many scriptures in many places; God saith he is a jealous God, who will have all honour, glory, and worship given to him only; and Christ saith, in the fourth of Luke, to Satan who tempted him, even to the same Satan, the same Beelzebub, the same devil, which hath prevailed against thee, It is written, Thou shalt honour the Lord thy God, and him only shalt thou serve.

These, and such-like, do prohibit thee and all christians, to worship any other god than He who was before all worlds, and laid the foundations both of heaven and earth; and wilt thou honour a detestable idol invented by Romish popes, and the abominable college of crafty cardinals? Christ offered himself up once for all, and wilt thou offer him up again daily at thy pleasure? But thou wilt say, thou doest it for a good intent!—O sink of sin! O child of perdition! Dost thou dream therein of a good intent where thy conscience beareth thee witness of God's threatened wrath against thee? How did Saul, who disobeyed the word of the Lord for a good intent, but was thrown from his worldly and temporal kingdom? Shalt thou then, that dost deface God's honour, and rob him of his right, inherit the eternal and heavenly kingdom?

Wilt thou, for a good intent, dishonour God, offend thy brother, and endanger thy soul wherefor Christ hath shed his most precious blood? Wilt thou, for a good intent, pluck Christ out of heaven, and make his death void, and deface the triumph of his cross, by offering him up daily? Wilt thou, either for fear of death, or hope of life, deny and refuse thy God, who enriched thy poverty, healed thy infirmity, and yielded to thee his victory, if thou couldest have kept it? Dost thou not consider that the thread of thy life hangeth upon Him that made thee, who can, as his will is, either twine it harder to last the longer, or untwine it again to break it the sooner?

Dost thou not, then, remember the saying of David, a notable king, to teach thee, a miserable wretch, in his hundred-and-fourth psalm, where he saith thus, When thou takest away thy Spirit, O Lord, from men, they die, and are turned again to their dust; but when thou lettest thy breath go forth, they shall be made, and thou shalt renew the face of the earth. Remember the saying of Christ in his gospel, Matt. x. Whosoever seeketh to save his life, shall lose it; but whosoever will lose his life for my sake, shall find it. And in the same place, Whosoever loveth father or mother above me, is not meet for me; he that will follow me, let him forsake himself, and take up his cross, and follow me. What cross?—The cross of infamy and shame, of misery and poverty, of affliction and persecution, for his name's sake.

Let the often falling of those heavenly showers pierce thy stony heart; let the two-edged sword of God's holy word shear asunder the sinews of worldly respects, even to the very marrow of thy carnal heart, that thou mayest once again forsake thyself, and embrace Christ; and like as good subjects will not refuse to hazard all in the defence of their earthly and temporal governor; so fly not like a white-livered milksop from the standing wherein thy chief Captain, Christ, hath set thee in array of this life. Fight manfully, come life come death; the quarrel is God's, and undoubtedly the victory is ours.

But thou wilt say, I will not break unity. What! not the unity of Satan and his members! not the unity of darkness, the agreement of antichrist and his adherents! Nay, thou deceivest thyself with the fond imagination of such a unity as is among the enemies of Christ. Were not the false prophets in unity? were not Joseph's brethren and Jacob's sons in unity? were not the heathen, as the Amalekites, the Perizzites, and Jebusites, in unity? were not the scribes and pharisees in unity? Doth not king David testify, They have taken counsel in unity against the Lord. Yea, thieves, murderers, conspirators, have their unity. But what unity? Tully saith of amity, There is no friendship excepting amongst good men. But mark, my friend, yea, friend, if thou be not God's enemy; there is no unity but where Christ knitteth the knot among such as be his. Yea, be well assured, that where his truth is resident, there is verified what he himself saith, I am not come to send peace on the earth, but a sword, &c. but to set one against another, the son against the father, and the daughter against the mother-in-law. Deceive not thyself, therefore, with the glittering and glorious name of unity; for antichrist hath his unity, not yet in deed, but in name.

The agreement of ill men is not unity, but conspiracy. Thou hast heard some threatenings, some curses, and some admonitions out of the scriptures, to those that love themselves above Christ. Thou hast heard also the sharp and biting words to those that deny him for love of life. Saith he not, He that denieth me before men, I will deny him before my Father in heaven? Matt. x. And to the same effect writeth Paul, Heb. vi. It is impossible that they which were once lightened, and have tasted of the heavenly gift, and were partakers of the Holy Ghost, and have tasted of the good word of God, if they fall and slide away, crucifying to themselves the Son of God afresh, and making of him a mocking-stock, should be renewed again by repentance. And again saith he, If we shall willingly sin after we have received the knowledge of his truth, there is no oblation left for sin, but the terrible expectation of judgment and fire which shall devour the adversaries. Thus St. Paul wrote, and this thou readest, and dost thou not quake and tremble?

Well, if these terrible and thundering threatenings cannot stir thee to cleave unto Christ, and forsake the world, yet let the sweet consolations and promises of the scriptures, let the example of Christ and his apostles, holy martyrs, and confessors, encourage thee to take fast hold by Christ. Hearken what he saith, Blessed are you when men revile you, and persecute you, for my sake; rejoice, and be glad, for great is your reward in heaven; for so persecuted they the prophets that were before you. Matt. v. Hear what Isaiah the prophet saith, Fear not the curse of men, be not afraid of their blasphemies, for worms and moths shall eat them up like cloth and wool; but my righteousness shall endure for ever, and my saving health from generation to generation. What art thou then that fearest a mortal man, the child of man, that fadeth away like a flower, and forgettest the Lord that made thee, that spread out the heavens, and laid the foundation of the earth? I am thy Lord thy God, that make the sea to rage, and be still, whose name is the Lord of hosts. I shall put my word in thy mouth, and defend thee with the turning of an hand. Isa. li.

And our Saviour Christ saith to his disciples, They shall accuse you, and bring you before princes and rulers for my name's sake, and some of you they shall persecute and kill; but fear you not, nor care you what you shall say, for it is the Spirit of your Father that speaketh within you. Even the very hairs of your head are all numbered. Lay up treasure for yourselves, where no thief cometh, nor moth corrupteth. Fear not them that kill the body, but are not able to kill the soul; but fear Him that hath power to destroy both soul and body. If ye were of the world, the world would love his own; but because ye are not of the world, but I have chosen you out of the world, therefore the world hateth you.

Let these, and such-like consolations, taken out of the scriptures, strengthen you toward God. Let not also the examples of holy men and women go out of your mind, as Daniel and the rest of the prophets; of the three children of Eleazarus, that constant father; of the seven of the Maccabees' children; of Peter, Paul, Stephen, and other apostles and holy martyrs in the beginning of the church; as of good Simeon, archbishop of Soloma; and Zetrophone, with many others under Sapor, the king of the Persians and Indians, who contemned all torments devised by the tyrants for their Saviour's sake.

Return, return again into Christ's war, and, as becomes

a faithful warrior, put on that armour which St. Paul teaches to be most necessary for a christian man. Eph. vi. And above all things, take to you the shield of faith, and be you provoked by Christ's own example to withstand the devil, to forsake the world, and to become a true and faithful member of his mystical body, who spared not his own body for our sins.

Throw down yourself with the fear of his threatened vengeance for this so great and heinous offence of apostacy, and comfort yourself on the other part with the mercy, blood, and promise of Him that is ready to turn unto you whensoever you turn unto him. Disdain not to come again with the lost son, seeing you have so wandered with him. Be not ashamed to turn again with him from the swill of strangers to the delicates of your most benign and loving Father, acknowledging that you have sinned against heaven and earth; against heaven, by staining the glorious name of God, and causing his most sincere and pure word to be evil spoken of through you; against earth, by offending so many of your weak brethren, to whom you have been a stumbling-block through your sudden sliding.

Be not abashed to come home again with Mary, and weep bitterly with Peter, not only with shedding the tears of your bodily eyes, but also pouring out the streams of your heart, to wash away out of the sight of God the filth and mire of your offensive fall. Be not abashed to say with the publican, Lord, be merciful to me a sinner. Remember the horrible history of Julian of old, and the lamentable case of Spira of late, whose case, methinks, should be yet so green in your remembrance, that being a thing of our time you should fear the like inconvenience, seeing you are fallen into the like offence.*

Last of all, let the lively remembrance of the last day be always before your eyes, remembering the terror that such shall be in at that time, with the runagates and fugitives from Christ, who, setting more by the world than by heaven, more by their life than by Him that gave them life, did shrink, yea, did clean fall away from Him that forsook them not; and contrariwise, the inestimable joys prepared for them, who fearing no peril, nor dreading

---

* Francis Spira was an Italian of rank, who having embraced the ctrines of the reformation, subsequently apostatized from the faith, shortly after died in the most bitter agonies of despair.

death, have manfully fought and victoriously triumphed over all power of darkness, over hell, death, and damnation, through their most redoubted Captain, Christ, who now stretches out his arms to receive you, ready to fall upon your neck and kiss you; and, last of all, to feast you with the dainties and delicates of his own precious blood, which undoubtedly, if it might stand with his determinate purpose, he would shed again, rather than you should be lost. To whom, with the Father and the Holy Ghost, be all honour, praise, and glory everlasting. Amen.

> Be constant, be constant; fear not for any pain;
> Christ hath redeemed thee, and heaven is thy gain.

## LETTER VII.

*A letter written by the Lady Jane, in the end of the new testament, in Greek, the which she sent unto her sister, lady Catharine, the night before she suffered.*

I HAVE here sent you, good sister Catharine, a book, which, although it be not outwardly rimmed with gold, yet inwardly it is more worth than precious stones. It is the book, dear sister, of the laws of the Lord: it is his testament and last will, which he bequeathed unto us wretches, which shall lead you to the path of eternal joy; and if you with a good mind read it, and with an earnest desire to follow it, shall bring you to an immortal and everlasting life. It will teach you to live, and learn you to die; it shall win you more than you should have gained by the possession of your woful father's lands. For as if God had prospered him, you should have inherited his lands, so if you apply diligently to this book, trying to direct your life after it, you shall be an inheritor of such riches, as neither the covetous shall withdraw from you, neither thief shall steal, neither yet the moth corrupt.

Desire with David, good sister, to understand the law of the Lord God. Live still to die, that you, by death, may purchase eternal life, or after your death enjoy the life purchased you by Christ's death. And trust not that the tenderness of your age shall lengthen your life; for as soon, if God call, the young goeth as the old; labour always to learn to die. Deny the world, defy the devil, and despise the flesh, and delight yourself only in the Lord. Be penitent for your sins, and yet despair not; be steady in faith, and yet presume not; and desire with St. Paul to be dissolved, and to be with Christ, with whom, even in death, there is life. Be like the good servant, and even at midnight be waking, lest, when death cometh, and stealeth upon you like a thief in the night, you with the evil servant be found sleeping, and lest, for lack of oil, you be found like the five foolish women, and like him that had not on the wedding garment, and then ye be cast out from the marriage.

Resist, as I trust you do; and seeing you have the name of a christian, as near as you can, follow the steps of your Master, Christ, and take up your cross, lay your sins on his back, and always embrace him. And as touching my death, rejoice as I do, good sister, that I shall be delivered of this corruption, and put on incorruption. For I am assured, that I shall, for losing of a mortal life, find an immortal felicity, the which I pray God grant you, and send you of his grace to live in his fear, and to die in the true christian faith, from the which, in God's name, I exhort you that you never swerve, neither for hope of life, nor for fear of death;[*] for if you will deny his truth for to lengthen your life, God will deny you, and shorten your days. And if you will cleave unto him, he will prolong your days to your comfort and his glory; to the which glory God bring me now, and you hereafter, when it pleases him to call you. Fare you well, good sister, and put your only trust in God, who only must help you.

*Here follows a certain effectual prayer, made by the lady Jane in the time of her trouble.*

O Lord, thou God and Father of my life, hear me, poor and desolate woman, which flieth unto thee only, in all troubles and miseries. Thou, O Lord, art the only defender and deliverer of those that put their trust in thee; and therefore I, being defiled with sin, encumbered with affliction, unquieted with troubles, wrapped in cares,

---

[*] In another copy this sentence appears to be "Pray God grant you and send you of his grace to live in his fear and to die in the love [of Christ from which I exhort you not to swerve, and which shall be] of joy to you when the hour shall arrive, neither for love of life, nor fear of death.'

overwhelmed with miseries, vexed with temptations, and grievously tormented with the long imprisonment of this vile mass of clay, my sinful body, do come unto thee, O merciful Saviour, craving thy mercy and help, without which so little hope of deliverance is left, that I may utterly despair of any liberty.

Albeit it is expedient, that, seeing our life standeth upon trying, we should be visited sometime with some adversity, whereby we might both be tried whether we are of thy flock, or no; and also know thee and ourselves the better; yet thou that saidst thou wouldest not suffer us to be tempted above our power, be merciful unto me now a miserable wretch, I beseech thee, who with Solomon* do cry unto thee, humbly desiring thee, that I may neither be too much puffed up with prosperity, neither too much pressed down with adversity, lest I, being too full, should deny thee, my God; or being too low brought, should despair, and blaspheme thee, my Lord and Saviour.

O merciful God! consider my misery which is best known unto thee, and be thou now unto me a strong tower of defence, I humbly require thee. Suffer me not to be tempted above my power; but either be thou a deliverer unto me out of this great misery, or else give me grace patiently to bear thy heavy hand and sharp correction. It was thy right hand that delivered the people of Israel out of the hands of Pharaoh, who, for the space of four hundred years, did oppress them, and keep them in bondage. Let it, therefore, likewise seem good to thy fatherly goodness to deliver me, sorrowful wretch, for whom thy Son Christ shed his precious blood on the cross, out of this miserable captivity and bondage, wherein I am now. How long wilt thou be absent? For ever? O Lord, hast thou forgotten to be gracious, and hast thou shut up thy loving kindness in displeasure? Wilt thou be no more entreated? Is thy mercy clean gone for ever, and thy promise come utterly to an end for evermore? Why dost thou make so long tarrying? Shall I despair of thy mercy, O God? Far be that from me. I am thy workmanship created in Christ Jesus; give me grace, therefore, to tarry thy leisure, and patiently to bear thy works; assuredly knowing that as thou canst, so thou wilt deliver me, when it shall please thee; nothing doubting or mistrusting thy goodness towards me, for thou knowest better what is good for me

* Or Agur, Prov. xxx.

than I do. Therefore, do with me in all things what thou wilt, and plague me what way thou wilt; only in the mean time arm me, I beseech thee, with thy armour, that I may stand fast, my loins being girded about with verity, having on the breast-plate of righteousness, and shod with the shoes prepared by the gospel of peace; above all things taking to me the shield of faith, wherewith I may be able to quench all the fiery darts of the wicked, and taking the helmet of salvation, and the sword of the Spirit, which is thy most holy word; praying always with all manner of prayer and supplication, that I may refer myself wholly to thy will, abiding thy pleasure, and comforting myself in those troubles that it shall please thee to send me; seeing such troubles are profitable for me; and seeing I am assuredly persuaded that it cannot be but well, all that thou doest. Hear me, O merciful Father, for His sake, whom thou wouldest should be a sacrifice for my sins; to whom with thee, and the Holy Ghost, be all honour and glory. Amen.

### *John Banks to Henry Bullinger.**

MOST EXCELLENT FATHER,—You will perhaps wonder that in these turbulent times I should write to you, who never before have done so—the rather as I never had any communication with you, and I am now about to write of matters which would endanger my safety, if these letters should be intercepted before the bearer leaves England. But I do not consider this a sufficient cause to delay what I am about to state, since it is not only right in itself that these details should be known, but especially by you, on account of your affection and kindness towards the Greys, that most noble of our families—which indeed it never hesitated to set forth. Although this family is now ruined, and almost become extinct, for the blessed name of our Saviour, and the sake of the gospel, yet those who are real christians, ought not so much to lament the ruin of that illustrious family, as to rejoice that its last act was a testimony to the name of Jesus.† The more so, since those

---

\* Ep. Helv. Ref. lxxx. In another letter of the same date, written by Banks, intended to be prefixed to a publication, containing the letters of lady Jane to her sister and Harding, and her conference with Feckenham, he gives an account of her short reign, and the cruel proceedings of the papists towards her.

† He refers to the execution of the duke of Suffolk, about three weeks before.

who rest with our Lord in the kingdom of the Father, no longer are occupied in witnessing the lamentable ruin of our nation. Wretched indeed are we, who daily hear contumelies heaped upon the name of the Saviour, and behold the dreadful slaughter of those who endeavoured to promote his glory, and extend his kingdom.

But to return to the Greys, of whom I intended to write to you, both on account of that great regard towards them, which is so plainly shown in your works, and for my affection towards them when dead, to whom, when living, I was anxious to show my respect. I send you some communications relative to Jane, the daughter of the duke—truly precious;* not so much for her incredible advances in learning, wherein she excelled other females, although but in the seventeenth year of her age, as for the singular courage with which this youthful female surpassed men in the warfare of Christ, so that she could not be subdued by any machinations of the papists, nor deceived by their snares, as may be understood from her conference, which I send to you.

This communication she had with that distinguished and crafty papist, Dr. Feckenham, upon certain controverted points of our religion, her opinion concerning which she explained with learning and ability. It is sufficiently apparent, from what she declared shortly before her execution, that she continued stedfast to the end in this confession of faith. I have joined it to other documents which appear to me worthy to be generally known.

How her precious mind was illumined by the true light of the word of God, may also be discerned from two letters—one which she wrote to her sister the lady Catherine, inciting her to study the sacred writings, the other to a certain apostate, to call him back to the Lord Jesus Christ. I have translated all these from our language into Latin, that you may not consider the labour to have been wholly lost, by which you endeavoured to enlighten that family, and excited them to the pursuit of religion. For I can be a witness, if not the fullest, still an eye witness, to the especial benefits which the whole family, particularly Jane, received from your works. She not only diligently marked all the heads of your second decade, but even committed them to memory.

* Filia vere gemmea.

The duke himself occupied in the study of religious works, as much time as he could gain from state affairs, particularly those written by you, with the pleasing style of which he often expressed himself to be much delighted. From this study he gained considerable advantage, when, during his imprisonment, some unreasonable men endeavoured to draw him from the faith and confession of the true Saviour —but they could not move him by any means. To the last breath he confessed the Lord Christ. Although when carried to execution, a papistical adviser, one of the swinish herd, clamoured concerning the catholic church, the mass, the fathers, and their customs confirmed by ancient usage, he would not acknowledge any other sacrifice, than that which is perfected in the death of Christ. By this faith he sustained himself, and in this faith he ended his life.

I would have written you farther concerning the entire subversion of religion, and the antichristian madness now prevalent in England, but those who daily arrive from England at Zurich, that seat of good literature, can better inform you the particulars. It therefore only remains for me, again and again, to beseech you to accept this my expression of duty, and that you would account me among the number of your friends, and pray to God that our England may at length be freed from that popish tyranny whereby it is now oppressed.—Farewell, excellent Bullinger, and whatever you do, continue to enlighten the kingdom of Christ by your writings. London, 15th March, 1554.

*Last hours of the Duke of Suffolk.*

The last hours of the dukes of Northumberland and Suffolk present a striking contrast. The duke of Northumberland professed himself a papist, and besought his life in the most abject terms, intimating that he never had really approved the protestant doctrines, but had promoted the reformation only to forward his political designs. The duke of Suffolk died openly professing his belief in the doctrines of truth, as appears from the account of his last hours given by Fox.

" On Friday, the 23rd of February, 1554, about nine of the clock in the forenoon, the lord Henry Grey, duke of Suffolk, was brought forth of the Tower of London, unto the scaffold on the Tower-hill, with a great company, &c. and in his coming thither, there accompanied him doctor Weston, dean of Westminster, as his spiritual father, notwithstanding, as it should seem, it was against the will of the said duke. For when the duke went up to the scaffold, Weston being on his left hand, pressed to go up with him. The duke with his hand put him down again off the stairs, and Weston taking hold of the duke, forced him down likewise. And as they ascended the second time, the duke again put him down. Then Weston said that it was the queen's pleasure he should so do. Wherewith the duke casting his hands abroad, ascended up the scaffold, and paused some time after. And then he said: 'Masters, I have offended the queen, and her laws, and thereby am justly condemned to die, and am willing to die, desiring all men to be obedient; and I pray God that this my death may be an example to all men, beseeching you all to bear me witness, that I die in the faith of Christ, trusting to be saved by his blood only, (and not by any trumpery,) the which died for me, and for all them that truly repent, and stedfastly trust in him. And I do repent, desiring you all to pray to God for me, that when you see my breath depart from me, you will pray to God that he may receive my soul.' And then he desired all men to forgive him, saying, that the queen had forgiven him.

"Then master Weston declared with a loud voice, that the queen's majesty had forgiven him. With that, divers of the standers-by said with audible voices, Such forgiveness God send thee, meaning doctor Weston. Then the duke kneeled down upon his knees, and said the psalm Miserere mei Deus, (Ps. li.) to the end, holding up his hands, and looking up to heaven. And when he had ended the psalm, he said, Into thy hands I commend my spirit. Then he arose and stood up, and delivered his cap and his scarf unto the executioner.

"Then the executioner kneeled down and asked the duke's forgiveness. And the duke said, God forgive thee, and I do: and when thou doest thine office, I pray thee do it well, and bring me out of this world quickly, and God have mercy to thee. Then stood there a man and said, My lord, how shall I do for the money that you do owe me? And the duke said, Alas, good fellow, I pray thee trouble me not now, but go thy way to my officers. Then he knitted a handkerchief about his face, and kneeled down and said the Lord's prayer unto the end. And then he said, Christ have mercy upon me, and laid down his head on the block, and the executioner took the axe, and at the first chop struck off his head, and held it up to the people."

Hollinshed observes, " Such was the end of this duke of Suffolk; a man of high nobility by birth, and of nature to his friends gentle and courteous; more easy, indeed, to be led, than was thought expedient. Of stomach stout and hard; hasty and soon kindled, but pacified strait again, and sorry, if in his heat aught had passed him otherwise than reason might seem to bear; upright and plain in his private dealings; no dissembler, nor well able to bear injuries; but yet forgiving and forgetting the same, if the party would seem but to acknowledge his fault, and to seek reconcilement. Bountiful he was and very liberal; somewhat learned himself, and a great favourer of those that were learned; so that to many he showed himself a very Mæcenas. As free from covetousness as void of pride and disdainful haughtiness of mind; more regarding plain-meaning men, than claw-back flatterers. And this virtue he had, that he could patiently hear his faults told him by those whom he had in credit for their wisdom and faithful meaning towards him. He was a hearty friend unto the gospel, and professed it to the last."

# A CERTAIN GODLY SUPPLICATION,

EXHIBITED BY CERTAIN INHABITANTS OF THE COUNTY OF NORFOLK, TO THE COMMISSIONERS COME DOWN TO NORFOLK AND SUFFOLK. APRIL, A. D. 1556.

Fruitful to be read and marked of all men.

---

THE reader will have seen from the preceding account of lady Jane Grey, that the opposition to the accession of queen Mary proceeded from political and party intrigues, and not from the English protestants at large, although they knew that she was a bigoted Romanist. But it should be further stated that Mary was chiefly indebted to the protestants for the timely support which placed her upon the throne. Strype and others relate, that the Suffolk men, when they resorted to queen Mary, promised her their aid and help, so that she would not attempt the alteration of the religion which her brother king Edward had before established by laws and orders publicly enacted, and received by the consent of the whole realm in that behalf. She agreed unto this condition, with such promise made unto them that no innovation should be made of religion, as that no man would or could then have misdoubted her.— It is hardly necessary to add that these promises were not kept by her.

---

IN most humble and lowly wise, we beseech your honours, right honourable commissioners, to tender and pity the humble suit of us poor men, and true, faithful, and obedient subjects; who as we have ever heretofore, so intend we, with God's grace, to continue in christian obedience unto the end, and, according to the holy word of God, with all reverend fear of God, to do our bounden duty to all those superior powers whom God hath appointed over us, doing as St. Paul saith, "Let every soul be subject to the superior powers. For there is no power but of God; but those powers that are, are ordained of God. Wherefore, whosoever resisteth the powers, the same resisteth God, and they that resist, get themselves judgment," Rom. xiii.

These lessons, right honourable commissioners, we have learned of the holy word of God, in our mother tongue.

First, that the authority of a king, queen, lord, and other their officers under them, is no tyrannical usurpation, but a just, holy, lawful, and necessary estate for man to be governed by, and that the same is of God, the fountain and author of righteousness.

Secondly, that to obey the same in all things not against God, is to obey God; and to resist them, is to resist God.

Therefore, as to obey God in his ministers and magistrates bringeth life; so to resist God in them, bringeth punishment and death. The same lesson have we learned of St. Peter, saying, "Be ye subject to all human ordinances for the Lord's sake, whether it be to the king, as to the most highest, or to the lieutenants sent from him to the punishment of evil doers, but to the praise of such as do well. For so is the will of God, that with well doing ye should stop the mouths of foolish and ignorant men; as free, and not as having the liberty to be a cloak to malice, but as the servants of God," 1 Pet. ii.

Wherefore, considering with ourselves, both that the magistrates' power is of God, and that for the Lord's sake we are bound to christian obedience unto them, having now a commandment, as though it were from the queen's majesty; with all humble obedience due to the regal power and authority ordained of God, which we acknowledge to stand wholly and perfectly in her grace, and with due reverence unto you her grace's commissioners, we humbly beseech you with patience and pity to receive this our answer unto that commandment, given unto us.

First, right honourable commissioners, we have considered ourselves to be, not only English men, but also christians, and therefore bound by the holy vow made to God in our baptism, to prefer God's honour in all things, and that all obedience, not only of us mortal men, but even of the very angels and heavenly spirits, is due unto God's word; insomuch that no obedience can be true and perfect, either before God or man, that wholly and fully agreeth not with God's word.

Then have we weighed the commandment concerning the restitution of the late abolished Latin service given unto us, to dissent and disagree from God's word, and to command manifest impiety, and the overthrow of godliness and true religion, and to import a subversion of the regal power of this our native country and realm of England, with the bringing in of the Romish bishop's supremacy, with all errors, superstitions, and idolatry, wasting of our goods and bodies, destroying of our souls, bringing with it nothing but the severe wrath of God, which we already feel, and fear lest the same shall be more fiercely kindled upon us. Wherefore, we humbly protest that we cannot be persuaded that the same wicked commandment should come from the queen's majesty, but rather from some other, abusing the queen's goodness and favour, and studying to work some feat against the queen, her crown and the realm, to please with it the Roman bishop, at whose hands the same thinketh hereafter to be advanced.

[They refer to Haman and others as examples of evil counsellors, and urge that every christian man must needs, if God will so call them, gladly suffer all manner of persecution, and lose their lives in the defence of God's word and truth.]

We humbly beseech the queen's majesty, and you her honourable commissioners, be not offended with us for confessing this truth of God, so straitly given us in charge of Christ. Neither bring upon us that great sin that never shall be forgiven, and shall cause our Saviour Jesus Christ in the great day of judgment, before his heavenly Father and all his angels, to deny us, and to take from us the blessed price and ransom of his blood-shedding, wherewith we are redeemed, Matt. x.

For in that day, neither the queen's highness, neither you, nor any man, shall be able to excuse us, nor to purchase a pardon of Christ for this horrible sin and blasphemy of casting aside, and condemning his word. We cannot agree or consent unto this so horrible a sin; but we beseech God, for his mercy, to give us and all men grace, most earnestly to flee from it, and rather, if the will of God be so, to suffer all extremity and punishment in this world, than to incur such damnation before God.

[They then refer to the scriptures, which state that the introduction of idolatry by Jereboam and and Manesseh brought wrath upon the Jews.]

This most heinous offence is now offered unto us, although the same be painted and coloured with the name of reformation, restoring of religion, ancient faith, with the name of the catholic church, of unity, catholic truth, and with the cloak of feigned holiness. These are sheepskins, under the which, as Christ saith, ravening wolves cover themselves. But Christ willeth us to look upon their fruits, whereby we may know them; and truly that is no good fruit, to cast aside God's word, and to banish the English service out of the churches, and in the place of it, to bring in a Latin tongue unknown unto the people. Which, as it edifieth no man, so it hath been occasion of all blindness and error among the people. For before the blessed reformation, it is known what blindness and error we were all in, when not one man in all this realm, unlearned in the Latin, could say in English the Lord's prayer, or knew any one article of his belief, or rehearse any one of the ten commandments. And that ignorance, mother of mischief, was the very root and wellspring of all idolatry, monkery, licentious unchastity of unmarried priests, of all whoredom, drunkenness, covetousness, swearing, and blasphemy, with all other wicked, sinful living. These brought in the severe wrath and vengeance of God, plaguing sin with famine and pestilence; and at last the sword consumed and avenged all their impiety and wicked living. As it is greatly to be feared, the same or more grievous plagues shall now again follow.

We cannot therefore consent nor agree, that the word of God and prayers in our English tongue, which we understand, should be taken away from us, and for it a Latin service, we wot not what, for none of us understand it, be again brought in amongst us; especially seeing that Christ hath said, My sheep hear my voice, and follow me, and I give to them everlasting life, John x.

The service in English teaches us, that we are the Lord's people and the sheep of his pasture, and God commandeth that we harden not our hearts, as when they provoked the Lord's wrath in the wilderness, lest he swear unto us, as he did swear unto them, that they should not enter into his rest. The service in Latin is a confused noise; which if it be good, as they say it is, yet unto us that lack understanding, what goodness can it bring? St. Paul commandeth, that in the churches all things should be done to edifying, which we are sure is God's commandment. But in the Latin service nothing is done to edifying, but contrarily all to destroy those that are already edified, and to drive us from God's word and truth, and from believing of the same, and so to bring us to believe lies and fables, that tempting and provoking God, we should be brought into that judgment which blessed Paul speaketh of, saying, Antichrist shall come according to the working of Satan, with all manner of power and signs, and lying wonders in all deceiveableness of unrighteousness in those that perish, because they have not received the love of the truth, that they might be saved. And therefore God will send them strong delusion, that they should believe lies and be damned, as many as have not believed the truth, but have approved unrighteousness.

Thus altogether drawn from God, we shall fall into his

wrath through unbelief, till he swear unto us, as to the unfaithful Jews, that such infidels shall not enter into his rest.

In the administration of the Lord's supper, which we confessed to be the holy communion, and partaking with Christ and his holy congregation, we have learned God's holy commandments, and at the rehearsal of every one of them to ask God mercy for our most grievous transgressions against them, and to ask grace of God, to keep them in time to come, that the same may not only outwardly sound in our ears, but also inwardly, by the Holy Ghost, be written in our hearts. We have learned the holy prayer made for the queen's majesty, wherein we learn that her power and authority is of God, therefore we pray to God for her, that she, and all magistrates under her, may rule according to God's word, and we her subjects obey according to the same.

Truly, most honourable commissioners, we cannot think these things evil, but think them most worthy to be retained in our churches, and we would think ourselves not to have true subjects' hearts, if we should go about to put away such godly prayers, as put us perpetually in memory of our bounden obedience and duty to God and our rulers. For, as we think, at this present, the unquiet multitude had more need to have these things more often and earnestly beaten and driven into them, now given in many places to stir and trouble, than to take from them that blessed doctrine, whereby only they may to their salvation be kept in quiet.

[They then urge the superior spiritual advantages of the sacrament of the Lord's Supper as lately administered in English, compared to the sacrament of the Latin mass.]

The priests complain that we laymen love them not, nor have them in honour; but it is their own fault. For how should we love them that only seek to keep us in blindness and ignorance, to damn our souls, to destroy our bodies, to rob and spoil our goods and substance under a colour of pretended holiness? We know, right honourable commissioners, what honour is due to such wolves, and how by the authority of God's word, such are to be fled, as pestilences to the Lord's lambs, whom they miserably daily murder.

But we have rather chosen, by this our meek supplication, humbly to desire the queen's majesty, and you her honourable commissioners, to render God's word again unto the churches, and to permit us freely to enjoy the same. For we certainly know, that the whole religion lately set out by the holy saint of God, our late most dear king Edward, is Christ's true religion, written in the holy scripture of God, and by Christ and his apostles taught unto his church. Wherefore, we cannot allow with safe consciences this refusal of it, and casting of it out of our churches; forasmuch as to refuse, cast off, and to reject it, is to cast off Christ himself, and to refuse our part in his blessed body broken for our sins, and his blood shed for our redemption. Which thing, whoso doth the same without repentance can look for no sacrifice for his sins, but most fearfully waits for the judgment and for that vehement fire that shall destroy Christ's adversaries. For if he that despised the law of Moses, was without mercy put to death under two or three witnesses, how much more grievous torments shall he suffer that treadeth under foot the Son of God, and esteemeth the blood of the testament, whereby he was sanctified, as a profane thing, and contumeliously useth the Spirit of grace?

Wherefore, we most humbly pray and beseech the queen's gracious majesty, to have mercy and pity upon us her poor and faithful subjects, and not to compel us to do that which is against our consciences, and so incurably wound us in heart, by bringing into the church the Latin mass and service that nothing edifieth us, and casting out of Christ's holy communion and English service, so causing us to sin against our redemption. For such as willingly and wittingly against their consciences shall so do, as it is to be feared many do, they are in a miserable state until the mercy of God turn them; which if he do not, we certainly believe that they shall eternally be damned; and as in this world they deny Christ's holy word and communion before men, so shall Christ deny them before his heavenly Father and his angels.

And whereas it is very earnestly required, that we should go in procession, as they call it, at which time the priests say in Latin such things as we are ignorant of, the same edifieth nothing at all unto godliness. And we have learned, that to follow Christ's cross, is another matter, namely, to take up our cross, and to follow Christ, in patient suffering for his love, in tribulations, sickness, poverty, prison, or any other adversity, whensoever God's holy will and pleasure is to lay the same upon us. The triumphant passion and death of Christ, whereby in his own person he conquered death, sin, hell, and damnation, hath most lively been preached unto us, and the glory of Christ's cross declared by our preachers; whereby we learned the causes and effects of the same more lively in one sermon, than in all the processions that ever we went, or shall go in.

When we worshipped the divine Trinity kneeling, and in the litany invocating the Father, the Son, and the Holy Ghost, asking mercy for our sins, and desiring such petitions as the need of our frail estate and this mortal life requires, we were edified; both to know unto whom all christian prayers should be directed, and also to know that of God's hand we receive all things, as well to the salvation of our souls, as to the relief of our mortal necessities. And we humbly beseech the queen's majesty, that the same most holy prayers may be continued amongst us, that our ministers pray in our mother tongue, and we, understanding their prayers and petitions, may answer, Amen, unto them. At evening service we understood our ministers' prayers, we were taught and admonished by the scriptures then read; which in the Latin evensong is all gone.

At the ministration of holy baptism, we learned what league and covenant God had made with us, and what vows and promises we upon our part had made, namely, to believe in him, to forsake Satan and his works, and to walk in the way of God's holy word and commandments.

The christian catechism continually taught and called to remembrance the same, whereas before no man knew anything at all. And many good men of sixty years, that had been godfathers to thirty children, knew no more of the godfather's office, than to wash their hands ere they departed the church, or to fast five Fridays on bread and water.

O merciful God, have pity upon us. Shall we be altogether cast from thy presence? We may well lament our miserable estate, to receive such a commandment, to reject and cast out of our churches all these most godly prayers, instructions, admonitions, and doctrines; and thus to be compelled to deny God, and Christ our Saviour, his holy word, and all his doctrine of our salvation, the candle to our feet, and the light to our steps, the bread coming down from heaven, the water that giveth life, which whoso drinketh, it shall be in him a well-spring streaming unto eternal life; whereby we have learned all righteousness, all true religion, all true obedience towards our governors, all charity one towards another, all good works that God would have us to walk in; what punishment abideth the wicked, and what heavenly reward God will give to those that reverently walk in his ways and commandments.

Wherefore, right honourable commissioners, we cannot, without impiety, refuse and cast from us the holy word of God which we have received, or condemn anything set forth by our most godly late king Edward and his virtuous proceedings, so agreeable to God's word. And our most humble suit is, that the commandment may be revoked, so that we be not constrained thereunto. For we protest before God, we think if the holy word of God had not taken some root amongst us, we could not in times past have done that poor duty of ours, which we did, in assisting the queen our most dear sovereign against her grace's mortal foe, that then sought her destruction. It was our bounden duty, and we thank God for that knowledge of his word and grace, that we then did some part of our bounden service.

And we meekly pray and beseech the queen's majesty, for the dear passion of Jesus Christ, that the same word be not taken away out of her churches, nor from us her loving, faithful, and true subjects; lest if the like necessity should hereafter befall, which God for his mercy sake forbid, and ever save and defend her grace and us all, the want of knowledge and due remembrance of God's word may be occasion of great ruin to an infinite number of her grace's true subjects. And truly, we judge this to be one subtle part of the devil, that enemy to all godly peace and quietness, that by taking God's word from among us, and planting ignorance, he may make a way to all mischief and wickedness; and by banishing the holy gospel of peace, he may bring upon us the heavy wrath of God, with all manner of plagues; as death, strange sickness, pestilence, murrain, most terrible uproars, commotions, and seditions.

[They then refer to the judgments, Isa. vi. Micah vii.]

The same plagues, we are afraid, will also fall upon us. For whereas heretofore, with the receiving of Christ's word and peaceable gospel, we had great benedictions of God, especially this christian concord and holy peace, so that all were at a full and perfect stay in religion, no man offended with another, but as the sons of peace, each of us with christian charity embraced other; now, alas for pity, the devil, riding upon the red horse, showed unto St. John in the Revelation, is come forth, and power is given unto him to take peace from the earth. For now a man can go to no place, but malicious busy-bodies curiously search out his deeds, mark his words, and if he agree not with them in despising God's word, then will they spitefully and hatefully rail against him and it, calling it error and heresy, and the professors thereof heretics and schismatics, with other odious and despiteful names, as traitors and not the queen's friends, not favourers of the queen's proceedings; as if to love God's word were heresy, and as though to talk of Christ, were to be schismatics. As though none could be true to the queen, that were not false to God. As though none were the queen's friends, but such as despitefully rail on her grace's father and brother, and on God's word that they set forth; as though none favoured the queen's majesty, but such as hate all godly knowledge.

They describe the things urged as inventions of popes.]

And we poor subjects, for speaking of that which is truth, and our bounden allegiance, are daily punished, railed upon, and noted for seditious, and not the queen's friends.

But God, who is blessed for ever, knoweth that they slander us, and pull the thorn out of their own foot, and put it in ours; for the Searcher of hearts knoweth, that we bear a faithful and true heart unto her grace, and unto all her proceedings that are not against God and his holy word And we daily pray unto the heavenly Father, to lighten her grace's royal heart with the glorious light of his gospel, that she may establish and confirm that religion that her grace's brother, our most dear king, did set out amongst us; and so governing and ruling this her realm in the fear and true way of God, she may long live, and with prosperity, peace, and honour reign over us.

But we cannot think that those men do seek either God's honour, or her grace's prosperity, or wealth of the realm, that take God's word from her grace's faithful subjects, which only is the root of all love and faithful obedience under her grace, and of all honesty, good life, and virtuous concord among her commons. And this we fear, lest the root being taken away, the branches will soon wither and be fruitless. And when the Philistines have stopped up the well-spring, the fair streams that should flow, shall soon be dried up. All our watchmen, our true preachers, have taught us, that as long as we retained God's word, we should have God our gracious merciful Father; but if we refused and cast off the Lord's yoke of his doctrine, then shall we look for the Lord's wrath and severe visitation to plague us, as he did the Jews for the like offences. And Paul saith, God gave to them the spirit of unquietness and uproar, eyes wherewith they should not see, and ears wherewith they should not hear, until this day, Rom. xi. And as David said, Let their table be made a snare to take themselves withal, a trap to catch them, and a stumbling block to fall at. Let their eyes be blinded, that they see not, and bow thou down their backs always, Ps. lxix.

O merciful God, all this is now come upon us, and daily more and more increased, and we fear at last it will so bow down our backs, that we shall utterly be destroyed. The troublesome spirit of uproars and unquietness, daily troubleth men's hearts, and worketh such unquietness in all places, that no man that loveth quietness, can tell where to place himself. Men have eyes, and see not how grievous offence it is, to cast off the yoke of God's doctrine, and to bear the heavy burden that unfaithful hypocrites lay upon us. We have ears, and hear not the warning of God's word, calling us to true repentance, nor his threats against our impiety. Our most sweet table of Christ's word and most holy communion is taken away, and turned to a most perilous snare, through the brawling disputations of men. And as the idol of abomination betokened final subversion unto the Jewish nation, so we fear this setting aside of the gospel and holy communion of Christ, and the placing in of Romish religion, betokens desolation to be at hand of this noble realm of England.

For the plagues of hunger, pestilence, and sword, cannot long tarry;* but except we repent, and turn again to the Lord, our backs shall be so bowed, that the like horrible plagues were never seen. And no marvel, for the like offence was never committed, as to reject and cast off Christ and his word, and in plain English to say, "We will not have him to reign over us." O Lord how terrible is it that followeth in the gospel! "Those mine enemies that would not have me to reign over them, bring them hither, and slay them before me." God be merciful unto us, and move the queen's majesty's heart, and the hearts of her honourable council, and your hearts, right honourable commissioners, to weigh these dangers in due time; and to call God's word into your council, and then you shall see how it agreeth with this bishoplike commandment, and be as wary to avoid the contempt of the eternal God, and dangers of the same, as you are prudent and wise in matters

* This anticipation of evils to come was speedily realized. The latter years of queen Mary's reign were marked by scarcity, pestilential diseases prevalent throughout the nation, and disasters in warfare.

of this world. Lest, if the Almighty be contemned, he stretch forth his arm, which no man can turn, and kindle his wrath, that no man can quench.

We have humbly opened unto you our consciences, doubtless sore wounded and grieved by this commandment; and we meekly pray and beseech the queen's majesty, for the precious death and bloodshedding of Jesus Christ our Saviour, to have mercy and pity upon us her gracious poor commons, faithful and true subjects, members of the same body politic, whereof her grace is supreme head. All our bodies, goods, lands, and lives, are ready to do her grace faithful obedience, and true service, of all commandments that are not against God and his word; but in these things that import a denial of Christ, and refusal of his word and holy communion, we cannot consent or agree unto it. For we have bound ourselves in baptism to be Christ's disciples, and to keep his holy word and ordinances. And if we deny him before men, he will deny us before his heavenly Father and his holy angels in the day of judgment, which we trust her benign grace will not require of us.

And we humbly beseech her majesty, that we be not enforced unto it; but as we serve her grace with body and goods, and due obedience, according to God's commandment; so we may be permitted freely to serve God and Christ our Saviour, and keep unto him our souls which he hath with his precious blood redeemed; that so, as Christ teacheth, we may render to Cæsar that which is due to Cæsar, and to God that which is due to God.

For, we think it no true obedience unto the queen's highness, or to any other magistrate ordained of God under her, to obey in things contrary to God's word, although the same be ever so straitly charged in her grace's name. The bishop of Winchester hath truly taught in that point, in his book of True Obedience, that true obedience is in the Lord, and not against the Lord;* as the apostles answered before the council at Jerusalem, commanding them no more to preach in the name of the Lord Jesus; "Judge you," said they, "whether it be right in the sight of God, to hear you rather than God." And again they said, "We must obey God rather than man." Wherefore, we learn that true obedience is to obey God, King of all kings, and Lord of all lords; and for him, in him, and not against

* Gardiner's book, "De vera obedientia," written in the time of king Henry VIII. against the pope's supremacy.

him and his word, to obey the princes and magistrates of this world, who are not truly obeyed when God is disobeyed, nor yet disobeyed when God is faithfully obeyed.

[They then refer to the examples of Daniel and others.]

Wherefore, we humbly beseech the queen's majesty, with pity and mercy to tender the lamentable suit of us her poor subjects, who are by this commandment sorely hurt, and wounded in our consciences, and driven to many miseries, and by the malicious attempts of wicked men suffer great wrongs and injuries, slanders, loss of goods, and bodily vexations. We think not good by any unlawful stir or commotion to seek remedy; but intend by God's grace to obey her majesty in all things not against God and his holy word. But unto such ungodly bishoplike commandments as are against God, we answer with the apostles, "God must be obeyed rather than man." If persecution shall ensue, which some threaten us with, we desire the heavenly Father, according to his promise, to look from heaven, to hear our cry, to judge between us and our adversaries, to give us faith, strength and patience, to continue faithfully unto the end, and to shorten these evil days for the sake of his chosen; and so we faithfully believe he will.

[They then fervently beseech the queen,] to permit the holy word of God and true religion, set forth by king Edward, to be restored again unto our churches, to be frequented amongst us. So shall we grow and increase in the knowledge of God and of Christ, in true repentance and amendment of life. So shall we exhibit true obedience to our lawful magistrates and all superiors ordained of God, so shall love and charity, of late through this commandment so decayed, be again restored, the honour of her regal estate the more confirmed and established, and godliness and virtuous life among her loving subjects increased and maintained.

And we most heartily pray you, right honourable commissioners, to be means unto the queen's highness, and to her honourable council, that this our humble suit may be favourably tendered, and graciously heard and granted. And we shall not cease, day and night, to pray unto the heavenly Father long to preserve her grace, and all other magistrates, in his fear and love, and in prosperous peace and wealth, with long life and honour. Amen.

Your poor suppliants, the lovers of Christ's true religion in Norfolk and Suffolk.

# PATRICK'S PLACES;

A TREATISE OF THE LAW AND THE GOSPEL.

WRITTEN IN LATIN BY PATRICK HAMILTON; TRANSLATED AND PUBLISHED WITH A PREFATORY LETTER BY JOHN FRITH.

TO WHICH ARE ADDED

THE ANNOTATIONS OF JOHN FOX.

---

LONDON:
PRINTED FOR
The Religious Tract Society,
AND SOLD AT THE DEPOSITORY, 56, PATERNOSTER-ROW;
ALSO BY J. NISBET, NO. 21, BERNERS-STREET;
AND OTHER BOOKSELLERS.

# A BRIEF ACCOUNT OF PATRICK HAMILTON,

Abbot of Fearn, in Scotland, and Martyr, 1528.

PATRICK HAMILTON, abbot of Fearn, was the first person burned in Scotland for the doctrines of the Reformation. He was of noble and royal descent, and not more than twenty-three years of age. He had travelled in Germany, and visited Luther, Melancthon, and other reformers, by whom he was instructed in the knowledge of the truth; and in the university of Marburg, he publicly advanced the conclusions respecting faith and works, which propositions are set forth in his treatise, called PATRICK'S PLACES.

Having thus received the truth, he became desirous to impart it to his countrymen, and returned home. On his arrival, wherever he came, he exposed the corruptions of the Church of Rome, and preached the gospel. Many listened to his discourses, and were inclined to adopt the doctrines of the Reformation. At this the popish clergy were alarmed; but as Hamilton had expressed his views with caution, so as not easily to afford them a pretext for proceeding against him, they enticed him to St. Andrews, to confer with archbishop Beaton, and appointed a Dominican friar, named Campbell, to converse with him, and draw forth the declaration of his opinions, under the pretence of desiring instruction. Having succeeded in this treacherous design, they caused Hamilton to be seized in his bed at midnight, and carried to the castle.

On the next day, February 28, 1528, he was brought before the bishops and clergy, accused of maintaining the doctrines of the Reformation, condemned to be burned, and almost immediately after led forth to the stake; his execution being hastened lest the king, who was then absent on a pilgrimage to Ross-shire, should interfere, and prevent the cruel designs of the popish ecclesiastics. Hamilton suffered with much constancy, desiring the people "to keep in mind the example of his death; for although bitter to the flesh, and fearful in the sight of men, yet it is the entrance to eternal life, which none can inherit who deny Christ!" The flame being kindled, he cried with a loud voice, "Lord Jesus, receive my spirit! How long shall darkness overwhelm this realm, and how long wilt thou suffer the tyranny of men?" Friar Campbell exhorted him repeatedly to recant, and call upon the Virgin Mary; upon which Hamilton reminded him of what had passed in their private conferences, and summoned him to answer for his conduct at the judgment-seat of Christ by a certain time which he named. The conscience-stricken friar expired in a frenzy of despair before that period arrived.

# A BRIEF TREATISE

CALLED

# PATRICK'S PLACES.

### JOHN FRITH UNTO THE CHRISTIAN READER.[*]

BLESSED be God, the Father of our Lord Jesus Christ, who, in these last days and perilous times, hath stirred up in all countries witnesses unto his Son, to testify the truth unto the unfaithful, to save, at the least, some from the snares of antichrist, which lead to perdition, as you may here perceive by that excellent and well learned young man, Patrick Hamilton, born in Scotland, of a noble progeny: who sought all means to testify the truth, and took upon him the priesthood, even as Paul circumcised Timothy, to win the weak Jews, that he might be admitted to preach the pure word of God. Notwithstanding, as soon as the chamberlain[†] and other bishops of Scotland had perceived that the light began to shine, which disclosed their falsehoods, which they conveyed in darkness, they laid hands on him, and because he would not deny his Saviour Christ, at their instance, they burnt him to ashes. Nevertheless, God, of his bounteous mercy (to publish to the whole world, what a man these monsters have murdered), hath reserved a little treatise, made by this Patrick, which, if you please, you may call "PATRICK's PLACES:" for it treateth exactly of certain common places, which being known, you have the pith of all divinity. This treatise have I turned into the English tongue, for the profit of my nation: to whom, I beseech God, to give light, that they may espy the deceitful paths of perdition, and return to the right way which leadeth to life everlasting. Amen.

[*] John Frith was burned in Smithfield, A.D. 1533.
[†] Or chancellor, archbishop Beaton.

## PATRICK'S PLACES.

### THE DOCTRINE OF THE LAW.

The law is a doctrine that biddeth good, and forbiddeth evil, as the commandments do specify, here following:—

*The ten commandments of God.*

1. Thou shalt worship but one God.
2. Thou shalt make thee no image to worship it.
3. Thou shalt not swear by His name in vain.
4. Hold the sabbath-day holy.
5. Honour thy father and thy mother.
6. Thou shalt not kill.
7. Thou shalt not commit adultery.
8. Thou shalt not steal.
9. Thou shalt not bear false witness.
10. Thou shalt not desire aught that belongeth to thy neighbour.

*All these commandments are briefly comprised in these two, here under ensuing.*

"Love thy Lord God with all thine heart, with all thy soul, and with all thy mind. This is the first and great commandment. The second is like unto this, that is, Love thy neighbour as thyself. On these two commandments hang all the law and the prophets." Matt. xxii. 37—40.

*Certain general propositions proved by the scripture.*

*The first proposition.*

He that loveth God, loveth his neighbour.

This proposition is proved, 1 John. iv. 20. "If any man say, I love God, and yet hateth his brother, he is a liar. He that loveth not his brother, whom he hath seen, how can he love God, whom he hath not seen?"

*The second proposition.*

He that loveth his neighbour as himself, keepeth all the commandments of God.

This proposition is thus proved: "Whatsoever ye would that men should do to you, even so do to them. For this is the law and the prophets." (Mat. vii. 12.)

He that loveth his neighbour, fulfilleth the law. "Thou shalt not commit adultery: Thou shalt not kill: Thou shalt not steal: Thou shalt not bear false witness: Thou shalt not desire, &c. And if there be any other commandments, all are comprehended in this saying; Love thy neighbour as thyself." (Rom. xiii. 8, 9.)

"All the law is fulfilled in one word, that is, Love thy neighbour as thyself." (Gal. v. 14.)

### Argument.

"He that loveth his neighbour, keepeth all the commandments of God." (Rom. xiii. 8, 9.)

"He that loveth God, loveth his neighbour." (1 John, iv. 20.)

Therefore, he that loveth God, keepeth all the commandments of God.

### The third proposition.

He that hath faith, loveth God.

"My father loveth you, because you love me, and believe that I came of God." (John, xvi. 27.)

### Argument.

He that keepeth the commandments of God, hath the love of God.

He that hath faith, keepeth the commandments of God.

Therefore, he that hath faith loveth God.

### The fourth proposition.

He that keepeth one commandment of God, keepeth them all.

This proposition is confirmed, Heb. xi. 6. "It is impossible for a man without faith to please God," that is, to keep any one of God's commandments, as he should do. Then, whosoever keepeth any one commandment, hath faith.

### Argument.

He that hath faith, keepeth all the commandments of God.

He that keeps any one commandment of God, hath faith.

Therefore, he that keepeth one commandment, keepeth them all.

### The fifth proposition.

He that keepeth not all the commandments of God, keepeth not one of them.

### Argument.

He that keepeth one commandment of God, keepeth all

Therefore, he that keepeth not all the commandments of God, keepeth not one of them.

### The sixth proposition.

It is not in our power to keep any one of the commandments of God.

### Argument.

It is impossible to keep any of the commandments of God, without grace.

It is not in our power to have grace (of ourselves.)

Therefore, it is not in our power to keep any of the commandments of God.

And even so, may you reason concerning the Holy Ghost and faith, for neither without them are we able to keep any of the commandments of God, neither yet are they in our power to have (of ourselves), " It is not of him that willeth," &c. (Rom. ix. 16.)

### The seventh proposition.

The law was given us to show our sin.

" By the law cometh the knowledge of sin," (Rom. iii. 20.) " I knew not what sin meant, but through the law. For I had not known what lust had meant, except the law had said, Thou shalt not lust. Without the law, sin was dead." That is, It moved me not, neither wist I that it was sin, which notwithstanding was sin, and forbidden by the law. (Rom. vii. 7, 8.)

### The eighth proposition.

The law biddeth us do that which is impossible for us.

### Argument.

The keeping of the commandments is to us impossible.

The law commandeth us to keep the commandments.

Therefore, the law commandeth us that which is impossible.

*Objection.* But thou wilt say, Wherefore doth God bid us do that which is impossible for us?

*Ans.* I answer, To make thee know that thou art but evil, and that there is no remedy to save thee, in thine own hand: and that thou mayest seek a remedy at some other, for the law doth nothing else but command thee.

## THE DOCTRINE OF THE GOSPEL.

The gospel, is as much as to say, in our tongue, GOOD TIDINGS: as these following passages, and others like them.

Christ is the Saviour of the world. (Luke ii. 11.)
Christ is the Saviour. (John iv. 42.)
Christ died for us. (Rom. v. 8.)
Christ died for our sins. (1 Cor. xv. 3.)
Christ bought us with his blood. (1 Pet. i. 18, 19.)
Christ washed us with his blood. (Rev. i. 5.)
Christ offered himself for us. (Heb. vii. 27.)
Christ bare our sins in his body. (Isa. liii. 4.)
Christ came into this world to save sinners.(1 Tim. i. 15.)
Christ came into this world to take away our sins. (1 John, iii. 5.)
Christ was the price that was given for us and for our sins. (Titus, ii. 14.)
Christ was made debtor for us. (2 Cor. v. 21.)
Christ paid our debt, for he died for us. (Mat. xx. 28.)
Christ made satisfaction for us and for our sins. (1 John, ii. 2.)
Christ is our righteousness.
Christ is our sanctification. } (1 Cor. i. 30.)
Christ is our redemption.
Christ is our peace. (Eph. ii. 14.)
Christ hath pacified the Father of heaven for us. (Rom. v. 1. Eph. ii. 16.)
Christ is ours and all his. (1 Cor. iii. 21, 22, 23.)
Christ hath delivered us from the law, from the devil, and from hell. (Col. i. 13.)
The Father of heaven hath forgiven us our sins, for Christ's sake. (Eph. iv. 32.)
Or any such others like them, which declare unto us the mercy of God.

### THE NATURE AND OFFICE OF THE LAW, AND OF THE GOSPEL.

The law showeth us our sin. (Rom. iii. 20.)
The gospel showeth us a remedy for it. (John, i. 29.)
The law showeth us our condemnation. (Rom. vii. 9.)
The gospel showeth us our redemption. (Col i. 14.)
The law is the word of wrath. (Rom. iv. 15.)
The gospel is the word of grace. (Acts, xx. 32.)

The law is the word of despair. (Deut. xxvii. 26.)
The gospel is the word of comfort. (Luke, ii. 14.)
The law is the word of unrest.* (Rom. vii. 13.)
The gospel is the word of peace. (Eph. ii. 17.)

*A disputation between the law and the gospel, where is showed the difference or contrariety between them both.*

The law saith, Pay thy debt.

The gospel saith, Christ hath paid it.

The law saith, Thou art a sinner, despair, and thou shalt be damned.

The gospel saith, Thy sins are forgiven thee, be of good comfort, thou shalt be saved.

The law saith, Make amends for thy sins.

The gospel saith, Christ hath made it for thee.

The law saith, The Father of heaven is angry with thee.

The gospel saith, Christ has pacified him with his blood.

The law saith, Where is thy righteousness, goodness, and satisfaction?

The gospel saith, Christ is thy righteousness, thy goodness, and satisfaction.

The law saith, Thou art bound and obliged to me, to the devil, and to hell.

The gospel saith, Christ has delivered thee from them all.

---

THE DOCTRINE OF FAITH.

Faith is to believe God, like as Abraham believed God, and it was imputed unto him for righteousness.

To believe God, is to believe his word, and to account as true what he saith.

He that believeth not God's word, believeth not God himself.

He that believeth not God's word, counteth him false and a liar, and believeth not that he may and will fulfil his word, and so denieth the might of God, and God himself.

*The ninth proposition.*

Faith is the gift of God.

*Argument.*

Every good thing is the gift of God.
Faith is good.

* Anxiety, disquietude.

Therefore, faith is the gift of God.

### The tenth proposition.

Faith is not in our power.

### Argument.

The gift of God is not in our power.
Faith is the gift of God.
Therefore, faith is not in our power.

### The eleventh proposition.

He that lacketh faith cannot please God.

" Without faith, it is impossible to please God." (Rom. xiv.) All that cometh not of faith, is sin, for without faith can no man please God. (Heb. xi. 6.)

### Induction.

He that lacketh faith, trusteth not God: he that trusteth not God, trusteth not his word: he that trusteth not his word, holdeth him false and a liar: he that holdeth him false and a liar, believeth not that he may do what he promiseth; and so he denieth that he is God.

Therefore, it followeth,—He that lacketh faith, cannot please God.

If it were possible for any man to do all the good deeds that ever were done, either by men or angels: yet being without faith, it is impossible for him to please God.

### The twelfth proposition.

All that is done in faith, pleaseth God.

" Right is the word of God, and all his works in faith." (Psal. xxxiii. 4.)

" Lord, thine eyes look to faith:" that is as much as to say, Lord, thou delightest in faith. (Jer. v. 3.)

### The thirteenth proposition.

He that hath faith, is just and good.

### Argument.

He that is a good tree, bringing forth good fruit, is just and good.

He that hath faith is a good tree, bringing forth good fruit.

Therefore, he that hath faith is just and good.

### The fourteenth proposition.

He that hath faith, and believeth God, cannot displease him.

### Induction.

He that hath faith, believeth God: he that believeth God, believeth his word: he that believeth his word, knoweth well that he is true and faithful and may not lie, knowing that he both may and will fulfil his word.

Therefore, he that hath faith, cannot displease God, neither can any man do a greater honour to God, than to count him true.

*Objection.* Thou wilt then say, that theft, murder, adultery, and all vices, please God.

*Ans.* Nay verily, for they cannot be done in faith: "for a good tree beareth good fruit." (Matt. vii.)

### The fifteenth proposition.

Faith is a certainty or assuredness.

"Faith is a sure confidence of things which are hoped for, and a certainty of things which are not seen." (Heb. xi. 1.)

"The same Spirit certifieth our spirit, that we are the children of God." (Rom. viii. 16.)

Moreover, he that hath faith, well knoweth that God will fulfil his word.

Whereby it appears, that faith is certainty or assuredness.

---

### A MAN IS JUSTIFIED BY FAITH.

Abraham believed God, and it was imputed unto him for righteousness." (Rom. iv. 3.)

"We suppose, therefore, that a man is justified by faith without the deeds of the law." (Rom. iii. 28. Gal. ii. 16.)

"He that worketh not, but believeth on Him that justifieth the wicked, his faith is counted to him for righteousness." (Rom. iv. 5.)

"The just man liveth by his faith." (Hab. ii. 4. Rom. i. 17.)

"We know, that a man is not justified by the deeds of the law; but by the faith of Jesus Christ: and we believe in Jesus Christ, that we may be justified by the faith of Christ, and not by the deeds of the law." (Gal. ii. 16.)

---

### WHAT IS THE FAITH OF CHRIST?

The faith of Christ is, to believe in him, that is, to believe his word, and believe that he will help thee in all thy need, and deliver thee from all evil.

Thou wilt ask me, What word?—I answer, The Gospel.

" He that believeth in Christ, shall be saved." (Mark, xvi. 16.)

" He that believeth on the Son, hath everlasting life." (John, iii. 36.)

" Verily, I say unto you, He that believeth in me hath everlasting life." (John, vi. 47.)

" This I write unto you, that believe on the Son of God, that ye may know that ye have eternal life." (1 John, v. 13.)

" Thomas, because thou hast seen me, therefore hast thou believed? Happy are they which have not seen, and yet have believed in me." (John, xx. 29.)

" All the prophets bare witness to him, that whosoever believeth in him, shall have remission of their sins." (Acts, x. 43.)

" What must I do, that I may be saved?" The apostles answered: " Believe in the Lord Jesus Christ, and thou shalt be saved." (Acts, xvi. 30, 31.)

" If thou acknowledge with thy mouth, that Jesus is the Lord, and believest with thine heart, that God raised him from death, thou shalt be safe." (Rom. x. 9.)

" He that believeth not in Christ, shall be condemned." (Mark, xvi. 16.)

" He that believeth not the Son, shall never see life, but the wrath of God abideth upon him." (John, iii. 36.)

" The Holy Ghost shall reprove the world of sin, because they believe not in me." (John, xvi. 9.)

" They that believe in Jesus Christ, are the sons of God." (1 John, v. 1.)

" Ye are all the sons of God, because ye believe in Jesus Christ." (1 John iii. 1.)

He that believeth that Christ is the Son of God, is safe.

" Peter said, Thou art Christ the Son of the living God; Jesus answered and said unto him: Happy art thou, Simon, the son of Jonas, for flesh and blood have not opened to thee that; but my Father, which is in heaven." (Mat. xvi. 16, 17.)

" We have believed, and know that thou art Christ, the Son of the living God." (John, vi. 69.)

" I believe, that thou art Christ the Son of God, which should come into the world." (John, xi. 27.)

"These things are written that ye might believe that Jesus is Christ the Son of God, and that ye, in believing, might have life." (John, xx. 31.)

"I believe that Jesus is the Son of God." (Acts, viii. 37.)

### The sixteenth proposition.

He that believeth the gospel, believeth God.

### Argument.

He that believeth God's word, believeth God.
The gospel is God's word.
Therefore, he that believeth the gospel, believeth God.
(See page 7—the doctrine of the gospel.)

### The seventeenth proposition.

He that believeth not the gospel, believeth not God.

### Argument.

He that believeth not God's word, believeth not God.
The gospel is God's word.
Therefore, he that believeth not the gospel, believeth not God himself, and consequently, he that believeth not those things above written, and such others, believeth not God.

### The eighteenth proposition.

He that believeth the gospel, shall be saved.

"Go ye into all the world, and preach the gospel unto every creature: he that believeth and is baptized, shall be saved: but he that believeth not, shall be condemned." (Mark, xvi. 16.)

---

## A COMPARISON BETWEEN FAITH AND UNBELIEF

Faith is the root of all good.
Unbelief is the root of all evil.
Faith maketh God and man good friends.
Unbelief maketh them foes.
Faith bringeth God and man together.
Unbelief sundereth them.
All that faith doth pleases God.
All that unbelief doth displeases God.
Faith only, maketh a man good and righteous.
Unbelief only, maketh him unjust and evil
Faith maketh a man a member of Christ.
Unbelief maketh him a member of the devil.

Faith maketh a man the inheritor of heaven.
Unbelief maketh him inheritor of hell.
Faith maketh a man the servant of God.
Unbelief maketh him the servant of the devil.
Faith showeth us that God is a sweet Father.
Unbelief showeth him as a terrible Judge.
Faith holdeth firm by the word of God.
Unbelief wavers here and there.
Faith counteth and holdeth God to be true.
Unbelief holdeth him false and a liar
Faith knoweth God.
Unbelief knoweth him not.
Faith loveth both God and his neighbour.
Unbelief loveth neither of them.
Faith only, saveth us.
Unbelief only, condemneth us.
Faith extolleth God and his deeds.
Unbelief extolleth herself and her own deeds.

OF HOPE.

Hope is a trusty (confident) looking after that which is promised us to come: as we hope after the everlasting joy, which Christ hath promised unto all that believe in him.

We should put our hope and trust in God alone, and in no other thing.

"It is good to trust in God, and not in man." (Psal. cxviii. 8.)

"He that trusteth in his own heart, is a fool." (Prov. xxviii. 26.)

"It is good to trust in God, and not in princes." (Psal. cxviii. 9.)

"They shall be like unto the images which they make, and all that trust in them." (Psal. cxv. 8.)

"He that trusteth in his own thoughts, doth that which is ungodly." (Prov. xii. 5.)

"Cursed be he that trusteth in man." (Jer. xvii. 5.)

"Bid the rich men of this world, that they trust not in their unstable riches, but that they trust in the living God." (1 Tim. vi. 17.)

"It is hard for them that trust in money, to enter into the kingdom of heaven." (Luke, xviii. 24.)

Moreover, we should trust in him only, that may help

us: God only can help us; therefore we should trust in him only.

Well are they that trust in God: and woe to them that trust not in Him.

"Well is that man that trusteth in God, for God shall be his trust." (Jer. xvii. 7.)

He that trusteth in him, shall understand the verity.

"They shall all rejoice that trust in thee: they shall ever be glad, and thou wilt defend them." (Psal. v. 11.)

### OF CHARITY

Charity is the love of thy neighbour. The rule of charity is this, do as thou wouldest be done unto: for Christ holdeth all alike, the rich, the poor, the friend and the foe, the thankful and unthankful, the kinsman and stranger.

### A COMPARISON BETWEEN FAITH, HOPE, AND CHARITY.

Faith cometh of the word of God: Hope cometh of faith: and Charity springeth of them both.

Faith believes the word. Hope trusteth in that which is promised by the word. Charity doth good unto her neighbour, through the love that she hath to God, and the gladness that is within herself.

Faith looketh to God and his word. Hope looketh unto his gift and reward. Charity looketh on her neighbour's profit.

Faith receives God. Hope receives his reward. Charity loves her neighbour with a glad heart, and that without any respect of reward.

Faith pertaineth to God only. Hope to his reward; and Charity to her neighbour.

### THE DOCTRINE OF WORKS.

*No manner of Works make us righteous.*

We believe that a man shall be justified without works. (Rom. iii. 28.)

No man is justified by the deeds of the law, but by the faith of Jesus Christ, and we believe in Jesus Christ that we may be justified by the faith of Christ, and not by the

*Treatise on the law and the gospel.*

deeds of the law · for if righteousness come by the law, then Christ died in vain. (Gal. ii. 16, 21.)

That no man is justified by the law, is manifest; for a righteous man liveth by his faith, but the law is not of faith.

Moreover, since Christ, the Maker of heaven and earth, and all that is therein, behoved to die for us; we are compelled to grant, that we were so far drowned and sunk in sin, that neither our deeds nor all the treasures, that ever God made or might make, could have holpen us out of them : therefore no deeds, nor works make us righteous.

### No Works make us unrighteous.

If any evil works make us unrighteous, then the contrary works should make us rightwise.* But it is proved that no works can make us rightwise : therefore no works make us unrightwise.

### Works make us neither good nor evil.

It is proved, that works neither make us rightwise nor unrightwise : therefore no works make us either good or evil; for rightwise and good are one thing, and unrightwise and evil likewise one.

Good works make not a good man, nor evil works an evil man; but a good man bringeth forth good works, and an evil man evil works.

Good fruit maketh not the tree good, nor evil fruit the tree evil; but a good tree beareth good fruit, and an evil tree evil fruit.

A good man cannot do evil works, nor an evil man good works ; for a good tree cannot bear evil fruit, nor an evil tree good fruit.

A man is good before he do good works, and evil before he do evil works ; for the tree is good before it bears good fruit, and evil before it bears evil fruit.

### Every Man, and the Works of Man, are either good or evil.

Every tree, and the fruits thereof, are either good or evil: either make ye the tree good, and the fruit good also, or else make the tree evil, and the fruit of it likewise evil. (Mat. xii. 33.)

A good man is known by his works ; for a good man doth good works, and an evil man, evil works. Ye shall know them by their fruits ; for a good tree beareth good

---

* Justify us.

fruit, and an evil tree, evil fruit. A man is likened to the tree, and his works to the fruit of the tree.

Beware of false prophets, which come to you in sheep's clothing, but inwardly they are ravening wolves: ye shall know them by their fruits. (Matt. vii. 15, 16.)

### *None of our Works either save us, or condemn us.*

If works make us neither righteous, or unrighteous, then thou wilt say, it maketh no matter what we do. I answer, If thou do evil, it is a sure argument that thou art evil, and wantest faith. If thou do good, it is an argument that thou art good, and hast faith; for a good tree beareth good fruit, and an evil tree, evil fruit. Yet good fruit maketh not the tree good, nor evil fruit the tree evil: so that a man is good, ere he do good deeds; and evil, ere he do evil deeds.

### *The Man is the Tree, his Works are the Fruit.*

Faith maketh the good tree, and unbelief the evil tree: as the tree, so is the fruit; as is a man, such are his works. For all things that are done in faith please God, and are good works: and all that are done without faith displease God, and are evil works.

Whosoever believeth, or thinketh to be saved by his works, denieth that Christ is his Saviour, that Christ died for him, and that all things pertain to Christ. For how is he thy Saviour, if thou mightest save thyself by thy works, or whereto should he die for thee, if any of thy works might have saved thee?

What is it to say, Christ died for thee? Verily, it is that thou shouldest have died perpetually, and that Christ, to deliver thee from death, died for thee, and changed thy perpetual death into his own death. For thou madest the fault, and he suffered the pain, and that for the love he had unto thee, before thou wast born, when thou hadst done neither good nor evil.

Now, seeing he hath paid thy debt, thou needest not, neither canst thou pay it, but thou shouldest be damned, if his blood were not shed. But since he was punished for thee, thou shalt not be punished.

Finally, he has delivered thee from thy condemnation and all evil, and desires nought of thee, but that thou wilt acknowledge what he has done for thee, and bear it in mind: and that thou wouldest help others for his sake, both

## Treatise on the law and the gospel.

in word and deed, even as he has helped thee for nought, and without reward.

O how ready should we be to help others, if we knew his goodness and gentleness towards us! He is a good and gentle Lord, for he does all for nought. Let us beseech you, therefore, follow his footsteps, whom all the world ought to praise and worship. Amen.

*He that thinketh to be saved by his Works, calleth himself Christ.*

For he calleth himself the Saviour, which name pertaineth to Christ only.

What is a Saviour, but he that saveth? and he saith, "I saved myself," which is as much as to say, "I am Christ;" for Christ only is the Saviour of the world.

*We should not do good Works for the intent to get the inheritance of Heaven, or remission of Sin.*

For whosoever believeth to get the inheritance of heaven, or remission of sin, through works, he believeth not to get the same for Christ's sake. And they that believe not that their sins are forgiven them, and that they shall be saved, for Christ's sake, they believe not the gospel. For the gospel saith, You shall be saved for Christ's sake; your sins are forgiven for Christ's sake.

He that believeth not the gospel, believeth not God. So it follows, that they which believe to be saved by their works, or to get remission of their sins by their own deeds, believe not God, but account him a liar, and so utterly deny him to be God.

*Object.* Thou wilt say, "Shall we then do no good deeds?"

*Ans.* I say not so, but I say, we should do no good works for the intent to get the inheritance of heaven, or remission of sin. For if we believe to get the inheritance of heaven, through good works, then we believe not to get it through the promise of God. Or, if we think to get remission of our sins, by our deeds, then we believe not that they are forgiven us, and so we account God a liar. For God saith, Thou shalt have the inheritance of heaven for my Son's sake: thy sins are forgiven thee for my Son's sake: and you say, It is not so, but I will win it through my works. Thus you see, I condemn not good deeds, but I condemn the false trust in any works; for all the works wherein a man putteth any confidence, are therefore poisoned and become evil.

Wherefore, thou must do good works; but beware that thou do them not to deserve any good through them. For if thou do so, thou receivest the good, not as the gift of God, but as a debt due to thee, and makest thyself fellow with God, because thou wilt take nothing of him for nought. And what needeth he any thing of thine, who giveth all things, and is not the poorer?

Therefore, do nothing to him, but take of him; for he is a gentle Lord, and with more glad will gives us all that we need, than we can take it of him. Then if we want aught, let us thank ourselves.

Press not therefore to the inheritance of heaven, through presumption of thy good works, for if thou do, thou countest thyself holy and equal to God, because thou wilt take nothing of him for nought; and so shalt thou fall, as Lucifer fell for his pride.

---

*Certain brief Notes or Declarations upon* THE PLACES OF PATRICK HAMILTON, *by John Fox.*

This little treatise of *Master Patrick's Places*, albeit, in quantity it is short, yet in effect, it comprehends matter, able to fill large volumes, declaring to us the true doctrine of the law, of the gospel, of faith, and of works; with the nature, and properties, and also the difference of the same. Which difference is thus to be understood—that in the cause of salvation, and in the office of justifying, these are to be removed and separated asunder; the law from the gospel, and faith from works: otherwise, in the person that is justified, and also in order of doctrine, they ought commonly to go necessarily together.

Therefore, wheresoever any question or doubt arises respecting salvation, or our justification before God, there the law and all good works must be utterly excluded and stand apart, that grace may appear free, the promise simple, and that faith may stand alone. Which faith alone, without law or works, worketh to every man particularly[*] his salvation, through the mere promise, and the free grace of God. This word, particularly, I add, for the particular certifying of every man's heart privately and peculiarly, who believes in Christ. For as the body of Christ is the *efficient* cause of the redemption of the whole world in general: so is faith the *instrumental* cause, by which every man applies the said body of Christ particularly to his own salvation. So that in the action and office of justification, both law and works are utterly secluded and exempted,[†] as things having nothing to do in this behalf. The reason is this: seeing that all our redemption universally springeth only from the body of the Son of God crucified; then there is nothing, that can stand us in stead, but that only, wherewith this body of Christ is apprehended. Now, forsomuch as neither the law nor works, but faith only, is that which apprehendeth the body and

[*] Or individually.     [†] Put out of question.

death of Christ, therefore faith only is that matter which justifies every soul before God, through the strength of that object which it doth apprehend. For the only object of our faith is the body of Christ, like as the brazen serpent was the only object of the Israelites' looking, and not of their hands' working; by the strength of which object, through the promise of God, immediately proceeded health to the beholders. So, the body of Christ, being the object of our faith, striketh* righteousness to our souls, not through working, but believing only.

Thus you see, how Faith, being the only eye of our souls, standeth alone with her object, in the case of justification: but yet, nevertheless, in the body she standeth not alone: for besides the eye, there are also hands to work, feet to walk, ears to hear, and other members more, every one convenient for the service of the body and yet there is none of them all that can see, but only the eye. So, in a Christian man's life, and in order of doctrine, there is the law, there is repentance, there is hope, charity, and deeds of charity: all which, in life, and in doctrine, are joined, and necessarily concur together, and yet in the action of justifying, there is nothing else in man, that hath any part or place but Faith only, apprehending the object, which is the body of Christ Jesus crucified for us, in whom consisteth all the worthiness and fulness of our salvation, by faith: that is, by our apprehending and receiving of him, according as it is written (John, i. 12.), "Whosoever received him, he gave them power to be made the sons of God, even all such as believed in his name," &c. Also (Isa. liii. 11.), "And this just servant of mine, in the knowledge of him shall justify many," &c.

*Argument.* Apprehending and receiving of Christ only, maketh us justified before God. (John, i. 12.)
Christ only is apprehended and received by faith.
*Therefore,* Faith only maketh us justified before God.

*Argument.* Justification cometh only by apprehending and receiving of Christ. (Isa. liii. 11.)
The law and works do not pertain to the apprehending of Christ.
*Therefore,* The law and works pertain nothing to justification.

*Argument.* Nothing, which is unjust of itself, can justify us before God, or help any thing to our justification.
Every work we do, is unjust before God. (Isa. lxiv. 6.)
*Therefore,* No works that we do, can justify us before God, or help any thing to our justification.

*Argument.* If works could any thing further our justification, then should our works profit us something before God.
No works, do the best we can, profit us before God. (Luke, xvii.10.)
*Therefore,* No works that we do, can further our justification.

*Argument.* All that we can do with God, is by Christ only. (John, xv. 5.)
Our works and merits are not Christ, neither any part of him.
*Therefore,* Our works and merits can do nothing with God.

*Argument.* That which is the cause of condemnation, cannot be the cause of justification.
The law is the cause of condemnation. (Rom. iv. 15.)
*Therefore,* It is not the cause of justification.

*A Consequent.* We are quit and delivered *from* the law. (Rom. vii. 4.)
Therefore, we are not quit and delivered *by* the law.

Forasmuch, therefore, as the truth of the Scripture, in express words, hath thus included our salvation in Faith only, we are enforced necessarily to exclude all other causes and means in our

* Imparts.

justification, and to make this difference between the law and the gospel, between faith and works; affirming with the Scripture and word of God, that the law condemns us, our works do not avail us, and that faith in Christ only justifies us. And this difference and distinction ought diligently to be learned and retained by all Christians, especially in conflicts of conscience, between the law and the gospel; faith and works; grace and merits; promise and condition, God's free election and man's free will. So, that the light of the free grace of God, in our salvation, may appear to all consciences, to the immortal glory of God's holy name. Amen.

### The Order and difference of Places.

| The Gospel. | Faith. | Grace. | Promise. | God's free election. |
| The Law. | Works. | Merits. | Condition. | Man's free will. |

The difference and repugnance of these places being well noted and expended,* it shall give no small light to every faithful Christian, both to understand the Scripture, to judge in cases of conscience, and to reconcile such places in the Old and New Testament, as else may seem to repugn,† according to the rule of Austin, saying; "Make distinction of times, and thou shalt reconcile the two Scriptures," &c. Contrariwise, where men are not perfectly instructed in these Places to discern between the law and the gospel, between faith and works, &c.; so long they can never rightly establish their minds in the free promises of God's grace; but they walk confusedly, without order, in all matters of religion. Example whereof we have in the Romish church, who, confounding these Places together without distinction, following no method, have perverted the true order of Christian doctrine, and have obscured the sweet comfort and benefit of the gospel of Christ, not knowing what the true use of the law, nor of the gospel meaneth.

### In the Doctrine of the Law three things are to be noted.

First, what is the true rigour and strength of the law, which is, to require full and perfect obedience of the whole man, not only to restrain his outward actions, but also his inward motions and inclinations of will and affection, from the appetite of sin: and therefore saith St. Paul: "The law is spiritual, but I am carnal," &c. (Rom. vii. 14.) Whereupon rises this proposition: that it is not in our nature and power to fulfil the law. Likewise, the law commandeth that which is to us impossible, &c. The second thing to be noted in the doctrine of the law, is to consider the time and place of the law, what they are, and how far they extend. For as the surging seas have their banks and bars to keep them in; so, the law hath his times and limits which it ought not to pass. If Christ had not come and suffered, the time and dominion of the law had been everlasting. But now, seeing Christ hath come and hath died in his righteous flesh, the power of the law against our sinful flesh doth cease. "For the end of the law is Christ." (Rom. x. 4.) That is, the death of Christ's body is the death of the law to all that believe in him: so that whosoever repent of their sins, and fly to the death and sufferings of Christ, the condemnation and time of the law is expired as to them. Wherefore, this is to be understood as a perpetual rule in the Scripture, that the law with all its sentences and judgments, wheresoever they are written, either in the Old Testament or in the New, ever includes a privy exception‡ of repentance and belief in Christ, to which it gives always place, having there its end, and can proceed no further, according as St. Paul says, "The law is our schoolmaster until Christ, that we might be justified by faith." (Gal. iii. 24, 25.)

* Considered.    † Differ, oppose.    ‡ Reservation.

Moreover, as the law hath its time, how long to reign, so also it hath its proper place, where to reign. By the reign of the law here is meant, the condemnation of the law: for as the time of the law ceases, when the faith of Christ, in a true repenting heart, begins: so the law hath no place in such as are good and faithful, that is, in sinners repenting and amending, but only in those who are evil and wicked. I here call all such evil men, as walking in sinful flesh, are not yet driven by earnest repentance, to fly to Christ for succour. And therefore saith St. Paul: " To the just men there is no law set, but to the unjust and disobedient," &c. (1 Tim. i. 9.) By the just man here is meant, not he, who never had a disease, but he, who knowing his disease, seeks out the physician, and being cured, keeps himself in health, as much as he may, from any more surfeits: notwithstanding, he shall never so keep himself, but that his health, (that is, his new obedience) shall always remain frail and imperfect, and shall continually need the physician. Where, by the way, these three things are to be noted. 1. The sickness itself. 2. The knowing of the sickness. 3. The physician. The sickness is sin. The knowing of the sickness is repentance, which the law worketh. The physician is Christ. And, therefore, although in remission of our sins, repentance is joined with faith, yet it is not the dignity or worthiness of repentance that causes remission of sins, but only the worthiness of Christ, whom faith only apprehends: no more than the feeling of the disease is the cause of health, but only the physician. For else when man is cast and condemned by the law, it is not repentance that can save or deserve life, but if his pardon come, then is it the grace of the prince, and not his repentance that saves.

The third point to be considered in the doctrine of the law, is this: that we mark well the end and purpose, why the law is given, which is, not to bring us to salvation, nor to work God's favour, nor to make us good: but rather to declare and convict our wickedness, and to make us feel the danger thereof, to this end and purpose, that we, seeing our condemnation, and being in ourselves confounded, may be driven thereby to have our refuge in Christ, the Son of God, and submit ourselves to him, in whom only is to be found our remedy, and in none other. And this end of the law ought to be pondered discreetly by all Christians. Otherwise, they that consider not this end and purpose of the law fall into manifold errors and inconveniences. 1. They pervert all order of doctrine. 2. They seek that in the law, which the law cannot give. 3. They are not able to comfort themselves, nor others. 4. They keep men's souls in an uncertain doubt and dubitation of their salvation. 5. They obscure the light of God's grace. 6. They are unkind to\* God's benefits. 7. They are injurious to Christ's sufferings, and enemies to his cross. 8. They stop Christian liberty. 9. They bereave the church, the spouse of Christ, of her due comfort, as if they took away the sun out of the world. 10. In all their doings they shoot at a wrong mark. For where Christ only is set up to be apprehended by our faith, and so freely to justify us, they, leaving this justification by faith, set up other marks, partly of the law, partly of their own devising, for men to shoot at. And here come in the manifest and manifold absurdities of the bishop of Rome's doctrine, which here we will rehearse, as in a catalogue here following.

*Errors and Absurdities of the Papists, touching the doctrine of the Law, and of the Gospel.*

1. They erroneously conceive opinion of salvation in the law, which is to be sought only in the faith of Christ, and in no other.

\* Ungrateful for.

2. They erroneously seek God's favour by works of the law, not knowing that the law in this our corrupt nature worketh only the anger of God. (Rom. iv. 15.)

3. They err also in this—that where the office of the law is diverse and contrary from the gospel, they, without any difference, confound the one with the other, making the gospel to be a law, and Christ to be a Moses. Thus opposing John, i. 17.

4. They err in dividing the law unskilfully into three parts; into the law natural, the law moral, and the law evangelical.

5. They err again, in dividing the law evangelical into precepts and counsels, making the precepts to serve for all men, the counsels only to serve for them that are perfect.

6. The chief substance of all their teaching and preaching rests upon the works of the law, as may appear by their religion, which wholly consists in men's merits, traditions, laws, canons, decrees, and ceremonies. Thus opposing Mark, xvi. 15.

7. In the doctrine of salvation, of remission, and justification, they either admix the law equally with the gospel, or else, quite secluding the gospel, they teach and preach the law; so that little mention or none at all is made of the faith of Christ.

8. They err in thinking, that the law of God requires nothing in us under pain of damnation, but only our obedience in external actions; as for the inward affections and concupiscence, they esteem them but light matters.

9. They, not knowing the true nature and strength of the law, erroneously imagine that it is in man's power to fulfil it Rom. viii. 3.

10. They err in thinking it not only to be in man's power to keep the law of God, but also to perform more perfect works than are commanded in God's law, and these they call the works of perfection. And hereof rise the works of supererogation, of satisfaction, of congruity, and condignity, to store up the treasure-house of the pope's church, and to be sold out to the people for money. Gal. ii. 21.

11. They err, in saying, that the monastical state is more perfect, for keeping the counsels of the gospel, than other states are, in keeping the law of the gospel.

12. The counsels of the gospel they call the vows of their religious men, as profound humility, perfect chastity, and wilful poverty.

13. They err abominably, in equalling their laws and constitutions with God's law, and in saying, that man's law bindeth under pain of damnation no less than God's law. See Mat. xxiii. 4.

14. They err sinfully, in punishing the transgressors of their laws more sharply than the transgressors of the law of God, as appears by their inquisitions and their canon law, &c.

15. Finally, they err most horribly in this, that where the free promise of God ascribes our salvation, only to our faith in Christ, excluding works, they contrarily ascribe salvation only, or principally, to works and merits, excluding faith. Whereupon riseth the application of the sacrifice of the mass, 'ex opere operato' (that is, by the work wrought) for the quick and dead; application of the merits of Christ's passion in bulls; application of the merits of all religious orders; and many other falsehoods. Matt. xv. 7—9.

*Here follow three Cautions to be observed and avoided in the true understanding of the Law.*

First, that we through misunderstanding of the Scriptures, do not take the law for the gospel, nor the gospel for the law: but skilfully discern and distinguish the voice of the one, from the voice of the other. Many there are, who reading the book of the New Testament, take and understand whatsoever they see contained in the said book, to be only and merely the voice of the gospel. And contrariwise suppose that whatsoever is contained in the compass of the Old Testament, that is, within the law, histories, psalms, and prophets, is only and merely the word and voice of the law ; wherein many are deceived. For the preaching of the law and the gospel, are mixed together in both the Testaments, as well in the old as the new. Neither is the order of these two doctrines to be distinguished by books and leaves, but by the diversity of God's Spirit, speaking unto us. For sometimes in the Old Testament, God comforts, as he comforteth Adam, with the voice of the gospel. Sometimes, also, in the New Testament, he threatens and terrifies, as when Christ threatened the Pharisees : in some places again, Moses and the prophets are as the evangelists. Insomuch, that Jerome doubted whether he should call Isaiah a prophet, or an evangelist. In some places, likewise, Christ and the apostles supply the part of Moses : and as Christ himself, until his death, was under the law, which law he came not to break but to fulfil, so, his sermons made to the Jews, for the most part all run upon the perfect doctrine and works of the law, showing and teaching what we ought to do by the right law of justice, and what danger ensues in not performing the same. All which places, though they are contained in the book of the New Testament, yet they are to be referred to the doctrine of the law, ever having in them included a privy exception of repentance, and faith in Christ Jesus. As for example, where Christ thus preached: "Blessed are they that are pure in heart, for they shall see God," &c. (Mat. v. 8.) Again : " Except ye are made like these children, ye shall not enter into the kingdom of heaven," &c. (Mal. xviii. 3.) Again : " But he that doeth the will of my Father, shalt enter into the kingdom of heaven," &c. (Mat. vii. 21.) Again : the parable of the unkind servant justly cast into prison for not forgiving his fellow, &c. (Mat. xviii. 23—35.) The casting of the rich glutton into hell, &c. (Luke, xvi.) Again ; " He that denieth me here before men, 1 will deny him before my Father," &c. (Luke, xii. 9.) With such other places of like condition. All these, I say, pertaining to the doctrine of the law, ever include in them a secret exception of earnest repentance, and faith in Christ's precious blood. For Peter denied, and yet repented. Many publicans and sinners were unkind, unmerciful, and hard-hearted to their fellow-servants, and yet many of them repented, and by faith were saved. The grace of Christ Jesus work in us earnest repentance, and unfeigned faith in him. Amen.

Briefly, this may serve for a mark to know when the law speaketh, and when the gospel speaketh, and to discern the voice of the one, from the voice of the other. When there is any moral work commanded to be done, either for eschewing* punishment, or upon promise of any reward temporal or eternal ; or, when any promise is made with condition of any work commanded in the law ; there is to be understood the voice of the law. Contrarily, where the promise of life and salvation is offered unto us freely without our merits, and simply without any condition annexed of any law, either natural, ceremonial, or moral ; all those places, whether they are read in the Old Testament, or in the New, are to be referred to the voice and doctrine of the gospel. And this promise of God freely made to us by the merits of Jesus Christ, so long before prophesied to us in the Old Testament, and afterwards exhibited in the New Testament, and now requiring nothing but our faith in the Son of God, is called properly the voice of the gospel, and differs from the voice of the law in this, that it has no condition adjoined of our meriting, but only respects the merits of Christ, the Son of God, by whose faith only we are promised of God to be saved and justified,

* Avoiding.

according as we read, (Rom. iii. 22.) "The righteousness of God cometh by faith of Jesus Christ, in all and upon all, that do believe."

The second caution or danger to be avoided is, that we, now knowing, how to discern rightly between the law and the gospel, and having intelligence not to mistake the one for the other, must take heed again, that we break not the order between these two, taking and applying the law, where the gospel is to be applied, either to ourselves, or towards others. For albeit, the law and the gospel, many times are to be joined together in order of doctrine; yet the case may happen sometimes, that the law must be utterly separated from the gospel. As when any person or persons feel themselves so terrified and oppressed, with the majesty of the law, and judgments of God, and with the burden of their sins overweighed and thrown down into utter discomfort, almost even to the pit of hell, as happens many times to soft and timorous consciences of God's good servants. When such mortified hearts hear, either in preaching, or in reading, any such example or place of the Scripture, which pertains to the law, let them think that the same belongs not to them, any more than mourning weeds belong to a marriage feast; and therefore removing utterly out of their minds all cogitation of the law, of fear, of judgment, and condemnation, let them only set before their eyes the gospel, the sweet comfort of God's promise, free forgiveness of sins in Christ's grace, redemption, liberty, rejoicing, psalms, thanksgiving, and a paradise of spiritual joyfulness, and nothing else. Thinking thus with themselves—that the law hath done its office in them already, and now must needs give place to its better, that is, must needs give place to Christ, the Son of God, who is the Lord and Master, the Fulfiller, and also the Finisher of the law; for the end of the law is Christ. (Rom. x. 4.)

The third danger to be avoided is, that we do not use or apply, on the contrary side, the gospel instead of the law. For as the other was like putting on a mourning gown, in the feast of marriage: so is this like casting pearls before swine, wherein is great abuse among many. For commonly it is seen that these worldly epicures and secure mammonists, to whom the doctrine of the law properly appertains, receive and apply to themselves, most principally, the sweet promises of the gospel; and contrariwise, the other contrite and bruised hearts, to whom belong only the joyful tidings of the gospel, and not the law, for the most part, receive and retain to themselves the terrible voice and sentence of the law. Whereby it comes to pass, that many rejoice, where they should mourn; and on the other side, many fear and mourn, where they need not. Wherefore to conclude, in private use of life,* let every person discreetly discern between the law and the gospel, and aptly apply to himself that which he seeth to be convenient.

And again, in public order of doctrine, let every discreet preacher put a difference between the broken heart of the mourning sinner, and the unrepenting worldling; and so conjoin both the law with the gospel, and the gospel with the law, that in throwing down the wicked, he may ever spare the weak-hearted: and again, so spare the weak, that he do not encourage the ungodly. And thus much concerning the conjunction and the difference between the law and the gospel, upon the occasion of MASTER PATRICK'S PLACES.

* Individually and for his private use.

# THE CONFESSION OF FAITH,

CONTAINING HOW THE TROUBLED MAN SHOULD SEEK REFUGE AT HIS GOD, THERETO LED BY FAITH; WITH THE DECLARATION OF THE ARTICLE OF JUSTIFICATION AT LENGTH. THE ORDER OF GOOD WORKS WHICH ARE THE FRUITS OF FAITH; AND HOW THE FAITHFUL AND JUSTIFIED MAN SHOULD WALK AND LIVE IN THE PERFECT AND TRUE CHRISTIAN RELIGION, ACCORDING TO HIS VOCATION.

COMPILED BY M. HENRY BALNAVES, OF HALHILL, AND ONE OF THE LORDS OF SESSION AND COUNCIL OF SCOTLAND, BEING A PRISONER WITHIN THE OLD PALACE OF ROANE.
IN THE YEAR OF OUR LORD, 1548.
DIRECTED TO HIS FAITHFUL BRETHREN, BEING IN LIKE TROUBLE OR MORE. AND TO ALL TRUE PROFESSORS AND FAVOURERS OF THE SINCERE WORD OF GOD.

---

He shall come, and shall not tarry, in whom who believe shall not be confounded.—Acts i. Hab. ii. Heb. x.

---

*Imprinted at Edinburgh by Thomas Vautrollier, 1584.*

HENRY BALNAVES, of Halhill, was born of poor parents in the town of Kirkaldy, in Scotland. When yet a boy he travelled to the continent. Hearing of a free school at Cologne, he procured admission, and received a liberal education with instruction in the principles of the Reformation. Returning to his native country, he studied the law, and was for some time in the family of the earl of Arran, by whom he was employed in public affairs, but was dismissed in 1542, for having embraced the protestant faith. In 1546, he took refuge in the castle of St. Andrew's with those who had put cardinal Beaton to death. Though he was not concerned in that act, he was declared a traitor, and excommunicated. During the siege which ensued, he went to England, whence he returned with supplies of provisions and money. Upon the surrender of the castle to the French, he was conveyed to Rouen with Knox and others, where they were detained prisoners contrary to the terms of capitulation. While in prison, Balnaves composed a treatise on Justification, which being conveyed to Knox, then a prisoner on board the gallies, the latter was so much pleased with the work, as to divide it into chapters, adding marginal notes, and an epitome of the contents. He prefixed a recommendatory preface, in which he gives an account of the treatise and its origin. There is reason to think that the manuscript was conveyed to Scotland about this time, but was mislaid, and for many years supposed to be lost. After the death of Knox, it was discovered by Knox's secretary, Bannantine, in the hands of a child, and was printed in 1584, under the title of A Confession of Faith.

Balnaves returned to Scotland in 1559, and was again employed in public affairs. In 1563, he was appointed one of the lords of session; he died at Edinburgh in 1579. Dr. M'Crie says that he raised himself, by his talents and probity, from an obscure station to the first honours of the state, and was justly regarded as one of the principal supporters of the reformed cause in Scotland

The treatise of Balnaves is now reprinted from the edition of 1584. Dr. M'Crie, in his life of Knox, has given several passages from it, considering that he could not give a more correct view of the sentiments of the great Scottish Reformer on the fundamental article of faith—the doctrine of Justification—than by quoting from a book which was revised and approved by him

THE

# CONFESSION OF FAITH.

**THE EPISTLE DEDICATORY BY THE PUBLISHER.**

*To the right honourable and virtuous lady Alison Sandi-*
*lands, lady of Ormistoun,\* Thomas Vautrollier, her*
*humble servitor, wisheth grace and peace, in Christ Jesus.*

WHILE I consider, noble lady, how that after the miserable sackage of Jerusalem, the utter wreck and overthrow of the city and temple thereof, the lamentable leading unto and being in captivity of the Jews; and to the eyes of men the unrecoverable desolation of that whole commonweal, having now, as it were, lain so many years buried; yet at the last, besides their deliverance which was most wonderful; how, I say, that wherein their greatest beauty and highest felicity ever did stand; yea, the only glory wherein any people could excel, that is, the law of God given by Moses, was found out amongst the desperate ruins, undestroyed, unviolated, and safely preserved, as is to be seen by the holy history, 2 Chron. xxxiv. 2 Kings xxii. I cannot but acknowledge the wonderful providence and exceeding great mercy of our God, in preserving from time to time his blessed law and word, (wherein only consists the glory and felicity of his church upon the face of this earth,) from depravation, corruption, and destruction, in whatsoever extreme dangers; howsoever the blind papists cannot see this without a visible and glistening succession of a church to do the same. The like persuasion whereof, now in the whole body of the scripture, now in some parts or portions of the same; the histories of times, and memories of men do record; so that God's careful providence and merciful preservation, hath always been bent hereto.

And if it be lawful to compare small, base, and little things, unto such as are great, high, and mighty; surely there was a certain pretty, learned, and godly treatise, com-

\* Knox in early life was tutor in the family of Ormiston, who favoured and protected him.

piled by a divine lawyer, and honourable sessioner of the king's majesty's session and public council, which through the injuries of time, negligence of keepers, great and careful distractions of the author, was so lost, and, to the opinion of all, perished, that being earnestly coveted, greatly desired, and carefully sought for and searched out by some good, godly, and learned, as having some intelligence of the author's travels in that part; yet it could never be had, as desperate at any time to have been able to be recovered, until to man's appearance of mere chance, but most assuredly by the merciful providence of our God, a certain godly and zealous gentleman,[*] privy to the desires of some that so earnestly coveted it, being in the town of Ormiston in Lothian, found the same in the hands of a child, as it were serving to the child to play him with! and so he received and recovered the same. And as this treatise was a pretty and gentle strand[†] of the abundant fountain of the scriptures, why might it not savour of its own source, spring, and beginning? Why might not the daughter this far even resemble the mother, or be of the same fortune, and as it were subject to the same fatality with her?

Wherefore, this treatise, coming to my hands, as a singular token of the finder's loving-kindness and liberal will and affection towards me; considering the worthiness, utility, compendious learning, and singular godliness thereof; I could not either be so unjust to the honourable fame of the godly author, either so ingrate to the loving offerer unto me, either envious to the commonwealth of christianity, or sacrilegious towards God, in suppressing his glory in this point, as not to commit the same, by my travail, to a longer and more lasting memory: that so, in this rarity of trusty and faithful handmaids, and great store of treasonable dealing of vile hirelings, this lawful and loving daughter might, after a manner, somewhat be an handmaiden and servant to the own mother, that is, to the scriptures, whereof she floweth and proceedeth.

And surely not a few nor small reasons moved me to utter the same, worshipful lady, under the shadow of your name, and as it were dedicate it, at least my pains and travails in setting it out, unto your honour. For, it being

---

[*] Richard Bannantine, servant, or rather secretary to John Knox, by whom an account of the last illness of that reformer was drawn up. The diary of Bannantine contains some interesting historical particulars of the times of the reformation.

[†] Interweaving, compilation.

found and recovered in your ground and holding, and, after a manner, being the birth thereof; who can so justly as you now and yours challenge the right of the same, after God's calling the author to his mercies? It is also a work bred and brought forth in that affliction and banishment for Christ's sake, in the which you did breed and bring forth your dearest children. It is the work of a faithful brother and most trusty counsellor, participant of all the afflictions, and continuing constant to the end, and in the end. It is such, that when as it was, I wot not how, let be amongst the hands of babes to play them with, it was through God's providence recovered by that godly gentleman, your ladyship's secretary.* It was by that notable servant of God, whom the laird, your husband, of godly memory, and you, did ever so dutifully reverence,† and he so fatherly and christianly love you, so earnestly cared for, and so diligently sought out and inquired of, that it might be preserved from perishing, as almost nothing more. And as the book of the law, found in the temple by God's providence, was presented to Josiah, to renew the covenant betwixt God and his people, and to bring them again under his right obedience, and to found them in his true knowledge and worshipping, which all now a long time had been put in oblivion—who knows but the like is resembled and shadowed to you, and given you to understand and learn in finding this pendicle‡ of God's law and word in your dwelling, that you and yours may be put in mind of your duty towards God, constantly to abide by his truth, and to see that he is truly served in your dominion: that you and yours, first seeking the kingdom of God and righteousness thereof, then all other things may be cast unto you. In case you or they fail in so doing, it may be a testimony against you or them, that God hath offered himself, even to be found by you and in your ground, and yet you have not rightly regarded him.

Surely these, with other reasons, besides my duty towards your honour, moved me to set out this small work chiefly under your name. The utility whereof, I doubt not, shall be found so profitable, the delight so pleasant, the dignity so excellent, that whosoever reads it, shall find themselves greatly benefited by the goodness of God, the fountain thereof, joyfully delighted by the author or writer, and

* Richard Bannantine. † John Knox.
‡ Compendium, summary.

honourably decored\* through your mean, whereby they enjoy the use of it.

Now as to that which remains, God ever preserve your ladyship, and yours, in his true fear, grant you good days and long life, to the furtherance and advancement of his glory, the helping to the building up of the work of his church, and your eternal comfort.

### ORIGINAL PREFACE BY KNOX.

JOHN KNOX, *the bound servant of Jesus Christ, unto his best beloved brethren of the congregation of the castle of St. Andrew's, and to all professors of Christ's true evangel, desireth grace, mercy, and peace from God the Father, with perpetual consolation of the Holy Spirit.*

BLESSED be God, the Father of our Lord Jesus Christ, whose infinite goodness and incomprehensible wisdom, in every age, so frustrates the purpose, and maketh of none effect the sleight of Satan, that the same things, which appear to be extreme destruction to the just, and damage to the small flock of Jesus Christ, beyond all men's expectation, yea, and Satan himself, by the mercy of our God are turned to the laud, praise, and glory of his own name, to the utility and singular profit of his congregation, and to the pleasure, comfort, and advancement of them that suffer. How the name of the only living God hath been magnified in all ages by them which were sorely troubled, by persecution of tyrants, exiled from their own country, it were long to rehearse. Yet one or two principal will we touch, for probation of our words aforesaid.

Satan moved the hatred of the rest of his brethren against young Joseph, to whom God promised honours and authority above his brethren and parents. To the impediment whereof Satan procured that he should be sold as a bondman or slave, carried into a strange country, where many years unjustly he suffered imprisonment. And Satan wrought this, to the intent that he who reproved the wickedness of his brethren, should perish altogether. For nothing is to Satan more noisome, than that those men in whom godliness, and in whom purity of life, and hatred of iniquity appear, should flourish in dominion or authority.

\* Adorned.

But all his counsels were frustrate, when, by the singular mercy and providence of God, Joseph was exalted in most high honours, made principal governor of Egypt by Pharaoh, the potent king thereof, who gave in charge, that all princes of his kingdom should obey his will, and that his senators should learn wisdom at the mouth of Joseph: who, no doubt, with all study set forth the true knowledge, worshipping, and religion of the only living God, which in that country was unknown before. And, after certain years, he received his father and brethren in this same country, whom he with all godliness and wisdom, in the years of hunger, sustained and nourished. And so was Satan frustrate, and all his deceit turned to nought.

When, after this, God of his great mercy, according to his own promise, sometime made to Abraham, had placed the people of Israel in the land of Canaan, Satan, to corrupt the true religion, which they had received from God by his faithful servant Moses, invented abominations of idolatry, under the pretext of the true worshipping of God. And albeit frequently they were reproved by true prophets, yet ever superstition prevailed; while God, of his righteous judgment, was compelled to punish, first Israel, and thereafter Judah, giving them into the power of their enemies, who translated them from their own countries—Salmanaser, Israel unto Assyria, and Nebuchadnezzar, Judah unto Babylon. Then Satan believed the true knowledge and worshipping of God, to have decayed for ever. But he was far deceived, when first Nebuchadnezzar, king of Babylon, and the mightiest prince in the earth, and after him Darius, the potent king of Media, received the true knowledge of the Lord God by Daniel the prophet, one of the same number, which were transported from their own country. And the kings, then having the whole empire in earth, not only received the true religion of God, but also commanded the same to be observed by their subjects. For after this manner it was written, "Then Darius wrote unto all people, nations, and tongues in the universal earth, saying, Peace be multiplied with you. A decree is ordained by me, that in my universal empire and kingdom, all men shall fear, dread, and honour the God of Daniel; for he is the living and eternal God for ever. He is a deliverer, and Saviour, working signs, and wonderful things in heaven and earth; who hath delivered Daniel from the den of lions." Secondly, after Darius, the most prosperous, valiant, and mighty Cyrus, the first monarch of the Persians and Medians, not only obtained knowledge of the true living God by the same prophet, but also for singular affection which he bare to the true religion, restored unto liberty the people of Israel, permitting them to build a new temple, and to repair the walls of Jerusalem, which by the Babylonians sometime were brought to ruin. And albeit that by the perpetual hatred of Satan, working by his members, some years they were impeded, yet at the last, to the great consolation of all the people, was the work finished, where, many years after, God's true religion was observed.

Satan never believed his purpose rather to take effect, than when, after the death of Jesus Christ, he moved the princes of the priests, who then were esteemed the true church of God, to persecute the apostles, and other professors of Christ's evangel. For, who believed not great damage to follow the congregation, when, after the death of Stephen, who was stoned to death, the professors were dispersed, banished, and exiled from Jerusalem? But what entries the church of God thereby took, the eleventh chapter of the Acts of the Apostles showeth, in these words: "And they which were scattered abroad, because of the affliction that arose about Stephen, went through till they came unto Phenice, Cyprus, and Antioch, preaching plainly the evangel of Jesus Christ."

Of these, and other testimonies of the scripture, we may consider, dearly beloved brethren, that the infinite goodness of our Father turned the same things, whereby Satan and his members intended to destroy and oppress the true religion of God, to the advancement and forthsetting thereof; and that no less in these latter, wicked, and dangerous days, than he did in any age before us. Which thing this godly work subsequent shall openly declare. The counsel of Satan in the persecution of us, first, was to stop the wholesome winds of Christ's evangel to blow upon the parts where we converse and dwell; and secondly, so to oppress ourselves by corporeal affliction, and worldly calamities, that we should find no place to godly study. But by the great mercy, and infinite goodness of God our Father, these his counsels shall be frustrate and vain. For in despite of him, and all his wicked members, shall yet that same word—O Lord, this I speak, confiding in thy holy promise—openly be proclaimed in that same country.*

* Scotland.

And how that our merciful Father, amongst these tempestuous storms, beyond all men's expectation, hath provided some rest for us, this present work shall testify; which was sent to me in Roan, I then lying in irons, and sore troubled by corporal infirmity, in a galley named Notre Dame, by an honourable man and faithful christian brother, M. Henry Balnaves, of Halhill, for the present holden as prisoner, though unjustly, in the old palace of Roan. Which work, after I had once again read, to the great comfort and consolation of my spirit, by counsel and advice of the aforesaid noble and faithful man, author of the same work, I thought expedient it should be digested into chapters; and to the better memory of the reader, the contents of every chapter proponed briefly unto them, with certain annotations, to the more instruction of the simple, in the margin. And also that an epitome of the same work should be shortly collected, we have likewise digested the same into chapters, which follow the work in place of a table. Which thing I have done, as imbecility of understanding and incommodity of place would permit; not so much to illustrate the work, which in itself is godly and perfect, as, together with the aforesaid noble man and faithful brother, to give my confession of the article of JUSTIFICATION therein contained. And I beseech you, beloved brethren, earnestly to consider if we deny any thing presently, or yet conceal or hide, which any time before we professed in that article.

And now we have not the castle of St. Andrew's to be our defence, as some of our enemies falsely accused us, saying, If we wanted our walls we would not speak so boldly: but we pray the eternal God, that the same affection, which now and then remained in us, remain with them eternally. The Lord shall judge if all which we spake was not of pure heart, having no respect either to love or hatred of any person, but only to the word of God and verity of his scriptures, as we must answer in the great day of the Lord, where no man shall have place to dissemble. But, blessed be that Lord, whose infinite goodness and wisdom hath taken from us the occasion of that slander, and hath shown unto us that the serpent hath power only to sting the heel, that is, to molest and trouble the flesh, but not to move the spirit from constant adhering to Jesus Christ, and public professing of his true word. O! blessed be thou, eternal Father, who by thy mercy alone hast preserved us to this day, and provided that the confession of our faith, which we ever desired all men to have known, should by this treatise come plainly to light. Continue, O Lord, and grant unto us, that as now with pen and ink, so, shortly we may confess with voice and tongue, the same before thy congregation; upon whom look, O Lord God, with the eyes of thy mercy, and suffer no more darkness to prevail. I pray you, pardon me, beloved brethren, that on this matter I digress: vehemency of spirit—the Lord knoweth I lie not—compelleth me thereto. The head of Satan shall be trodden down, when he believeth surely to triumph. Therefore, most dear brethren, (so call I all professing Christ's evangel,) continue in that purpose which ye have begun godly; though the battle appear strong, your Captain is inexpugnable: to Him is given all power in heaven and earth. Abide, stand, and call for his support; and so the enemies, who now affright you, shortly shall be confounded, and never again shall appear to molest you.

Consider, brethren; it is no speculative theologian who desires to give you courage, but even your brother in affliction, who partly hath experience what Satan's wrath may do against the chosen of God. Rejoice (yet I say) spiritually, and be glad; the time of the battle is short, but the reward is eternal. Victory is sure, without ye list to fly (which God forbid) from Christ. But that ye may plainly know whereby Satan and the world are overcome, and which are the weapons against whom they may not stand, ye shall read diligently this work following; which, I am sure, no man having the Spirit of God shall think tedious, because it contains nothing except the very scriptures of God, and meditations of his law, wherein is the whole study of the godly man both day and night, knowing that therein are found only wisdom, prudence, liberty, and life. And therefore, in reading, talking, or meditation thereof, he is never satiated. But, as for the ungodly, because their works are wicked, they may not abide the light. And therefore they abhor all godly writings, thinking them tedious, though they contain not the length of the Lord's Prayer. But according to the threatening of Isaiah the prophet, saying, Because they contemn the law of the Lord God, he shall contemn them. Their hearts shall be hardened, in the day of anguish and trouble they shall despair, and curse the Lord God in their hearts. They shall be numbered to the sword, and in the slaughter shall they fall. Then shall they know that their works were vain, and that they placed their refuge in lies. Their vestments of spiders' webs, which are their vain works, shall not abide the force of the Lord's wind; but they shall stand naked, and the works of iniquity in their hands, to their extreme confusion. And this shall apprehend and overtake them, because they call light darkness, and darkness light. That which was sweet, they called bitter; and, by the contrary, that which was bitter, they called sweet, seeking salvation where none was to be found. But you, most christian brethren, humbly I beseech, and in the blood of Jesus Christ I exhort, that you read diligently this present treatise. Not only with earnest prayer, that you may understand the same aright, but also with humble and due thanksgiving unto our most merciful Father, who of his infinite power hath so strengthened the hearts of his prisoners, that in despite of Satan they desist not yet to work, but in the greatest vehemency of tribulation seek the utility and salvation of others.

It is not my purpose to commend, or advance this work with words, as commonly writers of profane or human science do, seeing the verity is only to be commended by itself. But one thing boldly I dare affirm, that no man who cometh with a godly heart hereto, shall pass from the same without satisfaction. The firm and weak shall find strength and comfort, the rude and simple true knowledge and erudition, the learned and godly humble rejoicing, by the omnipotent spirit of Jesus Christ, to whom be glory before his congregation. Amen.

This work following contains three principal parts. The first part, How man, being in trouble, should seek refuge at God alone. And that naturally all men are subject to trouble, and how profitable the same is to the godly. Last, of the cruel persecution of Satan and his members against the chosen of God.

The second part contains, How man is released of his trouble by faith and hope in the promises of God, and therefore declares the article of justification, proving that faith only justifieth before God, without any deserving or merit of our works, either preceding or following faith; with a solution to certain contrary arguments made by the adversaries of faith and this article, with the true understanding of such scriptures as they allege for them.

The third and last part contains the fruits of faith, which are good works, which every man should work according to their own vocation in every estate.

All this plainly may be perceived in the life of our first parent Adam, who by transgression of God's commandment fell into great trouble and affliction. From which he should never have been released, without the goodness of God had first called him; and, secondly, made unto him the promise of his salvation. The which Adam believing, before ever he wrought good works, was reputed just. After, during all his life, he continued in good works, striving against Satan, the world, and his own flesh.

---

### *The Author, unto the faithful Readers.*

The love, favour, mercy, grace, and peace of God the Father, God the Son, with the illumination of God the Holy Ghost, be with you all, my beloved brethren, who thirst after the knowledge of the word of God; and most fervently desire the same to the augmentation and increasing of the church of Christ, daily to flourish in godly wisdom and understanding, through faith unfeigned, ever working by love. Amen.

# CONFESSION OF FAITH,

DECLARING

# THE ARTICLE OF JUSTIFICATION.

## CHAPTER I

*What should be the study of man; and what man should do in time of tribulation.*

As desirous as the wild hart is, in the most burning heat and vehement drought, to seek the cold fountain or river of water, to refresh his thirst; so desirous should we be, O Lord God, to seek unto thee, our Creator and Maker, in all our troubles and afflictions; and say with the prophet David, Psal. xlii. xliii. Wherefore art thou sad or sorrowful, O thou my soul or spirit, and why troublest thou me? Believe and hope surely in God—that is, confide in his mercy, and call to remembrance the time by-past, how merciful, helpful, and propitious he hath been to the fathers, and delivered them of their troubles, Psal. lxxvi. xxii. civ. Even so shall he do to thee if thou believest unfeignedly in him, and seekest him in his word; not inquiring his name,[*] what they call him, nor what similitude, form, or shape he is of, for that is forbidden thee in his law. He is that he is; the God of Abraham, Isaac, and Jacob; and the God of the fathers, to whom he made the promise of our redemption. He would show his name no other way to Moses, Exod. iii. but commanded him to pass to the people of Israel, and say unto them, He which is hath sent me to you—that is my name from the beginning, and that is my memorial from one generation to another.

## CHAPTER II.

*How man comes to the knowledge of God. Where should man seek God, and how he should receive him. And by whom we should offer our petitions.*

By faith we are taught to know God the Father, Maker, and Creator of heaven, earth, and all creatures; whom we should believe to be almighty, of infinite power, mercy, justice, and goodness; and that he created, in the beginning,

---

[*] That is, The manner how he will deliver.—Ed. 1584. These notes, it is supposed, were added by Knox.

all things of nought, as the scripture teacheth us, Gen. i. And that, by the Word, that is, the Son of God, he made all things which are made: who is equal to the Father in divine nature and substance, without beginning, in the bosom of the Father, who was with God in the beginning, and was also God. And at the prefixed and preordinate time, by God the Father was sent into the world, and made man, taking our human nature, and clothing himself with the same, and dwelled among us, John i. And after long time conversing among us, teaching and preaching the realm of heaven, being exercised in all troubles and calamities, in the which this our mortal body is subject, except sin only; finally, for our sakes, suffered the most vile death for our redemption; and rose from the same the third day for our justification; and after forty days ascended to the heavens, and sitteth at the right hand of the Father, our Advocate, as testify the holy scriptures of him, Luke xxiv. Acts i. ii. And thereafter he sent the Holy Spirit to instruct his disciples of all verity, as he had promised before, John xiv. xv. xvi. who, proceeding from the Father and the Son, the third person of the Trinity, descended upon the disciples in a visible sign of fiery tongues: by whom all creatures are vivified and have life; are governed, ruled, sustained, and comforted, without which all creatures would turn to nought, Gen. vi. Psal. ciii.

Of this manner know thy God, three Persons distinct in one substance of Godhead; confound not the persons, nor divide the Godhead. But believe firmly and undoubtedly as thou art taught in the creed of the apostles, and of the holy man Athanasius, confessed in the holy church of Christ. Ascend no higher in the speculation of the Trinity, than thou art taught in the scriptures of God. If thou wilt have knowledge of the Father, seek him at the Son;* if thou wilt know the Son, seek him at the Father. For none knoweth the Son but the Father, and none may come to the knowledge of the Father but by the Son. And also Christ, being desired of Philip, one of his apostles, to show them the Father, answered, This long time I have been with you, and ye have not known me, Philip, John xiv. He who hath seen me hath seen the Father:† believest thou not

* That is, Give credit to the doctrine which Jesus the Son of God hath taught.—Ed. 1584.

† That is, Though my Father were present, no other works should he work than I have wrought in your presence: nor yet other doctrine should he teach to you than I have done.—Ed. 1584.

that I am in the Father, and the Father in me? Therefore, whatever thou desirest which is good, seek the same at the Son; for the Father hath given all things in his power. For that cause Christ commandeth us all to come to him, Matt. xi. and seeing he hath all things given to him, and also commandeth us all to come to him, great fools we are which seek any other way, of the which we are uncertain, either in heaven or in earth; as concerning our salvation we are sure he loveth us, and will hear us, according to his promise. Greater love than this can no man show, but that he put his life for his friends. Yea, verily, we being his enemies, he willingly gave himself to the death to get us life, and to reconcile us to the Father. Therefore, if we will have our thirst and drought quenched and refreshed, seek unto Christ, who is the fountain of living water, John iv. of the which, whosoever drinketh, shall never thirst, but it shall be to him a fountain of running water to everlasting life.

## CHAPTER III.

*The fruit of tribulation unto the faithful. God is a peculiar Father unto the faithful. What care he takes of them, and wherefore. Tribulation the sign of God's love. The judgment of the wicked concerning tribulation; what they do, and why they despair therein.*

THIS vehement drought and thirst had David, the holy prophet, when he said, O God, thou art my God,[*] of most might and power; therefore I seek thee early in the morning; with most ardent desire my soul thirsteth after thee, and my flesh desires thee. Great and fervent was this desire of the holy man, as ye may read in the 62d Psalm, which teacheth us how profitable, wholesome, and commodious the troubles, afflictions, and incommodities of the world are to the faithful and godly men; insomuch that the flesh, which ever of its own nature is adversary and enemy to the spirit, Rom. viii. drawing and enticing the same from the true worshipping of God; with frequent troubles and calamities is so broken and debilitate, that it takes peace with the spirit, and altogether most fervently seeks God, saying, Better is thy goodness, mercy, and benignity, the which thou showest to thy faithful flock, than this corporeal life; therefore my lips shall never cease to

[*] That is, Thou alone art sufficient to save, though all men be enemies.—Ed. 1584.

praise thee. O happy is that trouble and affliction which teaches us this way to know our good God, and causes this thirst in our soul, that we may learn to cry unto God as the fathers did; O thou, my God! As Daniel and Paul say in divers places. I give thanks, saith Paul, to my God for you, my brethren, Rom. i. Howbeit he is God to all creatures by creation, yet to the faithful he is one special and peculiar God, Mal. iii. whose troubles and afflictions he seeth, and shall deliver them thereof, even as he did his people of Israel forth of the hands of Pharaoh, without all our deservings or merits, Exod. iii. Therefore let us not look upon our merits, worthiness or unworthiness, but only to his mercy and goodness, putting all our trust, hope, and belief into him, and into no other thing either in heaven or earth; and say with the prophet David, O Lord, my strength, I shall love thee. The Lord is my sureness, my refuge, and my deliverance. And after, Be unto me a God, defender, and a house of refuge, that thou mayest save me, for thou art my strength: and for thy name's sake thou shalt lead me and nourish me, Psal. xviii. xxxi. lxxi. That is, I put no confidence in my own strength, wit, or manly power, but only into thy mercy and goodness, by the which I am defended and preserved from all evils, and led and kept in all goodness. For thou takest care upon me, and art my only refuge, and strength unwinnable in all my troubles and adversities, Psal. xlii. and cxliii.

Therefore, my well beloved brethren, let us rejoice greatly of this our little trouble and afflictions, James i. and consider them to be good and not evil; the signs and tokens of the goodwill of God toward us, and not of ire nor wrath; and receive them forth of his hands, neither of chance, accident, nor fortune, but of his permission and certain purpose, to our weal, as the trial and exercise of our faith.* And that he punisheth us, not that we be lost thereby, but to draw and provoke us to repentance, according to that saying, Ezek. xviii. I will not the death of a sinner, &c. In the time of tribulation he requireth of us obedience, faith, and calling upon his name, as the prophet David teacheth us, saying, Call upon me in the day of thy trouble, and I shall deliver thee, and thou shalt honour me, Psal. l. That is, believe me ever present with them that unfeignedly call upon me, and I shall not abstract my

* Jer. xxxi. Prov. iii. Heb. xii. Rev. iii. Psal. cxviii. Isa. xxvi. and xxviii. —Ed. 1584.

favour, help, and supply from them; but shall so deliver them, that they may therefore give me great thanks and praise: for I desire no other thing of man. This manner of trouble brings patience, and patience proof, and proof hope, which frustrates not, but greatly comforts the faithful, Rom. v. .

The world hath another judgment of this trouble, and the wicked man, when the same happeneth to him, he grudges and murmurs against God, saying, Why hath God punished me? What have I done to be punished of this manner? Then gathers he in his heart, Had I done this thing, or that thing, sought this remedy or that remedy, these things had not happened to me. And so he thinks that they are come to him either by chance or fortune, or by neglecting of manly wisdom. Thus he flees from God, and turns to the help of man, which is vain; in the which finding no remedy, finally in his wickedness, he despairs, for he can do no other thing, because all things wherein he put his trust and belief have left him, and so rests no consolation, Psal. lix. lxii. cix.

## CHAPTER IV.

*What the faithful do in time of tribulation. What we have of our own nature, and what of Jesus Christ. What Adam did after his transgression. The goodness of God shewn unto Adam. What Adam wrought in his justification. To Abraham, being an idolater, was made the promise that he should be the father of many nations; and the conclusion thereupon.*

BUT the godly say, O my God, thanks and praise be to thee, who hast visited thy froward child and unprofitable servant, and hast not suffered me to run on in my wickedness, but hast called me to repentance. I know my offences: justly have I deserved this punishment, yea, and ten thousand times more for my sins, the which sorely repenteth me. Our wicked nature teaches us to fly from thee, to diffide or doubt of thy mercy and goodness. And to excuse in our selves our sin and vice, and to object the same in another, as our forefather Adam did; having no respect to person, or love of any creature more than he had; for against his own fellow, which was of his own flesh, he objected the crime, to excuse himself! Yea, and also against God, thinking that the good work of God, making the woman, and giving her to him in fellowship, was the cause of his sin and fall, as the scriptures say, Gen. iii. But faith in the blood of thy only begotten Son Christ Jesu, leadeth us to thy mercy-stool, and hope comforteth us that we are not overcome in this battle; knowing perfectly that the flesh is subject to these bodily afflictions, that the dregs of sin may be mortified in us, the which we have of our forefather Adam.

This corruption of nature teaches us what we have of our first parents, and what we are of ourselves; which, being considered, shall lead us to the knowledge of God, in whom we shall find goodness, mercy, and justice, as we may clearly perceive in our first parent. For after he had transgressed the law and commandment of God, he fled from him, whom God followed, moved of love toward his handiwork, and called him again; in the which he did show his goodness. And when he accused Adam of his sin, he was not penitent, nor trusted in the mercy of God, nor asked forgiveness, but excused his transgression and fault. Nevertheless, God of his infinite mercy made the promise of salvation before he would pronounce the sentence against the man or woman; saying to the serpent, I will put enmity between thee and the woman, and between thy seed and the woman's seed. The Seed of the woman shall tread down thy head, and thou shalt sting the same on the heel. Adam was comforted with these words, and through faith in this promise, was of wicked made just, that is, received again into favour, and through faith in the blood of Christ to be shed, was accepted as just. And thereafter God manifested his ire and wrath against sin, which of his righteous judgment he cannot suffer to be unpunished, Nah. i. Num. xiv. and pronounced the sentence first against the woman, and then against the man; and ejected them forth of paradise, clothing them with skin coats;* saying, Behold, Adam is made as it were one of us, knowing good and evil; that is as much to say, O miserable man! now thou mayest perceive thy state, and the fruits thou hast gotten for the transgression of my commandment; what is thy knowledge who hast learned nothing but to fly from thy Maker, to pass from life to death, from great pleasure to all misery? And so Adam is spoiled of all the noble gifts he was endued with in his creation, as hereafter in time and place

* Skin coats were the sign and remembrance of their mortality.—Ed. 1584.

at more length shall be shown. Read with order the third chapter of Genesis, and thou shalt understand this matter clearly.

Now ye may see what was our first parent's part in the obtaining of this promise of God. Verily, no more than he had of his creation, but rather less; for being but dust and clay, he made no evil cause, but being made man, he disobeyed his Maker, transgressed his law, usurped glory to himself, and knowledge which became him not to seek; for the which he deserved nothing but eternal damnation. Abraham, in his father's house, an idolater as he was, and the rest of his house, made no good cause to God, nor merit to obtain the promise, that he should be the father of a faithful; but only believed in the promise of God, as hereafter shall be discussed. But even as they were accepted as just through faith, without all their merits or deservings, so shall we be who are the sons of Abraham, and heirs of the promise, Gen. xi. xii. Josh. xxiv. No other way should we seek, but the order taught us in the scriptures of God, that is, if we will be sure of our salvation, and have passage to the Father, pass unto Christ, who saith, John xiv. I am the way, the truth, and the life; no man cometh to the Father but by me. If ye had knowledge of me, ye should also have knowledge of the Father. Therefore, ir we will walk right in the way, go with Christ and walk in him. If we will not be deceived, pass unto him; for he is the verity who can neither deceive, nor be deceived; and if we will not die the eternal death, he is the life. These gifts may we have of no other but of him, and by him only through faith in the mercy of God, by the operation of the Holy Spirit.

## CHAPTER V.

*The consolation of Adam when expelled from Paradise. The consolation of Adam, which he took of his two sons, turned into dolour. What Adam did when he received Seth for Abel, whom Cain slew. The comfort of Adam in all afflictions, and the example left to us therein.*

GREAT was the trouble and affliction both of body and spirit which was in Adam, standing trembling before God, whom he had so highly offended, perceiving himself deceived of the false promise, made by the serpent, which was, that he should not die, howbeit he ate of the apple, but should be like unto God, know good and evil; being therefore ejected forth of that pleasant garden of all delight and pleasure, into the miserable earth, to eat his bread with the sweat of his face. Trust well, he was sorely penitent now, and would have suffered great torment upon his body, to have satisfied for his offences; but that could not be, nor might it stand with the justice of God. What was his comfort then? Nothing but this promise, which he apprehended by faith, and believed him to be in the favour of God; for that promised Seed's sake. This comforted his spirit, or else in despair he had perished in this sorrow and trouble; for he found no remedy in himself. For his bodily consolation God sent him two sons, in his own image and similitude. This was no little consolation and comfort to Adam; but this bodily comfort* turned shortly into great displeasure, when one brother slew the other, of malice, by which Adam was destitute of all succession. Thus dolorously led he his life a long time, desiring ever at God succession in place of Abel. Of whom God had pity and compassion, and sent him a son named Seth, of whom descended the promised Seed, that God might be found true in his sayings; for rather would he have raised Abel from death to life, than his promise should not have been fulfilled. By this was the dolour and trouble of Adam converted into joy and gladness; for the which he gave thanks and praise unto God, saying, God hath sent me another seed for Abel, whom Cain hath slain. Here he saith not that he hath gotten a son in place of Abel, but saith, God hath sent me another seed for Abel, ascribing the same to the gift of God, and not to the work of man. This is a notable example to all the faithful, to receive all things of the hands of God, giving him ever thanks therefore, as the holy fathers did; not contemning the work nor help of man, whom God maketh the instrument to do that thing which is his godly will to perform.

Let us, therefore, take example of our forefather; that like as he was subject to troubles and afflictions all the days of his life in this miserable world; even so are we, and let us take therefore all things in patience, thinking us to have deserved the same justly, how just that ever we are, or appear to the world. Trust well there is, nor was ever man which descended of Adam by natural propagation, juster than he was after his fall: for there is no mention in the

* All pleasure of earthly things turns and ends in sorrow.—Ed. 1584.

scripture of any offence done by Adam, against the law of his God, after his expulsion forth of paradise. And as for his first rebellion and corrupting of his nature, we are all guilty of that as he was, and then also guilty of our sins proceeding of that rebellion; wherefore, we may well be worse than he, but no better. Think well, he confessed himself justly punished, and thought he deserved more punishment than ever was put upon him; taking ever consolation of the sweet promises of God, in the which he believed; and in all his troubles comforted himself with hope to be delivered of them, as all faithful do; and to be restored to the glory he was ejected from for his own foolishness; without all merits and deservings of himself, which were nothing in him, and much less in us.

There had been no difference between the expulsion of Adam forth of paradise, and Lucifer out of the heaven, if the promise had not been made to Adam; through faith in the which promise he ever hoped victory against the devil\* who had deceived him; and that by power and strength of the promised Seed, and not through any power or might of himself. Even so should we do, confiding in the promises of God, and the merits of the promised Seed, Christ Jesu, to be delivered from the tyranny of the devil, the calamities and troubles of this miserable world.

## CHAPTER VI.

*Wherefore we should rejoice in tribulation. Under what pretext the wicked pursues the just. Whereby riseth the dishonouring of God. The diversity of opinions touching the article of justification, and who are just before God. What is the substance of justification; and why the article thereof should be holden in memory.*

To the faithful, these bodily afflictions and troubles are marvellously necessary, for by them the faith is tried, and made more precious than gold, which is purified by the fire, 1 Pet. i. for by many troubles it is needful to us to enter in the realm of heaven, by firm and constant persevering in faith, as saith St. Peter. Acts xiv. And also, it behoved Christ to suffer, and so to enter into his glory; that is, not for himself but for us, Luke xxiv. Therefore the godly men, in their

---

\* This victory shall we obtain in the general resurrection, 'or th' both body and soul shall be glorified.—Ed. 1584.

troubles and afflictions, take great consolation and comfort, and anchor them upon God alone by faith; to whom they can come no other way, and think them no better nor greater than their master, Christ, but should take both comfort and consolation of his word, saying, Seeing the world hath persecuted me, they shall persecute you also, John xv. This persecution is a communion with the passions (sufferings) of Christ, in the which we have great matter to rejoice, so we suffer not as homicides, thieves, or evil doers, but for Christ's sake and his word, as St. Peter saith in the first epistle, fourth chapter.

But in this matter take no care what the world judge of thee, but to thy own conscience and the scriptures of God. For the judgment of the world pronounces contrary to the word of God; calling them which profess the same, heretics, seditious men, and perturbers of commonweals. Therefore they think they punish justly, in burning, slaying, banishing, and confiscating of lands and goods. And, howbeit the faithful suffer all patiently and undeserved, yet they say they suffer justly as traitors, heretics, homicides, perturbers of commonweals and evil doers. Let these sayings not move thee, faithful brother, but comfort thee with thy master Christ, who was called by the adversaries of verity, a seducer of the people, a drunkard, a devourer or glutton, an open sinner, conversant amongst them, and an authorizer of their sins, John vii. Matt. xxvii. Mark ii. Luke v. His apostles were called heretics, and their doctrine heresy. The prophets were called perturbers of commonweals, and traitors to their country; prophesying against the commonweal and liberty of the realm, as ye may read of Elijah, 1 Kings xviii. and Jeremiah in divers places of his prophecy, Jer. xx. xxi. xxv.—xxvii; which scriptures I pray you read, and ye shall perceive no difference between the blasphemations of the prophets, of Christ himself, and his apostles, and the faithful in these days; for all was and is done by the wicked under colour of holiness.

Therefore, let us seek refuge at our God, and stick fast to his word, who can neither deceive, nor be deceived. For the world is full of deceit, and judgeth ever the wrong part; of the which unjust judgment cometh all the diversity of opinions, and sects ruling this day in the church of Christ, to the dishonouring of the name of God, diminishing of his glory, and no little perturbation of commonweals. The cause hereof is the neglecting of faith, and taking from the same her due office, which is, to justify only by herself, without the deeds or works of the law. That is, man, of wicked is made just by the mercy of God, through faith in the blood of Jesu Christ, without the deeds or works of the law. This I dare affirm, because the scriptures of God testify the same to be true, as hereafter shall be declared at length.

Here rises the contention; for some brag and boast them to have faith, and have no works; and others rejoicing them to have faith, attribute and give the justification to works. Others have works, and look nothing to faith, as hypocrites: and others again there are, who have neither faith nor works, as the plain wicked and ungodly. My well beloved brethren, let us authorize neither of these persons; for all they impugn this article of justification. Against the first speaks St. James in his epistle. Against the next St. Paul speaks in his epistles to the Romans, Galatians, and divers other places. And against the other two kinds of men, the whole scripture speaks.

By these considerations moved, I thought necessary for my own erudition and your comfort, my well beloved brethren, to declare and show forth my belief concerning THE ARTICLE OF JUSTIFICATION, as the scriptures teach me, having no respect to man's opinion, that thereby we may have consolation through our mutual faith, Rom. i. and be more ready to give account and reckoning to all who ask of us any question of our faith, 1 Peter iii. Always in this and all other things submitting myself to the scriptures of God, and the authority of the faithful church of Christ, which is governed, ruled, kept and defended from all spot of heresy by the Holy Spirit; who moves this ardent thirst in our soul to seek Christ, the fountain of living water, John iv. love and charity in our hearts to Christ, our brethren's salvation as our own. The foundation and groundstone hereto is faith, and the shield or buckler to defend us with, against the fiery darts of Satan, at the which he ever shoots, because it is our victory against him, and gets dominion of the world, 1 John v. Eph. vi. But if he find us destitute or disarmed of our shield, he shall wound us so, that he may safely or lightly take us captive to his realm. Therefore, this our faith should never be idle, but ever working by love; that is, to be ever clad with our shield, being vigilant and watchful, because our said adversary Satan is ever going about us, as it were a roaring lion.

seeking for the prey to devour or swallow; against whom we should resist stoutly in faith, 1 Pet. v. taking in our hand tne sword of the Spirit, which is the word of God, with the rest of the armour pertaining to a christian knight, specified by St. Paul, Eph. vi.

The substance of the article of justification, is to cleave and stick fast by our God, knowing him our Maker and Creator, and to believe firmly and undoubtedly that we are not righteous, nor just, of ourselves, nor yet by our works, which are less than we; but by the help of another, the only begotten Son of God, Christ Jesu, who hath delivered and redeemed us from death, the devil, and sin; and hath given to us eternal life, as hereafter at length shall be declared. Above all things, the said article is to be holden in memory, recent among the faithful; and at every time and hour driven and inculcated in their ears as it were by a trumpet. Without the which faith, which is the foundation of the christian religion and church of Christ, is made so dark and misty, that no place shall be found, whereupon to build the perfect works of faith.

## CHAPTER VII.

*What Adam and Eve, seeking wisdom against God's commandment, obtained, and what they obtain which seek justification other ways than the scriptures teach. Whereby the wicked man is made just. Where Satan may enter, and where not. What the law wrought in Adam, and the office thereof unto us.*

THE ground-stone and sure firm rock, whereupon all godly works and virtues are builded, our adversary Satan vexed in the paradise; when in the beginning, he persuaded and enticed our forefather Adam, and Eve, to leave their faith in God, their Maker and Creator, and consent to his false persuasion, which was, that through their own wisdom, strength and power, they might be made equal and like unto God, who gave them life, and promised the same ever to endure with all pleasures and commodities in paradise. The devil, perceiving the woman void and without faith,*

* That is, Satan after he perceived the woman doubt of the faith and verity of God's word, durst affirm the contrary, saying, Though ye eat of the tree ye shall not die; whereto the woman giving credit, transgressed God's command. And so to doubt of God's promise, is root of all wickedness, Gen. iii.—Ed. 1584

love, and fear of God, said, Howbeit ye eat of the fruits oi this tree, ye shall not die the death. Ye know not wherefore God hath forbidden you to eat of the same, but I shall show you the cause. God knoweth that in whatsoever day ye shall eat of the fruit of this tree, your eyes shall be opened, and ye shall be like gods, knowing good and evil. The same persuasion have all the wicked, who persuade man to trust to his own works, merits, power, and strength, thereby to be made just, and to get great reward of God, for doing of works not commanded by God, but invented by man's vain conceit, thinking that God shall be pleased therewith. But surely, even as our forefather was deceived, so shall we be, if we consent thereto. Therefore, give trust to nothing in this case or matter, but to God and his word; keeping ever faith pure and clean, without any mixture of works, in the making of a wicked man just, and then our adversary shall get no place to enter to deceive us.

Ye shall understand that Adam knew good and evil, before the eating of the apple, (fruit,) for that was taught him by the law of nature, and the other great wisdom he was clothed with, as ye may read in the book of Ecclesiasticus xvii. saying, God created them with the spirit of knowledge and with wisdom, and understanding, he fulfilled the hearts of them, and showed unto them good and evil. His judgments and justice also he showed to them. What then was the knowledge Adam got of the eating of the apple? Only that he had offended his good God, transgressed his law, which showed to him his offences and sin. By this knowledge he understood that he was fallen from the good state in which he was created, and should have remained, if he had obeyed the law of his God, into the miserable state of sin, for he had never known what the transgression of the law had been, if he had not sinned. The law before taught him what he should do and leave undone, what was good and what was evil; and after he sinned, the law uttered the same to him, and brought him to knowledge thereof; for it can do no other thing to the sinner but trouble his mind, and bring upon him great fear and dread. This is proved by the sayings of God to Adam, inquiring, Who hath shown unto thee that thou wast naked? Hast thou eaten of the tree of the which I commanded thou shouldest not eat?

This hatred and enmity is old, which Satan hath moved against mankind, and it had beginning at the first creation of man, of malice conceived, to bring man into the same rebellion he was in. This persecution of Satan shall endure to the latter judgment; therefore let us be watchful and diligent, ever armed with our shield, faith, the word of God ever printed in our hearts, taking no care of worldly troubles, hoping speedily to be delivered therefrom, 1 Chron. xxix. considering we have no permanent city here, but are as pilgrims, travelling to and fro, beholding and looking for that heavenly city and place, prepared for us from the beginning of the world, 1 Pet. ii. Heb. xiii.

## CHAPTER VIII.

*Wherefore Cain slew Abel. How long God suffered the article of justification to be pursued by the seed of Cain. What pain he took at last, and how Satan reserved his seed. Whereof sprang the idolatry, which abounded between the days of Noah and Abraham; and under what pretext it was defended.*

SHORTLY hereafter, the said adversary, a mankiller and liar, 1 John iii. persuaded and enticed the one brother to slay the other, of malice, without any cause but that the one brother, Abel, being just and godly, offered in faith a more pleasant and acceptable sacrifice unto God, than the other, Cain,* who was wicked and a hypocrite, whose sacrifice pleased not God, because the person was not acceptable to him. Therefore God looked to Abel and to his works; unto Cain and his works he looked not.

There followed against the said article the perpetual persecution of Satan, intolerable by the sons of Cain, while God was compelled, provoked of his righteous judgment, to drown the whole world, and once to purge the same from sin; reserving and defending, through his mercy only, the preacher of faith and righteousness, Noah. Nevertheless, Satan kept his seed in the third son of Noah, Ham, as the history testifies. After this, the whole world, rising in madness and fury, impugning this article of justification, finding and inventing innumerable idols and religions, with which they pretended to please God; with their own

---

* Cain gloried he was the first begotten, and thought therefore he was acceptable. But Abel knew himself a sinner, seeking for God's favour by that promised Seed alone, Gen. iv.—Ed. 1584.

works and inventions, every one making to himself a particular or peculiar god or gods. The which is no other thing but to think, that without the help of Christ, of their own power, works, and inventions, they may redeem themselves from sin and all evils, and please God with their free will and natural reason.

From Noah unto Abraham, our adversary, Satan, so covered this article, that no outward testimony is found thereof in scripture. And, trust well, the fathers, all this while, had many pleasant works, invented of their own conceit, good intention, and natural reason, having some footsteps of the examples of the holy fathers, by which they believed to please God; but it was not so indeed, because they followed the examples of the fathers in the outward works and ceremonies, but not in faith, and so all became idolaters, Gen. iv. vi. And the same ceremonies and most shining works appear to be most excellent in the offspring and posterity of Ham ; because his grandson Nimrod began first to be mighty in the earth, and usurped to himself the kingdom of Babylon. It is not to be presumed that the preaching of Noah, and the word of God taught to him and his sons by the mouth of God, and his manner of sacrifice was passed from their memory; but man is lightly drawn from faith and the word, to his own conceit, and vain intention, to the exercising of the outward deed, in the which man will never be seen to do evil, so there appear any manner of outward holiness in his works; the which he defends to be holy and good, because the holy fathers did so; and have no respect to faith, which maketh the work acceptable and pleasant in the sight of God, without the which all is but idolatry, how holy that ever the work appear. And so enters Satan, and rules mightily, as he did amongst the fathers to the time of Abraham.

## CHAPTER IX.

*God renewed to Abraham the promise made to Adam of the blessed Seed, whereto Abraham believing is pronounced just. Though the just be ever persecuted, at last they prevail. Wherefore we are brethren to Jesus Christ. The wrong judgment of the fleshly man touching the chosen of God.*

GOD, of his infinite mercy and goodness, moved of love, which he bears to mankind, seeing our adversary ruling so mightily, would raise up this article of justification in Abraham, that his church should not perish, commanding him in these words, Pass forth of thy father's house, and from thy friends, and forth of thy own country, and come into the land which I shall show thee. That is as much to say, As thy father, his household, and the whole country in the which thou now makest dwelling, thy whole nation and kindred are all idolaters; therefore of my mercy and grace, without thy merits or deservings, I will call thee to the faith, and raise up in thee the ground-stone of my church, and make thee the father of all faithful. This exposition ye shall find in the book of Joshua xxiv. for the scripture is the best interpreter of itself. And God so stirred up this article in the person of Abraham in these words, saying, I shall make thee a great nation, and I shall bless thee. and shall magnify thy name, and thou shalt be blessed; I shall bless them that bless thee, and curse them that curse thee; and in thee shall all nations of the earth be blessed, Gen. xii. This is the renewing of the promise made to Adam in paradise, that the Seed of the woman should tread down the serpent's head. Here shall ye find the beginning of the faith of Abraham; who passed forward as God commanded him, to whom he gave credence, and surely believed in his promise; and left all worldly affections, committing him wholly into the hands of God, depending only upon his word, believing the same to be true, hoping to obtain all things which were promised him by the word of God, of the which he had deserved nothing; for the scriptures testify him to be no other but an idolater, as his father was. After this God drove and inculcated this article of justification into the ears of Abraham, saying, Dread not, Abraham, I am thy defender, and reward above measure, &c. Thou shalt have him to be thy heir that shall pass forth of thy bosom. Thy seed shall be as the stars of the heaven. Abraham believed God, and it was reputed to him for righteousness, &c. Gen. xv. Here ye see the proceeding of this article, from faith to faith, ever continuing in more perfection day by day.

Then began Satan, our adversary, newly to impugn this article, ever to annul the promise of God, and as he persuaded Cain to pursue Abel, even so persuaded he Ishmael to pursue Isaac; Esau, Jacob: and the rest of the brethren, young Joseph, whom they sold, as testifies the history. Thus still continued the old hatred and enmity between the seed of the serpent and the seed of the woman. That is, the wicked ever pursue the chosen and godly, which are the woman's seed that treadeth down the serpent's head. For even as Christ, the blessed Seed, hath obtained victory of our adversary; so shall we by faith in him, of whose flesh and bones we are, and he of ours; that is, we are members of his body, and brethren to him, by two reasons; the one is that he is made man and of our flesh, the natural begotten son of the glorious virgin Mary, and so of Adam, is said to be our brother. The other reason is, that by him, and through him, by faith in the mercy of God, we are the adopted sons of God, and so his brethren, and fellow-heirs of the heritage with him, John vii. Matt. xxvii. Mark ii. Luke iii.

The fleshly man and worldly judgment is deceived in the knowledge of this seed as our mother Eve was. For she said, after she had conceived and borne Cain, I have gotten or possessed a man by God, that is, according to the promise made by God; I have gotten the Seed that shall tread down the serpent's head. Here she looked not into faith, but took the fleshly reason of the first begotten Son. But when she saw he slew his brother, then she understood him to be the seed of the serpent. Therefore, when she bare Seth, she held her peace, because she knew herself deceived before in the opinion of Cain. And then she cleaved to faith as Adam did, saying, God hath given to me another seed, for Abel whom Cain hath slain.

Abraham believed of his fleshly judgment, that Ishmael was the promised seed; as appears by the answer he made to God, when he said to him, Sarai shall bear unto thee a son, whom I am to bless, &c. Abraham smiled in his heart, and said, Would to God Ishmael might live before thee.[*] But hereafter, admonished by the mouth of God to obey Sarai, and expel Hagar and her son, for he should have no part of heritage with Isaac, he understood spiritually, and obeyed the voice of his wife.

The seed of the serpent contended with the seed promised in the bosom of that noble and godly woman Rebecca, Gen. xxv. This contention moved the mother to say, Better I had remained still barren, than to have this displeasure. To whom God gave consolation, saying, There is in thy bosom two sundry nations, and two people shall be divided of thee That is, thou knowest not which of them is the

[*] As he would say, Sufficient have I received of thy mercy, in that thou hast given to me a son of whom I am content.—Ed. 1584.

seed of the promise; the youngest have I chosen, to whom the eldest shall serve. This is conformable to the saying of St. Paul, Rom. ix. But, trust well, she understood spiritually by faith that Jacob was the promised seed, when she procured and laboured so diligently that he should get the blessing of his father, and defrauded the eldest, Esau. This was not known to Isaac, for he would not only that Esau should succeed to the heritage, but to have gotten the blessing also, which Jacob obtained by persuasion of his mother. Nevertheless, Esau remained with the heritage in his father's house, and ceased not to pursue Jacob, who at last was compelled to fly for fear of his life. And so ever the seed of the serpent pursues the chosen, conformably to this beginning. Let Abel die and Cain live. But finally the seed of Jacob succeeded to the land of promise, and enjoyed the heritage; howbeit they were long troubled and afflicted in Egypt.

## CHAPTER X.

*The wrong opinion of the Jews of the promised Seed. Wherein the ungodly place justification. Satan moves his members against the true professors of faith. Jeremiah, the prophet of God, resisted the whole ecclesiastical power of the Jews. The head of the serpent trodden down by the death of Jesus Christ. The article of justification preached after the death of Christ.*

YE shall understand that the Jews had a fleshly opinion of this promised Seed: for they understood that the Messiah which was promised to them, should rule temporally as David did; and establish his realm with great quietness and rest with all pleasure and voluptuousness, as ye may learn by the desire of the mother of the sons of Zebedee. Her sons, being with Christ and his apostles, were of the same opinion, as the answer of Christ testified, saying to them, Ye know not what ye ask. But the spiritual knowledge which the fathers had, was far different therefrom; who understood in the spirit that the realm of Christ was spiritual and not temporal, to the which they were led by faith.

By this ye shall understand, not only that the fleshly judgment is deceived in knowledge of this Seed, but also of the persecution of Satan; ever persuading the wicked and ungodly, which are his seed, to persecute the woman's seed of the promise—that is, the chosen, who, according to the promise of God, obtain victory by faith in the blood of Christ. For Satan, intending to destroy this article of justification, may not suffer the preaching thereof; that is, that by grace, through faith, and not of our own righteousness and works, we are made safe, please God, are received into favour with him, and accepted as righteous and just, not of our merits or deservings; but through the merits of Christ Jesus our Saviour. By the contrary, the wicked trust in their own strength and merits, and will have their good works, invented by themselves, without the commandment of God, to be a part of their salvation; and those who will not authorize the same they persecute with deadly hatred, and must needs die as Abel did. So, Let Abel die and Cain live;—that is our law, say the ungodly.

In the church of the Jews, our said adversary ceased not to impugn this article, and persuade the wicked to persecute the godly, and kill the prophets for preaching the same; for the defence of which Jeremiah the prophet resisted the whole ecclesiastical power and authority of the church of the Jews—that is, the multitude of the wicked, there being but a few number of the chosen that assisted him, as ye may read, Jer. xxvi. Not the less afterward, he was stoned to death for the same cause, which is the reward of man, that is, which man giveth for the true preaching of this article. So, Let Abel die and Cain live.

Finally, the persecution of Satan, our adversary, persuaded the death of Christ, his apostles, and martyrs, and their true successors, all for this article. But Christ ever got victory, and triumphed by his word only; insomuch as he got victory of the devil, hell, and death, of the law, sin, the world, and the flesh, through his death and resurrection. So, by faith in his blood, all the prophets, apostles, martyrs, and confessors, with their blood have watered the church, and have left a sure testimony to us, for confirmation of this article, that in the blood of Christ, and not in their own blood, works, or deeds, they are made safe, and have gotten the realm of heaven, conquered and purchased to them by Christ, and not by themselves, nor their merits. The which confession is the cause that the godly are ever persecuted by the wicked. So, Let Abel die and Cain live;—that is our law.

## CHAPTER XI.

*How Satan hath deceived the world after Christ, and wherewith he hath clad himself. An evident argument, showing those which this day are called bishops, to be the church malignant. An exhortation to them which enter in the church by the pope's authority; and of his power to make bishops. Wherein the wicked Jews gloried, and wherein the pope and his kingdom.*

Now our adversary, perceiving by the death of Christ, that the promise made in paradise was fulfilled, and his head trodden down, that is, his power and strength by the shedding of the blood of Christ, this article of justification laid so abroad, and the church of Christ so strongly edged with the same, that all his imaginations, with which he deceived mankind, had no place to pervert the perfect faith. Then he invented a new manner of habit, which he found in the same church amongst the slothful ministers, whom, by process of time, seeing them idle, and not occupied in the reading, teaching, and preaching of the scriptures, he provoked to invent works of their own conceit. And also to abuse the holy sacraments, and good works of God, with vain superstitions, which they call good works. And by this means he hath so drawn them from faith, that they know not what the same is; nor what Christ is, but as it were, a thief hanged upon a gallows or gibbet innocently; or like another manner of profane history of Hector, or of the great Alexander; and therefore he hath provoked them to pursue this article more cruelly than ever it was pursued from the beginning of the world. Themselves by word confessing the same with their mouth, reading, singing, and, of their manner, daily teaching and preaching the same; and yet, nevertheless, daily burning, killing, and banishing the true faithful preachers of the said article and confessors thereof. And so ever shall Abel die and Cain live;—that is our law, say they.

Our said adversary, that he should not be perceived, hath transformed himself into an angel of light. That is, in form of holiness, he hath entered into the church in wonderful subtlety; for he hath clad himself with the most honest and shining works, invented this day by men's wit or reason;

yea, with the same works commanded by God, and by them he maintains and defends himself wholly; yea, verily, he had clad himself with the blessed sacrament of the body and blood of Christ; for he can well disguise himself in works, with pride, vain glory, hypocrisy, diffidence, despair, idle faith, as to believe the history only, presumption of their own merits, &c. But in perfect faith, which is the ground-stone of this article of justification, he can never enter. Therefore, under colour of holiness he has caused, and daily causes the prelates of the church as they call them, who should of their vocation have, to the shedding of their blood, defended this article, to pursue the same most cruelly with all torments invented by man's ingenuity under the false pretence of good works, having no respect to faith. And so shall Abel die and Cain live.

Ye shall understand, that the oft repeating of the death of Abel, and the life of Cain, is no vain story or purpose, but the true similitude of the church of Christ, which, first watered with the blood of Abel, remains an example to this hour, and shall to the second coming of Christ to the latter judgment. In the which two persons is set forth to us the perfect knowledge of the church, which consists in the godly and ungodly.* And ever the perfect and just church is pursued by the wicked, and never pursueth, by which the disciples and servants of Christ are known, as testify the holy scriptures.

I exhort you which are adversaries to this article of justification, consider with yourselves if ever ye read the history in canonical scriptures or profane histories, that ever the true and perfect church, from the beginning of the world unto this hour, persecuted any, but ever was persecuted, and the godly glad thereof. Therefore, the form and order of this tyrannical persecution used this day by those who have the ecclesiastical power in their hands, against the faithful professors of this article, I judge to be of the devil, and may say truly to them, as Christ said to the scribes and pharisees, All the blood which is shed, from the blood of Zacharias, whom they slew between the altar and the temple, shall come upon these cruel tyrants, which impugn this article, and slay the faithful professors thereof. Against these sayings, the adversaries of faith and

* Which shall be separate when the Lord God sends forth his angels in his harvest.—Ed. 1584.

verity cry, The canon law, the authority of the church, the long consuetude, the examples of the fathers, the bishop of Rome's authority, the general councils; heresy, heresy! So there is no remedy, but, Let Abel die and Cain live;—that is our law.

My hearts! ye which have entered in the church of Christ, by the bishop of Rome's law and authority, with his fair bulls, your shaven crowns, smearing you with oil or cream, and clothing you with all ceremonies commanded in your law; if ye think yourselves therethrough the successors of the apostles, ye are greatly deceived, for that is but a politic succession or ceremonial. The succession of the church is far otherwise, the which requires you to have knowledge in the scriptures of God, to preach and teach the same, with the other qualities and conditions contained in the scriptures, as hereafter shall be shown in the special vocations, 1 Tim. iii. Of the which, if ye are expert, and your vocation lawful, according to the word of God, doubtless ye are the successors of the apostles, and have the same authority they had committed to them by Christ. And, if ye want the said conditions and qualities, ye are but ravening wolves, clad with sheep skins, what authority soever the bishop of Rome give you. For it is no more in his power to make a bishop of him which cannot preach, nor hath the knowledge to rule the flock committed to his care, according to the word of God, than it is in his power to make an ass to speak, or to be a man, or yet to cause a blind man to see. Therefore, I pray you, learn the scriptures, that ye may walk in your vocation aright. For of your succession ye have no more matter to glory, than the Jews had to glory against Christ, calling themselves the sons of Abraham, whom he called the sons of the devil, John viii. They gloried in the carnal succession, and ye glory in the politic or ceremonial succession; and all is one thing. God send you knowledge and understanding of his word, that ye may cease from your tyranny, and the true faithful may live in rest and quietness.

## CHAPTER XII

*The division of justice\* in general, with the definition of every part thereof. The cause that no man is just by the law. Scriptures and examples proving all men, except Jesus Christ, to be sinners.*

LET us pass forward in the discussion of this article of JUSTIFICATION; for knowledge of which it is necessary to show what justice of man is, and what of the law, either of God or man; which being shortly discussed, we shall the more easily come to the knowledge of our christian justification; which is a thing far above all law, either of God or man; for it is the justice by which a wicked man is made just, through faith in the blood of Jesus Christ, without the works of the law; because of the deeds of the law no flesh shall be made just before God, as the apostle saith, Rom. iii. Gal. iii. This is as much to say as, because no man fulfilleth the law, nor doth the deeds and works of the same in the pure and clean estate, as the law required them to be done, according to the purity of the same, therefore the law can pronounce none just before God.

This word, justice or righteousness, generally by the philosophers is taken commonly for obedience and outward honesty, according to all virtues of moral manners, the which a man may do and perform of his own power and strength. This is called a universal or general justice after the philosophical definition. St. Paul called the same the righteousness of the law or works, because the transgressors of this justice are punished as wicked and unrighteous. For whom the law is made and ordinate, as St. Paul saith, 1 Tim. i. for the just needeth no law. These moral manners and discipline is the most excellent raiment or habit wherewith man may be clad. Nevertheless, they cannot make a man just before God, nor are they the justice which we speak of here in this treatise.

The politic or civil justice is, the obedience which every subject or inferior estate of man gives to their prince and superior, in all the world. The which proceedeth of the law of nature, and is a good work: without which obedience to the punishment of the wicked and defence of the just, no

\* Righteousness.

commonweal might be conserved and kept in rule and order; but all would run to confusion. Therefore princes and higher powers are commanded of God to be obeyed, as his good work, Rom. xiii. for they are the ministers of God unto good. Nevertheless, ye shall never find man so just in fulfilling this justice, but the law of nature shall accuse him that he hath not done his whole duty, which the same requireth. Neither the prince to the subject, nor the subject to the prince, nor equal to equal, that is, neighbour to neighbour. The knowledge of this law of nature is born with man, printed in his heart with the finger of God. And therefore, let every man consider his own estate, and he shall perceive, that if God will accuse him with this law, he shall not be found just, because of the deeds of the law no flesh shall be found just before God. Notwithstanding, he which doeth the deeds of this law, and is obedient thereto in doing and leaving undone, according to the external works, is so reckoned just before man, and liveth in the same; and therefore hath the name of justice.

The ceremonial justice is, the obedience and fulfilling of the statutes, ordinances, and traditions of man, made by the bishop of Rome and other bishops, councils, schoolmasters, and householders, for good rule, and order, and manners to be kept in the church, schools, and families. This is a good work, and necessary to be had with these conditions; that is, that they be made not repugnant to the law of God; and that through keeping of them, no man think himself the holier before God; nor yet therefore to obtain remission of sins, or to be found righteous before God: nor yet that the same may bind or oblige any man to the observing of them, under the pain of deadly sin. Nevertheless, how well that ever ye observe or keep them, that is, this law ceremonial, ye shall not be found just therethrough before God, because of the deeds of the law no flesh shall be found just before him.

The justice of the law moral, or Moses's law, which is the law of God, exceedeth and is far above the other two kinds of justice. It is the perfect obedience required of man, according to all the works and deeds of the same. Not only in external and outward deeds, but also with the inward affections and motions of the heart, conformable to the commandment of the same, saying, Thou shalt love thy Lord God with all thy heart, with all thy mind, with all thy power and strength: and thy neighbour as thyself, Deut. x. Matt. xxii. Mark xii. This is no other thing than the law of nature, printed in the heart of man in the beginning; now made plain, by the mouth of God, to man, to utter his sin, and to make his corrupted nature more plain to himself. And so the law of nature and the law of Moses are joined together in a knot, which is a doctrine teaching all men a perfect rule, to know what he should do, and what he should leave undone, both to God and his neighbour.

The justice of the law is, to fulfil the law, that is, to do the perfect works of the law as they are required from the bottom of the heart; and as they are declared and expounded by Christ, Matt. v.—vii. And whosoever transgresseth the same shall never be pronounced just of the law. But there never was man that fulfilled this law to the uttermost perfection thereof, except only Jesus Christ. Therefore, in the law can we not find our justice, because, of the deeds of the law no flesh shall be made just before God.

For the probation hereof, we will show the authorities of scripture from the beginning; how the most holy fathers were transgressors of the law, and therefore could never be made righteous by the same. And if they which were most holy could not be found just by the deeds of the law, much less may the wicked be pronounced just by the same? Therefore, we must take this conclusion, with the apostle St. Paul, All have sinned, and have need or are destitute of the glory of God;* and are made just, freely by grace, through faith in the blood of Jesus Christ.

Adam, first, in paradise transgressed the law, and therefore the same accused him, and condemned him, and all his posterity, as rebels and transgressors of the same, to the death. Nevertheless, the law remaineth still holy, just, and good; requiring the same holiness, justice, and goodness of us, as St. Paul testified, Rom. vii. And because we do not the same, the law ever accuseth us, and pronounceth us rebels and transgressors, as our forefather Adam was; who might never be pronounced just by the

* That is, By original sin all man is become blind, and is fallen from that image of God, (which was, integrity of nature, justice, and righteousness,) in which man was first created, and now is clad with the contrary, Rom. iii. Gen. iii.—Ed 1584.

law, because, of the deeds of the law no flesh shall be made just before God.

And seeing all men have descended from Adam, they are corrupted and rebels to the law as Adam was. For he might get no better sons than his nature was. This corruption is so infixed in the nature of man, that he is never clean purged thereof, so long as this mortal body of sin and the spirit remain together. And this is the cause why we fulfil not the law, in the pure and clean form as the same requireth the deeds thereof to be done. For this cause St. Paul saith, Rom. vii. Now I work not this evil, but the sin which dwelleth in me; for I know there dwelleth in me, that is, in my flesh, no good: for the good which I would, that do I not, but the evil which I would not, that do I. As St. Paul would say, so rebellious is my wicked nature to the affections of my spirit, that the very things which I know to be good, and would do, for weakness I may not complete. I would love, fear, honour, and thank God with all my heart and all my strength, and adhere to his promise in every hour and all tribulation; but by the wicked flesh I am impeded to do the same. For howbeit I have fear and love begun in me, yet natural security and concupiscence are impediments that they are not pure and perfect as the law requireth. And albeit I have faith begun in me, which teacheth that God is true in all his promises, yet natural dubitation and imbecility cause me frequently to doubt if God shall deliver.* And so the flesh sometimes murmurs, and loves not God with all the heart. Here, my hearts, ye may learn of the apostle to know this corruption of nature: for he gives the example in himself and in no other, teaching every one of us to judge ourself and not our neighbour.

This corruption of nature is called original sin, which is the wanting of original justice, that should have been in man according to his first creation. This corruption of nature followed the fall of Adam, in all men, that the nature of man may not truly obey the law of God, nor fulfil the same, for the inherent faults and concupiscences in the heart of man, engendered of this corrupted nature, and so cannot be pronounced just by the law, because, of

---

* Let every man judge if in time of tribulation he find not this battle within himself.—Ed. 1584.

the deeds of the law no flesh shall be made just before God.

From Adam to Noah, from Noah to Abraham, and from Abraham to Moses, during which space and time we can find none of the holy fathers, who lived under the law of nature, pronounced just by the deeds of the law; but all were sinners and transgressors of the law, as Adam was, as the whole history of Genesis testifies. Therefore, the justice of a christian man shall we not find in the law, because, of the deeds of the law no flesh shall be found just before God.

Moses, who was mediator between God and his people of Israel, in giving the law of the two tables, which is but a declaration of the law of nature rightly understood, fulfilled not the law, as ye may read in the book of Numbers, ch. xx. where Moses and Aaron are both reprehended of God for their diffidence and incredulity, the which is the breaking of the first commandment of God; and a great and mighty sin, howbeit the reason of man cannot consider it; yea, verily, greater and weightier before God than either slaughter or adultery. In the sight of man the crime appears but small; for God gave commandment to speak to the stone or rock in presence of the people, and charged the same to give water; but they spake to the people with a doubt, saying, May not God give you water out of this rock? and then struck upon the stone twice, which gave water abundantly. But God would not pretermit the punishment of their unfaithfulness, saying, they should never enter in the land promised to the people of Israel. And Moses also testified no man to be innocent before God, but by favour and imputation of grace through faith, Exod. xxxiv. And howbeit Moses repented sorely the said offence, and prayed fervently that he might enter into the land of promise, he was not heard; for God would not alter his sentence, as ye may collect of the saying of Moses, Deut. iii. where God saith to him, Speak no more to me of that matter; thou shalt not pass over the water of Jordan. Here we may see that man can find no justice in the law which is of value before God.

Job, who was commended by the mouth of God, the most just in the earth, could find no justice in the law. For howbeit he was innocent in the sight of man, he might not enter into judgment with God; because the justice of man is nothing before God, as ye may read in his book,

Job vi. xv. and he alleges the stars of heaven not to be pure in the sight of God, much less are men to stand in judgment with his law, to be pronounced just. Therefore the holy man Job concluded his book with confession and repentance, granting himself to be a foolish sinner, Job xlii. And so by faith in the promised Seed he was received in the favour of God, and accepted as righteous, the which is the justice that is of value before God.

David, a figure of Christ, of whom God speaketh, saying, I have found a man according to my heart's desire, 1 Sam. xiii. xvi. saith, Enter not into judgment with thy servant, O Lord; for in thy sight no man living shall be made just or righteous, Psal. cxliii. that is as much to say, after the mind of the prophet, If ye will be justified by the law, ye must enter into judgment with God. Who is he that liveth so godly and holy in the earth, who may or can defend his cause, being called to the justice seat of God to give account and reckoning of all things which he ought to God, and by his law justly he may require? There is not one, as the prophet saith. Therefore, O Lord, if thou shalt call us to judgment, and ask questions of our life and manners according to the rigour of thy law, there shall be to us no hope of salvation. St. Augustine, expounding the said verse, saith, "There is no man living upon earth excepted in this cause, no, not the apostles;" and he concludeth with these words, "Let the apostles say and pray, O Father of heaven, forgive us our debts, as we forgive our debtors. And if any would say unto them, Why say ye so? what is your debt? They would answer, saying, Because no living creature shall be found just in thy sight." And in another place, expounding the said words, Enter not in judgment with thy servant, O Lord, that is, stand not in judgment with me, asking from me all things which thou hast commanded, and given me charge to do and to leave undone; for thou shalt find me guilty if thou enter in judgment with me. Therefore, saith he, "I have need of thy mercy, rather than to enter with thee in judgment."

And St. Bernard, in the sermon which he made for the day of All Saints, speaks after this manner, "But what may all our justice be before God? Shall it not be reputed or esteemed like unto a filthy cloth, according to the saying of the prophet? And if it be sharply accused, all our justice shall be found unrighteousness. What then shall be our sins, when our justice may not answer for itself? Therefore, let us cry with the prophet, Enter not in judgment with thy servant, O Lord; and with all humility run to the mercy of God, which only may save our souls." Here ye may clearly understand by the holy fathers' saying, that they understood the scriptures, and article of justification, as we do, finding no righteousness in the law, but only through faith in the mercy of God.

The said prophet saith, If thou, O Lord, shalt keep our iniquities, and lay up our sins in store, O Lord, who shall sustain or abide? Psal. cxxx. St. Augustine, expounding these words, saith, "The prophet said not, I shall not sustain; but, Who may sustain or abide thy judgment, if thou wilt accuse? He saw the whole life of man circumvolved with sins, all consciences to be accused with their own thoughts; and no clean, pure, or chaste heart to be found, presuming in his own righteousness. Therefore, if a clean or chaste heart cannot be found, presuming in his own justice, let all men, with the heart, in faith, unfeignedly presume in the mercy of God, and say unto him, If thou, O Lord, shalt keep or lay up in store our iniquities, O Lord, who shall or may abide it?" Where then is the hope of our salvation? With thee, O Lord; for the help and satisfaction or sacrifice for our sins is with thee; as it followeth in the next verse of the same psalm. What is this sacrifice, but the innocent blood of Christ shed, which hath blotted out and put away our sins, the only price given to redeem all prisoners and captives forth of the enemy's hands.[*] Therefore, help and satisfaction is with thee, O Lord; for if it were not with thee, but that thou wouldest be a just judge, and not merciful, and wouldest observe and keep all our iniquities, and seek them of us, who might abide it? Who should stand in thy judgment, and say, I am innocent? Therefore our only hope is, that help, mercy, and favour is with thee!

O ye which are adversaries to faith, print these words in your hearts which ye read with your mouths but take no care of them; and then ye shall not impugn this article of JUSTIFICATION, but say with us the words of the prophet, Enter not into judgment with thy servant, O Lord, for in thy sight no living creature shall be found just.

[*] Sacrifice for our sins, Isa. liii. Heb. ix. Gal. iii. iv. Eph i Titus ii. Rev. v.—Ed. 1584.

## CHAPTER XIII.

*The justice of a christian. The questions of the wicked against the manifest will of God, taught in the scriptures. Tokens declaring the serpent's seed.*

Now, since our forefathers, who lived most just, could not be made just in the deeds of the law, or in no law could find this justice by which a wicked man is made just; of necessity we are compelled to seek the justice of a christian man without all law, or works of the law; and of another than ourselves, who is just and innocent, that no law may or can accuse; and through his justice we must be made just, for of ourselves we are not just, nor any man, as the prophet saith, Psal. xiv. And the apostle, Rom. iii. All men have left God, and altogether have become unprofitable, none of them is found good, except one, which is the man Christ Jesus, the only begotten Son of God; by whom, and by his merits, through faith in his blood, we are all received into the favour, grace, and mercy of God the Father; accepted as righteous and just, without all our merits or deservings, to everlasting life. This is the justice of a christian, which shall be declared at length, by God's grace, hereafter.

Here the adversaries will move three questions to see if they may impugn the truth; the first is, Wherefore gave God the law to men, or what availed the giving of the same, if man of his own power and strength may not fulfil the same? The second question is, If man may not be made just through the deeds and works of the law, wherefore should man do any good works? The third is, How were the fathers made just, and by what means? As to the first question, concerning the giving of the law, the cause wherefore it was given, and why we fulfil not the same, I will answer unto it presently. And the other two questions shall be discussed with the article of Justification; that is, with the discussing of the justice pertaining to a christian man; and in the setting forth of good works, which follow faith as the true fruits thereof.

But first, ye shall note and keep well in memory, that the wicked ever object questions and causes unto God, on this manner; when any thing occurs which transcends their fleshly knowledge and reason, then say they, Wherefore did God this or that thing? The which sayings declare them to be the serpent's seed, of whom they learned that lesson. For it was his first proposition, made unto our mother Eve in paradise, saying, Wherefore hath God commanded you that ye should not eat of all the trees in the paradise? Thus he persuaded the woman to give him answer of the cause not pertaining her to know, and so brought her to confusion. Even so do the ungodly and sons of the devil, inquiring at God the causes of his secret judgments; as, Wherefore hath God chosen one and rejected another? with other such unprofitable questions of the predestination and forescience of God. But in all such matters which are above our capacity and reason, let us say with the apostle, Oh highness! Oh deepness! Oh profoundness! of the riches, of the knowledge, and of the wisdom of God! How incomprehensible are the judgments of him, and unsearchable are the ways of him! For who hath known the mind of the Lord, or who hath been his counsellor? or who hath first given to him, that he should give again to them? For of him, and by him, and in him are all things; to whom be honour, praise, and glory, for ever, Rom. xi.

Therefore, my well beloved brethren, inquire ye nothing of the works of God, and of his secret judgments, but as his word teaches you; and seek no cause of his works more than of his divinity, but be content to know those things which are in your capacity, and under judgment of the reason of man. For, as Job saith in his book, If God hastily inquire of us, who shall answer him, or who may say unto him, wherefore doest thou so? He is God, whose ire no man may resist, Job ix. Read the whole tenth chapter for confirmation of this matter. And I exhort you, by the mercy of God, to read the scriptures, not as though they were a profane history of Hector, Alexander, or other gentile histories, nor yet as the manly* science of Plato, Aristotle, the bishop of Rome's law, or others, which are but the science of men, and may be judged by the reason of man; but with an humble heart, submit you to God and his Holy Spirit, who is Schoolmaster of his scriptures, and will teach you all verity necessary to your salvation, according to the promise of Jesus Christ, John xiv. xvi. For the understanding of the scriptures is not of man's wisdom

* Human.

or knowledge, but the godly men, moved by the Holy Spirit, have spoken and shown forth the perfect knowledge of the scripture, as St. Peter saith, in his second epistle, chap. i. Therefore think the scriptures not difficult, but to the fleshly man which shall get no understanding thereof. They deceive you who say, The scriptures are difficult, and that no man can understand them but great clerks. Verily, those whom they call their clerks know not what the scriptures mean. Fear not and dread not to read the scriptures, as ye are taught here before. Seek nothing in them but your own salvation, and that which is necessary for you to know. And so the Holy Spirit, your teacher, shall not suffer you to err, nor to go beside the right way, but shall lead you in all verity. And so will we pass forward to the question before rehearsed, Wherefore God gave the law? as we are taught by his scriptures.

## CHAPTER XIV.

*An introduction to answer the first question of the wicked. To what creatures God gave law, and why he gave the law to man. Of Adam's gifts before his fall no man hath experience. The law given to Moses, and why man may not fulfil the law.*

There can nothing be perfectly understood without the ground and foundation be sought and known. So, for the true knowledge of this question, ye must begin at God, and know him as he hath commanded in his scriptures, and seek him no other ways; and by him ye shall get knowledge of yourself. God, being without beginning, as he is without ending, in the beginning made all creatures perfect, right, and good; and, last of all, man, to his own image and similitude, male and female he made them; whom he endued and clad with most excellent gifts of nature and godly virtues, with original justice, full integrity, the law of nature imprinted in his heart, with power to do the same of his own free will; and put him in the paradise of pleasure, that he should labour, and keep the same, with commandment to eat of the fruit of all the trees of paradise, and forbade him to eat of the fruit of the tree of knowledge of good and evil, standing in the midst of the paradise, joining the pain if he transgressed this commandment, saying, Whatsoever day thou eatest of the same thou shalt die the death.

Not only gave God a law to man, but also to beast, sun, moon, elements, and all his creatures in their kinds, the which they should not transgress nor overpass. That in his creatures he might be glorified and have obedience of them, to that effect he made them, and gave them the law. This exposition ye shall find in Psalm cxlviii. where the prophet exhorts all creatures, animate and inanimate, to preach and forthshow the glory of God, because he said the word and they were made, and he gave commandment and they were created. So the law was given to man, to the effect that he should know his Maker, glorify him, and obey him; for obedience is the fulfilling of the law. To obey God, is to love God, with all thy heart, with all thy mind power, and strength; and thy neighbour as thyself. This law was printed pure and clean in the heart of Adam, who had free will and power of himself to do the same. For God made man in the beginning, and left him in the power of his own counsel; he gave to him his precepts and commandments, saying, If thou wilt keep the commandments, they will keep thee, &c. He put before him fire and water, that he might put his hand to which of them he liked. He laid before him life and death, good and evil, saying, Whatever shall please him shall be given to him, &c.

The perfection of Adam, and knowledge of the law, the righteousness and integrity of him in his creation, with the excellent gifts and godly virtues he was endued with, are unspeakable, as saith the book of Ecclesiasticus, "God created man of the earth, and made him after his own image and similitude, turned and converted him again in the same. And clad him with virtues according to himself," &c. Read the whole seventeenth chapter, which will instruct you of these noble virtues and qualities of Adam. What might he want, being participant in virtues to the godly nature? Nothing at all. And so all the works of God were made perfect; the which he never altered nor changed. No more did he his law; but, after the fall of man, by his prophets and holy preachers he set forth and uttered his law in the same form and pure state as it was created; that man, thereby, might the more perfectly know his weakness and imperfection. Therefore the apostle saith, By the law is the knowledge of sin. The law is not sin but sin is not known but by the law. That is the cause why the law works anger and hatred, Rom. iii. iv. vii.

The law of Moses of the two tables, was but an uttering and declaration of the law of nature. And that the sayings of Christ prove; for when he had made a long sermon teaching his disciples and the people the perfection of the law of Moses, as ye may read, the fifth, sixth, and seventh chapters of St. Matthew, he concludes on this manner, All things whatsoever ye will men do to you, do ye the same to them: for this is the law and prophets. Here you see the law and all the preaching of the prophets joined in a knot to the law of nature, which teacheth us what we should do, and what we should leave undone. This law was perfectly printed in the heart of Adam, who wanted no perfection to fulfil, observe, and keep the same, to the uttermost perfection thereof.

For transgression of the commandment of God, our forefather Adam was exiled and banished forth of paradise, and spoiled of the integrity, perfection, and all the excellent qualities, dignities, and godly virtues with which he was endued by his creation, made rebel and disobedient to God in his own default; and therefore he might not fulfil the law to the perfection, as the same required. For the law, remaining in its own perfection just, holy, and good, requireth and asketh the same of man to be indeed fulfilled. But all men, proceeding from Adam, have the same imperfection that he had: which corruption of nature resists the will and goodness of the law, which is the cause that we fulfil not the same, nor may we of our power and strength, through the infirmity and weakness of our flesh, which is enemy to the spirit, as the apostle saith, Rom. vii. viii.

Oh miserable man! accuse not God but thyself, because thou fulfillest not the law. For howbeit thou in thy default fall from thy goodness and perfection of nature, by the which of thy own free will and power thou mightest have fulfilled the law, into evilness and imperfection, and hath corrupted thy nature—nevertheless, God remained just, good, true, and unchangeable, and his law also, which requireth of thee duty, not according to the fragility of thy nature, but to the purity of its nature, according to the good will of God. Therefore impute no fault to God, nor yet to his law, that thou fulfillest not the same; but to thyself, and thy corrupted nature, which obeyed the will of the devil, and resisted the good will of God.

## CHAPTER XV.

*What remained in man after his fall, and what man may do thereby. The opinion of the philosophers touching the wickedness of man. The office of the law, and what shall man, accused thereby, do. The conclusion of Paul, and evasion of sophisters therefrom; with arguments convincing them as liars.*

NOTWITHSTANDING, after the fall of man, there remained with our first parent some rest and footsteps of this law, knowledge, and virtues* in which he was created, and of him descended in us; by the which, of our free will and power, we may do the outward deeds of the law, as is before written. This knowledge deceived and beguiled the philosophers; for they looked but to the reason and judgment of man, and could not perceive the inward corruption of nature; but ever supposed man to be clean and pure of nature, and might of his own free will and natural reason, fulfil all perfection. And when they perceived the wickedness of man from his birth, they judged that to be by reason of the planet under which he was born, or through evil nourishing, upbringing, or other accidents; and they could never consider the corrupted nature of man, which is the cause of all our wickedness. And therefore they erred and were deceived in their opinions and judgments. But the perfect christian man should look first in his corruption of nature, and consider what the law requireth of him; in the which he findeth his imperfection and sins accused; for that is the office of the law, to utter sin to man, and it giveth him no remedy; then of necessity he must either despair, or seek Christ, by whom he shall get the justice that is of value before God; which cannot be gotten by any law or works, because, by the deeds of the law no flesh shall be justified before God.

Ye shall not marvel of the oft rehearsing of these words, that OF THE DEEDS OF THE LAW NO FLESH SHALL BE MADE JUST, that is, declared, reputed, found, or pronounced just before God; for they are rehearsed before the forth setting of THE ARTICLE OF JUSTIFICATION, that it may seem the more clear; and to that effect the same words were spoken by the apostle, Rom. iii. of this manner, We know

* Powers.

whatever the law speaketh, to them it speaketh which are in the law, that all mouths may be stopped, and all the world made subject unto God, because by the deeds of the law no flesh shall be made just before him. And therefore I have repeated them so oft, because they lead all men to the perfect knowledge of their justification which is in Christ.

This proposition of the Holy Spirit is so perfect, that it excludes, (if ye will understand the same aright,) all the vain, foolish arguments of sophistry, made by the justifiers of themselves, which pervert the words of St. Paul, as they do the other scriptures of God, to their perversed sense and mind, saying, that the apostle excludes by these words the works of the ceremonial law, and not the deeds of the law of nature, and moral law of Moses. The which shameless sayings are expressly done away by the words of the apostle; insomuch that no man of righteous judgment can deny, but he shall feel the same, as it were in their hands; by this probation, the law speaketh to all, that is, accuses all men that are under the law. All men are under the law of nature or the law of Moses. Therefore the apostle speaks of the law of nature and Moses, and of all men, whom he comprehends under Jew and Gentile, as he proves by his arguments in the first and second chapters to the Romans; and concludes in the third chapter, All men are sinners. If all men are sinners, none is just: if none be just, none fulfil the law: if none fulfil the law, the law can pronounce none just. Therefore he concludes, that of the deeds of the law, no flesh shall be found just before God. The same is proved by David in Psalm xiv.

Here you see by the words of the apostle, he intends to prove and declare all men sinners. That is, to stop all men's mouths, and to drive them to Christ, by the accusation of the law. No law may make or declare all men sinners, and subdue the whole world to God, but the law of nature and Moses. Therefore under that word LAW, the apostle comprehended the law moral, and not the law ceremonial only; because it follows in the text, The knowledge of sin is by the law: and also, I knew not sin, saith St. Paul, but by the law; nor had I known that lust or concupiscence had been sin, had not the law said, Thou shalt not lust. Therefore ye cannot help but confess that the apostle speaks of the moral law; yea, and of all laws, and of all men, because he excepts none, Rom. iii. Therefore let us conclude with the apostle and the Holy Spirit, that the justice of God is without the law, made plain and forthshown by the law and prophets. And then shall we come to our justice, which is CHRIST, as St. Paul saith, 1 Cor. i.

If ye will say of your vain conceit, as ye which are adversaries to faith ever object vanities, that the apostle in his conclusion comprehends not all men proceeding from Adam, but that some just men are excepted; ye shall not find that exception in scripture of any man except Christ, who, being both God and man, is expressly excepted, because he never contracted sin; fraud or deceit was never found in his mouth, Isa. liii. 1 Pet. ii. 1 John iii. By this exception, all others are excluded, because there is no other who can be found just but he. For that cause he only fulfilled the law, and satisfied the same. By whom all which believe are accepted as just, without the deeds of the law, through faith in the blood of Jesus Christ. Let us pass forward, therefore, in the scriptures for to find the justice of a christian man which cannot be found in the law, nor the deeds thereof.

## CHAPTER XVI.

*The diversity of names of that justice which is acceptable before God. Justice is plainly revealed in the gospel. What it is to live in faith, or by faith.*

THE justice whereof we have made mention in the beginning, and that is so cruelly and tyrannously persecuted by our adversary Satan, is called the justice of God; the justice of faith; and the justice of a christian man: the which is all one thing, glued and joined together, that by the same we are in CHRIST, and he in us, by the mercy of God, purchased by Christ, through faith in his blood, without all our deservings either preceding or following the same. And it is as far different from the other justice of the law, as darkness from light, and heaven from earth; because it will be alone, and not participant with any other thing, that Christ may have his due honour, who obtained this justice from the Father, and is the price thereof.

And first, it is called the justice of God because it proceedeth only of the mercy of God. Secondly, the justice of faith, because faith is the instrument, whereby in Christ we obtain the mercy of God, freely given to us for Christ's sake.

And thirdly, it is called ours, because by faith in Christ, without all our deservings, we receive the same, and are made, reputed, and counted just, and accepted into the favour of God. And all three are one justice, divided by sundry names, as is before said, which is this ARTICLE OF JUSTIFICATION. As, by example, almsdeed is but one name, and yet after the common manner of speaking it is appropriated truly to three; that is, to the giver, to God, and to the receiver. In alms, the poor and indigent have no part but only to receive and give thanks. The giver freely giveth of his liberality and substance; and for God's sake. So it is properly called the alms of the giver, and justly attributed unto God, because for his sake it is given; and also to the receiver, because he is made rich therewith. In the like manner, this justice of God proceedeth of his abundant mercy and grace, favour and goodness, which he beareth toward mankind, that is poor, yea, beyond all poverty, laden with sin, having need of the grace and mercy of God, destitute of all comfort and consolation; and therefore is called his justice, by reason of the giving. And it is called the justice of faith, or the justice of Christ, because faith is the instrument, and Christ the purchaser of the same. And it is called ours, by reason of participation of all Christ's merits, which we have through faith in his blood, without our merits or deservings.

Therefore, even as the sick man receiveth his health, the poor his alms, and the dry earth the rain, without all their merits or deservings; so receivest thou of God this justice, which is of value before him, by such instruments as God provideth mediately thereto, He being the immediate cause. The physician giveth thee his counsel in thy sickness, exercises his labours upon thee, by the creatures of God, according to his vocation; thou doest nothing but suffer to work in thee till thou be healed. And then, at commandment of the good physician, thou keepest good diet, not to get thy health, but that thou fall not again in sickness. The poor man, receiving his alms, hath no part thereunto, only but to receive; the man that giveth being the instrument, whom God hath made the steward of that his gift. The earth receiveth the rain, and hath no part thereinto, but only to receive; the labourer or ploughman being the instrument to open the pores of the earth, that the rain may descend into it, and then it bringeth forth fruit in due time. Even so it is with man.

It is called the justice of God, and not of man or of free will, but of God. Not that justice by which God is just, but the justice with which man is clad, and, by the mercy of God, of wicked made just; as St. Augustine saith in his book of the spirit and the letter, (ch. xx.) in obtaining of which, we neither work nor give any thing to God, but receive, and suffer God to work in us. Therefore, it is far above all justice of the law which man doeth and worketh, the which are also the works of God, both because they are of the law, and man may do them of his own free will and power; as to the external work. And also they are the gift of God; but always they may have no place in this article of justification before God, except ye will exclude the merits of Christ, which God forbid!

This justice was covered in the Old Testament under ceremonies and sacrifices, but is made known and plain unto us now by the gospel of Jesus Christ, from faith to faith, Rom. i.—that is, not from one faith to another faith, but from that faith by which we receive the gospel of God, through hearing of his word, and with gladness accept the same, in continual perseverance growing daily in more perfect knowledge of God, through faith in Christ, till we give up the spirit into the hands of the Father of heaven; never doubting for whatsoever temptation or trouble in adversity; but receiving all things from God, and of his hands, as our forefather Abraham did, and judging all for the best. Then follows the formal conclusion, THE JUST SHALL LIVE IN FAITH, that is, ever continue in sure trust, hoping to obtain the thing he looketh for, which is remission of sins, the gift of the Holy Spirit, and everlasting life, all purchased by Christ, without our merits or deservings.

This is the faith of which the prophet Habakkuk speaketh: The just shall live by his faith. The just man and faithful hath never respect to any thing, but only to faith in Christ; and whatever he work or do, he referreth all to Christ, and so remaineth he in Christ and Christ in him, conformable to the saying of St. Paul, I live now, no, not I, but Christ liveth in me; forsomuch as I live in the flesh, I live in the faith of the Son of God, who hath loved me, and given himself for me, Gal. ii. Here ye may see to live in the faith is to believe in Christ, joined unto him continually by faith; then live we in Christ and Christ in us, from faith to faith, having no respect to works or merits, but only to the merits of Christ. And so the just liveth by his faith.

## CHAPTER XVII.

*The definition of faith. What faith the fathers had before Christ's incarnation, and whereby they were safe. Good works are a testimony to faith. Wherefore works please God. The method of St. Paul in writing and teaching, and the necessity of good works. Wherefore justice is ascribed unto man. Who spoileth God of his glory.*

THE apostle defines and declares what faith is, saying, Faith is the substance of things hoped or looked for; the argument or matter of things not seen, without which it is impossible to please God, Heb. xi. That is, faith is the true and perfect thought of the heart, truly thinking and believing God, the which a man doth when he believeth his word, and putteth his sure trust in the mercy of God; which is to believe that his sins are forgiven him for Christ's sake only, the wrath of the Father pacified, and he received in favour and accepted as just; and firmly and undoubtedly believeth the Father of heaven to be ever merciful, gentle, helpful, and favourable unto him, for Christ's sake, without all deservings of his deeds or merits, either preceding faith, or following the same. This is the justice of God, which is made plain and revealed by the Son of God, Christ Jesus, in his gospel, as is said before.

In this faith only in Christ were all the fathers, to the coming of Christ in the flesh, made just without the deeds of the law, Jer. xxiii. and xxxiii. Isa. iv. and xlv. Ezek. xxxiv. And, therefore, all the promises of the coming of Christ are to be referred to that promise made in Gen. iii. that the seed of the woman shall tread down the serpent's head, &c. And so the faith of the fathers in the Old Testament, and our faith in the New Testament, was and is one thing; howbeit, they had other external rites, objects, ceremonies, and signs than we have. And they believed in the coming of Christ, to fulfil all promises and prophecies spoken of him. And we believe he is come already, and hath fulfilled all which was spoken of him in the law and prophets; and hath ascended to the heavens, and sitteth at the right hand of the Father, our advocate. And as the fathers believed the first coming of Christ, ever desiring and looking for the same by faith; even so now we believe and look for his second coming, and most fervently desire the same, to be delivered of this mortal body of sin, that we may rule eternally with him in glory. That the fathers were safe by faith, without the deeds of the law, St. Peter testifies, saying, Wherefore now tempt ye God to put a yoke upon the necks of the disciples, the which neither we nor our fathers might bear; but by the mercy of Jesus Christ, we believe to be made safe, as they were. And St. Augustine, in the 157th epistle, saith, "Therefore, if the fathers, being unable to bear the yoke of the old law, believed them to be made safe by the mercy of our Lord Jesus Christ; it is manifest that the same mercy or grace made the old fathers to live just by faith." Now ye may see clearly that the old fathers were all made safe through the mercy of God, without all the deeds of the law. Then, how will you make yourself safe with works, who never did such good works as the fathers? So there can be no better conclusion to exclude your works in the article of justification than St. Paul maketh, saying, that a man is made just by faith without the deeds of the law. Therefore faith only justifieth before God. Ye shall understand that it is all one thing to say, faith only justifieth, and to say, faith without works justifieth. As by example, if one say, The good man is in the house alone, or he is in the house without any body with him. This is all one manner of speaking. The scripture saith, Man is made just by faith, without the works of the law; therefore we may well say, that faith only justifieth.

For confirmation hereof ye shall read Hebrews xi. before rehearsed, in the which ye shall find the histories briefly repeated by the apostle, testifying the fathers to be made safe by faith, referring nothing to works; except only that the works bear an outward testimony of the faith. Abel, by faith, or in faith, offered to God a more acceptable sacrifice than Cain did, by the which he obtained witness that he was just; God bearing witness of the offerings; and by the same he hitherto speaketh, being dead. God looketh first to the heart of man, before he looketh to his works; as testifieth the voice of God, saying, I judge not after the sight of man; for he seeth the thing which appeareth outwardly, but I behold the heart, 1 Sam. xvi. That is, the man is first made just by faith, and accepted in the favour of God, as Abel was; and then his works are acceptable and please God, because they are wrought in faith. That it is the mind of the apostle St. Paul to exclude all works either going before or following faith, to be of the substance of the article of justification, the arguments and matter of his epistles prove clearly; especially to the Romans, Galatians, and Hebrews: in which he labours so diligently, that all the sophisters and workers, that are justifiers of themselves, may not get a corner to hide them into, from his conclusions, without they deny Christ and his office, at the least in effect, as they do after their manner. But the wisdom of God and his Holy Spirit deceiveth them;* for when they wrest and throw the scriptures to their mind in one place, they are compelled in another place of the same scripture to confess themselves liars. In the epistle to the Romans, from the beginning to the twelfth chapter, and in the epistle to the Galatians, to the fifth chapter, with all labour and diligence the apostle setteth forth the justice of God to be through faith in Jesus Christ, without all works of the law. And when he hath established the same article of justification, then he setteth forth the works of righteousness, in the which a christian man shall live, because the just shall live in faith. This order ye may see in the said epistles; and in the epistle to the Hebrews he declareth the office of Christ, his priesthood and sacrifice, and giveth faith her place, Heb. xi. All his labour was to exclude the mixture which these feigned workers now would have joined in with faith, and the benefit of Christ; which is no other thing than the work of the devil our adversary to make the death of Christ in vain; as the apostle saith, Therefore if justice be of the law, or by the law, Christ's death is in vain, Gal. ii.

But think not that I intend through these assertions to exclude GOOD WORKS. No, God forbid! for good works are the gift of God, and his good creatures; and ought and should be done of a christian, as shall be shown hereafter at length in their place. But in this article of justification, ye must either exclude all works, or else exclude Christ from you, and make yourselves just, which is impossible to do, because we are wicked and can do no good at all which can be of value before God, or pacify his wrath; except Christ first make our peace, for that is his office, for which he came in the world, and suffered death.† So, if ye will not

---

* Cannot be overcome of them.

† The office of Jesus Christ is to pacify the wrath of God, which our orks may not do.—Ed. 1584.

exclude Christ, exclude your works : for in this case there is no concurrence, more than there is between darkness and light. For what participation hath righteousness with iniquity? or what fellowship hath light with darkness? 2 Cor. vi. The definition of this justice is made plain by St. Paul, Rom. iii. which I exhort you to read. Consider word by word, conceive and print them well in your hearts; then shall ye be able to contend and fight valiantly against Satan and his sophists, of whom ye shall have victory by faith, which is our victory that overcometh the world, 1 John v.

The justice of God is, by the faith of Jesus Christ, in all and upon all which believe in him; there is no distinction or exception. All have sinned, and have need, or are destitute, of the glory of God; but they are made just by his mercy, freely without the works, by the redemption which is in Christ Jesus; whom God hath proponed or laid before a sacrifice or satisfaction by faith in his blood, to the forthshowing of his justice for the remission of the sins by-past; the which God hath suffered to the forthshowing of his righteousness at this time; that he may be just, and justify him which is of the faith of Jesus Christ. Where then is thy glory or vaunting? It is excluded. By what law? Of works? No, but by the law of faith. Therefore we believe surely, a man to be made just by faith, without the deeds of the law.

Now, I pray you tell me what plainer words may be spoken, or terms invented, to exclude ALL our works, merits, or power, to be participant with God in this article of justification? They are as plain and clear as the sun in mid-day. Nevertheless, because the words are so precious, and necessary above all things to be imprinted and continually kept in the heart of man, I will make some declaration of every part and particle of this definition; and prove by authority of scripture, this justice of God, by the which a man is made just, to be without all works or power of man, only by faith in the mercy of God.

Of this justice David speaketh, saying, Lead me in thy justice, O Lord, because of my enemies; direct my way in thy sight, Psal. v. That is, O Lord, my God, for thy great goodness, singular kindness, and natural love, thou wast ever wont to show unto sinners and mankind, be to me a governor, guider, and convoyer in all perils and dangers; never suffer my mind to decline from the right way, for any manner of strength or fear of mine enemies. And also, In thy justice, O Lord, deliver me, that is, for thy goodness and mercy, Psal. xxxi. And after, Judge thou me, O Lord, and discuss my cause; that is, take my defence upon thee, for I am not able of myself to resist. Therefore, in thy justice deliver me, and be unto me a strength invincible, Psal. xliii. lxxi. So shall ye find in divers and sundry psalms and other places of scripture; as Dan. ix. Justice and righteousness unto thee, O Lord, but unto us confusion, and shame of face. In the which chapter, ye may read, what justice or holiness, that holy prophet ascribeth unto him, or to the most holy of the people, amongst whom assuredly there were many good punished with the wicked, but none which might ascribe righteousness to themselves.

Sometimes ye shall find in scripture this word, justice, ascribed unto man; as David saith, Psal. iv. Hear me, who called on thee, O Lord, of my justice, &c. That is, God, the author, giver, and keeper of my innocency, hath looked upon me. And, Judge me, Lord, after my justice, and according to my innocency, which is in me, Psal. vii. Here he forthshoweth, not his virtues or his righteousness which are in him, with these words; because he saith in another place, Enter not in judgment with thy servant, O Lord, for in thy sight no living thing shall be found just, Psal. cxliii. And the Holy Ghost is never contrary to himself. But here he called the justice of God his, by imputation. And also, he was innocent of the thing that was laid to his charge by king Saul, who ever accused him of treason, and usurping of the crown of Israel. In Psalm xvii. he saith, Hear my justice, O Lord, and give attendance to my desire and prayers. Here he calleth his justice, his petition. And, in innumerable places of scripture, ye shall find this word, JUSTICE, sometime ascribed to God, and sometime to man; because of the receiving of the same from God. But ever the scripture makes itself plain by the sentence which goeth before, or else follows, or in some other place. Therefore, take good heed upon the reading of the scriptures, that ye deceive not yourselves, ascribing any deed or power of yours to the article of justification; for it may suffer none, but only Christ's merits, because the merits of man are impure and imperfect, and may not abide the justice of God, nor stand in his sight.

It follows in the definition of this justice, By the faith of

Jesus Christ, in all and upon all which believe in him. Here ye may see our faith, that we believe in Jesus Christ, called HIS faith, as it is indeed. And the faith also of God, and by the same reason as the justice is called before, because it is the gift of God, as St. Paul saith, Eph. ii. and is the instrument by the which we obtain the mercy of God, remission of our sins, the gift of the Holy Spirit, and everlasting life, all for Christ's sake, without our deservings; by the which we are joined in Christ, and Christ in us, as the precious stone is joined in the gold ring. So let all our delight and pleasure be to embrace Christ in our heart, by faith in his blood. For faith is the thing which Christ desireth of a sinner. Believe, Son, thy sins are forgiven thee, Matt. ix. And also, All which believe in me, saith Christ, shall not die eternally, John xi. And to the woman, in St. Luke vii. Thy faith hath made thee safe.

It follows in the definition, that there is no distinction or exception; All have sinned, and have need of the glory of God; that is, all want that justice which God approved or judged to be glory, 1 Kings viii. 2 Chron. vi. 1 John i. Eccles. vii. And so all men are sinners and rejected from God, and cannot be made just by the law, because the same accuseth of sin, and is like a mirror in thy hand to consider the form of thy face, which can do no other thing but show thee thy deformity. God hath concluded all under sin, that he may have mercy upon all. The scripture hath concluded all under sin, that the promise may be given, through the faith of Jesus Christ, to all which believe, Rom. iii. Gal. iii.

It followeth in the definition, that they are made just FREELY, by the grace of God, through the redemption which is in Jesus Christ. Here ye see the apostle purposes to exclude all your merits in deserving of this justice; to the effect that he may, as in all his epistles and labours he intended, set forth the glory of God, and the benefit of Christ; the which can no wise be more highly set forth, than in the making of a wicked man just, and freely, that is, for nothing and without deserving. For that cause, Christ is made to us from God, wisdom, justice, holiness, and redemption; that he which rejoiceth may rejoice in the Lord. And that means the apostle Paul, 1 Cor. i. and the prophet Jeremiah, Jer. ix. who will have all our virtues given unto God, as wisdom, strength, and riches, which are in our power to use and exercise, as the gifts of God;

much more justice, which is not in our power. For we are made, and make not ourselves, the which we do if we deserve it, either for works preceding or following the justification, to have any part of the substance thereof. And so would ye draw the glory of God to you in one part, the which God will not suffer, as the prophet Isaiah saith, My glory will I give to no other, Isa. xlii. Either must ye make yourselves just, or else be made just by God. If ye make yourselves just, ye are not allowed of God; so the glory redounds to yourself of your own work. This the Holy Spirit will never approve and consent unto, as ye read, 2 Cor. x. Col. iii. Phil. iii. Gal. vi.

That we are made just freely by the mercy of God, St. Paul declares for confirmation of this his assertion; By grace, saith he, ye are made safe, through faith; and that not of yourselves, it is the gift of God. Not of works, that none have matter to glory or rejoice, Eph. ii. This same he affirms in his epistle to Titus, ch. iii. and Rom. xi. where he saith, If it be of grace, then it is not of works; otherwise grace were no grace.* Here ye may see, this justice is of mercy, freely, without all our merits or deservings.

Ye are made just by the redemption which is in Christ Jesus, and not in yourselves. For Christ hath redeemed us from the curse of the law, and is made for us accursed. That is, he suffered the pain which the curse of the law enjoined to us by sin. In whom we have redemption by his blood, remission of our sins, according to the riches of his mercy and grace, Gal. iii. Eph. ii. What words may be more plain to prove this justice only by faith in Christ, excluding our merits. Ye have the same assertion in the epistle to Titus, the second chapter, Gal. iv. and Rev. v. where it is written, Thou art worthy, O Lord, to take the book, and to open the seals of it; for thou art slain, and hast redeemed us to God in thy blood. He saith not, in our works, but in thy blood. Here ye may see and consider our sins were no light things; considering there was no other thing which might pacify the wrath of the Father, but the blood and death of his only begotten Son Christ Jesus, to be made man for that cause. And now for vain invented imaginations of ignorant sophisters, who will not only be their own redeemers, but also redeem others, this precious blood is reputed in vain, or a light thing!

* That is, Remission of sins were not freely given.—Ed. 1584

It follows, Whom God hath laid before as a sacrifice or satisfaction, through faith in his blood, to the forthshowing of his justice, for remission of the sins by-past, which God hath suffered, or in the suffering of God, to the forthshowing of his justice at this time; that he may be just, and justify him which is of the faith of Jesus Christ. Here the apostle abounds in words to exclude all sophistry and vain conceit of works, which men intend, and would intend to make satisfaction for sin. For he setteth forth Christ here, the full sacrifice and satisfaction for sin; and therefore he calleth him the Mediator of the new testament, by intercession of his death, Heb. ix. And also, Christ offered a sacrifice for sins, and for ever sitteth at the right hand of God, beholding till his enemies be made his footstool, Heb. x. And St. John saith, If any shall sin, we have an Advocate before the Father, Jesus Christ, who is just, and he is satisfaction for our sins; not only for ours, but for the whole world's, and that through faith in his blood, 1 John ii. For there is nothing may bring us thereto, but faith only. And no satisfaction may be but Christ's death, who hath once died therefore, and shall not die again; death shall have no more dominion of him. Rom. vi. In the which he hath declared him just, in fulfilling the promise made of him in the law and prophets; that is, that He was to make us just, who could not make ourselves just.

And where he saith, For remission of sins by-past, the which God hath suffered, &c. understand not that of the sin by-past, before the coming of Christ only, but also of all sins committed to the world's end. For these words are spoken forth of the mouth of God, with whom all things are present, as ye may consider by the words of Christ, speaking to the Jews on this manner, Before Abraham was, I am, John viii. Howbeit Abraham was dead a thousand years before his incarnation. So to the penitent all sins are by-past; therefore the remission of sins by-past, in Christ's blood, endureth to the end of the world.

This is necessary to know for two causes principally. The one is, for confounding of the heresy of the Novatians,[*] who pervert the sayings of the apostle, whereupon they would infer that man, once being justified, and thereafter falling in sin, may have no place of repentance; which

[*] See the History of the Church of Christ, vol. i. Cent. 3. ch. xi. Cent. 4. ch. iii. xix.

were the perverting all the scriptures of God, and his promise in the blood of Christ, who is the Lamb of God, that taketh away the sins of the world, John i. and our Advocate, Sacrifice, and Satisfaction, 1 John ii. Howbeit the apostle speaketh plainly, that it is impossible to be renewed to repentance through renewing of baptism; for that were to crucify Christ again, not in his flesh, but in thy flesh, which would be new baptized. The other cause is, to exclude their opinion, which think that Christ satisfied but for original sin only, and that baptism giveth, or hath purchased grace to man, after the baptism, that he may satisfy for his own sins by recompensation, as though God were a merchant, to chop and change with man; and that if Christ was the first merchant, they shall be the next! And this is as great a heresy as the other, by which they would make the death of Christ but a vain trifle, and change faith into works of man's making, the which is the work of the devil, who ever intended to impugn this article of justification by the mixture of works. This opinion St. John confoundeth in his first epistle, ch. i. ii. where he declares, first, If a man say he hath no sin, he deceiveth himself; and then, if a man sin, as doubtless all men do, he saith, We have an Advocate, Christ Jesus, who is just, and is a satisfaction for our sins. Moreover, all men, how just that ever they be, need daily to pray, Forgive us our debts, as we do our debtors; which prayer were not necessary, nor had Christ ever taught the same, if we might have satisfied for our own sins at any time. So, Christ is ever our satisfaction, and we are daily sinners; and therefore we ought ever to pray, Forgive us our debts, as we forgive our debtors.

It follows in the definition, Where is thy glory? by what law is it excluded? Of works? No; but by the law of faith; and concludeth man to be made just without the deeds of the law. Ye shall understand that glory in this place, is taken for the sure trust and belief which men put in their own works and merits; the which the apostle will have cleanly excluded forth of this article, and given wholly to Christ, who deserveth the same, because he is obtainer thereof to us, through faith in his blood. The which faith will have nothing participant with it in this case, more than the sight of the eye will have or suffer the finger in it to help the sight. No, it cannot suffer a mote, but ever waters, being hurt till the mote be taken forth. Even so faith forthshoweth all things to the glory of God, and merits of Christ, without all works or merits of man.

If Abraham had been made just of works, then had he wherein to rejoice, but not before God, Rom. iv. And also he had not obtained that name to be called the father of the faithful, but the father of workers, Gen. xv. Therefore the scripture saith, Abraham believed God, and it was reckoned to him for righteousness, Rom. iv. Gal. iii. Heb. xi. In the which scriptures, ye shall not only find this justice which is of value before God, attributed and given wholly to faith in the mercy of God; but also the works expressly excluded. For either we must be made just by faith only, or by works only; because they may not be mixed, without Christ's death be in vain: for to him that worketh, saith Paul, the reward is not imputed according to grace or mercy, but according to debt. But to him which worketh not, that is, confideth not in his own merits, but believeth in Him which justifieth the wicked, his faith is counted to him for righteousness, according to the purpose of the mercy of God; and that without works. For the probation and sure understanding of this assertion, ye shall read the whole of Rom. iv. Gen. xv. Gal. ii. iii. iv. and Eph. ii. which words shall be shown in the subsequent chapter.

## CHAPTER XVIII.

*The cause wherefore God loveth us. Whereby cometh the heritage. The constancy of Abraham in faith, and his obedience. Jesus Christ payeth for us that which the law requireth. Who spoileth Christ of his office.*

By grace ye are made safe, by faith, and not of ourselves; it is the gift of God; not of works, that no man rejoice. We are his handiwork, created in Christ Jesus unto good works, the which God hath prepared that we should walk in them, Eph. ii. Verily, these words are worthy to be written in letters of gold, and ever imprinted in the heart of man, because they contain the whole sum of the gospel of Christ; and also exclude all the vain sophistical arguments made against this article of justification, because in this epistle there is no question of the law, as in the epistles to the Romans and Galatians, but it is written to the Gentiles, being confirmed in the faith, and also persevering thereunto; whom the apostle certifies of their justification in the first three chapters; and then sets forth to the end of the epistle, the works of righteousness, in which true christians should live, according to their vocation; upon which words, I will make some short declaration, according to the scriptures.

By grace ye are made safe—that is, by the grace and mercy of God, and abundant love he hath to mankind; because he hath made us, he would not that we should perish; for he loveth his own work. He saith, I will not the death of a sinner, but that he convert and live, Ezek. xviii. xxxiii. He made us, that he should love us; for no man hateth or envieth his own work. This grace we get by faith in Jesus Christ, the which is not our work, but the gift of God, Eph. ii. For we are not of ourselves able or sufficient, as of ourselves, to think a good thought, but all our ability is of God, as the apostle saith, 2 Cor. iii. and Gal. iii. If the heritage be of the law, then it is not of the promise; but by the promise God gave it to Abraham. Ishmael and Esau, who were the eldest sons, succeeded not to the heritage, but Isaac and Jacob, who were heirs of the promise, succeeded.

We are not made safe through works, that none should glory, because God will not have us rejoicing in ourselves in any part of his gifts, as the apostle saith; What hast thou that thou hast not received? And if thou hast received it, why rejoicest thou, more than if thou hadst not received it? 1 Cor. iv. Ye see works excluded forth of this article, that man hath no matter to glory, but to refer all the glory unto God, as is before rehearsed. And that man hath nothing to glory into, but in the cross of Jesus Christ, by whom we should crucify the world to us. That is, we should esteem all that is in the world wicked, as the apostle saith to the Galatians, ch. vi.

Ye shall not marvel that our salvation is ascribed and attributed to the mercy of God through faith, excluding all works, because the reason is here shown by the apostle, in these words; For we are the handiwork of God created in Jesus Christ unto good works. That is, forsomuch as we live, have life, and understanding, and belief, it is of God, and not of ourselves; because he is our Maker and Creator, Acts xvii. Psal. c. Isa. xlv. Jer. xviii. Rom. ix. Why should the earthen or clay pot extol itself against the potter, of whom it hath all which it hath? Or the branch against the tree, of which it hath all the substance to bring forth the fruit? as Christ giveth the parable in the gospel of St. John, ch. xv. the which ye shall read that ye may understand the words of Christ, and the similitude in which the Father is declared to be the husbandman, or the labourer; and Christ the wine tree, and us christians to be the branches or the bearers. For the branch hath two offices, the one is, if it remain with the tree, fresh and green, it bringeth forth good fruit of the substance of the tree, and not of itself; the other is, if it wither, and bring forth no fruit, it must be cut off and burnt. Therefore, if thou wilt be a christian, and remain in Christ, by faith ever joined to him, thou shalt bring forth good fruit of his substance, and not of thine; of which the glory pertaineth to him, and not to thee. And, if thou wilt be the withered branch, that is, wicked, and bring forth no fruit, thou art prepared for the fire, there to serve with the devil and his angels. And this is sure, if thou wilt either glory in thy works, or yet that thou art thy own saviour, or any part thereof, as concerning this article of justification. But to remain in Christ by faith, and to suffer him to work in thee, which thou doest when thou workest the works commanded in the scriptures of God, and attributest them to Christ, to be his works working in thee; then shall he make thy imperfection perfect, that neither the devil nor the law dare accuse them, because they are the works of Christ, and for his sake received of the Father by faith. So there is here nothing to thee to glory of, but to say with the apostle, He that will glory, let him glory in the Lord, &c. 1 Cor. i. 2 Cor. x. Jer. ix.

This glory of works is excluded by the law of faith; of which law the apostle maketh mention, Rom. viii. saying, The law of the Spirit of life in Christ Jesus, hath delivered me from the law of sin and death. That is, the mercy of God, the gift of the Holy Spirit, remission of sins, and everlasting life, purchased to us through faith in Christ; by which we live in righteousness, free from sin and death. And so it is called the law of faith, which excludeth all glory of works, because we receive, and give nothing but glory and honour unto God, which is the sacrifice of praise and thanksgiving. In this we should live in righteousness, and work the works of God; and not become thrall again to sin and death, from which we are freed freely, without our merits or deservings, through faith in the blood of Christ, our Saviour and Advocate.

Therefore let us conclude with the apostle, and establish for an infallible conclusion, man to be made just by faith, without the deeds of the law, as the scriptures before rehearsed prove, and by the example of Abraham, who had no mixture of works in his justification. The which we must affirm to be true, because the scriptures affirm the same, and testify him to be justified by imputation through faith, because he believed God, and gave sure trust to his promise, howbeit the same appeared not possible, as indeed it was not to the judgment of man, nevertheless he doubted not in his faith, but believed hope against hope;* and therefore it was counted to him for righteousness. Not only to him, but of the same manner to us who believe, and are sons to Abraham by faith. And trust well Abraham did many noble and heroical works of the law of nature; but none of these works were participant of his justification before God, but only bear witness to his faith, and obedience to God in his righteousness, as shall be shown hereafter.

The most excellent work amongst the Jews was circumcision, which was given to Abraham, and commanded to be used in all his posterity for the sign and token of the band and covenant between God and him; which was long after the justification of Abraham, as ye may read, Gen. xvii. And the apostle saith, Abraham received the sign of circumcision, the seal of the justice of faith, &c. Rom. iv. Therefore this work made him not just, nor yet had any part of his justification. Nevertheless, God rehearsed to him at that time the promise, saying, Abraham, walk before me, and be perfect; and I shall put my covenant between me and thee; and shall multiply thy seed exceedingly; and thou shalt be the father of many nations. And after this God tempted Abraham, Gen. xxi. that is, searched or espied out his faith; commanding him to take his son Isaac, whom he loved, and offer him in a sacrifice, &c. Consider this command, and ye shall perceive it a great temptation of the faith of Abraham. And confer the same with the scriptures going before, where God gave command to him that he should put away his son Ishmael; for the seed of the promise should be fulfilled in Isaac.

* That is, He believed the promise of God, albeit the same appeared impossible to nature or manly power, Gen. xv. Rom. iv.—Ed. 1584.

Nevertheless, the faith of Abraham was so firm and constant, that he rather hoped and surely believed, that God was to raise Isaac from death to life, than that his word should be false, or of none effect. And therefore God said unto him, and confirmed the same with an oath, saying, Because thou hast done this thing, and hast not spared thy only begotten son, I will bless thee, and multiply thy seed as the stars of the heaven, and sand of the sea shore, because thou hast obeyed my voice and charge. Here ye see and find the promise repeated again, which was made to him long before. But it is not said here, that because Abraham did this work, it was counted to him for righteousness; but that he was commended by the mouth of God for his obedience and perseverance in faith; for the faithful should live by faith, daily persevering and increasing, day by day, more and more perfect, which is from faith to faith; giving ever thanks and praise unto God, and obeying his command.

Ye shall take this conclusion, that no man can be called just, who liveth wickedly; but he who is godly and liveth well, is called just. Nevertheless, his good life or works have no participation of this article, because they are excluded by the apostle, in the words before rehearsed for a conclusion; that man is made just before God by faith, without the deeds of the law. Upon which words St. Augustine saith, "These words are not to be understood so, that a man receiving the faith, if he live afterward wickedly, shall be called just; but he is made just without all his works, that he may live in righteousness and work well."

Christ is the end of the law unto righteousness, to all that believe; that is, Christ is the consummation and fulfilling of the law, and that justice which the law requireth; and all they which believe in him are just by imputation through faith, and for his sake are reputed and accepted as just. This is the justice of faith, of which the apostle speaketh, Rom. x. Therefore, if ye will be just, seek CHRIST, and not the law, nor your invented works, which are less than the law. Let HIM be the mark whereat ye shoot, and let him never pass forth of your heart—whereto seek ye that thing which already hath taken an end? Is it not written in the gospel by St. Luke, ch. xvi. The law and the prophets are unto the time of John, from the which time the kingdom of God is preached and forthshown, &c. And St. John, ch. i. saith, The law is given by Moses; but grace and verity are given by Jesus Christ. These two words are expounded by St. Paul; Grace—that is, the mercy of God whereby we are made safe through faith in Christ, and not of works, Eph. ii. Verity—is the fulfilling of the promises of God, for the which Christ was made servant to circumcision, for the verity of God, to confirm the promises of the fathers. Here ye see Christ will have no mixture with the law, nor works thereof, in this article of justification, because the law is as contrary to the office of Christ as darkness to light, and is as far different as heaven and earth. For the office of the law is to accuse the wicked, to fear them, and to condemn them, as transgressors of the same. The office of Christ is to preach mercy, remission of sins, freely in his blood, through faith, give consolation, and to save sinners. For he came not into this world to call them which are just, or think themselves just, but to call sinners to repentance, Luke v. The office of Christ, John the Baptist declares, saying, Behold the Lamb of God! behold him, which taketh away the sins of the world! John i. It is not I, saith John, nor the law, repentance or works of repentance, which I preach, that taketh away your sins; but it is Christ, that innocent Lamb of God, to whom I send you. And also Christ saith, God sent not his Son into the world that he should accuse, condemn, or judge the world, but that the world should be made safe by him, John iii. And after, It is not I, saith Christ to the Jews, that judgeth you, it is Moses which accuseth you, John v. And so the scriptures testify that the law accuseth, and Christ saveth. He sendeth none to the law; but rather the law driveth and compelleth man to seek Christ, if ye will understand it aright. The woman accused of adultery, he sent her not to the law, but said to her, Pass thy way, and sin no more, John viii. And to the man which had been diseased thirty-eight years, &c. Behold thou art made whole, now sin no more, that some worse thing happen not to thee, John v. Christ called all to himself, saying, Come unto me, all ye which labour and are laden with sin, and I shall refresh you, Matt. xi. And Peter saith, There is no salvation but in Jesus Christ; nor any other name given under heaven by the which man may obtain salvation, Acts iv.

Therefore, since no other may save but He, we should put all our trust and hope in him, and in his mercy only, and neither in the law nor works. For to all them which think they may be safe by works, or made just, Christ's death is in vain. Or, if there had been given a law which might have given life, then righteousness surely had been of the law, Gal. iii. But it is manifest that by the law no man is made just before God, because the just shall live by faith. What words may be more plain than those are, to exclude works forth of this article? Now, since the scripture teacheth us so plainly that Christ is our Justice, our Saviour, our Redeemer, satisfaction for our sins, the end and consummation of the law; and hath freed us from the law, sin, and death, and from the kingdom of Satan our adversary, and bought us to the kingdom of righteousness, without our merits or deservings: why will we usurp his office to ourselves, and spoil Christ of his glory, or become thrall again to that thing from which Christ hath freed us? The which we do, if we will be participant with Christ in the making of ourselves just, or mix any works with the article of justification.

## CHAPTER XIX.

*As the good tree beareth good fruit, so the good man worketh good works. But as the fruit maketh not the tree good, so works make not the man just. For, as the tree is before the fruit, so the man is just before the work be good. The cause why we should work good works. The captains in the kingdom of Christ, his subjects, and reward: and of his adversary Satan.*

THIS faith, which only justifieth and giveth life, is not idle, nor remaineth alone; nevertheless, it alone justifieth; and then it works by charity. For unfeigned faith may no more abide idle from working in love, than the good tree may from bringing forth her fruit in due time, and yet the fruit is not the cause of the tree, nor maketh the tree good; but the tree is the cause of the fruit; and the good tree bringeth forth good fruit, by which it is known to be good. Even so it is of the faithful man. The works make him not faithful, nor just, nor yet are the cause thereof. But the faithful and just man bringeth forth and maketh good works, to the honour and glory of God, and profit of his neighbour, which bear witness of his inward faith, and testify him to be just before man. Therefore, ye must be just and good, or ever\* ye work good works, for Christ saith, Matt. vii. May ye gather grapes of thorns, or figs of thistles? No, no; it is contrary to their nature. Even so it is with man; till he be made just by faith, as it is before written, he may never do a good work, but whatever he doeth is sin; for all which is not of faith is sin; and Christ saith to the pharisees, How can ye speak good, while ye are yet evil? Rom. xiv. Matt. xii. Therefore, or ever we speak good or do good, we must be made good, and that by the mercy of God, through faith in Christ, without all our deservings. Then shall we work all good works in the kingdom of Christ as his faithful subjects.

There are two kingdoms, and two kinds of subjects, which are directly contrary each to the other, because their princes are as contrary as light and darkness; that is to say, the kingdom of Christ, and the kingdom of the devil, Eph. ii. 1 Peter iv. To the kingdom of the devil, man is of his own nature a perfect subject, and the son of ire and wrath. To the kingdom of Christ, man is made subject through his second birth or regeneration, which is by baptism in the blood of Christ. To this kingdom, man is bought, neither with gold nor silver, but with the precious blood of the Son of God, Christ Jesus, and so is made servant to righteousness to serve unto life. Therefore, who is made just by faith, through the mercy of God, and merits of Christ Jesus, must, in faith which is not idle, but ever working in love, serve Christ and embrace him in his heart. Then shall he remain in Christ and Christ in him, by the which joining, through faith, sin shall have no dominion, nor shall it rule as a prince; howbeit the dregs remain in us, they shall not be imputed to us, if we persevere in faith, as our forefather Abraham did, ever working by love and charity. And this is the cause why we should work good works, because we are bought to the kingdom of Christ, in the which rule, as valiant captains, faith, hope, and charity, working ever righteousness unto life.

The kingdom of the devil hath three valiant captains, which govern the same, that is, incredulity, despair, and envy, ever working sin and unrighteousness unto death, because the reward of sin is death. In this kingdom, sin ruleth as a prince having dominion; therefore, if ye will serve sin, and obey the same, ye are servants to that thing which ye obey, whether it be of sin unto death, or

\* Before.

righteousness unto life. But Christ hath redeemed us, and bought us from this realm; that even as Christ hath risen from death to the glory of the Father, right so we should live in a new life, and let not sin have more dominion over us. There is no man so foolish, who will think, he being delivered of a vile prison, by the grace and mercy of a great prince, and brought to serve in his hall, and so made tender to the prince that he is made participant of his son's heritage, will say, I will pass again to prison, because he is not a part of his own deliverance. Verily, it is even so of their sayings, which say, I will do no good, because Christ hath delivered me; and being delivered, I will sin and follow all liberty of flesh: wherefore should I do any good works, since Christ hath delivered me without my deservings?

My hearts, ye which object these sayings, read the scriptures, and ye shall find another lesson taught you. And attend upon your schoolmaster, which is the Holy Spirit, who shall teach you the right way, that ye pass neither to the right hand nor to the wrong, but the right kingly way; that is, to confess, and ever to have printed in your hearts, that by faith only, of the mercy and grace of God, ye are made safe. And then follow the example of our Lord Jesus Christ, giving your whole study and care to love, charity, and all manner of righteous living, to the glory of God, and the profit of your neighbour. Not that therethrough ye are made safe, but that ye may be found thankful unto God, whom ye know to be favourable, gentle, kind, and merciful to the godly; and to the wicked, wrathful and angry. This is the solution to the argument made in the beginning, which proveth wherefore we should do good, if we are free from the law, and freely justified by the mercy of God, through faith, without our deservings. Therefore, choose you now, if ye will be servants to sin, or servants to righteousness; subjects of the kingdom of Christ, or of the kingdom of the devil. For we are made free and just by grace through faith, that we should live in righteousness to Christ, who hath died for all; that they which live, live not now to themselves, but to him which hath suffered death for them, and hath risen again from the same. Keeping this order, ye shall never cease to do good works as occasion requireth.

## CHAPTER XX.

*An answer to all scriptures which our adversaries allege for themselves, against the justification of faith. Wherefore works are commended in scripture. An argument proving that no works justify.*

Now because there are some scriptures which our adversaries would cause to be seen, either contrary to the scriptures before rehearsed for probation of this article of justification; or else, they would mix this article with them; so that faith justifieth not only, without works,—therefore I will rehearse some of the most principal of them, and cause you to understand by the same scriptures, that they are neither contrary to this article, nor yet have any entresse* with faith, in the making of a wicked man just; but follow faith, as the due fruits thereof; in the which the christian man should live, as is said before.

In the epistle of St. James, ch. ii. it is said, Brethren, what profit is it, if a man say he hath faith, but hath no works? may his faith save him? And again, Ye see, saith he, that a man is justified of works, and not of faith only. Here the adversaries of faith make a great feast, but they understand this saying of the holy apostle, as they do the other scriptures, ever working with the devil to make the Holy Spirit contrary to himself, which is impossible. But if ye will understand, take heed, and read the text, ye shall see clearly that the apostle speaketh of the historical or idle faith; that is dead without works, to the confusion of the wicked christians, which have no faith but in the mouth; and not of the faith which maketh a man just before God, and obtaineth remission of sins; by the same examples and words that he rehearseth. For he saith, The devil troweth,† believeth, and dreadeth; but the devil can never believe that Christ hath redeemed him, and purchased to him the mercy of God, remission of sins, and eternal life, which is the faith to which St. Paul ascribeth justification only. And also he reproved the evil christian, who saith he hath faith, and neglecteth the deeds of charity, in clothing the naked, and feeding the hungry, which deeds

---

\* Intromission, entrance.
† Knoweth.

are the fruits of faith, of which St. Paul speaketh. Therefore, there is no contrariety in the scriptures before rehearsed, but concurrence.

And also the offering of Isaac, as mention is made before, was done above thirty years after the justification of Abraham, to the forthshowing of his obedience, as the text proves, Gen. xv. and xxii. In which offering, the scripture was fulfilled; as saith St. James, Abraham believed God, and it was counted to him for righteousness. Here ye may see clearly St. James speaketh nothing of the justification before God, but of the justification before thy neighbour, because of the examples and authorities of the scriptures alleged by him, which are of works done in faith by the faithful, long after their justification. For faith only justifieth before God, as St. Paul saith, without works. And works justify before men outwardly, and declare a man just before his neighbour, in exercising the deeds of charity, which are approved before God, and acceptable to him, in them which are reconciliate by faith in the mercy of God, and bear witness that a man is just. Therefore, ye who would allege this authority of St. James to impugn the article of justification which we confess, understand not the scriptures, nor have any foundation for you but ignorance and babbling of words.

They allege another text, Acts x. of Cornelius, whose prayers and alms-deeds passed up in the sight and memory of God: by which words they would infer, his works made him just, or at the least provoked God to call him to the faith, which is all one thing. For if we, by our deeds, may provoke God to love us, or to have mercy upon us, through our merits, by the same reason we may make ourselves just: and so we need no other Saviour, but let Christ's death be in vain. But, my well beloved brethren, ye shall understand that God first loved us, and provoked us to love him, we being sinners unworthy of love, yea, enemies also, as the scriptures of God teach you, 1 John iv. and in his gospel, ch. iii. and Rom. v. And therefore, God first preveened\* us with love and all goodness, and not we him. And so shall ye understand this text following, of Cornelius. The text saith, There was a man named Cornelius, a captain, &c. a devout man, and one that feared God with all his household; who gave great alms to the people, and prayed to God continually, &c. To whom the angel sent

\* Went before.

from God, said, Thy alms and prayers are passed up in the sight of God, &c. Here ye see this man was faithful and just, by the first two proprieties for the which he is commended, which cannot stand without faith; that is, devout and fearing God. Devout, is to say, a true worshipper of God. No man truly can worship God or please him but in faith, because it is impossible to please God without faith. Cornelius worshipped God truly, and so pleased him, therefore he was faithful,\* he feared and dreaded God, by love, for that is the fear whereof the text speaketh. Therefore Cornelius was faithful, because that love cannot be without faith. The works which Cornelius wrought were the fruits of faith, and pleased God, because God approved the same, which he had never allowed except they had been done in faith; for all which is not of faith is sin. Therefore, ye must confess that Cornelius was faithful and just before God, or else ye must deny the scriptures; which God forbid!

And then will ye say, To what effect was Peter sent for? To instruct him in the faith, and teach him what he should do? If he was faithful, what faith was it he had? To that I shall answer, Cornelius had the same faith that Adam, Noah, and the fathers had; for he believed the promised seed, which was Christ, and knew not that he was come; but believed in one God, and that the same God had promised a Saviour to redeem the world. So, God looking upon the faithful, humble, and simple heart of Cornelius, and the fervent desire of his prayers, which desire doubtless was conformable to the sayings of the prophet Isaiah, lxvi. Oh, if thou wouldest break asunder the heavens, that thou might come down! would not have him deceived, to look for Him who was already come. Therefore, he caused him to send for Peter to instruct him in the present faith; and to certify that Christ was come, whom he looked for so ardently. Ye may read the text, then shall ye perceive the sermon Peter made unto him, which was only of the opening of the scriptures, testifying the coming of Christ in the flesh; and fulfilling of all the promises and prophets' sayings, spoken of him before. And that he was risen from death, and had given Peter and the rest of his disciples and apostles, command to preach repentance and remission of sins to all which would believe in his name, &c. Matt. xxviii. Mark xvi. Luke xxiv. To the which words and preaching of St. Peter, Cornelius and his

\* Cornelius had faith, and thereby wrought good works.—Ed. 1584.

whole household gave firm faith, and received by a visible sign the Holy Spirit. The which is no other thing but this article of justification. For he believed the word of God, and by faith in Christ, through the mercy of God, received the Holy Spirit, without all working of any deed of the law of Moses, but only being under the law of nature; and so was baptized, &c. Therefore, ye cannot prove, by the authority of scripture, that either the works preceding or following the gift of the Holy Spirit, were the cause of his justification, or yet any part thereof. But, first, being just through the faith which the fathers had, who had also the Holy Spirit, he truly worshipped God, and feared him of love, and so he was just; and in that righteousness wrought the fruits of faith in prayers and almsdeeds. And, secondly, being taught by Peter, he believed that Christ was come, the sure Saviour of the world, and had fulfilled all which was spoken of Him by the prophets. By this faith was he, by the mercy of God, made just, and received the Holy Spirit visibly, without all works or deservings. And then, in the kingdom of Christ and righteousness, he wrought the fruits of faith unto life, as all perfect christians should do.

They allege another text, Gal. v. Faith, which worketh by love, &c. Of these words they would infer, of their corrupted manner, that faith only, justifieth not before God, but faith which worketh by love. By this manner of understanding, they not only make the apostle false, but also cast all down, and destroy the same thing which he hath builded.* For in the fourth chapter of the same epistle, with great labour and invincible arguments he setteth forth the article of justification, proving faith only to justify, without all deeds or works of the law. And then in the fifth chapter he beginneth to set forth the fruits of faith, saying, Ye are abolished from Christ who would be made just by the law; ye have left grace; for we, by the Spirit of faith, behold or look for the hope of righteousness; for into Christ Jesus neither is circumcision nor uncircumcision any thing worth, but faith which worketh by love. In these words shortly, and in brief terms, the apostle excludes all works and laws, sacrifices and worshippings, both of Jew and Gentile, to have any mixture with Christ in the justification of a christian. For if there had been any more

* Sophists would make the Holy Spirit speaking in St. Paul contrary to himself.—Ed 1584.

excellent work, or greater in estimation among the Jews, who were the chosen people of God, than circumcision, no doubt but the apostle would have excluded the same. And so the principal work, commanded by God, and given by him as the seal of the promise and covenant made to Abraham, being excluded forth of this article, how can any other work of less or equal estimation have part thereinto? Therefore the apostle concluding shortly, and comprehending the whole estate of a christian man, saith, Neither is circumcision nor uncircumcision any thing worth in Christ, but faith which worketh by love. He saith not, love which worketh by faith, but faith which worketh by love; that is, faith inwardly maketh a man just before God, who hath no need of our works; for the whole world, and all that is therein is his. And love outwardly testifieth of thy inward faith toward thy neighbour, who hath need of thy works; for whose utility and profit thou art commanded to do good works; to whom thy faith availeth nothing. And so this text impugns not the article of justification, but fortifies the same.

Ye read love greatly extolled by St. Paul, 1 Cor. xiii. as it is worthy, but ye never find justification before God attributed to love, for that is not the office thereof. But love followeth faith in the third degree, whose office the apostle sets forth in the said chapter. Especially, how that love suffereth all things, believeth all things, hopeth all things, and endureth all things. Yea, verily, some things which faith may not suffer, nor will in any ways suffer; as a light\* superstition repugning to the will of God, love will, or may suffer the same to be in it, for the weakness of the infirm brother. But faith may in no manner suffer the same, because it may be prejudicial to the article of justification, and induce the mixture of works.

Also faith, hope, and charity being reckoned, the apostle exalteth charity to be the most excellent of the three, but giveth her none of their offices. But, if ye will understand the text well, ye shall know the apostle's mind by the conclusion: saying, Now we see through a glass darkly, but then we shall see face to face: now I know in part, but then shall I know even as I am known. And now abideth faith, hope, and charity, but the chiefest of these is charity. As he would say, Now we are imperfect, but then we shall be perfect. Faith and hope shall both perish, and vanish

\* Trifling.

away, but charity shall remain in her perfection; for then she is in her perfection when the others have taken effect, and are vanished away: for in the heaven there is neither faith nor hope, but charity is in her most excellent degree there, which never hath an end. The cause wherefore the apostle extolleth charity ye shall consider in 1 Cor. xii. the which I pray you to read. For in that whole epistle there is no question of the article of justification, nor of the office of faith, but an instruction how the christian man should live; reproving hatred, envy, dissensions, and opinions amongst the Corinthians, which became not to be amongst christians. Therefore, he exhorted them above all things to charity, which is the band of peace, and the most excellent virtue to be had, and ever kept among the christians; for by that men shall know you, saith Christ, to be my disciples, John xiii. Therefore, howbeit charity is the most excellent virtue, and that the whole life of a perfect christian is faith and charity, or faith working by charity; nevertheless charity justifieth not before God, nor yet hath any mixture with faith in the making of the wicked just; but followeth faith as the due fruits thereof, conformable to the order of scripture before rehearsed, and as also hereafter shall be shown.

To impugn this article, they allege this text, If thou wilt enter into life, keep the commands; by the which they would infer that the keeping of the commands is in our own power of free will; and that we, fulfilling the same according to our power and strength, may thereby obtain the kingdom of heaven by our works; the which is as agreeable to the saying of Christ, as black and white are; as ye shall clearly understand by the scriptures. Christ, being asked and inquired of by the young man, what he should do or work that he might have eternal life, answered on this manner, saying, If thou wilt enter into life, keep the commands. Which are they? said the young man. Jesus answered, Thou shalt not kill; thou shalt not commit adultery; thou shalt not steal; thou shalt speak no false witness; thou shalt honour thy father and mother; and, thou shalt love thy neighbour as thyself. Here ye see Christ teacheth the young man the works of the second table, which concern our neighbour only; and speaks nothing of the first table, which pertaineth properly to God, and consisteth into faith. Therefore, by these words of

Christ it may not be inferred that he sendeth any to the law, to obtain perfection therein, that is to say, justification or salvation; but only to let them know what the law requireth of them, and what they were obliged to do; that they, seeing no remedy thereinto, might seek Christ, who came into the world to call all unto him, and not to send them to the law, for that was the office of Moses. What availed Christ's coming in the flesh, if he would have sent man to the law to get salvation? But Christ declareth plainly hereafter in the same text, that there was no perfection to be had in the deeds of the law of man's doing; as appears by the answer made to the young man, and the precept given to him. When the young man said, he had observed all the said deeds of the law from his youth, &c. howbeit he made a lie, Christ accused him not, because it was not his office; but said unto him, If thou wilt be perfect, go thy way, and sell all that thou hast, and give it to the poor, and come and follow me. But when the young man heard that saying, he went away sorrowful and left Christ, because he had great possessions. These words of Christ are no other thing but the declaration of the feigned man, to let his heart be known, who believed that through fulfilling of the outward deeds of the law, he might be found just before God; and also to teach us the duty which we are bound to do to our neighbour. For, howbeit Christ hath freed us from the thraldom and malediction of the law, he wills that we work the works of charity, to the utility of our neighbour, and nothing draws us so much therefrom as avarice and covetousness. Therefore, Christ opened the young man's covetous heart, which he would have hidden, as all hypocrites do, and taught him, if he would be perfect, to follow him in whom is all perfection. And so this text makes nothing for them which impugn this article of justification, but rather against them, because the matter of which Christ speaketh doth concern the neighbour only, and works to be wrought to his weal and utility, which of necessity follow the article of justification, as the fruits of faith done by the justified man, who may or can find no better works to do than those which are commanded in the law of God. The adversaries of faith reading the scriptures, wherever they find mention made of works, that part they collect not to the effect as it is spoken by the Holy Spirit, but to the intent they may impugn thereby the Holy

Spirit as contrary to himself. This proceeds of the devil, to empoison the article of justification; that is, to mix the same with works, that he may enter and obtain his place, by the which he may abolish faith, or at the least the perfect office thereof, and diminish the glory of God. But for showing of this, ye who well know the perfect estate of a christian man, wherever ye find mention made of faith in the scripture, without any addition thereto, ye shall understand it of perfect faith unfeigned, which, without all works, either preceding or following the same, justifieth. And upon this faith St. Paul groundeth all his arguments, to prove that faith only justifieth before God, without the law or works, which he ever excludeth, as is proved by the scriptures before rehearsed.

And wherever ye find mention made of works in the scriptures without any addition, ye shall understand them of perfect works wrought into faith. Of these works St. Paul maketh mention in all his epistles, after he hath set forth the article of justification. Therefore, the works are but the witnessing of faith, and the obedience which is required of the just and faithful man, to the glory of God and profit of his neighbour, by which the just obtaineth witnessing of his faith, as is proved clearly by St. Paul to the Hebrews, ch. xi. where he reckoned from the just and faithful Abel, and their works in special, till he come to Gideon, Barak, Samson, Jephthah, David, Samuel, and the prophets in general, declaring them all to have done many great and excellent works into faith; and yet he ascribeth nothing to works, but to faith only, showing the works to be the testimony and witnessing of their faith outwardly, and no part of their justification; concluding in this manner: The which by faith have subdued and overcome realms, have wrought righteousness, obtained and gotten the promise, have stopped the mouths of lions, quenched the violence of fire, and escaped the edge of the sword, &c.

Here is a clear solution to all the objections of works, made by the adversaries of faith: for, seeing the apostle saith, It is impossible to please God without faith, where then are the works which precede faith, and move God to give grace and favour, which ye call "De congruo."* And then ye work of your own strength and power, as ye say, the works which deserve remission of sins and everlasting life: yea, not only sufficient to yourselves, but also superabundant to

* Grace of congruity. See History of Church of Christ, vol. iv. ch. v.

save others, which ye call, "De condigno et opera supererogationis."*

The scriptures are plain against your false superstitions and sophistical arguments; concluding that neither works preceding nor following faith have entrance in making of a wicked man just, nor yet may save you. It is written, All which is not of faith is sin; how then can ye do any work preceding faith, that it may please God, or provoke him to love you, considering all that ye do out of faith is sin? Will ye say that he delighteth in sin? No, no; it is a thing most abominable in his sight. Therefore, all that ever ye do, how excellent the work be in your sight, it is sin before God; and ye 'heap sin upon sin, which is abomination in his sight, as saith the prophet Isaiah. The works which follow faith make you not just, because or ever ye work good works ye must first be made just, and thereafter in faith ye work the works of justice. Nevertheless, the said works may not save you, nor merit the kingdom of heaven to you, much less may they merit to others. But ye are made safe by the mercy of God, and not of works, as St. Paul saith, Titus iii. Not of works of righteousness which we have done, shall we be saved; but according to his mercy, God hath saved us.

Here ye see not only works excluded in general forth of this article, but also the works of justice, which cannot be done but by the justified man. Where are then your works, which deserve the kingdom of heaven of their worthiness, not only to yourselves, but superabundant to others? They are excluded by the scriptures of God. Therefore I exhort you to exclude them also and cleave to faith.

## CHAPTER XXI.

*The opinion of the wicked, seeking their own glory. The works commanded by God and done without faith, are abomination before him. Whereby cometh the new birth. Paul refuseth his works, seeking no justification thereby. The conclusion of all the scriptures. What is given to man who hath true faith.*

I MARVEL greatly of your blindness who are adversaries to this article and would ever mix it with works, especially of your own making; that ye may be a part of your own salvation. But I ought not to marvel thereat, because ye

* Of your deserving, and works of superorogation.

seek your own glory, and not the glory of God: for ever ye cry, The law, the law; Good works, good works; the which ye never do, nor yet is it in your power of yourself to complete according to the perfection, that ye may set them before the judgment seat of God, Rom. x. And this same thing did your forefathers, the scribes and pharisees, against Christ; and now ye, against his faithful little flock, of the same blindness and ignorance. For, to establish your own justice, ye neglect the justice of God, and will not be subject thereto, as the apostle saith. And Christ saith, Ye are they which justify yourselves before men, but God knoweth your hearts; because that which is of great estimation in men's eyes, is abominable before God, Luke xvi. Isa. lvi.—lviii. Zech. i. Even so it is of your works not commanded by God; how honest and shining that ever they are in the sight of man; for verily God will be pleased with no works of man's invention, but with the works commanded by himself. And the same should be done in faith, according to his will and not ours; for the which we are commanded, and should daily pray- Thy will, O heavenly Father, be fulfilled, and not ours. What better works can man do, than the works commanded by God, as prayers, alms-deeds, fastings, and keeping of holy days, and others, as ye may read, Isaiah i. the which God, by the mouth of the prophet, calleth abomination? And Christ called prophesying, preaching, casting forth of devils, miracles, wonders, and signs, and many other great and excellent virtues done in his name, the works of iniquity; and the doers of them the workers of iniquity. Saying, Pass away from me all ye which are workers of iniquity; for not all which say unto me, Lord, Lord, shall enter in the kingdom of heaven; but they which do the will of my Father which is in heaven. These works are contemned by God for no other cause, but that they are wrought by the wicked without faith. or mixed with the article of justification; thinking therethrough to be made just, or to be a part of their own justification; and therefore cannot please God, but greatly displease him, because the good work is converted into sin through the iniquity of man. Nevertheless, they appear in the sight of man to be most excellent good, and should have a great reward, after the judgment of man; but ye see here what reward God giveth them.

And seeing the works commanded by God to be done, are so displeasing in his sight, wrought by the wicked without faith, what shall be of your works which are not commanded by God, or have no authority in his scriptures, but invented by yourselves, of your good zeal, and intention to make yourselves just by them, having no respect to faith; but to the working of them of the self deed, yea, verily, expressly contrary to the scripture, and plain idolatry! Nevertheless, he that doth them ye make just; and he that doth them not ye condemn. Is this any other thing but to make the death of Christ in vain, and to be justifiers of yourselves? For, seeing the justice which is of value before God is not of the deeds of the law, how can it be of your deeds? Therefore Christ will say unto you, Pass from me, all ye workers of iniquity; I know you not. Notwithstanding, in other places of the scripture ye shall find the same works greatly commended by God, where they are done by the just man as the fruits of faith; and reward promised to the workers of them. So they confess themselves unprofitable servants when they have done all that they can; for Christ said to his disciples, When ye have done all which is commanded you to do, then say, we are unprofitable servants, we have done that which we were bound to do, Luke xvii.

And if they which fulfil all the commandments of God, are counted or reputed by him unprofitable servants, what have we to glory in, who fulfil not one of his commandments? Now, I pray you, lay this text to your assertion, If thou wilt enter into life, keep the commandments, and ye shall think shame of your sayings, insomuch as ye would impugn the article of justification therewith, and mix works with faith to the making of a wicked man just.

Now I trust it is sufficiently proved by authority of the scripture, as is before rehearsed at length, to the satisfaction of a christian and godly man, that works are excluded forth of this article of justification, and have no participation therewith, but follow faith as the due fruits thereof, that all glory may redound to God. Howbeit, the wicked hypocrites and justifiers of themselves will never be satisfied by any authority of the scripture; for they cannot and will not be content with God, nor his word, but ever impugn the same, to establish their own authority and glory; Isa. xlviii. and therefore are never at rest nor quietness in their conscience with God, because they reject the mercy, grace, and peace of God, which are the substance of the estate of a christian, wherein the just liveth by faith, and are so necessary that they should ever be blown in at the ears of the faithful by the ministers of the word. Therefore, wherever the apostle St. Paul wrote or preached, howbeit there was no question of the law, nor works thereof, he never omitted in the beginning of his epistle, as the other apostles in like manner used, to certify the christian congregation of the substance of this article, saluting them with grace and peace; which is as much as to say, the mercy of God, by the which ye are made just, and accepted as righteous in the favour of God the Father, through faith in Jesus Christ, our only Lord and Saviour. Rest and quietness in your conscience I desire to be with you, and to remain with you continually, that thereby ye may work the fruits of faith, by charity or love, in righteousness, to the glory of God, and profit of your neighbour, through Jesus Christ, by whom we have this mercy and grace, and entrance to the Father, Rom. v. and the same grace; the which grace is given to us by God in Jesus Christ, that no flesh should rejoice in his sight, 1 Cor. i. who hath given himself for our sins, that he might deliver us out of this present wicked world, according to the will of God the Father, and according to the riches of his mercy, the which he hath abundantly shed forth upon us, by whose mercy we are made safe. He hath called us by his holy vocation, not according to our works, but according to his purpose and mercy, the which he hath given to us by Jesus Christ, Gal. i. Eph. i. and ii. 2 Tim. i.

And St. Peter saith, Blessed be God, the Father of our Lord Jesus Christ, who according to his great mercy hath begotten us of new, into a lively hope by the rising of our Lord Jesus Christ from the death, 1 Pet. i. Therefore, if we are born and begotten of new by mercy, it is not of works nor of our deservings, but freely given us by the grace and mercy of God through faith in Jesus Christ. Nor have we righteousness of the law nor works, as is before clearly proved by the scriptures at length. And St. Paul testifieth in his own body the same to be true, who wrought many excellent works of the law, Phil. iii. Nevertheless he reputeth all but filthiness, that he may win Christ and be found in him, not having his own justice or righteousness which is of the law, but that justice which is of the faith of Jesus Christ. And, seeing the holy apostle, the chosen vessel of God, might not obtain righteousness in the law nor works, but in the mercy of God, through faith in the precious blood of Jesus Christ, alas, what blindness is in us wicked and miserable sinners, who will ever glory and cry, Good works, which we never do, and will have them mixed with this article of justification: insomuch that Christ, after our judgment, is not sufficient to save us and make us just; howbeit, it be the only cause wherefore he was made man for us.

Therefore, let us conclude with the apostle and the holy scriptures, that by faith only in Christ we are made just, without the law and works thereof. And after man is made just by faith, and possesseth Christ in his heart, knowing perfectly him to be his justice and his life, then shall he not be idle; but even as the good tree shall bring forth good fruit; because a man truly believing, hath the Holy Spirit, and where he is he suffereth not man to be idle, but doth move and provoke him to all godly exercises of good works; as the love of God, patience in troubles and afflictions, calling upon the name of God, and thanksgiving, and to the forthshowing of charity and love unto all. This is the order of a christian's life, and the substance of good works, as hereafter followeth, and as we have also touched something in the beginning concerning the trouble and patience thereof.

## CHAPTER XXII.

*What works christians should do. The life of man is a perpetual battle. What is the law of the members, and what the law of the spirit. What sacrifice we should offer to God, and what is required that our sacrifice be acceptable. Who followeth Christ, who goeth before him, and who is equal with him.*

BECAUSE good works are the fruits of faith, and necessarily must follow the same, and proceed of the justified man as the good fruit of the good tree, without which no christian man may get witnessing of his faith, therefore, after the forthsetting of the article of justification, mention should ever be made of good works, and all the faithful be taught to do the same. The which method St. Paul uses in all his epistles, but specially in the epistles to the Romans and Galatians. For being justified by faith we are at peace with God, by our Lord Jesus Christ. But then hastily rises the battle and strife with the world and persecution, because all who will live godly in Christ Jesus shall suffer persecution. Then shalt thou begin to rejoice of thy trouble, knowing surely that thou art the son of God, because he chasteneth all sons whom he loveth. This affliction, whether it be in spirit or body, brings patience to thee, which is the proof of thy faith. Then conceive thou hope, whose office is to comfort thee that thou be not overcome in thy affliction; and so then faith and hope being joined together, the love, favour, and grace of God are by his Holy Spirit shed abroad in our hearts; by which, we, as valiant knights, pass to a new battle against the devil, the world, and the flesh, of whom we obtain victory by faith, and suffer not sin to rule over us, 1 John v. This method to good works the apostle teaches, Rom. v. and vi. exhorting us, that as we before gave our members to be weapons of unrighteousness unto sin to the death; that now we, being justified by faith, give to God our members, weapons and armour of righteousness, unto life. For the reward of sin is death, but the grace of God is eternal life by our Lord Jesus Christ. Then let us surely believe he that hath begun the good work in us, which is God, shall perform the same to the day of our Lord Jesus Christ. And so, to begin good works is not to suffer sin to rule in this mortal body, that we obey not the lusts and concupiscence of the same.

The whole life of man is but a battle upon the earth, Job vii. and whosoever will pass forward in the service of God, he must prepare himself for temptation and trouble. This battle St. Paul had, and, as a knight of great experience, taught us the same; how he found a law in his members repugning to the law of his mind; which is no other thing but the tyranny of the devil, drawing and provoking man to follow the lusts and concupiscence of the flesh; not only in external works, but also in the inward affections of the mind, as to doubt or diffide of the goodness and mercy of God, or to be slothful, void, and empty, of the love and fear of God. The law of the mind is the law of God provoking and calling men to do all justice and righteousness, which the faithful man consenteth to in his mind, to be good and just; and yet findeth no power in himself to perform the same. For which the holy apostle, with an exclamation, saith, Oh unhappy man that I am, who shall deliver me of this mortal body, which is no other thing but a mass of sin? These words he saith, not as of a doubt in his faith, but of a fervent desire to be dissolved and separated from this vile life, to be with Christ; because he giveth thanks to God, by Jesus Christ, by whom he is delivered of the said battle. Read Romans vii. where ye shall clearly perceive this matter at length. Therefore, the saints and holy men vehemently lament these motions and affections of the flesh, which they feel in their inward mind; reason, and human wisdom, repugning against the spirit, and will not be subject thereto, nor may so be of their own power or strength, but by the Spirit of God, which beareth witness with our spirit that we are the sons of God, Rom. viii. There are none which perceive this battle, or valiant fighting, but the just men, who confide not in their own works, merits, or deservings, but only in the mercy of God through faith in Jesus Christ, by whom they obtain victory and thank God.

But because this mortal body of sin is ever repugning unto the spirit, and our greatest enemy, daily borne about with us, the apostle exhorts us most fervently, by the mercy of God, to give and offer the same a quick, lively, holy, and pleasant sacrifice unto God. And that our service and worshipping of God be reasonable; not conforming ourselves to this world, but to be renewed and reformed into a new knowledge and understanding; that we may have proof how the will of God is, how good, how acceptable, and how perfect, Rom. xii. The which is, that we mortify our bodies and members which are upon earth; not only to abstain from external, outward, and gross sins, as from fornication, uncleanness, avarice, indignation, wicked lusts, and concupiscence, ire, filthy communications, and the like unto these, reckoned by St. Paul; but also to conceive in our hearts the true and perfect fear of God, which moveth and causeth us to abhor sin, and to detest our wicked corrupt nature, which ever resists the will of God, and entices us to follow our own will, mind, reason, and honest appearance of good zeal, and intention; the which we should not obey, but the will of God, which is, to believe in him, and in Jesus Christ whom he hath sent. And also it is the work of God, for the which we should ever pray to God, Thy will be fulfilled, and not ours.

This doing, the kingdom of heaven is within us, as Christ saith, Luke xvii. and the old man mortified in our bodies, and crucified with Christ; the body of sin abolished and destroyed, that we serve no more to sin. Which is no other thing but to cast off all our affections of the fleshly man, and submit us wholly to Christ; and as he hath risen from death, that we likewise rise with him from sin, and live a new life in the kingdom of righteousness; no more being under the law nor sin, but under grace; that is, Christ and his word, which will never teach us to sin, but to all virtue in faith. The order hereof St. Paul teacheth, Rom. xii. and so forth to the end of the epistle. And St. Peter, 1st Ep. ii. teaches the same.

' This quick and lively sacrifice which God desireth of us, and which is so pleasant and acceptable in his sight, is a contrite and broken heart, a troubled spirit, humiliate and subject unto God, Psal. v. 1. These the prophet calls the affections of the mind, or thoughts of the heart, which are broken, afflicted, and cast down, by the knowledge of sin, and place their whole hope and confidence only in the mercy of God. The same affections of the heart he calls the sacrifice most acceptable unto God; and commandeth the same to be offered unto him, as it is written, Give unto the Lord the sacrifice of righteousness, and put your whole hope into him. And in Psalm l. he called the same the sacrifice of praise and thanksgiving. For we should ever praise God, that is, preach and forthshow in all things his infinite goodness; and whatever we think, speak, or do, direct the same to his glory. This is a worthy sacrifice to be done by a christian. On this manner we are taught by St. Paul to the Hebrews, and in divers other places of the scriptures.

To the fulfilling of this sacrifice is required that we spoil ourselves of the old man, that is, our first conversation in sin, which we have of our first father Adam, wherewith we are clad, and bear the same so long as we live after the example of Adam, ever rebels to God and his law; and clothe us with new Adam, that is Christ, with whom we are clad when we reform our life to the similitude of him who restoreth again to us the image and similitude of God, to the which we were created. This is the right and true holiness, integrity, and justice, to which in Christ we are renewed, by the Holy Spirit; that we should live in all justice and holiness of life; in that we were created by God in the beginning, that we should walk before him.[*] Therefore, the apostle commandeth us to be renewed with the pirit of the mind, and to clothe us with the new man. The mind is the fountain and beginning of all things; so it

[*] That is, love and extol his magnificence in all kinds of godly life. Eph. iv —Ed. 1584.

must be renewed, if any good works should follow. And that the prophet Isaiah teaches in these words, Put away the evil of your thoughts from my eyes, &c. And so to do good works according to the pleasure of God and order of the scripture, is to begin to mortify this sinful body, as is before rehearsed. Then are we the good tree whose fruit is sweet and pleasant in the sight of God, and acceptable to him.

Therefore, let us deny ourselves, take our own cross upon our backs and follow Christ, as he hath commanded us in his gospel. For which he suffered death for us, leaving to us an example that we should follow his footsteps, and neither go before Christ, nor yet aside from him; but let us follow him. The which we do when we cast from us all our wisdom, righteousness, holiness, and redemption, and receive them from Christ, who is made to us, by God, our wisdom, justice, holiness, and redemption, 1 Cor. i. and confess us to have nothing of ourselves but evil, and all our goodness to be from God; as St. James saith in his epistle, first chapter. This our cross is no other thing but the troubles and afflictions, both spiritual and corporal, that we have in this present life; the which are the probations and exercises of our faith, whereby the same is tried and searched by our heavenly Father, to our weal; and testify us to be the sons of God and not bastards, Heb. ii. And therefore we shall gladly accept the same, with thanksgiving from the bottom of our heart, thinking them to come to us for the best, and that we are the beloved of God, so accepting them, Rom. viii. And then in the greatest troubles and afflictions raise up our hearts with faith and hope, Psal. xxxi. and lxxi. believing surely our good God to be so faithful and true that he will not suffer us to be overcome or confounded, and tempted above that we are able, but will even give the issue with the temptation, that we may be able to bear it; because our weak and fragile nature is known to him. He will have compassion upon us for Christ's sake, by whom we are reconciliate to his favour. So let us not go astray, but follow Christ's footsteps; that is, suffer all things patiently, and think that we have deserved more for our sins. Also remembering that Christ our Saviour hath suffered ten thousand times more for us. On this manner we follow Christ's footsteps, who hath borne our sins in his own body upon the cross; that, being dead from sin we should live in righteousness. My hearts, ye that are adversaries to the article of justification, learn to read the scriptures with effect, to the perfect understanding thereof; and then ye shall obtain knowledge to begin to do good works, in faith, pleasant and acceptable to God.

Since we have made mention of three kinds of persons, that is, of them which go before Christ, of them which go astray from Christ, and of them which follow Christ's footsteps, it is necessary to let them be known by themselves, that the true and faithful may be known by their deeds. They which confide in their own works, merits, and deservings, thinking therethrough to obtain the kingdom of heaven, and satisfy for their own sins, not only for themselves, but also, of the superabundance of their merits, for others; of the which they make merchandise—these are they which go before Christ; and are called antichrists, or contrary to Christ, because they usurp his office, and will be justifiers of themselves and others. They which think faith not sufficient to justify without works, but will have their own good deeds joined, to help Christ in their justification; these are they which go astray from Christ, and will be equal with him in their own justification—for none of these hath Christ suffered death. Therefore he shall abstract from these two kinds his wisdom, righteousness, holiness, and redemption; and shall suffer them to contend with the law in the latter judgment, whose works being accused, and the purity and cleanness required, according to the perfection of the law, all their noble works and deeds of good zeal and intention shall be found abomination in the sight of God, how excellent or shining that ever they be before men; to whom it shall be said, Pass your way from me, ye workers of iniquity. Lucifer was thrown down out of the heaven, because he would have made himself equal with God. Adam was cast forth of paradise, because he pretended to know more than was given him in commandment to know, &c. The pharisee of whom Christ maketh mention, pretended no other thing but a great reward for his good works. The same thing pretend all they which impugn this article of justification; for will ye compare these sayings and doings, it is the self-same thing, but of another arrayment. Nevertheless they are as like as one egg is like another. And so they are not of Christ's little flock, which he hath chosen, and which follow him.

The third kind of persons are they who put all their

trust, hope, and confidence in Christ, take his cross upon their backs, and daily follow Christ in his footsteps, neither declining to the right hand, nor to the left; that is, grounded in faith, ever working by charity, abstaining from evil, and doing good works, in which they put no confidence; but when they have done all which is commanded them to do, nevertheless they think themselves but unprofitable servants. They lay their sins upon Christ's back, and follow him by faith, ascribing all their wisdom, justice, holiness, and redemption to Christ, and nothing to themselves nor their merits; because they are sinners, and through the dregs of sin left in them, of the old corrupted man, their works are not perfect according to the perfection which the law requireth. Therefore, they may not stand in judgment with them, of their own power and strength, but believe the same works, through faith in Christ, to be accepted as obedience to the law, and through Christ's merits made perfect. These are they to whom it shall be said, Come unto me, ye blessed of my Father, and possess the kingdom of heaven, prepared unto you from the beginning of the world. Against which the law hath no place to accuse, nor condemn their works of any imperfection, because they are Christ's works, made perfect by him, through faith in his blood.

## CHAPTER XXIII.

*What the reason of man persuadeth to be done in the matter of religion. Arguments against good zeal and good intention. The papistical church this day is worse than the external church of the Jews, in the days of the prophets and Christ. What fruit the good zeal of man brings.*

THE blind reason, knowledge, and understanding of man, which is but the desires and appetites of the fleshly man, is the cause why we misknow the good and perfect order to do good works taught us in the scriptures, neglecting the word of God, and following our own will, which teacheth us good zeal and good intention.* This our reason affirms to be good, and thinks that God shall approve the same, according to our desire, which is but flesh, I mean of the whole man, and all that is in him. But the Spirit

* All men depending upon their own reason are deceived.—Ed. 1584.

and word of God teach us to walk in the spirit and not to perform the desires and lusts of the flesh. For the flesh ever contendeth against the spirit, and the spirit against the flesh. Therefore, we are commanded to fight valiantly against the desires of the flesh, and to abstain from the lusts and appetites thereof; and to follow the will of God, which is to walk in the Spirit, and clothe us with Christ Jesus. This order the apostle teaches, Gal. v. Rom. viii. xiii. and St. Peter in his first epistle, second chapter.

Oh miserable, blind, and ignorant man! why dost thou neglect the good work of God, to invent a good work of thy own making? thinking therethrough to please God, saying thou doest it of a good zeal and intention; which is as much to say as, that thy mind and intention are good in themselves. And, because thou thinkest the same good, God, after thy judgment, should approve the same as good. Thou art deceived, because thou understandest not the scriptures, or wilt not understand the same. It is written that the whole thought of man, and all the cogitations of his heart, are ready given and bent upon evil at all times. And also the understanding and conceit of man, and the thought of his heart, are prone, ready, and inclined to evil, from his youth and young age. And David saith, The Lord knoweth the cogitations of man's heart that they are vain. Now, my hearts, where will ye find your GOOD ZEAL AND GOOD INTENTION? Either it is evil of itself, or else God is false, which cannot be. Ye may call it good, but God, who hath better knowledge thereof than ye have, by his word testifieth all that is in you to be but evil, as he hath declared by the mouth of Moses, Deut. xii. commanding that we do not that thing which we think good; but that thing which he hath commanded us to do, that should we do; and neither add to his word, nor take therefrom, but walk in the way which the Lord hath commanded. This showeth thee that thou shouldest not follow thy "good zeal and intention," thinking therethrough to please God, or fulfil his will, which thou canst not fulfil but by his word. For all men of themselves are but liars, and full of vanity, Psal. cxvi.

Great is the difference betwixt the will of God, and the will of man; the thought of God, and the thoughts of man; the ways of God, and the ways of man. As saith the prophet in the person of God, Isa. lv. My thoughts and cogitations are not yours, nor your ways mine; but as the heavens are exalted above the earth, even so are my ways and cogitations from yours. This is no other thing but to teach us to follow the will and command of God, and not ours, who hath declared in his scriptures, plainly, what we should do and leave undone, that we need to seek no further, Mic. vi. So doing, we shall procure the blessing of God, if we take his erudition and teaching. As David saith, Blessed is the man whom thou, O Lord, instructest, and of thy law teachest him, Psal. xciv. And if we will follow our own teaching, doing works of our own intention, which we think good, we shall procure the plagues and punishments threatened by the prophet Jeremiah, ch. xv. xix. because we do the thing which he hath not commanded nor spoken to us, nor yet hath ascended in his heart. Trust well, the people thought they did a great excellent work to God and sacrifice to please him, when they spared not their own children, to kill and offer sacrifice unto God of their innocent blood! This was their good zeal and good intention. But they had no command of God for them; and verily ye have less for you to make such sacrifice as ye do daily, to deceive the poor people, and to purchase to yourselves great riches, goods, and possessions. Therefore, I exhort you, by the mercy of God, to cast away that " good zeal and intention;" and to follow the word of God, as he hath commanded you in the scriptures; for they bear witness of him, and show to man what is his will. Seek no further, nor confound the works of God with thy own vain thoughts.

Through the vain conceit of man, used in these words, " good zeal and intention," have all the abuses, now ruling in the church of God, risen so, that the sayings of the prophet spoken to the people of Israel, are complete this day in the church of Christ, and may be said to us as they were said to the Jews. Even as the thief is ashamed when he is taken, even so is the house of Israel ashamed; they, and their kings, their princes, priests, and prophets, saying unto the tree or stock, Thou art my father, and to the stone, Thou hast begotten me. They have turned their back to me, saith the Lord, and not their face. And in the time of their trouble and affliction, they shall say, Rise and deliver us. Then shall the Lord say unto them, Where are thy gods, which thou hast made thee? let them arise and deliver thee in the time of thy trouble. Thy gods were verily in number according to the number of thy cities, O Judah!

What! wilt thou contend with me in judgment? Ye have all left me, saith the Lord. Now I pray you, confer these words of God, plainly spoken, with the doings of these days now ruling in the church, and then ye shall perceive the abuse of God's word. We commonly pray the paternoster, that is, the Lord's Prayer, to the image of this or that saint, made of tree or stone! And especially to this or that altar we kneel, which is by ourselves or our predecessors founded upon such a saint's name, whose picture is well graved in a stock or stone, and painted with costly colours. And the blessed sacrament of the body and blood of Christ, after their manner, is offered daily to this or that saint, and called, " his mass;" for doing of which there is not a syllable in God's word for you, but the contrary expressly commanded; both that ye should have no graven images, nor worship them; nor yet invent any manner of worshipping of God, but as God hath commanded by his word, Exod. xx. Lev. xxvi. Deut. v. Psal. lxxxi. xcvii. cxv. And for your defence ye have only these words, " good zeal and intention," the which is expressly contrary to the first commandment of God. For even as we are forbidden and inhibited to have strange gods, so are we inhibited to have strange worshippings of God.

Blessed be God, the matter is so open and plainly set forth in these days concerning the said vain works invented by man, to the confusion thereof, by the godly men which labour day and night in his scriptures, to the edification of Christ's chosen little flock, that it is not needful to abide long upon the discussing of these matters; but only to remit you to the scriptures, and the said godly declarations made thereupon; against the superstitious worshipping of saints; going in pilgrimage; purging in purgatory; hallowing of water, or other elements; foundation of masses to public or private idolatry; offering or sacrifices making, not commanded in the word of God; choice of meats; forbidding of marriage in the church of God; and abominable abuses of the whole christian religion, by the shaven, anointed, or smeared priests, bishops, monks, and friars; having only their vocation of man, and by man. Therefore, we let the specialities of them pass, and refer the same to thy judgment, good reader. Thanks be to God, these abuses and grounds are not unknown; and we will pass forward to the knowledge of the works commanded us to do and work by the scriptures of God, as the fruits of faith.

## CHAPTER XXIV.

*What works pastors should teach unto their flocks. Wherefore the yoke of Christ is sweet, and his burden light to christians. Vocation mediate and immediate. Vocation in general, by the which all true christians are equal, made kings and priests in Christ's blood.*

If any will ask or inquire, what works the faithful should do; I can find no more perfect answer to make thereto, than the gospel teaches us. As St. Luke saith, John the Baptist preaching repentance in the remission of sins; the people inquired of him what they should do. To whom he answered, saying, He that hath two coats, give to him that hath not one; and he that hath meat, let him do in like manner. This is no other thing but to exercise the deeds of mercy and charity towards thy neighbour, as the prophet Isaiah saith, Break thy bread to the hungry, and needy; and the poor who are cast out bring into thy house; when thou seest the naked, clothe him; contemn or despise not thy own flesh. This is the forthshowing of thy faith, which St. James desireth of thee in his epistle. Thou art taught the same, with the other works of charity to thy neighbour, Ezek. xviii.

The publicans and open sinners inquired in like manner, what they should do. To whom he answered, saying, Ye shall do no further than that which is commanded you to do; as if he would say, Decline and cease to do evil, and learn to do good, as ye are taught by the prophet Isaiah, ch. i. And David teaches you the perfection of religion, saying, Come to me, my sons, and hear me, and I shall teach you the fear of the Lord. Who is he that liveth and loveth to see good days, let him refrain his tongue from evil, and his lips that they speak no fraud. Decline from evil, and do good; seek peace, and follow the same, Jer. vii. and xxvi. Ezek. xviii. Psal. xxxiv. 1 Peter iii. James i.

Therefore, pass your way, and sin no more; for I will not send you to the law to get remedy of your sins. But look in the law, and behold what is ordained you to do; which will declare you to be sinners and transgressors. And then ye shall seek Christ for remedy, whose forerunner I am. It is he in whom ye shall find remedy. Therefore, I say unto you, Behold the Lamb of God, which taketh away the sins of the world.

And John Baptist, being inquired of by the soldiers, what they should do, he answered, saying, Ye shall strike or hurt no man; nor yet do wrong nor injury to any person; but be content with your wages, Luke iii. Which is as much as to say, Oppress none; take no person's geare* violently; ye are public officers, deputed by princes and magistrates for keeping of good rule and order amongst the people, for rest and quietness of the commonweal; for the which cause ye have your wages. Your office is honest, and the good work of God; therefore, look on your own vocation, and do that justly which is commanded you, and exceed not your bounds.

Here is a good order taught you, who are ministers of the word, to teach the auditors in general or special, to do good works; that is, to show them the works commanded by God, the right fruits of repentance and faith; to the which ye should send them, and not to vain works invented by man, which is no other thing but to heap sin upon sin.

And Christ, being asked by the Jews, "What shall we do, that we might work the works of God?" answered them, saying, This is the work of God, that ye believe in Him whom he hath sent, John vi. Here he sent them not to the law, howbeit the law be the work of God, but to faith, which is not the work of man, but the work of God, which he worketh in man. Therefore, Christ saith to us, Believe, and ye shall be safe. And so let us say with St. Peter, Lord, to whom shall we pass? thou hast the words of life, we shall seek no other, but believe in thee. Ye shall consider, that Christ, after he had refreshed the people with their corporal food, then he taught them the perfection of a christian man, and fed them with the spiritual food; and they which received the same, followed him. The rest left him, who had no faith, but took his doctrine carnally, and of external and outward works; as did the young man, to whom Christ made the answer, as is before rehearsed, Matt. xix. By the which scriptures, we are taught to follow Christ, because there is no perfection but in the following of him.

Therefore, as we have received our Lord Jesus Christ, let us walk in him, being rooted and builded in him, and confirmed in the faith as we have learned, abounding in the same with giving thanks, as the apostle saith, Col. ii. For he is the fountain of all goodness, and the head of our

* Property.

felicity; and let us have respect to no other thing, nor lay any other foundation. For as the apostle saith, 1 Cor. iii. No man may lay another foundation than that which is already laid, the which is Jesus Christ. Let us build upon this foundation, gold, silver, and precious stones, which are the works of God, commanded in the holy scripture, to be wrought into faith;[*] every one according to his vocation, in which we should walk worthily, as we are called, with all humility, and meekness, and patience, supporting one another in love and charity; careful to keep the unity of the spirit in the band of peace, as we are taught by the apostle, Eph. iv.

And Christ saith, Take my yoke on you, and learn of me, that I am meek and lowly in heart; and ye shall find rest unto your souls. For my yoke is easy, and my burden light, Matt. xi. The which words Christ would never have spoken, if he had laden us with the law. For that burden is so weighty, that neither we nor our fathers might bear it; as St. Peter saith in the Acts of the Apostles, ch. xv. But verily the yoke of Christ is easy, and his burden is light, to the faithful and chosen; for they lay all upon Christ's back, and follow him through faith; confiding nothing in their own works or merits; but ever working all good according to their vocation, giving all glory and honour unto God. Not exceeding the bounds of their vocation, which is the best rule that the faithful can have to do good works; to the knowledge thereof, we will make some short declaration, and then make an end.

Ye shall understand that there are two kinds of godly vocations. The one is immediate by God, as the prophets were called in the Old Testament; yea, and as David to be a king, and Moses a governor to the people; and as the apostles in the New Testament. The other is mediate by man, and immediate by God, as Joshua in the Old Testament was called by Moses to be governor to the people, at the commandment of God. And as Timothy and Titus were called by St. Paul to be bishops; and as all they which now are called to bishops, which are lawfully made, according to the word of God, and authority of the magistrates. Therefore, for the knowledge of every man's vocation, I remit him to the word of God, and his own conscience, which are his inward and most sure judges.

[*] Christ is the head and foundation of our felicity, upon whom we should build good works, Col. iv.—Ed. 1584.

There is a general vocation, by which we are called by Christ and his word, to a christian religion, through the which we are made one body and one spirit; even as we are called in one hope of our vocation. For, that charity is required of us by the word of God which maketh and bringeth us together in one body, through mutual conjunction of faith, working by charity; therefore charity is called the band of peace. There is but one fellowship of all the faithful, and one body; that is, one church, whose only head is Christ. In this church there neither is, nor should be, any division; for there is in this vocation and christian religion but one body, one faith, one baptism, which is the seal of our religion, marked by God with the blood of his only begotten Son, Christ Jesus our Lord, in whose blood we are baptized; one God and one Father of all, which is upon all, and by all, and in us all. And therefore the apostle testifieth all to be but one body, that is, one church in Christ, 1 Cor. xiii. Eph. iv. v. For into one Spirit, and by one Spirit, the whole universal congregation is governed, ruled, strengthened, and kept. There is but one mark or end, which all the faithful contend or shoot at, that is, eternal life. We are all the sons of one Father, and participant of one heritage, as we are called in one hope of our vocation.

And, seeing we have but one Lord, which is Jesus Christ; it is convenient that his servants be of one mind, and not divided through discord and envy. There is but one profession of faith in all this christian religion and vocation; for howbeit we see in these our days many sundry professions and opinions of faith, there is but one true faith; which is that faith which the apostles of our Lord Jesus Christ, together with the patriarchs and prophets, have professed, and given to all nations through their teaching and preaching, as testify the holy scriptures.\* Upon the which foundation, the whole church of Christ is builded. Therefore, by one baptism, we are all made clean and purified, and by which we are ingrafted in Christ, and made the people of God, purified from our sins, and altogether buried with Christ. There is amongst us all but one power or strength of baptism; and in one name, of the Father, Son, and the Holy Spirit, we are baptized. And so are we made one body into Christ, being many members, compacted and joined together into him. For the more perfect

\* 1 Cor. iii. Eph. ii. Acts ix. xiv. and xx. Rom. v. 1 Cor. xii.

understanding of this body, ye shall read the whole of 1 Cor. xii. and Eph. iv. v. in which ye shall find this matter declared by the apostle at length.

In this general vocation there is no distinction of persons, for all men are equal before God, of one estate; by one general promise all are called to the faith, under our Lord and King, Jesus Christ, who hath shed his blood for all which believe in him. Therefore, all scriptures which make mention that there is no exception of persons before God, are referred to this general vocation in the christian religion, as Romans ii. where the apostle, under Jew and Gentile comprehending all men, intending to prove them sinners, saith, Before God there is no acception of persons. And Peter saith, In verity I have found that God is not an accepter of persons; but in all nations and people he is accepted unto him, which feareth him and worketh righteousness, Acts x. And St. James saith, My brethren have not the faith of our glorious Lord Jesus Christ in respect of persons, James ii. And St. Paul saith, to the confounding of the false apostles who seduced the Galatians through great authority, and also to show himself equal in power with James, Peter, and John, that God is not a respecter of the person of man; but in this vocation of christian religion by baptism, through faith in the blood of Christ, all men are equal, both Jew and Gentile, servant, free man and woman, all are one in Christ Jesus—the sons of Abraham by faith, and, according to the promise, heirs; that is to say, all which believe are the sons of God, therefore are they free, and heirs of eternal life. To this general vocation pertains the saying of St. Peter in these words, Ye are a chosen generation, a royal priesthood, a holy nation, and a people set at liberty; that ye should forthshow the virtues of Him that hath called you forth of darkness into a marvellous light, &c. The same is said by Moses, Exod. xix. Here ye see in this vocation there is no acception of persons. We are all the holy people of God who believe unfeignedly; yea, kings anointed in baptism by the Holy Spirit; and priests, making sacrifice to God daily of this our sinful body, mortified from sin, and offer a holy and acceptable sacrifice, after the manner above written, conformable to the teaching of the apostle, Rom. xii. But beware ye call not yourselves kings in office and dignity, nor priests in the administration of the word and holy sacraments; for that pertaineth to a special vocation, or office by itself.

Therefore, I exhort you which read the scriptures, take heed that ye confound not the works of God, for if ye do ye shall not escape error. These special vocations shall follow in their own places.

If we look daily to this christian vocation, we shall have perfect knowledge what works we should do, and what works we should leave undone. The neglecting hereof is the cause of all the enormities and abuses now ruling in the church or Christ through the whole world. For, considering we are all members of one body, and all members have not one office, but every one serveth other in their own place; as when the ears hear any thing, the eyes cast the sight to what it should be; then the feet and hands prepare them to pursue or defend, to stand or flee. And all these members and whole body obey the head, and wait upon the direction of the same. Even so, we being all members of one body, which is the church, whose head is Christ, should, in our estate and office, according to the gift of God, and grace given to us, differing one from another, serve, in our special vocation, every one another in our own estate, not envying the gift of God in our neighbour, but as the apostle saith, Let us love brotherly fellowship, in going before another in honour and reverence. In doing hereof, there would be no strife in the body; but if a member were troubled, hurt, or had any disease, all the other members would have compassion of it. And if one member were glad or joyful, all the other members would rejoice with the same, as the apostle saith, 1 Cor. xii. If we knew this perfectly, none would usurp another's office or dignity, to the which he were not called, but would be content of his own vocation, and give to every man his duty; tribute to whom tribute is due, custom to whom custom pertaineth, fear to whom fear belongeth, and honour to whom it pertaineth. The which are all complete by this saying, Love thy neighbour as thyself; for the love of thy neighbour worketh no evil. Therefore the apostle saith, Owe nothing to any man, but that ye love together, Rom. xiii. These words being observed, ye fulfil the whole law. Therefore this love, one to another, is ever a debt, and should ever be paid. For, if the prince and superior will do his duty to the subject, and the subject his duty to the superior, there would be no disobedience. The minister of the word to the auditor, and to the flock committed to his care; the auditor to the minister of the word, then there would be no division in the church. The father and mother to the children, and the children to the parents, then there would be no dishonouring. The lord to the servant, and the servant to the lord, then there would be no contempt nor trouble in the commonweal. And so would we all look upon Christ our head, and be ruled with his word, and seek no other way beside it, nor mix the civil or politic estate with the word of God, but every one to serve in their own room and place; then should there be no question of politic works, nor works of any other law to be mixed with faith, which justifieth only before God, as it is before written; but every faithful person should, by the word of God, know their own vocation, and diligently exercise them therein; and seek no farther knowledge nor wisdom, but that which is needful to them to know; and that with meekness and soberness, ever working the works of God, which are the fruits of faith, to the honour of God and profit of our neighbour.

## CHAPTER XXV.

*All estates of man are contained within one of four special vocations. The offices of princes, magistrates, and judges. Wherefore judges are called the sons of God; wherefore, and in what case they should be obeyed.*

To the more perfect knowledge and understanding of our special vocations in the which we should walk, according to the word of God, and gift of the Holy Spirit; we will divide all the estate of man in four offices, dignities, or special vocations; that is to say, in the office of a prince, under whom we comprehend all kinds of men having general administration in the commonweal, or jurisdiction of others. In the office of the administration of the word of God, under which we comprehend all ecclesiastical power. In the father and mother, under whom we will comprehend all householders, having special families. And in the subject or servant, under whom we will comprehend all states of men subject to others.

If thou art called to the office, estate, or dignity of a king, prince, or any supreme power, having jurisdiction of people in the civil ordinance, consider thy estate, and know thee perfectly to be the creature of God, equal to the poorest of thy kingdom or dominion, his brother by creation and natural succession of Adam, and of nature a rebel to God; the son of wrath and ire, as he was, as the apostle saith, Eph. ii. And the innocent blood of Christ, shed for thy redemption, as for him; and thou, called by faith, and born new by baptism in his blood, the son of God by adoption, and made fellow-heir with Christ of the kingdom of heaven, without respect of persons, the son of favour and grace. Therefore, the poorest and most vile within thy jurisdiction, is thy brother, whom thou shouldest not despise nor contemn, but love him as thyself. This is thy debt and duty, because it is the commandment of God, whom thou shouldest love and fear, for that is the beginning of wisdom, as Solomon saith, Prov. i. The right way to rule in thy office is to know God, of whom thou canst have no knowledge, but by his word and law, which teacheth thee what thou shouldest do, and leave undone, according to thy vocation.

And as to thy princely estate, and dignity, and office, thou art father to all thy kingdom, their head in the place of God, to rule, govern, and keep them; upon whom thou shouldest take no less care than the carnal father taketh upon his own best beloved son. For they are given by God to thee in government. Therefore thou shouldest begin to know the will of thy God, and take the book of his law in thy hand, to read upon it, which teacheth thee the will of God. It should never pass forth of thy heart, nor depart from thy mouth, day and night having thy meditation thereinto, that thou mayest keep all which is written therein; then shalt thou direct thy way, and have knowledge and understanding of the same, Deut. xvi. Josh. i. This being done, thou shalt get the blessing, of which David speaks, saying, Blessed is the man which delighteth in the law of the Lord, and hath his meditation thereinto day and night. Then ask of God wisdom and understanding, which is the knowledge of his godly will, and a heart that may receive teaching, that thou mayest judge thy people, and discern betwixt good and evil, as thou art taught by the example of Solomon, 1 Kings iii. For if thou lack wisdom, ask the same of God, who giveth abundantly. And doubt not, for he that doubteth in his faith shall obtain nothing from God, James i. Confide not in thy own wisdom, for God maketh wise men blind, who are wise in their own conceit; his witnessing is faithful which giveth wisdom to young babes, Psal. xix. that is, to simple hearts, bearing themselves lowly and humbly before God, not presuming in their own wisdom. For there is no place to wisdom in the proud breast, as is said in the Book of Wisdom. For God resisteth the proud, but to the meek and humble he giveth grace, 1 Peter v. The mighty and proud he casteth down off their seat, and exalteth the humble and lowly in heart, as testifieth the song of the glorious virgin Mary, Luke i. Therefore, humbly and lowly submit thyself in the hands of thy God, and take thought of him, being governed by his word. Begin at him, and set forth the true and perfect worshipping of God in thy kingdom. Restore the true, pure, and sincere christian religion; abolish, destroy, and put down all false worshippings and superstitions, contrary to the word of God, and not commanded therein; according to the example of the noble kings of Judah, Hezekiah and Josiah as thou mayest read, 2 Kings xviii. xxiii. This is thy vocation, in the which thou shouldest walk, and orderly proceed in guiding of thy people, as thou art taught by the word of God; and decline not therefrom, neither to the right hand nor to the left, but walk in the kingly way taught thee in the holy scriptures, Deut. xvii.

To you, which are princes, judges, and superior powers upon earth, pertain wisdom, knowledge, understanding, and learning, that ye may justly and truly exercise the office and charge committed to your care by God. Therefore David exhorts you, saying, Understand and know, O ye kings; and be learned, O ye which judge the earth. And serve the Lord in fear and reverence, and rejoice in him with trembling, Psal. ii. This is your wisdom and understanding taught you in the law of God, Deut. iv. For the godly man needeth not to seek wisdom, but in the scriptures of God, where he shall find how he shall behave him both to God and man, in prosperity and adversity, in peace and war. Therefore, to seek wisdom any other way, it is nothing but foolishness before God, 1 Cor. i. Since ye are the ministers of God unto good, created and ordained by him, (as the apostle saith, Rom. xiii.) it becometh you of your office to guide and rule your subjects in all goodness and sweetness; not seeking from them their lands or goods, but seek righteous judgment; help the oppressed; judge righteously the people and widows' cause; justify the needful, humble, and poor, as the scriptures of God teach you, Psal. lxxxii. Zech. vii. Isa. i. Defend them from the injuries, and oppressions of the wicked, and being unjustly pursued judgment absolve them. Take from them your duty, and no more; have no respect of persons, nor take any bribes or rewards, which blind the eyes of the wise, and pervert the words of the just. These two things, that is to say, respect of persons and rewards, pervert all righteous judgments. The first comprehends in it the fear and reverence of great, mighty, and rich men; love of friends, favour of kin or affinity, contempt of the poor, humble, and sober persons, mercy of the wicked and guilty, peril of thy own life, tinsel, or loss of fame, and loss of goods or worldly honours. The second, that is, rewards, comprehends in it lucre, profit, hope, and all that infinite and insatiate gulph of avarice. Therefore Jethro counselled Moses to provide, for administration of justice and good order in the civil policy, wise men which feared God, and were true, who hated and detested avarice, which is the root and beginning of all evil. And so learn, yea, above all things, to detest avarice, vain glory, and particular affection of persons, if ye will walk right in the christian religion, according to your vocation.

Your estate and office is great, and not to be contemned, but to be praised and commended of all men; of your subjects feared, reverenced, and also loved, because ye are as it were gods, and are so called in the scriptures, by reason of participation of the power of God, committed unto you, whose judgments ye exercise; and are called the sons of God; as David saith, I have said, Ye are gods, and sons of the Most Highest; that is, for the excellent dignity of your office, I have called you my sons. Nevertheless, know yourselves to be but men, and to suffer death as other men do, and in like manner as princes of earthly kingdoms, or tyrants, which have the ruling of commonwealths, as ye have. Therefore be just and righteous, exercising yourselves in all godliness, according to your vocation; being sure ye shall shortly die, and give account and reckoning of your administration. For ye are but flesh, and all flesh is but grass, and all the glory of the same, as it were the flower of the field; the grass is withered, and the flower falleth, but the word of God remaineth for ever, Isa. xl. 1 Peter i. James i. Therefore know Christ to be your king, ruler, guider, and governor, who shall rule you with an iron rod, and break you asunder, as it were a clay pot, or vessel of fragile earth. If ye will not understand the will and commandment of God, his ire and wrath shall rule above your head at all times. These sharp threatenings are shown you in the scriptures, Isa. i. Jer. v. David in

Psalms ii. lxxxii. and Zechariah vii. where ye are taught the chief points of your office, and works which ye are bound to do; for the neglecting of the which, being left undone, ye shall be accused before God. But never for neglecting of pilgrimages, offering to images, praying to saints, founding of masses and abbeys, of monks and friars; making of images, bells, copes, and other such vain superstitions; because the same are not commanded you to do, but rather the contrary. This dare I affirm, because God's word affirmeth the same.

Ye should be pure and clean of life, without crime, because ye are deputed by God, and ordained to the punishment of crimes. How can ye judge justly being corrupted? A thief shall never punish theft; an oppressor, manslayer, adulterer, a false liar, a dishonourer of father and mother, a disobeyer of his superior, a covetous or avaricious man, a blasphemer of the name of God, shall never punish these crimes in others. Therefore, the scriptures of God teach you to abstain from all such vices and crimes. For in you which are great men, and have the care of others, your crimes and sins are not so much to be lamented in you, as the evil example your subjects take thereof; and therethrough follow you in the same and other crimes, heaping sin upon sin, ever, till God of his righteous judgments take vengeance, yea, and cause another as wicked as ye are to punish you; as ye may read of the punishment of the people of Israel by the open enemies of God, and manifest idolaters, because they neglected the law of God, as the whole history of the kings and judges of Israel and Judah testifies.

And the greatest judgment is sent by God for doing of the most excellent work, after the judgment of man, because it was not commanded by God; for nothing from the beginning of the world hath ever been so displeasant in the sight of God as to invent any manner of worshipping of him which he hath not commanded. For this cause king Saul was ejected, and all his posterity lost and fell from the kingdom. In the which example ye shall consider, that the works wrought by king Saul were right excellent in the sight of man, and also done by him of a good intent, and for a good cause. He offered sacrifice for fear that the people should pass from him, he being prepared for battle against the enemies of God. He did show the deed of mercy in saving of the life of an aged and impotent king. And for the love he had to the worshipping of God, he assented to the people, and kept the fattest beasts, the most precious clothing, and jewels of gold and silver, to offer the same to God in a sacrifice. Was this not a good zeal and intention? But ye may read the great punishment which God laid upon him, which shall remain an example in all ages to come.

## CHAPTER XXVI.

*The office of a bishop. Bishops should not mix them with worldly matters. If the flock perish, their blood shall be required of the bishop. Bishops should exhort their flock to frequent the reading of the scriptures. Bishops can do no good works, without they preach the word of God. The punishment of bishops which leave that undone which God commandeth, and attend upon their own superstitions.*

If thou art called to the office of a bishop or minister of the word of God, preach the pure and sincere word to the flock committed to thy charge, counsel and comfort the weak and feeble, minister the sacraments in their due form, according to the word of God. Exceed not the bounds of thy vocation, but walk thereinto, conformably to the ordinance of the Holy Spirit, taught thee in the two epistles of St. Paul, written to the first bishop that he made, called Timothy, and to another called Titus—there thou shalt find the works which thou art bound to do, and what is thy office; specially in 1 Tim. iii. and Titus i. There is nothing left unexpressed, that is necessary for thee to work, in the scriptures of God. Thou art commanded to be a mirror, or example to thy flock, in teaching of the word, in good life, and honest conversation; in love and charity, in faith and chastity; ever exercising thyself in reading, exhorting, and teaching; the which if thou do, thou shalt save thyself and others, 1 Tim. iv.

Thou shalt not meddle thee with secular affairs or business, for that is not thy vocation, 2 Tim. ii. Follow the example of the apostles in all righteousness and godly living; in faith, love, patience, meekness, and sweetness, as thou art taught, 1 Tim. vi. If ye will remember daily upon the office ye are called to which are bishops, ye shall find you have a great charge and work to do, and not a great dignity or lordship. But, alas, now ye take thought of the lordship, dignity, rent, and profit, and look never to the work ye should do ; the cause thereof is, the neglecting of your vocation ; the which, if ye will understand perfectly, ye would not omit the charge and commandment given to you by God, and invent vain superstitious works, not commanded. The principal work ye should do is to preach and teach; which ye never do because ye cannot; and to excuse you, ye have, as ye say, others to whom ye commit the cause and charge. Ye are blind, and know nothing : they to whom ye commit the charge know as little or less. So the poor people perish in ignorance ; for ye are blind, and leaders of the blind, and therefore both fall into the mire. Nevertheless, the blood of them shall be required at your hands, as the prophet saith, Jer. xxiii. and Ezek. xxxiv. the which I pray you read ; for there ye shall see clearly your deeds laid before you, with sore threatenings.

Ye should not only yourselves continually read and teach the scriptures, but also ye should command the flock in your charge to seek their spiritual food in the same. This was the order in the church of Christ in the beginning ; the minister of the word to teach and preach, and the auditors to read, that thereby they might take the teaching the better ; as the Thessalonians did at the preaching of the apostle, as ye may read and consider in the Acts of the Apostles, xvii. And Christ teacheth us to search the scriptures, for they bear witness of him. And St. Paul saith, All things which are written, they are written to our learning, that through patience and consolation of scriptures, we may have hope, that is, of eternal life. The which is the mark whereat all the faithful shoot; for in the scriptures of God all things are contained necessary for our salvation, Alas ! think ye not shame, who are bound and obliged, under the pain of eternal damnation, to teach your flock this manner of doctrine, to inhibit and forbid them to look upon the scripture, either to hear or read them? This is far different from the order of the apostles, yea, and of the holy fathers of the church long time after, as appears clearly by the teaching of Chrysostom, writing upon Matthew i. where he, with a great lamentation, reproves the secular men and householders, who alleged that the reading and teaching of scriptures pertained not to them ; exhorting them to give attendance to the scriptures, that they might instruct their families and household, how they should live according to the order of the scripture, and as becometh christians. But by the contrary, ye would that none of your flock or auditors should know them, lest your misdeeds were espied.

The feeding of your flock, the attendance and care ye should take thereupon, is so necessary, that without the doing thereof ye can do no good works at all according to your vocation, which can please God; because in neglecting of this, ye neglect faith, out of which all good works should spring. So should all your good works follow faith. And this principal point of your vocation is the cause that St. Paul, departing from Ephesus to Jerusalem, called before him the ministers of the word in the congregation, certifying them, that he would not return again in bodily presence; and therefore he left to them this legacy, saying, Attend, and take heed unto yourselves, and to the whole flock, in the which the Holy Spirit hath put you as bishops to guide and rule the church of God, the which he hath redeemed with his blood. For I know, after my departing, there shall enter in amongst you ravening wolves, which shall not spare the flock. And of yourselves there shall rise men, speaking wickedness, that they may lead disciples to follow them. Therefore, be diligent and vigilant, keeping in memory that by the space of three years, I ceased not, day and night, with tears and weeping, warning and admonishing every one of you, &c.

If the apostle had known any better work or more excellent, to be left in memory or legacy to the ministers of the word, he would, no doubt, have expressed the same. And even so St. Peter, 1st Pet. v. exhorts you to feed the flock of Christ committed to your charge; even as Christ said to him thrice, Feed my sheep; so saith he to you, Feed the flock committed to you, every one within his bounds, according to your vocation. This food is the word of God, and wo be to you who do not the same, for it is your vocation. For the apostle saith, Wo be to me if I preach not the gospel, &c. 1 Cor. ix. For the neglecting of this good work undone, ye shall be accused before God, but not for the neglecting of the other vain superstitious works invented by man; but rather ye will be accused for the doing of them. And it will be said unto you, Wherefore have ye left the command of God undone for your statutes and traditions?

Ye should teach every estate of man, how they should behave them in their conversation; the poor to the rich, and the rich to the poor; the servant to the master, and the master to his servant. And give yourselves forth for an example in deed, to be followed, as ye are taught by the apostle; and play not the tyrant or the lord upon the inferior ministers and estates of the church; 1 Tim. vi. Titus i. but, from the bottom of your heart, be as it were a form or rule to the flock, as St. Peter teacheth you in the 1st Pet. v. Labour continually in your vocation, as the good knights of Christ, being ready, if need require, to suffer death for the flock; resisting the unfaithful, and eschewing profane and worldly trifles, as ye are taught by the apostle, 2 Tim. ii. If ye will attend upon these works, which are good, taught and commanded you to do, as the fruits of faith, ye should find yourselves so well occupied in the scripture, that there shall be no place found to your vain superstitions above written, which are not commanded by God or his word. For in the using of them, ye do that which is not commanded you, and leave that undone which is commanded. For this cause God suffereth you to be contemned and cast off, Mal. ii. Because ye have left him, he hath left you, and will punish you after the same manner as ye have sinned. For the contempt of God, and neglecting of his word, Eli the chief priest was deposed, and all his posterity, of the priesthood; his sons killed in battle; the ark of God put in the hands of his enemies; and the people also heavily tormented, as the history testifies. The holy king David, for the slaughter of Uriah, and adultery of Bathsheba, suffered much, as ye may read the 2nd book of Samuel, the xiii. xv. xvi. and xviii. chapters. This example of David pertains as well to you as to princes, and to all estates of the world, that they may learn not to sin. And, if they fall in sin, that they despair not, but turn to repentance, and come unto God, whose will is that all be safe, and come to the knowledge of the verity.

## CHAPTER XXVII.

*The office of the fathers to the sons; householders to their families; and of husbands to their wives. What kind of men were chosen to be bishops in the primitive church.*

IF thou art a householder, rule and guide thy family and household; bring up thy children in all godliness and honesty, exercising thyself in thy occupation faithfully and truly, without deceit or fraud to thy neighbour, either in word or deed. Love thy wife, even as Christ hath loved the church, for thou art debt-bound to love thy wife, even as thine own body, Eph. v. Col. iii. There is no man which hateth or detesteth his own body, but nourisheth and feedeth the same, as Christ the church. For we are members of his body, of his flesh, and of his bones; for that cause man shall leave father and mother, and cleave unto his wife, and they shall be two in one flesh, 1 Pet. iii. And, in like manner, thou woman, be subject to thy husband, as if it were to the Lord; for the man is thy head, even as Christ is the head of the congregation. And, as the church is subject to Christ, even so be thou subject to thy husband, in all lawful things. This is your vocation, in the which ye should walk, according to the commandment given to you by the apostle, Eph. v. and Col. iii. in these words, Let every man love his wife as himself, and let the woman fear and dread the husband: this is the commandment of God.

If ye, men and women, would take care upon your vocation, how honourable the estate of the same is, and what ye ought to do every one unto another, there were none of you who would commit adultery, nor abstract one from another that mutual love which ye are commanded to have together, Col. iii. 1 Pet. iii. This doing, ye exercise the good work of God. Be not outrageous nor froward upon the woman, but teach her with meekness and sweetness, forbearing her somewhat, as the weakest vessel. And thou, woman, pretend no dominion upon thy husband, but obey him as thy lord, taking example of the obedience of that noble woman Sarah. If ye would keep this order and rule in your own vocation, there would be no strife betwixt you, but all godliness and love. No man would contemn or disdain his wife, nor any woman her husband; but every one love other, as their own body, and take care one for another in all things.

Thou, man, shouldest daily and hourly exercise thee according to thy vocation; and labour diligently for sustentation of thy wife, children, and family; that thou mayest minister unto them their necessities; for if a man take no thought of his own, and specially of his household and family, he hath denied the faith, and is worse than an infidel, 1 Tim. v. Suffer not thy children or servants to be idle, but see ever that they are employed in some good and virtuous occupation. For that is the right way to keep them from vice and sin, because idleness is the beginning of all evil. Teach them the law of God, use all things with discretion, and provoke not your children to anger, but bring them up i good teaching, discipline, and correction, and in the erudition of the Lord. Give unto your servants that which is just and right: what ye promise, pay them, knowing well that ye have a Lord in heaven, Col. iii. iv. Eph. vi.

And thou, woman, exercise thee in nourishing and upbringing of thy children; in ruling all things within thy house, as thou hast commandment of thy husband, take care upon his direction, as thy head, and transgress not his commandment, for that is the will of God. I mean not of evil, but of all goodness; because I speak of the fruits of faith, and works of righteousness. Ye are all bound to do the works which God hath commanded you to do, in his holy scripture, of mercy, love, and charity, by reason of your vocation in the christian religion; and these other works in your special vocation. In doing which, think that ye do the good work of God, and please him, if ye work them in faith, albeit hypocrites commend not the same. Being occupied on this manner daily, there shall be no place to vice, for your mind is occupied upon other business.

It is but idleness to you, to pass in pilgrimage to this or that saint, to sit the half of the day in the church, babbling upon a pair of beads, speaking to stocks or stones, the thing which neither thou nor they know; and neglecting the good work of God, the which thou art bound to do. If thou wilt pray right, learn the Lord's prayer in the tongue thou understandest; thy creed, that is, the articles of thy belief; the ten commandments of God. And daily at thy rising and downlying at night, have some space to thy contemplation thereinto, and teach thy household the same manner. And occupy the rest, as is before said, according to thy vocation, not exceeding the bounds thereof, nor seeking any other works but those which are commanded in the holy scriptures, and are necessary to be done; as is written to Titus. Let the faithful which are of our number be ever ready, and learn to do good works to all necessary uses, that they be not unfruitful, Tit. iii. For the faithful can never be idle, because unfeigned faith worketh ever by charity. But they which know not their own vocation, can never be faithful, Rom. xiv. Therefore they can never work good works, but all is evil, whatsoever thing they do, or work without faith; because all which is not of faith is sin. Therefore, if thou wilt work well, be faithful, and look ever to thy vocation; and thou shalt find thy conscience teaching thee both to do good, and eschew evil, at all times.

Ye should be pure and clean in your conversation, for

good example giving to your children and family. For as they see you do, so shall they learn; and are ever rather inclined to do evil than good, by reason of this corrupted nature of man. Therefore, teach them to love and fear God, to know his law, being ever yourselves an example to them, and, as it were, a mirror to look into, in all godly life and conversation. For if they behold you living together in great love and charity, chastity and temperance; being merciful to the poor; supporting the indigent after the quantity of your riches; at love and charity with your neighbour; ever speaking good of all creatures, detracting none, they shall follow the same doings; by the which ye shall be called the faithful fellowship of Jesus Christ, and true subjects of his realm. Your vocation is good and holy, and it becometh you to know the scriptures; for in the primitive church, the bishops were chosen commonly forth of your number. A godly and honest householder, who lived in chaste matrimony, ruled and guided his household well, brought up his children in subjection and reverence, in all manner of godly teachings. He, having this outward witnessing, is commanded by the apostle to be chosen to the office of a bishop, 1 Tim. iii. When this order was kept in the church of Christ, the word of God flourished.

Therefore, wo be to you which say, that laics, or secular men and householders, should not know the scriptures, read them, or teach their household the same. Ye impugn the Holy Spirit, and dishonour the old fathers of the church, who taught the contrary; as by example of Chrysostom before rehearsed. It is even alike to you to say that temporal or secular men should not hear the word of God, read, and teach their families the same, as to say they have not a soul; and if ye will abstract the food, without which the soul must perish, ye shall make man as a brutish beast, Deut. viii. Matt. iv. And, if ye will admit them to hear the word, ye should admit them to read the same, and talk thereupon; for what availeth the hearing, if a man should not conceive, and keep in memory that which he heareth, and live thereafter. For Christ saith, Blessed are they which hear the word of God, and keep the same. The oft reading of the word, and communication thereof, keepeth the same ever recent in memory; and digesteth in thy heart, by continual meditation, some comfort and consolation; and abstracteth thee from vice and sin, leadeth and convoyeth thee to all godly living. Therefore

David calleth that man blessed, which delighteth in the law of God, and hath his meditation therein day and night.

Wo, wo, be unto you therefore, who would abstract this blessing from any man or woman, the which God pronounceth with his mouth. These doings of yours bear witness of you, that ye are not the ministers of the word of God, or true successors of the apostles; but false teachers, subverters of the word, and very antichrist. Wherefore, I exhort you who are the faithful, whatsoever estate or vocation ye be called to, that ye both gladly hear the word of God, read it, teach your children, family, and subjects the same; and conform your life thereto, ever working the deeds of charity and mercy in all godliness, according to your vocation; and give no credit to them which teach you the contrary, for they are false teachers and members of the devil, who withdraw you from that which is your salvation.

## CHAPTER XXVIII.
*The duty of the master unto the servant, and the contrary. Of the subject to the prince. Of the son to the father. The honour which the sons ought to give the parents. The devilish doctrine of pestilent papistical priests, in the contrary thereof.*

IF thou art a subject, servant, son, or daughter, be obedient to thy superior: first unto thy prince, as the supreme power, and to every one having power from him, for they are the ministers of God, whom thou shouldest obey and not resist, ordained by God to the revenge of evil doers, and loving of the good doers; which is the will of God, as ye are taught, Rom. xiii. and 1 Pet. ii. Your duty is, to honour all men, love brotherly fellowship, fear God, and honour the king; to be obedient to him, not only for fear and dread of his ire, but also for hurting of your conscience, because it is the will of God, in all things not repugning to his command. Give to thy prince and superior his duty; or whatever he chargeth thee with concerning temporal riches, inquire not the cause, for that pertaineth not to thy vocation. He is thy head, whom thou shouldest obey; transgress not his laws. Be not a revenger of thine own cause, for that is as much as to usurp his office. So thou walkest not aright in thy vocation. Look not to his faults or vices, but to thy own; disobey him not; howbeit he be evil, and doeth thee wrong, which becometh him not of his office, grudge not thereat, but pray for him, and commit thy cause to God. Be not a perturber of the commonweal, but live with thy neighbour at rest and quietness, every one supporting others, as members of one body; forgiving gladly and freely one another, if there be any complaint amongst you, even as the Lord hath forgiven you. Be sweet, meek, benign, humble, and patient one with another, as becometh the saints and well beloved of God, having compassion one of another. Above all these have love and charity, which is the bond of perfection. For charity coupleth together many members in one body. This are ye taught by the apostle, Col. iii. and in other places before rehearsed.

Here ye find abundance of works commanded you by God to do, and ye need to seek no others. There is none which can work these good works but the faithful; from doing of which, the faithful and justified man cannot cease; but ever worketh as he findeth occasion, according to his vocation: he looketh ever to his own faults and sins, and not to his neighbours. But if he perceive any fault or vice in his neighbour, he laments the same, and considers greater vices to be in himself; and therefore he hath compassion of his neighbour, and neither blasphemes, backbites, nor dishonours him; but counsels and comforts him, as his own body, of brotherly love and affection.

Ye children, obey your parents with great humility; love, fear, and honour them; for that is the command of God, and the first which hath promise, as concerning thy neighbour, that it may be well to thee, and that thou live long upon earth. This obedience and honour consists not in words only, nor in salutations, but also in ministering all things necessary unto them; remembering, as they ministered unto you in your tender, feeble, and poor youth, even so do ye to them in their tender, impotent, and poor age. Neglecting this good work undone, ye can do no good work that can please God. There is no colour of godliness which may excuse you from this good work. Howbeit your wicked and ungodly pastors have taught you to found a soul mass with your substance, and to suffer father and mother to beg their bread. This is a devilish doctrine, to convert the good work of God into idolatry. The scribes and pharisees, their forefathers, taught the same, as testify the words of Christ.

Ye servants, obey your carnal lords and masters, with fear and trembling, with simpleness of heart, as it were unto Christ; not in eyeservice, as it were to please men, but as servants of Christ; doing the will of God, not only to them which are good, and well instructed in manners, but also to the wicked and evil. Whatever ye do, work the same with your heart, as it were to the Lord, and not to man, knowing surely ye shall receive from the Lord the reward of the heritage; therefore, serve the Lord Jesus Christ. Be not flatterers nor liars, backbiters nor detracters; serve not your masters only in their presence, but also in their absence, without deceit or dissimulation. Take thought of the things given you in charge, and obey their will, even as to God, who looketh upon your inward minds. Pretend not to be equal with your lord or master, because ye are both of one christian religion, but serve him the better. Have love and charity with your equal fellow servants, all as members of one body, exercising you in all good works, according to your vocation in the christian religion.

Now ye see that we which profess the true faith of Jesus Christ, and ascribe the justification of man before God, only to faith, without any works, merits, or deservings on our part, are not the destroyers of good works, but the maintainers, defenders, and forthsetters of the same, as the fruits of faith; as I have before at length showed.

Therefore, I exhort you which blaspheme us, saying, we would destroy all good works, because we affirm with the scriptures of God, faith only to justify before God, to re-mord\* your conscience; and read the scriptures with an humble heart and spirit, which shall teach you the right way, by the grace of the Holy Spirit, who will lead you in all verity. And then I doubt not but ye shall agree with us, and contemn and despise the vain superstitious works, not commanded in the scripture, but invented of man's vain conceit, as we do; and altogether, as it becometh the faithful members of Jesus Christ, work the works of God, which are commanded us in his holy scriptures; every one according to his vocation, proceeding of love, forth of a clean and pure heart, of a good conscience, and of faith unfeigned, which worketh by charity, to the profit of thy neighbour, and glory of God. To whom be all praise, honour, and glory, for ever and ever. Amen.

### TO THE READER.

IF it please thee, good reader, of these pleasant flowers, amongst the which thou hast walked at large, again to take a taste or smelling; thou shalt read these short abbreviations subsequent. Exhorting thee, that where any obscu-

\* To excite to remorse.

rity appears, thou make recourse unto the preceding places, where every thing is manifestly expressed. Thou shalt do well, if earnestly thou shalt pray that Lord only, to whom the harvest pertaineth, that it would please him to send true workmen thereto; to the manifestation of his own glory before his congregation, by Jesus Christ; whose omnipotent Spirit satiate the hearts of them which thirst after righteousness. Amen.

## A BRIEF SUMMARY OF THIS BOOK.

Ch. I.—Our whole study should be to adhere unto God; running to him in the time of tribulation, as doth the wild hart in the burning heat to the cold river, with sure hope of deliverance by him alone; not inquiring his name, that is, the manner how he shall deliver us.

Ch. II.—By faith have we knowledge of God, whom we should seek in his scriptures, and receive him, as he is offered to us thereinto; that is, a Defender, Protector, Refuge, and Father, inquiring no further speculation of him. For to Philip, desiring to see the Father, Christ answered, Whoso hath seen me, hath seen the Father. Meaning that the love, goodness, and mercy, which God the Father beareth unto mankind, he had expressed in doctrine and works; and also should show a most singular token of love, giving his own life for his enemies. And therefore would all men come to him, to whom the Father hath given all power.

Ch. III.—Tribulations are profitable to the faithful, for thereby the strength of the flesh somewhat is dantoned,* and ceases to rebel against the spirit; and beginneth to seek God, who is a peculiar Father to the faithful, delivering them from all tribulations, not for their worthiness, but for his own mercy. Worldly tribulations are the signs and tokens of God's love; albeit the wicked and unfaithful judge otherwise, who in time of tribulation run from God, seeking help of man, which is but vain, whereof they, being frustrate and deceived, fall into desperation.

Ch. IV.—The faithful thank God in tribulation; and, albeit our wicked nature teacheth us to fly from God, as did our first parent Adam, after his transgression; yet faith in Jesus Christ leadeth us to the throne of our Father's grace, where we find goodness, mercy, and justice, given to us freely by Jesus Christ, as they were given to Adam; who, albeit he fled from God, yet He, moved of love toward his own handiwork, followed him. And albeit Adam, at the voice of God, repented not, but obstinately excused his sin, yet God made to him the promise of salvation, before he pronounced his wrath against sin, which of his righteous judgment he must punish. And so Adam wrought nothing which might move God to make this promise, more than he wrought that of dust and clay, he should be made a living creature, to the image and similitude of God. And to Abraham, being an idolater, was the promise made, that he should be the father of many nations, which he merited not, to which promise Abraham giving credit, was reckoned just. By the which it is plain that the mercy of God, and not our works, is the cause that he calleth us by his word, whereto we giving credit are reckoned just, all our deservings or merits being excluded.

Ch. V.—Adam, expelled forth of paradise, had no consolation, except in the blessed Seed promised; by whom he believed himself to stand

* Weakened, damned.

in God's favour; for all bodily consolation which he had of his two sons, was turned into dolour when Cain killed Abel. In which dolour Adam many years remained, till God, having compassion upon him, gave him another son named Seth, of whom descended the blessed Seed. For this son, Adam gave thanks unto God, taking all afflictions in patience, knowing himself worthy of greater punishment. By whose example, we should patiently, with thanksgiving unto God, suffer all tribulation. For none descending of Adam by natural propagation, are juster than he was after his fall, who all his life suffered trouble, having no comfort, but that he should overcome all worldly calamity, yea, and also the sleights of Satan, which had deceived him, by the blessed Seed promised. And this same should be our comfort in all tribulations.

Ch. VI.—By bodily afflictions our faith is tried, as gold by the fire. They are also a communion with the sufferings of Jesus Christ. And, therefore, in them have we matter and cause to rejoice, considering we suffer without cause, committed against man. Notwithstanding, the wicked persecute the faithful in all ages, as if they had been mischievous or evil doers; as may be seen in the persecution of the prophets, apostles, and of Jesus Christ himself. The cause hereof is the neglecting of God's word, and taking from faith her due office, whereof riseth all dishonouring of God; for none may or can honour God, except the justified man. And albeit in divers men there are divers opinions of justification, yet they alone, in whom the Holy Spirit worketh true faith, which never wanteth good works, are just before God. The substance of justification is, to cleave fast unto God, by Jesus Christ, and not by ourselves, nor yet by our works. And this article of justification should be holden in recent memory, because without the knowledge thereof, no works are pleasant before God.

Ch. VII.—As by persuasion of Satan, Adam and Eve, seeking wisdom against God's commandment, were deceived, and fell in extreme misery; so they, seeking justification otherwise than the scriptures teach, remain under the wrath of God. For faith alone reconcileth man to God, which the law, whose office is only to utter sin, and trouble the conscience, as it did to Adam after his transgression, may not do. Therefore, whoso desireth to resist Satan, let him cleave to faith, for it is the only shield which his darts may not pierce.

Ch. VIII.—Cain, a wicked hypocrite, killed his brother Abel, for no other cause but that his brother's sacrifice pleased God because it was offered in faith. And the posterity of Cain pursued perpetually those who depended upon the blessed Seed. While God was compelled to drown the whole world, eight persons being reserved, amongst whom yet was kept the seed of Satan in the third son of Noah, Ham. From the days of Noah to Abraham, this article of justification altogether was obscured, idolatry spreading over all. The cause thereof was, they followed the external works of the holy fathers in sacrifice, but had no respect to faith, without which all sacrifices are idolatry.

Ch. IX.—God, of his mercy, providing that his church should not perish altogether, renewed to Abraham the promise of the blessed Seed, made to Adam; whereto Abraham giving credit, is, without his works, reckoned just. But shortly after, Satan began newly to pursue the just by his members, stirring up Ishmael against Isaac, Esau against Jacob. But the just, at the end, shall prevail, as Jesus Christ hath done, whose brethren we are, by reason that he is very man of the seed of Adam; and also because in him we are adopted and made the sons of God. The fleshly man is ever deceived, judging the wicked to be the chosen, as Abraham believed Ishmael, and Isaac believed Esau, to have been their heirs. But faith judged righteously, which caused Rebekah to labour with diligence, that Jacob the youngest son should be blessed by his father.

Ch. X.—The Jews, having a carnal opinion of the promised Seed, that their Messias should rule temporally as David did, refused Jesus Christ, appearing simple and poor. But the cause which moved Satan to stir up his members against Christ was, that he plainly taught, that by faith, without all works, man is reckoned just. For the wicked, thinking to make their foolish works a part of their justification, may never suffer them to be condemned. And the true preacher can never but exclude them from the justification of man; as did the prophets, Jesus Christ himself, and his apostles, for which they suffered death; leaving to us a sure testimony for confirmation of this article, which after Christ's death was plainly preached.

Ch. XI.—Satan, perceiving that his crafts, wherewith he deceived mankind, were discovered, and his head trodden down by the death of Christ, clad himself in a new arrayment; and, finding those idle who should have truly preached, persuaded man to invent new works, by which they should seek justification, neglecting true faith. Which pestilent works have so abolished the effect of perfect faith, that they which are called bishops understand nothing thereof, but pursue all those who truly preach or defend the same; by which they show themselves to be the church malignant. For the chosen never pursue, but ever are pursued.

Ch. XII.—Justice, in general, is an outward obedience or honesty, which a man may perform of his own power: and is divided in the justice of man, that is, which cometh of the law which man maketh; and in the justice of the law of God. The justice of man is divided into politic and ceremonial. Politic justice is, an obedience which the inferior estates give to their superior; which should be kept, because it is the command of God that princes be obeyed. Ceremonial justice is, observing of statutes and traditions commanded by the bishops of Rome, councils, or schoolmasters; which are to be kept, so that they repugn not to the law of God, nor yet that by them men seek remission of sins. The justice of the law of God is, to fulfil the same as it requireth; that is, to love, fear, serve, and honour God, with all thy heart, and strength thereof. Which because no creature in earth doeth, there is no man justified by the works of the law; for in all men, Jesus Christ excepted, is found sin; as the examples of Abraham, Moses, Noah, and other most holy fathers prove, in all of whom sin was found. For, by the transgression of Adam, all his posterity became rebels to the law, and are compelled to pray with David, Enter not into judgment with thy servant, O Lord; for in thy sight no living creature shall be found just.

Ch. XIII.—Seeing then our forefathers were not just by the law, nor works thereof, of necessity must we seek the justice of another, that is, of Jesus Christ, which the law may not accuse. In whom if we believe, we are received into the favour of God, accepted as just without our merits or deserving. But here object the wicked (as their use is when anything transcends their capacity in understanding) these questions. First. Wherefore gave God the law, if man may not fulfil the same? Second. Wherefore should we work good works, seeing by them we are not made just? Third. Whereby were the fathers made just?

Ch. XIV.—For understanding of the first question—Man should learn to know God as he is declared in the scriptures; That is, to know him Creator and Maker of all; who also made all his creatures, in their first creation, good and perfect; who not only gave a law to man, but also to the rest of his creatures; as to beasts, sun, moon, sea, and elements; that thereby he might be glorified and known to be Lord. And so to man he gave a law to the effect he should know his Maker and obey him; which law when Adam transgressed, he lost his perfection and righteousness. And so the cause why man may not fulfil the law is, that the law remaineth in its own perfection, in which it was first created by God. But man, by his disobedience and foolishness fell from his perfection; and therefore he should accuse himself and not God, that he may not fulfil the law which is perfect.

Ch. XV.—In Adam, after his transgression, remained a little of that knowledge and power, with which he was endued by God, and from him it descended in his posterity; whereby man may work the outward works of the law; but the whole obedience thereto no man giveth. For these words prove all men (Jesus Christ excepted) to be sinners by the law. Of the deeds of the law shall no flesh be justified before God. Which words sophists would abolish, saying, Paul speaketh of the ceremonial law, and not of the moral or law of nature. But the plain words of Paul prove them to be liars. He saith, The law speaketh to all which are under the law. And all men are under the moral law; and therefore Paul speaketh of the moral law, which condemneth all men, Jesus Christ excepted.

Ch. XVI.—The justice which is acceptable before God hath divers names. First, it is called the justice of God, because it proceedeth only of the mercy of God. Secondly, it is called the justice of faith, because faith is the instrument whereby we apprehend the mercy of God. And last, it is called justice, because by faith in Christ, it is given us freely without our deservings; but even as the dry earth receiveth the rain without all deservings of the self, so receive we the justice which is of value before God, without all our works. But yet we must suffer God to work in us. And this justice is plainly revealed in the gospel, from faith to faith, that is, we should continue in this faith all our life. For the just live by faith, ever trusting to obtain that which is promised, which is eternal life, promised to us by Jesus Christ.

Ch. XVII.—The faith of the fathers, before Christ's coming in the flesh, and ours in the New Testament, was and is one thing. For they believed themselves to stand in the favour of God, by reason of that promised Seed which was to come, who we believe is come already, and hath fulfilled all which was spoken of him in the law and the prophets. By this faith were the fathers made safe, without all their works, as Peter testifies. And where our adversaries ask, What availed works? we answer, that works are an outward testimony to faith, by which only man is first made just, and thereafter his works please God, because the person is acceptable. And so, no godly man forbiddeth good works; but of necessity must they be excluded from the justification of man; for Paul saith, If justice be of the law, Christ's death is in vain. For albeit justice sometimes is ascribed to man, that is not because it proceedeth of man, but because it is given to man freely by God. Like as our faith is called the faith of Jesus Christ, because by him we are reputed just; for he is made to us from God, wisdom, justice, holiness, and redemption. And so all the scripture testifieth us to be made just, sely, by the mercy of God, that all glory may be given to him. And therefore, whoever make works a part of their own justification, spoil God of his glory.

Ch. XVIII.—God loveth us because we are his own handiwork, created unto good works in Christ Jesus; in whom we remain as branches in the vine root, bringing forth good fruits, not of our own strength, but of the power of the Spirit of Jesus Christ, remaining in us by true faith; which works the law may not condemn, because they are the works of Jesus Christ, and not ours. And so the glory of works is excluded by the law of faith. For in our justification, we only receive, as did our father Abraham, (whose sons we are by faith,) who was reckoned just before he wrought any good works. The verity of the scripture proveth that the heritage cometh not by the law: for by the law Ishmael and Esau, the eldest sons, should have succeeded to the heritage, and not Isaac and Jacob, who were younger. And so, by the promise cometh the heritage, and not by the law; for the law ever accuseth, and craveth more of us than we are able to pay. And therefore, damnation abideth us, without we apprehend Jesus Christ, who payeth for us that which the law requireth. For he alone taketh away the sins of the world. He calleth all to himself, and sendeth none to the law to seek justification; and therefore, whoso seek any part thereof by their works, spoil Christ of his office.

Ch. XIX.—As the good tree beareth good fruits, so the just man worketh good works; but neither does the fruit make the tree good, nor yet the works the man just. For as the tree is before the fruit, so the man is just before the work is good. We should work good works, because, we, being sometime the sons of God's wrath, and subjects to Satan, are bought by the blood of Jesus Christ to serve in his kingdom. In the which rule, are faith, hope, and charity, ever working righteousness unto life. By the contrary, in the kingdom of the devil rule incredulity, despair, and envy, ever working unrighteousness. And so we owe obedience to him, whose servants we are. There are divers princes, realms, subjects, and rewards, no man can serve both, and of both the rewards no man shall be participant. But whoso serveth sin, receiveth eternal death for his reward; and whoso serveth righteousness, receiveth life everlasting by Jesus Christ.

Ch. XX.—Works are commended in the scripture; not that they justify before God, but that they are the fruits of a justified man, wrought to testify his true faith; which only justifieth, without works either preceding or following the same. And that proveth Paul, saying, Without faith it is impossible to please God: and also, All which is not of faith is sin. Whereof it is plain, that sophists alleging that works preceding faith deserve the grace of God from congruity, say as much as, Sin deserveth the grace of God. For all works preceding faith, are sin. And that works following faith justify not, testifieth the same apostle, saying, Not of the works of righteousness which we have wrought, shall we be safe, but according to his mercy God hath made us safe. And so neither works preceding nor following faith justify.

Ch. XXI.—The wicked, by works of their own invention, would be a part of their own salvation, because they seek their own glory, as did the scribes and pharisees, and not the glory of God. But, seeing the works commanded by God, done without faith, to deserve remission of sins, are abomination before God, as Isaiah testifieth; what shall be of the vain works of man, set up without the command of God, by which hypocrites would be made just? And if we should confess, as Jesus Christ commandeth, when we have done all, yet that we are but unprofitable servants, where is the merits of works of supererogation, which hypocrites would sell to others? And if Paul, who had right excellent works, esteemed them all to be but filthiness, that he might win Christ, and be found in him, not having his own justice, which is of the law, but the justice which is of the faith of Jesus Christ; if Paul, I say, sought no justice in his own works; how shall we, whose works are in no manner equal to the works of Paul, be justified thereby? And therefore, with the scriptures and apostles, we conclude, that by faith only in Christ, we are made just, without all law or works. And after man is made just by faith, and possesseth Jesus Christ in his heart, then can he not be idle. For with true faith is also given the Holy Spirit, who suffereth not man to be idle, but moveth him to all godly exercise of good works.

Ch. XXII.—After the article of justification, christians should be instructed to do good works; not these which are invented by man, but which are commanded by God; amongst which the principal is, to rejoice in tribulation, giving thanks to God in all things, with sure hope and patience, abiding his deliverance; knowing that the life of man is a perpetual battle upon earth; the law of the members ever rebelling against the law of the mind. The law of the members we call the tyranny of the devil, ever drawing us to the lusts of the flesh, not only in external works, but also in the inward affections of the mind: as, to doubt of the goodness and mercy of God, to be slothful, and not to love and fear him with our whole heart. The law of the mind, or of the spirit is, the motion of the Holy Ghost, stirring us up to all justice and righteousness; which we know to be good, and yet find no power in ourselves to perform the same. And this battle is most vehement in the most holy, as Paul witnesseth. And therefore, to kill this outward man, which is our wisdom, reason, and will, we should offer our bodies unto God in a quick, lively, and holy sacrifice. But before this sacrifice is pleasant to God, must the mind, which is the fountain of all good works, be renewed with the Spirit of God, and made clean; which is, when we cast from us our wisdom, righteousness, holiness, and redemption, and receive the same from Jesus Christ. Some there are who put their whole trust in their own works, thinking thereby to obtain eternal glory. And these men go before Christ, and are called antichrists. Others there are, who think faith not sufficient, but will have their works joined to help Christ, and these go astray from him. For none of these two kinds did Jesus Christ suffer death; but for those only who follow him, laying all their sins upon him.

Ch. XXIII.—The foolish reason of man persuades us to leave the works commanded by God; and to set up works of our own invention, thinking God to be pleased therewith, because they are done of good zeal and intention. The scriptures of God show all the thoughts and cogitations of man to be evil at all times. And if so be, what is our good intention? But whether the intent of man be good or not, the fruits proceeding therefrom shall testify. For, as sometime in Israel all idolatry abounded, they having gods according to the multitude of their cities, so now, amongst those who are called christians, carved images are set up, defended, adorned, and worshipped, against the express commandment of God. The blessed sacrament of Christ's body and blood is abused and profaned before them. And all this, and much more abomination proceeds from that zeal, which we call good. But how good soever it appear in our sight, the adherers thereto shall receive the malediction of God.

Ch. XXIV.—No better works can there be, than John the Baptist taught to the people, which are the works of mercy, and to desist from fraud, injury, and oppression. And these works, and not the vain inventions of man, pastors should teach their flocks, instructing them first in perfect faith. For Jesus Christ, being asked by the Jews, what they should do that they might work the works of God, that is, that they might please God, answered, This is the work of God, that ye believe in Him whom he hath sent. By the which words our Master understandeth, that without faith, which is the work of God, and not of man, no work pleaseth God.

The yoke of Christ is easy, and his burden is light to the faithful, because they lay all their sins upon Christ's back, and follow him, every man in his own vocation. There are two manner of vocations, one immediate by God, as the prophets and apostles were called to be preachers without authority of man. The other is, mediate, or when one man called another; as Paul called Timothy and Titus to be bishops. There is a general vocation, by which all the chosen are called to a christian religion, having one Lord, one faith, one baptism. In this vocation there is no difference of persons, but all are equally loved by God; because we are all the sons of one Father, and all bought with one price; all servants to one Lord, all guided with one Spirit, all tending to one end, and all shall be participant of one heritage; that is, the life eternal of Jesus Christ, by whom we are all made priests and kings. But let no man therefore usurp the authority of a king in dignity, nor the office of a priest in administration of God's word and sacraments; for that pertaineth to a special vocation.

Ch. XXV.—All estates of man are contained within one of these four special vocations; either is he prince or subject, pastor or one of the flock, father or son, lord or servant. In the prince is contained all magistrates having jurisdiction in a commonweal; whose duty is, First. To know God, and his law, which hath placed them in that authority; Second. To guide, feed, and defend their subjects; knowing themselves to be no better of their nature than the poorest in their realm; Third. To defend the just, and punish the wicked, without respect of persons, having their hearts and eyes clean and pure from all avarice. They are called the sons of God, and should be obeyed in all things not repugning to the command of God; because they are ordained and placed by God to punish vice and maintain virtue. And therefore their own life should be pure and clean; first, because otherwise they cannot punish sin; and second, because the wickedness of princes provokes their subjects to the imitation thereof. And therefore the life of princes should be pure and clean, as a mirror to their subjects; and they should admit into their kingdoms no worshipping of God, except that which is commanded in the scriptures. For God, being commoved by idolatry and strange worshipping, hath destroyed many kingdoms, as all prophesyings witness.

Ch. XXVI.—The principal office of a bishop is, to preach the true gospel of Jesus Christ; knowing that if the flock perish, the blood shall be required at his hands; and that he, neglecting the preaching of the gospel, is no bishop, nor can he do any work pleasant before God. And therefore, no bishop should mix himself with temporal or secular business, for that is against his vocation; but he should continually preach, read, and exhort his flock to seek their spiritual food in the scriptures. And so the tyrants in these days, forbidding men to read the scriptures, declare themselves wolves and no pastors; who

God shall shortly punish, because they have contemned his command, attending altogether upon their own vain superstitions, as he did Eli and his two sons under the law; and the whole priesthood after Jesus Christ.

Ch. XXVII.—The office of the father, under whom is comprehended all householders, is, to rule and guide his children, family, and servants in all godliness and honesty, instructing them in the law and word of God. For honest householders, who lived in chaste matrimony, ruled and guided their households well, nourished their children in the fear and reverence of God, were chosen to be bishops in the primitive church. And therefore they are blasphemous to the Holy Spirit, who inhibit the laics (so style they the chosen of God) from learning, reading, or teaching of the holy scriptures, wherein is contained the food of the soul; whereof antichrists willing to deprive them, would also kill the soul. For the soul, without God's word, neither hath nor may have any life. The office of the husband is, to love and defend his wife, giving himself to her only. The office of the wife is likewise to love and obey her husband, usurping no dominion over him. And the office of them both is, to instruct their children in God's law; ever giving to them example of good life, and holding them at godly occupations; labouring also themselves faithfully for the sustentation of their families.

Ch. XXVIII.—The office and duty of a lord is, to pay unto his servants the reward promised. And the office of the servant is, faithfully to work and labour, to the profit and utility of his lord, without fraud or simulation, as he would serve Jesus Christ. The office of the subject is, to obey his prince, and rulers placed by him; giving unto them honour, custom, and tribute, not requiring the cause why they receive the same; for that pertaineth not to the vocation of a subject. The office of the son is, to love, fear, and honour his parents; which honour standeth not in words only, but in ministering of all things necessary unto them; which if the son do not to the father and mother, he can do no good work before God. And therefore, devilish doctors are they, which teach men to found soul masses of their substance, suffering father and mother to labour in indigence and poverty.

The works before written, are they in which every christian should be exercised, to the glory of God, and utility of his neighbour.

---

THE following extract from Dr. M'Crie's observations on this work of Balnaves is very important.

"In reading the writings of the first reformers, there are two things which must strike our minds. The first is, the exact conformity between the doctrine maintained by them, respecting the justification of sinners, and that of the apostles. The second is, the surprising harmony which subsisted among the reformers as to this doctrine. On some questions respecting the sacraments, and the external government and worship of the church, they differed; but upon the article of FREE JUSTIFICATION, Luther and Zuinglius, Melancthon and Calvin, Cranmer and Knox, spoke the very same language. This was not owing to their having read each other's writings, but because they copied from the same divine original. The clearness with which they understood and explained this great truth is also very observable. More learned and able defences of it have since appeared; but I question if ever it has been stated in more scriptural, unequivocal, decided language, than it was in the writings of the early reformers."

May we not say, that more *learned* defences of the doctrine of justification by faith perhaps have since appeared, but it would be difficult to point out any of equal *ability*, in all essential respects.

## Date Loaned

| 27Mr'61 | | | |
|---|---|---|---|

Demco 292-5

B89085204048A

CPSIA information can be obtained
at www.ICGtesting.com
Printed in the USA
BVHW030727070622
638997BV00018B/286